Fathers and
Developmental
Psychopathology

Fathers and Developmental Psychopathology

Vicky Phares

John Wiley & Sons, Inc.

New York • Chichester • Brisbane • Toronto • Singapore

Library of Congress Cataloging-in-Publication Data:

Phares, Vicky.
    Fathers and developmental psychopathology / Vicky Phares.
        p.   cm. — (Wiley series on personality processes)
    "A Wiley-Interscience publication."
    Includes bibliographical references and index.
    ISBN 0-471-59940-9 (cloth : alk. paper)
    1. Father and child.   2. Child psychopathology—Etiology.
I. Title.   II. Series.
RJ507.P35P48   1995
618.92'89071—dc20   95-20363

Printed in the United States of America

10 9 8 7 6 5 4 3 2 1

To the man with the child in his eyes

Preface

When I was an undergraduate student at the University of California-Los Angeles, I worked as a research assistant on a project that investigated clinically referred children and their mothers. Often when I went to the waiting room to pick up the mothers and children for data collection, I would have to explain to fathers that they were not required for the data collection and then I would leave them in the waiting room with a stack of magazines. When I had to identify a topic for a 5-page paper that academic quarter, I chose to look into whether or not fathers were included in other research projects. At the time, I found Michael Lamb's (1975) landmark article entitled "Fathers: Forgotten Contributors to Child Development" and his edited volume entitled *The Role of the Father in Child Development* (Lamb, 1976). This work suggested that fathers were included in a limited amount of research projects—but the focus was on normal child development as opposed to abnormal child development.

About 4 years later when I was in my first year of graduate school at the University of Vermont, I again had to identify a topic for a paper. Because the paper was for a class in child psychopathology, I decided to revisit the research literature on fathers and child psychopathology. Caplan and Hall-McCorquodale's (1985a) excellent article on mother-blaming in clinical journals had just been published, and Lamb's (1981) revised edited volume of *The Role of the Father in Child Development* had already received a lot of attention. Although there was still very little investigation into fathers' roles in child psychopathology, a fair amount of attention had been paid to paternal influences on normal child development. Nevertheless, I was surprised to see that no researchers had taken up the cause of fathers and child psychopathology in an attempt to move the field in this important direction.

A few years later, Bruce Compas and I decided to try to review what was known about fathers and child psychopathology. After what felt like years in the library and in front of the PsycLIT CD-ROM screen, we were able to identify a core body of research in which paternal influences on child psychopathology had been identified. This review culminated in the article "The Role of

Fathers in Child and Adolescent Psychopathology: Make Room for Daddy" (Phares & Compas, 1992) and was used to discuss the issues related to research on fathers in "Where's Poppa?: The Relative Lack of Attention to the Role of Fathers in Child and Adolescent Psychopathology" (Phares, 1992). These reviews became the cornerstone of this book.

There are two primary purposes for this book: to provide a comprehensive review of what is known currently about fathers and developmental psychopathology and to encourage researchers and clinicians to pay more attention to paternal characteristics in relation to the development of psychopathology. To borrow Biller and Solomon's (1986) phrase, this book can be considered "a manifesto for research, prevention, and treatment." I hope that it has the greatest impact at the stage of research design—when clinical researchers are jotting down notes and discussing with colleagues the important variables, sample characteristics, and hypotheses that they wish to explore. At the most basic level, I want to encourage researchers at least to pose the question, "Hey, what about including fathers in this study?"

As most writers note, no book can be written without the help of many people. My mother and father provided me with a stable family environment in which I could grow and feel safe to explore less stable family environments on a professional level. My siblings and their children continue to keep me amused and appreciative of family bonds. My friends from the undergraduate and graduate years continue to make me realize that water can be just as thick as blood. A special note of thanks goes to my mentors in graduate school, Bruce Compas and Tom Achenbach. I owe much of my professional success to their high standards, warm support, and an occasional kick in the butt. My colleagues and friends from these years as a faculty member have helped me to see that playing hard really is the best remedy to working hard. A special note of thanks goes to the graduate students and secretaries who have been sensitive to the "deer caught in the headlights" look that I sometimes exhibit when I am up against deadlines. I am proud to work with such fine (and tolerant) folks. Finally, I would like to thank Herb Reich and the staff at John Wiley & Sons, Inc. for their support, encouragement, and humor throughout this process.

VICKY PHARES

Tampa, Florida

Contents

Introduction

To provide the reader a context with which to understand research on developmental psychopathology, the book will cover topics of normative development as well as abnormal development. In addition, both clinical and research issues will be discussed as they relate to fathers and developmental psychopathology. The book is organized around fundamental questions related to fathers.

I have tried to start at the beginning by addressing, in Part I, the question: *Who are fathers these days?* With all the changes in the American family, it is important first to establish the existence of fathers in children's lives. Chapter 1 presents the current demographics of American families and discusses the amount and type of contact that fathers have with their children, whether or not the fathers and children live in the same house any longer. In addition, specific sections address the effects of paternal and maternal employment, adolescent fatherhood, noncustodial fathers, and single fathers with custody. Chapter 2 focuses on the current research knowledge about fathers and the normative developmental process. This chapter discusses the process of becoming a father, paternal influences in infancy, fathers and gender role socialization, and paternal characteristics and the intellectual development and achievement of their children. Because, historically, it is such a salient research paradigm in studies on fathers, there also is a section on the effects of paternal absence.

Part II focuses on the question: *Why study fathers and developmental psychopathology?* I have approached this question in two ways. First, Chapter 3 looks at the history of mother blaming. By understanding the influences of mother blaming on psychological research and practice, the importance of studying fathers and developmental psychopathology should become clearer. Mother blaming is examined in relation to theories of the development of psychopathology, clinical research, and clinical practice. The final section of this chapter provides suggestions for the prevention of mother blaming in the future. Chapter 4 reviews current theories of the development of psychopathology. The discussion of fathers in theories of psychopathology should underscore the importance of actually studying paternal influences in the development of psychopathology. The chapter begins with a section on the role of theories in research and then progresses to discussions of genetic influences, behavioral genetics, behavioral models, social learning theories, family systems theories, and psychosocial influences in the development of psychopathology.

The third question, raised in Part III of this book, constitutes its primary focus: *What is known about fathers and developmental psychopathology?* Answers to this question are organized around different research strategies (related to target populations) and around different types of psychopathology or maladjustment. In Chapter 5, I explore the characteristics of fathers who have children who were referred for psychological services or who have met criteria for a psychiatric diagnosis. The focus of Chapter 6 is on the characteristics of children who have fathers who were referred for psychological services or who have met criteria for a psychiatric diagnosis. Chapter 7 looks at the clinical characteristics of nonreferred fathers and children. Throughout Chapters 5, 6, and 7, paternal characteristics are reviewed in relation to maternal characteristics.

After reading the chapters in Part III, it should be evident that research on fathers and developmental psychopathology is both important and feasible. However, there continues to be a lack of attention to the clinical characteristics of fathers and their children. Therefore, Part IV raises the question: *How should investigators study fathers and developmental psychopathology?* Chapter 8 covers methodological issues in research with fathers and provides specific suggestions for conducting research with fathers. Methodological issues are addressed from the perspective of the research participants (e.g., willingness of fathers vs. mothers to participate in research) and the perspective of the researcher (e.g., how research designs encourage vs. discourage paternal participation in research). The practical tips on implementation of research with fathers include issues of scheduling data collection, sample selection, family constellation issues, and measurement issues. A number of resources (e.g., specific questionnaires, interviews, and behavioral observation systems that include paternal characteristics) are provided for researchers who are interested in conducting research on fathers and developmental psychopathology.

Part V, the final part in this book, considers the question: *Where do we go from here?* In Chapter 9, I examine future directions in therapy and clinical practice. This review includes the relative effectiveness of inclusion versus exclusion of fathers in child and family-oriented therapy and the rates of paternal involvement in therapy. These issues are discussed for fathers who still live with their children as well as for fathers who no longer live with their children due to parental separation or divorce. The chapter ends with suggestions from clinicians and researchers about how to increase paternal involvement in the therapeutic process and how to increase the therapeutic effectiveness of paternal inclusion in therapy. The focus of Chapter 10 is future directions in empirical research. This chapter covers issues related to theory-driven research, gender differences within families, and developmental issues of both children and fathers. In addition, political and social concerns are discussed in relation to paternal payment of child support after divorce, and differing family constellations of various ethnic groups.

PART I

Who Are Fathers These Days?

CHAPTER 1

Demographics and Trends

After a research colloquium on fathers and developmental psychopathology, a well-respected psychologist asked me, "How exactly do you define 'father'?" Although this is a legitimate question regarding the definition of characteristics of a research sample, it is hard to believe that a researcher would ever be asked, "How exactly do you define 'mother'?" after a similar talk on mothers and developmental psychopathology. It seems that we all intuitively know what a mother is, and yet we struggle with the issue of what a father is. This struggle is not surprising given the frequency of divorce followed by maternal custody, but it also may reflect a hesitation that many people have about exploring the role of fathers in child and adolescent psychopathology. For nearly 20 years, fathers' roles in normal child development have been explored in rigorous empirical studies. Although the amount of research on fathers and normal child development does not come close to the amount of research on mothers and normal child development, it appears that the research community has been able to acknowledge that fathers may have some impact on normal child development. However, there continues to be a significant lack of attention to fathers' roles in abnormal child development. It is as if we are saying that fathers can help their children grow and flourish, but when it comes to problems, we still point to mothers and assume that fathers have little or no impact. The purpose of this chapter is to establish that fathers are present in children's lives and to explore how fathers are involved in their children's lives currently.

FATHERS DEFINED

Dinosaurs, a popular children's television show created by Jim Henson's production company, provides an interesting and enlightening definition of a father. The infant dinosaur calls its father, "Not the momma." Along with being a cute idiosyncracy of the infant in the show, this comment on fatherhood is meaningful. It reflects the perceived importance of the mother as the primary parent and the relegation of fathers to a secondary status vis-à-vis the mother. "Not the momma" implies that the father serves some type of parental role but can be defined primarily by what he is not rather than what he is.

Lest we get too carried away with interpreting a children's show, we can also seek out a more formal definition. The most obvious place to find a formal definition of "father" is in the dictionary. According to *Webster's New World Dictionary* (Neufeldt, 1994), father is defined as "a man who has begotten a child; esp., a man as he is related to his child or children . . . a person regarded as a male parent; protector" (p. 493). Based on this definition, fathers can be identified because of their biological contribution to the creation of a child (begetting a child), and they can be identified because of their parental role in the child's life (being regarded as a male parent). This broad definition encompasses biological fathers, stepfathers, and any other male who serves a parental function for the child. Interestingly, the definition of mother is comparable to the definition of father with the exception of mothers being said to act in a nurturing role rather than a protective role. Hence lies one of the original dichotomies between male and female parents: Fathers are said to protect; mothers are said to nurture. This dichotomy not only is present in the dictionary definition of fathers and mothers but is also evident in anthropological and sociological writings on the historical influences of fathers and mothers.

Although there have been suggestions that fatherhood was a manufactured role that does not exist in nature (Kraemer, 1991) and thus is a social invention (Garbarino, 1993), there is evidence that a number of different roles for fathers exist in both nonhuman and human groups (Hill & Hill, 1990; Silverstein, 1993a). According to cross-cultural anthropological research, there is consistent evidence that mothers (and adult women) are usually responsible for nurturance and provision of resources to children, whereas fathers (and adult men) are usually responsible for protection of children and defense against attack from within or outside their own community (Mackey, 1985). However, when fathers and other adult men produce or acquire food from the environment, they are usually socially sanctioned to redistribute the food to the children (Mackey, 1985). From a sociological point of view, fathers have been seen traditionally as breadwinners and authority figures (Robinson & Barret, 1986).

The "traditional father" has a limited role in the family other than providing a solid economic base and assisting in punishment of inappropriate behaviors, especially sons' inappropriate behaviors (Robinson & Barret, 1986). Parsons and Bales (1955) labeled the mother's role in the family as "expressive" and the father's role in the family as "instrumental." They noted that mothers show expressive characteristics in providing empathy and emotional security for their children, whereas fathers show instrumental characteristics in protecting the family and in providing economic stability by working outside the home at jobs that require skill and intelligence. The focus on mothers' duties within the family and fathers' duties outside the family has allowed, and possibly encouraged, the omission of fathers from research on families (Robinson & Barret, 1986).

Although these dichotomies between the roles of mothers and fathers have existed for centuries, during the 1970s there was a new focus on fathers' changing roles in American families (Fein, 1978; Lamb, 1975, 1979). This change in focus brought attention to the "new father" who was said to be highly nurturing toward his children and to show increasing amounts of participation in child care and housework duties (Robinson & Barret, 1986). Lewis and O'Brien (1987), however, seriously question the existence of the "new father." They noted that there was sufficient rhetoric about new fathers but very little empirical investigation as to whether the new father really exists. For example, Coverman and Sheley (1986) investigated fathers' child care and housework involvement from 1965 to 1975 to ascertain whether there were any noticeable increases over this 10-year period. When comparing time use in 1965 and 1975, men did not show significant differences in time spent in housework or child care, but they did show significant decreases in paid work and significant increases in leisure time. Women also did not show significant changes in time spent in child care, but they showed significant decreases in housework and paid work, and significant increases in leisure time. Overall, this study suggested that the emergence of the "new father" had not yet become evident in the mid-1970s. This same type of analysis of time spent has not been conducted in more recent years to investigate the existence of the new father.

Regarding the possible existence of the new father, Furstenberg (1988) noted that there is a bimodal distribution of fathers, with some fathers seeming to be "good dads" and some fathers appearing to be "bad dads." He argued that good dads are highly nurturant and involved in their children's lives. These fathers are represented in best-selling books such as *Fatherhood* (Cosby, 1986) and in empirically based books such as *How Fathers Care for the Next Generation* (Snarey, 1993). Conversely, bad dads provide little or no financial support for their children and little emotional support for and involvement with their children. Furstenberg argued that, although both types of fathers exist, it is up to social and political forces to help transform bad dads into good dads.

Overall, a question still remains as to the accurate definition of a father. In addition to the issues already addressed, there is the issue of genetic versus social paternity (Marsiglio, 1986). Although genetic paternity can now be proven with 99.8% certainty (Tripp-Reimer & Wilson, 1991), social paternity (the adult male who serves a role in the child's life) may still be the most important feature of fatherhood (Marsiglio, 1986; Simonds, 1974). To address these remaining questions about who fathers are in the current culture, the following sections will describe the demographic characteristics of families as well as current research of fathers' involvement in their children's lives. Interested readers are also referred to two issues of *Journal of Family Issues* (December 1993, March 1994) that were devoted solely to fatherhood (Marsiglio, 1993, 1994; see review and extension of this work in Marsiglio, 1995).

FAMILY DEMOGRAPHICS

It would be an understatement to say that demographics of families have changed over the past three decades (Glick, 1988). Whereas 87.1% of children were reported to live in two-parent households in 1970, it is currently estimated that approximately 61.1% of U.S. children under 18 years old live with both biological parents (Roberts, 1993). A total of 10.8% of children live in stepfamilies, 24.2% live in a single-parent household headed by the mother, and 3.9% of U.S. children under the age of 18 live in a single-parent household headed by the father. These family demographic distributions vary according to ethnic groups, with 56.3% of African American children living in single-parent households headed by mothers.

With all these changes in family structure over the past three decades, a lot of attention has been paid to the potentially negative impact of dual-employed couples, divorce, and single-parent families. Demo (1992) argued that these are not the most salient issues that researchers should investigate, but rather that more attention should be paid to economic hardship and high levels of interparental and family conflict in all types of family constellations.

PATERNAL INTERACTIONS WITH CHILDREN WHO LIVE WITH BOTH BIOLOGICAL PARENTS

Although these current family demographics indicate the living situations of U.S. children under 18 years old, they do not elucidate the amount of involvement that children have with their fathers. The majority of research in this area has been conducted with two-parent families who were recruited from the community rather than from any specialized referral source (such as mental health clinics). Therefore, this section will address the involvement of fathers and their children in two-parent families based in the community. The amount and type of contact with noncustodial parents will be addressed in a later section in this chapter. Two issues will be addressed here for two-parent families: (a) Do mothers and fathers differ in the time spent with their children? and (b) What impact does differential time involvement have on children and their parents?

Lamb (1986) noted that parental time involvement with children can be conceptualized in three ways: (a) parental engagement/direct interaction with the child, (b) parental accessibility to the child (time when the parent is accessible to the child but not necessarily engaged in one-on-one interactions with the child) and (c) parental responsibility for the child (extent to which the parent takes responsibility for the child rather than just "helping out"). All three of these types of involvement can be assessed in absolute terms (e.g., how many hours per day) or in relative terms (e.g., proportion of time father spends with the child in relation to time mother spends with the child). Lamb argues that relative proportions are more meaningful than absolute hours spent. In addition, all three types of involvement can be assessed with a variety of methods, including daily diaries or time charts to be filled out soon after the interactions take place, retrospective estimates of time involvement, direct observation of time involvement, and time-sampling methods.

Across all these different methodologies and different definitions of parental time involvement, a clear picture has emerged about the involvement of mothers and fathers in two-parent families. Regardless of employment status of mothers and assuming fathers are employed, there is consistent evidence that most mothers spend more time with their children than most fathers (Ahrentzen, Levine, & Michelson, 1989; Barnett & Baruch, 1987; Baruch & Barnett, 1986b; Demo, 1992; Grossman, Pollack, & Golding, 1988; Lamb, 1986; Levant, Slattery, & Loiselle, 1987; Thompson & Walker, 1989). This pattern is also present in other countries such as India (Suppal, 1994). In two-parent families in the United States where both parents are employed, fathers spend approximately 33% as much time as mothers in direct interaction with their children and fathers spend approximately 65% as much time as mothers being accessible to their children (Lamb, 1986). Fathers carry less than 10% of the burden of responsibility toward children, as distinguished from their ability to "help out" (Thompson & Walker, 1989). Mothers' greater involvement in the parental role appears to be associated with greater risk for the development of maternal anxiety, depression, and psychosomatic syndromes (Lampert & Friedman, 1992).

When mothers are employed, fathers provide a somewhat higher proportion of care for children than do fathers whose wife is a full-time homemaker (Jones & Heermann, 1992). Data from the Census Bureau suggest that the incidence of fathers taking primary care of children when mothers are at their place of employment is increasing. For example, 20.0% of married fathers in two-parent families and 7.0% of unmarried fathers in two-parent families took care of their preschool children when their wife was at her job (U.S. Bureau of the Census, 1987). This increase in paternal care appears to be due to a number of factors, including the increase of paternal unemployment, the high cost of out-of-home child care, parents' ability to work night shifts or to work part-time, and changing social attitudes that enable fathers to participate more fully in their children's daily lives (Chira, 1993).

To quantify the amount of time that fathers and mothers spend with their children, Barnett and Baruch (1987) conducted a study with 160 Caucasian middle-class families with children ranging from kindergarten to fourth grade. They found that fathers spent an average of 29.48 hours per week and mothers spent an average of 44.45 hours per week in total interaction time with their children. However, the difference between fathers and mothers was more pronounced when only "solo" time was compared. Fathers spent an average of 5.48 hours per week alone with their children, whereas mothers spent an average of 19.56 hours per week alone with their children. These figures did not vary significantly when maternal employment status was considered. This study suggested that whether or not mothers are employed, they spend far more time than do fathers interacting with their children.

Evidence also suggests, however, that dual employment has an impact on the types of activity that fathers and mothers engage in with their children. For example, Fish, New, and VanCleave (1992) compared the proportion of time that fathers and mothers were involved in 15 different child-care activities. They compared these proportions for dual-income families and traditional families in which the father was employed and the mother had primary responsibility for the children. Not surprisingly, mothers in traditional families showed significantly more time involvement and responsibility than fathers in all 15 of the child-care duties. In the dual-income families, however, mothers showed greater responsibility for four activities (food preparation, caring for sick children, nurturing, and shopping for children), fathers showed greater responsibility for one activity (playing), and mothers and fathers showed approximately similar levels of responsibility in 10 activities (bathing, bedtime, dressing, disciplining, feeding, night-time care, outings, school liaison, teaching, and transportation). Therefore, the study by Fish and colleagues suggests that it is important to assess the specific child-care activities of fathers and mothers when comparing paternal and maternal interactions with children.

Crouter and McHale (1993) provided an interesting study of the changing patterns of paternal and maternal involvement with their children based on the season of the year. They studied school-age children and interviewed the family at three time points across 18 months (winter, summer, winter). They categorized families into one of three types of families based on the employment status of fathers and mothers during these three seasons: consistently dual-earner (both father and mother were employed at all three points in time), consistently single-earner (father was employed and mother was a full-time homemaker at all three points in time), and dual-earner during winter with single-earner during the summer (father was employed during all three time points, mother was employed at both winter data collections but was a full-time homemaker during the summer). Fathers in the consistently dual-earner families were significantly more aware of and knowledgeable about their children's activities during the summer than were fathers in the other two groups. Crouter and McHale pointed out that seasonal changes in employment status should be considered when conducting research on paternal and maternal employment.

Involvement in children's health care and arrangements for out-of-home day care are two important aspects of taking care of children, especially when both parents are employed. Bailey (1991) studied 50 Caucasian, middle-class families of young children (mean age of 4.6 years) with regard to taking children to doctor and dentist appointments and staying home when children were sick.

In both dual-income and single-income (only father employed) families, mothers were more likely than fathers to take children to doctor and dentist appointments and were more likely to stay home with a sick child. However, fathers in dual-income families were significantly more likely than fathers in single-income families to take children to doctor and dentist appointments and to stay home when their children were sick. This pattern was true regardless of the gender of the child. Bailey suggested that when mothers had less time for children's health care because of their employment, fathers were more likely to become involved.

Regarding the use of day care, Atkinson (1987, 1991) found that 38% of the fathers in her sample reported visiting their child in family day care, 83% reported that they discussed the day-care arrangements with the day-care provider, and 71% reported that they provided transportation for their children to day-care. In addition, 58% of the fathers reported caring for their children when they were ill. Although a greater percentage of mothers reported taking part in these activities, this study suggested that a large percentage of fathers have some level of involvement in the out-of-home day-care arrangements for their children. Overall, these studies suggest that mothers spend more time with their children than do fathers, but fathers do spend a substantial amount of time interacting with their children.

Fathers or mothers engage in different direct interactions with their children. In general, mothers tend to act as comfort-givers and as caretakers, whereas fathers tend to act as playmates with their children (Fagot & Hagan, 1991; Fish et al., 1992; Lamb, 1981; Parke & Tinsley, 1981; Roggman, 1992; Stevenson, Leavitt, Thompson, & Roach, 1988; Tiedje & Darling-Fisher, 1993). Even when fathers are conducting caretaking activities, such as feeding or dressing their child, they tend to be playful in their interactions (Yogman, Cooley, & Kindlon, 1988). In a study of fathers and mothers of preterm infants, Levy-Shiff, Sharir, and Mogilner (1989) found that differences in paternal and maternal behavior were more pronounced immediately after birth than after a few weeks. Specifically, they found that soon after birth, mothers talked with, held, and provided more caregiving to their neonates than did fathers. As time passed, however, (and before the infant was discharged from the preterm nursery at the hospital), fathers did not show significant differences from mothers in speaking to, caring for, or holding their infants. Fathers continued to show higher levels of playing and stimulating behaviors with their infants than did mothers.

Differences between fathers and mothers in playing and caretaking behaviors are especially pronounced when both parents are in the child's presence. Mothers' emotional support and fathers' playfulness seem to be more salient when mothers and fathers are interacting with their children at the same time (Daniels & Weingarten, 1988). Conversely, parenting behaviors of fathers and mothers when they are alone with their children are more similar than different. When either parent is the sole caretaker, even for a limited time, he or she exhibits similar behaviors such as feeding, clothing, and playing with his or her children (Thompson & Walker, 1989).

Although popular culture seems to portray greater paternal involvement when children reach older childhood and adolescence, the amount of time that both mothers and fathers spend with their children decreases with children's age (Lamb, 1986). Both mothers and fathers spend the largest amount of time with infants and toddlers, less time with school-age children, and even less time with adolescents. In unobtrusive observations of families in a park, fathers and mothers showed greater proximity to and touching behavior with their infants and toddlers than with their older children (Sigelman & Adams, 1990). Across all age groups, however, mothers continue to spend more time with their children than do fathers (Thompson & Walker, 1989). This trend continues into adulthood, with fathers primarily giving advice to their offspring and mothers primarily lending emotional support (Miller & Lane, 1991).

Popular beliefs about fathers' greater involvement with their sons than their daughters are correct (Barnett & Baruch, 1987; Starrels, 1994). Fathers tend to report more interest in their sons' activities, and across all age groups, fathers tend to spend more time with their sons than with their daughters (Lamb, 1986). Fathers are more likely to go on outings, to be involved in leisure activities, and to talk to their sons than to their daughters (Marsiglio, 1991). Interestingly, mothers perceive less risk for separation and divorce when there is at least one son in the family as opposed to when there are only daughters (Katzev, Warner, & Acock, 1994), and there is evidence to suggest that fathers are more likely to be present in the home when they have at least one son (Mott, 1994). These findings appear to be related to fathers' greater involvement with their sons than with their daughters.

The majority of the studies on paternal involvement have been conducted with primarily Caucasian, middle-class families. However, there are no known differences in patterns of time involvement based on ethnicity, regional location, or religious affiliation (Lamb, 1986). For example, Wilson, Tolson, Hinton, and Kiernan (1990) investigated child-care duties in African American families that were either dual-parent or single-parent families, with an additional emphasis on the presence or absence of grandmothers. Similar to the research with Caucasian families, they found that African American mothers were responsible for the majority of child care regardless of family constellation. However, they found that the presence of other adults, such as the father or the grandmother, led to a decrease in mothers' child-care duties. Wilson and colleagues also noted that noncustodial fathers were often listed as contributors to child-care duties by single mothers. Overall, this research suggests that African American mothers, like Caucasian American mothers, have a greater responsibility for child-care duties. This research also shows, however, that many African American fathers, like many Caucasian American fathers, show significant levels of involvement in their children's lives.

Studies in other cultures show similar patterns. For example, in an interesting study of Efe (pygmy) fathers in northeastern Zaire, Morelli and Tronick (1992) found that fathers' interactions with their children were very similar to their children's interactions with other adult men. Children between the ages of 1 and 3 years old were equally as likely to participate in social activities and to watch the adults' activities whether the adult male was their father or another adult male in the community. Much like fathers in studies of Western cultures (Lamb, 1986), Efe fathers showed decreasing levels of social engagement with their children as they grew older. Morelli and Tronick suggest that there are a fair number of similarities, with a few notable differences, between Efe fathers and fathers in Western cultures.

DETERMINANTS OF PATERNAL INVOLVEMENT

There have been a number of investigations into the factors within the family that influence fathers' involvement with their children. Grossman and Vollkner (1984) found that fathers who expressed interest in attending the delivery of their child showed greater paternal involvement when their child was 1 year old, regardless of whether they had been allowed to attend the birth. This suggests that paternal attitudes toward involvement at birth influence involvement later in the child's life.

Grossman and colleagues (1988) conducted a comprehensive study of the predictors of quantity of fathers' time involvement with their children. Their sample included families at a variety of socioeconomic levels ranging from working class through upper middle class, all of whom were married. Fathers' time involvement was reported for four dimensions: average time playing, average time caretaking, average weekday time in both playing and caretaking, and average weekend day time in both playing and caretaking. When the children were 5 years old, fathers' time playing with their children and fathers' weekend time with their children were inversely correlated with paternal job satisfaction: The higher the job satisfaction, the less time fathers spent playing with their children and the less time fathers spent on the weekends with their children. Paternal education, occupation, and socioeconomic status were also inversely related to duration of paternal play with children. No other paternal characteristics (age, life adaptation, anxiety, job involvement, marital adjustment, support for autonomy, support for affiliation) were significantly related to fathers' time playing with their children or weekend time with their children. Fathers' time caretaking and fathers' weekday time spent with their children were not significantly related to any paternal characteristics that were measured. Overall, fathers' who were lower in educational level, occupational level, socioeconomic status, and job satisfaction were shown to have higher amounts of play with their 5-year-old children. Fathers' weekend time with their children was also higher for fathers who were less satisfied with their jobs.

Four maternal variables were significantly correlated with fathers' time involvement with their 5-year-old children. Maternal education was inversely related to paternal caretaking of the child, which suggested that mothers with fewer years of education had husbands who spent more time providing childcare. Mothers' occupational level was inversely related to fathers' time playing with their children and fathers' time involvement on weekdays. Maternal age was inversely related to paternal caretaking, play, and weekend time with children. Mothers' support for affiliation with the child (e.g., warmth, attention, and responsiveness to the child as measured by direct observation) was negatively correlated with paternal playing, caretaking, and weekend time spent with the child. Thus, mothers who showed lower levels of support for affiliation had husbands who spent more time playing with their children, taking care of their children, and spending time with their children on weekends. No other maternal variables (life adaptation, anxiety, marital adjustment, support for autonomy) were related to paternal time spent with children. It should also be noted that maternal time spent with children was unrelated to paternal time spent with children for all four dimensions of time spent that were measured (playing, caretaking, weekday time, and weekend time). Overall, this study suggests that fathers' quantity of time spent with their children is influenced by a variety of paternal and maternal characteristics. Although the sample size was small ($N = 23$ families), the study by Grossman and colleagues represents a comprehensive investigation of factors related to fathers' time spent with their children.

In a study of intact families with children in kindergarten or fourth grade, Barnett and Baruch (1987) found that the determinants of fathers' participation in caretaking were different for dual-income versus single-income families. In dual-income families, the more hours mothers worked outside the home, the more time fathers spent interacting with their children. Employed mothers' attitude toward the male role was also related to fathers' interaction time with their children. Mothers with less traditional sex-role attitudes about the male role (e.g., disagreement with statements such as "It bothers me when a man does something that I consider feminine") had husbands who showed a higher proportion of interaction time with their children. Due to the correlational nature of this research, causality cannot be determined to suggest whether maternal sex-role attitudes influenced paternal interaction with children or vice versa. No other variables (flexibility of mothers' employment schedule, gender of child, child's grade, fathers' attitude toward the male role, fathers' attitude toward the quality of fathering he received) were significantly related to fathers' interaction time and caretaking of children in dual-income families.

The pattern of determinants of fathers' participation was somewhat different in single-income families in which only the father was employed. A number of characteristics were related to fathers' interaction with their children, including number of hours fathers worked outside the home, child's grade, number of children in the family, mothers' attitude toward the male role, and fathers' attitude toward the quality of fathering they received. Higher levels of paternal-child interaction were evidenced when fathers worked fewer hours outside the home, when children were in lower grades, when there were more children in the family, when mothers had a less traditional sex-role attitude about the male role, and when fathers had lower opinions of the fathering they had received. Of all these variables, the most consistent predictor of fathers' participation with children in single-income families was fathers' attitudes toward the quality of fathering they received. Fathers in single-income families who were somewhat dissatisfied with the fathering they had received when they were children spent more time with their own children than did fathers who were relatively satisfied with the fathering they had received. This factor may be related to fathers' attempts to compensate for perceived deprivation from their own childhood. In single-income families, fathers' education, gender of child, and fathers' attitude toward the male role were not significantly related to the amount of paternal interactions with children. Barnett and Baruch suggest that maternal employment status served as a moderating variable that allowed different determinants to emerge as significant predictors of paternal interaction and caretaking.

These studies suggest that a variety of maternal and paternal characteristics influence the amount of interactions and level of responsibility that fathers have with their children. Cowan and Cowan (1988) suggest that barriers in the family may limit fathers' involvement with their young children. Given the decrease in mothers' employment outside the home at the birth of their first child, and the concomitant loss of a major source of self-esteem, mothers may be reluctant to give up some of their parental role to fathers. Atkinson (1991) also noted that many mothers might not support greater paternal involvement because of the assumption that fathers would be incompetent at caretaking or that fathers' involvement would imply maternal incompetence. The issue of paternal interaction with children versus paternal responsibility for children should be noted here (Lamb, 1986). Pleck (1985) found that most mothers want their husbands to spend more time with their children, not to decrease the amount of maternal contact with children nor to increase fathers' responsibility for their children, but rather because mothers felt that greater father-child interactions would be good for fathers as well as children. Lamb and Oppenheim (1989) summarized a number of surveys that showed most fathers desire more involvement with their children at the same time that most mothers (between 60% and 80%) do not want their husbands to be more involved with their children.

In addition to barriers within the family that may limit fathers' involvement and responsibility for their children, barriers outside the family also may limit fathers' participation in caretaking. Most businesses are reluctant to provide paid paternity leave beyond the first few weeks after the birth of a child, and therefore fathers' involvement may be limited due to employment-related constraints (Cowan & Cowan, 1988). The enduring image of motherhood (women who enjoy their children every minute of the day and who intuitively know how to keep their children happy and healthy) and the enduring image of fatherhood (men who provide monetary support to the family but who do not desire physical or emotional closeness with their children) may also continue to limit fathers' participation with and responsibility for their children (Thompson & Walker, 1989).

Some of the factors that limit paternal involvement may need to be addressed through social policy. For example, support for paternity leave and greater availability of paternity leave (such as through the Family and Medical Leave Act) might encourage fathers to become more active in their children's lives. Certain countries, such as Sweden, have actively supported paternal involvement. Since the early 1970s, the Swedish government has conducted a comprehensive campaign to encourage fathers to become more involved in the daily care of their children. In a chapter about the changing roles of fathers, Lamb (1986) included reproductions of brochures and posters published by the Swedish government to show that masculinity and active parenting are not diametrically opposed (e.g., three burly men apparently taking pleasure in strolling their young infants in carriages). In the United States, the multitude of barriers against increased paternal involvement will need to be addressed on the personal, familial, and social policy levels if any noticeable changes are to be expected in fathers' roles in the family.

Regardless of the reasons, there is strong evidence that fathers tend to spend less time than mothers with their children. The next logical step is to investigate the impact of this differential time involvement on children and their parents. Like the consistent findings in research on fathers' time spent with their children, there is also consistent evidence about the impact of parental time involvement on children's development. Overall, the amount of parental time involvement with children is less important than its quality as well as the mothers', fathers', and children's evaluation of the amount of time involvement (Lamb, Pleck, & Levine, 1985; Wenk, Hardesty, Morgan, & Blair, 1994). For example, Baruch and Barnett (1986b) found that fathers' time involvement had almost no relation to their children's sex-role attitudes. Grossman and colleagues (1988) investigated the relation between quantity of fathers' time involvement and quality of interaction with their children (as defined by support for child's affiliation, support for child's autonomy, warmth, attention to child, and responsiveness to child). They found no relation between quantity of fathering and quality of fathering. Quantity and quality of fathering appear to be orthogonal dimensions, and it is *quality* rather than *quantity* that seems to have a greater impact on children's well-being. Overall, it appears that the type of interactions children have with their mothers or fathers is more impactful than the amount of those interactions.

FAMILY WORK AROUND THE HOME AND AWAY FROM THE HOME IN TWO-PARENT FAMILIES

Nonpaid Household Work

Along with the investigation of fathers' and mothers' caretaking, there have been numerous investigations of fathers' and mothers' involvement in household tasks other than child care (see Goodnow & Bowes, 1994, for review). Again, most of these studies have included only two-parent households, although some studies have investigated differences in involvement in household work based on whether or not both parents were employed. Overall, the pattern of fathers' and mothers' involvement in household work follows the somewhat traditional pattern of fathers' and mothers' involvement in child-care activities. Fathers continue to be more involved in "masculine" household tasks, such as mowing the lawn, taking out the trash, and repairing the car, whereas mothers continue to be more involved in "feminine" household tasks, such as doing the laundry, sweeping, and preparing meals (Coltrane & Ishii-Kuntz, 1992; Levant et al., 1987; McKenry, Price, Gordon, & Rudd, 1986).

These patterns are evident whether or not both parents are employed. For example, Fish and colleagues (1992) found that fathers were significantly more likely than mothers to be responsible for car maintenance, car repair, financial investment, taking out the garbage, and yardwork. Mothers were significantly more likely than fathers to be responsible for cooking, grocery shopping, laundry, and sewing. These patterns were true for families in which both parents were employed as well as "traditional" families in which the father was employed and the mother was a full-time homemaker. When the patterns of household work were compared for dual-income families and "traditional" families, fathers in "traditional" families took significantly more responsibility for financial investment and income tax preparation than fathers in dual-income families, whereas mothers in "traditional" families took significantly more responsibility for car maintenance (although still less than fathers in traditional families), cooking, and light household cleaning than mothers in dual-income families. This study suggests that the households continue to reflect what can be considered a traditional division of labor.

Baruch and Barnett (1986a) discussed the characteristics of household work in which fathers versus mothers are engaged, and they noted that traditionally masculine chores tend to be done only sporadically (e.g., car repair), whereas traditionally feminine chores tend to be done on a daily basis (e.g., cooking). In a time analysis of families in which both parents were employed full time, Baruch and Barnett found that fathers spent an average of 11.75 hours per week and mothers spent an average of 29.88 hours per week in both masculine and feminine household chores, not including direct child-care tasks. These studies suggest that the burden of household work continues to fall primarily on mothers; however, fathers do contribute to household work.

Although a number of researchers have noted that the traditional division of labor becomes more pronounced after the arrival of the first child (e.g., Belsky, Lang, & Rovine, 1985; Coltrane & Ishii-Kuntz, 1992), there is also evidence that families show a combination of more traditional and less traditional division of labor after the birth of the first child (Cowan & Cowan, 1988). In a comprehensive, longitudinal study of transitions to parenthood, Cowan and Cowan (1988) found that when compared with activities before birth, at 6 months after birth of the first child, fathers showed decreased involvement in doing the laundry and increased contributions to family income (both of which can be considered moving toward the "traditional" division of labor). However, fathers also showed increased involvement in meal preparation, housecleaning, and grocery shopping (which can be considered a move toward a "nontraditional" division of labor). From 6 months to 18 months after birth, fathers continued to show increased involvement in shopping and gardening, although they showed decreased involvement in meal preparation, housecleaning, and taking out the garbage. At the same time, mothers showed increased contributions to family income; two-thirds of the mothers in the sample returned to paid employment. This study suggests that the transition to parenthood shows both traditional and nontraditional patterns of division of labor within the household.

Coltrane and Ishii-Kuntz (1992) provided an interesting investigation into the determinants of greater paternal involvement in housework. They compared couples who had children "early" (before the father was 28 years old) with couples who "delayed" childbirth (when the father was 28 years old or older). They found that for early-birth families, fathers showed more involvement in household tasks when mothers contributed more money to family income, when mothers held less traditional ideology about gender and family roles, when fathers had greater time available to do housework, when mothers had less time available to do housework, and when there were more child-care demands. The pattern was similar in delayed-birth families except that mothers' financial contribution was no longer related to fathers' involvement in household chores. Fathers' less traditional ideology about gender and family roles was significantly related to their greater participation in housework. Overall, time availability and mothers' ideology about gender and family roles seemed to be most strongly related to fathers' participation in household chores.

Perceptions within the family of what household tasks are appropriate for different family members may also influence fathers' and mothers' involvement in household work. In a study entitled, "Would you ask someone else to do this task?" mothers, fathers, and 8- to 14-year-old children were asked which household tasks they would complete themselves and which tasks they would ask another family member to complete (Goodnow, Bowes, Warton, Dawes, & Taylor, 1991). Based on the participants' responses, Goodnow and colleagues identified four categories of household tasks: Tasks that were seen as most appropriate for fathers or sons (e.g., cutting the grass, doing small repairs, and washing the car), tasks that were seen as most appropriate for mothers only (e.g., cleaning the toilet, doing small sewing repairs, and doing regular grocery shopping), tasks that were appropriate for anyone in the household except the father (e.g., ironing, vacuuming, and tidying others' things), and open tasks that were seen as appropriate for any family member (e.g., tidying one's own things, setting the table, or helping buy a gift). Similarly, children from the second, fourth, and sixth grades reported preferences in their help-seeking behavior from their fathers versus their mothers (Barnett et al., 1990). Specifically, both boys and girls were more likely to ask their father for help with opening a jar and finishing a puzzle, whereas they were more likely to ask their mother for help in writing a story for school, bandaging a skinned knee, and removing a splinter. However, children were more likely to ask their same-sex parent (girls asking mothers and boys asking fathers) for help to fix a broken game and to select a gift for a teacher. Overall, these studies show perceptions of appropriate household tasks that are consistent with the actual participation in household tasks by fathers and mothers.

It is difficult to establish the causal direction between perceptions of appropriate household work and the actual household work itself, and the two issues may be completely confounded at this point. The work by Coltrane and Ishii-Kuntz (1992) suggests that mothers' ideology, and to a lesser extent fathers' ideology of gender roles within the family influences fathers' involvement in household tasks. It seems reasonable that mothers' and fathers' perceptions of the appropriateness of the chore may also influence their participation in different household tasks (Goodnow et al., 1991). Future research will also need to be cognizant of who is reporting on the completion of different tasks within the family. For example, Bird and Ratcliff (1990) found that fathers' and mothers' reports of their children's participation in family tasks were influenced by familial factors such as family size, sibling structure, and the age of the oldest sibling. In addition, fathers and mothers were found to differ significantly in their reports of shared child care (Goldberg, 1990). Specifically, fathers reported greater rates of child care that was shared by both father and mother, whereas mothers reported higher levels of having primary responsibility (and not shared responsibility) for child care. In future studies of nonpaid household work and child-care responsibilities, researchers must attempt to assess the perspectives of multiple informants within the family to gain a better understanding of work patterns within the family home.

Wage Work Outside the Home

The previous section established the continuation of relatively traditional division of labor within the household. This section will explore the differential involvement and impact of fathers' and mothers' paid employment outside the family home. Labor statistics suggest that maternal and paternal employment is a fact of life for most families in the United States. For example, in 1987, 48.2% of married mothers and 72% of divorced mothers with children under the age of 18 were employed outside the home (Holder & Anderson, 1989). More recently, 75% of mothers with children between the ages of 6 and 17 were employed (Roberts, 1993). It is estimated that less than 7% of families in the United States fit the traditional family constellation in which the married father works outside the home for paid employment and the married mother works inside the home for unpaid household and child-care duties (Braverman, 1989). Although many people still consider maternal employment a choice, empirical evidence suggests that the majority of employed mothers (and employed fathers) are wage earners because of economic necessity (Thompson & Walker, 1989). However, there is also evidence that the majority of employed mothers (and employed fathers) would continue in their jobs even if it was not necessary for economic reasons (Scarr, Phillips, & McCartney, 1989). To discuss the area of wage work outside the home, the issues of other-than-parent child care, maternal employment and most importantly, the effects of paternal employment will be considered.

Parental Employment and Child Care

When parents work outside the home, the issue of what to do with young children is prominent. Although it is beyond the scope of this chapter to cover research on other-than-parent child care and the effects of such care, child care continues to be a topic surrounded by debate and controversy. Some researchers continue to find that infants who are placed in other-than-parent child care show increased risk for emotional insecurity (Barglow, Vaughn, & Molitor, 1987; Belsky & Rovine, 1988), but most research on child care has suggested that infants and children placed in child care are not at increased risk for emotional or behavioral problems (Scarr et al., 1989). Rather than child care having deleterious effects on children, the important issues appear to be the quality of the child care, the economic circumstances of the family, and the quality of time that parents spend with their children when they are together (Grossman et al., 1988; Scarr et al., 1989).

A number of questions have also been raised about traditional research designs that investigate the attachment styles of children who are cared for by people other than their parents (McCartney, Phillips, & Scarr, 1993). Infants are sometimes found to be more "avoidant" when their attachment to their parents is evaluated through the Strange Situation procedure. However, Clarke-Stewart (1989) questions the usefulness of this procedure, given that the "avoidance" may actually be "independence" that the infants have developed from the daily separations and reunifications with employed parents. This area of research has led to interesting discussions of the overlap between research and social policy. For example, Silverstein (1991, 1993b) argued that researchers should help transform the debate about other-than-parent child care into a call for social policy reform, whereas other researchers (e.g., Maddux, 1993; NICHD Early Child Care Network, 1993) have expressed concern over the loss of boundaries between social science research and social policy.

Because of the data presented earlier suggesting that maternal (and paternal) employment is not a choice but a necessity, many psychologists have argued that other-than-parent child care should not be considered a choice but a necessity (e.g., Scarr, Phillips, & McCartney, 1990; Silverstein, 1991; Thompson & Walker, 1989). The question of whether women (and men) will choose to be employed and will need child care is irrelevant—it is now economic necessity rather than a whim that leads most parents to work outside the home. Because of the important yet controversial nature of the subject, debate of this issue is likely to continue for quite some time.

Maternal Employment

The research on other-than-parent child care is often discussed in relation to maternal employment rather than paternal employment or dual-income families (Silverstein, 1991). Maternal employment has been referred to as "maternal absence" in a study of infant-mother attachment (Barglow et al., 1987) whereas "paternal absence" usually refers to fathers who have little or no contact with their children (Phares, 1993a). Paternal employment is rarely investigated except to investigate fathers' loss of employment and the impact on child and family functioning (McLoyd, 1989). Gilbert and Rachlin (1987) pointed out that when employment and children are discussed together, the focus continues to be on mothers who must "choose" between love and work and who will undoubtedly perceive role conflict when attempting motherhood and employment simultaneously. Historically, men and women were said to have had "two worlds"—the male world that focused on achievement through employment and the female world that focused on nurturing through emotional involvement with the family (Bernard, 1982; Voydanoff, 1988). Based on employment and family constellation statistics, this separation is no longer accurate, and yet many researchers continue to assume that maternal employment is aberrant rather than a normative reality. Although there are many high-quality investigations of the effects of maternal employment (e.g., Greenberger & O'Neil, 1992; Paulson, Koman, & Hill, 1990) and perceptions of the positive and negative consequences of maternal employment (Greenberger, Goldberg, Crawford, & Granger, 1988; Spitze, 1988), increased attention should be given to the effects of paternal employment and perceptions of the positive and negative consequences of paternal employment because both maternal employment and paternal employment are the norm rather than the exception. In addition, Baruch, Biener, and Barnett (1987) argued that research into maternal employment has been replete with a misunderstanding of the duties of full-time homemakers. Researchers often suggest that the out-of-home workplace is a "stressful" environment in contrast to the "stress-free" sanctuary of the home.

Baruch and colleagues noted that full-time homemaking and child care is far from stress-free and the assumption of the home as a sanctuary from stress is misguided and harmful to the research enterprise. Thus, there is a need for more objective investigations into the effects of multiple roles (e.g., parent, worker, spouse) for both fathers and mothers.

Paternal Employment

In spite of the long tradition of investigating maternal *employment* (e.g., Barglow et al., 1987) and paternal *unemployment* (McLoyd, 1989), there have been some excellent programmatic investigations into the impact of paternal employment on children and families. Most notably, Barling (1990) provided a comprehensive documentation of the effects of paternal employment on children, fathers, and mothers. After reviewing the literature on maternal employment, Barling noted that the research literatures on maternal employment and paternal employment are very different. For example, investigations of maternal employment tend to investigate negative effects on children, whereas investigations of paternal employment tend to investigate positive effects on children. Barling also noted that, with only a few exceptions, most researchers have looked at the effects of maternal employment and paternal employment separately, as though they are two separate and independent issues. Therefore, researchers have not been able to directly compare the effects of maternal and paternal employment status within the same families.

Overall, fathers' absence due to "ordinary" work hours (e.g., 8-to-5 job hours) do not seem to impact on paternal behavior with children (Piotrkowski & Gornick, 1987). However, there is consistent evidence that when fathers are involved in shift work that necessitates absence from the house in the evenings (Volger, Ernst, Nachreiner, & Hanecke, 1988) or when fathers are involved in prolonged absences from the home due to out-of-town job responsibilities, such as military service (Hiew, 1992; Hillenbrand, 1976), the father-child relationship is adversely affected and children often show increased emotional and behavioral problems. It is not clear whether children are adversely affected because of paternal absence per se, or whether the decrements in functioning are due to some other factor such as economic hardship, marital conflict, or lack of stability in the family (Piotrkowski, Rapaport, & Rapaport, 1987). A study by Hiew (1992) suggested that adverse effects of prolonged paternal absence (in this case, due to military duties) may be related to mothers' perceptions of loss of social support. Children reported the most intense experience of stress during the actual time of paternal absence. Thus, a variety of factors may relate to the adverse effects of prolonged paternal absence due to employment duties.

With regard to fathers' subjective experiences of their employment, job satisfaction has been found to be positively associated with children's adjustment. Even though fathers who enjoy their jobs spend less time with their children, the time they spend together is associated with a closer father-child relationship and decreased emotional/behavioral problems in children (Barling, 1990). However, paternal dissatisfaction does not appear to have a direct link to child maladjustment; rather, the father-child relationship seems to moderate the effects of paternal job dissatisfaction (Barling, 1986). Specifically, when fathers are dissatisfied with their jobs and when they have a close relationship with their children, children show heightened levels of hyperactivity or conduct disorder according to teachers' reports. Conversely, when fathers are dissatisfied with their jobs, and the father-child relationship is not very close, children do not show higher levels of teacher-reported hyperactivity or conduct disorder. Piotrkowski and colleagues (1987) suggest that information about paternal job dissatisfaction is transmitted through a close father-child relationship, and therefore rather than the close father-child relationship buffering adverse effects on the child, it may actually be the source of transmission.

Barling (1990) noted that the findings regarding paternal employment and child functioning are remarkably similar to the findings regarding maternal employment and child functioning. More research is needed that directly compares employment experiences within the same family; there is growing evidence, however, that employment of either fathers or mothers serves a similar role in relation to children's psychological adjustment.

A few interesting studies have evaluated the effects of dual-employed parents. In a study of dual-employed parents of preschool-age children, Greenberger and Goldberg (1989) found that fathers' and mothers' investment in the parental role and not their investment in the worker role was associated with their greater expectations for mature behavior in their children. Greenberger and O'Neil (1990) also found that fathers' well-being was strongly related to their children's behavioral adjustment. Specifically, fathers who rated their preschool child as having increased behavioral problems also showed greater amounts of role strain, depression, and physical symptoms. In addition, fathers who perceived the quality of out-of-home child care to be poor were more likely to report low levels of organizational commitment to their place of employment. Relatively similar results were found for mothers in dual-employed families.

With regard to role strain between employee and parental roles, O'Neil and Greenberger (1994) found that fathers who showed low employment commitment and high parental commitment felt the least amount of role strain. Mothers' levels of commitment to employment and parenting were not associated with role strain. Simon (1992) found that the majority of fathers (73%) and mothers (84%) showed high commitment to their parental identity. For both fathers and mothers, high parental commitment was associated with greater psychological symptoms when there were higher levels of parental strains. Role strain and guilt were also associated for both fathers and mothers (Shaw & Burns, 1993). Specifically, fathers felt more guilt than mothers regarding role conflicts between employment and marriage and between marriage and their own needs, whereas mothers experienced more guilt than fathers regarding role conflicts between parenting and their own needs. Fathers and mothers showed similar levels of guilt when there were role conflicts between employment and parenting, marriage and parenting, and employment and their own needs. In a national sample of African American fathers, provider role strain was associated with lowered satisfaction within the family (Bowman, 1990).

The impact of maternal and paternal employment status was investigated in regard to parental monitoring (the degree to which parents monitor their children's daily activities as reflected in the parents' ability to answer questions correctly about their children's daily activities). Crouter, MacDermid, McHale, and Perry-Jenkins (1990) found that both boys and girls between the ages of 9 and 12 were monitored to a similar degree regardless of whether they lived in a dual-income family or a single-income family. The primary difference was that mothers were significantly better at monitoring their children's daily activities than were fathers, regardless of parental employment status.

Fathers involvement with their children vis-à-vis parents' employment status may also be related to the gender of the children. Crouter and Crowley (1990) compared children in single-and dual-employed families and found that patterns of involvement and perceptions of closeness to fathers were somewhat dependent on the child's gender. For example, in single-employed families, fathers spent significantly more time with their sons than their daughters, whereas there were no differences based on child gender for fathers in dual-employed families. Regardless of parental employment status, girls felt closer to their fathers when there were increased levels of dyadic interactions but boys' feelings of closeness to their fathers were not related to the amount of father-son interaction.

Barnett and Marshall (1993) argued that fathers' concerns about their parental role have been largely ignored in studies of paternal employment and stress. They suggested that studies of employed fathers should include measures of the quality of men's parental role, the quality of men's spousal role, and the quality of men's job role in relation to children's adjustment.

PATERNAL VISITATION AND INTERACTIONS WITH CHILDREN WHO DO NOT LIVE WITH BOTH BIOLOGICAL PARENTS

Based on the numbers presented earlier on family demographics, a large number of children appear to have "absent" biological fathers. The question remains, however, as to whether "absent" can be equated with "uninvolved." Further differentiation of involvement of absent fathers should be broken down into financial involvement, physical presence with children, and emotional involvement with the children. First, parental visitation will be discussed for children who do not live with both biological parents. It is important to note that perceptions of the frequency of visitation vary according to who is asked. Seltzer and Brandreth (1994) found that noncustodial fathers reported greater frequency of visitation and more extended visits with their children than did custodial mothers.

Seltzer and Bianchi (1988) utilized the Census Bureau's National Health Interview Survey and the Child Health Supplement to investigate the amount of contact that absent (noncustodial) parents have with their children. Based on the reports of the custodial parent, they found that the majority of noncustodial parents have at least some contact with their biological children. Regarding children who live with their biological mothers, 19% have at least weekly contact with their biological fathers, 42% have some contact (up to 2 or 3 times a month), and 35% have no contact with their biological fathers (the remaining 4% showed missing data regarding paternal contact). Regarding children who live with their biological fathers, 22% have at least weekly contact with their biological mothers, 54% have some contact, and 19% have no contact with their biological mothers (the contact patterns of the remaining 5% were unknown). There were few differences in contact between noncustodial parents and their children when race and ethnicity were analyzed. Different patterns of contact emerged for two different living constellations that were investigated. Children who had recently lived with the absent parent showed more frequent contact than children who had not lived with the absent parent for many years. In addition, children who lived with an unmarried parent had more frequent contact with their absent biological parent than children who lived with their biological parent and their stepparent. Based on these patterns of visitation, Seltzer and Bianchi concluded that children appear to have sequential relationships with their parents and tend not to maintain close relationships with more than two parents or caretakers at any one time.

Mott (1990) provided gross indicators of father presence and absence in a cohort that was born between 1979 and 1983. He found that 21.5% of African American children had a father who was always present, 55.7% had a father who was always absent, and 22.8% had a father who was sometimes present and sometimes absent. The figures for non-African American children were 70.35, 8.6%, and 21.1%, respectively. For those children who did not live with their biological father, a total of 59.3% of African American children had access to a father figure (e.g., their mother's significant other or a grandfather) and a total of 61.9% of non-African American children had access to a father figure. Mott used these data to highlight that the classification of children in father-absent homes due to the nonresidential status of their biological father is erroneous due to the involvement of father figures.

Because of the different patterns of paternal involvement that are based on family constellation and custody arrangements, issues related to divorced fathers without custody, stepfathers who live with custodial mothers, single fathers with custody, and adolescent fathers will be discussed separately. To set the stage for the father-child relationships in these different family environments, first a discussion of the separation and divorce process will be provided.

Custodial Arrangements after Separation and Divorce

Although it is easy to refer to children of divorced parents as one group (e.g., research studies that involve a group of children from divorced parents and still-married parents), a variety of factors leading to separation and divorce may have an impact on the parent-child relationships after the divorce. Corley and Woods (1991) found that several factors were related to the length of time before married couples divorced. They identified a sample of over 600 couples who had recently married and collected basic demographic data from these couples. When these couples were reinterviewed seven years later, a total of 105 couples had gotten divorced. The researchers tried to determine which factors were related to length of marriage before divorce (the "tempo" of the divorce). They found that four variables accounted for 62% of the variance in length of marriage before divorce: (a) wife's employment status (whether or not she was employed), (b) husband's level of employment based on socioeconomic ratings, (c) wife's age at marriage, and (d) the number of children. A number of other factors that were assessed while the couples were still married, such as education at the time of marriage, family income, and desired number of children, did not appear to be related to length of marriage before divorce. With regard to the four factors that were related to the length of marriage before divorce, the researchers found that marriages were maintained longer when wives were not employed, when husbands' jobs were higher in status, when the couple had married at an older rather than younger age, and when there was at least one child from the marriage. Corley and Woods pointed out that these factors are consistent with most previous research into the timing of divorce.

Once the divorce proceedings are instituted, most divorcing parents have to consider custody and visitation arrangements. Because of the potential emotional turmoil due to acrimonious divorce proceedings, there has been growing interest in mediation rather than litigation when considering child custody. Emery, Matthews, and Wyer (1991) investigated the effects of mediation versus litigation, with special attention to the differing effects based on fathers' versus mothers' perspectives. In this study, divorcing parents with custody disputes were randomly assigned to either a traditional litigation process or to a mediational process. After parents had completed the proceedings (by either completing mediation—with or without an agreement, had a court-ordered decision rendered, or settled their disputes outside of court), they were interviewed by the researchers about their satisfaction with the court process, satisfaction with the court outcome, and impact of the court proceedings on parents personally, on the children, and on the father-mother relationship. At postintervention interview, fathers showed a preference for mediation over litigation in 16 of the 19 variables that were assessed. Fathers who received mediation rather than litigation were more satisfied with the court's role, more satisfied with the final decision, felt that their feelings were understood, perceived that more concern was shown for their children, and felt that more issues were settled with their former spouse. Conversely, mothers who received mediation showed no significant differences from mothers who received litigation in their ratings of any of the 19 variables.

However, these results should not be interpreted as showing that mediation is good for fathers and bad for mothers. Most of the mothers' ratings from both the mediation and the litigation groups showed relatively good satisfaction with the outcome and process of the court process. On a scale of 1 to 5 (where 1 denotes very low satisfaction and 5 denotes very high satisfaction), mothers in the mediation group showed an average of 3.7 and mothers in the litigation group showed an average of 3.9 with regard to their satisfaction with the court decisions. Also, when fathers and mothers were compared directly (collapsed across both the mediation and the litigation groups), mothers showed more favorable reactions to the custody process than fathers on 11 out of the 19 variables that were compared. Mothers showed significantly more satisfaction than fathers with the court's role, with the decision, with the amount of concern that was shown toward them, and with the decrease in problems with their former spouse. There were no significant differences on the remaining 8 variables (such as the impact of the court process on the children, having feelings understood, and reaching a lasting agreement). There were mixed findings on the impact on psychological health due to the type of court proceeding (mediation or litigation), and these results were determined to be inconclusive.

This study suggests that mediation of custody disputes has beneficial effects for fathers and has neither beneficial nor deleterious effects for mothers. Emery and colleagues suggested that alternative forms of resolution of custody disputes will need to be found that are also perceived to be advantageous for mothers. They highlighted that this study focused on resolution of custody disputes, and more work is needed to protect the interests of mothers and children with regard to payment of child support after the court decisions are made. In addition, further research needs to be conducted on the ramifications of the court process for children's well-being. It would not be unusual to find that any process that helps decrease interparental conflict would eventually have beneficial effects for children. For example, if mediation increases fathers' satisfaction with the court proceedings, decreases fathers' perceptions of conflict with their former spouse, and does not impact negatively on maternal perceptions of court proceedings, it might be expected that children would adjust better to the custody arrangements determined through mediation. However, more research is needed to test this hypothesis directly.

A step in the direction of this type of research was published by Emery, Matthews, and Kitzmann (1994) in a one-year follow-up to the Emery et al.

(1991) study. One year after mediation or litigation, fathers who participated in mediation continued to be significantly more satisfied and to provide more child support than fathers who participated in litigation. Conversely, at one-year follow-up, mothers who participated in mediation were significantly less satisfied with the settlement than mothers who participated in litigation. However, Emery and colleagues (1994) noted that this finding may have been due to the selective attrition of mothers who were initially satisfied with mediation. Unfortunately, measures of children's functioning were not included in the follow-up to this study, so the impact of mediation or litigation on children remains unclear.

Facchino and Aron (1990) conducted a study that addressed some of these issues in a sample of fathers who had been divorced for an average of 4.9 years. All the fathers had at least one-third custody of the child (at least 10 nights per month in the home), and the average custody arrangement within this sample was 66.8% physical custody for the child. Custody arrangements had been arranged by either mutual agreement ($N = 24$), mediation ($N = 16$), or litigation ($N = 16$). When paternal adjustment measures were analyzed, there were no significant differences between these three methods of custody arrangement. Fathers from the three groups did not differ significantly in their physical symptoms, their perceptions of self-worth, or their social trust of others. Unfortunately, no data were collected about the children's adjustment based on these three types of custody arrangements. Facchino and Aron pointed out that many mental health professionals have assumed that mediation is advantageous for fathers both immediately after the settlement and for many years after the settlement. However, their study suggests that there are few differences in fathers' adjustment based on these three types of custody negotiation. Because this was a relatively homogenous and actively involved group of fathers, it may be that differences would be found for these three methods of custody arrangements if the sample were more heterogenous with regard to fathers' involvement in their children's lives.

Another controversial issue regarding custody disputes involves allegations of sexual abuse by the father. Eastman and Moran (1991) reviewed the research literature on the effects of divorce and the effects of child sexual abuse for children under the age of 6 and noted that children can be traumatized both by an acrimonious divorce process and by sexual abuse. They also noted however, that a number of well-publicized cases have suggested that allegations of sexual abuse have been fabricated to gain leverage in a custody or visitation battle. They provide a thoughtful discussion of the issues related to sexual abuse allegations. When assessing these cases, Eastman and Moran suggested that the history of the parent-child relationship must be evaluated, the adjustment to separation and divorce for both children and parents must be considered, and the timing and context of disclosure of abuse must be evaluated. Whether or not there is adequate evidence of sexual abuse having occurred, they noted that therapists must become actively involved in the crisis resolution phase to help children and their parents deal with the allegations and effects of sexual abuse.

The other side of the abuse issue is what to do when children are physically abused or maltreated by their mothers. Greif and Zuravin (1989) identified the court records of 14 mothers who had been found guilty of maltreatment of their children and whose children had been placed with their biological father. There were 17 biological fathers who gained custody from these mothers (some mothers had children with more than one man). When records were reviewed, the researchers found that there were primarily three reasons fathers would get custody of their children rather than the children being put into foster care or being cared for by another relative: The mother wanted to give up custody, the child protective services agency sought out the father and encouraged his involvement, or the child chose the father. Caucasian children were more likely than African American children to be placed in the custody of their biological father. Often when fathers were given custody of their children, problems still remained. Greif and Zuravin noted that many of the fathers who were given custody of their children were themselves violent to female partners in their life or were abusing substances. They noted that only one of the 17 custodial fathers was judged by social workers to be a competent parent. Given this pessimistic outlook, Greif and Zuravin tentatively suggested that fathers continue to be considered as placement resources when mothers maltreat their children. However, social service agencies must carefully consider the strengths and weaknesses of pursuing custody with fathers who may be ill-equipped to handle full-time caretaking duties at short notice.

Although court settlements are the first step in custody disputes (with or without allegations of abuse) and financial support disputes, it is not surprising to find that not all families live by the settlement that was determined through the court system. The next sections will deal with financial support and fathers' involvement with their children after divorce, regardless of the court mandate. The primary focus will be on what type of involvement (including financial, physical, and emotional involvement) fathers have with their children depending on the family constellation after divorce or separation.

Separated or Divorced Fathers without Physical Child Custody

A number of authors have noted the abysmal rates of payment of child support from fathers who no longer reside with their children (Ellwood, 1988; Weitzman, 1988). This lack of financial support appears to be true for many fathers regardless of ethnicity and socioeconomic status. For example, in 1985, 82% of mothers with physical custody were awarded child support; however, only 54% of the noncustodial fathers paid the amount of support that was awarded (Ellwood, 1988). In 1989, 51.4% of mothers with sole custody were paid the full amount of child support that was awarded to them (U.S. Bureau of the Census, 1992). This figure differed significantly depending on the way in which child support was awarded. Whereas 70.6% of mothers who had been awarded child support on a voluntary basis received the full payment, only 42.3% of mothers who were awarded court-ordered child support received full payment of child support from the child's father (U.S. Bureau of the Census, 1992). Across both types of child support awards, the average amount of child support received was $200 a week (Weitzman, 1988). For fathers who have yearly incomes that exceed $50,000, the rate of payment of court-ordered child support payment is 90% (Okin, 1989). With the exception of these fathers with well-paying jobs, the payment of child support (whether court-mandated or not) leaves much to be desired. Failure to pay child support has been noted as one of the reasons that noncustodial fathers seem to make financial gains after divorce whereas custodial mothers and their children are harmed financially by divorce (Emery et al., 1991).

Aside from poor payment of child support, there are also low levels of other types of paternal assistance. Teachman (1991) asked divorced mothers to report on their former husbands' contributions to their children and found that 40% of divorced fathers never bought their children presents, 65% of fathers never took their children on vacation, 61% of fathers did not carry medical insurance for their children, 85% of fathers never helped their children with homework, and 75% of fathers never attended their children's school events. This lack of contribution to their children's lives has led some researchers to suggest that many fathers do not have any involvement with their children, financial or otherwise (Silverstein, 1993a). However, low payments of child support do not necessarily mean that fathers are not involved with their children in other capacities (Phares, 1993a). In addition, a number of factors appear to be related to fathers' payment of child support as well as their involvement with noncustodial children.

To ascertain patterns of payment of court-mandated child support, Paasch and Teachman (1991) analyzed factors that influence financial assistance from separated or divorced fathers who do not live with their children. They found that absence of father visitation, geographic distance between father and child, and a poor relationship with the exspouse at divorce were associated with little or no payment of child support. In contrast, higher amounts of payment and more consistent payment of child support were associated with joint physical custody, higher paternal earnings, and a voluntary child support agreement between exspouses. Additionally, fathers who consistently paid child support were likely to provide additional financial support and physical involvement, such as buying presents for the child, carrying medical insurance for the child, and attending the child's school events. Sonenstein and Calhoun (1990) interviewed both custodial and noncustodial parents and found nearly identical results as Paasch and Teachman (1991). In a comprehensive investigation of joint legal custody, Arditti (1992) found that fathers with joint custody felt closer to their children, had more contact with them, and showed greater satisfaction with custody arrangements than did fathers without joint custody. Shrier, Simring, Shapiro, Greif, and Lindenthal (1991) also found that fathers were significantly more satisfied with joint custody arrangements than sole (mother) custody arrangements.

A number of researchers have investigated fathers' involvement with their children after divorce and have attempted to understand correlates between predivorce and postdivorce father-child relationships. Ahrons and Miller (1993) found that high levels of interparental conflict and low levels of interparental cooperation were associated with low levels of father-child contact after divorce. In a national survey of over 1,000 families in the United States, Seltzer (1991) assessed three aspects of parenting after separation or divorce: Social involvement, economic involvement, and authority in child-rearing decisions. She found a wide range of visitation (social involvement), with 28.8% of fathers reporting no visits with their children in the past year, 11.7% visiting with their children once a year, 18.0% seeing their children several times a year, 14.5% reporting visits from once to three times per month, 12.2% having face-to-face contact once a week, and 15.1% of noncustodial fathers reporting having contact with their children several times a week. With regard to economic involvement, 47.0% of fathers paid some amount of child support during the previous year. With regard to fathers' authority in child-rearing decisions, 64.4% of fathers reported that they had talked with the child's mother about the child during the past year. Of the fathers who reported talking with the child's mother, 52.6% felt that they had no influence, 30.0% reported having some influence, and 17.4% reported having a great deal of influence in decisions about the child. Seltzer noted that these patterns differed for fathers who had been married to their children's mother versus fathers who had not been married to their children's mother. Divorced fathers had more social involvement, greater economic involvement, and more perceived authority in child-rearing decisions than did never-married fathers.

With regard to the factors associated with different visitation patterns after divorce, McKenry, Price, Fine, and Serovich (1992) found that noncustodial fathers of young children were more likely to have continued contact with their children when they were more satisfied with the parental role, had greater perceptions of influence over their children's lives, lived closer to their children, and had more nonconflicted contact with their children's mother. Wall (1992) found that noncustodial fathers were more likely to have greater contact with their children when there was low interparental conflict, when the original marriage was lengthy, when they were remarried, and when they rated the father-child relationship as low in conflict. In a multistate investigation, Pearson and Anhalt (1994) found that when visitation problems arose after divorce, fathers and mothers perceived the problems to be more easily resolved when there was a history of consistent payment of child support and frequent visitation between fathers and children.

Kruk (1991, 1992; reviewed in 1994) provided an intriguing discussion of the familial and personal factors that influence the father-child relationship after divorce. In a cross-national survey of 80 noncustodial fathers in Canada and Scotland, Kruk (1991, 1992) found that fathers who showed the most involvement and most attachment with their children before divorce were the most likely to lose contact after divorce. Fathers who were less involved with their children before divorce and who showed low amounts of attachment with their children before divorce tended to maintain a fair amount of contact after divorce. Although these findings might be counterintuitive, Kruk (1991, 1992) argued that psychological constraints seem to be related to highly involved fathers' disengagement from their children after divorce. Kruk (1991) noted that the majority of fathers who disengaged from their children after divorce showed signs of grief reactions including depression and resignation. Before the divorce, many of these fathers had a large part of their self-identity invested in the paternal role; after divorce, they felt that this part of themselves was gone. Many fathers perceived a threat of loss of their children, and they tended to disengage to prepare themselves for this loss, even if the loss was avoidable (Kruk, 1992). Overall, these results shed light on the psychological process that divorcing fathers appear to go through, which may be related to the decrease in involvement in their children's lives (see Arendell, 1995, for further discussion).

In addition to considering fathers' adjustment after divorce, it is important to view children's adjustment. Overall adjustment of children after parental divorce has been the subject of numerous studies and debates that are beyond the scope of this chapter. Interested readers are referred to Chapter 2, which discusses the effects of paternal absence after divorce, and Chapter 7, which discusses children's functioning after divorce. However, children's adjustment and paternal involvement with children after parental divorce has been studied and will be discussed briefly here. With regard to specific patterns of involvement and the impact on children, Healy, Malley, and Stewart (1990) conducted a comprehensive study of fathers' involvement with children after parental separation/divorce and found that the issue cannot be answered with any blanket statements of what is best for the children and parents involved. They found that although younger children and boys of any age showed higher self-reported self-esteem when paternal visitation was frequent and regular, older children and girls of any age who had regular visits with their fathers actually showed lower self-esteem according to children's self-reports. In contrast, when maternal reports of children's behavior were assessed, girls who had frequent and regular visits with their fathers showed low levels of behavior problems, whereas boys who had regular visits with their fathers showed higher levels of behavior problems.

In a study of young adolescents whose parents were divorced, Forehand and colleagues (1990) found that paternal visitation could serve as a protective factor depending on the level of interparental conflict. Based on teachers' ratings of adolescents' cognitive and social competence, adolescents in families with low levels of interparental conflict showed adequate amounts of cognitive and social competence, regardless of the level of visitation by noncustodial fathers. However, when there were high levels of interparental conflict, adolescents with low levels of paternal visitation showed low levels of cognitive and social competence, whereas adolescents with high levels of paternal visitation showed similar levels of adequate cognitive and social competence as those adolescents in low interparental conflict families. Forehand and colleagues suggested that when there are high levels of interparental conflict, frequent visitations between adolescents and their noncustodial fathers can promote cognitive and social competence in these adolescents. Conversely, when paternal visitation is low and there are high levels of interparental conflict, teachers report decrements in the young adolescents' levels of social and cognitive competence. Taken together, these studies suggest that the impact of paternal involvement after parental divorce is extremely complex and may be affected by whose perspective is investigated (who is the informant of child functioning), what type of child adjustment is measured, and the level of interparental conflict.

Another important issue in the visitation process is the quality or acrimony of the father-mother relationship after the separation and divorce. Maccoby, Depner, and Mnookin (1990) interviewed parents during the divorce process and interviewed them again 18 months after the first interview. They assessed living arrangements of the children (live with mother and visit father, live with father and visit mother, or "dual residence" where the child spends substantial time in each household), cooperation and communication between parents, and the level of conflict and hostility that remained between parents. They identified 415 families in which children lived with their mother and visited their father, 73 families in which children lived with their father and visited their mother, and 168 families in which children spent substantial amounts of time in both households. Parental dyads were categorized on one of four categories based on their pattern of coparenting: Cooperative, conflicted, disengaged, or mixed. When pattern of coparenting was analyzed to see whether there were differences based on the children's living arrangements, no significant differences emerged. Interparental discord also did not differ according to children's residential status. In other words, there were relatively equivalent rates of interparental discord in all three types of residential arrangements. Interparental discord was associated with type of coparenting relationship and this relation seems to be stable over time. Notably, parents who showed high levels of hostility at the time of divorce were significantly more likely to show conflicted coparenting patterns 18 months later. Parents who showed low levels of hostility at the time of divorce were likely to show either cooperative coparenting at follow-up or were likely to show disengaged coparenting at follow-up. Cooperative communication differed according to children's residential status. Fathers and mothers whose children had dual residence showed significantly higher amounts of cooperative communication than did fathers and mothers in mother-residence families and father-residence families. These data suggest that although parents whose children have dual residence showed greater levels of cooperative communication with each other, they also showed levels of high interparental conflict and hostility similar to that of parents whose children live in mother-residence or father-residence households.

Another issue that must be considered is what happens to the father-mother and father-child relationship when the noncustodial father remarries. Schuldberg and Guisinger (1991) interviewed noncustodial fathers who had recently remarried and asked them about their former spouse (their children's biological mother) and their current spouse (their children's stepmother). Participants had been married to their current spouse for an average of 1.9 years after having been divorced from their former spouse for an average of 4.7 years. As expected, fathers rated their former spouse more negatively than their current spouse and themselves in nearly every characteristic that was assessed, including being more aggressive, less affiliative, less nurturant, less achievement oriented, and as a more critical and less nurturing parent. With the same sample, Guisinger, Cowan, and Schuldberg (1989) reported that remarried fathers did not perceive their children to be a major source of stress in their new marriage. Rather, the remaining conflict and bitterness with their former spouse tended to be the most salient stressor that remarried fathers reported.

Along with the problems encountered by children of divorced fathers, children of divorced gay fathers face additional difficulties. It is estimated that there are between 6 and 14 million gay fathers and lesbian mothers in the United States, and these numbers may be an underestimate because of the "hidden" nature of these families (Bozett, 1987a). In her review of the functioning of children of homosexual parents, Patterson (1992) noted that the majority of children of homosexual parents were born into male-female marriages and then at some point (often after a divorce) one of the parents acknowledges a homosexual orientation. Patterson also noted that the majority of research on children of homosexual parents has been completed with children of lesbian mothers. Regardless of the sexual orientation of the parents, mothers continue to be awarded custody and to have physical custody to a greater extent than do fathers. Thus, it is even more difficult to complete research on children of gay fathers because gay fathers seem to be invisible (Bozett, 1987b).

A groundbreaking study was completed by Bozett (1987a, 1988), who interviewed 19 children of gay fathers. Six of the children were male and 13 of the children were female, with ages ranging from 14 to 35. Although Bozett (1987a) did not directly assess visitation patterns, he did assess children's strategies for interacting with their fathers, their friends, and themselves in relation to their father's sexual orientation. In another study of gay fathers, Bigner and Jacobsen (1992) found that gay fathers and heterosexual fathers showed similar parenting styles and attitudes toward fathering. Thus, gay and nongay fathers were found to have more similarities than differences in their roles as fathers. Sexual orientation of adult sons of gay fathers was found to be similar to sexual orientation of adult sons of nongay fathers (Bailey, Bobrow, Wolfe, & Mikach, 1995). Bozett (1987a) argues that further research is needed to ascertain the struggles and strengths of families with a gay father.

Stepfathers Who Live with Custodial Mothers

Aside from considering the involvement of biological fathers with their children, it is important to consider what type of involvement stepfathers have with their children. Based on vignettes of stepfathers and fathers participating in similar parenting roles, college students rated stepfathers who instituted disciplinary techniques as being more negative than biological fathers and stepfathers' appropriate affection toward their stepchildren (such as a hug) was rated as more uncomfortable to the child in the vignette than was affection from a biological father (Claxton-Oldfield, 1992). Turning to actual perceptions of stepfathers, Marsiglio (1992) studied 195 stepfathers and found that the majority (52%) reported that it was no more difficult to love their stepchildren than to love their biological children. Stepfathers were more likely to have fatherlike perceptions regarding their stepfather role if they lived with their stepchildren as well as their biological children in the same house, if they had become a father figure when the stepchildren were relatively young, and if they were happy with their relationship with their stepchildren's mother (their wife or cohabitating partner). Overall, Marsiglio found that stepfathers who reported stronger fatherlike perceptions were more likely to have a positive relationship with their stepchildren.

With regard to stepchildren's functioning, Clingempeel and Segal (1986) conducted a study of children, aged 9 to 12, who lived in either a biological mother-stepfather family or a biological father-stepmother family. To investigate these family constellations thoroughly, analyses were conducted separately for boys and girls. The researchers did not find any significant main effects for family type or child gender with regard to children's emotional/ behavioral functioning or children's self-concept. When correlations were completed within each family type, stepfather families with either boys or girls did not show significant relations between the stepfather-child relationship and child adjustment. However, stepmother families showed a number of correlations with regard to the stepmother-child relationship and child adjustment. For example, girls showed higher self-esteem when the stepmother-child relationship was more positive. For both boys and girls, a positive stepmother-child relationship was associated with lower aggressiveness and lower inhibition in children. For girls, a poor stepmother-child relationship was associated with greater numbers of visits from the noncustodial biological mother. It is unclear why the relations within stepmother families were significant whereas the majority of relations within stepfather families were not significant. Clingempeel and Segal noted that stepmother families are somewhat unusual, especially for daughters (given that the biological father would have been awarded sole custody). Therefore, these families may be more salient in their uniqueness, whereas stepfather families are more like many other types of family constellations. The researchers note the need for more research into stepfather families as well as stepmother families to assess the impact of these family constellations on children's functioning.

One other study was identified that investigated family constellations, with specific attention to stepfather families. The adjustment of seventh- and ninth-grade students was evaluated and compared for those adolescents who lived with either both of their biological parents, their biological mother and their stepfather, or their divorced, single mother (Kurdek & Sinclair, 1988). The majority of the sample (91%) was Caucasian American. Adolescents in the three family constellations did not differ significantly in their level of psychological symptoms, goal directedness, or number of school problems. Across all three types of family constellations, adolescents' showed more maladjustment when there was more family and interparental conflict, and low peer support from outside the family. Kurdek and Sinclair noted that there were more similarities than differences across these three family constellations. What appears to be important to adolescents' adjustment is the quality of familial and parental relationships, regardless of the particular living arrangement.

Because these studies have focused primarily on Caucasian stepfamilies, Fine, McKenry, Donnelly, and Voydanoff (1992) sought to establish whether similar results would be found in African American stepfamilies. Four groups were evaluated: African-American stepfather families, African-American intact families, Caucasian stepfather families, and Caucasian intact families. In general, there were more similarities than differences between these four types of families with regard to parental adjustment and child adjustment. However, African American and Caucasian stepfathers tended to rate their own lives as less satisfying, rated their stepchildren as more psychologically distressed, and rated pcorer relationships with their stepchildren than did biological fathers. When race of respondent was considered as a main effect, the analyses suggested that Caucasian stepfathers and biological fathers rated their children as more psychologically distressed than did African American stepfathers and biological fathers. Fine and colleagues surmised that there were enough similarities between African American stepfathers and Caucasian stepfathers to suggest that the previous empirical literature that used primarily Caucasian samples might reflect functioning within African American stepfather families. However, caution should be taken not to dismiss important differences between families based on race, and further studies should continue to investigate similarities and differences between stepfather families of all races and ethnicities.

Single or Divorced Fathers with Physical Child Custody

Greif and DeMaris (1990) estimated that by the end of the 1990s, nearly one million fathers will be raising their biological children by themselves. Although significantly lower than the number of single mothers who will be raising their children, this figure suggests that a substantial percentage of men are taking the majority of responsibility for the care of their children. Greif and DeMaris conducted a study of over 1,000 single fathers and found that 72% of the fathers reported feeling comfortable as a custodial parent whereas 28% reported having mixed feelings or overt feelings of discomfort in the role of a single custodial parent. Greater comfort in the role of a single father was associated with more years of sole custody and greater satisfaction with the father's social life, whereas greater discomfort was associated with a deteriorating relationship with the children. Unfortunately, this study did not include single mothers as a comparison group. However, the study does suggest that some single fathers with custody may need supportive services to help them deal with the role of primary caretaker. Greif (1987, 1992) and Pruett (1989) provided suggestions for clinicians who work with single custodial fathers. One issue that therapists must be aware of is the need for men to adjust to their status as a single parent (rather than a married parent) and to help them with their perceptions of inadequacy. In general, human fathers (Risman, 1987) as well as nonhuman primate fathers (Silverstein, 1993a) have been found to have the same potential for parental involvement as do mothers, and to have similar abilities as mothers when they are the primary caretakers of their offspring.

Greif and DeMaris (1991) also investigated payment of child support by noncustodial mothers to custodial fathers. They found that mothers were more likely to pay child support when they earned more than the custodial father, when the children were younger, when all the children were living with the father, and if the father had been actively involved in parenting during the marriage.

A salient aspect for children living in different households is what type of rules are enforced in their different households. When single fathers and mothers are compared with married fathers and mothers in families with adolescents, single fathers and mothers are found to be less restrictive than their married counterparts (Thomson, McLanahan, & Curtin, 1992). When interactions are assessed, stepfathers, stepmothers, and cohabiting male partners interacted less frequently with adolescents and reported less positive responses to adolescents than did their biological parents.

With regard to children's functioning in father-custody families, Santrock, Warshak, and Elliott (1982) reviewed early research in this area and found that children's placement with the same sex seemed to be advantageous. Specifically, girls were found to have lower competence in social behaviors when they were raised in father-custody families, and boys were shown to have more social development problems than girls in mother-custody families. In contrast, DeMaris and Greif (1992) found that fathers who had sole custody of preadolescent daughters reported fewer problems with their children than did fathers of sons only or fathers who were raising both sons and daughters. Santrock and Warshak (1986) noted that across many types of family constellations, more robust results were found for parenting strategies rather than family constellation, with authoritative parenting being associated with children's better adjustment in terms of self-esteem, maturity, sociability, social conformity, anger, and demandingness. Further research is needed to establish whether the same-sex parent-child dyad was actually advantageous or whether other factors (such as quality of the parent-child relationship) might account for the early findings in this area of research.

Adolescent Fathers

Approximately 10% of adolescent girls become pregnant each year and the majority are impregnated by boys under 20 years old (Hamburg, Nightingale, & Takanishi, 1987). Approximately 40% of the girls choose to abort the pregnancy (Cullari & Mikus, 1990). If the teenage girl decides to carry the pregnancy to term, she must decide whether to give the infant up for adoption or to raise the child. Dworkin, Harding, and Schreiber (1993) found that teen fathers and the mothers of the pregnant girls had a substantial impact on whether the girls decided to keep the child or give it up. They found that the girls' mothers were most influential in the initial plan for the pregnancy, and the birthfathers' preferences were most influential in the consistency of the plan (staying with the initial decision to keep the child or give it up for adoption). Unfortunately, these adolescents were not followed up to assess paternal involvement based on the adolescent father's wishes regarding the pregnancy.

To establish educational antecedents of teen fatherhood, Dearden, Hale, and Alvarez (1992) compared the academic and familial histories of boys who became fathers before the age of 20 and those who did not. They found that teen fathers were significantly more likely to have experienced academic problems in elementary and junior high school, to have parents who were not interested in their education, to have been evaluated negatively by teachers, and to have wanted to discontinue their education at an early age. The researchers noted that academic difficulties predated the onset of fatherhood and that these factors could be targeted for prevention efforts with young boys.

In Great Britain, adolescent boys who were raised in economically disadvantaged homes and who had older siblings were at risk for becoming teen fathers (Dearden, Hale, & Blankson, 1994). Boys raised by a single mother, boys with a relatively uninvolved father, or boys from conflicted family environments were not at greater risk to become a father in their teen years.

Danziger and Radin (1990) investigated adolescent fathers' involvement with their infants and children and reported their findings in an article entitled, "Absent Does Not Equal Uninvolved." They surveyed adolescent mothers who received Aid to Families with Dependent Children (AFDC) and who either lived alone with their children or who lived with their own parents. They did not investigate adolescent mothers who were married to or were living with their child's father. Adolescent mothers reported on paternal involvement regarding the degree to which they discussed the child with the father, the diversity of caretaking chores in which the father engaged, and the overall quality of the father-child relationship. The mean of each of these variables fell between 2.3 and 2.5, based on a 4-point scale (with 4 representing high interaction). For each of the characteristics that were assessed, significantly higher paternal involvement was found in families with younger children, in families with younger fathers, in families in which the father was employed, and in ethnic minority families. Therefore, the younger the child and the younger the father, the greater the father's involvement with the child. Regarding the findings for fathers who had been employed during the past year, it is unclear whether the greater involvement of employed fathers was due to the adolescent mother's greater likelihood of permitting employed fathers to be involved in fathering, or whether it was due to the father's increased desire and financial ability to maintain the role of a father.

The finding of greater paternal involvement in ethnic minority families was unexpected and may have been influenced by the research design. As previously noted, the research design for the presentation of results in this study only called for analysis of data for families in which adolescent mothers were not living with or married to the child's father. To further address the meaning of the findings of greater paternal involvement in ethnic minority families, Danziger and Radin conducted additional analyses and included adolescent mothers who were living with the child's father, regardless of the parents' marital status. They found that Caucasian adolescent mothers were more likely to live with (and marry) the child's father than were ethnic minority adolescent mothers. Therefore, Danziger and Radin concluded that father "absence" from the home was associated with less paternal contact for Caucasian children, but not necessarily for African American, Latino/Latina, or Native American children. These different patterns of paternal participation and involvement were found regardless of whether or not the adolescent mothers were living with their own parents. This null result means that the availability of children's maternal grandfathers and grandmothers did not seem to impact on teenage fathers' involvement with their children. Although this study added a significant amount of knowledge about the involvement of fathers who have children with adolescent mothers, the study relied on adolescent mothers' reports of fathers' contact rather than interviewing the fathers themselves. Danziger and Radin acknowledged that this was a limitation to the study and suggested that other research should also include fathers' reports of their own involvement with their children.

One such series of studies was conducted by Christmon (1990a, 1990b), who interviewed unwed African American adolescent fathers about their self-image, their image of their family of origin, and their involvement with their children. Christmon (1990b) found that adolescent fathers with higher self-esteem showed greater willingness to take responsibility for their child's care and were more psychosocially prepared to handle fatherhood. Additionally, adolescent fathers who had more positive feelings toward their family of origin showed greater parental responsibility for their own children (Christmon, 1990a).

Hendricks (1980) provided pilot data on social support networks from interviews with 20 unwed African American adolescent fathers. In response to the question, "Who would you go to first with a problem?" nearly all the adolescents (95%) reported that they would seek out the support of their family (most notably their mother and less frequently their father) in a time of need. Friends were rarely mentioned as a source of support in response to a problem and only one out of the 20 adolescent fathers mentioned that he would go to a friend first to deal with a problem. As secondary sources of social support, community resources such as teachers or the clergy were often noted by the adolescent fathers. It appeared that unwed African American adolescent fathers were aware of a variety of social supports; however, they often were not able to access support from resources outside the family.

In McAdoo's reviews (1988, 1990) of the research literature on African American adolescent fathers, he argues that economic and educational barriers often prevent adolescent fathers from becoming more involved with their children. Adolescent fathers who were economically stable and served as a provider to the family were found to be more nurturing in their interactions with their children (McAdoo, 1988). The author describes a number of effective community-based programs across the country that attempt to help African American adolescent fathers in a variety of ways (McAdoo, 1990). Programs range from teaching fathers parenting skills, to working with adolescents to change their attitudes toward women and sexuality, to helping with job training and job placement. McAdoo (1990) noted that many of these programs have been successful, but lack of funding and community support often limits the ability to maintain these programs.

Taken together, these studies show that a variety of factors appear to influence adolescent fathers' involvement in their children's lives. Many adolescent fathers express willingness to be involved with their children (Cervera, 1991; Robinson, 1988b) and to participate in outreach programs, such as parenting classes, if these were available (Bergman, 1989; Hendricks, 1980). In fact, Hendricks (1980) found that 95% of the adolescent fathers he interviewed reported that they would be interested in teenage parenting services if offered. Adolescent fathers expressed interest in services for improvement in parenting skills, sex education, job training, and job placement. Silverstein (1993a) noted that although many adolescent fathers are interested in becoming more involved with their children, community and social forces often impede their doing so. Similarly, Kiselica and Sturmer (1993) argued that far too few services are provided for adolescent fathers. In effect, society presents a mixed message by suggesting that adolescent fathers should be actively involved in their parental role without providing the resources or skills that would help them to do so.

Summary of Paternal "Absence"

Regardless of whether fathers live with their children, paternal absence does not necessarily mean that fathers and children have no contact (Mott, 1990; Phares, 1993a). There can be different levels of paternal involvement whether children live with their biological father or not. Interestingly, the labels applied to the same amount of paternal involvement from absent fathers vary widely according to the researcher. For example, Silverstein (1993a) described weekly dinners and bimonthly weekends spent together as "relatively limited" contact between noncustodial fathers and their children. Similar levels of father-child contact have been categorized as "frequent" by Healy et al. (1990) and as "very frequent" by Seltzer and Bianchi (1988). It will be important to have the children, fathers, and mothers involved in visitation arrangements help researchers label patterns of paternal involvement so that those labels reflect families' perceptions of the arrangements. In addition, further research is needed into the personal, familial, and societal forces associated with increased versus decreased paternal involvement with children whether the fathers are residential or noncustodial fathers.

CHAPTER 2

Fathers and Normative Development

This chapter will review research literature on the roles of fathers in normative development (in contrast to problematic development). Although it will cover the primary issues regarding fathers and normative child development, a thorough review of this literature is not feasible within the constraints of a single chapter. Interested readers are referred to an excellent book entitled *Fathers and Families* (Biller, 1993), which provides in-depth coverage of the roles of fathers in normative child development and to the third edition of *The Role of the Father in Child Development* (Lamb, in press).

HISTORY OF RESEARCH ON FATHERS AND NORMAL CHILD DEVELOPMENT

The fields of anthropology and sociology predated psychology in thoroughly evaluating the impact of fathers on their children and on the family. From an anthropological perspective, Mead (1949) explored the impact of fathers in the family and largely negated it. She argued, "Human fatherhood is a social invention (p. 183)," and believed that the father's role in the family was largely a biological one to enable procreation. In the field of sociology, Bernard (1981) noted that theory and research on fathering in the 1950s suggested that men provided children's role models of power and authority but that they should have little to do with the actual parenting of young children. During the 1960s, fathers were seen as important and therefore a new goal of fathering was the successful development of their children, especially their sons. During the 1970s, fathering was considered important for both the child and the adult male and therefore the impact of fathering on *fathers* became a major issue for consideration (Bernard, 1981).

In 1965, Nash published an article in *Child Development* that provided a comprehensive discussion of fathers in "contemporary culture" and the role of fathers in children's psychological development. Although the article largely has been ignored, it covered many of the issues that continue to face researchers interested in fathers and the family. Nash reviewed the limited research on fathers' and children's psychological development and argued that fathers should be included in more research studies of "parent"-child relationships. Although most of the points he made would seem reasonable (if somewhat dated) to most current-day researchers, Nash felt the need to include the following disclaimer at the end of the article: "The author, in discussing the ideas expressed in this paper, often finds himself accused of underestimating the mother's role. This paper is not to be interpreted as an attack on motherhood, but merely as a suggestion that there are other aspects of parent-child relationships than those included in the widely discussed interaction between mother and child" (p. 292). It appears that even the suggestion that fathers were important to study was taken by some as a challenge to the importance of motherhood. Nash summarized the review by suggesting that fathers appeared to have an impact on both normal and abnormal child development, and he provided an eloquent argument for the inclusion of fathers in research that investigated children's psychological development.

It wasn't until many years later that the field was again challenged to include fathers in research and theory of child development. In the early 1970s, Biller published three books about fathers and their children: One focused on fathers and children's sex roles (Biller, 1971); the second one focused on the effects of paternal deprivation (Biller, 1974); and the third investigated fathers' influences and power within families (Biller & Meredith, 1974). In 1975, Lamb published an article entitled "Fathers: The Forgotten Contributors to Child Development," and in 1976 he edited a book entitled *The Role of the Father in Child Development*. Also in 1976, Earls published an article entitled, "The Fathers (Not the Mothers)," which reviewed the sparse literature on bidirectional father-infant influences. In 1980, Henderson (1980a, 1980b) continued to call for increased attention to the nature and purpose of the roles of fathers. Since that time, the importance of fathers (as well as mothers) in the normal development of children has been highlighted in empirically based books (Berman & Pedersen, 1987; Bozett & Hanson, 1991; Bronstein & Cowan, 1988; Gerson, 1993; Hanson & Bozett, 1985; Lamb, 1981, 1986, 1987; Lewis, 1986; Lewis & O'Brien, 1987; Lewis & Salt, 1986; Mackey, 1985; Parke, 1981; Robinson, 1988a; Robinson & Barret, 1986; Rosenthal & Keshet, 1981; Russell, 1983; Youniss & Smollar, 1985), case-study oriented books (Boose & Flowers, 1989; Scull, 1992; Secunda, 1992), and even magazine articles in the popular press (Gibbs, 1993; Ingrassia, 1993; O'Reilly, 1992; Shapiro, 1987; Whitehead, 1993). For a fascinating first-person account of the development of a programmatic research career investigating fathers, interested readers are referred to Parke's (1990) eloquent description of his odyssey into research on fathering.

Although there has been a noticeable increase in research and theory regarding the roles of fathers in normative child development, many of the same issues that Nash discussed in 1965 still apply. For example, Russell and Radojevic (1992) found that only 22% of the family articles published in *Child Development* in 1985 and 1986 included fathers and this percentage was down to 20% in 1990. In 1965, Nash noted that a textbook that was touted to give "a complete account of child development from birth to maturity (p. 264)" devoted less than 3 of its 300 pages to the father's role in child development. The same underrepresentation of fathers in textbooks of child development continues. For example, fathers were mentioned specifically on only 4 out of 575 pages of text in one book of child psychology (Vasta, Haith, & Miller, 1992) and on 11 pages out of 691 pages of text in a book of developmental psychology (Berger, 1994). These two textbooks seem to be representative of other textbooks in the field. The progress that has been made in the research area of paternal influences on normative child development has not yet been thoroughly represented in textbooks. This chapter will review the research literature on the roles of fathers in normative child development, with the caveat that much more research needs to be completed and disseminated more effectively.

THE PROCESS OF BEING A FATHER

Education for Fatherhood

Before becoming parents, most women have more experience with child-care duties and are willing to spend more time caring for infants than most men (Buffo & Gustafson, 1994). A number of researchers have suggested that once men become fathers, they may intentionally spend longer hours at their place of employment to avoid family duties because they feel ill prepared and inadequate in the knowledge and skills needed for the role of a father (Levant, 1988; Price-Bonham & Skeen, 1979; Sawin & Parke, 1979). Until recently, most "parent" educational material was geared toward mothers (Bloom-Feshbach, 1981). Most books on birth and child rearing in the popular press were geared toward mothers, with little attention to fathers and the skills they needed to acquire. DeFrain (1977) noted that most popular books on child-rearing were sexist in the focus on traditional, sex-role stereotyped roles of mothers and fathers. As described earlier, in the mid-1970s when researchers were discovering the importance of fathers, books were being written for fathers to purchase in their local bookstore (e.g., Biller & Meredith, 1974; Dodson, 1974). By the 1980s and early 1990s, there was a plethora of books aimed at teaching men how to father, such as *The Father Factor* (Biller & Trotter, 1994), *Pregnant Fathers* (Heinowitz, 1982), *Black Fatherhood: The Guide to Male Parenting* (Hutchinson, 1992), *Teen Dads: Rights, Responsibilities and Joys* (Lindsay, 1993), *How to Father a Successful Daughter* (Marone, 1988), *Expectant Father* (Marshall, 1992), *How to Be a Pregnant Father* (Mayle, 1990), *The Measure of a Man: Becoming the Father You Wish Your*

Father Had Been (Shapiro, 1993), and *The Father's Almanac—Revised* (Sullivan, 1992); and aimed at describing the experience of fatherhood, such as *Fatherhood* (Cosby, 1986) and *Good Morning, Merry Sunshine* (Greene, 1985).

Most books on parenting now are geared toward both mothers and fathers, and even the revision of the classic *Dr. Spock's Baby and Child Care* (Spock & Rothenberg, 1992) emphasizes that fathers should share the daily care of the children from birth onward to establish a strong father-child relationship. Spock and Rothenberg (1992) include a section entitled "Men Need Liberating, Too" (p. 31) and suggest that when it comes to care of children and the home, "There is no reason why fathers shouldn't be able to do these jobs as well as mothers, and contribute equally to the children's security and development" (p. 27).

It is interesting to note that this "new" emphasis on teaching fathers how to care for their children is actually a rediscovered trend, albeit for different reasons. Up until the mid-1700s, books and manuals on child rearing were geared toward fathers. Families in Europe as well as in America were largely patriarchal in structure (Bloom-Feshbach, 1981; Stearns, 1991). Because fathers were seen as having the ultimate responsibility for nearly all aspects of the family, and because most preindustrial work was conducted around the home, child-rearing manuals were geared toward fathers (Griswold, 1993). However, industrialization created a separation of work and home life, and most fathers began spending more and more time away from the family home to earn a living. Historians have referred to family life in the 1800s as a time for feminization of the domestic sphere and the marginalization of fathers' involvement with their children (Griswold, 1993). By the mid-1800s, child-rearing manuals were geared toward mothers, and this trend continued for the most part until the mid-1970s.

Even with the increased focus on fathers in popular press books and child-rearing manuals, many fathers feel ill prepared to fill the role of a father. For this reason, Levant (1988) suggests that more needs to be done to help young boys and men learn about child care and children's development. He described a number of preparent, new-parent, and child-rearing programs that are offered across the United States in elementary schools, universities, community mental health agencies, health care clinics, and hospitals (especially for birthing classes and transition-to-parenthood classes). Cowan (1988) also provided a detailed description of group intervention for men who were about to become fathers. McBride (1991a) described a parent education and support program for fathers and empirically tested the effectiveness of this program. Fathers were assigned randomly to either the parent education and support program or a "wait list" control group. The education/support group met for 2 hours on 10 consecutive Saturday mornings. After the intervention was completed, fathers who participated in the education/support group reported significantly more perceived competence in the parental role, greater perceived responsibility for caretaking duties, greater personal value for child-care activities, more nonworkday interactions with their children, and more nonworkday accessibility to their children than did fathers in the control group. Fathers in the education/support group also showed lower levels of social isolation and depression than fathers in the control group (McBride, 1991b).

In addition to the assessments of perceptions and time-spent between fathers and their infants that were completed in the McBride (1991a, 1991b) study, Pfannenstiel and Honig (1991) also analyzed direct observations of postintervention father-infant interactions to assess the effectiveness of their intervention program. The study involved low-socioeconomic-status, first-time fathers whose partner was considered to be having either a high-risk or a low-risk pregnancy. The majority of the father participants were not married to the expectant mother (54% were single and 46% were married). Approximately 70% of the participants were Caucasian and the remaining 30% were not Caucasian. Within the high-risk and low-risk groups, fathers were randomly assigned to participate in a prenatal intervention program or to be in the comparison control group, which received no intervention. For those who were assigned to the intervention group, fathers received two 90-minute intervention sessions that focused on information and insights about infants. These fathers were taught what to expect from their infants and how to be sensitive to their infant's needs. The intervention consisted of didactic dissemination of information, modeling of behaviors, and role-playing of newly learned behaviors. After the birth of the infant, fathers were videotaped feeding the infant while the infant was still in the hospital (usually within 48 hours of birth) and again after the infant was discharged from the hospital (usually within 1 month after discharge). At the time of the first videotaped feeding, fathers who had received the intervention showed significantly greater overall parenting skills than fathers who had not received the intervention. Specifically, fathers in the intervention group showed greater sensitivity to their newborn, and were able to hold, feed, and respond to their newborn in a more responsive and effective manner than fathers in the control group.

At 1 month follow-up, the main effect for overall parenting skills no longer showed significant differences between the intervention and control group ($p < .06$). However, there were still significant differences in specific parenting behaviors. Fathers who received the intervention showed greater skills in holding style, verbal tone, verbal content, visual interaction, caregiving, and mood/affect than fathers who did not receive the intervention. It should also be noted that fathers in the control group showed some strengths compared with fathers in the intervention group. Fathers in the control group showed better modulation of infant distress and better response to infant satiation than did fathers in the intervention group. Overall, this intervention study showed that a relatively brief intervention (3 hours total) with fathers from low socioeconomic backgrounds, many of whom were not married to the mother of the infant, helped fathers become more responsive and sensitive to their infant's needs. Honig and Pfannenstiel (1991) provided an interesting discussion of the process of conducting this program with low-income expectant fathers.

The findings from Pfannenstiel and Honig's (1991) study that showed a few strengths of fathers in the control group suggest that learning can occur outside intervention programs. It would be interesting to conduct studies to find how fathers (and mothers) acquire skills in the caretaking of their infants and children and how these skills relate to the time involvement of both parents. Parke and Tinsley (1981) suggest that acquiring early parenting skills is greatly dependent on the amount of time that parents spend with their infant and child. Therefore, the findings of greater paternal involvement from McBride's (1991a) intervention study and the findings of fathers' greater beginning level parenting skills from the Pfannenstiel and Honig (1991) study suggest that preventive interventions with fathers can have a significant impact on the father-child relationship. McBride (1991a) argued that parent education and support programs for fathers can be an effective way of increasing involvement with their children. However, such programs are still rare. More educational efforts are needed to reach a larger number and a wider variety of fathers. In addition, Levant (1988) noted that few of these educational efforts have been tested empirically to ascertain the effects of the training sessions and to determine the methods to which fathers respond best. Therefore, efforts must continue both on the empirical research side and the educational service delivery side to ensure that fathers and prospective fathers (as well as mothers and prospective mothers) who wish to learn more about parenting are given the chance.

Transition to Becoming a Father

Before discussing fathers' transition into the parental role, it is important to consider why men become fathers. A group of working-class men were asked to provide their motivations for becoming a father (Mackey, White, & Day, 1992). The percentage of fathers and nonfathers was not provided for this study, although both were in the sample. The researchers provided nine statements (and an "other" category) that described men's motivation to become fathers, and participants were asked to rank order these nine reasons from the most important to the least important. Results of the study showed the following overall rank order that participants provided (from most important to least important reason): Children bring love and emotional satisfaction to the family; Children carry on name or bloodline; Children are fun; Children are accidents—the pregnancy just happened; Children are wanted by the wife; Children are expected by the potential grandparents; Children are expected by friends of the potential parents; Children earn money for the family and they complete chores; and Children help parents in their retirement years. There were no significant differences based on the men's age, ethnicity, or parental status.

Women also were asked to report on why they thought that men became fathers, and the distribution of answers was nearly identical to the rank order provided by men themselves. Overall, Mackey and colleagues suggested that psychological reasons, and to a lesser extent social reasons, motivate men to become fathers. An important extension of this research would be to investigate whether men's initial motivations to become fathers change over the course of their child's development.

During their partner's pregnancy, a number of expectant fathers experience couvade syndrome, in which fathers experience multiple physical discomforts that parallel the pregnant woman's physical complaints. The experience of couvade syndrome has been documented in fathers from a number of regions including the United States (Behrman, 1992) and Thailand (Khanobdee, Sukratanachaiyakul, & Gay, 1993).

Turning to the emotional and psychological transition to fatherhood, in 1957 LeMasters published a study that showed 83% of the couples in his sample could be considered in "crisis" due to the birth of their first child. The results were based on retrospective interview data with couples who recalled joy and happiness at the birth of their first child but also focused mainly on the stress and strain that it caused. This study was attacked from a variety of different angles and the findings were minimized by suggesting that the transition to parenthood might be somewhat difficult for some couples, but that it did not warrant being referred to as a crisis (Hobbs, 1965; Hobbs & Cole, 1976).

Since that time, a number of studies have been conducted to document empirically the personal and interpersonal changes that accompany the birth of a first child. Many of these studies are longitudinal, with prospective parents being identified in birthing classes and recruited into the study before the birth of their child, and then followed through until after the birth of their child (Entwisle & Doering, 1988). Often these studies have continued on for many months or years to investigate fathers' and mothers' transitions to different developmental levels of the child (see Berman & Pedersen, 1987, for a description of eight of these research projects). These studies have found that the transition to parenthood is a time of turmoil associated with risks for the fathers and mothers as individuals as well as for the marital relationship (Cowan, Cowan, Heming, & Miller, 1991). Specifically, marital satisfaction decreases from the time of pregnancy through the first year postpartum, and this decrease is not simply a function of time because childless couples do not show the same decrease over the same period (Cowan et al., 1985). Crawford and Huston (1993) found that after the birth of the first child, fathers spent less time in independent leisure activities that they had previously enjoyed, fathers and mothers spent more time in joint leisure activities that the mother had previously enjoyed, and spent less time in joint leisure activities that the father had previously enjoyed but that the mother had not previously enjoyed. With regard to sexual satisfaction after the birth of a child, Moran (1992) found that couples who gave birth at home rather than in a hospital reported greater desire for sex, frequency of sex, and greater closeness toward their spouse than did couples who gave birth in a hospital setting. These findings were consistent based on the reports of both fathers and mothers. In a sample of fathers in Greece, fathers who attended the birth of their child reported feeling emotionally closer to their infant and to the infant's mother (Dragonas, 1992).

Turning to psychological consequences associated with pregnancy and the birth of a child, there is evidence to suggest that fathers and mothers have more similarities than differences in anticipation and in response to the birth of their first child. Both fathers and mothers have been found to show emotional attachment to the fetus (Condon, 1993). In a study of couples who were experiencing either a high-risk or low-risk pregnancy, Aradine and Ferketich (1990) found that both fathers and mothers in the high-risk group showed significantly more depression and anxiety before the birth of their child than did their counterparts in the low-risk group. After the birth of the infant, however, fathers and mothers in the high-risk group did not differ significantly from their counterparts in the low-risk group. Mothers' coping with a preterm infant appears to be related to fathers' coping with the preterm birth (Chatwin & MacArthur, 1993). Both fathers and mothers showed elevated levels of anxiety and stress when their preterm infant was in the neonatal intensive care unit, and mothers showed higher levels of stress than fathers (Miles, Funk, & Kasper, 1992).

Regardless of the risk status during pregnancy, both fathers and mothers show higher levels of psychological distress (including "the blues," clinical depression, and less frequently psychosis) after the birth of their first child (Fedele, Golding, Grossman, & Pollack, 1988; Lacoursiere, 1972; Retterstol & Opjordsmoen, 1991). For fathers but not mothers, greater satisfaction with child-care arrangements when the infant is 6 months old appears to be associated with lower levels of depression and lower levels of stress (Leventhal-Belfer, Cowan, & Cowan, 1992). Mothers', but not fathers', marital satisfaction was significantly related to satisfaction with child-care arrangements when the firstborn child was 42 months old (Leventhal-Belfer et al., 1992). There is evidence that support from the new father's and new mother's own parents (i.e., the infant's grandparents) can help significantly in the transition to parenthood (Hansen & Jacob, 1992).

Along with the investigation of the impact of a firstborn child on marital satisfaction and on fathers' and mothers' psychological functioning, there has also been interest in the changing perceptions of paternal competence due to the birth of the first child. Entwisle and Doering (1988) interviewed first-time fathers and mothers about the father's abilities. Fathers and mothers were interviewed approximately 1 month before and 1 to 2 months after the birth of their child. Entwisle and Doering found that mothers rated fathers as significantly more competent than fathers rated themselves at both points in time. However, both fathers' and mothers' ratings of paternal competence decreased from the prenatal to the postnatal assessment. This drop in perceived competence as a father is similar to decreases in perceived competence that have been shown in new mothers (Reilly, Entwisle, & Doering, 1987).

After summarizing research on paternal and maternal parenting skills with infants, Parke and Tinsley (1981) concluded that there are no differences in infant caretaking skills when the infant is born. Fathers and mothers appear to do equally well or equally poorly. However, through providing daily care of infants, mothers acquire more skills in what might be considered "on-the-job training." This perceived skill, therefore, appears to be due to mothers' greater time involvement and caretaking responsibilities for their infants (Parke & Tinsley, 1981). Both fathers and mothers have been found to gain sensitivity and competence in determining their infants' needs over the first year of the child's life, which suggests that fathers and mothers become more competent with experience (Belsky, Gilstrap, & Rovine, 1984). By the child's third year of life, fathers who are more involved in their children's daily lives report higher levels of competence as a father and higher levels of commitment to the family (Roopnarine & Ahmeduzzaman, 1993). Overall, the research on transition to fatherhood and fathers' skills suggests that although there are a number of positive aspects of the transition to fatherhood, there are also a number of personal and interpersonal risks associated with becoming a father (as well as becoming a mother).

The majority of the studies conducted on the transition to fatherhood have been conducted with primarily middle-class, Caucasian samples. For example, in the eight transition-to-fatherhood research projects described in Berman and Pedersen (1987), six of the studies utilized solely white samples, with the other two studies including less than 15% ethnic minorities in their samples. Out of these eight projects, four samples could be categorized as middle to upper-middle class, three samples were categorized as middle to lower-middle class, and one sample showed a wide range of SES. In an effort to investigate differing levels of SES on the transition to fatherhood, Entwisle and Doering (1988) recruited a sample in which half the participants were from working-class backgrounds and half the participants were from middle-class backgrounds (based on the social class in which the mothers in the study were raised). However, even in the working-class sample, mothers' and fathers' average education was over 13 years (suggesting at least some college). In addition, all the participants in the study were Caucasian. Obviously, there is a need to investigate the transition-to-fatherhood process for more ethnically and socioeconomically diverse samples. To date, this research is similar to far too many other areas of research in which the participants' section says, "Most of the subjects were white and middle class" (Graham, 1992).

The Psychological Consequences of Being a Father

In keeping with traditional patterns of research that emphasize men as wage earners rather than as fathers, there has been a significant amount of research on the relation between men's subjective experiences of their employment and their psychological health but little work that investigates the relation between men's experiences of being a father and their psychological health. One study that did investigate this issue was conducted by Barnett, Marshall, and Pleck

(1992b) outside the Boston area with 300 married couples. The sample consisted of parents as well as nonparents, all of whom were employed and most of whom were middle class. Because of the towns in which participants were recruited, the majority of the sample (97%) was Caucasian, with only a small number of participants who were Latino/Latina, African American, and Native American. Barnett and colleagues investigated the differential impact of job-role quality, marital-role quality, parental-role quality, and parental status (being a father or not) on men's level of psychological symptoms. They found that lower job-role quality, lower marital-role quality, and lower parental-role quality were all significantly related to greater levels of psychological distress with similar magnitudes (all correlations were between .35 and .38). Marital-role quality and parental-role quality were significant predictors of men's psychological distress above and beyond the level of job-role quality. This was true for fathers as well as nonfathers given that parental status was not related to men's psychological distress. This study suggests that men's perceived quality of their marital role and their parental role moderates the relation between job-role quality and psychological distress. It will be important to conduct this type of study with samples that are more heterogeneous in socioeconomic status and ethnicity. Nevertheless, this study is a step in the direction of determining the psychological impact of fatherhood on fathers.

Another line of research that has investigated the psychological consequences of being a father has focused on families in which the traditional roles of father and mother have been reversed so that fathers take primary responsibility for taking care of the children and the household. Pruett (1993) found that highly involved fathers showed higher levels of self-esteem and had spouses who were more satisfied with their marriage. In a study of nontraditional families in Australia, Russell (1983) found that many fathers reported difficulty with adjusting to the demands of child care and housework. Like most traditional mothers, 45% of the fathers in Russell's sample had difficulty with the monotony, boredom, physical work, and lack of adult contact that is associated with being a full-time caretaker. Another factor that was often cited by both fathers and mothers in nontraditional families was the social disapproval that they felt from friends and extended family members. However, there were also positive personal benefits to being highly involved fathers, including increased self-esteem, greater confidence and comfort with the fathering role, a closer father-child relationship, and a change in attitudes toward the importance of children's welfare and the family.

Similar results have been found for highly involved fathers in a number of other countries, including the United States (Radin, 1981a), Israel (Sagi, 1982), and Sweden (Lamb, Frodi, Hwang, Frodi, & Steinberg, 1982). There appear to be mixed results regarding marriages in which the husband is primary caretaker. Approximately 45% of the parents in Russell's (1983) sample reported positive changes in their marital relationship due to their nontraditional lifestyle, including greater sensitivity, understanding, and equality. However about 40% of the parents reported negative consequences, such as greater conflict, dissatisfaction with the marriage, and problems due to a rushed lifestyle (e.g., being tired, irritable, and not having enough time to spend together as a couple). In summarizing the somewhat limited research on nontraditional families, Russell (1986b) noted that there are both positive and negative personal and interpersonal consequences to greater paternal responsibility and involvement in children's lives. Further research will be needed to ascertain the factors that lead to positive versus negative consequences of greater paternal involvement in children's day-to-day care.

PATERNAL INFLUENCES IN NORMATIVE CHILD DEVELOPMENT

Infancy

Fathers and Infant Temperament

Research on infant temperament largely has been influenced by Bates's (1980) suggestion that difficult infant temperament is a social perception that has both objective and subjective components. In keeping with this suggestion, much of the recent research on infant temperament has focused on the possibility that prenatal expectancies of the infant influence later reports of infant temperament and has explored factors that affect parents' perceptions of infant temperament. Although the bulk of research continues to be completed with mothers (e.g., Zeanah, Keener, & Anders, 1986), a growing number of studies have included fathers in the investigation of perceptions of infant temperament. For example, paternal alcohol use and maternal depression were found to be associated with parental perceptions of negative infant temperament (Eiden, Leonard, & McLaughlin, 1994). Evidence is accumulating that both fathers' and mothers' expectancies of infant temperament before the birth of their child are significantly related to fathers' and mothers' ratings at 3 months postpartum (Mebert, 1991; Wolk, Zeanah, Garcia-Coll, & Carr, 1992). When parents' ratings of infant temperament are compared with observers' ratings, both fathers' and mothers' ratings are significantly related to observers' ratings of unsoothable and negative dimensions of infants' behavior but not of the sociable and positive dimensions of the infants' behavior (Wolk et al., 1992). Factors such as maternal prenatal perceptions of temperament and paternal attachment to the fetus seem to influence postnatal perceptions of temperament above and beyond the behavior that is evident from observers' ratings of the infant (Wolk et al., 1992). Overall, fathers' and mothers' ratings of infant temperament appear to be influenced both by the infant's actual temperament and by the parents' earlier perceptions of the infant. These findings are in keeping with Bates's (1980) argument that infant temperament is influenced by both objective and subjective aspects and that infant temperament is best considered a social perception.

Research on infant temperament has been extended into research on child and adolescent temperament. For example, preschoolers' temperament was rated similarly by fathers, mothers, and preschool teachers (Jewsuwan, Luster, & Kostelnik, 1993). With older children, Bezirganian and Cohen (1992) conducted a longitudinal study that followed families over a 10-year period (from the time the children were an average of 6 years old until they were an average of 16 years old). With regard to the development and maintenance of difficult temperament, low father-daughter closeness, high mother-son punishment, and high mother-son control were associated with increases in difficult temperament. No significant relations were found for difficult temperament and the father-son or mother-daughter relationship. In general, boys showed greater levels of difficult temperament than girls during late childhood and early adolescence, but this gender difference was no longer evident in later adolescence. This study suggests that the research on fathers and temperament in infancy can be extended to the child's temperament during later stages of development.

Infant-Father Attachment

Infants as young as 6 weeks appear to act differently with their fathers and mothers than they do with strangers, as reflected by their facial expression and limb movements (Dixon et al., 1981). This differentiation between parents and strangers suggests the early groundwork for attachment. Most research on parent-infant attachment has been conducted when infants are between 6 and 24 months old, and the exploration and definition of attachment primarily has been informed by the work of Bowlby (1969) and Ainsworth, Blehar, Waters, and Wall (1978). In general, attachment research has focused on whether infants greet, seek proximity with, and protest separations from their parents. Work specific to fathers and infant attachment primarily has investigated whether infants show attachment to their fathers, and if so, how infant-father attachment differs from infant-mother attachment. In a comprehensive review of infant-father relationships, Lamb (1981) concluded that infants in two-parent families show strong attachments to both mothers and fathers. However, when infants are placed in a stressful situation, they sometimes show preferences for mothers rather than fathers, depending on the infant's age. In a stressful situation, 12- and 18-month-old infants present a hierarchy of attachment preference that shows a stronger attachment to their primary caretaker (usually the mother). This stronger attachment to mothers is not evident in 8- or 24-month-olds, even in a stressful situation with access to both parents. The hierarchy of attachment figures appears only during a brief period, and at other times it appears that infants can show similar levels of attachment to their fathers as well as their mothers. Lamb also highlighted that this hierarchy of attachment figures depends on the types of behavior being assessed in the infant.

The research just described shows infant preference for mothers when the infants are distressed during a certain developmental period. However, when affiliative behavioral measures are used (e.g., measuring the infant's smiling and vocalizing behaviors), infants tend to show a preference for their fathers throughout the first 2 years of life (Clarke-Stewart, 1978). This higher level of affiliative behaviors has been attributed to the relative novelty of fathers (all of whom were employed full-time in this sample) and the tendency for fathers to elicit more affiliative interactions with their infants than do mothers (Lamb, 1981). This series of research studies suggests that it is important to distinguish between attachment behaviors and affiliative behaviors when discussing infants' responses to their fathers and mothers.

Since Lamb's (1981) review, research on infant-father and infant-mother relationships has continued, with an emphasis on infant attachment styles and the meaning of attachment rather than on affiliative behaviors toward their parents (MacDonald, 1992). The question of whether infants show similar or different attachment to their fathers versus their mothers has remained a central issue in research on infancy. To address this question, Fox, Kimmerly, and Schafer (1991) conducted a meta-analysis of the 11 studies that investigated the concordance of infant-father and infant-mother attachment styles using the Strange Situation classification paradigm to assess infant attachment. Early proponents of the Strange Situation classification system argued that the lack of concordance between infant-father and infant-mother attachment styles supported the use of the Strange Situation as a measurement of attachment style and also argued against the idea that infant temperament influenced the quality of attachment security (Main & Weston, 1981). In the eleven studies that Fox and colleagues (1991) utilized for the meta-analysis, sample sizes ranged from 32 to 132, most of the infants were 12 months of age, and there was a relatively equal distribution of male and female infants. Although maternal and paternal employment were not mentioned in many of the original studies, it appears that some of the mothers were employed and the assumption is that nearly all the fathers were employed. Six studies were based in the United States, and the other studies took place in Sweden, Israel, Germany (two samples), and the Netherlands. Ethnicity and socioeconomic status were not described for the samples in the 11 studies. Parental marital status also was not explicitly stated, although it is assumed that all the parental dyads were married.

The results of the meta-analysis showed consistent evidence for concordance between infant-father and infant-mother attachment styles. Fox et al. analyzed this issue in a variety of ways and found that infants who were classified as secure with one parent were unlikely to be classified as insecure with the other parent; the type of insecurity that was evident with one parent was similar to the type of insecurity that was evident with the other parent; and when an infant was classified as secure, the subcategory classification of security was similar for both parents. These results suggest that infants show the same kind of attachment to both fathers and mothers. Similar results have been found when comparing full-term and very low birthweight preterm infants (Easterbrooks, 1989).

Fox et al. discussed two plausible explanations for these results that suggest concordance between infant-father and infant-mother attachment styles. First, parental dyads may show similar types of parenting behaviors (including responsivity and sensitivity to their infants), and these behaviors increase the likelihood of similar attachment to both parents. In essence, parental concordance of parenting style would lead to concordance in infant-parent attachment style. This hypothesis is supported by Belsky and Volling's (1987) findings that paternal and maternal responsive behavior was significantly correlated when infants were 1, 3, and 9 months of age. Fox et al. also suggested that the results of the meta-analysis may be due to the infant's temperament rather than the infant's attachment style per se. The Strange Situation paradigm actually may be strongly influenced by the infant's temperament (e.g., tendency to cry on separation regardless of from whom the infant is being separated), and therefore the concordance between infant-father and infant-mother attachment is really based on the infant's temperament. This hypothesis is supported by findings that infants react to frustrating stimulus situations in similar ways throughout their first year of life. For example, 2-day-old infants who cried in response to mildly frustrating situations were more likely to cry when presented with a novel situation when they were 5 months old (Stifter & Fox, 1990). Fox and colleagues noted that both of these hypotheses may help explain the results of the meta-analysis. They suggested that further research is needed to ascertain why infants show concordant attachment styles to their fathers and mothers. It will also be important to investigate how paternal or maternal absence influences the concordance between infant-father and infant-mother attachment styles.

Not all researchers have come to the same conclusion of concordant infant attachment styles with their fathers and mothers. For example, Cox, Owen, Henderson, and Margand (1992) found that there was a small but insignificant correlation ($r = .32$ with a sample size of 32 families) between infant-father and infant-mother attachment scores. Although they noted a similar distribution of infant-father and infant-mother scores, they concluded that infant-father and infant-mother attachments within marital dyads are independent from each other. Probably because of the overlapping lag time for publication and the time that it takes for articles to appear in print, Cox et al. (1992) did not include the Fox et al. (1991) meta-analysis in their review of infants' attachment to their fathers and mothers, and therefore they did not comment on the evidence in support of infants' similar attachment to their fathers and mothers. The Fox et al. meta-analysis appears to provide strong evidence that infants show similar types of attachment to their fathers and mothers; however, the debate on this issue will undoubtedly continue. Volling and Belsky (1992b) noted that, although there may be high concordance between infant-father and infant-mother attachment, there may be different precursors to these attachment styles for fathers versus mothers. They argued that even when concordance is found between infant-father and infant-mother attachment, researchers should not automatically assume that the antecedents of infant-mother attachment can be generalized to explain the antecedents of infant-father attachment.

Along with the investigation of concordance of infant-father and infant-mother attachment, researchers have also investigated the factors that influence attachment. Factors such as marital harmony and personal stress have been found to affect both fathers and mothers in the way that they interact with their infants and hence influence the style of attachment exhibited by the infant. Cox, Owen, Lewis, and Henderson (1989) assessed marital closeness and intimacy prenatally and then assessed parental attitudes and behaviors when the infant was 3 months old. They found that when fathers were in close/confiding marriages, they had more positive attitudes toward their infants and toward their paternal role than fathers in distant/nonconfiding marriages. Mothers in close/confiding marriages were warmer and more sensitive with their infants than mothers who were in distant/nonconfiding marriages. Cox et al. pointed to the importance of paternal and maternal attitudes and behavior on the security of infant-father and infant-mother attachment. Parental stress that is exhibited prenatally can also influence the quality of parent-infant interactions. Noppe, Noppe, and Hughes (1991) assessed fathers' and mothers' vulnerability to stress, expectations for parenting stress, and low power attributions during pregnancy and then conducted in-home observations of infant-father and infant-mother interactions when the infants were 4 months old. They found that fathers and mothers did not differ in prenatal levels of stress vulnerability, expectations for parenting stress, attributions of low power, observed levels of noninvolvement, distress, and basic care when the infants were 4 months old. The only observed difference between fathers and mothers was that fathers showed significantly more reciprocal interaction with their infants during the 30-minute observations.

With regard to prenatal stress predicting the quality of parent-infant interactions, Noppe et al. (1991) found that fathers' prenatal stress more consistently influenced infant-father interactions than did mothers' prenatal stress on infant-mother interactions. For example, prenatal stress, expectations for stress, and attributions of low power significantly predicted fathers' basic care interactions during the observation sessions and accounted for 43% of the variance for basic care. For mothers, the same three variables measured prenatally only accounted for 2% of the variance in basic care interactions during the observation sessions. Noppe and colleagues concluded that prenatal stress seems to influence infant-father interactions to a greater extent than infant-mother interactions, although there was never a direct test of the differential impact of paternal versus maternal prenatal stress.

Postnatal parental stress also has been found to be related to both infant-father and infant-mother attachment. In a study of attachment styles of 18-month-old infants, Jarvis and Creasey (1991) found that fathers' and mothers' parenting stress was significantly associated with insecure attachments in infants. In addition, fathers' and mothers' use of positive reappraisal as a coping strategy served as a mediator to decrease the likelihood of insecure infant-father and infant-mother attachment in the presence of high levels of paternal and maternal stress. Jarvis and Creasey concluded that psychological separation (inferred from higher levels of parental stress) was more impactful than physical separation (due to out-of-home child care on a daily basis) on infant-father and infant-mother attachment security.

Not surprisingly, parenting behavior and attitudes that are evident early in the infant's life also appear to influence attachment style that is assessed a number of months later. Cox and colleagues (1992) investigated paternal and maternal attitudes and behaviors that were assessed when the infant was 3 months old and sought to predict infant-father and infant-mother attachments that were assessed when the infant was 12 months old. For both fathers and mothers, security of attachment when infants were 12 months old was predicted from the quality of interactions when infants were 3 months old. Fathers and mothers who showed positive and physically affectionate behaviors with their 3-month-old infants tended to have infants who were securely attached to them when the infants were 12 months old. Additionally, fathers' positive attitudes about the infant and the parental role were predictive of infants' greater security of attachment when the infants were 12 months old. Mothers' attitudes about the infant and the parental role were not significantly related to later attachment security. This study suggests that security of parent-infant attachment when infants are 12 months old is related to earlier paternal and maternal behaviors, as well as paternal attitudes. Although some differences were found in the associations for infant-father and infant-mother attachment, Cox and colleagues noted many similarities in early parenting behaviors and later infant-parent attachment security. Child-father and child-mother attachment has also been investigated beyond the period of infancy into toddlerhood (Fagot & Kavanagh, 1993; Rosen & Rothbaum, 1993), the preschool years (Cohn, Cowan, Cowan, & Pearson, 1992), and even into late adolescence (Benson, Harris, & Rogers, 1992).

There is overwhelming evidence that infants show attachment to their fathers in the same ways that they show attachment to their mothers (Fox et al., 1991). Based on the large number of studies that have compared infant-father and infant-mother interactions, there appear to be more similarities than differences in the ways that fathers and mothers interact with and connect with their infants.

Gender Role Socialization

Gender roles are considered the extent to which an individual exhibits behaviors and attitudes that are consistent with the societal expectations for that gender. Gender roles can be considered the degree of sex-typing that is present in a child, which is also sometimes referred to as a child's sex role (Basow, 1992). Gender roles are distinguished from gender identity in that gender identity refers to children's knowledge of their gender, awareness that their gender is unchangeable, and psychological satisfaction with their gender (Money & Ehrhardt, 1972). Although Lamb and colleagues (1985) argue that gender identity is of greater importance than gender role, the majority of research in parental influences in this area has been conducted on parental impact on gender role rather than gender identity.

The majority of research on fathers' influences on children's gender role development and sex-typing has utilized the "father-absent" research paradigm, which compares children who do not live with their fathers with children who do live with their fathers (Stevenson & Black, 1988). The results of gender role socialization research based on father-absent homes will be discussed later in the chapter. In this section, the scant research that directly investigates paternal influences on children's gender role socialization will be reviewed.

Bronstein (1988) noted that fathers and mothers can influence gender role socialization through both direct and indirect processes. Parental direct effects on gender role socialization can take the form of direct communication of cultural norms and values (e.g., teaching sons to drive a tractor and teaching daughters to sew), verbally communicating and reinforcing appropriate gender-role behaviors (e.g., telling sons not to cry and praising daughters who sit in a "ladylike" manner), and structuring children's environment to elicit gender-specific behaviors and self-perceptions (e.g., providing sex-typed toys and assigning sex-typed chores to their sons and daughters). Parents' indirect effects on gender role socialization can include the ways in which parents relate to their children (e.g., amount of time spent and types of activities engaged in with sons vs. daughters) and the ways in which parents model gender-based behaviors (e.g., fathers providing prototypes of male behavior and mothers providing prototypes of female behavior for their children). Biller (1981b) and Lamb and colleagues (1985) also note that children's gender roles are influenced by socializing agents other than parents, such as peers, teachers, and the media.

Early research on parental socialization of gender roles appeared to be concerned with fathers' and mothers' abilities to raise gender-appropriate sons and daughters, and most of the studies addressed gender roles of children in preschool or early elementary grades (Biller, 1981b). A number of studies investigated paternal masculinity in relation to sons' masculinity and daughters' femininity, with the assumption that greater masculinity in sons and greater femininity in daughters were desirable outcomes. Contrary to what might be expected from a straight social learning perspective, fathers who scored high on masculinity did not necessarily have sons who showed high levels of masculinity. Rather, significant associations between fathers' and sons' masculinity were found only when fathers also showed warmth and nurturance toward their sons (Mussen & Rutherford, 1963; Payne & Mussen, 1956). In fact, paternal nurturance and involvement in child rearing appeared to be more important than paternal masculinity in the development of masculinity in sons (Sears, Maccoby, & Levin, 1957). Paternal masculinity was also associated with greater femininity in daughters (Deutsch, 1944; Heilbrun, 1965; Mussen & Rutherford, 1963), although paternal warmth, nurturance, and involvement in child rearing were associated with greater femininity in daughters regardless of the level of paternal masculinity (Johnson, 1963). Overall, the early research on gender-role socialization suggested that paternal masculinity and paternal nurturance were associated with greater sex-typing in sons and daughters.

In the mid-1970s (Bem, 1974), researchers began to focus on paternal characteristics that were related to children's androgyny and lower levels of sex-stereotyped behaviors. Although there are still research projects that investigate only the associations between masculinity in fathers and sons, and femininity in mothers and daughters (Juni & Grimm, 1993), the majority of research has moved on to investigate parental behaviors that are related to children's gender-related behaviors. Research on paternal influences on gender-role socialization suggests that highly involved, nurturant fathers have children who hold less stereotyped gender beliefs (Pruett, 1987; Weisner, Garnier, & Loucky, 1994; Williams, Radin, & Allegro, 1992). Nurturant, nontraditional fathers have also been found to have school-age daughters with higher self-esteem than do traditional fathers (Levant, Slattery, Loiselle, Sawyer-Smith, & Schneider, 1990). In addition, when fathers and mothers convey egalitarian beliefs in both their attitude and their behavior, their 6-year-old children show increased knowledge of diversity of job opportunities and increased awareness of non-sex-typed objects than children of nonegalitarian parents (Weisner & Wilson-Mitchell, 1990). In an Israeli sample, Barak, Feldman, and Noy (1991) found that mothers' but not fathers' traditionality of occupation was related to greater traditionality of sons' and daughters' interests in future occupations. In a study of retrospective reports of parenting received when growing up, Binion (1990) surveyed 123 African American women about their own current level of psychological androgyny. She found that androgynous women were more likely to report positive identification with both their father and their mother than women characterized by other gender roles.

An important issue in the investigation of parental socialization of gender role is the extent to which fathers and mothers treat their sons and daughters in similar or different ways. To review this issue through quantitative rather than qualitative means, Lytton and Romney (1991) conducted a meta-analysis of parents' differential socialization of boys and girls. They identified 172 studies that analyzed paternal and maternal socialization practices for boys and girls separately. Contrary to other narrative reviews (e.g., Bronstein, 1988; Siegal, 1987), Lytton and Romney found very few significant differences in parental treatment based on the child's gender. Most effect sizes were small and insignificant. In studies from the United States and from other Western countries, the following areas of parental socialization were found not to differ for boys and girls: amount of interaction, encouragement of achievement, warmth, encouragement of dependency, restrictiveness, and discipline. Additionally, clarity/reasoning was found not to differ based on studies in the United States, and there were no studies of clarity/reasoning from other Western countries. The only primary area of socialization that was found to differ for boys and girls is the encouragement of sex-typed activities. Although this area was not studied in other Western countries, the findings from 20 studies conducted in the United States provided evidence that fathers and mothers are likely to encourage their sons and daughters to engage in sex-typed activities. Although the finding of differential encouragement of sex-typed activities was robust (it withstood a number of secondary analyses), it was considered a fairly modest difference. Specifically, the magnitudes of the effect sizes ranged from one-third to one-half of a standard deviation, and therefore parental encouragement of sex-typed activities should not be seen as an overwhelming tendency.

Lytton and Romney also provided a micro-analysis of areas of socialization and found that in studies conducted in the United States, parental socialization practices did not differ between boys and girls for amount of verbal interaction, motor stimulation, joint-combined play, encouragement of achievement in mathematics, material rewards, nonphysical discipline, physical discipline, and discouragement of aggression. No subsidiary areas of socialization showed significant differences in studies conducted in the United States. In studies from other Western countries, there was no difference in nonphysical discipline of boys versus girls; however, there was a significant difference that showed greater paternal and maternal physical punishment of boys when compared with girls. This difference was found only for studies conducted in other Western countries and not for studies conducted in the United States. This finding suggests that American parents are more egalitarian in their use of physical punishment, whereas fathers and mothers in other Western countries are more likely to use physical punishment on their sons than their daughters. This meta-analysis investigated only parents' differential use of physical punishment on boys versus girls, not the actual amount of use of physical punishment in the United States versus in other Western countries.

It should be noted that when no differences were found in the differential treatment of boys and girls, it may have been because of variability of results in opposite directions. Because the meta-analytic technique combines effect sizes from a variety of different studies, if some studies found positive effects in a particular area of socialization but other studies found negative effects in that same area of socialization, then the result would show nonsignificant differences that would mask the diversity of results from those studies. Four areas of socialization were noted by Lytton and Romney to have relatively equal amounts of studies showing results in opposite directions. When comparing the amount of studies in the boys-more-than-girls direction versus the girls-more-than-boys direction, amount of interaction (35 vs. 39), encouragement of achievement (14 vs. 8), warmth (27 vs. 36), and clarity of communication (4 vs. 9) were the four areas in which a null result may have been due to the variability of results in opposite directions. This is not to suggest that the findings of the meta-analysis are not valid, but rather to point out the extreme fluctuation of findings in these areas of parental socialization.

When fathers' and mothers' behaviors were compared for each area of socialization, fathers were found to make greater gender distinctions than mothers in their behavior toward their children. This tendency was evident in a number of areas of socialization, but the only significant difference was in the area of restrictiveness. Specifically, fathers were more restrictive with their children than were mothers. The suggestion that fathers make greater differentiations between their children based on gender is consistent with other reviews of fathers' and mothers' behavior with their children (Bronstein, 1988; Siegal, 1987).

Other factors about the studies were analyzed to ascertain whether there were any "moderating variables" that would influence the interpretation of results in parents' differential socialization of boys and girls. These variables can be categorized into three general areas for discussion: (a) characteristics of the research participants (age and social class/educational level), (b) characteristics of the research design (sample size and method of data collection—observational vs. self-report), and (c) characteristics of the presentation of research results or of the researchers themselves (publication status, year of publication, quality of the article, and gender of the first author).

Regarding characteristics of the research participants, there was a trend toward greater differential treatment of younger boys and girls versus older boys and girls. There was a nonsignificant trend in this direction for overall socialization, and there were significant differences based on the age of children for the individual socialization areas of disciplinary strictness and encouragement of sex-typed activities. Overall, effect sizes decreased with child's age, suggesting that parents tend to decrease the amount of differential treatment of their children as the children grow older. No significant differences or nonsignificant trends were found based on research participants' social class or educational level. Lytton and Romney noted that they were not able to analyze for same-gender effects (mother favoring daughter, father favoring son) or cross-gender effects (mother favoring son, father favoring daughter) due to the complexity of the meta-analytic procedures. However, they suggested that these same-gender and cross-gender effects will need to be analyzed in future studies of parents' differential socialization of boys and girls.

With regard to characteristics of the research design, sample size was not related to effect sizes in any area of parental socialization. This suggests that sample size was not a primary factor that influenced the results of the study. However, there were some significant differences based on the method of data collection. The authors had hypothesized that larger effect sizes would be found in observational or experimental studies (as opposed to studies based on interviews or questionnaires) because parents might minimize their self-reported differences in gender-based treatment of their children while still showing these differences in direct observational tasks. The meta-analysis provided tentative support for this hypothesis by showing nonsignificant trends in the expected direction for most of the areas of socialization, and significant differences based on the areas of restrictiveness and disciplinary strictness. These findings suggest that for many areas of parental socialization practices, and especially for parental restrictiveness and disciplinary strictness, researchers may find greater differences in treatment of boys and girls when using direct observations rather than self-report measures.

There were mixed results regarding the moderator variables that were related to the presentation of research results or characteristics of the researchers themselves. Across all areas of socialization, publication status (whether the study was published in a journal or book vs. being an unpublished dissertation or conference presentation) was not related to effect size. That effect sizes did not differ according to publication status was heartening because meta-analyses of gender differences have been criticized for primarily utilizing published research that may bias the results in the direction of finding gender differences rather than null results (Hyde & Linn, 1988). Across all areas of parental socialization, the year of publication was not related to effect size. This null result suggests that no changes in socialization practices were discernible over the time period that was investigated (1950–1987). Although Lytton and Romney had hypothesized that smaller effect sizes would be found in more recent years due to a greater emphasis on egalitarian child-rearing practices, no such trend was found. Effect sizes were found to increase as the quality of the study increased. Determination of the quality of the study was based on its internal validity, which included ratings of the carefulness and appropriateness of data collection methods and the appropriateness of statistical analysis. Although there was a tendency toward larger effect sizes in higher quality studies, Lytton and Romney concluded that the lack of significant findings in the overall study was not due to poor-quality articles. Gender of the first author was found to be somewhat related to the effect sizes that were found. There was a near-significant trend for females to be first authors on studies that showed larger effect sizes. This tendency was significant for the socialization areas of encouragement of dependency and encouragement of sex-typed activities. This suggests that female first authors were more likely than male first authors to publish studies that showed greater encouragement of girls' dependency and that showed significant differences in parental encouragement of sex-typed activities. This finding must be viewed with great caution because the majority of the studies in this meta-analysis had multiple authors and research teams were often made up of females as well as males, regardless of who was listed as the first author.

Even though the analysis of moderator variables provides interesting insights and details to the meta-analysis, Lytton and Romney pointed out that none of the primary findings of the meta-analysis were altered by analyses of moderator variables. Therefore, the findings of few significant differences in parental socialization of boys and girls can be considered robust. Because so few differences could be found in the way that parents treat their boys and girls, Lytton and Romney speculated as to what other factors might lead to the gender differences that are evident in children and adults. They suggested that factors other than parental socialization, such as imitating same-sex adult models, influences of peers and larger society, and biological predispositions may account for some of the documented gender differences. However, they stressed that their meta-analysis serves to refute one hypothesis (parental socialization leads to gender differences) rather than to support other possible hypotheses. This meta-analysis showed that, with the exception of encouraging sex-typed activities, neither fathers nor mothers show strong differential socialization practices with their boys and girls. Further, although fathers tend to be more restrictive than mothers with their sons and daughters, fathers and mothers showed strikingly similar patterns of parental behavior. This meta-analysis is consistent with other work that suggests, while there are differences between fathers and mothers, there seem to be more similarities than differences in the parental role.

As might be expected, gender-role socialization remains a controversial and constantly changing area of research (Lamb et al., 1985; Lamb & Oppenheim, 1989). It appears that researchers have recently moved away from the investigation of children's gender roles per se, to focus on paternal and maternal treatment of sons and daughters, as reflected by Lytton and Romney's (1991) meta-analysis and an empirical study by Werrbach, Grotevant, and Cooper (1992). Because of the constant societal changes regarding gender roles, it is expected that the controversy over whether or not to investigate gender roles, and how exactly to investigate gender roles in relation to paternal and maternal influences will continue. For a more thorough discussion of these issues, interested readers are referred to Beal (1994).

Intellectual Development and Academic Achievement

The behaviors that fathers exhibit with their children have been found to influence the intellectual development of children (especially boys). Radin (1976) summarized a series of observational studies that she conducted with fathers and their preschool-age children. Fathers were interviewed at home while their children were present, and the way in which fathers handled their children's interruptions to the interview were observed and coded. Fathers who showed nurturing behaviors (e.g., praising, helpful, and kind behaviors) toward their child during the interview had sons who scored higher on tests of intelligence and verbal ability than sons who had fathers who showed nonnurturing behaviors (e.g., being cool and aloof). Restrictive behaviors by fathers were also associated with lower cognitive scores for their sons. Few significant patterns were found for fathers' behavior and their daughters' intellectual functioning. In fact, too much paternal warmth may limit the intellectual growth of girls. Honzik (1967) found that 7- to 9-year-old girls showed higher intellectual functioning when their fathers showed overt friendliness toward them, but not when fathers showed a close bond or a high degree of expressions of affection. For boys, a close bond between father and son was associated with higher intellectual functioning. Conversely, other studies have shown that paternal authoritarian behavior and intense involvement in children's problem-solving activities are associated with lower intellectual functioning for both boys and girls (Radin, 1981b).

To investigate the impact of varying degrees of paternal involvement on children's intellectual functioning, Radin (1982) compared preschool children of highly involved fathers with children whose fathers showed "traditional" levels of involvement with their children. Based on the Peabody Picture Vocabulary Test, both boys and girls who had highly involved fathers showed higher levels of verbal intellectual skills than boys and girls who had fathers with lower levels of involvement. Although there were significant correlations between fathers' level of involvement and children's intelligence, the findings were stronger for boys than for girls. Radin suggested that highly involved fathers were instrumental in encouraging cognitive development of their children, and especially of their sons. As with other studies of highly involved fathers, these findings should be viewed cautiously because the characteristics of families in which fathers would choose to be highly involved may differ from more traditional families.

Fathers' educational level has been found to be associated with children's intelligence, especially for girls. Honzik (1963) provided correlations between fathers' education and children's IQ according to how old the children were when they were tested. For boys, correlations were not significant from 21 months through 6 years old. However, when boys were tested from the ages of 7 through 15, significant associations emerged. Correlations between father's education and boy's IQ ranged from .27 to .41 during this period and all these correlations were statistically significant. The pattern was even more consistent for girls. Although intellectual level of 21-month-old girls was not associated with paternal education, the IQ of girls who were tested between the ages of 3 and 15 showed strong and significant associations with paternal education.

The correlations ranged from .32 to .44, and all the correlations were significant. Although the Honzik study showed consistent associations between paternal education and children's intellectual functioning, Radin (1981b) pointed out that less than 25% of the variance in children's intellectual functioning was accounted for by paternal education. Thus, over 75% of the variance in children's intellectual functioning appears to be related to something other than paternal education. Also of importance is that the Honzik study showed only associations between children's IQ and paternal education and therefore could not speak to the causal factors that influence children's intellectual functioning. Radin pointed out that the significant associations may have been due to genetic factors, environmental factors, or some combination of both genetic and environmental factors.

Overall, fathers' nurturing behaviors appear to be more strongly associated with intellectual development in their sons than in their daughters (Radin, 1981b). A close father-son relationship is associated with greater analytic cognitive skills in sons, granted that the father's behavior is focused on encouraging the son's mastery efforts rather than intimidating the son. The relation between paternal behavior and daughters' intellectual development is more complex and contradictory findings have yet to be resolved. For example, higher intellectual proficiency in girls is associated with some degree of autonomy and distance from their fathers; however, fathers' specific interest in their daughters' academic progress is associated with greater proficiency (Radin, 1981b). These differences may be due to the way in which fathers interact with their children around cognitive tasks and to the different expectations that fathers seem to have about their sons versus their daughters. Both fathers and mothers have been found to emphasize achievement and competition in boys more than in girls (Barry, Bacon, & Child, 1957), and paternal encouragement of intellectual performance has been found to be related to children's academic achievement (Crandall, Dewey, Katkovsky, & Preston, 1964). In a review of this research, Hoffman (1977) concluded that fathers focus more on achieving the goals of cognitive tasks when they interact with their sons, whereas they focus on the interpersonal aspects of the task with their daughters (e.g., whether their daughters are enjoying the activity rather than whether they are completing the task correctly). When describing cognitive tasks, both fathers and mothers have been found to focus on the achievement aspects with their sons as opposed to with their daughters (Hoffman, 1977).

Although many of these studies were conducted over a decade ago, more recent reviews of this literature (Biller, 1993; Lamb & Oppenheim, 1989) continue to cite this research as the strongest evidence of paternal influences on their sons' and daughters' intellectual and academic achievement. Researchers have now moved away from the basic questions of investigating paternal influences on sons' and daughters' intelligence toward investigations of interpersonal and familial factors that relate to sons' and daughters' academic achievement (Biller, 1993).

In a sample of high-achieving third graders, Wagner and Phillips (1992) found that fathers' warmth was positively related to children's perceived academic competence. In a sample of ninth graders, Paulson (1994) found that students' but not parents' ratings of paternal and maternal involvement were associated with higher levels of academic achievement. In a comprehensive longitudinal study, Williams and Radin (1993) found that maternal employment was a better predictor of adolescents' academic achievement than was paternal involvement in child rearing. Specifically, maternal part-time employment was associated with children's and adolescents' higher levels of academic achievement and academic expectations. In a sample of families in India, mothers' but not fathers' school attendance was related to their children's performance in school (Bhatnagar & Sharma, 1992).

To investigate indirect effects between parental behavior and children's academic achievement, two studies conducted path analyses. In a sample of Caucasian American young adolescents, Grolnick and Slowiaczek (1994) found that fathers' higher levels of behavioral involvement and intellectual/cognitive pursuits were associated with their children's greater perceived academic competence, which in turn was associated with higher grades at school. The same pattern was true for mothers, with the addition that mothers' behavioral involvement was also related to children's control understanding, which in turn was related to children's higher grades at school. Mothers' greater behavioral involvement also had a direct path to children's grades. This study suggested that there were both indirect and direct relations between fathers' and mothers' characteristics and their children's academic achievement. Similar results were found in a study of African American young adolescents. Brody and colleagues (1994) found that fathers' cocaregiving support received from mothers, mothers' cocaregiving support received from fathers, and low levels of cocaregiver conflict were significantly related to greater levels of adolescents' self-regulation (such as thinking ahead about consequences before acting), which in turn were related to adolescents' reading proficiency, mathematics proficiency, and decreased externalizing and internalizing emotional/behavioral problems. Together, these studies suggest that parental characteristics have indirect relations to children's academic competence; and children's perceptions of competence, control, and self-regulation may serve to mediate the relation between parental behavior and children's academic achievement.

Henggeler, Cohen, Edwards, Summerville, and Ray (1991) provided an interesting study of academic achievement of third graders, television watching, and paternal and maternal perceptions of life events stress, psychological distress, and marital satisfaction. The researchers found that children's academic achievement was inversely related to the amount of television the children watched on weekdays, even after verbal intelligence was statistically controlled. In addition, paternal reports of marital satisfaction were inversely related to children's television watching and maternal reports of life events stress were related to increased weekday television viewing by children. Henggeler and colleagues suggested that the association between children's television watching and lower academic achievement must be considered in the context of greater marital dissatisfaction and greater stress within the family.

In a study of female adolescents who were academically advanced, Callahan, Comell, and Loyd (1990) studied the relations between fathers' and mothers' communication with their daughters and adolescents' perceived competence in academic and nonacademic domains. Based on zero-order correlations, adolescents' perceived competence varied in relation to paternal and maternal communication. Fathers who showed higher levels of communication had daughters who perceived themselves to have significantly higher levels of academic competence, lower levels of social competence, lower levels of athletic competence, higher levels of conduct/morality competence, higher levels of competence with peers, and higher overall global self-worth. With regard to mother-daughter associations, mothers who showed higher levels of communication had daughters who perceived themselves to have significantly higher academic competence, higher competence in paid employment, higher romantic appeal, higher conduct/morality competence, higher competence with peers, and higher overall global self-worth. This study suggests that, even within a sample of high-achieving adolescent girls, communication styles with their father and mother had a significant relation with the girls' perceived competence in a variety of domains.

Parents' and children's appraisals of academic abilities and expectations for educational attainment have also been investigated. In a study of preschoolers and their families, fathers reported higher academic expectations for their children than did mothers, and both fathers and mothers had higher academic expectations for their daughters than for their sons (McBride & Ferguson, 1992). In a study of elementary school and middle school students, Felson (1990) found that fathers' appraisal of their child's academic performance was significantly correlated with the child's own appraisal of academic performance in middle school students but not elementary school students. The pattern was reversed for mothers: Mothers' appraisal of their child's academic abilities was significantly correlated with the child's own appraisal of academic abilities in elementary school but not in middle school. The patterns of results were similar for both sons and daughters. Interestingly, at both the elementary school level and the middle school level, children provided more negative ratings of their own academic abilities than did fathers or mothers. When fathers' and mothers' appraisals of their child's academic performance were compared, no significant differences were evident.

With regard to parents' educational goals for their children, Smith (1991) conducted a study with 988, an ethnically and economically diverse sample of seventh- and ninth-grade students. Students were asked to provide their own educational expectations (e.g., How far do you actually expect to go in school?) and to report their perceptions of their fathers' and mothers' expectations for their educational goals (e.g., How far do you think your father/mother wants you to go in school?). Agreement between students' own expectations and their perceptions of their fathers' and mothers' goals were calculated. Overall, there was a high level of agreement between students' own goals and their perceptions of their fathers' and mothers' expectations. In addition, adolescents' educational goals were significantly associated with their fathers' and mothers' own levels of educational attainment, but not with their fathers' and mothers' occupational attainment. Smith interpreted these data as supporting the hypothesis of intergenerational transmission of educational goals. He suggested that further research will be needed to ascertain the mechanisms for such transmission and to establish a better understanding of the directionality between adolescents' and parents' educational goals for the adolescent.

The same issues hold true for children's occupational goals. For example, Trice and Knapp (1992) found that fifth- and eighth-grade boys and girls were more likely to aspire to their mother's career than to their father's career. This pattern was especially strong when mother and father had equal status in their careers or when the mother had higher status in her career than the father did. Further research is needed to ascertain the effects of children's occupational and career aspirations for their eventual employment levels as adults and also to ascertain the mechanisms within the family that relate to children's eventual employment status.

Father-Child Relationships from Infancy through Adulthood

Fathers' Behavior with Their Infants

Much of the research completed with fathers and their infants has explored how fathers' behavior is similar to or different from mothers' behavior with their infants. As noted in Chapter 1, throughout children's lives, fathers tend to act more as a playmate to their children whereas mothers tend to act more as a caretaker (Fagot & Hagan, 1991; Levy-Shiff et al., 1989; Roggman, 1992; Stevenson et al., 1988; Tiedje & Darling-Fisher, 1993; Yogman et al., 1988). Although this difference is evident even in infancy, there appear to be many more similarities than differences in how fathers and mothers interact with their infants. For example, Parke and Tinsley (1981) summarized their work showing that during a 10-minute observation session within the first 3 days of the infant's life, fathers and mothers showed comparable levels of touching the infant, kissing the infant, imitating the infant, and vocalizing to the infant. Fathers tended to rock the infant in their arms and hold the infant more than mothers during these observations, and mothers tended to smile at the infant more than did fathers. When fathers and mothers held their infant, they did similar things, such as appearing interested in the infant, showing nurturance, and providing stimulating interactions with the infant. In a study of unstructured play, Dixon and colleagues (1981) found that fathers and mothers were equally able to engage their infants in games and to maintain the infant's attention. Fathers and mothers of 3-month-old infants were able to successfully interact with their infants in a mutually regulated, reciprocal pattern where both parents and infant showed cycles of affective involvement followed by brief withdrawal (Dixon et al., 1981). Both fathers and mothers alter their speech pattern by using shorter phrases, with greater repetition of phrases, when talking with their neonates and their infants who are 3 months old (Parke & Tinsley, 1981). By the time their infants reach toddlerhood, both fathers and mothers seem to use directives in ways that are more similar than different from each other (Yogman et al., 1988).

Because most of these studies were based in the laboratory, and all were completed when the parents knew they were being observed, the results may have been influenced by reactivity related to the research setting. As noted previously, mothers spend significantly more time with infants outside the laboratory (Lamb, 1981). Therefore, the solitary time that fathers spend with their infants due to the research observations may be somewhat artificial. However, most of the preceding research results have been replicated by a number of different researchers in both laboratory and home-based observational settings, in both high and low SES samples, and in a number of countries (Parke & Tinsely, 1981). Thus, the comparability of paternal and maternal behavior with their infants seems to be a relatively robust finding. Overall, there is strong evidence that fathers and mothers show more similarities than differences in the way they treat their infants (Lamb, 1981; Parke & Tinsley, 1981; Yogman et al., 1988). Lamb (1981) and Kotelchuck (1976) argued that there is no innate gender difference in the way that adults relate to infants, nor that there is any genetic predisposition for infants to interact differently with their fathers than with their mothers. In a review of men's and women's responses to the young, Berman (1980) also concluded that social determinants appear to be more important than hormonal or biological determinants of response to infants. The quality of the infant-father or infant-mother relationship seemingly is more important than the gender of the parent who is interacting with the infant (Yogman et al., 1988).

Father-Child Interactions with Preschool Children

Bentley and Fox (1991) compared the parenting behaviors of fathers and mothers of children aged 1 through 4 years. In this primarily middle- to upper-middle-class sample, fathers and mothers did not differ in their reports of developmental expectations of their children nor did they differ in their choice of disciplinary techniques with their children. However, fathers and mothers did differ in their level of nurturing. Specifically, mothers rated themselves as significantly more nurturing than fathers with regard to caring for the child and trying to promote the child's psychological growth. Because these ratings were based on parents' self-reports rather than on observations of behavior, it is unclear whether these perceptions of greater maternal nurturing behavior are based on parental perceptions or based on actual behavior. Continuing with the assessment of fathers' and mothers' beliefs about parenting and about children's behavior, Mills and Rubin (1990) found relatively similar patterns for fathers and mothers of 4-year-olds in their reactions to hypothetical vignettes of child aggression and social withdrawal. Both fathers and mothers reported high levels of concern about peer-directed child aggression and child social withdrawal. In addition, fathers and mothers reported a great deal of negative reactions to child aggression and a great deal of confusion and puzzlement about child social withdrawal.

Another method of investigating parental behavior with children has been to assess the agreement between parents' and child development experts' ratings of child-rearing values. Deal, Halverson, and Wampler (1989) investigated how fathers' or mothers' perceptions of child-rearing values and parenting behavior agreed or disagreed with the idealized perceptions of parenting behavior and child-rearing values of child development experts. They found that the agreement between fathers' and mothers' child-rearing values and experts' ratings did not add significantly more information after parenting effectiveness was already established (parental agreement did not show increased utility). The researchers also found that fathers and mothers who showed good agreement with experts tended to be effective parents who agreed with other effective parents. Conversely, fathers and mothers who showed high levels of disagreement with experts regarding parenting techniques tended to be ineffective parents who disagreed with other parents, regardless of the other parents' effectiveness or ineffectiveness. Overall, the patterns of parental agreement were relatively similar for both fathers and mothers.

Because the development of language is of great importance during the preschool years, Becker and Hall (1989) chose to investigate fathers' and mothers' reports of their influence over their children's pragmatic development. The development of pragmatic skills allows the child to use language appropriately in different social contexts. Pragmatic skills include such behaviors as saying "please" and "thank you," saying "hello" and "good-bye" at the appropriate times, taking turns in conversations, not interrupting when someone else is talking, and using appropriate volume and tone in a specific context. In a sample of 50 Caucasian, middle-class families of preschoolers, fathers and mothers were asked to rate the importance of specific pragmatic skills and to rate their influence on their child's use of these skills. Fathers and mothers did not differ significantly in their ratings of the importance of the use of pragmatic skills. However, mothers reported being more influential than fathers in their child's use of pragmatic skills. In general, fathers and mothers reported that they would prompt their child when he or she neglected to use a pragmatic skill, but fathers also showed a greater tendency than mothers to ignore such errors. It would be interesting to extend this research to ascertain whether the similarities and differences in fathers' and mothers' reports of their influence over their children's use of pragmatics are actually documented in direct observations of families of preschoolers. The limited studies in this area suggest that there are more similarities than differences in fathers' and mothers' speech with young children (Barton & Tomasello, 1994).

Parenting style has been evaluated through direct observations in relation to style of speech with young children. Pratt, Kerig, Cowan, and Cowan (1992) conducted a study with fathers and mothers and their 3½-year-old children. The sample was predominantly Caucasian (85%) and middle class. Language usage and style of speech with children were assessed in videotaped dyadic play interactions between children and their fathers and their mothers. Fathers and mothers also provided reports of their own parenting style with their children, which were categorized as either authoritative or authoritarian. Overall comparisons between fathers and mothers showed that there were no main effects or interaction effects for parental language usage and child gender. Thus, fathers and mothers did not show significant differences in their speech patterns to their sons or daughters. Associations were found between parents' style of parenting and parents' speech patterns with their children. Fathers who were authoritarian in parenting style showed high levels of directive speech in interactions with their young child. No other associations were found for fathers' parenting style and language usage (e.g., responsiveness, use of questions, parental monologues, and total utterances). Mothers who were authoritarian in their parenting style also showed higher levels of directive speech, in addition to lower levels of responsiveness, and lower levels of mean length of utterance. Mothers who were authoritative in their parenting style showed lower levels of directive speech and higher responsiveness in play interactions with their young child. Overall, fathers' and mothers' patterns of speech with their children were relatively similar.

The ways in which fathers, mothers, and preschoolers communicate about daily experiences, emotions, and past experiences has also been studied. Mothers, more often than fathers, initiated conversations with their preschoolers about the child's daily experiences (Bradbard, Endsley, & Mize, 1992). However, fathers and preschoolers also initiated quite a few conversations. Fathers and mothers were found to talk in similar ways about past events with their preschool children, but both fathers and mothers showed a greater diversity in their use of emotion-ladened words with their daughters as opposed to their sons (Kuebli & Fivush, 1992). Fathers and mothers also participated in more elaborative conversations with their daughters (e.g., by providing more narrative structure and longer conversations) than with their sons even though daughters' and sons' linguistic skills were similar (Reese & Fivush, 1993). It appears that both fathers and mothers change their style of conversation based on the gender rather than the language abilities of their child.

Leinbach and Fagot (1991) conducted an interesting study to evaluate the impact of young children's attractiveness on their fathers' and mothers' interactions with them. The researchers had independent adult judges rate the attractiveness (based on facial photographs) of children aged 1 to 3 years old. After the attractiveness ratings were ascertained, children and their fathers and mothers were observed directly to code parents' interactions with their young child. Research assistants who coded the parent-child behavioral observations were blind to the attractiveness ratings of the independent judges. There were no significant differences between girls' and boys' attractiveness ratings nor in their parents' behavior with them. Results of the correlational analyses show strikingly different patterns for boys and girls. Boys' attractiveness was not significantly associated with their fathers', mothers', or play group caregivers' interactions with them. Conversely, a number of significant association between girls' attractiveness and adults' interactions were identified. Girls' attractiveness ratings were significantly correlated with their fathers', mothers', and caregivers' higher level of instructional activity and with their mothers' (but not their fathers' or caregivers') lower levels of positive reactions to the girls. In terms of bidirectional influences, girls' and boys' attractiveness ratings were also associated with certain child behaviors. For example, girls' attractiveness ratings were associated with their increased likelihood to attempt to communicate in both the home and the play-group setting, and children's attractiveness ratings were inversely related to boys' passive behavior in the home setting and girls' passive behavior in the play-group setting. Overall, this study provides evidence that girls' attractiveness appears to be more of a factor in adults' responses to them. Again, fathers and mothers showed relatively similar patterns in their interactions with their children in relation to their child's attractiveness.

Father-Child Interactions with School-Age Children

Two primary areas of research have been conducted regarding fathers' interactions with their school-age children. First, investigations have been completed that ascertain the similarities and differences in fathers' and mothers' reports of their children's behavior. For example, Duncan and Kilpatrick (1991) found that parents of nonreferred 6- to 12-year-olds showed relatively high levels of agreement in their reports of their sons' problematic and prosocial behavior. For daughters, there were no differences between fathers' and mothers' reports of problem behavior; however, fathers consistently reported lower rates of prosocial behavior in their daughters when compared with mothers' reports of their daughters' prosocial behavior. With a sample of second- and fifth-grade students, Miller, Davis, Wilde, and Brown (1993) assessed fathers' and mothers' accuracy in reporting their children's preferences. Mothers were significantly more accurate at reporting their children's preferences than were fathers, and fathers and mothers of fifth graders were significantly more accurate in their knowledge of their children's preferences than were parents of second graders.

The area of research that has received somewhat more attention is the parent-child relationship in middle childhood. For example, Mullis and Mullis (1990) investigated the problem-solving behaviors of 9-year-old children when they were involved in either dyadic or triadic interactions with their parents. In the sample of 18 rural, two-parent families, Mullis and Mullis found that the context of interactions (i.e., whether they were dyadic or triadic) seemed to influence the interactions that children had with their father and mother. For boys' interactions with their fathers, boys showed lower location cues, reminder of task completed, and verbalization of a strategy when in a dyadic context as opposed to a triadic context. The opposite pattern was evident for girls' interactions with their fathers. Girls showed higher location cues, reminder of task completed, and verbalization of a strategy when in a triadic context versus a dyadic context. With regard to mothers' interactions with their children, both boys and girls showed higher levels of reminder of task completed and verbalization of a strategy within a dyadic context as opposed to the triadic context. No differences in fathers' behavior were found in analyzing context or gender of child. Mothers showed significantly higher levels of location cues and form, shape, and direction relationships with both their sons and their daughters in the dyadic context as opposed to the triadic context. Overall, this study suggests that any interaction behaviors that are assessed between parents and their sons and daughters should take into account the context and whether or not the other parent is present during the interactions. These issues are also discussed in Chapter 8 regarding behavioral observations using clinically referred children and parents.

Bronstein (1984) conducted an interesting study in Mexico to ascertain differences in fathers' and mothers' behavior with their school-age children. Children ranged in age from 7 to 12 years, and there were 19 families from lower- and middle-socioeconomic backgrounds involved in the study. She found that fathers showed more play behavior with their children and mothers showed more nurturant behavior that was related to caring for the immediate physical needs of the children. Overall, Bronstein found a great deal of similarities between family interaction patterns in Mexico and family interaction patterns in the United States.

As previously noted, fathers have been found to interact with their children using a context of play more so than mothers. This pattern has been found in middle childhood as well. For example, McBride-Chang and Jacklin (1993) found that fathers' earlier level of play, but not mothers' earlier level of play, was associated with sons' level of rough-and-tumble play in first grade. In another study, Russell and Russell (1987) recruited a sample in Australia in which married fathers and mothers had an eldest child who was either 6 or 7 years old. All the fathers were employed and the majority of mothers were either full-time homemakers or were employed part-time. The researchers observed parent-child interactions during a 90-minute interview conducted in the family's home. Overall, a larger portion of fathers' time was spent interacting with their children in a playful manner, whereas mothers' time was more often involved with caregiving activities. When the amount of time during interactions was compared, mothers spent significantly more time interacting with their children and provided more directive responses to their children than did fathers. There was no difference between fathers and mothers in their amount of responsiveness, negativity, or restrictiveness with their children. These patterns were similar for both sons and daughters, and there were no significant interactions between gender of parent and gender of child. Overall, the study by Russell and Russell provided further evidence that the patterns of paternal play and maternal caretaking that are often found in infancy, continue on through middle childhood.

In a review of studies of father-child and mother-child relationships in middle childhood and adolescence, Collins and Russell (1991) concluded that these differences between fathers and mothers appear to become somewhat more pronounced as the child moves from middle childhood to adolescence. They suggested that father-child and mother-child relationships must be considered within a developmental framework that takes into account not only the child's developmental level but also the developmental level of the father and the mother.

Parent-child relationships in middle childhood have also been investigated regarding parental warmth, acceptance, and negativity. Families with a fourth- or fifth-grade child were assessed for children's coping with parental negativity (Herman & McHale, 1993). Boys were more likely than girls to report "forgetting" about their fathers' or mothers' negativity. Girls were more likely to talk to their mother than their father about parental negativity. Both boys and girls coped with paternal negativity by talking with someone else (not their father or their mother) about their father's negativity. Overall, both fathers' and mothers' warmth were associated with boys' and girls' likelihood of talking with them about children's concerns. In a sample of preadolescents in Israel, Shulman, Collins, and Dital (1993) found that 11-year-olds perceived less acceptance by their fathers than did 9-year-olds. There were no significant age differences in perceptions of maternal acceptance.

Another important factor in the father-child relationship is the father's initial preference for the gender of the child. Stattin and Klackenberg-Larsson (1991) provided compelling evidence that suggests fathers whose gender preference for their child was not fulfilled (e.g., fathers who wanted a son but had a daughter or fathers who wanted a daughter but had a son) show greater levels of conflict with their children, especially their daughters. The father-child relations of girls aged 4 to 18 years showed greater rates of conflict when the father's preference for the gender of the child was incongruent with the child's actual gender. When fathers had expressed a preference prenatally for a son and then had a daughter, the father-daughter relationship showed significantly higher rates of conflict than father-daughter relationships in which fathers had wanted a daughter. For fathers who had wanted a daughter but had a son, the father-son relationship only showed significantly greater levels of conflict when the sons were less than 4 years old. Mother-child relationships were rarely influenced by maternal preference for gender of the child. Mothers of daughters (who had wanted a son) showed greater conflict with their daughters when the daughters were between the ages of 10 and 12. Mothers of sons (who had wanted a daughter) showed greater conflict with their sons when the sons were younger than 4 years old and when the sons were between the ages of 7 and 9 years. Overall, Stattin and Klackenberg-Larsson suggest that the father-child relationship, especially the father-daughter relationship, is significantly influenced by paternal preferences regarding gender.

Father-Child Interactions with Adolescent Children

A number of studies have investigated various facets of the father-adolescent relationship (see Youniss & Smollar, 1985, and Shulman & Collins, 1993, for review). As a transition into this research, a study will first be discussed that evaluated the father-child relationship from preschool through adolescence. DeLuccie and Davis (1991) surveyed fathers of children aged 4, 8, 12, and 16 years old and asked about parenting practices, parenting attitudes, parental role involvement, and parental role satisfaction. The sample consisted of approximately equal numbers of boys and girls, all of whom were first born children. The fathers were well educated (with over 75% of them having completed a college or graduate degree) and all were married to the child's mother. Data from mothers were not included in this study. Results of the study showed that fathers' reports of their own parenting behavior, the modifiability of their children's behavior, their frequency of involvement with their children, and their role satisfaction all showed significant changes from fathers of preschoolers to fathers of adolescents. Specifically, fathers of preschoolers reported greater levels of acceptance of their preschool child than fathers of a child aged 8, 12, or 16 years old. Fathers of preschool children (4 years old) and adolescents (16 years old) perceived their children's behavior as significantly less malleable or modifiable than fathers of school-age children (8 years old) and young adolescents (12 years old). Fathers of preschool children reported greater frequency of involvement with their children than did fathers of school-age children, young adolescents, and adolescents, with fathers of adolescents showing significantly less frequency of involvement than fathers with children in any of the other age groups. However, fathers of adolescents showed greater levels of task sharing than any of the other groups of fathers. Fathers of adolescents also showed greater levels of role satisfaction than other fathers. There was not a main effect for child gender, which suggests that these patterns were similar for both sons and daughters.

This study suggests that fathers' perceptions of their own and their child's behavior change as the child and the father continue development. Other researchers have found that children's and adolescents' perceptions of the congruence of their father's and mother's parenting styles change as a function of time, with adolescents reporting significantly less congruence between father-mother parenting style (e.g., father used authoritarian parenting style and mother used authoritative parenting style) than younger children (Johnson, Shulman, & Collins, 1991). These types of study highlight the importance of investigating families over time. However, because both of these studies were cross-sectional in nature and studied fathers of children at different ages, rather than following the same set of fathers and children at different time points, results must be interpreted cautiously because of the possibility of cohort effects. It will be important to conduct a prospective study that follows children, their fathers, and their mothers from the child's preschool years through adolescence to ascertain whether these patterns of changes in the father-child and mother-child relationship are seen as the child, father, and mother develop.

A number of studies have investigated the similarities and differences in characteristics of fathers and their adolescent children. For example, younger adolescent males' decision-making self-esteem was significantly related to their father's and their mother's decision-making self-esteem, and young adolescent females' decision-making self-esteem was significantly related to their father's but not their mother's decision-making self-esteem (Brown & Mann, 1991). For older adolescents (aged 15 to 17 years), none of these correlations were significant. With regard to individuation from parents, adolescents (aged 12 to 19 years) were found to show similar patterns of individuation from both their father and their mother (Bartle & Anderson, 1991). When intergenerational patterns of individuation were analyzed, adolescents' individuation from their father and mother was significantly correlated with their mother's individuation from her father and mother (the adolescent's grandparents) but not correlated with their father's individuation from his father and mother.

A large percentage of the research into the father-child relationship during adolescence has focused on adolescents' perceptions of their father. For example, seventh graders showed more differentiation of their perceptions of attachment to their fathers than to their mothers (Papini, Roggman, & Anderson, 1991). Boys reported significantly lower attachment to their fathers than did girls, whereas there were no gender differences in the reports of perceived attachment to mothers. Both boys and girls showed significantly lower perceived attachment to their father but not to their mother after the onset of puberty. In another study of seventh graders, Paulson, Hill, and Holmbeck (1991) found that both boys and girls reported greater levels of closeness with their mother than with their father, but there were no significant differences when adolescents reported on their father's and mother's level of warmth. The same pattern of perceived closeness was found when fathers and mothers reported on their relationships with their sons and daughters. Specifically, fathers reported significantly lower closeness with both their sons and their daughters than did mothers. When gender differences in the parent-adolescent relationship are investigated, more gender differences (based on adolescent's gender) seem to occur in the father-adolescent relationship than in the mother-adolescent relationship. Bezirganian and Cohen (1992) found few differences between adolescent boys and adolescent girls in their identification with mother, closeness to mother, and involvement with mother. However, when these differences were analyzed for fathers, significant differences emerged due to adolescent gender. Boys showed greater identification with their father than did girls, and boys perceived greater involvement with their father than did girls. Boys perceived more punishment than did girls from both their father and their mother.

With regard to communication, Nolin and Petersen (1992) found that adolescent girls receive more information about sexuality and sex education from their parents (most notably their mothers) than do adolescent boys. In a study that looked at all types of communication in families of adolescents, Noller and Callan (1990) recruited almost 300 adolescents aged 13 to 17 years and asked adolescents to report on the nature of communication with their father and their mother. The researchers found that adolescent females reported more self-disclosure to their mother than to their father and greater satisfaction in their conversations with their mother than with their father. Adolescent males perceived their self-disclosure to be approximately equal with their father and their mother and were equally satisfied with conversations with either parent. Overall, mothers were perceived to initiate more conversations with adolescents than did fathers, and mothers were seen as more interested in adolescents' opinions. When adolescent females and males were compared directly, adolescent females reported talking with their mother more frequently than did adolescent males, and adolescent males talked more frequently and self-disclosed more with their fathers about sexual issues and general problems than did females.

This study suggests that adolescent girls have somewhat more communication with their mother, whereas adolescent boys have approximately equal levels of communication with both their father and their mother. These results are interesting because other researchers (Wierson, Armistead, Forehand, Thomas, & Fauber, 1990) found that mothers of 11- to 15-year-old adolescents report a greater number of conflicts, a less positive relationship, and more intense discussions about conflict with their adolescent children than do fathers. This pattern of greater conflict between mothers and their adolescent children was consistent for both boys and girls and for adolescents of all ages (11–15 years). It appears that the mother-adolescent relationship may be characterized by more communication, in both positive and negative terms, than the father-adolescent relationship. Successful programs have been established to help fathers and mothers learn how to communicate more effectively with their sons and daughters (Riesch, Tosi, Thurston, & Forsyth, 1993).

A study was conducted by Oz and Fine (1991) to compare the father-daughter and mother-daughter relationships for teenagers who had become pregnant during high school and teenagers who had never been pregnant. In retrospective reports of their childhood years, teenage mothers perceived fewer positive qualities and greater negative qualities in their relationship with their father than did teenagers in the control group. Conversely, teenage mothers reported more positive qualities and fewer negative qualities in their relationship with their mother than did teenagers in the control group. The same pattern of significant differences was found when teenagers reported on their current relationship with their father and their mother. Teenage mothers also reported more positive qualities in the relationship with their sisters but fewer positive qualities in the relationship with their brothers than did the other adolescent girls. Overall, this study suggested a pattern of poor relationships with males (fathers and brothers) but better relationships with females (mothers and sisters) for adolescents who became pregnant in high school.

Transferring back to adolescents in general, adolescents' perceptions of their fathers' and mothers' prosocial and empathic characteristics have been evaluated. McDevitt, Lennon, and Kopriva (1991) found that adolescents (12–18 years) reported significantly more promotion of prosocial behaviors from their mothers than from their fathers. Specifically, in contrast to fathers, adolescents perceived that their mothers were more likely to encourage adolescents to help others outside the family, to expresses emotions appropriately, to be kind and responsible, and to not be callous. When gender differences were evaluated, adolescent girls reported being encouraged by their mother more than adolescent boys to show prosocial behaviors and to be empathic. Girls and boys did not differ in their reports of their fathers' encouragement of prosocial behaviors and empathic responses.

With regard to adolescents' perceptions of their parents, there appears to be a connection between adolescents' feelings of closeness to their parents and their own level of self-esteem. Adolescent girls who perceived their father to be warm and supportive, and adolescent boys who perceived their mother to be warm and supportive showed higher levels of self-esteem than their peers (Richards, Gitelson, Petersen, & Hurtig, 1991). In addition, adolescents' perceptions of the family environment appear to be significantly associated with adolescent self-esteem and adolescent-parent incongruence in perceptions of the family environment (Carlson, Cooper, & Spradling, 1991). Specifically, in a sample of sixth graders (mean age 11.5 years), adolescents, fathers, and mothers were asked to complete measures of family environment. After these measures were compared, father-adolescent and mother-adolescent incongruence ratings were calculated and these incongruence ratings were correlated with adolescents' reports of their own perceived competence and self-esteem. Higher levels of incongruence between father-adolescent dyads were associated with boys' perceptions of higher scholastic ability, higher social acceptance, better physical appearance, and better behavioral conduct. For girls, higher father-adolescent incongruence ratings were associated with perceptions of lower scholastic ability, lower social acceptance, and poorer behavioral conduct. With regard to mother-adolescent incongruence, boys' reported higher physical appearance, better behavioral conduct, and lower global self-esteem when there were higher rates of mother-adolescent incongruence. For girls, higher mother-adolescent incongruence was associated with lower social acceptance. Carlson and colleagues interpreted these data as suggesting even more complexity within families of adolescents than previously thought, especially with regard to different patterns of parent-adolescent incongruence and adolescent self-esteem for boys versus girls.

Parents and teachers have been surveyed to ascertain their opinions about the developmental stages of adolescence. In one study (Buchanan et al., 1990), parents of young adolescents (sixth and seventh graders) and junior high and high school teachers were asked their perceptions of the difficulty of adolescence and the degree of impact adults can have with adolescents. Fathers, mothers, and teachers all reported that although they perceived adolescence to be a difficult developmental period, they firmly believed that adults can have an impact during this period. When fathers' and mothers' beliefs were compared, mothers reported the period of adolescence to be more difficult than did fathers. Both fathers and mothers of adolescent daughters reported that adolescence is more difficult than did fathers and mothers of adolescent sons. For teachers, the amount of teaching experience with adolescents was positively correlated with teachers' perceptions of greater difficulty. Buchanan and colleagues suggested that bidirectional processes may be at work, with parents' and teachers' expectations of greater difficulty during adolescence probably altering their behavior with adolescents and conversely more experience with adolescents providing greater expectations of difficulty.

Another study that investigated fathers' perceptions of their adolescent children suggested that a variety of factors contribute to fathers' perceptions of the father-adolescent relationship. Julian, McKenry, and McKelvey (1991) collected data from middle-aged men who had an adolescent child. All the fathers were employed in a professional capacity and the majority (95%) were Caucasian. Mothers and adolescents were not invited to participate in the study. Fathers reported on their own midlife developmental stress, the quality of their marital relationship, their emotional expressiveness, their level of trait anxiety, and their perceptions of the father-adolescent relationship. Fathers were also asked to have blood drawn to ascertain testosterone levels. Results of the study showed that a positive father-adolescent relationship was associated with lower paternal midlife developmental stress, greater paternal emotional expressiveness, lower quality of the marital relationship, and lower levels of paternal testosterone. Julian and colleagues noted that all these significant relations were expected and were consistent with past research, except for the negative relation between quality of marital relationship and father-adolescent relationship. They suggested that this inverse relation may be because middle-aged men often begin to differentiate more between their role as a father and their role as a husband. Aside from this unanticipated finding, this study suggests that fathers' experience of greater levels of midlife developmental stress seem to be related to a more problematic father-adolescent relationship. This study also highlights the need to take into account the father's developmental level as well as the child's developmental level.

Father-Child Interactions with Young Adult Children

As noted in Chapter 1, mothers continue to spend more time with their adult children than do fathers (Miller & Lane, 1991). When younger adults have been asked to report on their perceptions of closeness to their parents, somewhat different patterns emerge for males and females. When reporting retrospective recollections of closeness to parents, both adult sons and daughters report greater closeness to their mother than to their father (Goldsmith, Hoffman, & Hofacker, 1993; Nydegger & Mitteness, 1991; Saarnio, 1994). However, when reporting current relationships with their parents, daughters report greater closeness to their mother, whereas sons report approximately equivalent levels of closeness to both their father and their mother. Nydegger and Mitteness concluded that, whereas the mother-daughter relationship remains close into adulthood, the mother-son relationship tends to weaken over time with a slight strengthening of the father-son relationship. Conversely, when the quality of the relationship is assessed, different patterns emerge. Vitulli and Holland (1993) asked male and female college students to rate their current relationship with their father and their mother as great, good, average, poor, or awful. Overall, relationships with mothers were reported to be of a higher quality than relationships with fathers. However, daughters rated their relationship with their father as about the same quality as their relationship with their mother, whereas sons rated their relationship with their mother as significantly better than their relationship with their father. In another study, adult sons who reported a high-quality relationship with their father or their mother appeared to experience lower levels of psychological distress than adult sons with poor relationships with their parents (Barnett, Marshall, & Pleck, 1992a). It is unclear how the two constructs of closeness and quality of relationship are related, given that these two studies did not address both constructs at the same time (Nydegger & Mitteness, 1991; Vitulli & Holland, 1993). However, the quality of the relationship with fathers or mothers appears to be related to the fathers' or mothers' parenting behavior. Specifically, fathers and mothers who were perceived by their young adult children as warm and permissive were rated as having higher quality parent-child relationships than parents who were rated as hostile or restrictive (Parish & McCluskey, 1992).

Retrospective recollections of parenting behavior during childhood were assessed in a group of young adult college women. Using structural equation modeling, Arditti, Godwin, and Scanzoni (1991) found that young women's level of instrumentality was significantly predicted from higher levels of paternal and maternal encouragement, lower levels of maternal control, and higher levels of paternal control that the young women reported receiving in childhood. Young women's expressiveness was significantly predicted from higher levels of maternal encouragement and control, but was not significantly associated with any paternal parenting characteristics. Arditti and colleagues concluded that maternal behavior in childhood seemed to have a stronger association to gender role traits that daughters exhibited in young adulthood.

A retrospective study was also completed in China to ascertain the relations between young adults' recollections of the parenting that they received and their perceptions of family harmony. In a sample of over 900 Chinese young adults, Lau, Lew, Hau, Cheung, and Berndt (1990) found that paternal dominating control and warmth were inversely related, that greater paternal warmth was positively related to greater perceptions of family harmony, and that greater levels of paternal control were associated with lower levels of perceived family harmony. The same pattern of findings was evident for retrospective reports of maternal control and warmth. Lau and colleagues suggested that these patterns of family interactions appear to be relatively universal, given the consistency with which similar results have been found in many other cultures and many other countries.

In a study that investigated parents' influences in their adult children's ideology regarding crime, Dunaway and Cullen (1991) surveyed over 150 father-mother-adult child triads about their perceptions of what should be done about crime. Conservative crime ideology was identified when respondents endorsed punitive policies that focused on "getting tough" on crime. Liberal crime ideology was conceptualized as a focus on rehabilitation and prevention, rather than punishment. Results of the study showed that fathers and mothers had more significant influences in their adult sons' and daughters' conservative crime ideology than in their liberal crime ideology. Fathers' and mothers' political party affiliation and political participation did not appear to be related to their adult children's beliefs in these areas. Dunaway and Cullen suggested that there was a stronger connection between parents' conservative ideology related to crime, but this influence did not appear to be as strong in other ideological areas.

Turning to adult children's contact with their aging parents, mothers continue to have more contact with their adult children than do fathers (Miller & Lane, 1991). This pattern was found in a sample of African American middle-aged and elderly fathers and mothers who were over 55 years old (Spitze & Miner, 1992) and in a national, multiethnic sample in which fathers and mothers were over 65 years old (Spitze & Logan, 1989). In addition, older mothers receive more instrumental help (such as household duties, shopping, transportation) from their children than older fathers (Spitze & Logan, 1992). There appear to be different reasons for contact between adults and their fathers and mothers. Lawton, Silverstein, and Bengtson (1994) found that there was a reciprocal relationship between frequency of contact with mothers and affection between mothers and their adult children. With fathers, however, the relationship was not reciprocal. Whereas greater frequency of contact with fathers led to greater affection between fathers and their adult children, the reverse pattern was not true—greater affection from one's father did not lead to greater frequency of contact. The researchers suggest that the mother-adult child relationship may be a more mutually reinforcing relationship, whereas the father-adult child relationship may be based on more instrumental or obligatory concerns.

Ward and Spitze (1992) noted the importance of investigating coresidence between adult children and their parents. Coresidence is often necessitated by the housing needs of the adult child and is less often due to the physical needs of an elderly parent. The limited research that has been conducted with adult children who live with their parents suggests that these living arrangements have a greater tendency to be satisfactory than unsatisfactory. However, further research is needed to ascertain fathers' and mothers' separate perceptions of these living patterns and to investigate whether different patterns of satisfaction depend on the gender of the adult child who is living with the elderly parents.

Overall, many patterns evident in the father-child and the mother-child relationships at earlier developmental periods were found after the children reach adulthood. Researchers need to follow children and their parents longitudinally all the way into adulthood to ascertain whether these patterns are consistent across the development of the same sample of families. As it is now, much of the research that is known about the stability of father-child and mother-child relationships is based on adult children's retrospective reports of the parenting received in childhood (e.g., Nydegger & Mitteness, 1991). Although this is a legitimate way of assessing parenting behavior, adult children's recollections may be influenced by their current relationship with their parents. Therefore, it will be important to conduct longitudinal studies in which parenting behaviors have been assessed when the child was still in childhood and then analyze those parenting behaviors in relation to children's functioning once they reach adulthood.

Children's Relationships with Significant Others

The majority of research reviewed to this point has focused on fathers and to a lesser extent on mothers. This has been necessary given the focus of this book; however, it is also important to gain an understanding of children's involvement with other people (e.g., siblings, peers, grandparents) in addition to their parents. In addition, Parke, MacDonald, Beitel, and Bhavnagri (1988) noted the importance of the family's role in the development of relationships outside the family, especially peer relationships. Studies that include investigations of children's relationships with significant others (including fathers) will be reviewed to gain a better understanding of the context of the father-child relationship.

In a sample of children and adolescents aged 9 to 13, Bigelow, Tesson, and Lewko (1992) investigated how children conceptualize their interactions with their father, mother, brother, sister, close friend, other friend, other kid, and teacher. Children and adolescents reported significantly greater compliance, information management, prosocial behavior, loyalty, and managing of feelings with their father, mother, and close friend than with "other kids." Social facilitation was used with close friends more often than with any family member, other child, or teacher. Fathers, mothers, and teachers were all rated as receiving similar levels of loyalty and compliance from children and adolescents.

Furman and Buhrmester (1992) surveyed over 500 children and adolescents (in the 4th, 7th, and 10th grades, and in college) to study their perceptions of their relationships with their father, mother, teacher, sibling, same-gender friend, romantic friend, and grandparent. They found a variety of developmental changes in children's and adolescents' reports of their relationships. With regard to supportiveness, 4th-grade students perceived their fathers and mothers to provide more support than any of the other respondents. In 7th grade, adolescents reported that their primary support was from their father, mother, and same-gender friend. By 10th grade, same-gender friends were perceived as a more crucial support than any of the other relationships. College students reported that their mother, romantic friend, and same-gender friend were more of a support than any of the other relationships. This study suggests that younger children find their father and mother to be more central to their needs, with same-gender friends and romantic partners becoming increasingly important as adolescents develop.

Clark-Lempers, Lempers, and Ho (1991) conducted a study to ascertain adolescents' perceptions of their relationships with their father, mother, teacher, sibling, and best friend. The sample was predominately Caucasian (98%) and from working-and middle-class families. Results of the study showed that in nearly all the aspects of the relationships that were evaluated (including admiration, affection, companionship, conflict, instrumental aid, intimacy, nurturance, reliable alliance, and satisfaction with the relationship) and for all of the relationships that were evaluated (father, mother, teacher, sibling, and best friend), early adolescents (aged 11–13) reported greater levels than did middle adolescents (aged 14–16) or late adolescents (aged 17–19). For all three age groups, boys reported higher levels of companionship, instrumental aid, intimacy, nurturance, and satisfaction with their fathers than did girls. With regard to the mother-child relationship, girls reported greater levels of companionship, conflict, and intimacy with their mothers than did boys. For the other relationships that were assessed, boys reported more conflict with teachers than did girls, girls reported more admiration and intimacy with their siblings than did boys, and girls reported more admiration, affection, companionship, instrumental aid, intimacy, nurturance, reliable alliance, and satisfaction with their same-gender best friend than did boys.

With regard to the functional importance of these relationships, fathers and mothers were perceived as the most important sources of instrumental aid, reliable alliance, and affection but also were associated with high levels of conflict (Lempers & Clark-Lempers, 1992). Teachers were not perceived to be important providers of any of the evaluated resources. Best friends and siblings were perceived to be very important for intimacy and companionship. Siblings were also associated with high levels of nurturance and conflict. This study (reported in Clark-Lempers et al., 1991 and Lempers & Clark-Lempers, 1992) sheds light on the important dimensions of relationships that are perceived by adolescents with their fathers, mothers, teachers, siblings, and friends.

In a sample of Yugoslavian adolescents, Lackovic-Grgin and Dekovic (1990) found that adolescents' perceptions of their fathers, mothers, teachers, and friends were related to their own reports of self-esteem. Adolescents were asked to report on their own self-esteem and were also asked to provide their perceptions of their fathers', mothers', teachers', and friends' reports of the adolescents' self-esteem. These data were then analyzed to determine the relative contributions of others in the adolescents' perceptions of their own self-esteem. Because of different patterns of findings depending on adolescent age, adolescents were grouped into three age groups: Early adolescents (mean age 13.4), middle adolescents (mean age 15.5), and late adolescents (mean age 17.5). For early adolescent boys, fathers', teachers', and friends' (but not mothers') perceived opinions about adolescents' self-esteem were significantly related to adolescents' self-reported self-esteem. For middle adolescent males, mothers', teachers', and friends' (but not fathers') perceived opinions about adolescents' self-esteem were significantly related to adolescents' self-esteem. For late adolescent males, only fathers' perceived opinions about the adolescents' self-esteem were significantly related to adolescents' reports of their own self-esteem. For females, none of the three age groups showed significant relations between their perceptions of their fathers' opinions about their self-esteem and their own reports of self-esteem. For early adolescent females, teachers' perceived opinions were the only significant predictor, and for both middle and late adolescent females, mothers', teachers', and friends' perceived opinions about the adolescents were significantly associated with the adolescents' reports of their own self-esteem. Overall, girls reported higher self-esteem than did boys, and younger adolescents reported significantly higher levels of self-esteem than did older adolescents. Lackovic-Grgin and Dekovic suggested that this study showed the relative importance in self-esteem of different significant others in the lives of girls and boys at different developmental time periods.

Two recent studies (Creasey & Koblewski, 1991; Oyserman, Radin, & Benn, 1993) were identified in addition to a number of chapters (Baranowski, 1985; McCready, 1985; McGreal, 1994; Radin, Oyserman, & Benn, 1991; G. Russell,

1986a; Tinsley & Parke, 1987, 1988) that focus on the grandfather-grandchild relationship. In a study of adolescent mothers, their babies, and the babies' grandfathers and grandmothers, Oyserman and colleagues (1993) found that grandfathers', but not grandmothers', level of nurturance had a direct influence on their grandchildren's well-being. In a study of older adolescents' perceptions of their grandfathers and grandmothers, Creasey and Koblewski (1991) found that adolescents did not perceive their grandfathers or their grandmothers as important sources of instrumental aid or intimacy. However, grandfathers and grandmothers were perceived to be important attachment figures in the lives of the older adolescents. Paralleling the research on older adolescents' relationships with their father and mother, older adolescents reported better relationships with their grandmothers than with their grandfathers, and females reported better overall relationships with their grandparents than did males. Tinsley and Parke (1987) found that the timing of grandfatherhood influenced how involved grandfathers were with their grandchildren. Early-timed and late-timed grandfathers showed significantly less involvement with their grandchildren than did grandfathers who were considered "on time." Overall, McGreal (1994) noted that research on relationships with grandfathers continues to be a neglected area of research that has still not caught up to the level of developmental research on fathers and their children. Given that 5% of children in the United States live with at least one grandparent, and 30% of these children had no biological parent present (Roberts, 1993), research that focuses on the grandparent-grandchild relationship is of increasing importance.

THE IMPACT OF FATHER "ABSENCE"

History of Father Absence Research

Psychological research on paternal absence was initially popularized during World War II, when fathers' absence was studied with the assumption that the absence would be temporary. During the 1950s and 1960s, a large number of father absence studies were begun for the investigation of long term paternal absence due to parental separation and divorce (summarized in Anderson, 1968). These studies were intended to investigate paternal influences on children's development in general. Lamb (1986) described the rationale behind the father absence research design in the following way: "The assumption was that by comparing the behavior and personalities of children raised with and without fathers, one could—essentially by a process of subtraction—estimate what sort of influence fathers typically had" (p. 15). In 1976, Pedersen noted that the research design that was most frequently used to investigate paternal influences on children's development was the father absence research paradigm. At that time, Pedersen (1976) argued that "the conventional father absence research paradigm has outlived its usefulness" (p. 463). However, Pedersen's suggestions were not heeded, and the father absence research paradigm continues to dominate much of the research that is meant to investigate fathers' influences on their children.

Findings Based on Father Absence Research

Based on the early work using the paternal absence research paradigm, a number of differences were found between children who did or did not live with their fathers (for reviews, see Biller, 1981a; Biller & Solomon, 1986; Hamilton, 1977). Boys from father-absent homes were found to either show low levels of masculinity (Hetherington, 1966) or to show "compensatory" hypermasculinity, aggressiveness, and delinquency (Bacon, Child, & Barry, 1963; McCord, McCord, & Thurber, 1962). Father absence was also associated with children's personality disturbance, lower intellectual functioning, and impaired academic performance (Hamilton, 1977). However, further investigation of most of these findings suggests that the deficits of children in father-absent homes were actually due to greater stress and economic difficulty in those homes, rather than being due to the lack of a father in the household (Biller, 1981a). Radin (1976) found that father absence did not influence academic achievement in financially advantaged populations.

More recently, children from father-absent homes have been found to be at increased risk for suicide (Andrews & Lewinsohn, 1992) and for personality disturbance (Nelson & Valliant, 1993). African American children who do not have a father or a father figure in their lives appear to show lower adaptive functioning than those with fathers in the household (Dunn & Tucker, 1993) and to be more at risk for the development of posttraumatic stress disorder as a result of the chronic community violence to which they are exposed (Fitzpatrick & Boldizar, 1993).

Stevenson and Black (1988) conducted a meta-analysis of paternal absence and sex-role development because of the continued concern that children (especially boys) growing up without their fathers might show confusion in their gender roles. Again, the controversy over gender role research should be noted, given the confusion about what a healthy gender role should be for boys and girls. The meta-analysis included 67 studies, which yielded 222 estimates of effect size that compared the sex-typing of children in father-present and father-absent households. Father absence was due to a variety of factors, including parental divorce, paternal death, and paternal military involvement, with the majority of studies evaluating father absence due to parental divorce. Overall, significant differences were found for boys at different developmental levels, although the effect sizes were not large. Few differences were found for girls. Specifically, there was a slight tendency for girls in father-absent homes to be less feminine than girls in father-present homes. Stevenson and Black noted that the small effect size that suggested this difference was unlikely to be used to categorize girls in father-absent homes as pathologically unfeminine. In fact, the lower levels of femininity found for girls in father-absent homes might even be considered more psychologically healthy (Basow, 1992). For boys, there was stronger evidence of sex-typing effects, but the effects were in opposite directions depending on the age of the boys at the time of the study, and the effect sizes continued to be small. Preschool boys who lived with their fathers were found to make more sex-typed choices of toys and activities than preschool boys who did not live with their fathers. Thus, for young boys, there was evidence of stronger sex-typing for father-present boys when compared with father-absent boys. The reverse pattern was true for boys who were older at the time of the study. Older boys who lived in father-absent homes showed significantly more sex-typed overt behavior, especially with regard to aggression, than did older boys who lived in father-present homes.

The different results for different-aged boys may be due to developmental changes; however, prospective studies that follow the same children over many years would need to be conducted to reach this conclusion. In addition, these age differences were based on the age of the children at the time of the study, without regard for how old children were when their parents separated. Obviously father-absent boys who were in preschool at the time of the study had already experienced parental separation at a relatively young age, but boys' ages at the time of parental separation were unclear for father-absent boys who were studied when they were older. Therefore, further meta-analyses need to be completed to evaluate possible differences based on how old children are at the time of parental separation. Overall, this meta-analysis suggested that paternal absence had a stronger impact on boys than girls, and that younger boys showed lower levels of masculine-typed behavior whereas older boys showed higher levels of masculine-typed behavior.

Gabel (1992) discussed the increased emotional/behavioral problems that many children show due to paternal absence when their father is incarcerated. He noted, however, that rather than the absence serving as the main stressor to children, it may be that the psychological meaning of the incarceration, the quality of the parenting skills of the remaining caretaker, and the resources within the family all have an impact on children's adjustment to paternal absence due to incarceration. Gabel's discussion highlights the need to consider the reasons for paternal absence and the child's interpretation of the father's absence.

Limitations of Father Absence Research

Pedersen (1976) argued that the father-absent design was not capable of providing information about fathers' influences on children, just as the early research on "maternal deprivation" of children raised in institutions was not capable of providing information about mothers' influences on children. He suggested that children who are raised by single mothers may be affected by a number of factors other than their father's absence, including altered family structure, differences in maternal behavior, the presence of surrogate caregivers due to maternal employment, and changes in economic status. With regard to changes in economic status, there is strong evidence that custodial mothers and children usually experience a drop in financial resources after a divorce while noncustodial fathers experience a gain. Weitzman (1988) found that wives experience a 73% decrease in their standard of living during the first year after a divorce, whereas husbands experience a 42% increase in their standard of living during the same period. In addition, a substantial amount of court-ordered child support is never paid by noncustodial fathers, which further exacerbates the financial stress in single-mother households (Ellwood, 1988). Therefore, the financial stress in father-absent households could certainly be a factor that influences children's functioning. In addition, because African American children are more likely than Caucasian American children to be in a single-mother home at some time during their lives, the comparison of father-absent and father-present homes may be confounded by race and ethnicity.

Another limitation to the father absence research paradigm is the type of information that it yields about fathers and their children. If differences are found between children in father-absent homes and father-present homes, we must then ask why the differences emerged and how the differences should be interpreted (Lamb, 1986). The father absence research paradigm rarely enables researchers to answer these questions. In addition, when differences are found, they are often misinterpreted to mean that every child who grows up without a father is different from every child who grows up with a father. Even though research findings are based on group differences (e.g., the mean scores of 50 children from father-absent homes shows lower functioning in a certain area when compared with the mean scores of 50 children from father-present homes), there may be a tendency to assume that all children from father-absent homes will show decrements in that particular area of functioning (Lamb, 1986). This problem is not unique to the father absence research paradigm, but it seems to be a particular problem in the interpretation of results based on this paradigm. Kotelchuck (1976) argued that clearer information about paternal influences would be gained in investigations using direct methods, such as observation of father-child interactions, rather than the indirect, inferential methods of the paternal absence research paradigm.

The final limitation to the father absence research paradigm that will be discussed is the problem with the definition of "father absence." Most studies consider fathers absent if they do not live with their children. However, as discussed in Chapter 1, fathers' involvement with their children exists on a continuum regardless of their living arrangements (Danziger & Radin, 1990; Phares, 1993a; Seltzer & Bianchi, 1988). To use an artificial dichotomy of absence versus presence based on living arrangements neglects the vast diversity of fathers' involvement in their children's lives. In addition to being physically present with their children, there is also the issue of fathers' psychological presence or absence with their children (Fleck, Fuller, Malin, Miller & Acheson, 1980). When fathers are physically absent, attention should be paid to why they are physically absent. For example, Arendell (1992) found that a large percentage of absent divorced fathers actively chose to remain physically absent from their children to control conflict, tension, and undesirable emotions. It would be interesting to investigate whether similar rationales are given by fathers who are physically present in their children's lives, but emotionally absent from involvement with their children.

Whether or not fathers live with their children, there is a broad range of possible levels of physical and emotional involvement with children. Rather than the global categorization of absent versus present that the father absence research paradigm has utilized, researchers should specifically address the level of fathers' as well as mothers' involvement in their children's daily lives when investigating parental influences on normative child development.

PART II

Why Study Fathers and Developmental Psychopathology?

CHAPTER 3

Mother Blaming

The *FarSide* cartoon by Gary Larson shows the following: We see a client and a therapist in a nice private practice office, with the requisite diplomas on the wall and the couch for psychoanalysis. The client is wearing a clown hat, trench coat, flippers, and a rubber duck swimming pool flotation device around his waist, and he is sitting on the top of the coatrack. The therapist, with pen and paper in hand, says, "So, Mr. Fenton. . . . Let's begin with your mother." Certainly this is an amusing and harmless cartoon, and yet it reflects the assumptions about the etiology of psychopathology that are evident in both the lay public and the profession of psychology. Mothers are blamed for their children's behavior, whether their children are still young or fully grown adults. This chapter will discuss the existence of mother blaming, the possible reasons for mother blaming, and the ramifications of mother blaming. In addition, steps to prevent mother blaming in research and treatment will be outlined.

HISTORY OF MOTHER BLAMING

In clinical research, *mother blaming* has been defined as a sexist bias toward studying maternal contributions to children's emotional/behavioral problems while ignoring possible paternal contributions (Caplan & Hall-McCorquodale, 1985a). Mother blaming is also evident in clinical practice when maternal culpability for the client's psychological problems is explored without the concomitant exploration of paternal culpability (Caplan, 1989). The mother blaming that is evident in clinical research and practice may be associated with the mother blaming in society at large. It is difficult to say which one came first, but it is clear that professionals have helped to exacerbate the tendency toward mother blaming among the lay public. Before addressing the mother blaming that is currently present in clinical research and clinical therapeutic writings, the history of mother blaming will be discussed in relation to the sociology of motherhood and "professional" knowledge related to mothering.

Maternal Instinct

Much of the presumed connection between mother and child, and hence maternal culpability for both positive and negative aspects of the child, stems from the assumption of a maternal instinct. For example, Hobhouse (1916) reported that maternal instinct was a "true" instinct and no corresponding paternal instinct was evident based on the fact that few men were naturally skilled at taking care of infants. In 1923, Reed thoroughly discredited the existence of a maternal instinct through use of empirical research and previously collected demographic data. She asked 87 women in a maternity hospital "Are you glad that you are going to have a baby?" based on the premise that if there were a maternal instinct then the resounding answers would be "yes." Yet, 65 of these mothers-to-be reported that they were not happy to be having a baby. Many of the mothers reported that they could not afford another child or that they had been forced to forfeit employment due to the pregnancy. Reed argued that there was no empirical support for a maternal instinct, and she further called for a discontinuation of the perpetration of the maternal instinct myth. Watson (1926) also discredited the concept of a maternal instinct by noting that new mothers were often awkward and lacked skills in taking care of their newborns.

However, the idea of maternal instinct has remained very much in existence, even when there is direct evidence to the contrary. For example, in their studies of rhesus monkeys raised without monkey parents, Harlow, Harlow, and Hansen (1963) reported that "all five females (motherless mothers) were totally hopeless mothers, and none of the infants would have survived without artificial feeding in the first days or weeks of life" (p. 275). These data argue against a maternal instinct, and yet Harlow and colleagues (1963) go on to conclude that "the maternal affectional system is one of a number of affectional systems exhibited by rhesus monkeys" (p. 280). This conclusion is especially ironic given that many of the research assistants who so carefully nurtured the infant monkeys were undoubtedly male. These data could have been interpreted in many different ways, but the focus remained on the "maternal instinct" of the inadequate monkey mothers rather than on the "paternal instinct" of the male researchers.

With regard to humans, Bettelheim (1965) stated, "As much as women want to be good scientists or engineers, they want first and foremost to be womanly companions of men and to be mothers" (p. 15). Even though there is strong evidence to the contrary, maternal instinct is a concept that has remained ingrained in both the professional and lay communities (Shields, 1975). The myth of maternal instinct may help to explain why mothers are so often blamed for their children's problems. Because mothers are expected to have the instinctual abilities to care for their young, anything that goes wrong must be the mother's fault due to her overriding instinctual abilities (criticism noted by Caplan, 1989).

Motherhood Mandate

A number of authors have noted that a motherhood mandate exists that necessitates motherhood for most women in Western culture. For example, Russo (1979) argued that the motherhood mandate centralizes the role of motherhood in a woman's identity and that motherhood is seen as incompatible and in conflict with other roles in the woman's life (e.g., employed worker). However, the role of fatherhood allows men to serve in multiple roles, with little or no conflict (e.g., employed worker and parent). The motherhood mandate can be considered to be a product of an affluent society that can afford to expect women to care for a few children rather than using their resources in a larger workforce (Bernard, 1975). The motherhood mandate pervades social institutions and emphasizes that motherhood is not merely one life option that women can choose (Bernard, 1974, 1982; Russo, 1979). Chesler (1972) noted that women are conditioned to need and want motherhood more than men are conditioned to need and want fatherhood. A man who is a lifelong "bachelor" with no children is rarely looked down on, whereas a woman who is a childless "spinster" is considered tragic regardless of her choice of a life path (Chesler, 1972).

"Good" Mother/"Bad" Mother

The definition of a "good" mother (and conversely a "bad" mother) can change dramatically from time to time. For example, Reed (1923) noted that in ancient Sparta the practice of infant exposure and infanticide were common practices because of the wish for a strong and hardy population. Therefore, mothers were expected to allow their weak or ill infants to die for the presumed betterment of that society. Mothers who refused to part with their sickly infants were considered bad mothers and were ostracized socially, just as present-day mothers who participated in infanticide might be.

A number of writers have noted the "good" mother/"bad" mother dichotomy in current Western culture (Goodrich, 1991; Welldon, 1988). These myths of the "good" mother and the "bad" mother imply that mothers can only be all good or all bad, with little room for the complexity of human emotion and behavior. In describing these myths, Swigart (1991) noted the good mother knows and fills every need for her children, is constantly nurturing and caring, never gets bored with her children, and fills this role effortlessly and without any sense of self-sacrifice. Conversely, the bad mother is so self-absorbed and narcissistic that she is indifferent to her children's needs and is also unaware of the harm she constantly inflicts on them. Swigart argued that, except in extremely rare cases, this dichotomy does not represent real mothers. Most mothers are not perfect, as reflected by the "good" mother, and yet most do not deserve to be called "bad" mothers either. The myth of the good mother/bad mother dichotomy has been a way of negating the real work that goes into mothering. It has served to blame mothers for their children's problems, with the underlying assumption that when children have problems it must be because of their bad mother.

In addition, there have been mixed messages from professionals as to what constitutes good or bad mothering. Bernard (1975) noted that mothers are considered pathogenic if they are possessive and overprotective, and yet they are also pathogenic if they are somewhat withdrawn and do not provide constant attention to their children. It is truly a no-win situation. In discussing the myths related to good mothers and bad mothers, Caplan (1989) noted, "If someone offered you a job saying 'If *anything* goes wrong, even sixty or seventy years from now, you will be blamed,' you'd tell them forget it. But that is what motherhood is" (p. 67). Yet, the search for the good mother continues, as reflected in a recent article entitled "What Is a Good Mother?" (Fairbanks, 1993).

Mother Blaming

It would be impossible to discuss all of the examples of mother blaming throughout the history of psychology because it has been so pervasive. One of the most infamous examples of mother blaming in the history of psychology was Wylie's (1946) book entitled *Generation of Vipers*. Wylie appeared to be reacting to the myth of the good mother and argued that "megaloid momworship has got completely out of hand" (p. 185). He further coined the term "momism" to reflect mothers' excessive domination of their children that leads to maladaptive functioning (Wylie, 1946; also see Sebald, 1976). In the same mother-bashing vain, Rheingold (1967) stated, "Even if men performed the caretaking duties of the mothering person, it is doubtful that they would exert comparable harmful influence, because very few men have the destructive drive toward children common to mothers (p. 107)." He suggested that if all mothers could be made nurturant (with no unconscious aggressive impulses), then in subsequent generations there would be no mental illness or social disorganization. In response, Bernard (1975) argued that the message is painfully clear, "Cure mother, cure the social order" (p. 219).

Wylie and Rheingold represent just a few examples of unabashed mother blaming in professional writing. Undoubtedly, their writing was influenced by, and in turn has influenced theories of developmental psychopathology, clinical research investigating developmental psychopathology, and clinical therapeutic work that has been conducted.

MOTHER BLAMING IN THEORIES OF THE DEVELOPMENT OF PSYCHOPATHOLOGY

The "professional" knowledge that has blamed mothers for their children's psychopathology has been strongly influenced by psychological theories of normal and abnormal development throughout the history of psychology and psychiatry. Originally, many of the theories were used to describe normal development where mothers were seen as the primary caregiver to infants, but these theories also were used to implicate mothers when their infants and children did not show a normal course of psychological development. The focus on mothers in theories of child development led to a research focus on mothers to the exclusion of fathers. Ironically, although the role of fathers in normal child development was unjustly ignored, the lack of attention to fathers also kept them safe from being blamed for their children's psychological problems. The major theoretical perspectives that will be explored are psychodynamic theories, attachment theories, and family systems theories.

Psychodynamic Theories

A variety of psychodynamic theories have implicated mothers in the normal and abnormal development of their children, the most notable ones being those developed by Freud and Mahler. Although in his early work Freud focused attention on the father's role due to the importance of resolution of the oedipal conflict, the majority of Freud's career was focused on the mother's importance as it related to the mother-child relationship (Freud, 1949). Freud believed that the mother-child relationship was the prototype of all the child's future romantic relationships, and therefore the mother-child relationship was of utmost importance in the child's development. Although he believed that infants and children could identify with both parents, Freud argued that the mother-child relationship was of primary importance for the child's psychological development. Freud's focus on the importance on the mother-child relationship led to a significant amount of mother blaming when the child's development did not turn out as originally planned (Caplan, 1989).

Mahler also focused her attention on the mother-infant relationship, although she acknowledged that the father played an important role in the separation and individuation of the child from his or her mother (Mahler, 1952). Mahler and her students argued that the infant's first and primary relationship is with the mother, whereas the father serves to break this "symbiotic" relationship once the infant reaches toddlerhood. Much of Mahler's work was used to implicate the mother's responsibility for childhood autism due to the "state of symbiosis" between mother and child, and yet little attention was given to the father's role. As discussed in Chapter 5, recent research has suggested that neither mothering nor fathering behaviors are associated with the development of autism (Sanua, 1986a, 1986b).

It is interesting to note that Jung (1949) wrote a book entitled *The Significance of the Father in the Destiny of the Individual,* in which he explored the father's role in human development. However, most of his other writings focused on the mother and only on archetypal representations of the father (Von Der

Heydt, 1964) and therefore Jung's followers tend to focus on the mother's role in children's psychological functioning.

Many psychodynamic theorists highlighted the importance of mothers because of their ability to breast-feed the infant. The bond between mother and infant primarily was due to breast-feeding and the sustenance and physical gratification that the infant received from his or her mother. However, this hypothesis was shown to be incorrect by Harlow's (1958) work with infant monkeys. Harlow found that infant monkeys were more likely to cling to a soft terrycloth "mother" surrogate rather than a wire-mesh "mother" surrogate, even if it was the wire-mesh surrogate that fed the infant. These studies suggested that contact comfort was more crucial than food sustenance to the attachment process of infant monkeys. Therefore, the psychodynamic hypothesis that food and physical gratification from an infant's mother were more critical than other aspects of caretaking that could be provided by other caretakers (including fathers) was questioned severely.

Although the work by Harlow was crucial in questioning the importance of mothers as primary caretakers, the language used in Harlow's research may have inadvertently reinforced the focus on mothers and infants. The surrogate monkeys were built from wire, terrycloth, and a plastic bottle, but they were still referred to as "mother" surrogates, rather than "parent" or "caretaker" surrogates (Harlow et al., 1963). Thus, even though these surrogates were gender-neutral and were being used to question the importance of maternal feeding, the language used to describe the results may have inadvertently maintained the focus on the mother-infant relationship, rather than a more generic caretaker-infant relationship. These studies continue to be referred to as studies of "mother love" (e.g., Vasta et al., 1992), which seems to focus more attention, rather than less attention, on the importance of mothers just as had been proposed by psychodynamic theorists. Although there is little evidence to support psychodynamic theories that highlight the importance of the mother-child relationship to the near exclusion of the father-child relationship (Schaffer, 1971), these theories have had a long-lasting impact on psychological research and thinking.

Attachment Theories

An outgrowth of psychodynamic theories was the development of attachment theories by object relations theorists such as Winnicott (1958), Klein (1957), and Bowlby (1951). Both Bowlby (1951) and Ainsworth et al. (1978) focused on the biologically based tendency for newborn infants to seek contact with adults. Although they acknowledged that infants could develop meaningful attachments with any primary caregiver, the primary focus of early work in attachment investigated the process of mother-infant attachment. Much of children's later social relationships were attributed to the early attachment with their mother. Although Bowlby's work highlighted the need for humane care of infants, it also served to lay the blame on mothers for children's minor behavioral problems as well as more severe problems such as juvenile delinquency and schizophrenia (Chess & Thomas, 1982).

Proponents of the more strict bonding hypothesis suggested that unless there was skin-to-skin contact between mother and infant within a critical period (usually within hours after birth), the child would be unable to develop meaningful relationships later in life (Klaus & Kennell, 1976). There is little support for a strong version of the bonding hypothesis (Rode, Chang, Fisch, & Sroufe, 1981). However, infants' attachment is not limited to the mother; they can be similarly attached to their fathers, or other stable caretakers. In a meta-analysis of maternal and paternal attachment, Fox and colleagues (1991) found that infants tended to have similar attachment styles to both their mothers and their fathers, and that this pattern seemed to be due to the similar parenting styles of parental dyads.

Family Systems Theories

Although more recent family systems theorists point to problems in the structure of the entire family rather than in a maladaptive mother-child relationship (e.g., Minuchin, 1974), original theories of family malfunctioning still placed the burden of guilt on mothers of emotionally disturbed children. Many theories of family malfunctioning were originally influenced by psychodynamic thought and therefore focused on problematic mother-child interactions as the cause of children's emotional problems (Brodkin, 1980). For example, Fromm-Reichmann (1948) argued that schizophrenia was due to the child's cold and dominant "schizophrenogenic mother." Similarly, Bateson, Jackson, Haley, and Weakland (1956) argued that schizophrenia was due to mothers who put their children in a "double bind" by providing contradictory communication about the need for emotional closeness versus emotional distance.

Ackerman (1958) originally practiced traditional child psychiatry and worked with the child alone or with the child and his or her mother. To address the social basis of children's problems within the family, he then moved to working with the child and both parents and eventually to working with the entire family. Bowen (1965) originally worked with schizophrenic clients based on the assumption of a "schizophrenogenic mother." He believed that mothers of schizophrenic clients showed overinvestment and symbiosis with their offspring, and therefore schizophrenic clients and their mothers were hospitalized for treatment. Eventually, however, he came to believe that the larger family system played a role in schizophrenia and later began hospitalizing the entire family of a schizophrenic client. More recently, Bowen (1966) moved toward only treating the client's parents due to the assumption of problems within the marital system.

Although original family theories implicated mothers for their children's maladaptive functioning, more recent theories have moved toward a focus on the entire family or on the marital dyad (Becvar & Becvar, 1993; Brodkin, 1980; L'Abate, 1994). However, the old mother-blaming terminology of the schizophrenogenic mother and double bind continue to influence research and practice even today.

MOTHER BLAMING IN CLINICAL RESEARCH LITERATURE

Mother blaming in the clinical research literature has been investigated in three ways: (a) research that has documented mother blaming in the way in which mothers are discussed in clinical research, (b) research that has documented the concomitant lack of attention to the father's role in child and adolescent psychopathology, and (c) research that has investigated directly subjects' perceptions of maternal and paternal culpability for children's and adolescents' emotional/behavioral problems.

Caplan and Hall-McCorquodale (1985a) conducted a comprehensive review of major clinical journals to investigate how mothers are discussed in clinical research. They surveyed nine journals for three different years (1970, 1976, 1982) and analyzed articles in five different domains:

1. Number of words to describe mother versus father.
2. Information-gathering techniques such as collecting data from mother versus father.
3. Attribution of blame such as discussing the impact of mothers' versus fathers' psychopathology on children's functioning.
4. Implications of psychological treatment such as only including mothers but not fathers in treatment.
5. Whether or not previous literature was discussed in such a way as to blame mothers for their children's psychological problems.

A total of 125 articles were identified for inclusion representing a mix of empirical research on clinical topics and clinical writings related to professionals' experiences rather than empirical data. Within these 125 articles, the word "mother" was used 2,151 times, whereas the word "father" was used 946 times. Case examples or illustrations of clinical problems showed that mothers were described more often than fathers at a 5:1 ratio. Data on maternal psychological functioning were collected in 82% of the studies, whereas data on paternal psychological functioning were collected in 54% of the studies. When paternal absence was noted, 24% of the articles stated that the absence had no impact on child functioning, but when maternal absence was noted, only 2% of the articles stated that the absence had not contributed to the child's maladaptive functioning. Maternal psychopathology was said to contribute to children's functioning in 64% of the articles, whereas paternal psychopathology was noted as a contributing factor in only 34% of the articles. In terms of psychological treatment, mothers were the only parent involved in treatment in 18% of the studies and fathers were the only parent involved in treatment in 2% of the studies. In 53% of the articles, unquestioned assumptions about maternal culpability for child psychopathology were presented based on previous research literature. Overall, Caplan and Hall-McCorquodale documented a strong tendency toward mother blaming in clinical and research literature. They further noted that the frequency of mother blaming did not appear to vary based on the year of publication nor the gender of the author(s). In other words, mother blaming did not appear to decrease between 1970 and 1982, and female authors were just as likely as male authors to blame mothers for children's psychopathology.

To update this review of mother blaming in research literature and also to investigate the concomitant lack of attention to fathers in developmental research on psychopathology, Phares and Compas (1992) reviewed empirical research published from 1984 through 1991 in eight clinical and developmental journals (*Child Development, Developmental Psychology, Journal of Abnormal Child Psychology, Journal of Abnormal Psychology, Journal of the American Academy of Child and Adolescent Psychiatry, Journal of Child Psychology and Psychiatry and Allied Disciplines, Journal of Clinical Child Psychology,* and *Journal of Consulting and Clinical Psychology*). They reviewed empirical studies (not clinical case studies) that involved information relating to at least one parent and that addressed psychopathology in either the child or the parent(s) or both. Because the intended focus on abnormal rather than normal development in human beings, articles were excluded if they dealt solely with normative developmental processes or if they dealt with nonhuman research participants. A total of 577 articles that fit these criteria were identified. Of these 577 articles, 48% (277 articles) included mothers only, 26% (151 articles) included both mothers and fathers and analyzed them separately for maternal and paternal effects, 25% (141 articles) either included "parents" without noting the gender of the parent or included both mothers and fathers but did not analyze for separate maternal and paternal effects, and just 1% (8 articles) included fathers only. Based on a chi-square analysis, these data showed that mothers were significantly more likely to be included in research on child and adolescent psychopathology than were fathers. Further, this review showed that the lack of attention to fathers and child psychopathology that Caplan and Hall-McCorquodale (1985a) noted was still evident. Although it was exciting to see that 26% of the articles included both maternal and paternal characteristics *and* analyzed them separately, Phares and Compas (1992) noted a clear need to include fathers in more studies of developmental psychopathology.

An alternate method for investigating mother blaming has been to investigate empirically subjects' perceptions of maternal and paternal culpability for children's and adolescents' emotional/behavioral problems. Because mother blaming had been well documented in research literature (Caplan & Hall-McCorquodale, 1985a), Der-Karabetian and Preciado (1989) investigated the mother-blaming tendencies of a nonprofessional sample. They asked college students to choose whether mother, father, individual, or society was most responsible for 45 emotional/behavioral problems of childhood. They found that the individual child him- or herself was held most responsible for his or her problematic behavior, followed by societal responsibility for children's maladaptive behavior. Mothers were significantly more likely than fathers to be held responsible for their children's emotional/behavioral problems. There was a tendency for mothers to be blamed for internalizing child problems such as shyness, whereas fathers were somewhat more likely to be blamed for externalizing child problems such as alcohol abuse. This study suggested that when mothers and fathers were directly compared, mothers were more likely to be held responsible for their children's emotional/behavioral problems. However, this study also raised the issue of alternate sources of responsibility for children's problems (e.g., the child or society in general) as well as the issue of differential blame given to different types of child problems.

To further investigate these issues, Phares (1993b) conducted a study in which college students were asked to use a 1-to-7 scale to rate the responsibility of mother, father, child, and society for a variety of internalizing, externalizing, and prosocial behaviors. Overall, mothers were rated as significantly more responsible than fathers, children, and society for children's internalizing behavior problems. Fathers were rated as significantly more responsible than mothers and children, but not society, for children's externalizing problems. Both mothers and fathers were seen as more responsible than children or society for prosocial, adaptive child behaviors. This study suggested that there is a need for greater specificity when investigating mother blaming. Although this college student sample showed evidence of blaming mothers for their children's internalizing problems, there was also evidence of blaming fathers for their children's externalizing problems. Therefore, future research into mother blaming should investigate the specificity of child problems. Thus far, this specificity of mother versus father blaming has been shown in college student samples, but it has not yet been explored in samples of researchers.

MOTHER BLAMING IN CLINICAL PRACTICE

In 1964, Stella Chess began an editorial by repeating an often-heard comment when children are referred for clinical services: "To meet Johnny's mother is to understand his problem" (p. 613). Chess went on to argue eloquently that when clinicians assume maternal responsibility for children's problems, clinicians are likely to only investigate the mother-child relationship and are likely to ignore other factors in the child's life. When mothers are initially blamed for their children's emotional problems, "Other questions go unasked, hence unanswered" (Chess, 1964, p. 613). In 1982, Chess revisited the "blame the mother" ideology and acknowledged that although mother blaming was not as blatant as in 1964, it was still evident. She again documented the tendency to blame mothers for their children's problems when children are referred for services and again argued that it is irresponsible for professionals to automatically assume maternal culpability for children's problems. Caplan (1989) noted that mother blaming, and on a more global level woman blaming, is an insidious aspect of many clinicians' training and current perspective. She argued that, whereas in some families mothers may have some responsibility for their children's problems, it is just as likely that there are other etiologic factors for children's problems. It is clear that mother blaming occurs in clinical practice, just as it does in theory development and empirical research. A related topic is the issue of whether fathers are even involved in clinical practice when their children are referred for services.

Many clinicians have acknowledged the "well-known" fact that fathers are reluctant to become involved in therapy for child and family problems (Berg & Rosenblum, 1977; Doherty, 1981; Gaines, 1981; Guillebeaux, Storm, & Demaris, 1986; Horton, 1984; LeCroy, 1987; Sachs, 1986). Although empirical data are rarely cited to establish this fact, data are available to support the notion of fathers' comparatively lower involvement in child and family treatment. For example, in an investigation of the effect of initial family assessments conducted in the home, Churven (1978) found that all mothers attended the first clinic visit, but few fathers attended the first clinic visit. Only 6.5% of the fathers in the control group (no preclinic home visit) attended the first clinic appointment and 43.5% of the fathers in the preclinic home visit group attended the first clinic appointment. This study suggested that low paternal involvement in therapy could be because fathers are often not required or even overtly encouraged to be involved in child and family treatment.

In a review of outcome studies of parent training over a 12-year period (from 1970 to 1981), Budd and O'Brien (1982) found that fathers were involved in only 13% of the families treated in these studies, and there was a decline over time in the percentage of these studies that included fathers. It is unclear whether this low involvement was due to the fathers' reluctance to participate or due to the researchers' and therapists' reluctance to have them participate. It could be that the "well-known" fact of fathers' lower therapeutic participation rates at least partially reflects therapists' and clinical researchers' lower expectations for paternal involvement. Feldman (1990) argues that the most important barrier to paternal involvement in therapy is the therapist's failure to include fathers in the initial stages of therapy. Doherty (1981) noted that when the fathers' participation in treatment was explained as "automatic" at the time of the initial intake phone call, fathers nearly always participated in treatment. Regardless of the underlying reasons, there is consensus on the limited participation rates of fathers in treatment from both empirical research and clinical writing.

It is interesting to note that in literature describing the father's overt resistance to therapy, mothers are often given the blame for not involving the father in treatment (Gaines, 1981; Kaslow, 1981; Sachs, 1986; Szapocznik et al., 1988). Doherty (1981) noted that if the mother is not able to get the father to agree to therapy, then the mother herself is ambivalent about therapy. Although this may be true in some families, it may be inaccurate for other families, especially in view of the power and status differentials that exist in many families. This type of unquestioned belief in mothers' culpability may be further evidence of the mother blaming in clinical journals that was documented by Caplan and Hall-McCorquodale (1985a). Ironically, although the clinical and research literature on child sexual abuse may neglect mothers as perpetrators due to inadequate assessment techniques (Banning, 1989), there is still a noticeable amount of mother blaming for maternal culpability in father-child incest (Pierce, 1987; Ringwalt & Earp, 1988). Assumptions of maternal culpability for child and family problems, especially those that are perpetrated by the father, need to be examined empirically.

An additional avenue of research into mother blaming has been to assess fathers' and mothers' own sense of responsibility for their children's emotional and behavioral problems. Penfold (1985) and Watson (1986) both recruited families in which a child was receiving outpatient mental health treatment for an emotional or behavioral problem. Fathers and mothers were both asked the extent to which they felt responsible for their children's problems and the extent to which the other parent was responsible for their children's problems. Given the extensive mother blaming that exists in psychological theory, research, and practice, it was not surprising to find evidence of mother blaming in these clinically referred families. Fathers tended not to take personal responsibility for their children's problems, whereas mothers were likely to attribute their children's problems to themselves significantly more than to external sources. Interestingly, fathers showed a significant tendency to blame mothers for their children's emotional and behavioral problems.

PREVENTION OF MOTHER BLAMING

Although some might say that the answer in preventing mother blaming is to just start blaming fathers at an equal rate as mothers, this would be neither a productive nor an admirable solution. Caplan (1989) elaborated ways in which individuals can discontinue their own personal mother blaming. At the professional level, a number of tactics can be used to decrease and eventually prevent mother blaming.

Acknowledge the Problem of Mother Blaming

The first step to reducing mother blaming is to acknowledge that it exists. This chapter has discussed the many forms of mother blaming that have been documented. There are also anecdotal examples of psychologists who have begun acknowledging the problem of mother blaming. For example, in an excellent review of children of depressed mothers, Downey and Coyne (1990) noted the "mother bashing" that was apparent in much of the research on depressed mothers. A number of textbooks on abnormal psychology have raised the issue of mother blaming in theories of etiology for abnormal behavior. For example, after discussing theories of the etiology of schizophrenia, Davison and Neale (1990) added a footnote that stated, "It is noteworthy that most theories implicating family processes in the etiology of abnormal behavior focus almost exclusively on the mother. Sexism?" (p. 396). In the popular press, Caplan (1986, 1989) has attempted to make people outside academia aware of the issue of mother blaming. Although acknowledging the problem is the first step to decreasing its incidence, other more direct steps will need to be taken to significantly decrease and eventually prevent mother blaming in clinical research and treatment.

Question Sexist Theories and Outdated Assumptions about Motherhood

Theories that only hypothesize maternal culpability for children's problems must be questioned and thoroughly investigated (Phares, 1992). Research on fathers' roles in normal child development has shown that fathers have a significant impact on their children's development (Biller, 1993; Bronstein & Cowan, 1988; Lamb, 1981). This research was conducted because researchers finally questioned theories that focused only on mothers' roles in child development. Research studies that investigate only one gender due to unexamined assumptions about that gender are considered sexist (Denmark, Russo, Frieze, & Sechzer, 1988). In the history of psychological research, there was a trend for primarily using male subjects and then applying the results to females (e.g., Kohlberg & Kramer, 1969; McClelland, 1955). However, when parenting is concerned, the focus has been almost exclusively on mothers (Phares, 1992). Although these trends are less evident in current research, we need to remain vigilant about conducting nonsexist research (Gannon, Luchetta, Rhodes, Pardie, & Segrist, 1992). This requirement is especially true in questioning sexist theories of the etiology of child and adolescent psychopathology.

There is also a need to question assumptions about motherhood and the role of mothers in children's lives these days. Most people are well aware of the changing family constellations over the past few decades and recognize the economic necessity of maternal employment. However, research on parental influences on children rarely reflects this common knowledge. Even though the majority of mothers in the United States with children under the age of 18 years are employed (Matthews & Rodin, 1989), researchers still seem to expect mothers but not fathers to make themselves available for research participation. This expectation may be a current-day reflection of the motherhood mandate. Mothers are still supposed to make themselves available for research projects (and school conferences and after-school activities), whereas the same expectation is not true for fathers. These assumptions need to be questioned.

Maternal responsibility for children's well-being may simply be one aspect of a global belief that women are more responsible for the development and maintenance of social relationships (Goodrich, Rampage, Ellman, & Halstead, 1988). Bernard (1981) noted that mothers are assumed to have responsibility for family well-being and child caretaking, whereas fathers seem to have been given a dispensation against any familial participation other than financial responsibility. Mothers' parenting contributions are seen as mandatory, whereas fathers' parenting contributions are seen as optional (Bernard, 1987). This may be why there seems to be a taboo against father blaming that is not evident for mother blaming. Caplan (1989) noted a number of case examples where fathers were not held responsible for their lack of fathering activities because their job was so important. Mothers rarely receive this kind of reprieve, even when they are employed for the same amount of time as are their husbands. Fathers' behaviors tend to be excused, whereas mothers are held responsible for nearly every aspect of their child's well-being (Gilbert, 1981). For example, a plethora of studies have investigated single mothers, and yet there has been very little research investigating fathers who leave the family (Gilbert, 1981). Bernard (1981) argues that professionals should not allow these inequities to be mirrored in research and practice.

Conduct Research on Fathers as Well as Mothers

Research into outdated assumptions about motherhood and sexist theories should lead to the obvious conclusion that fathers should be investigated to the same degree that mothers have been in developmental research on psychopathology. Almost any research that has been conducted on the maternal-child relationship can be conducted on the paternal-child relationship. In addition, fathers who are not physically present in the home still undoubtedly have an impact on their children's well-being (Biller, 1981a), and therefore they should be studied. At a minimum, fathers provide a genetic contribution to their child's functioning that is evident regardless of whether they are present or not (Simeonsson & Rosenthal, 1992).

Once a substantial body of research literature has been amassed on the fathers' role in developmental psychopathology, researchers can move into research that investigates the overall impact of parenting, rather than fathering and mothering separately. Parenting will always occur against a contextual background and not in a vacuum, so researchers need to focus eventually on the context of the family rather than on individual dyads. For example, in studies of maternal nurturing, anthropologists studied women in six cultures around the world and found that mothers were more nurturing when they received more help with child care (Bernard, 1975). The help often came from fathers, elders in the community, or relatives. This suggests that nurturing is not an individual or a dyadic variable, but occurs within a context of familial and social support for parenting. Similar investigations should include paternal nurturing within the familial and social context.

Related to the issue of conducting research on parenting behaviors (rather than mothering behaviors or fathering behaviors) is the issue of research on gender differences and gender similarities. There has been a heated debate among feminist psychologists as to whether research into gender differences can help the status of American women (e.g., by pointing out how gendered the society is and how these social forces influence women's and men's behavior) or whether it in fact hurts women's status (e.g., by finding differences between females and males, and assuming that male characteristics are more valued, the research into gender differences may in fact point out what might be perceived as female "weaknesses"). Eagly (1990, 1993, 1995) argues that research into gender differences is not inherently disadvantageous for the well-being of women, but she points out that political and scientific agendas can influence the interpretation of results of research into gender differences.

The investigation of fathers and mothers can be conceptualized as research on male and female parents. Because so little is known about male parenting in contrast to female parenting, it is necessary initially to determine how male parenting and female parenting are different and similar. Once these basic processes are established, however, it will be important to move beyond the research into main effects of parent gender to investigate contextual and familial characteristics of parenting.

Work toward Greater Equality within the Family

Although professionals alone cannot change the status and roles for mothers and fathers in the family, professionals can help work toward a greater respect for mothering and fathering within the family. Bernard (1975) noted that it is easier to work toward equality in the workplace than equality at home because objective criteria can be evaluated in the workplace. The large percentage of mothers who carry a double burden of paid work in the workplace and unpaid work at home may only feel appreciated for their paid employment. The undervaluing of what has traditionally been "women's" work (e.g., raising children, maintaining the household, preparing meals) has been well documented (Bernard, 1974, 1975; Caplan & Hall-McCorquodale, 1989b; Welldon, 1988). Because employed women still carry the brunt of household work even when both parents are employed (Thompson & Walker, 1989), mothers do a significant amount of work that goes unappreciated and often unnoticed. Caplan (1989) noted that it is extremely rare to hear a mother thanked for a good week's worth of dusting, and yet if she were doing the same work within the context of employment, at least she would receive a paycheck that acknowledged her contribution. How often have full-time mothers been referred to as "women who do not work" when in fact they work 24 hours a day, 365 days per year (Caplan, 1989)?

This speaks to the larger sexist practice of devaluing activities that have traditionally been considered within the female realm. If children were raised to respect expressive qualities as well as instrumental qualities, the accomplishments of mothers might be valued more and mothers would be blamed less (Pogrebin, 1980). Although Firestone (1971) argued that true equality can only be achieved through a biological revolution that would free women from the birth process and allow fetuses to develop outside the human body, it is hoped that equality within the family and throughout society at large can be achieved through less radical means. It may be that with a growing awareness of the importance of fathers, and the simultaneous increase in fathers' participation in child care, a new respect for parenting behaviors of both mothers and fathers will emerge. Professionals can help in this venture by discontinuing mother blaming and by highlighting the importance of both fathers and mothers in the caretaking and expressive aspects of the family.

CHAPTER 4

Models and Theories of
Developmental Psychopathology

The preceding chapter discussed psychodynamic, attachment, and early family systems theories of abnormal development in relation to mother blaming and the lack of attention to paternal influences. This chapter will cover various theories of developmental psychopathology with special attention to the role of fathers. Although this is not an exhaustive discussion of theoretical frameworks, these theories represent the primary work in the investigation of paternal influences. Before discussing these individual theories related to developmental psychopathology, a more general discussion of the importance of theories and the use of theories will be provided.

THE ROLES OF THEORIES IN RESEARCH

At the most basic level of scientific inquiry, theories should serve a number of purposes:

1. Understanding of the phenomena under investigation.
2. Prediction of future associations related to the phenomena under investigation.
3. Organization and interpretation of research findings that result from investigation into the phenomena.
4. Generation of further research into the phenomena of interest (summarized in Bordens & Abbott, 1988).

Characteristics of a good theory include:

1. The ability to account for most of the existing research data in the domain of interest.
2. Explanatory relevance that shows good grounds for believing that the phenomena would occur under the given conditions.

3. Testability that suggests the theory is capable of being refuted.
4. Prediction of novel events so that predictions of new phenomena are included in the theory.
5. Parsimony so that there are simple descriptions and deductions in the theory with the fewest possible assumptions made regarding the phenomena of interest.
6. Logical consistency that suggests the theory is internally consistent and does not contradict itself in different predictions of different events related to the phenomena under investigation (Bordens & Abbott, 1988; Miller, 1989; Shaw & Costanzo, 1982).

With regard to theories of development, Miller (1989) noted that theories must focus on change over time and should include a description of changes *within* the area of behavior, a description of changes in the relations *among* several areas of behavior, and an explanation of the course of development for the phenomenon under investigation. These principles can be extrapolated to consider developmental psychopathology; however, rather than focusing on the individual's behavior, a more thorough understanding of the individual's environment (e.g., family, school, social, etc.) is required. Simeonsson and Rosenthal (1992) suggested that theories of developmental psychopathology should be evaluated on a commonsense basis, the empirical base, the inclusiveness of normality-abnormality variance, the developmental comprehensiveness, and the applied relevance.

It is important to remember that a particular theory can never be "proved" as this would necessitate an investigation of every possible instance of the variables to be studied, which is obviously impossible. Theories can be disproved, but usually this results from a number of negative findings related to the theory rather than only one or two studies that contradict the theory (Shaw & Costanzo, 1982). However, Achenbach (1982) noted that because theories usually consist of inferences, they rarely can be fully disproved. Instead, theories earn credibility when most of the deductions are verified and lose credibility when most of the deductions are called into question (Achenbach, 1982).

In nearly any domain, and especially in relation to developmental psychopathology, no one theory can be expected to encompass all extrapolations of a particular phenomenon. Achenbach (1982) put it succinctly when he wrote, "There is not now (and probably never will be) a *single* developmental theory of *all* psychopathology" (p. 1). In addition, Simeonsson and Rosenthal (1992) noted that because of the diversity of clinical needs of children and adolescence (e.g., depression, anxiety, hyperactivity, abuse) and the diversity of domains that require explanation (e.g., cognitive, familial, psychosocial, etc.), a matching number of theoretical frameworks may be required to fully understand the development of psychopathology in children and adolescents. Further, they noted that an eclectic approach that integrates a variety of theories may be most helpful in explaining a particular phenomenon related to developmental psychopathology.

As noted in the previous chapter, many theories of the development of psychopathology in children and adolescents have focused on the role of mothers. However, even with a well-researched topic such as maternal depression, the theories and models of transmission continue to be unclear. For example, Dodge (1990) noted that the effects of maternal depression on children appear to have multiple pathways, including (a) genetic transmission, (b) dyadic interactions between mothers and children such as modeling processes (c) maternal parenting practices such as teaching practices or structuring the child's social environment, and (d) marital conflict between parents. In addition, Gelfand and Teti (1990) noted that research with the children of depressed mothers has encompassed a variety of theories, most of which have received some support, including coercive family process models, cognitive theories, interactional models, social cognitive theories, mutual regulation models, and attachment theories. Because theoretical investigation into such a well-researched area as maternal depression continues to be cloudy, it is not surprising to discover that the theoretical formulation of paternal psychopathology is still quite limited.

At a general level of theoretical conceptualization, Sigel and Parke (1987) noted that models for investigating father-child interactions and relationships could include noninteractive models, unidirectional models, dyadic models that include bidirectional processes, dyadic models that include the impact of third parties, and family network models. Parke and colleagues (1988) also highlighted the importance of considering reciprocal or mutual processes of father-child and child-father effects. With these frameworks in mind, a number of theories related to the development of psychopathology in children and adolescents will be reviewed.

BEHAVIORAL GENETICS

This section will cover three primary areas of work regarding behavioral genetic influences in the development of psychopathology: (a) genetic factors, (b) nongenetic biological influences, and (c) behavioral genetic influences. Genetic influences in the development of psychopathology are discussed most often without reference to maternal versus paternal influences. For example, in a review of etiologies of child psychopathology, Willis and Walker (1989) discussed genetic influences related to dominant genes, recessive genes, chromosomal disorders, and inherited vulnerability to psychopathology without any discussion of separate maternal or paternal contributions to the genetic makeup of a child. Undoubtedly, this is because it is understood that mothers contribute

50% of the genetic material and fathers contribute 50% of the genetic material; thus there is no need to discuss maternal and paternal influences separately (Plomin, DeFries, & McClearn, 1990).

In some ways, the discussion of purely genetic influences in the development of psychopathology has been quite unbiased with regard to the treatment of mothers and fathers. Parents are rarely referred to separately in empirical discussions of genetic influences, and the focus is on the genetic contribution of both parents rather than a specific search for culpability from one parent versus the other (Vandenberg, Singer, & Pauls, 1986). Interestingly, there are a limited number of examples of disorders that may be sex-linked and therefore may have stronger associations with maternal versus paternal genetic material. For example, there is some evidence (deLong & Roy, 1993; McCord, 1988; Pihl, Peterson, & Finn, 1990) that alcoholism is linked through the Y chromosome and therefore shows a stronger association between fathers and sons. Overall, there is some evidence that certain psychological disorders (such as schizophrenia, alcoholism, bipolar affective disorder) have a genetic linkage (Vandenberg et al., 1986; Willis & Walker, 1989). The genetic contributions for the likelihood of divorce (McGue & Lykken, 1992), personality characteristics (McGue, Bacon, & Lykken, 1993) and proneness to sensation seeking (Resnick, Gottesman, & McGue, 1993) have even received empirical support. Even with the empirical support for genetic linkages to psychiatric disorders and personality characteristics, most researchers believe that the effects of genetic predisposition can be lessened or exacerbated by biological and environmental influences (Vandenberg & Crowe, 1990).

The major focus on nongenetic biological influences on the development of psychopathology has been on teratogenic agents (such as nicotine or toxic drug substances) that the fetus is exposed to in utero. Because of the obvious biological process of pregnancy, mothers have received nearly all the attention with regard to teratogens during pregnancy. Maternal alcohol use has been linked to fetal alcohol syndrome; maternal smoking has been linked to low birth weight in infants, which in turn is linked to delayed cognitive development and increased emotional/behavioral difficulties; and maternal cocaine use during pregnancy has been linked to infant addiction and physiological distress as well as prolonged cognitive delays, attentional difficulties, and behavioral maladjustment in childhood (Behrman, 1992; Roberts, 1986). Although less attention is paid to the impact of fathers during pregnancy, some studies suggest that fathers' actions can influence the biological course of pregnancy and influence the development of psychopathology through biological processes. For example, paternal smoking (which can affect the pregnant mother and the fetus through secondhand or "passive" smoke) has been linked to low birth weight in infants (Martin & Bracken, 1986; Schwartz-Bickenbach, Schulte-Hobein, Abt, Plum, & Nau, 1987), which in turn has been linked to intellectual delays and behavioral problems (Achenbach, Phares, Howell, Rauh, & Nurcombe, 1990; Behrman,

1992). Exposure of fetuses to passive smoke by their fathers' smoking has been documented through the analysis of nicotine and cotinine in the hair of neonates at delivery. Specifically, Eliopoulos and colleagues (1994) found that infants born to mothers who did not smoke and fathers who smoked showed significantly higher levels of nicotine and cotinine in their hair at birth than did infants who had mothers and fathers who did not smoke. Although the overwhelming evidence continues to point to the importance of maternal cautiousness during pregnancy with regard to teratogens, there is accumulating evidence that fathers have an impact on the biological process during pregnancy, which in turn can have an impact on the development of psychopathology.

Although the genetic and biological linkages just discussed have been relatively well established, to date, no one-to-one correspondence has been found between genetic or prenatal deficits and the development of subsequent emotional/behavioral problems (Wachs & Weizmann, 1992). Because of this lack of specificity regarding genetic and prenatal influences, many behavioral geneticists have moved away from a unidirectional model of the development of psychopathology and have begun utilizing a bidirectional model. For example, there is evidence that genes can mediate environmental influences, but there is also evidence that the environment can mediate genetic influences (Wachs & Weizmann, 1992). Hammen (1991) noted that although some children are born with genetic risk for certain types of psychopathology, further work is necessary to examine environmental and contextual factors that exacerbate the genetic risk for child maladjustment. In a clever reframe of these interdependent factors, Hebb (1980) concluded that children's maladaptive behavior is determined 100% by heredity and 100% by environment. Genes are never expressed directly in behavior. Therefore, the way in which heredity is expressed depends on the environment in which the individual lives. A particular genetic influence may be expressed behaviorally in different ways in different environments just as different environments can have varying impacts on individuals with different genetic compositions (Miller, 1989). Garmezy and Tellegen (1984) provided a simple yet eloquent example of the interdependence between genetically determined factors and the environment. In response to a jack-in-the-box, a placid or resilient infant would probably show delight at the sudden occurrence of the clown, but a nervous, reactive infant might be upset by this sudden change in his or her environment. This interplay between genetically determined factors and the environment constitute the study of human behavioral genetics.

Plomin and Daniels (1987) noted that in the early days of behavioral genetics, it was necessary to highlight genetic influences on behavior because of the strong emphasis on environmental influences in the research literature. More recently, behavioral geneticists have had to emphasize environmental contributions to behavior because of the strong emphasis on genetic influences. In addition, most behavioral genetics research has been able to document that no more than half of the variance for different types of psychopathology can be attributed to genetic influences (Plomin et al., 1990). For example, twin adoption studies have suggested that approximately 40% of the variability evident in the development of schizophrenia is due to genetic influences, with the remaining 60% of the variance most likely due to environmental influences and measurement error (Dunn & Plomin, 1990).

When considering environmental influences, it is important to acknowledge that children raised in the same household are not necessarily exposed to the same environment (Daniels & Plomin, 1985). They experience some aspects of the environment that are identical, such as shared meals or bedrooms. These aspects of the family environment that affect all the children in the same way are referred to as "shared environment." Other aspects of the environment are not identical for each child in the family and are referred to as "nonshared environment" (Plomin & Daniels, 1987). These experiences affect children in different ways, depending on individual and interpersonal differences. Examples of the nonshared environment vary for different sibling dyads, but common examples include the way in which parents interact with each sibling, the discipline that is used with each sibling, or the age and developmental status of different siblings. There is evidence to suggest that the bulk of "environmental" influences for children in the same family can be considered nonshared rather than shared environmental influences (Plomin & Daniels, 1987). In the development of schizophrenia, whereas 40% of the variance can be accounted for by genetic factors, 45% of the variance can be attributed to nonshared environmental influences, 5% of the variance can be accounted for by shared environmental experiences, and 10% of the variance is apparently due to error (Dunn & Plomin, 1990). In the case of schizophrenia, nonshared environmental influences appear to contribute somewhat more than genetic influences. Therefore, it is important to move beyond the classic question of nature versus nurture and to realize that "nurture" is a complex and multifaceted variable.

Most of the recent research in behavioral genetics has utilized twin adoption studies and sibling adoption studies to investigate genetic, shared environment, and nonshared environmental influences (reviewed in Plomin et al., 1990). Unfortunately, when "parents" are used in many of these studies, only mothers are recruited into the research study. For example, to ascertain the genetic versus environmental influences on parent and sibling interactions, Rende, Slomkowski, Stocker, Fulker, and Plomin (1992) investigated mother-child-child triads from adoptive and nonadoptive families. A few studies, however, have investigated father-child-child and mother-child-child triads in relation to environmental and genetic influences on interpersonal functioning. Fathers' equal treatment of siblings (Brody, Stoneman, & McCoy, 1992; Brody, Stoneman, McCoy, & Forehand, 1992; McHale, Crouter, McGuire, & Updegraff, 1995) and facilitative and affectionate behavior toward siblings (Volling & Belsky, 1992a) were associated with greater prosocial behavior and lower conflict between siblings (see Hetherington, Reiss, & Plomin, 1994, for review of nonshared environments of siblings). In a comprehensive investigation of genetic contributions to the family environment, Plomin, Reiss, Hetherington, and Howe (1994) found that there was evidence of significant genetic influences on 15 out of 18 composite measures of family characteristics, including paternal and maternal positive behavior and monitoring of children's activities.

Overall, the current research in behavioral genetics provides promising new directions in the investigation of developmental psychopathology. Although there has been some neglect of paternal influences in comparison with maternal influences, interesting new studies are attempting to tease apart genetic, shared environment, and nonshared environmental influences with attention being paid to paternal as well as maternal factors in the development of psychopathology.

BEHAVIORAL AND SOCIAL LEARNING THEORIES

The most basic interpretation of the behavioral theory in the development of psychopathology in children and adolescents suggests that a history of inadequate reinforcement accounts for inappropriate behavioral deficits and excesses (Bandura, 1977). Thus, although current behavioral functioning is assessed and treated, the past history of inappropriate reinforcement schedules is assumed to be at the root of children's emotional and behavioral difficulties.

To expand the tenets of behavioral theory, Rotter (1954) proposed a type of social learning theory in which the probability of the occurrence of a specific behavior in a given situation was a function of expectancy (the degree of expectancy that the person will receive the reinforcement) and reinforcement value (the value of the reinforcer to the person). By adding expectancy to the basic behavioral principles, Rotter helped to include social-cognitive aspects of human behavior to better determine the development of normal and abnormal behavior. In 1977, Bandura furthered Rotter's work in social learning theory and suggested that self-efficacy (a person's belief that he or she is competent and capable) also impacts on a person's behavioral repertoire. Both Rotter and Bandura focused on the fact that children learn not only through direct reinforcement and punishment of their own behavior but also through imitation and observation of others' behavior. Thus, children's socialization and behavioral development can be influenced by imitation of others' behavior.

Bandura (1977) also emphasized that observational learning can occur when the child observes someone else receiving reinforcement or punishment for a particular behavior. Observational learning involves four aspects: (a) attentional processes that determine what will be observed, (b) retention processes that determine what will be remembered, (c) motor reproduction processes that determine the conversion of symbolic representations into appropriate actions, and (d) motivational processes that determine which observed behavior will be performed. Thus, there was a focus on the situational determinants of modeling and an emphasis on why observation of a model in one situation may not lead to a child exhibiting those behaviors whereas in other situations the behavior is modeled. Bandura used the term "reciprocal determinism" to suggest that mutual effects between behavior, other personal factors, and the environment (cognitive, observation, and modeling factors) influence each other. Rather than reinforcement playing only a direct role in strengthening a particular behavioral response, reinforcement can help influence behavior through a feedback loop that provides information about consequences of different behaviors.

A specific application of the social learning theory was originally discussed by Patterson (1982) and updated by Patterson (1990), who referred to the model as a transactional model of the determinants of antisocial behavior. He argued that normal disobedience or unsocialized behavior of a child might be responded to by a parent with inappropriate discipline or with an inappropriate response, thereby leading to an escalation of the child's behavior, which then escalates the parents' coercive behavior, which then is followed by an increase in the child's coercive or antisocial behavior. The question that remains is why some parents might first respond inappropriately and why others do not. In keeping with the basic tenants of social learning theory, there is evidence that parent-child interactions are regulated by expectations and beliefs that are held by both the parents and the child (Field, Adler, Vega-Lahr, & Scafidi, 1987; Tronick, 1989).

So how do fathers fit into behavioral and social learning theories? Early behavioral and social learning theorists did not specifically argue that mothers were any better at rewarding or modeling appropriate behaviors compared with fathers or any other adult model around the child. In fact, Bandura and Walters (1963) suggested that children's behavioral difficulties and poor adjustment were often due to the lack of good parental models, including poor maternal and paternal models. Bandura (1977) argued that fathers were especially important for the observational learning of masculinity and of achievement for their sons. Other early social learning theorists (e.g., Mowrer, 1950; Mussen & Rutherford, 1963) also noted the importance of fathers as a model for their children's development of masculine behaviors. Sears (1957) suggested that fathers display typical masculine behaviors so that their sons and daughters could learn what men are like. More recently, Bjorkqvist and Osterman (1992) found that fathers played a significant role in inappropriate modeling of aggressive behavior that was then expressed by both their adolescent sons and daughters. Ullman and Orenstein (1994) argued that children of alcoholic fathers model their fathers' drinking behavior when they perceive their fathers as powerful.

In discussing the use of rewards and punishments, Lamb (1981) suggested that, although mothers spend more time with their children than do fathers and therefore are more likely to administer more consequences to children's behavior, fathers' responses may be more salient to children because of fathers' somewhat limited time spent with their children. However, Hart, DeWolf, Wozniak, and Burts (1992) found that maternal disciplinary styles had stronger associations with preschool children's behavior than did paternal disciplinary styles. In a study of fathers and not mothers, Ritchie and Ross (1992) found that fathers' disciplinary responses to children's behavior were influenced by the particular child behavior rather than a pattern of disciplinary action. Overall, fathers' and mothers' levels of harsh discipline were significantly correlated (Feldman & Wentzel, 1990).

Given the different family constellations in which children live, it is important to consider factors that relate to the different types of punishment and rewards that children receive. Amato (1987) found that children receive similar levels of punishment and support from their mothers regardless of whether they live with both biological parents, their biological mother and their stepfather, or their single biological mother. However, fathers' use of punishment and support varies according to family constellation. Children who live with their single mother and children who live with their mother and their stepfather reported receiving less punishment and less support from their noncustodial biological father. Stepfathers also provided less punishment and less support than biological fathers in two-parent families. However, stepfathers' behavior began to approximate biological fathers' behavior (in two-parent families) as the length of time of the stepfathers' involvement in the stepfamily increased. This study suggested that punishment and support from fathers and stepfathers, but not mothers, varies according to the family constellation.

Conversely, evidence suggests that mothers' disciplinary practices may be influenced by the presence or absence of the father in the home. In a sample of working-class and middle-class African American mothers, Kelley, Sanchez-Hucles, and Walker (1993) found that mothers were more likely to use social/material control practices when a father was present in the home and were more likely to use restrictive disciplinary practices when the father was absent. In a sample of older adolescents, fathers' use of rewards was related to positive personality traits in their offspring (Gussman & Harder, 1990). These studies show the inconsistency in research findings regarding paternal and maternal disciplinary actions with children and suggest that parents' disciplinary actions may be dependent on family constellation, ethnicity, and SES.

There is still controversy about fathers' differential treatment of their sons and daughters when it comes to sex-role appropriate behaviors as well as the response to inappropriate behaviors in general. As noted in Chapter 2, a recent meta-analysis by Lytton and Romney (1991) suggested that fathers are no more likely to treat their sons and daughters differently than are mothers when it comes to socialization practices. However, other researchers (Siegal, 1987) have suggested that fathers treat their sons and daughters more differently than do mothers and this differential treatment may have an impact on the development of appropriate and inappropriate behavior in children and adolescents.

There appears to be a fair amount of support for behavioral and social learning theories regarding the development of psychopathology in children and adolescents, especially the development of antisocial and coercive externalizing behaviors (Kendziora & O'Leary, 1993; Patterson, 1990). Although the majority of research continues to be conducted with mothers and their children with maladaptive behaviors, there is reason to believe that the processes of observational learning, modeling, and providing consequences to behavior are similar for both fathers and mothers.

FAMILY SYSTEMS THEORIES

Family systems theory has numerous variations, and no one family systems theory dominates the field (Peters & McMahon, 1988). When Levant (1984) set out to review family systems theories, he identified 20 variants. Despite these differences, all family systems theories have several characteristics in common. Most importantly, family relationships and family structure are considered at the root of psychopathology rather than individual deficits of the identified patient. Therefore, the family system, rather than the individual client, is perceived to be the focus of therapeutic intervention. Families are assumed to have attained a certain amount of homeostasis, and therefore any interventions to change the family system are likely to meet with resistance. Most family systems theories propose that if individual interventions are attempted and are successful with the identified patient, symptom substitution at the family or systems level will occur because the underlying problem within the family system was not addressed (Peters & McMahon, 1988). The variations in different family systems theories have to do with the role of the therapist in family therapy (e.g., does the therapist try to "join" the family as an active participant in the family system or does the therapist serve a more passive role as a consultant or observer), the degree to which individual factors are seen to influence the family system, and the degree to which existential-phenomenological concepts are utilized in therapy (Levant, 1984). Aside from these conceptual idiosyncrasies, the underlying tenets of a family systems theory focus on the development of psychopathology being rooted in the family system rather than in the individual child or adolescent.

In Chapter 3, early family systems theories were discussed in relation to mother blaming and lack of attention to paternal influences. More recently, some attention has been paid to fathers in the context of families (e.g., Jurich, White, White, & Moody, 1991), but the research designs in family research often do not address paternal factors separately from family contextual factors (e.g., Hahlweg & Goldstein, 1987). Sigel and Parke (1987) noted that there are three primary levels of analysis in family research: individual, dyadic, and family. Much of the research at the level of the individual has focused on children or mothers (Phares, 1992). The same is true when dyadic relationships are studied: The mother-child relationship has been investigated to a much greater extent than the father-child relationship (Phares, 1992). When the family is investigated, by definition, individual or dyadic relationships are not addressed and therefore paternal influences are not considered separately from family contextual factors. For example, when research measures such as the Family Environment Scale (FES; Moos, 1990) or the Family Adaptability and Cohesion Evaluation Scales (FACES; Olson, 1986) are used, perceptions of the family unit as a whole, rather than individuals within the family, are assessed. Therefore, although the level of family analysis is undoubtedly the most useful and important level to analyze, these analyses do not provide separate information about paternal versus maternal influences within the family. Thorough investigations of family functioning influences and the development of psychopathology should include all three levels of analysis (individual, dyadic, and family) to add to the limited information that is known about fathers in families, and the family as a system.

Steinhauer (1987) presented a process model of family functioning in which an attempt was made to integrate multiple factors into the realm of family influences on the development of psychopathology. Steinhauer noted that there were six categories of influences on family functioning:

1. Contributions from the father, both genetic and psychodynamic.
2. Contributions from the mother, both genetic and psychodynamic.
3. Contributions from the nature of the marital subsystem.
4. Contributions from the subsystem of the individual child, including genetic, biological, and constitutional factors in the child.
5. Contributions from the nature of the family system.
6. Contributions from the nature of the social system and any other relevant subsystems.

This framework provides a comprehensive view of family functioning as it relates to the development of psychopathology given that it includes individual, familial, and social system contributions.

From a developmental perspective, it is also important to consider that fathers and mothers are developing individuals, just as are their children (Cicirelli, 1994; Sigel & Parke, 1987). Cusinato (1994) noted that parenting and parent-child relations change over the family life cycle. The marital relationship also shows a life cycle that must be considered in relation to the family life cycle (Fuller & Fincham, 1994). In addition, the family as a unit is in a constant state of change and it develops and changes over time. Thus, research on family factors that contribute to the development of psychopathology cannot treat families as static entities that can be thoroughly captured and assessed at one point in time (Sigel & Parke, 1987).

Another important process within the family system is the role of parenting behavior. Abidin (1992) argued that child adjustment and parenting behavior are influenced by environmental, sociological, behavioral, and developmental factors. To provide a comprehensive understanding of parenting behavior as it relates to child adjustment, Abidin presented a model of the determinants of parenting behavior. Individual and contextual factors for parents and children (e.g., environment, work, parents' marital relationship, life events, daily hassles) influence the parenting role, the parents' perceived relevance of their role, and the perceived harm or benefit in that role. According to the author, the "parental role" refers to a parent's commitment to that role and can be considered the parent's internal working model of the "self as parent." The parenting role influences parenting stress, which in turn has both a direct impact on parenting behavior as well as an indirect impact on parenting behavior through the influence on parents' resources (e.g., social support, parenting alliance, parenting skills and competencies, material resources, and cognitive coping). Abidin suggests that this model of the determinants of parenting behavior is important because it focuses not only on overt parental behavior but also on parental perceptions of their parental role.

As will be examined more thoroughly in Chapter 6, parental psychopathology also influences functioning within the family. In keeping with the focus on family systems and the interconnection between family members, it is important to recognize that parental psychopathology is not a static occurrence that affects only the disturbed individual (Forehand, 1987; Hahlweg & Goldstein, 1987). Instead, paternal or maternal psychopathology can influence and in turn be influenced by child, spouse, and family factors. Martin (1987) reviewed research that suggested mothers are more adversely affected by their husband's disorder than vice versa. In addition, there is evidence to suggest that when one parent is psychologically disturbed, patterns of assortative mating may cause significant psychopathology in the other parent (McLeod, 1993; Merikangas, Weissman, Prusoff, & John, 1988).

Children appear to be at an even greater risk for the development of psychopathology when both parents have a psychiatric disorder as opposed to when only one parent has such a disorder. Merikangas and colleagues found that when neither parent was diagnosed, one-third of their children received a psychiatric diagnosis. When one parent was diagnosed, the numbers increased to over one-half of the children who were diagnosed. When both parents were diagnosed, the numbers increased to three-quarters of children who met diagnostic criteria. This pattern of increased risk was found for a variety of parental as well as child psychiatric diagnoses. These studies suggest that there is an increased risk for psychopathology in children based on the number of parents who are psychiatrically disturbed. Taken together, this area of research would suggest that the individual assessment of psychopathology in parents does not capture the complexity of psychological symptoms within families.

When considering psychological symptoms within the family, it is important to take into account reciprocal processes rather than assuming that parent-child interactions are unidirectional (parental behavior impacting on the child). Cook,

Kenny, and Goldstein (1991) provided a social relations model analysis to investigate adolescents who were at risk for severe psychopathology. They found that adolescents' expression of negative affect toward their parents in turn elicits negative affect from their parents. This reciprocity effect suggests that adolescents serve a role in eliciting the negative affective style from their parents that results in greater risk for severe psychopathology in the adolescents. Overall, Cook and colleagues suggested that parent-child behavior related to the development of psychopathology must be considered in the broad context of the family system rather than individual or dyadic relationships within the family.

In addition to parenting behavior and parental psychopathology influencing the development of psychopathology, there is strong evidence that interparental discord is associated with child maladjustment (Grych & Fincham, 1990). Overt marital conflict appears to be associated with higher levels of children's problem behaviors than reports of marital dissatisfaction, and the association between overt marital conflict and child behavior problems appears to be stronger in clinical samples of children than in nonclinical samples. Marital conflict may act as a mediating factor in the development of child maladjustment in the presence of parental psychopathology, although maternal versus paternal effects have yet to be investigated. Downey and Coyne (1990) argued that in families with a depressed mother, current parental depressive symptoms are associated with increases in child depressive symptoms, whereas marital conflict is associated with increases in child externalizing behavior problems. These studies suggest that interparental conflict is an important factor in the development of psychopathology in children and adolescents. Further research will need to explore the bidirectional nature of interparental conflict: What characteristics of children seem to decrease or exacerbate interparental conflict? The assessment of interparental conflict is consistent with the attention that must be paid to contextual factors in relation to the impact of the family environment on child and adolescent psychopathology.

In addition to the work on risk factors for the development of psychopathology, there is growing interest in protective factors that decrease the likelihood of adverse effects due to parental psychopathology or interparental conflict (Beardslee & Podorefsky, 1988). In adverse environments, two mediating characteristics that have consistently been identified are higher child intellectual skills and parental competence, such as providing emotional support and stability. Garmezy (1989) found that children with higher intelligence and children whose parents were more competent tended to be protected from the adverse effects of their environment. Parents' social competence and global self-worth have been found to be inversely related to their self-reported psychological symptoms (Phares, in press). In addition, fathers', but not mothers', global self-worth was found to be predictive of lower levels of psychological symptoms in their children. Parental social competence and global self-worth may serve a protective function against the adverse effects of parental psychopathology, interparental conflict, and adverse family environments. Therefore, in the study of family functioning, it is important to consider protective factors, as well as risk factors, that are associated with the development of psychopathology.

The strength of family systems theories is the focus on the context and interdependence of functioning within the family. Although this focus sometimes obscures differential maternal and paternal effects, it will undoubtedly lead to a better understanding of the development of psychopathology within the family.

PSYCHOSOCIAL INFLUENCES

A number of psychosocial influences in the development of psychopathology have been identified. Rather than providing a comprehensive theory of psychosocial and environmental influences, most of this work has been investigated in a somewhat atheoretical manner and has been used to support various theories that include environmental factors in the development of psychopathology. It is extremely rare in the current research literature to find researchers who espouse a solely environmental focus with regard to the development of psychopathology (Plomin & Daniels, 1987). However, certain environmental factors have been identified that are associated with increased risk for psychopathology in children and adolescents. Because much of this research has been "genderless" with regard to parents (it lacks a focus on maternal and paternal influences), the overview of these factors will be brief. In addition, most of these psychosocial factors are discussed in other sections of this book, and therefore interested readers are referred to the appropriate chapters for discussions of these factors in greater detail.

Willis and Walker (1989) identified six psychosocial factors that are related to the development of psychopathology in children and adolescents: Divorce, teenage pregnancy, death of a parent, child abuse, low socioeconomic status (SES), and school peer pressures. First of all, parental divorce has received a significant amount of attention in relation to children's increased risk for emotional/behavioral problems and the development of psychopathology (Amato & Keith, 1991; Heavey, Shenk, & Christensen, 1994). Kurdek (1981) noted that divorce is a "complex cultural, social, legal, economic, and psychological process" (p. 856) that influences children's development in myriad ways. Because divorce rates are higher in African American families and in economically disadvantaged families (Amato & Keith, 1991; Dickson, 1993), the risk for psychopathology associated with divorce may be confounded with issues of racism and the impact of poverty. The roles of fathers in the divorce process and after divorce are discussed in greater detail in Chapters 1 and 7.

The second and third psychosocial influences that have received attention in relation to children's risk for maladjustment involve children living in single-parent households. Teenage pregnancy and the death of one parent both result in children living in single-parent households for some period of time and both have been identified as increasing the risk for the development of psychopathology in children. Teenage pregnancy and adolescent fatherhood were discussed in Chapter 1. In addition, interested readers are referred to an intriguing series of articles (Belsky, Steinberg, & Draper, 1991; Hinde, 1991; Maccoby, 1991) that discuss an evolutionary theory of socialization that predicts alternative reproductive strategies leading to single-parent versus dual-parent families. Research on death of a parent is somewhat limited because the lack of attention to the effects of the loss of a father as opposed to the loss of a mother (Bloom-Feshbach & Bloom-Feshbach, 1987; Plimpton & Rosenblum, 1987). Although there are case studies that describe the individual effects of losing a parent (e.g., Ziller & Stewart-Dowdell, 1991), few comprehensive empirical studies have been conducted that investigate the differential effects of losing a father versus a mother. When the effects of the loss of a father are compared with the effects of the loss of a mother, inconsistent results are found (Krupnick & Solomon, 1987). Although some research suggests that the loss of a same-sex parent is more detrimental to the child's well-being, an equal number of studies have found that there are no consistent patterns in the loss of a father versus a mother regardless of the child's gender (reviewed in Krupnick & Solomon, 1987). Loss of a mother or a father appears to be related to greater risk for panic disorder and phobias, but there is less consistent evidence about risk for major depression (Kendler, Neale, Kessler, Heath, & Eaves, 1992).

The fourth psychosocial factor associated with child maladjustment is child abuse. Child abuse can be expressed in many forms, including severe or harsh parenting, physical abuse, sexual abuse, emotional maltreatment, and neglect (Wolfe, 1991). Because of the intergenerational links in certain types of abuse (e.g., harsh parenting, physical abuse), the need to treat and eventually prevent child abuse is of utmost importance (Wolfe, 1991). A more detailed discussion of the role of fathers in child abuse and the impact of child abuse is included in Chapter 6.

The fifth psychosocial factor that Willis and Walker (1989) reviewed was low SES. They noted that race and ethnicity are not directly linked to child maladjustment, but rather that low SES is associated with increased risk for emotional/behavioral problems and the development of psychopathology. For example, Suinn (1984) concluded that children who live in impoverished inner-city environments are 10 times more likely to develop psychopathology than children living in residential areas outside the inner city. Additionally, urban children show higher rates of psychopathology than rural children (Zahner, Jacobs, Freeman, & Trainor, 1993). Urban and inner-city environments are associated with a host of problems other than low SES, including chronic violence and frequent malnutrition. Therefore, although the connection between SES and increased risk for maladjustment in children has been well established, it is not clear which aspects of low SES most strongly influence the development of psychopathology.

The final psychosocial influence that Willis and Walker (1989) discussed in relation to the development of psychopathology is pressure from peers at school. For example, peers have been found to reinforce aggressive and coercive behavior in young adolescence (Coie & Jacobs, 1993) and to encourage substance use in later adolescence (Bahr, Hawks, & Wang, 1993). Among other important variables, Kazdin, Mazurick, and Bass (1993) found that conduct-disordered children aged 5 to 13 were more likely to drop out of treatment when they were actively involved with peers who showed similar levels of antisocial characteristics. In their multisystemic therapy for serious juvenile offenders, Henggeler, Melton, and Smith (1992) work with adolescents to decrease their contact with maladaptive peers and to increase their contact with well-functioning peers in addition to working with the therapeutic needs of the family and the individual juvenile offender. The negative influences of peers in both the school and the neighborhood setting are increasingly of interest given the increase in violence within schools and neighborhoods (Youniss & Smollar, 1985). These psychosocial factors suggest that along with genetic, behavioral, and familial factors, environmental factors must be considered when attempting to determine the etiology of child and adolescent psychopathology.

SUMMARY

Although the various theories that were just discussed are quite divergent, there are also certain commonalities. Most current theories are becoming much more specific to certain psychopathologies (Gelfand & Teti, 1990), and many are becoming more integrative rather than separatist (Collins & Thompson, 1993). For example, Biller (1993) presented a biopsychosocial-interactional model that delineates the interconnections between family functioning, the child's individual characteristics and biological predispositions, the adequacy of fathering and mothering, sociocultural influences, and the child's short-term and long-term developmental outcomes. In keeping with this model, Simeonsson and Rosenthal (1992) suggested that researchers and clinicians should seek convergence and rapprochement between a variety of models and theories to best understand the development of psychopathology. They noted that an eclectic approach is not atheoretical, but rather reflects the necessity to specify the conditions in which different theories have greater relevance than others. Because of the complexity of developmental psychopathology, and the possible role that fathers play in its development, it is necessary to consider an array of conceptual models and frameworks through which to understand the clinical needs of children.

PART III

What Is Known about Fathers and Developmental Psychopathology?

CHAPTER 5

Referred Children and
Characteristics of Their Fathers

Chapters 5 through 7 will review the empirical research regarding fathers and developmental psychopathology. As noted by Phares and Compas (1992), research in developmental psychopathology varies on a number of different dimensions including the choice of a target population that is to be sampled. Research regarding fathers and developmental psychopathology has focused on three different methodologies regarding target populations:

1. Investigation of referred or diagnosed children and the characteristics of their fathers.
2. Investigation of referred or diagnosed fathers and the characteristics of their children.
3. Investigation of the characteristics of fathers and children who have not been referred for services nor diagnosed with a psychiatric disorder.

The current chapter will focus on the research findings from the first targeted population: Referred or diagnosed children and adolescents and their fathers. Chapter 6 will review research on referred fathers and characteristics of their children, and Chapter 7 will review the empirical literature on nonreferred fathers and children.

This chapter will review the empirical research that has investigated the fathers of children who have been referred for psychiatric or psychological services or who have received a psychiatric diagnosis. The diagnostic terminology used will reflect the nomenclature found in the studies that are reviewed. For example, although the *Diagnostic and Statistical Manual of Mental Disorders, Fourth Edition* (DSM-IV), now utilizes the notation AD/HD to signify Attention Deficit/Hyperactivity Disorder (American Psychiatric Association, 1994), the majority of the studies reviewed in this chapter utilized the notation of ADHD based on DSM-III-R criteria. This chapter will follow the convention of noting significance when the p-level is equal to or below .05. This means that sometimes the chapter will review research findings that were written up as "significant" when in fact the significance level was higher than .05 (e.g.,

$p < .07$ or $p < .10$). If the authors of the research used statistical corrections for the number of analyses that were conducted (e.g., a Bonferroni correction), those results will be reported as the authors reported them.

ATTENTION DEFICIT/HYPERACTIVITY DISORDER

Compared with the huge research literature that has investigated mothers of children diagnosed with attention deficit/hyperactivity disorder (ADHD), there has been relatively little investigation into the fathers of ADHD children. However, the few research studies that have been completed show relatively consistent trends. When fathers of ADHD children are compared with fathers of nonclinical children, they show a variety of differences in cognitive and social characteristics, but very few differences in psychological functioning. More specifically, fathers of children diagnosed with ADHD differ from fathers of nonclinical control children in showing lower expectations for future compliant child behavior (Sobol, Ashbourne, Earn, & Cunningham, 1989), poorer perceptions of parenting behavior and parental self-esteem (Margalit, 1985; Mash & Johnston, 1983), poorer behavioral interactions (Tallmadge & Barkley, 1983), and shorter attention span (Alberts-Corush, Firestone, & Goodman, 1986). Conversely, there are few differences in levels of psychological symptoms when fathers of ADHD children are compared with fathers of children in a nonclinical control group. Fathers of ADHD children and nonclinical children did not differ in their perceptions of affective functioning within the family (Cunningham, Benness, & Siegel, 1988), in the rates of alcoholism or antisocial personality disorder (Reeves, Werry, Elkind, & Zametkin, 1987), or in the levels of depressive symptoms (Cunningham et al., 1988).

Although fathers of ADHD children reported significantly more drinks per week than did fathers of nonclinical children (Cunningham et al., 1988), a laboratory-based study by Lang, Pelham, Johnston, and Gelernter (1989) suggests that this drinking behavior may be due to the maladaptive behavior of ADHD children rather than a predisposition toward alcoholism in the fathers of ADHD children. The researchers had boys act as confederates in the study and role-play either "normal" or "ADHD/Conduct Disorder" childhood behavior with young adult subjects in the study. Subjects interacted with a confederate child for approximately 18 minutes and then they were separated from the child and were allowed to drink as much alcohol as they desired during a 20-minute period while they awaited more interaction with the child. Mood data were collected before and after the interactions with the confederate child. Both male and female subjects showed greater distressed mood in response to interactions with the "ADHD/CD" confederate boys when compared with subjects who interacted with the "normal" confederate boys. Although women did not show differences in their drinking behaviors in response to the boys in the two different conditions, men did. Men who interacted with an "ADHD/CD" confederate boy drank significantly more (as measured by blood-alcohol level) than men who interacted with a "normal" confederate boy. Lang and colleagues (1989) suggested that this laboratory-based study may help explain the higher rates of drinking in fathers of children diagnosed with ADHD.

These studies suggest that fathers of ADHD children show differences in various cognitive and social characteristics, but they do not show differences in levels of most psychological symptoms. Similar patterns are found for mothers of ADHD children when compared with mothers of nonclinical children (Alberts-Corush et al., 1986; Lahey et al., 1988; Margalit, 1985; Mash & Johnston, 1983; Reeves et al., 1987; Sobol et al., 1989; Stewart, deBlois, & Cummings, 1980; Tallmadge & Barkley, 1983). The primary difference between fathers and mothers was evidenced in depressive symptoms. Whereas the level of depressive symptoms did not differ between fathers of ADHD children and nonclinical children, mothers of ADHD children reported significantly more depressive symptoms than mothers of nonclinical control children (Cunningham et al., 1988).

Given the parallel findings for fathers and mothers of ADHD children when compared with fathers and mothers of nonclinical control children, it is not surprising that there are few differences between fathers and mothers of ADHD children when they are compared with each other. Significant differences were not found between fathers and mothers of ADHD children in perceptions of parenting behavior and parental self-esteem (Margalit, 1985; Mash & Johnston, 1983), behavioral interactions (Tallmadge & Barkley, 1983), attention span (Alberts-Corush et al., 1986), perceptions of family affective functioning (Cunningham et al., 1988), and attributions about their children's behavior (Johnston & Patenaude, 1994). When fathers and mothers of ADHD twins were studied, high paternal and maternal malaise, high paternal and maternal criticism, and low maternal warmth were associated with fathers' and mothers' reports of higher levels of hyperactive behavior in their children (Goodman & Stevenson, 1989). The life satisfaction in the family of children diagnosed with ADHD was predicted by paternal support, paternal discipline, paternal indulgence, and maternal support (Margalit, 1985). Because so many of these studies have recruited primarily boys into their samples (undoubtedly because of the higher prevalence of ADHD in boys), no direct comparisons of fathers and mothers of ADHD boys versus ADHD girls can be discussed.

Although the majority of studies comparing fathers and mothers of ADHD children have not found differences, three studies identified differences between fathers and mothers of ADHD children. Cunningham and colleagues (1988) found that fathers of ADHD children reported more drinks of alcohol per week but fewer symptoms of depression than did mothers. Mothers reported feeling more stress than fathers regarding their ADHD child's behavior (Baker, 1994). Regarding attributions of children's behavior, Sobol and colleagues (1989) found that fathers of ADHD children rated their children's noncompliant behavior as less external than did mothers. Although there are some differences between fathers and mothers of ADHD children, there appear to be more similarities than differences in cognitive, social, and psychological functioning.

In an interesting study of behavioral observations of 6- to 12-year-old ADHD boys, their fathers, and their mothers, Buhrmester, Camparo, Christensen, Gonzalez, and Hinshaw (1992) found that family interactions differed based on whether dyadic or triadic interactions were evaluated. In dyadic interactions, ADHD boys and nonclinical boys showed significantly more negative behavior (e.g., resistance-avoidance) toward their mothers than toward their fathers. In triadic interactions (consisting of son, father, and mother), fathers appeared to increase their demands on their sons, whereas mothers appeared to decrease their demands. Thus, fathers and sons behaved more negatively toward each other in triadic interactions (in the presence of the mother) when compared with father-son dyadic interactions. Bhurmester and colleagues highlighted the importance of considering dyadic and triad interactions within the families of ADHD boys, in addition to observing the behavior of ADHD boys in other contexts such as school and the playground.

Only three studies were identified that have compared fathers of ADHD children with fathers of non-ADHD clinically referred children, and all these studies had to struggle with the issue of comorbidity (Frick, Lahey, Christ, Loeber, & Green, 1991; Lahey et al., 1988; Stewart et al., 1980). Because ADHD tends to co-occur with conduct disorder for a large number of children (estimates range from 41% to 75%; Lahey et al., 1988; Hinshaw, 1987), it is important to identify the paternal characteristics of children diagnosed solely with ADHD when comparing them with paternal characteristics of children diagnosed with another disorder. The studies by Frick et al., Lahey et al., and Stewart et al. were able to identify samples of ADHD children who did not meet diagnostic criteria for conduct disorder (CD). When comparing the childhood psychiatric histories of fathers and mothers of ADHD children and clinic controls, Frick and colleagues found that fathers and mothers of ADHD children were more likely to have a history of ADHD, but not antisocial behavior or substance abuse, than were fathers and mothers of clinic control children. When comparing parents of ADHD children with parents of conduct-disordered children, Lahey and colleagues found that there were no significant differences between the two groups in parental antisocial personality disorder or substance abuse. Fathers of ADHD children were significantly less likely than fathers of CD children to have experienced an episode of major depression within the last year. Although the sample included both boys and girls, there was a preponderance of boys in the solely ADHD group (72%), the ADHD plus CD group (91%), and the CD group (73%). Similar results were found by Stewart and colleagues in a sample of boys diagnosed with solely ADHD, CD, or major depression. They found that rates of antisocial personality disorder, substance abuse, and affective disorders did not differ between fathers of ADHD boys and fathers of clinically referred, nonhyperactive boys.

Nearly all the mothers in the studies by Frick et al. and Lahey et al. and over half the mothers in the study by Stewart and colleagues provided diagnostic information for their children's fathers. Very few fathers were interviewed directly about their own psychiatric history, but rather the mothers were used as informants about their own and their spouses' (or exspouses') psychiatric functioning. Based on these three studies, it appears that there are few differences between fathers of ADHD children and fathers of non-ADHD, clinically referred children.

Across these different methodologies, a relatively clear picture emerges for fathers of children diagnosed with ADHD. When fathers of ADHD children and nonclinical children are compared, there are some differences in nonpsychiatric variables, but few differences in psychological functioning or in affective functioning within the family. In addition, when compared with fathers of children referred for problems other than ADHD, fathers of ADHD children do not show elevated levels of psychiatric disorders. Finally, when comparing fathers and mothers of ADHD children, there appear to be more similarities than differences in a number of cognitive and psychological characteristics.

CONDUCT DISORDER

Two studies were identified that compared fathers of conduct-disordered children with fathers of children in a nonclinical control group. Because of the high rates of comorbidity among children diagnosed with conduct disorder (CD), both studies had samples with large percentages of children who met criteria for another psychiatric disorder in addition to CD. Reeves et al. (1987) identified a sample of primarily boys (89% of the sample) who ranged in age from 5 to 12 years. Along with meeting criteria for CD, 89% of the children met criteria for ADHD. When compared with fathers of nonclinical children, fathers of CD children were significantly more likely to meet diagnostic criteria for antisocial personality disorder and for alcoholism. There was no difference between these groups with regard to maternal anxiety disorders.

Similar results were found by Schachar and Wachsmuth (1990) in a study of fathers of boys who ranged in age from 7 to 11 years. A total of 77% of the CD boys also met criteria for ADHD and 5% met criteria for an emotional disorder (such as separation anxiety, overanxious, affective, phobic, or somatization disorder). When fathers of CD boys were compared with fathers of nonclinical control children, a number of significant differences emerged. Fathers of CD children were significantly younger than fathers of normal children. CD children were more likely to have been separated from their fathers for at least 1 month than were nonclinical children. Regarding paternal psychopathology, fathers of

CD children were significantly more likely to have a history of psychopathology than were fathers of nonclinical children. Although there were not separate analyses for different psychiatric disorders, Schachar and Wachsmuth noted that substance abuse, alcoholism, and antisocial personality disorder were the most common disorders in fathers of CD boys. As was found in the study by Reeves and colleagues, no significant differences were found in the psychiatric functioning of mothers of CD children when compared with mothers of nonclinical children.

Parental psychiatric information was obtained by directly interviewing parents in 83% of the cases and by interviewing the "available" parent in 17% of the cases. Schachar and Wachsmuth noted that directly interviewing the parent resulted in fewer diagnoses (56%) than when interviewing the other parent about the "unavailable" parent's psychiatric history (73%). However, because the rates of self-report and other-report interviews were similar for both the CD and nonclinical groups, the results based on group comparisons did not appear to be affected by who was interviewed about parental psychiatric status.

Although both these studies compared parents of CD and nonclinical children, neither of them compared the psychiatric status of fathers and mothers of CD children directly. Only one study could be identified that directly compared fathers and mothers of CD children, and this study was designed to investigate CD girls rather than CD boys. Because the majority of studies that investigate CD in children focus on samples of predominantly boys, Johnson and O'Leary (1987) wished to investigate the parental characteristics of CD girls. Their sample consisted of 42 girls between the ages of 9 and 11, 25 of whom displayed conduct problems and 17 of whom did not. All the girls were from intact families and the two groups were similar in family income, parental education, and number of children in the family. Parental behavior and marital satisfaction were investigated in relation to the girls' conduct disorder behavior and their social competence. Overall, there were more significant associations for mother-daughter associations than father-daughter associations. Of the 10 correlations for father-daughter associations, none were significant whereas 5 of the 10 correlations for mother-daughter associations were significant. Specifically, maternal overt hostility and aggression were positively correlated with daughters' conduct problems, maternal reports of marital satisfaction and positive behavior were positively related to daughters' social competence, and maternal reports of negative behavior (based on hypothetical vignettes) were inversely related to daughters' social competence. Based on these results, Johnson and O'Leary suggested that there was a stronger connection between maternal behavior and conduct problems in girls than for paternal behavior and conduct problems in girls. Although this pattern suggests that there are stronger father-son and mother-daughter links in conduct disorder, this hypothesis has yet to be tested in a single, comprehensive study.

The bulk of the research that investigates fathers in relation to conduct disorder has compared fathers of CD children with fathers of children with other psychiatric disorders. Relatively consistent evidence was found that fathers of CD children (primarily boys) show greater psychiatric disturbance than fathers of children referred for problems other than conduct disorder. Fathers of children diagnosed with both CD and ADHD showed higher rates of antisocial personality disorder and alcoholism than did fathers of solely ADHD children and fathers of children with anxiety disorders (Reeves et al., 1987). In addition, fathers of children comorbid with both CD and ADHD showed higher rates of arrests, imprisonments, and aggression than did fathers of children referred for problems other than CD (Lahey et al., 1988). Fathers of aggressive CD boys (Frick et al., 1992; Jary & Stewart, 1985; Stewart et al., 1980) as well as fathers of CD children (most of whom were boys; Lahey et al., 1988) showed higher rates of antisocial personality disorder and alcohol abuse than fathers of children referred for other problems such as ADHD and depression. Frick and colleagues found that fathers of CD boys as a group showed higher levels of antisocial personality disorder than fathers of boys with oppositional defiant disorder (ODD), but there was no difference in rates of alcoholism between fathers of CD boys and ODD boys. In a comparison of boys who showed either pervasive aggressive conduct disorder (PACD), situational aggressive conduct disorder (SACD), or a non-CD problem (such as ADHD or an anxiety disorder), Hamdan-Allen, Stewart, and Beeghly (1989) found that fathers of PACD boys showed a greater likelihood of antisocial personality disorder than fathers of SACD boys or fathers of boys referred for other problems, but fathers in both conduct-disordered groups (PACD and SACD) showed higher rates of alcoholism than fathers in the clinically referred control group. In a study that investigated levels of paternal depression, Dean and Jacobson (1982) found that fathers of CD children showed higher levels of depression than fathers of children with a learning disability or a personality disorder.

Along with the analysis of paternal psychopathology, some of these studies also investigated maternal psychopathology. For example, Hamdan-Allen et al. (1989) found that maternal alcoholism and drug abuse were significantly higher in mothers of boys who showed pervasive aggressive conduct disorder when compared with mothers of boys who showed situational aggressive conduct disorder or other clinical problems. Mothers of CD children also had a greater likelihood than mothers of other clinically referred children to be diagnosed with antisocial personality disorder (APD) or depression (Lahey et al., 1988). Both fathers and mothers of CD boys showed higher levels of CD symptoms and APD symptoms, which were related to the number of CD symptoms that their son showed (Vanyukov, Moss, Plail, & Blackson, 1993).

In a fascinating study of interactions within the family, Dumas and Gibson (1990) studied families of children diagnosed with CD and compared interactions with their parents depending on whether or not their mother showed elevated levels of depression. They found that CD children whose mothers showed elevated depressive symptoms were more compliant and less aversive in interactions with their mothers than with their fathers. CD children whose mothers did not show elevated levels of depression were more compliant and less aversive in their interactions with their fathers than with their mothers. This study suggests that the behavior of children diagnosed with CD must be considered within the family context, rather than assuming that the majority of CD children show similar behavioral patterns.

The majority of studies of children diagnosed with CD investigated paternal antisocial personality disorder, alcoholism, and substance abuse to the exclusion of other psychiatric disorders. Overall, there is strong evidence that fathers of CD children (primarily boys) show greater psychiatric disturbance than fathers of other clinically referred children. Certain types of aggressive conduct disorder in children, as well as comorbidity of CD and another disorder in children, are also associated with a greater likelihood of paternal psychopathology. These associations tended to be more evident for paternal psychopathology than for maternal psychopathology when CD boys were investigated.

Aggression and assaultive behaviors are related to the diagnosis of CD, but certainly are not exclusive to CD. A number of studies have investigated aggressive and assaultive behaviors in children receiving clinical services, and mixed results have emerged. In a sample of boys seen on an outpatient basis at a child psychiatry clinic, Stewart and deBlois (1983) found that fathers' aggressive and antisocial behaviors were significantly related to their sons' aggressive, antisocial, and noncompliant behaviors. The remaining studies investigated aggressive behavior in children and adolescents who were receiving inpatient psychiatric services. Lewis, Shanok, Grant, and Ritvo (1983) compared the fathers of homicidally aggressive children and nonhomicidal children and found that the former group showed more physical violence and alcoholism than the latter group. Mothers in the former group had a greater likelihood of receiving psychiatric inpatient services than mothers in the latter group. Truscott (1992) found that male adolescents who were admitted to a Young Offenders Unit were more likely to have experienced violent abuse from their father than were nonclinical adolescents. Experience of maternal violence and witnessing paternal or maternal violence were not associated with violent behavior in the adjudicated male adolescents.

In a series of studies investigating assaultive behavior in children and adolescents who were receiving psychiatric services, there were somewhat stronger associations between paternal behavior and children's assaultiveness when studies were conducted with children who were receiving outpatient services as opposed to inpatient services. Pfeffer, Newcorn, Kaplan, Mizruchi, and Plutchik (1989) found no significant differences in paternal or maternal alcoholism or affective disorders when comparing four groups of adolescent inpatients (nonassaultive-nonsuicidal, assaultive-only, assaultive-suicidal, suicidal-only). Similarly, children's assaultiveness ratings on a psychiatric inpatient unit were not significantly related to their fathers' or mothers' rates of assaultiveness, psychiatric hospitalization, alcoholism, depression, or suicidal behavior (Pfeffer, Solomon, Plutchik, Mizruchi, & Weiner, 1985). The lack of association between fathers' and mothers' assaultiveness and their children's assaultive behavior on a psychiatric inpatient unit was replicated by Pfeffer, Plutchik, Mizruchi, and Lipkins (1987), but they also investigated children who were receiving outpatient services and children in a nonclinical control group. In the noninpatient groups of children (who evidenced lower levels of assaultive behavior), fathers' and mothers' assaultiveness ratings were significantly related to their children's assaultive behavior. These series of studies suggest that lower levels of assaultive behavior in community settings show a stronger link with paternal and maternal assaultiveness and aggression than do the higher levels of assaultive behavior that are evidenced in psychiatric inpatient settings.

The research on conduct disorder in children and adolescents shows strong links between fathers' psychopathology (especially antisocial disorder and alcoholism) and their children's CD. There appears to be a stronger link between fathers and sons rather than fathers and daughters or mothers and sons regarding parental psychopathology and conduct-disordered behavior in children and adolescents. The link between fathers' and children's behavior seems to be stronger when the children show lower levels of assaultive behavior as opposed to higher levels.

DELINQUENCY

In addition to the studies of conduct disorder just discussed, a number of studies investigate juvenile delinquency without using the specific diagnostic criteria for CD. Therefore, studies that use derivations of the term *juvenile delinquency* (JD) will be reviewed here. However, there is a high degree of overlap between children and adolescents diagnosed as CD and those identified as JD (Johnson & Fennell, 1992). The primary difference in this review may be the age ranges because, the samples in the CD section tended to be children, whereas most of the samples discussed in this section consist of adolescents. This distinction is maintained to reflect the state of the research literature and to provide consistency between the research literature and this discussion.

A huge research literature exists that has investigated father absence in relation to juvenile delinquency. In keeping with the focus of reviewing paternal characteristics that were measured, rather than the mere absence of the father, this research will not be reviewed here. Interested readers are referred to a comprehensive review by Free (1991). In this review, Free summarized that father absence is associated more strongly with adolescents' minor offenses than with adolescents' serious offenses. He also noted that it is unclear whether absence of the father is any more significant than absence of the mother. Free (1991) noted that when maternal absence from the home has been documented, it is often associated with disrupted behavior in adolescents. However, small sample sizes preclude full analyses of the impact of maternal versus paternal absence from the home. Therefore findings from the paternal absence literature may be more generally related to absence of a parent, or to other confounding characteristics, such as socioeconomic status, ethnicity, or interparental conflict.

A wealth of studies have investigated the relations between paternal characteristics and juvenile delinquency. Adolescent delinquency has been found to be associated with poor paternal and maternal relationships (Atwood, Gold, & Taylor, 1989); inconsistency in family communication patterns (Lessin & Jacob, 1984); high levels of paternal and maternal defensive communication (Alexander, Waldron, Barton, & Mas, 1989); unaffectionate, conflicted father-son interactions and unsupportive, conflicted mother-son interactions (Borduin, Pruitt, & Henggeler, 1986; Hanson, Henggeler, Haefele, & Rodick, 1984); low rates of facilitative information exchange (Henggeler, Edwards, & Borduin, 1987); high levels of paternal and maternal social desirability and high levels of maternal neuroticism (Borduin, Henggeler, & Pruitt, 1985); high levels of parental aggressiveness, parental conflict, and paternal deviance, and low levels of maternal affection, supervision, and self-confidence (McCord, 1979); and lack of paternal and maternal supervision combined with a history of parental criminality (for reviews, see Goetting, 1994; Loeber, 1990; Loeber & Dishion, 1983).

In a direct observation study of chronic offenders who had either committed assaultive crimes, been arrested for stealing, or had no court contact, Loeber, Weissman, and Reid (1983) found surprisingly few differences in the paternal and maternal behavior within the three groups. When total aversive behavior (TAB) was assessed from an in-home observation, group differences did not reach significance for either fathers or mothers. This lack of significance may have been due to sample size (11 families in each group), but given that other analyses regarding adolescent behavior showed significance, the lack of differences in TAB for parents across the three groups may be an accurate reflection within these families.

With regard to psychopathology and abuse in the families of delinquents, Lewis, Pincus, Lovely, Spitzer, and Moy (1987) compared the families of delinquents and the families of nondelinquents. They found that delinquents were significantly more likely to have a mother with a prior psychiatric hospitalization, to have witnessed severe family violence, and to have been physically abused by their father or mother. The families of delinquents and nondelinquents did not differ in prior paternal psychiatric hospitalizations, paternal alcoholism, or maternal alcoholism. Delinquents who had been physically abused were significantly more likely than delinquents who had not been physically abused to have a father or mother who was alcoholic (Tarter, Hegedus, Winsten, & Alterman, 1984). In addition, paternal alcohol use was associated with delinquents' attentional problems when the delinquents were 11 years old and with the number of arrests by the time the delinquents were 18 years old (Wallander, 1988).

Although the majority of the research with delinquents is conducted with males, Henggeler and colleagues (1987) were able to compare the families of male delinquents with the families of female delinquents. When compared with parents of male delinquents, fathers and mothers of female delinquents evidenced significantly more overt conflict toward each other and fathers of female delinquents were significantly more neurotic.

Runaway behavior is related to juvenile delinquency and has been investigated in samples of both females and males. Englander (1984) obtained self-reports from 52 adolescent girls who had run away from home and compared them with the self-reports of girls who had not run away from home. Girls who had run away reported that their fathers and mothers were significantly less accepting and less restrictive than did the girls who had not run away. A significant number of runaways have experienced sexual and/or physical abuse by their father or stepfather (Warren, Gary, & Moorhead, 1994). Fry (1982) recruited over 200 runaways, with approximately equal numbers of girls and boys, and asked them to report on their fathers' personality characteristics and social orientation behavior. For both girls and boys, running-away behavior was associated with fathers' greater tolerance of deviance, greater depression, greater detachment, less child-centeredness, less communicativeness, less affection, and less consistency. Overall, it appears that adolescents who run away perceive their fathers to be unsupportive and to serve in an adversarial, rather than a supportive, role.

In summary, as was noted in the section on CD, juvenile delinquency seems to be related to a number of paternal, as well as maternal, factors. There are more similarities than differences in the roles that fathers and mothers seem to play in relation to delinquent behavior, but there have been few direct comparisons of the characteristics of fathers and mothers of delinquents.

Moving beyond juvenile delinquency, extreme violence in adulthood and the associations with retrospective reports of paternal behavior in childhood deserve mention here. Lisak and Roth (1990) investigated recollections of paternal behavior in young adult men who committed rape but who were not apprehended. The study compared 15 undetected rapists and 15 matched control subjects who did not show evidence of a history of rape. The rapists showed greater hostility toward women, underlying anger motivations, and hypermasculinity than did the nonrapists. In retrospective reports of parenting behavior during childhood, the rapists endorsed more negative statements about their fathers and their mothers, and endorsed fewer positive statements about their mothers than did participants in the control group. Correlational analyses showed that the father-son relationship was more strongly associated with sexual aggression than was the mother-son relationship. That is, a poor father-son relationship during childhood was significantly associated with hostility toward women, hypermasculinity, dominance over women, and underlying power motivations. None of these associations were significant for the mother-son relationship during childhood. Lisak (1991) provided a compelling discussion of the connections between fathering behaviors (or lack thereof) and sexual violence in sons.

Another related area of study deals with men who were incarcerated for child molestation or rape. Seghorn, Prentky, and Boucher (1987) compared the history of childhood sexual abuse in sexually aggressive offenders. They found that 7% of rapists and 33% of child molesters had been sexually assaulted during childhood by someone outside the family and 9% of the rapists and 7% of the child molesters had been sexually assaulted by a family member during childhood. Unfortunately, they did not provide data as to the identity of the family members (e.g., fathers, mothers, uncles). When rapists who had been sexually abused and rapists who had not been sexually abused were compared, there were no significant differences in their fathers' or mothers' psychiatric history, crime history, drug history, or alcohol abuse history. However, a number of significant differences were evident when the family histories of child molesters were compared. Child molesters who had been sexually abused as children were significantly more likely than child molesters who had not been sexually abused to have fathers and mothers with a psychiatric history, fathers with a criminal history, fathers with a drug history, and fathers with a history of alcohol abuse. This study suggested that a history of childhood sexual abuse was associated with a number of other disorders within the families of origin for child molesters but not rapists.

Patricide is the third area of extreme violence that has received attention regarding retrospective reports of fathering behavior during childhood. Singhal and Dutta (1990) identified 10 men who had killed their father (2 of whom also killed their mother) and compared them with 10 men who were diagnosed with schizophrenia and who had not been convicted of any crimes. Of the 10 men who killed their father, 8 had a diagnosis of schizophrenia and 2 had a personality disorder diagnosis. Nine of the 10 men who committed patricide reported that they had experienced a "cruel and unusual" relationship with their father. All the men in the study were receiving psychiatric services on an inpatient basis. Results of the study showed that men who committed patricide were more likely than control subjects to report that their fathers had been punitive, shaming, less depriving, and not stimulating when the men were younger. Men who committed patricide were more likely than controls to report that their mothers had been overinvolved and tolerant when the men were boys. When reports of fathers and mothers were compared, men who committed patricide reported that their fathers were more punitive, were more likely to favor siblings, were less protective, and were less tolerant than were their mothers. Singhal and Dutta summarized this study by suggesting that there are connections between patricide and paternal behavior during childhood. They noted that because these were retrospective reports, and because the participants were receiving psychiatric services, the recollections of fathering behavior may not have been accurate. They suggested that a study of people who committed patricide, but who were serving time in a prison rather than receiving psychiatric services, may help to clarify some of these issues.

Heide (1993) found that fathers were more likely to be killed by their offspring who were under 30 years old, whereas mothers were more likely to be killed by their offspring who were over 30 years old. A higher percentage of fathers who were killed by their children were African American (33% African American; 65% Caucasian). In contrast, Heide (1993) found that a higher percentage of mothers who were killed by their children were Caucasian (25% African American; 73% Caucasian). Through in-depth case studies, Heide (1992) illustrated the possibility of a connection between severe childhood abuse and patricide or matricide.

NONSPECIFIC BEHAVIOR PROBLEMS

A variety of studies have been conducted with samples of children and adolescents who experienced nonspecific behavior problems. Rather than studying samples of children and adolescents who meet criteria for specific diagnoses such as ADHD or CD, some researchers have studied samples of clinically referred children without attempting to diagnose their emotional or behavioral problems. More often, these researchers treat child and adolescent functioning as a continuous variable (e.g., the differing number of behavior problems) rather than a dichotomous variable (e.g., either they do or do not meet diagnostic criteria for a particular disorder). The advantages and disadvantages of conceptualizing children's behavior as a continuous variable rather than a dichotomous variable are beyond the scope of this chapter. However, interested readers are referred to discussions of this issue by leading researchers in the field of developmental psychopathology (Achenbach, 1990–1991; Caron & Rutter, 1991).

In a sample of children showing conduct problems, Schaughency and Lahey (1985) found that fathers' levels of self-reported depression were not significantly related to fathers' reports of their children's conduct problems or externalizing problems. However, mothers' levels of self-reported depression were significantly related to their reports of children's behavior problems. Johnston (1991) found similar results in that fathers' reports of child behavior problems were not related to paternal depression or fathers' reports of marital adjustment, whereas mothers' reports of child behavior problems were significantly related to maternal depression. In a study with a similar sample of children, Webster-Stratton (1988) also found that fathers' functioning had little to do with their behavior toward their children, whereas mothers' functioning was related to their behavior toward their children. Fathers' behaviors toward their children (e.g., criticism and physically negative behaviors) were unrelated to fathers' personal adjustment (e.g., parenting stress, depression, marital adjustment, and negative life events). However, mothers' personal adjustment was significantly related to higher levels of criticism and to higher levels of physically negative behaviors toward their children. When the personal adjustment of fathers and mothers was compared directly, Webster-Stratton found that fathers reported less depression, fewer negative life events, and lower parenting stress than did the mothers of children referred for unspecified conduct problems.

In contrast to the work by Webster-Stratton (1988), Christensen, Phillips, Glasgow, and Johnson (1983) found that both paternal and maternal depression were associated with poor marital adjustment and with a less positive approach to children. In addition, fathers' personal discomfort was positively correlated with intolerance of their children's bad behaviors and inversely correlated with a positive approach toward their children. A stronger connection between fathers' rather than mothers' functioning and children's deviant behavior was found by Johnson and Lobitz (1974). In a sample of children exhibiting disruptive behavior or obsessive compulsive behavior, Hibbs and colleagues (1991) found that both fathers' and mothers' psychiatric status was associated with their children's psychological functioning. In addition, fathers' and mothers' psychiatric status was significantly related to fathers' and mothers' high levels of expressed emotion (EE). Hibbs and colleagues concluded that high EE in fathers was primarily associated with paternal psychiatric diagnosis (for a variety of diagnostic categories including substance abuse, antisocial personality disorder, and histrionic personality disorder) although mothers' high levels of EE were associated with both their children's psychological functioning and maternal psychiatric diagnosis (primarily affective disorders, anxiety disorders, and borderline personality disorder).

Based on results using the original version of the Minnesota Multiphasic Personality Inventory (MMPI), all paternal clinical scales were significantly related to children's behavior problems but only one maternal clinical scale was significantly related to children's behavior problems (Johnson & Lobitz, 1974). In an interesting analysis of change over time in parents' MMPI scores, Holmes, Sabalis, Chestnut and Khoury (1984) compared the MMPI results of parents whose children received outpatient psychiatric services from 1970 to 1974 with the MMPI results of parents whose children received services from 1975 to 1979. They found that the latter group of mothers were significantly more disturbed than the former group of mothers, but there were no differences between the two groups when fathers' MMPI scores were analyzed.

A number of other studies that have investigated nonspecific behavior problems in children might also be considered studies of systemic family functioning. For example, Roehling and Robin (1986) used the Family Beliefs Inventory to compare unrealistic beliefs about parent-adolescent relationships in distressed families who were receiving family therapy services and nondistressed control families who were not involved in therapy. They found that fathers in distressed families held more unreasonable beliefs about obedience, perfectionism, ruination, and the malicious intent of their children than did fathers in nondistressed families. When comparing the beliefs of mothers from distressed families with the beliefs of mothers from nondistressed families, no significant differences emerged.

Sawyer, Sarris, Baghurst, Cross, and Kalucy (1988) used the Family Assessment Device (FAD) to compare families of adolescents in Australia who were receiving mental health services and families of adolescents who were not receiving services. They found that fathers, mothers, and adolescents in clinical families reported significantly greater distress than fathers, mothers, and adolescents in nonclinical control families on nearly all scales of the FAD, including communication, role, and general functioning. Within clinical families, Sawyer and colleagues found that adolescents reported higher levels of dysfunction than their fathers and their mothers on a number of scales, including problem solving, communication, affective responsiveness, behavior control, and general functioning within the family. When fathers and mothers were compared in the clinical group, only one significant difference emerged. Fathers reported greater levels of inappropriate affective responsiveness within the family than did mothers.

In a study of African American families in which an adolescent had been referred for mental health services, Berg-Cross, Kidd, and Carr (1990) found that fathers' and mothers' perception of cohesion were influenced by different interpersonal characteristics within the family. Fathers who reported higher levels of family cohesion tended to experience higher levels of anxiety when disclosing thoughts or feelings to family members. The reverse pattern was found for mothers. Mothers who reported higher levels of anxiety while self-disclosing (as well as lower levels of depression and higher levels of anger while self-disclosing) tended to report lower levels of family cohesion.

Family patterns of communication were assessed directly in a study of families with an adolescent who was receiving clinical services and families with a nonreferred adolescent (Krinsley & Bry, 1991). The Response Class Matrix coding system was used to quantify dyadic interactions within families while they discussed a problem or planned something together. When families were discussing a problem, there were no differences in fathers', mothers', or adolescents' levels of negative behaviors between families in the clinical and control groups. Adolescents in the clinical group (but not fathers or mothers) showed lower levels of problem-solving behaviors than their counterparts in the nonclinical control group when discussing a problem. With regard to planning something together, fathers, mothers, and adolescents in clinical families showed higher levels of negative behaviors than their counterparts in nonclinical families. Clinical mothers (but not fathers or adolescents) showed significantly less problem-solving behaviors than their counterparts in nonclinical families when the family attempted to plan something together. Krinsley and Bry discussed the results in relation to the aversive nature of the family environment in families of clinically referred adolescents, and they pointed out that different assessment techniques (e.g., having families discuss a problem vs. plan something together) were needed to provide a full assessment of the functioning within clinical and nonclinical families.

Overall, there is conflicting evidence as to the associations between fathers' and mothers' emotional functioning, family functioning, and children's and adolescents' problematic behavior. Although there were somewhat more significant associations between maternal functioning and child behavior problems, there were also significant associations between paternal functioning and child behavior problems.

ALCOHOL AND SUBSTANCE ABUSE

The research on paternal characteristics of children and adolescents who abuse alcohol and other substances is relatively limited and is somewhat equivocal. In a study of adolescent substance abusers, half of whom were recruited through community newspaper advertisements and half of whom were receiving inpatient treatment for substance abuse, Tarter, Laird, and Bukstein (1991) investigated the likelihood of paternal substance abuse in the family history of these adolescents. In the community sample of substance-abusing adolescents, 11 participants had a father with a history of substance abuse and 36 participants had a father without a history of substance abuse. In the inpatient sample, 55 adolescents had a father with a history of substance abuse and 31 had a father without such a history. When severity of the adolescent's substance abuse was considered in light of paternal substance abuse, the pattern was somewhat different between the community and inpatient samples. When comparing scores on a variety of psychosocial and mental health indexes (e.g., behavior patterns, psychiatric disorder, family system, school adjustment, peer relationships), there were no differences in the community sample of substance abusers who had fathers with or without a history of substance abuse. When the inpatient sample of adolescent substance abusers was evaluated, substance abusers who had a father with a history of substance abuse showed significantly more severe problems in the family system than did substance-abusing inpatient adolescents who had a father without a history of substance abuse. Based on results from these two samples, Tarter and colleagues suggested that having a father with a history of substance abuse was not necessarily associated with greater psychosocial maladjustment. Conversely, given that a large number of substance-abusing adolescents had a father or a mother without a history of substance abuse, this study suggested that a history of substance abuse within the immediate family was not a prerequisite to developing substance-abuse problems during adolescence.

In a study of 12- to 17-year-old, substance-abusing inpatients, Klinge and Piggott (1986) found that paternal and maternal substance abuse was not related to adolescents' substance abuse. Alcohol and drug abuse were tallied together for the determination of the substance-abuse status of fathers, mothers, and adolescents. Neither fathers' nor mothers' self-reported substance abuse was significantly correlated with their sons' or daughters' clinic-documented substance abuse. In addition, neither fathers nor mothers believed that their own use of substances was related to their adolescents' substance abuse problems. Fathers' and mothers' self-reported substance abuse scores were significantly correlated with each other ($r = .37$). Adolescents' perceptions of their fathers' and mothers' substance abuse were related to certain attitudes about their parents. For example, the greater the level of adolescents' reports of maternal substance abuse, the more adolescents reported that they had a negative attitude toward their mothers' substance abuse. This correlation was not significant for fathers. However, adolescents did report feeling that their own substance abuse was significantly influenced by their fathers' but not their mothers' substance abuse. This study suggested that adolescents' substance abuse was not significantly related to their parents' substance abuse directly, but that adolescents' attitudes about their parents' substance abuse showed some relation to their own substance abuse.

Other studies have suggested that adolescents' perceptions of their parents may be related to adolescents' substance abuse and other psychological symptoms. Gantman (1978) conducted a study with three groups of adolescents:

1. Drug-abusing adolescents who were referred for treatment at an outpatient drug and alcohol clinic.
2. Emotionally disturbed adolescents who were receiving services for a variety of psychiatric disturbances that were not related to alcohol or substance abuse.
3. Nonreferred adolescents in a control group who were recruited from the same geographic area as the other two groups.

These three groups did not differ on family socioeconomic status, parental age, size of the family, or adolescents' age or birth order within the family. The primary set of analyses investigated group differences in the level of paternal and maternal scapegoating of adolescents based on direct observations of a verbal family task. In families with a drug-abusing adolescent and families with an emotionally disturbed adolescent, fathers and mothers were significantly more likely to scapegoat their adolescent and to inaccurately blame the adolescent for problems with the task than in families with a nonreferred adolescent. There were no differences in scapegoating and blame between the families of drug-abusing and emotionally disturbed adolescents. The results were consistent for both paternal and maternal scapegoating and blame of the adolescent.

Similar results were found from the perspective of the adolescent in a study of heroin abusers. Jiloha (1986) compared adolescent heroin addicts and non-addicts and found that addicts reported that their fathers were significantly less able to communicate effectively than the fathers of nonaddicts. No significant differences were found in communication effectiveness between the mothers of heroin addicts versus nonaddicts. Although Jiloha did not assess the scapegoating or blame that fathers and mothers expressed toward their adolescents, heroin-addicted adolescents reported higher levels of fear and guilt than nonaddicted adolescents. In a study of adolescents who were abusing alcohol or drugs, fathers' ratings of problematic marital and family boundaries were associated with more severe problems in the adolescent (Marett, Sprenkle, & Lewis, 1992). Deykin, Buka, and Zeena (1992) studied chemically dependent adolescents, some of whom also met diagnostic criteria for major depression. They found that adolescents who were comorbid for chemical dependence and major depression were more likely to have a father who experienced some type of psychopathology, were more likely to have been victimized as a child, and were more likely to be female than those adolescents who were abusing substances but who were not also depressed.

These different findings should be considered in light of the specific methodology that was employed. Downs and Robertson (1991) conducted an interesting study that suggested different conclusions may be drawn depending on the research methodology. They recruited a clinical sample of adolescents who were receiving services for alcohol or drug abuse and a stratified random sample from the community. Based on adolescents' reports, Downs and Robertson evaluated family functioning, adolescents' delinquent behavior, and parental alcohol use separately for each of the two groups and then compared the different findings. For the stratified random sample, regression analyses revealed that family conflict was the only statistically significant predictor of delinquent behavior. In the clinical sample, adolescents' delinquent behavior was predicted by paternal alcohol use, family intellectual-cultural orientation, and familial organization. Downs and Robertson suggested that these different patterns of results should serve as a warning to researchers who try to generalize data from a random community to a clinical sample. The lack of common patterns may be due to different processes in clinical versus subclinical levels of delinquent behavior, the veracity with which the different samples answered the interviewers questions, or differences in some other confounding variable that was not assessed. Because no common predictors of delinquency were found between the clinical and nonclinical samples, Downs and Robertson suggested that data from one type of sample should not be applied to another type. This study highlights the need to conduct further research on the impact of different research methodologies and the use of different sampling techniques on research with substance-abusing adolescents.

Overall, these studies suggest that although adolescents' substance abuse was not directly related to their fathers' and mothers' self-reported substance abuse, there were significant relations between paternal and maternal attitudes and adolescents' substance abuse. There is a great need to conduct more studies of adolescents and their families to ascertain the relations between parental substance abuse and adolescents' substance abuse. However, a number of studies have investigated the retrospective reports of paternal characteristics by adults who were referred for treatment of their substance abuse.

The majority of retrospective studies that have been conducted with substance-abusing adults have focused on alcohol abuse somewhat more than abuse of other substances. As is reflective of the base rates of these problems, most research samples have consisted of more males than females and some researchers have focused solely on male participants. For example, three studies investigated the drinking behavior of parents of alcoholic men. Hill (1992) studied 29 alcoholic men and split them into two groups: sociopathic and nonsociopathic. All these alcoholic men had a brother who also showed evidence of alcoholism. In the sociopathic alcoholic group, 72.2% of the fathers had a history of alcoholism, 22.2% of the mothers had a history of alcoholism, and in 16.7% of the families there was evidence of both paternal and maternal alcoholism. In the nonsociopathic alcoholic group, 37.5% of the fathers had a history of alcoholism and none of the mothers showed evidence of alcoholism. None of the fathers or mothers in either group showed a history of antisocial personality disorder. Because of the severity of symptoms in the absence of paternal sociopathy, Hill suggested that this sample may reflect another type of alcoholism that has not yet been studied.

In a study of men diagnosed with alcohol dependence, Schuckit (1984) found that 32% of the sample of alcoholic men had fathers who were alcoholic, 6% had mothers who were alcoholic, 6% had both fathers and mothers who were alcoholic, and 56% reported that neither of their parents was alcoholic. In comparing the functioning of these four groups, the highest levels of earlier problems during adolescence with alcohol and antisocial behavior occurred for men with a father and mother who were both alcoholic. The lowest levels of problems were reported for men with neither parent showing alcoholic problems. There were few differences in current level of functioning or earlier problems during adolescence for alcoholic men whose fathers were alcoholic in comparison with those whose mothers were alcoholic. The primary difference that occurred between alcoholic sons with an alcoholic father versus an alcoholic mother was that sons with an alcoholic mother showed significantly more drug abuse than sons of an alcoholic father.

Mulinski (1989) conducted a study of alcoholic men and assessed their perceptions of their fathers' alcoholism, their perceptions of the importance of their fathers in their lives, and their perceived similarity to their fathers. Participants were not asked about their perceptions of their mothers. Results of the study showed that 37.9% of the participants reported that their fathers were alcoholic and 62.1% reported that their fathers were not alcoholic. In comparing these two groups, Mulinski found that sons with alcoholic fathers were less likely to perceive their fathers as serving an important role in their lives and were less likely to perceive their fathers as similar to themselves than were sons without alcoholic fathers.

In a rare study that investigated female alcoholics' perceptions of their fathers and mothers, Haver (1986) specifically addressed the familial characteristics that were associated with good versus poor outcome of a substance-abuse treatment program. This was a follow-up study to ascertain the functioning of 44 female alcoholics who had been out of treatment from 3 to 10 years. The women were all under 40 years old at the beginning of treatment. Four variables were used to measure outcome based on current functioning: amount of alcohol consumption, level of psychosocial functioning, amount of use of illicit drugs, and total outcome based on the summation of the first three outcome measures. Haver found that a number of characteristics of the participants' childhood were associated with poor treatment outcome in adulthood. Women who had been abused by their father showed greater levels of drug use after treatment, women who had been abused by their mother showed greater levels of alcohol consumption as well as lower overall outcome, women with a psychiatrically disturbed father showed higher levels of drug use and lower levels of psychosocial and overall functioning after treatment, and women with an alcoholic mother showed higher levels of drug use after treatment. Conversely, fathers' alcoholism and mothers' psychiatric disturbance were not significantly associated to their daughters' long-term treatment outcome.

Haver suggested that the history of paternal and maternal physical abuse, psychiatric disturbance, and alcoholism may have been related to the women's choice in romantic partners when they reached adulthood, which was also related to treatment outcome. Poorer total treatment outcome was seen in women who had partners who were violent and who had partners who abused alcohol. This study suggests that it is important to take paternal and maternal behavior during childhood, as well as current living situation, into account when treating women for alcohol abuse.

Hesselbrock (1991) recruited a sample of alcoholic men and women who had received inpatient services for the treatment of alcoholism and assessed participants for antisocial personality disorder (APD) and depression. The participants, all of whom were alcoholic, were placed in one of four groups: No APD or depression, APD but no depression, depression but no APD, and both APD and depression. Parental history of alcoholism was compared between these four groups for both male and female alcoholics. Across the four groups, female alcoholics reported a higher prevalence of paternal alcoholism than did male alcoholics. For example, 67% of the female alcoholics who also met criteria for APD and depression had alcoholic fathers, whereas 42% of male alcoholics who also met criteria for APD and depression had an alcoholic father. For both men and women, when APD co-occurred with alcoholism, there was a greater likelihood of paternal alcoholism than for men and women alcoholics who also met criteria for depression or who did not meet criteria for any other disorder. No consistent pattern could be ascertained regarding maternal alcoholism.

Pollock, Schneider, Gabrielli, and Goodwin (1987) conducted a meta-analysis to determine the relation between sex of parent and sex of offspring in the transmission of alcoholism. With combined data from 32 studies of familial transmission of alcoholism, they found that both men and women who were alcoholic were more likely to have a father, rather than a mother, who was alcoholic. This finding remained significant even after controlling for the overall prevalence rates of alcoholism in males and females. Women who had an alcoholic mother showed greater likelihood of developing alcoholism compared with women in nonclinical control groups. Men who had an alcoholic mother did not show elevated risk for the development of alcoholism.

A number of other studies have included both men and women in their samples and have investigated participants who were referred for both alcohol and drug abuse. In a comprehensive study of alcohol- and drug-abusing adults in the Netherlands, DeJong, Harteveld, and van de Wielen (1991) sought to establish differences in retrospective reports of paternal and maternal child-rearing behaviors that might differentiate between alcohol abusers and drug abusers. Over 70% of the sample was male. The mean age of alcohol abusers was 37.6 years, and the mean age of the drug addicts was 24.7 years. Participants reported on their memories of their fathers and mothers regarding the behaviors of rejection, overprotection, emotional warmth, and favoring participants over their siblings. Paternal and maternal parenting behaviors were compared, as were the behaviors of parents of alcohol abusers and drug abusers.

Results of the study showed that drug addicts had a greater perception of their fathers and mothers having been rejecting and overprotective than did alcoholics. Mothers of drug addicts were perceived to show more favoring during childhood than mothers of alcoholics. There were no differences between drug addicts and alcoholics in their reports of paternal favoring, paternal emotional warmth, or maternal warmth during childhood. When fathers and mothers were compared directly, mothers were perceived as showing greater emotional warmth and more overprotectiveness than fathers of both alcoholics and drug addicts. Mothers of drug addicts were also perceived as showing more favoritism than fathers of drug addicts. There were no significant differences between mothers and fathers regarding the favoritism that alcoholics reported, or the rejection that any of the participants reported. DeJong and colleagues summarized these data by suggesting that drug addicts have more negative memories of the parenting they received when compared with alcoholics.

Lesieur, Blume, and Zoppa (1986) conducted a study to ascertain the co-occurrence of gambling in inpatients who were receiving services for alcohol and drug abuse. However, they did not analyze alcohol abusers and drug abusers separately. They found that inpatients' pathological gambling was associated with retrospective accounts of paternal gambling, maternal gambling, and sibling gambling. In addition, fathers' but not mothers' abuse of alcohol was associated with their adult children's problematic gambling. Lesieur and colleagues argued that pathological gambling should be treated concurrently with alcohol and drug abuse because of the common co-occurrence and because of the similarities in family histories with these problems.

In a study of heroin addicts who were receiving methadone to treat their dependence on heroin, Metzger and Platt (1987) investigated the personal and familial characteristics that were related to the dose levels of methadone that were given to the recovering addicts. No mention was made of the use or abuse of alcohol by these clients. Clients had an average age of almost 32 years old, an average length of treatment of almost 3 years, and an average length of addiction of nearly 9 years. The sample was primarily male (61%), and primarily African American (66%), with an average length of education of 11.48 years. The purpose of the study was to determine which client characteristics accounted for the variation in methadone dose levels. Metzger and Platt noted that daily dosages of 40–60 mg per day have been established as the most effective and the safest dosage range for the majority of recovering addicts. However, they noted that there continues to be wide variability in the dosages that are given to clients. In this study, methadone dosage levels ranged from less than 20 mg per day up to 100 mg per day.

Results of the study suggested that a variety of client characteristics were associated with the methadone dosage levels that clients received. The researchers investigated client demographics (age, gender, race, education, marital status, employment, contacts with father, contacts with mother, having a father who was living, and having a mother who was living), client involvement in treatment (time in clinic, time on methadone, length of abuse prior to treatment, and prior attempts at treatment), client psychosocial factors (locus of control, self-evaluation, thrill and adventure seeking, general sensation seeking, boredom susceptibility, and disinhibition), and interpersonal problem-solving skills (means-ends ratio, alternatives, causality, consequential thinking, number of problems, problem categories, and transgressions).

Regression analyses with methadone dose entered as the criterion variable showed that current client contacts with father, client gender, client race, employment, having a mother who was living, and client interpersonal problem solving all accounted for a significant amount of the variance in the methadone dosage levels. Higher methadone dosages were associated with a greater number of current contacts with clients' fathers, male clients, Caucasian clients, being employed, having a mother who was living, and the ability to use causality and alternative reasoning in interpersonal problem solving. The variable that accounted for most of the variance in methadone dosage level was number of contacts with the father. Metzger and Platt suggested that clients who continue to have a lot of contact with their father may be able to better develop successful relationships with the clinic staff who might serve in a paternalistic or authoritarian role. Clients who had at least weekly contact with their father received methadone dosage levels that were in the optimal range according to Metzger and Platt. Clients who never saw their father or who saw their father only a few times a year received less than the optimal dosage of methadone. This study suggests that even with adult substance abusers, the father-child relationship seems to be associated with the type of treatment that adult substance abusers receive.

Taken together, these studies suggest that retrospective reports of paternal and maternal parenting behavior, as well as certain reports of current contact with fathers, seem to be associated with alcohol and substance abuse in adults. When the characteristics of both fathers and mothers were measured, there were more similarities than differences in the role of fathers and mothers in their offsprings' substance abuse. Although there were somewhat stronger associations between retrospective reports of parental substance abuse and parenting behaviors with current level of substance-abuse problems in adults than was seen in research on adolescent substance abusers, there were not enough studies to provide firm conclusions.

The research literature on adolescent substance abusers may be limited because of the age of onset for many types of addictions. Although alcohol and substance abuse are evident in samples of adolescents, researchers who focus on "addicted" populations may necessarily seek out samples of older clients. For example, in their sample of adult alcohol and substance abusers, DeJong and colleagues (1991) found that the mean age of the start of addiction to alcohol was 23.2 years and the mean age of the start of addiction to drugs was 18.5 years. Therefore, it is somewhat understandable why researchers would conduct more retrospective research on adult addicts than concurrent research on adolescent alcohol and substance abusers. This review, however, highlights the need for further research into paternal and maternal characteristics related to adolescent substance abusers. In addition, prospective analyses of the course and outcome of substance abuse and the treatment of substance abuse as it relates to paternal and maternal characteristics would help in bridging the gap between the research literature on substance-abusing adolescents and adults.

DEPRESSION

As in the research on substance abuse, two research designs have been used to investigate the relations between childhood depression and paternal functioning: concurrent research and retrospective research.

Concurrent Studies

Somewhat inconsistent findings have emerged from studies that have directly investigated depressed children and their fathers. Children diagnosed with dysthymia reported more maladaptive relationships with their fathers and their mothers compared with nonclinical children (John, Gammon, Prusoff, & Warner, 1987). The same study, however, found that children diagnosed with major depression reported maladaptive relationships with their fathers, but not their mothers, when compared with the reports of nonclinical children. In a study that utilized direct observations to assess father-child and mother-child interactions, Cole and Rehm (1986) did not find any differences in the interactions of fathers and their depressed children, fathers and their nondepressed clinically referred children, or fathers and their nonclinical children. Differences were found in the observations of mother-child interactions. Depressed children received fewer verbal rewards such as praise from their mothers than did nonreferred children or clinically referred children who were diagnosed with a disorder other than depression. Similarly, Puig-Antich and colleagues (1985a, 1985b) found that mothers' poor communication and mothers' low affection were associated with their children's higher levels of depression. Father-child interactions were not significantly associated with childhood depression. When children diagnosed with major depression reported a problematic relationship with their father and their mother, they were also likely to report problems with their peers and with their academic performance (Puig-Antich, Kaufman, Ryan, & Williamson, 1993).

With regard to depression in the parents of depressed children, two studies showed no differences in paternal depression but higher incidence of depression in the mothers of children who were depressed. Using the Schedule of Affective Disorders and Schizophrenia to diagnose depression, Kaslow, Rehm, Pollack, and Siegel (1988) found that fathers' diagnosis of depression did not differ between groups of children who were depressed, children who were clinically referred for a disorder other than depression, and children who were not referred for any psychological problems. In contrast, mothers of depressed children and mothers of nondepressed clinically referred children were significantly more likely to meet diagnostic criteria for depression than mothers of children in the normal control group. Cole and Rehm (1986) also found these results. Similar patterns were found in measures of depressive symptoms (without categorization into a diagnostic group) in a group of children who received outpatient services for a variety of disorders. Jensen, Bloedau, Degroot, Ussery, and Davis (1990) found that maternal psychological symptoms were significantly related to children's self-reported depression and anxiety but that paternal psychological symptoms were related only to children's anxiety, not depression. However, fathers' depressive symptoms were related to their reports of their children's depressive symptoms.

Ivens and Rehm (1988) found that fathers' depressive symptoms but not mothers' depressive symptoms were related to clinician-parent discrepancies in reports of children's depressive symptoms. Fathers with higher levels of depression rated their children as having more depressive symptoms than did clinicians when using a structured diagnostic interview. Mothers' depressive symptoms were not related to discrepancies between mothers and clinicians. Counter to many of these findings, Mitchell, McCauley, Burke, Calderon, and Schloredt (1989) found that neither fathers' nor mothers' rates of major depression differed between the two groups when comparing parents of depressed children and parents of nondepressed clinical children.

Turning to other psychiatric problems in the parents of depressed children, again there are mixed findings. When comparing fathers and mothers of depressed children directly, Mitchell and colleagues (1989) found that fathers were significantly less likely than mothers to have a lifetime diagnosis of depression but fathers were significantly more likely than mothers to have a lifetime diagnosis of substance abuse or antisocial personality disorder. However, Cole and Rehm (1986) did not find significant differences in any paternal or maternal diagnoses that were evaluated (e.g., alcohol abuse, anxiety disorder) when comparing parents of depressed children, parents of nondepressed clinically referred children, and parents of nondepressed nonclinical children.

Fathers of depressed children were more likely to be diagnosed with antisocial personality disorder than were fathers of clinical controls (Weller et al., 1994). However, there were no differences in rates of mood disorders, anxiety disorders, or psychotic disorders. Mitchell and colleagues (1989) found that fathers of depressed children and fathers of nondepressed clinically referred children did not differ on a variety of psychiatric diagnoses (such as anxiety disorders, alcoholism, schizophrenia, and antisocial personality disorder). However, mothers of depressed children were significantly more likely than mothers of nondepressed clinically referred children to have tried to commit suicide and to be diagnosed with an anxiety disorder, alcoholism, or the combination of alcoholism and drug abuse. Mitchell, McCauley, Burke, and Moss (1988) compared the parents of children with coexisting depression and anxiety disorders with the parents of children who only exhibited depression. They found that fathers and mothers in the two groups did not differ in rates of diagnosis of an anxiety disorder. Also, in a comparison of parents of children with coexisting depression and conduct disorder with parents of children who only exhibited depression, there were no differences between the two groups in paternal or maternal diagnosis of substance abuse or antisocial personality.

Overall, there does not appear to be a strong association between fathers' characteristics and childhood depression when the studies are conducted during childhood. There appears to be a stronger link between mothers' characteristics and childhood depression in contrast to fathers' characteristics and childhood depression. However, studies that were conducted with depressed children suggest a number of important areas for further research, such as children's self-reported paternal-child relationship. Although few studies of this kind have been conducted with depressed children while they are still children, more studies have been conducted that investigate depressed adults' retro-spective accounts of fathering and mothering behaviors that were evident while they were children.

Retrospective Studies

A variety of studies have investigated retrospective reports of paternal and maternal factors in the childhood histories of clients who experienced major depression in adulthood. Crook, Raskin, and Eliot (1981) compared the early parenting received by adults who were in treatment for depression and adults in a control group who were in treatment for a medical (nonpsychiatric) prob-lem. There was an attempt to match the clinical and control groups on race and gender. Slightly over 20% of the sample was African American and ap-proximately 70% of the sample was female. Between-group comparisons were done for the entire sample to test for main effects and then additional analy-ses were completed to investigate interaction effects based on race and gen-der. When comparing the parenting received by depressed clients and nonclinical adults, a number of differences were found for both paternal and maternal parenting. Depressed clients recalled their fathers as showing sig-nificantly more rejection, enforcement, control through guilt, hostile control, instillment of persistent anxiety, hostile detachment, withdrawal of relations, and extreme autonomy, and significantly less positive involvement than fa-thers of participants in the nonclinical control group. The same differences were found between mothers of depressed adults and mothers of nondepressed adults.

In addition to the differences found between fathers of adults in the two groups, mothers of depressed adults were also reported to have shown less ac-ceptance, less child centeredness, less acceptance of individuation, and more lax discipline than the mothers of nondepressed adults. Social workers who were familiar with the participants also provided ratings of parental affection, involvement, and tolerance of child rearing while the participants were grow-ing up. Based on the social workers' ratings, both fathers and mothers of de-pressed clients showed lower levels of affection and involvement than the fathers and mothers of nondepressed participants. No group differences were based on the social workers' ratings of paternal or maternal tolerance of child rearing. These analyses showed that there were strong main effects for pater-nal and maternal parenting behavior based on the participants' own reports and social workers' reports.

These main effects must be considered tentative because significant inter-action effects emerged when race and gender were investigated. Based on the analysis of 36 parenting subscales (18 paternal subscales and 18 maternal sub-scales), five significant second-order interaction effects were found when an-alyzing group $\times$ gender $\times$ race. Four subscales of parenting behavior were found to be significant for fathers (lack of acceptance, lack of child centeredness, low positive involvement, and low acceptance) and one subscale of parenting behavior was found to be significant for mothers (intrusiveness). The interaction effects suggested that, among African Americans, fathers' overall rejection was more closely associated with depression in males as opposed to females, whereas among Caucasian Americans, fathers' overall rejection was more closely associated with depression in females as opposed to males. For both African American and Caucasian American participants, mothers' intrusiveness seemed to show a stronger association with depression in their female children rather than their male children. This study suggested that there is a link between fathers' and mothers' parenting behavior and their children's depression in adulthood. As with any study that utilizes retrospective reports of parenting behavior, the caveat must be acknowledged that current level of depression in adults may have altered recall of parenting behavior from childhood. However, because group differences were found for fathers' and mothers' parenting based on social workers' reports, the results based on the participants' retrospective reports of parenting behavior should not be dismissed.

Alnaes and Torgersen (1990) compared the parental representation in clients with major depression, anxiety disorder, and mixed anxiety-depression. They found that clients with pure major depression did not recall their fathers' or mothers' care and protection any differently than clients with a pure anxiety disorder, or with other psychiatric disorders. However, clients with pure major depression reported significantly higher paternal care than did clients with mixed anxiety-depression. This study points to the detrimental fathering that was received by clients who ended up developing a combination of depression and anxiety disorder.

To provide a comprehensive review of retrospective reports of parenting, Gerlsma, Emmelkamp, and Arrindell (1990) conducted a meta-analysis of studies that used depressed adults' retrospective reports of the parenting behavior they received from their fathers and mothers during childhood. Although there were inconsistent findings from the meta-analysis, studies with the largest effect sizes found that depressed adults reported less affection and more control from their fathers and mothers than did nondepressed adults. This suggests a parenting style that could be referred to as "affectionless control." The overall findings from the meta-analysis were inconsistent and inconclusive with regard to the parenting that depressed adults had received while growing up, which may have been due to the comparison of different measures, the use of different methodologies, and the combination of data from different countries. Therefore, the meta-analysis by Gerlsma and colleagues suggested the need for more consistent research methodology in this area.

An interesting side note should be considered in regard to the retrospective accounts of psychiatrically disturbed adults, especially when depression and anxiety disorders are the primary diagnosis. Kendler, Silberg, Neale, Kessler,

Heath, and Eaves (1991) sought to establish the validity of family history reports of psychiatric disturbance based on the reporter's own psychiatric status. They interviewed over 1,000 pairs of female adult twins and assessed the lifetime psychiatric status of the twins themselves as well as the twins' reports of their fathers and mothers. A subsample was identified in which one twin met criteria for a psychiatric disorder and the other twin did not meet criteria. The primary diagnostic groups that were analyzed based on the status of at least one of the twins were major depression, generalized anxiety disorder, and alcoholism. The primary question in this study was whether or not the twin's own psychiatric status would influence her recollection of paternal and maternal psychiatric status. Results of the study showed that when a twin was diagnosed with major depression or generalized anxiety disorder, but not alcoholism, she was more likely to report psychiatric disturbance in her father or mother than was her twin. Based on these results, Kendler and colleagues suggest that depressed and anxious clients' reports of their family history of psychiatric disturbance must be used with caution because their reports may be influenced by their own level of distress. This caution does not appear to be necessary when using the family history reports of clients who are dependent on alcohol. To attenuate potentially invalid reports of family psychiatric status and gain convergence, Kendler and colleagues suggest that clinicians and researchers should use multiple informants of family psychiatric history.

In summary, a limited number of studies have been conducted with depressed children or with depressed adults' retrospective reports of their fathers' behavior when they were children (Burbach & Borduin, 1986). Although similar criteria are used to diagnose depression in children and depression in adults (American Psychiatric Association, 1994), the research findings regarding fathers' characteristics and their children's depression vary according to the research methodology that is used. Overall, there are somewhat stronger findings for paternal effects when retrospective reports are used as compared with the findings for paternal effects when concurrent reports of paternal behavior and childhood depression are used.

SUICIDAL BEHAVIOR

A limited number of studies were identified that investigated fathers' characteristics in relation to their children's suicidal behavior. Although none of the studies directly compared paternal and maternal characteristics, two studies (Garfinkel, Froese, & Hood, 1982; McKenry, Tishler, & Kelley, 1982) compared parents of suicidal children with parents of nonsuicidal children in a nonclinical control group; two studies (Myers, Burke, & McCauley, 1985; Pfeffer et al., 1989) compared parents of suicidal children with parents of nonsuicidal children in a clinical control group; one study (Lester, 1991b) investigated retrospective reports of parental behavior in adult prison inmates who had attempted suicide; and three studies (Bron, Strack, & Rudolph, 1991; Lester, 1991a; Tomlinson-Keasey, Warren, & Elliott, 1986) analyzed retrospective accounts of early paternal loss in adult women who had attempted suicide.

The studies by Garfinkel and colleagues (1982) and McKenry and colleagues (1982) used an emergency room setting to identify children and adolescents who had attempted suicide and children and adolescents in a matched control group who were brought to the emergency room for minor injuries that were not related to a suicide attempt. The study by Garfinkel and colleagues (1982) provided a number of analyses to compare the family diagnostic histories of the two groups (e.g., family history of a psychiatric disorder, family history of suicide attempts), but these variables were not analyzed separately for paternal and maternal effects. Only two variables (employment status and presence in the home) were analyzed for specific paternal and maternal effects. In the comparison of suicide attempters and controls, Garfinkel and colleagues found that fathers of suicide attempters were more likely to be unemployed and were more likely to be absent from the home. In contrast to mothers of nonsuicide attempters, mothers of suicide attempters were more likely to be employed and more likely to be absent from the homes.

The study by McKenry and colleagues (1982), which focused on adolescent suicide, was more comprehensive with regard to paternal and maternal characteristics. Adolescents ranged in age from 12 to 18 years, and the average family socioeconomic status was lower middle class. Fathers, mothers, and adolescents were asked to report on parental marital adjustment, their satisfaction with time spent with the family, and their own suicidal ideation. Fathers and mothers were also asked about their own feelings of depression, anxiety, and satisfaction with their spouse. Adolescents were asked about their perceptions of how much their fathers and mothers were interested in them. Compared with their counterparts in the nonclinical control group, fathers but not mothers of suicidal adolescents, and adolescents themselves reported lower marital adjustment in the parental dyad. Fathers, mothers, and their suicidal adolescents all reported less satisfaction with the time they spent with the family. Mothers and their suicidal adolescents, but not fathers, acknowledged greater suicidal ideation than their counterparts in the control families. Fathers of suicidal adolescents reported significantly more depression than fathers of nonsuicidal adolescents and mothers of suicidal adolescents reported significantly more anxiety than mothers of nonsuicidal adolescents. Suicidal adolescents reported less interest from their mothers than did nonsuicidal adolescents. No differences were evident in adolescents' reports of their fathers' level of interest. Although this study suggested that families of suicidal adolescents differ from families of nonsuicidal adolescents in a number of ways, McKenry and colleagues cautioned that a causal link in these analyses should not be assumed. They highlighted that the data were collected at a time of crisis that may have had more emotional meaning for families of suicidal adolescents than for families of adolescents who were being treated for minor injuries.

Rather than interviewing families in crisis about a suicide attempt, Myers and colleagues (1985) sought to find premorbid variables that might be related to children's suicidal behavior. Through use of chart review, they identified 61 preadolescent children who evidenced suicidal behavior and were admitted to an inpatient child psychiatry unit of a pediatric teaching hospital. For comparison, the researchers identified an equal number of matched clinical controls who were also admitted to the same unit during the same time span but who did not show any evidence of suicidal ideation or suicidal behavior. Children ranged in age from 5 to 13 years, and there were somewhat more boys than girls (66% and 34%, respectively). The sample was ethnically diverse, representing primarily lower socioeconomic status. A number of family history and child history variables were compared for suicidal children and nonsuicidal children.

Results of the study showed that suicidal children were more likely than nonsuicidal children to have a family history of suicidality, to have a mother who was physically abused by their father, and to have a father who showed physical abuse toward the family. This difference was only significant when general abuse toward the family by biological fathers (and not stepfathers) was considered. There were no group differences based on physical child abuse at the hands of the father or the mother. No differences were found between the two groups in parental history of alcoholism, parental depression, parental antisocial activities, personality disorders, or psychosis. It should be noted that these variables were analyzed for the "family history" of these disorders and were not analyzed separately for paternal versus maternal history. This study suggests a connection between family suicidal behavior and certain types of family violence in relation to preadolescents' suicidal behavior. In a comparison of the parents of suicidal adolescent inpatients with the parents of nonsuicidal adolescent inpatients, Pfeffer and colleagues (1989) also found few differences in parental psychiatric symptoms. The fathers and mothers of adolescent inpatients representing four types of behavior (suicidal-only, assaultive-only, assaultive-suicidal, nonassaultive-nonsuicidal) did not show group differences in their alcohol abuse, affective disorder, or suicidal behavior.

Lester (1991b) used chart reviews of adult prison inmates' records to investigate reports of parenting behavior and perceived closeness to parents when the inmates were growing up. These variables were compared for inmates who had attempted suicide, inmates who had suicidal ideation but who had not attempted suicide, and inmates who had no history of suicide attempts or suicidal ideation. Of the 454 inmates, 441 were men and 13 were women. Lester found that inmates who had attempted suicide had received more physical punishment from their fathers and felt less close to their fathers than did nonsuicidal inmates. There were no differences based on reports of maternal punishment or feelings of closeness to mothers. Inmates who had attempted suicide were more likely than nonsuicidal inmates to have been physically abused by their parents. However, the effects of paternal versus maternal physical abuse were not analyzed. This study suggested that paternal physical punishment and a lack of paternal closeness were associated with greater likelihood of suicidal behavior in a sample of adult prison inmates.

Tomlinson-Keasey and colleagues (1986) used longitudinal data from the Terman Genetic Studies of Genius to determine which family and personal characteristics were more likely to predict suicides in their sample of gifted women. They investigated seven characteristics in relation to the eventual suicide completions of the gifted women: signatures of mental health (e.g., anxiety, depression, conspicuous instability), temperament, mental health ratings, early loss of the father due to death or abandonment before the age of 20, stress in the family of origin, physical health, and self-reported alcohol use. When using these seven risk factors, discriminant function analysis correctly distinguished all the women who committed suicide from women who had died in ways that were not self-inflicted and from women who were still alive. In other words, this seven-factor model was able to correctly classify 100% of the women who had committed suicide. Although Tomlinson-Keasey and colleagues did not provide analyses to distinguish between the relative importance of these seven risk factors, the study did provide evidence of a possible link between early paternal loss and eventual suicide in a sample of gifted women. In an extension of this study, Lester (1991a) analyzed factors that related to the individual's age when he or she committed suicide in this sample of gifted women and gifted men. He found that suicide at a younger age was associated with paternal loss by either death or divorce during the child's adolescence. Loss of the father during adolescence through death was the characteristic that was most strongly associated with suicide at an earlier age.

Early paternal loss (by death or by separation) was also associated with a somewhat greater likelihood for suicide attempts in a sample of depressed men and women in Germany (Bron et al., 1991). More specifically, 26.5% of depressed clients who did not experience any paternal or maternal loss during childhood attempted suicide as an adult, 18.2% of depressed clients who experienced a maternal loss during childhood attempted suicide as an adult, and 46.5% of depressed clients who experienced a paternal loss during childhood attempted suicide as an adult. Bron and colleagues argued that there was an increased risk for suicide in depressed adult clients who had experienced the loss of their father during childhood.

Taken together, these studies suggest that fathers of suicidal children and adolescents are in greater distress than fathers of nonsuicidal, nonclinical children and adolescents. This distress is expressed through greater levels of depression, less enjoyment in time with the family, and lower enjoyment of the marital relationship. In addition, early paternal loss was associated with suicide attempts and completions in depressed adult clients. The differences between fathers of suicide attempters and fathers of nonclinical controls did not hold up when comparing fathers of suicidal children with fathers of nonsuicidal, clinically referred children. With the exception of greater levels of physical abuse toward their wife and their children, fathers of suicidal children and adolescents did not show any more distress than fathers of nonsuicidal, clinically referred children and adolescents. Although none of these studies directly compared fathers and mothers of suicidal children, it should be noted that the patterns of paternal and maternal findings were relatively similar.

ANXIETY DISORDERS

Only a limited number of studies have investigated the characteristics of fathers of children and adolescents with an anxiety disorder. Clark and Bolton (1985) conducted a study of adolescents diagnosed with obsessive compulsive disorder (OCD) and clinically referred anxious adolescents who showed no signs of obsessional thoughts. Based on an inventory of obsessional thoughts that was given to the parents of OCD and anxious adolescents, Clark and Bolton found that there were no differences between fathers and mothers of OCD and anxious adolescents. However, when comparing the level of fathers' and mothers' obsessional thoughts with the normative data available for the measure, fathers and mothers of OCD and anxious adolescents showed significantly higher levels of obsessional thoughts than adults in the normative control group. Lenane and colleagues (1990) conducted a study to ascertain the diagnostic status of the fathers and mothers of OCD children and adolescents ranging in age from 6 to 18 years (with a mean age of 13.87). The sample consisted of 29 boys and 17 girls. Based on structured psychiatric interviews, the researchers found that 25% of the fathers and 9% of the mothers received a primary diagnosis of OCD themselves. This is in contrast to the rate of 2% diagnosis of OCD found in the general population. Lenane and colleagues also found an additional 45% of fathers and 65% of mothers received one or more Axis I diagnoses other than OCD. Although they did not directly compare the rates of disorders for fathers and mothers, the authors noted that fathers (as well as male siblings of the OCD children and adolescents) were twice as likely to be diagnosed with OCD or obsessive compulsive personality than were mothers (and female siblings). Lenane and colleagues argued that the data provide support for a genetic link, rather than a social or cultural link, in the transmission of OCD.

In an investigation of panic disorder, Last and Strauss (1989) analyzed the likelihood of panic disorder in fathers and mothers of children and adolescents diagnosed with panic disorder. Of the nine sets of parents who completed structured psychiatric interviews, none of the fathers met criteria for panic disorder, whereas three of the mothers (33.3%) met criteria for a lifetime diagnosis of panic disorder. No other parental diagnoses were analyzed.

The researchers noted that the maternal rate of panic disorder was higher than had been found previously with mothers of children diagnosed with anxiety disorders (non-panic-disordered) or diagnosed with ADHD. However, the small sample size suggests that these findings will need to be replicated in larger samples before a clear link between maternal panic disorder and child panic disorder can be established.

In a study of children who were referred for school phobia, Bernstein, Svingen, and Garfinkel (1990) investigated fathers' and mothers' reports of family functioning. The sample consisted of 76 children and adolescents, with a mean age of 13.5 years. Boys and girls were represented in approximately equal numbers (55% and 45% of the sample, respectively). Fathers and mothers completed a measure of general family functioning and the parent-child relationship that consisted of seven subscales: Task accomplishment, role performance, communication, affective expression, involvement, control, and values and norms. Neither fathers nor mothers reported significantly elevated levels of family dysfunction based on the general family functioning factor. However, two of the seven subscales did show elevated dysfunction in the families of children referred for school phobia when compared with the normative data available for the measure. Both fathers and mothers reported greater dysfunction in role performance (role integration, role definition, and role adaptation) and in values and norms (degree of disagreement in the family's value system and degree to which this value system is in conflict with the culture to which the family belongs). Fathers' and mothers' ratings on the general family functioning factor and the seven subscales did not differ significantly. The results of this study suggest that there is somewhat greater dysfunction in families with children and adolescents referred for school phobia, but the father-child and mother-child relationship showed similar levels of dysfunction.

Two studies were identified that investigated fathers of children and adolescents with a variety of anxiety disorders. These studies did not provide separate analyses for the different types of disorders; however, they provide meaningful information about children and adolescents with anxiety disorders. Reeves et al. (1987) assessed the diagnostic status of fathers and mothers of 5- to 12-year-old children who were diagnosed with a variety of anxiety disorders, including overanxious disorder, separation anxiety disorder, avoidant disorder, and phobic disorder. They compared the diagnoses of antisocial personality disorder (APD) and alcoholism for fathers and the diagnosis of an anxiety disorder for mothers. When compared with the nonclinical control group, fathers of children with an anxiety disorder did not show a greater likelihood of receiving a diagnosis of APD or alcoholism. Approximately 10% of fathers in both groups received diagnoses of APD and alcoholism. Diagnosis of a maternal anxiety disorder did show significant differences based on group status. Mothers of children with an anxiety disorder were significantly more likely than mothers of nonclinical children to be diagnosed with an anxiety disorder. Approximately 48% of the mothers with an anxiety-disordered child were diagnosed with an anxiety disorder, and only 5% of the mothers of non-clinical children received an anxiety disorder diagnosis.

These findings are inconsistent with the study by Lenane and colleagues (1990) who found that fathers as well as mothers of children diagnosed with OCD were more likely than adults in the general population to show psychiatric disorders. Because Reeves and colleagues (1987) did not provide separate analyses based on the specific anxiety disorder with which the children were diagnosed and because they only analyzed two disorders in fathers (APD and alcoholism) and one disorder in mothers (anxiety disorder), it is unclear whether these conflicting results are based on the type of child anxiety disorder, the type of parental disorder, or some other factor such as demographic differences in the two samples.

Turning from parental psychiatric status to parental behavior, Alnaes and Torgersen (1990) conducted a study that investigated the retrospective reports of parental behavior from adults diagnosed with a variety of anxiety disorders. This study, which was mentioned briefly in the section on depression, took place in Norway and assessed outpatient adults from four diagnostic groups: anxiety disorder, mixed anxiety-depression, major depression, or another nonpsychotic psychiatric disorder. Participants ranged in age from 18 to 59 years, with a mean age of 35. The sample comprised 206 females and 92 males. Participants reported on their retrospective recollections of the paternal and maternal care and protection that they received when growing up. When comparing the four diagnostic groups, only paternal care proved to discriminate significantly between the groups. Clients who were diagnosed with mixed anxiety-depression reported significantly lower paternal care than clients in the other three diagnostic groups. The other three diagnostic groups did not differ significantly on recollections of paternal care, nor did any of the four groups differ on reports of paternal protection, maternal care, or maternal protection. Alnaes and Torgersen summarized the study by suggesting that the mixed anxiety-depression group may have a different etiologic path to psychiatric disorder than the other groups. In addition, they highlighted the importance of considering fathers in the development and maintenance of mixed anxiety-depression.

In a retrospective study of parenting behavior in Colombia, Leon and Leon (1990) compared the reports of adults diagnosed with panic disorder, adults diagnosed with generalized anxiety disorder, adults diagnosed with depression, and adults who did not meet criteria for any psychiatric diagnosis. Based on participants' retrospective reports of parenting behavior, the researchers categorized participants into one of four groups for both the paternal and maternal parenting behavior they had experienced: high care-low protection, high care-high protection, low care-low protection, and low care-high protection. When paternal parenting behavior was analyzed, fathers of participants in all three clinical groups were more likely to have shown a low care-high protection parenting style than any other parenting style. The parenting styles of fathers in the nonclinical group did not show a greater likelihood of any one parenting style. Mothers of participants diagnosed with generalized anxiety disorder or depression were more likely to show the low care-high protection parenting style. There were no significant differences in the parenting styles of mothers whose adult children were in the panic disorder group or the nonclinical control group.

Frost, Steketee, Cohn, and Griess (1994) compared the retrospective reports of parenting behavior from undergraduate and graduate students who showed subclinical levels of obsessive compulsive disorder. When compared with their nonclinical counterparts, fathers and mothers of obsessive compulsives showed greater levels of overprotection, and mothers showed lower levels of care when the participants were growing up. Based on the parents' own reports of their parenting behavior, fathers of obsessive compulsives reported greater criticism of their children and greater personal expectations of perfectionism than fathers in the control group. There were few differences based on mothers' self-reports.

Based on studies with a similar design to the research design used by Alnaes and Torgerson (1990) and Leon and Leon (1990), Gerlsma and colleagues (1990) conducted a meta-analysis of studies that investigated anxiety-disordered adults and their retrospective reports of parenting behavior they had received from their fathers and mothers while growing up. Adult clients who experienced phobias reported less affection from their fathers and mothers, and more control from their fathers when compared with adults who did not experience phobias. The parenting that fathers had exhibited with their children who later developed phobias was described as "affectionless control." There were no differences in the retrospective reports of adults who were experiencing OCD when compared with retrospective reports of nonclinical adults.

Posttraumatic stress disorder (PTSD) was investigated in a sample of Vietnam veterans (McCranie, Hyer, Boudewyns, & Woods, 1992). The researchers wished to establish whether certain men were at greater risk of developing PTSD because of premilitary experiences, such as parenting behavior received when they were growing up. They found that fathers' negative parenting behaviors, but not mothers' negative behaviors, were more predictive of development of PTSD than amount of combat exposure. Thus, there appeared to be a person-event interaction that left some men more vulnerable to the experience of PTSD, even with lower levels of combat exposure. It is unclear why fathers' negative parenting but not mothers' negative parenting was associated with a greater risk for the development of PTSD.

In summary, these studies provide evidence for greater psychopathology and poorer parenting behaviors in fathers of children diagnosed with an anxiety disorder when compared with fathers of nonreferred children. Overall, there were more similarities than differences between fathers and mothers of children and adolescents diagnosed with an anxiety disorder. The results are not consistent, however, and some studies have provided conflicting findings. Because of the limited number of studies that have investigated fathers of children with an anxiety disorder, it would be premature to reach any conclusions based on these studies.

EATING DISORDERS

The majority of studies that have included an investigation of fathers in relation to their eating-disordered offspring have found differences in the characteristics of the parents or the characteristics of the families when comparing the families of eating-disordered adolescents and noneating disordered adolescents. Most studies have compared families of eating-disordered females with families of nonclinical control females. Only one study was identified that investigated fathers of eating-disordered females with fathers of females experiencing other clinical disorders (Russell, Kopec-Schrader, Rey, & Beumont, 1992).

   Different patterns of significance often emerge depending on the informant (whether the father, the mother, or the adolescent is reporting on the characteristics of interest). Waller, Slade, and Calam (1990) found a number of differences between the families of eating-disordered young women and the families of non-eating-disordered young women, but these differences were evident mainly with the young womens' reports rather than paternal and maternal reports. This research took place in England, and the mean ages of the eating-disordered groups (and therefore the matched control group) fell between 25 and 26 years. Therefore, this sample is somewhat older than the samples of adolescents that are often recruited in the United States. Using the Family Assessment Device (FAD; Epstein, Baldwin, & Bishop, 1983), Waller and colleagues compared families who had a daughter diagnosed with anorexia nervosa, a daughter diagnosed with bulimia nervosa, or a daughter who had no evidence of an eating disorder or any other psychiatric disorder. Based on the daughters' reports, both eating-disordered groups reported greater problems in their families regarding problem solving, communication, roles, affective responsiveness, affective involvement, and behavior control than did the daughters in nonclinical families. There were no significant differences between the two eating-disordered groups. Only two of the six scales on the FAD were significantly different when mothers' reports were analyzed. Mothers in both eating-disordered groups reported that their families showed more problems with affective responsiveness and affective involvement than did the mothers in the nonclinical control group. There were no differences between groups when fathers' reports on the FAD were analyzed, but this may have been due to the lower response rate from fathers. The total sample consisted of 78 daughters and 78 mothers, but only 39 fathers. Waller and colleagues suggested that this study showed the greater utility of using reports on family functioning from the eating-disordered clients themselves rather than using reports from their mothers or their fathers.

Using a similar design and sample, the same research group as just discussed (Calam, Waller, Slade, & Newton, 1990) compared reports of young women who were anorexic, young women who were bulimic with a history of anorexia, and young women who were bulimic with no history of anorexia. They used the Parental Bonding Instrument (PBI; Parker, Tupling, & Brown, 1979), which measures retrospective reports of paternal and maternal care and protection during childhood. Collapsing across the three eating-disordered groups, Calam and colleagues found that eating-disordered young women reported significantly less maternal care, less paternal care, and more paternal protection during their childhood than did young women in the nonclinical control group. There were no differences in retrospective reports of maternal protection. When analyzing group differences between the three groups of eating-disordered young women and comparing them with young women in the control group, bulimics without a history of anorexia reported significantly less maternal care than the other clinical and nonclinical groups and bulimics with a history of anorexia reported significantly less paternal care than the other clinical and nonclinical groups. None of the four groups differed in their reports of paternal or maternal protection. Calam and colleagues interpreted these results as showing the importance of paternal and maternal care and overprotection in the childhood and adolescence of young women who develop eating disorders. In addition, fathers of daughters diagnosed with anorexia nervosa appear to be more emotionally uninvolved than fathers of daughters without an eating disorder (Telerant, Kronenberg, Rabinovitch, & Elman, 1992).

Using the Family Environment Scale (FES; Moos, 1990) to compare the families of adolescent girls who were hospitalized for anorexia and the families of normal-weight adolescent girls in a nonclinical control group, Leon, Lucas, Colligan, Ferdinande, and Kamp (1985) found that the pattern of results was dependent on whose responses were used. Anorexic and normal-weight adolescents did not show significant differences in their reports of the family environment. Fathers of anorexic adolescents reported less family cohesion and less expressiveness than fathers of normal-weight adolescents, but there were no differences in their reports of conflict, independence, achievement orientation, intellectual-cultural orientation, active-recreational orientation, moral religious emphasis, organization, or control. Mothers of anorexic adolescents reported less family cohesion, less expressiveness, and less family independence than mothers of normal-weight adolescents, but the two groups did not differ on the other seven subscales of the FES. Leon and colleagues noted that it was not clear whether the differences that emerged between families of anorexics and families of normal-weight adolescents were due to premorbid differences in the families or due to the stress associated with having a daughter who was starving herself.

Using the Family Assessment Measure (FAM; Skinner, Steinhauser, & Santa-Barbara, 1983), Garfinkel and colleagues (1983) compared families with an anorexic adolescent daughter and families with a nondisordered adolescent daughter. The samples combined families from Canada and Ireland. Anorexic adolescents reported significantly more difficulty with task accomplishment, role performance, and social desirability than did adolescents in the nonclinical control group. Similar results were found based on mothers' reports, with mothers of anorexic daughters reporting greater difficulty with task accomplishment, role performance, communication, affective expression, and social desirability than did mothers of daughters in the nonclinical control group. There were no significant differences between the two groups when fathers' reports on the FAM were analyzed.

Garfinkel and colleagues also investigated dieting habits and psychological functioning in fathers and mothers and found few differences between the two groups. Parents in the two groups did not differ in their own eating restraint, symptoms of anorexia, or other psychological symptoms. The only significant difference that emerged with regard to psychological functioning was that fathers of anorexic adolescents reported higher levels of conscientiousness on a personality measure than fathers of nonclinical adolescents. Mothers in the two groups did not differ on any other measure of personality functioning.

In a comprehensive series of studies, Humphrey and colleagues (Humphrey, 1986, 1987, 1989; Humphrey, Apple, & Kirschenbaum, 1986) used structural analysis of social behavior to investigate the families of eating-disordered adolescents and nondisordered adolescents. Based on direct observations of family interaction, Humphrey (1989) found that fathers and mothers of bulimics appeared to undermine their daughters' attempts at separation and self-assertion, and they also appeared to be hostilely enmeshed with their daughters. Fathers and mothers of anorexics gave conflicting messages of neglect for their daughters' needs combined with nurturance and affection. In the nonclinical control group, fathers and mothers showed higher levels of trusting, protecting, approaching, helping, and enjoying one another. These patterns were found for both fathers and mothers in each of the groups mentioned; however, there were fewer unique differences across the groups for fathers' behavior than for mothers' behavior.

In contrast, Humphrey (1986) found more consistent relations within the families of bulimic adolescents for the father-daughter relationship (significant results on all eight clusters) than for the mother-daughter relationship (significant results for only two of the eight clusters). Bulimic and bulimic-anorexic adolescents rated their parents as less understanding, nurturing, affirming, and comforting toward them than did nonclinical adolescents. Bulimic adolescents also rated their parents as less nurturant than adolescents who were bulimic-anorexic,

anorexic, or non-eating-disordered. These patterns were more consistent for the father-daughter relationship than for the mother-daughter relationship.

In a cross-sectional study of young adult female twins, Kendler, MacLean, Neale, Kessler, Heath, and Eaves (1991) assessed retrospective reports of paternal and maternal parenting behavior in relation to the likelihood of a bulimia diagnosis. They found that young women who were diagnosed with bulimia were significantly more likely to report low levels of paternal care when they were growing up than were young women who were not bulimic. The bulimic and nonbulimic groups did not differ in their reports of paternal overprotectiveness, maternal care, or maternal overprotectiveness.

Bulik and Sullivan (1993) chose to study young women who were bulimic and who were also abusing alcohol. The two comparison groups were bulimic women who were not abusing alcohol and young women who were in a nonclinical control group. Few differences were found between the two groups of bulimic young women. Fathers of daughters in both bulimic groups were rated as having been more seductive with their daughters than fathers of daughters in the nonclinical control group. Both groups of bulimic women rated their mothers as more neurotic and as less satisfied with the maternal role than did women in the nonclinical control group. The primary difference between the two groups of bulimic women was that bulimic women who also abused alcohol reported that their mothers, but not their fathers, were more concerned about their weight, exercise, and appearance than reported by the bulimic women who were not abusing alcohol.

With regard to parental attitudes toward their daughters' weight, Moreno and Thelen (1993) conducted a study that compared fathers' and mothers' encouragement of dieting, their opinions on their daughters' weight, and the values that they placed on thinness. Older adolescent females from an undergraduate sample were categorized as either bulimic, subclinical bulimic, or nonbulimic. When fathers from daughters in these three groups were compared, there were no significant differences in fathers' attitudes about their daughters' weight or need for dieting. In contrast, mothers attitudes differed across the three groups in terms of encouragement of dieting, restriction of food intake, encouragement of exercise to lose weight, and beliefs that daughters were overweight. Specifically, mothers of bulimic daughters were significantly more likely than other mothers to encourage their daughters to lose weight and to attempt to restrict their daughters' food intake. Mothers of bulimic daughters and mothers of daughters who showed subclinical levels of bulimia were more likely than mothers of nonbulimic daughters to encourage their daughters to use exercise as a means of weight control and to think that their daughters were overweight. Fathers and mothers in the three groups did not show different patterns of their own need for weight control. Overall, Moreno and Thelen suggested that mothers' attitudes about their daughters' weight seemed to have a stronger impact than fathers' attitudes about their daughters' weight, although they cautioned that paternal differences may exist that were not assessed directly in the study. It is interesting to note that in a community sample of 15-year-old girls and their parents, the fathers, mothers, and adolescents themselves were likely to significantly underestimate their own weight and to overestimate their own height (Tienboon, Wahlqvist, & Rutishauser, 1992). This pattern was evident regardless of body size of the fathers, mothers, or adolescents.

In another study that investigated daughters' perceptions of their parents' attitudes, Forston and Stanton (1992) utilized a nonclinical sample of college undergraduate young women to ascertain the relation between their perceptions of their parents' attitudes about physical appearance and their own level of psychological distress. Daughters who reported a large discrepancy between themselves and their mother with regard to their actual physical appearance and their ideal physical appearance showed higher levels of depression than other young women who did not report this discrepancy. Daughters who reported a large discrepancy between themselves and their father with regard to their actual appearance and what their appearance ought to be reported higher levels of anxiety. Thus, perceived discrepancies with mothers were more highly associated with depression, and perceived discrepancies with father were more highly associated with anxiety.

The only identified study that investigated fathers of eating-disordered daughters and daughters with another psychiatric disturbance utilized three groups: Adolescents diagnosed with anorexia nervosa, adolescents who were not anorexic but who were referred for psychiatric evaluation at an outpatient clinic, and nonclinical adolescents in a control group (J. D. Russell et al., 1992). Adolescents, who ranged in age from 12 to 19, completed the Parental Bonding Instrument (PBI; Parker et al., 1979) to report on their fathers' and mothers' levels of care and overprotection. In general, anorexic adolescents were more similar to adolescents in the nonclinical control group than psychiatrically referred adolescents in their ratings of their parents' behavior. Adolescents who were anorexic reported that their fathers and mothers were more caring than reported by the psychiatrically referred adolescents. In addition, anorexic adolescents reported that their mothers showed lower levels of overprotection than did the psychiatrically referred adolescents. This study points out the need for more studies that compare the parental functioning of fathers and mothers of adolescents with eating disorders, adolescents with other psychological disturbances, and adolescents with no apparent psychological distress.

Overall, these studies suggest relatively consistent differences in the families of adolescents with an eating disorder and adolescents without any psychological problems. In addition, different patterns appear to emerge for different subtypes of eating disorders. Further research is needed to clarify the different patterns that emerge from different informants (e.g., fathers' reports, mothers' reports, and adolescents' reports). Further research also is needed to investigate whether these patterns are specific to families with an eating-disordered adolescent or whether the patterns are more globally reflected in families with an adolescent experiencing any type of psychological distress. For a discussion of clinical issues in working with the families of eating-disordered clients, see Maine's (1991) book entitled *Father Hunger: Fathers, Daughters and Food.*

LEARNING DISABILITIES AND LANGUAGE DISORDERS

A variety of familial and interpersonal factors have been found to distinguish between the parents of learning disabled (LD) children and non-LD children. Fathers and mothers of LD boys reported significantly higher levels of anxiety than fathers and mothers of non-LD boys; and mothers, but not fathers, of LD boys perceived the family environment to stress system maintenance more so than did the mothers of non-LD boys (Margalit & Heiman, 1986a, 1986b). Fathers of LD boys reported higher interpersonal values of independence and leadership, and lower conformity and support; and mothers of LD boys showed greater authoritative attitudes than mothers of non-LD boys (Miletic, 1986). Mothers of LD children reported greater stress associated with their children's behavior problems than fathers of LD children (Konstantareas & Homatidis, 1989b).

In comparing parents of LD children with parents of children diagnosed either conduct disorder (CD) or a personality disorder (PD), Dean and Jacobson (1982) found that mothers of LD and PD children were more defensive than mothers of CD children; mothers of CD children were significantly more introverted, depressed, and interpersonally sensitive than mothers of either LD or PD children; and mothers of PD children reported more physical complaints than mothers of CD children. Fathers of LD children scored higher on the Lie scale on the MMPI than fathers of either CD or PD children, and fathers of CD children were more depressed than fathers of either LD or PD children.

Language disorders in childhood have also received a small amount of attention in relation to paternal characteristics. Schodorf and Edwards (1983) compared parent-child interactions of language-disordered and linguistically normal children and found few differences between mothers' and fathers' linguistic interaction styles in either group of children. They did, however, find linguistic differences between the parents of language-disordered and parents of linguistically normal children in all areas that were studied. However, rather than suggesting any etiologic role of parental use of speech, the differences between groups of parents may have been due to parents' attempts to compensate for their children's language differences.

Overall, there continues to be a dearth of studies that investigate paternal characteristics in relation to learning disabilities and language disorders. Although there may be little reason to investigate the fathers' role as an etiologic factor, research continues to be neglected in how fathers deal with their learning-disabled and language-disordered children. In addition, it may be helpful to investigate the father's role in the remediation of children's problems with learning and language.

PERSONALITY DISORDERS

Very little research has been conducted on paternal factors in relation to children's personality disorders, primarily because personality disorders in childhood or adolescence only recently have been receiving empirical attention (Brent, Johnson, Bartle, & Bridge, 1993; Caplan & Guthrie, 1992). However, a limited number of studies have provided retrospective accounts of fathering from adults diagnosed with personality disorders. Standage (1986) investigated adult inpatients who were diagnosed with at least one of the following personality disorders: narcissistic, borderline, antisocial, and histrionic. All these personality disorders are considered to correspond to a dramatic, emotional, and erratic cluster of personality disorders. Participants completed the socialization scale of the California Personality Inventory and also completed retrospective reports of paternal and maternal protection and care when they were growing up. Standage found that poor paternal, but not maternal, care and protection were associated with low socialization scores. These findings were established for all personality disorders combined together, and no separate analyses were conducted for different personality disorders.

Zweig-Frank and Paris (1991) conducted a study to address specifically the retrospective reports of parenting by clients who were diagnosed with borderline personality disorder (BPD). Clients were recruited from a general hospital psychiatric clinic and a student mental health clinic in Montreal, Quebec. Retrospective reports of paternal and maternal protection and care were compared for clients diagnosed with BPD and for clients who did not meet diagnostic criteria for BPD. Both fathers and mothers of BPD clients were rated as significantly less caring and significantly more controlling than fathers and mothers of non-BPD clients. These findings were quite robust, given that the results were consistent for both male and female clients as well as clients at both clinical sites.

To date, the research on retrospective accounts of the parenting received by clients with personality disorders—although it is limited—suggests a somewhat stronger link between overprotective and uncaring fathers rather than mothers.

SCHIZOPHRENIA

As noted in Chapter 3, the history of research on schizophrenia has been replete with examples of mother blaming. A few early writings discussed the role of fathers in the development and maintenance of schizophrenia (Lidz, Parker, & Cornelison, 1956; Nash, 1965; Sanua, 1961, 1963), but the majority of research was and is conducted with mothers of schizophrenic offspring. In addition to the work that investigates mothers to the exclusion of fathers, a number of research projects include both fathers and mothers in investigations of family factors related to schizophrenia, but do not investigate paternal and maternal characteristics separately. For example, there is an excellent line of research into communication styles within families of schizophrenics that focuses on expressed emotion and communication deviance (e.g., Hahlweg et al., 1989; Miklowitz et al., 1986; Miklowitz et al., 1989; Strachan, Feingold, Goldstein, Miklowitz, & Nuechterlein, 1989). Although most of these studies included both fathers and mothers, the data analyses did not involve separate analyses for paternal versus maternal communication styles within the family.

A limited number of studies, however, investigated both fathers and mothers of schizophrenic offspring and presented separate analyses for paternal and maternal characteristics. One study from India compared the fathers of schizophrenics with fathers in a nonclinical control group (Menon, Balakrishnan, Sujatha, Rajalakshmi, & Lulla, 1982). Unfortunately, the ages of the schizophrenic "children" were not provided, so it is unclear whether the fathers' children were still in childhood or whether they were already grown adults. Because of the dearth of research on fathers and the concomitant abundance of research on mothers, Menon and colleagues chose to focus the investigation on fathers of schizophrenics, but they also included limited analyses of mothers of schizophrenics. Results of the study showed that, when compared with fathers in the control group, fathers of schizophrenics evidenced greater abnormality in their interactions with their children and showed greater problems in their personality profiles. Fathers of schizophrenic children showed lower intelligence, lower superego strength, higher sensitivity, and higher tension than fathers in the control group. When fathers and mothers of schizophrenics were compared, fathers showed higher sociability, higher dominance, higher suspiciousness, lower shrewdness, and higher tension than mothers of schizophrenics. This study suggests that fathers of schizophrenics show greater deviance than fathers of nonclinical offspring.

A number of studies have investigated retrospective accounts of paternal and maternal characteristics in samples of adult schizophrenics. Kinnell (1983) investigated the hypothesis that parents of schizophrenics were older at the birth of the infant who later developed schizophrenia than parents of infants who did not later develop any psychiatric disorder. Based on samples collected from psychiatric hospitals in England, Kinnell found that fathers of schizophrenics were significantly older than fathers of nonclinical controls at the time of their child's birth. Likewise, mothers of schizophrenics were also found to be older than mothers of nonclinical controls at delivery. Kinnell used these data to suggest that the personality trait that leads parents to delay marriage and childbearing, is associated with the development of schizophrenia in offspring.

Because Kinnell did not investigate any parental factors other than age, it is difficult to rule out other possible etiologic factors in the development and maintenance of schizophrenia.

Yesavage and colleagues (1983) investigated the assaultive behavior of adult schizophrenic inpatients in relation to the paternal and maternal discipline and family conflict that they experienced during childhood. In an ethnically diverse sample of adult schizophrenic inpatients with a mean age of 32.3 years, the researchers found that severity of paternal discipline during childhood was strongly associated with assaultiveness and dangerousness evidenced on the inpatient unit, including physical assaults, verbal assaults, need for seclusion, need for restraint, and involuntary admission/legal status. Severity of maternal discipline during childhood was only entered as a significant predictor of the inpatients' legal status. Greater recollections of family conflict and fights between parents were also significantly related to the assaultive and dangerous behavior of adult schizophrenic inpatients.

In another investigation of the family atmosphere of adult male schizophrenic inpatients, Angermeyer (1982) examined whether paternal and maternal behaviors at the time of discharge of the inpatients would predict the likelihood of readmission 2 years later. At the time of discharge from an inpatient unit, fathers and mothers of schizophrenic sons were invited to participate in a family discussion that related to questionnaires they had completed about daily problems within the family. The technique, known as revealed differences, allowed a comparison of each individual's report of their own desires for family problem solving and the final outcome of problem solving that was evident after the family discussion. Behaviors and verbal comments that reflected anxiety or hostility were coded. Two years after this data collection, discharged patients were followed up to ascertain whether they had been readmitted to any psychiatric inpatient facility during the intervening 2 years. A total of 13 of the 30 former patients had been readmitted for inpatient treatment within the 2-year period.

In a comparison of those who were readmitted and those who were not, Angermeyer found that fathers' hostility and mothers' anxiety were related to the readmission status of their sons. Fathers who showed greater overt hostility that was directed outward or who showed greater ambivalent hostility were more likely to have sons who were readmitted to an inpatient unit. The sons of mothers who showed greater levels of inwardly directed hostility were also more likely to be readmitted within the 2-year follow-up period. Fathers' levels of anxiety that were observed during the family discussion did not significantly differentiate between sons who were and were not readmitted. Mothers who showed greater levels of guilt anxiety and shame anxiety were more likely than other mothers to have sons who were rehospitalized. These results speak to the relevance of paternal hostility and maternal anxiety in the maintenance of schizophrenia in adulthood and the need for family interventions.

In an Australian sample, Hafner and Miller (1991) investigated readmission rates within the first year after discharge in a sample of schizophrenic adults who were released to their parents' care after discharge from inpatient treatment. A total of 10 participants were readmitted for inpatient treatment within 1 year of discharge and 8 participants were not readmitted within 1 year of discharge. Hafner and Miller compared the readmitted participants and the non-readmitted participants on a variety of demographic, parental, and familial measures. They found that the readmitted group reported significantly lower protection and higher care from their mothers than did the non-readmitted group. Mothers' reports of their own criticism of others were higher in the readmitted group than in the non-readmitted group. None of these variables were significantly different for fathers. Correlations were calculated to ascertain which variables were related to the number of days that were spent in the hospital following initial discharge. Fathers' moral-religious emphasis and mothers' less traditional values were significantly related to greater length of stay by their offspring on an inpatient unit.

In a study of twins who were discordant for schizophrenia, Onstad, Skre, Torgersen, and Kringlen (1993) attempted to identify early parental behavior that was associated with the development of schizophrenia. Schizophrenic adults reported receiving less care and more overprotection from both their father and their mother than did their nonschizophrenic twin. These findings were consistent regardless of the age and gender of the schizophrenic individual. The single most important factor that distinguished between schizophrenic individuals and their nondisordered twins was paternal overprotection. Because these were retrospective findings, it is unclear whether the schizophrenic twin had actually experienced greater levels of paternal overprotection as they were growing up, or whether their retrospective reports of paternal and maternal parenting were influenced by their current psychiatric distress.

Separate from the issue of early parenting of schizophrenics, one study investigated the personal and interpersonal impact of fathers' and mothers' caretaking of adult children who were severely psychiatrically disturbed (Cook, Hoffschmidt, Cohler, & Pickett, 1992). Fathers were more likely than mothers to report that they were satisfied with their marital relationship. In addition, both fathers and mothers reported higher levels of marital satisfaction when there were a larger number of nondisturbed siblings of the disturbed individual, when they felt higher levels of mutual comfort from their spouse, and when they reported lower levels of interpersonal inadequacy. This study represents an important line of research that can help identify stressors and strengths in families that are dealing with a family member who is experiencing severe psychiatric disturbance.

These studies suggest that a number of paternal and maternal characteristics may be related to the development and/or maintenance of schizophrenia. Although these studies investigated parental characteristics in relation to schizophrenics' behavior, an important caveat is that schizophrenic children's and adults' behavior may be influencing their parents' behavior in a direct or reciprocal manner. For example, the greater connection between paternal hostility or maternal anxiety and adult children's readmission to inpatient treatment may have been due to greater severity of symptoms in the sons who were later rehospitalized (Angermeyer, 1982). Thus, although significant relations were found between paternal characteristics and their offspring's behavior related to schizophrenia, a causal link has yet to be established.

AUTISM

There has been a fair amount of conflicting evidence as to whether there are paternal and maternal factors related to childhood autism. In a study based in India, Rangaswamy (1983) found that fathers of autistic children were more neurotic than fathers of nonautistic children, but fathers did not differ on the psychoticism or introversion scales. Conversely, mothers of autistic children had higher psychoticism and introversion scores than mothers of nonautistic children, but mothers did not differ on the neuroticism scale. In a study in Edinburgh (Scotland), Wolff, Narayan, and Moyes (1988) found that both fathers and mothers of autistic children were significantly more likely to show schizoid traits when compared with fathers and mothers of children with other handicaps (e.g., deafness, epilepsy, developmental disabilities).

Based on a sample of autistic children in Israel, Dor-Shav and Horowitz (1984) found that fathers, but not mothers, of autistic children had significantly higher intelligence than their counterparts in a clinically referred nonautistic sample. They also found that mothers of autistic children were more neurotic but not more introverted or extroverted than mothers of nonautistic children. Dor-Shav and Horowitz did not administer any personality measures to fathers in this study, even though fathers were administered the Wechsler Adult Intelligence Scale and Raven's Progressive Matrices. No explanation was given for these procedural inequities. Although these three studies found problems in the psychological functioning of parents of autistic children, there is growing evidence that there are few differences in the psychological functioning of parents with autistic children when compared with parents of nonautistic children.

In comprehensive reviews of studies conducted in England (Sanua, 1986a) and the United States (Sanua, 1986b), Sanua concluded that fathers and mothers of autistic children do not show differences in psychological adjustment or personality characteristics when compared with fathers and mothers of nonclinical children. In addition, fathers and mothers of autistic children were found not to differ from fathers and mothers of nonautistic children who showed evidence of organic brain damage or other abnormalities. Overall, Sanua (1986a, 1986b) concluded that parents of autistic children did not differ from parents of nonautistic children in their psychological functioning and personality characteristics. When specifically assessing the use of language in a U.S. sample, Wolchik (1983) also found that few differences existed between the language of parents of autistic and nonclinical children. These studies suggest that paternal and maternal psychological and language characteristics do not play an etiologic role in the development or maintenance of autism in children. These conclusions clearly refute the dated beliefs about "refrigerator" parents (e.g., Kanner, 1943).

Aside from the psychological functioning and use of language by fathers and mothers of autistic children, increasing attention has been paid to the stress levels experienced by parents of autistic children. Freeman, Perry, and Factor (1991) argued that autistic children can represent significant stressors for their fathers and mothers, and therefore they argued that research should be completed to clarify the level of stress in families with an autistic child. Because parents' ratings of the symptoms experienced by their autistic children are often used, it is important to establish how fathers' and mothers' ratings of their autistic children's symptoms compare with clinicians' ratings.

Two studies that addressed this issue provide conflicting data. The studies were conducted by two different research groups in Ontario, Canada. In a comparison of fathers', mothers', and clinicians' symptom ratings of autistic children, Konstantareas and Homatidis (1989a) found that clinicians generally reported higher levels of symptoms than did fathers or mothers. Clinicians reported higher levels of five symptoms and the total symptom score than did fathers and mothers; clinicians and mothers reported higher levels of two symptoms than did fathers; clinicians reported higher levels of one symptom than did fathers; and on only one symptom did fathers and mothers report higher levels than clinicians. No significant differences were found for five symptoms of autism. Overall, Konstantareas and Homatidis concluded that clinicians were more likely than fathers and mothers of autistic children to acknowledge the symptoms of autistic children. However, using the same measures and the same research design, Freeman et al. (1991) did not find differences between fathers, mothers, and clinicians in their symptom severity ratings of autistic children. Freeman and colleagues suggested that the difference in results may have been due to differences in the ages of the two samples. The autistic children in the study by Konstantareas and Homatidis ranged in age from 2 to 12 years, whereas the children in the study by Freeman and colleagues ranged from 3 to nearly 21 years. It may be that agreement in symptom ratings between fathers, mothers, and clinicians is influenced by the age of the child as well as the experience that each of the informants has with the child. The issue of correspondence between parents' and clinicians' ratings of autistics children's symptoms remains unresolved.

Somewhat inconsistent results were also found when parental stress was considered in these two studies. Konstantareas and Homatidis (1989a) found that fathers and mothers of autistic children rated their level of stress similarly, with no significant differences between fathers and mothers on the total stress score or on 12 of the 14 subscales of the stress index. In contrast, Freeman and colleagues (1991) found that mothers reported significantly more stress over their autistic children's symptoms than did fathers. This finding was based on a comparison of fathers' and mothers' total stress score; individual subscales were not analyzed. Thus, it is not clear as to the extent that fathers and mothers report similar or different degrees of stress related to their autistic children's behavior and symptoms. If the age of the samples accounted for the differences in results it may be that as autistic children get older, the disparity between maternal and paternal stress increases. This would explain why significant differences between fathers' and mothers' stress were found in the older sample of autistic children and adolescents.

The associations between parental stress and children's symptoms in these two studies provide information about the impact of dealing with an autistic child. Konstantareas and Homatidis found that fathers' stress was best predicted by child self-abuse, whereas mothers' stress was best predicted by the combination of child self-abuse, hyperirritability, and older age in children. Freeman and colleagues found that fathers' and mothers' specific ratings of stress about their children's autistic behavior were significantly related to their global ratings of stress as a parent. In addition, fathers' ratings of stress over their autistic child's behavior were significantly related to fathers' reports of greater parent and family problems, pessimism, and child problems. The same relations were found for mothers. One additional study found that mothers of autistic children reported experiencing significantly more stress than fathers (Moes, Koegel, Schreibman, & Loos, 1992). In addition, the higher amount of stress mothers felt was related to the higher amount of child-rearing duties in which mothers engaged.

In summary, there is strong evidence that fathers and mothers of autistic children do not differ in their personality features or psychological functioning when compared with fathers and mothers of nonclinical children or fathers and mothers of nonautistic clinically referred children. The research on parental stress suggests that mothers may experience more child-related stress than fathers as their children grow older.

REFERRAL STATUS

A fair amount of research has combined a variety of diagnostic categories and has investigated maternal and paternal correlates to referral status and child placement. For example, Quinton and Rutter (1984a, 1984b) compared parental correlates of children in residential care ("in-care") with nonreferred children. They found that mother-child interactions of the in-care group were significantly less warm, sensitive, and playful than those of the control group. No significant differences were found in father-child interactions. Both mothers and fathers of the in-care children were more likely to have a current psychiatric disorder and to be experiencing greater malaise at the time of interview than their counterparts in the control group. Additionally, mothers of the in-care children were more likely to have a history of psychiatric treatment and of inpatient psychiatric treatment than control mothers. Fathers of in-care children were more likely to have a personality disorder, a history of criminal convictions, and a history of probation or prison than the control fathers (Quinton & Rutter, 1984a). Mothers, but not fathers, of psychiatrically hospitalized adolescents had significantly lower ego development than the parents of nonclinical adolescents (Hauser et al., 1984).

Regarding correlates to psychiatric hospitalization, Garralda (1983) found that disturbed father-child, but not mother-child, relationships and parental depression were the only family variables that distinguished child psychiatric emergency admissions from child psychiatric nonemergency admissions. Holmes and colleagues (1984) found that the group of mothers, and to a lesser extent the group of fathers, who had their children seen for psychological services in the latter half of the 1970s (1975–1979) were significantly more psychologically distressed than the mothers and fathers of children referred from 1970 to 1974. In comparing parents of outpatient and inpatient adolescents, Archer, Stolberg, Gordon, and Goldman (1986) found that mothers and fathers of inpatient adolescents had significantly higher mean scores on numerous MMPI scales when compared with the mothers and fathers of outpatient adolescents.

In an analysis of primary care utilizers, Schor (1988) found that 72% of children who had two parents with a psychological diagnosis were themselves diagnosed. Both mothers' and fathers' psychological diagnoses were associated with their children's likelihood of being diagnosed, although mothers' psychological diagnoses and fathers' heightened use of general health care services were more strongly associated with children's diagnoses. Overall, the psychological functioning of both mothers and fathers is associated with their children's use of inpatient, outpatient, psychiatric emergency, and residential services.

PHYSICAL ILLNESS

In addition to the studies of fathers and their children referred for psychological services, there are a number of studies of fathers and their children with special needs or their physically ill children. A number of personal and familial characteristics have been investigated in these populations.

McLinden (1990) recruited a sample of families who attended an early intervention program for their young children with special needs (e.g., motor impairments, developmental disabilities, cerebral palsy). Fathers and mothers did not differ in their reports of family cohesion, family support, acceptance, social relations, or financial problems. However, when the frequency of problems was compared, mothers reported more problems with time demands and feelings of well-being and fewer problems with the use of positive coping strategies than did fathers. McLinden suggested that these data should be used to develop more appropriate service programs for fathers and mothers of young children with special needs. In a sample from an Israeli kibbutz, Margalit, Leyser, and Avraham (1989) found that fathers of disabled children reported less encouragement of personal growth, less satisfaction from family life, and lower cohesion in their families than did fathers of nondisabled children. Again, Margalit et al. recommended special interventions and supportive services for fathers with disabled children.

A number of differences have been found when fathers of physically ill and physically healthy children have been compared. For example, Hilliard, Fritz, and Lewiston (1985) found that fathers of asthmatic children were less accommodating and more rigid in goal setting for their children than were fathers of healthy children. Fathers of asthmatic children and fathers of diabetic children had higher and less realistic goals for their children than did fathers of healthy children. Mothers' goals for their children did not differ across the healthy and chronically ill groups. Direct observations of fathers with asthmatic children and healthy children were compared (Schobinger, Florin, Zimmer, & Lindemann, 1992). Fathers of asthmatic children showed significantly more critical attitudes, made more critical comments toward their child, and had longer sequences of negative verbal communication with their child than did fathers of physically health children.

When parental psychological functioning was investigated, fathers of children with recurrent abdominal pain reported significantly more anxiety than fathers of behaviorally disordered children and fathers of nondisordered healthy children (Hodges, Kline, Barbero, & Woodruff, 1985). Mothers of children with recurrent abdominal pain and mothers of children with behavior disorders reported higher levels of anxiety than mothers of healthy children. Fathers and mothers of children with end-stage renal failure were found to show higher levels of anxiety and depression than men and women who provided normative data for the measures of anxiety and depression (Fielding et al., 1985). Contrary to these results, Speechley and Noh (1992) found that fathers and mothers of children who survived childhood cancer did not show any differences in depression or anxiety when compared with fathers and mothers of physically healthy children. However, when social support was further investigated, a complex pattern of interactions emerged. When fathers and mothers of children with cancer experienced medium to high levels of social support, they did not show elevated levels of anxiety or depression. However, when fathers of children with cancer experienced low levels of social support, they showed higher levels of depression and trait anxiety than fathers of healthy children. When mothers of children with cancer experienced low levels of social support, they showed higher levels of state and trait anxiety than mothers of healthy children. Speechley and Noh used these results to highlight the importance of social support for the families of children who were fighting cancer. In addition, prevention of parental psychopathology related to childhood cancer is important because of the relation between parental psychopathology and children's experience of psychological symptoms. In a study of families in which one child had leukemia, Brown, Kaslow, Madan-Swain, and Doepke (1993) found that fathers' and mothers' levels of psychopathology were significantly related to their children's higher levels of psychological distress.

Another research strategy in families of physically ill children has been to compare the functioning of fathers and mothers in these families, rather than comparing them with fathers and mothers in families with physically healthy children. In families of children with hemophilia, fathers were significantly less accepting of their hemophilic children than were mothers, but there were no significant differences between fathers and mothers in overprotection, overindulgence, or rejection of their children (Klein & Nimorwicz, 1982). Because of a small sample size of both fathers and mothers ($N = 10$), the researchers did not provide direct analyses of paternal and maternal psychological functioning and knowledge about hemophilia. However, they were able to conduct correlational analyses to ascertain the relation between psychological functioning and knowledge about hemophilia. The researchers found that there were no significant correlations between fathers' knowledge about hemophilia and fathers global psychological distress, depression, state anxiety, or trait anxiety. All these correlations, however, were significant for mothers. Therefore, mothers with lower levels of knowledge about hemophilia showed higher levels of global psychological distress, depression, state anxiety, and trait anxiety. These results highlight the importance of education for the parents, especially mothers, of hemophilic children (Handford, Mayes, Bagnato, & Bixler, 1986; Klein & Nimorwicz, 1982).

Another area that has received a lot of attention in pediatric psychology has been parents' experience of stress and their ability to cope with their children's chronic illnesses. Fathers and mothers of children diagnosed with cystic fibrosis reported greater levels of illness-specific stress, higher global parenting stress, and more depressive symptoms than parents with healthy children (Quittner, DiGirolamo, Michel, & Eigen, 1992). Mothers also reported more difficulty and strain with regard to their caretaking duties. In another study, nearly 28% of fathers and 25% of mothers whose child had just received a diagnosis of cancer reported significant marital distress (Dahlquist, Czyzewski, Copeland, & Jones, 1993). It appears that the illness-related stress that fathers and mothers experience may in turn influence the child's experience of greater adjustment problems to the illness. For example, Auslander, Bubb, Rogge, and Santiago (1993) found that fathers' reports of higher family stress and reports of lower family coping resources were significantly related to their children's poorer metabolic control of recently diagnosed diabetes. In a sample of children with juvenile rheumatic disease, fathers' and mothers' higher levels of depression and lower levels of functioning were related to their children's higher levels of functional disability, pain, and psychosocial problems (Timko, Stovel, & Moos, 1992).

With regard to coping mechanisms, fathers' and mothers' use of avoidance-coping strategies were related to poorer parental adjustment to their children's juvenile rheumatic disease (Timko et al., 1992). In a sample of children experiencing a variety of chronic illnesses (such as diabetes, asthma, cardiac conditions, epilepsy, or leukemia), fathers who reported greater child-related difficulties found that use of autonomy as a coping strategy was more helpful than seeking out medical care and advice, especially compared with fathers who reported fewer child-related difficulties (Eiser & Havermans, 1992). For mother, the greater the length of time since diagnosis of illness in their child, the less they found social support and information to be helpful.

In a study of children who experienced normal childhood illnesses (such as colds or otitis media), but not severe illnesses, Frank and colleagues (1991) found that mothers' but not fathers' functioning was related to the history of illness in their children. Mothers of children who showed greater amounts of normal childhood illness reported higher levels of role restriction, social isolation, and health problems. None of these correlations were significant for fathers. However, parenting alliance (e.g., support from spouse, respect for spouse) was found to relate meaningfully for fathers in their experience of parenting stress. Fathers with lower levels of parenting alliance reported greater difficulty in attaching to their child, less competence with their child, more restriction in the parenting role, more stress in relation to their spouse, and more social isolation. None of these correlations were significant for mothers. In discussing these results, Frank and colleagues pointed out that even minor childhood illness can be a source of stress for parents, although this source seemed to have a different impact on fathers versus mothers.

SUMMARY

Fathers of children referred for psychological problems showed greater levels of psychopathology than fathers of children who were not experiencing significant psychological distress. As can be seen in Table 5.1, the relations between paternal psychopathology and children's psychological problems are more consistent for externalizing problems (e.g., ADHD, conduct disorder, delinquent behaviors) than internalizing problems (depression, anxiety disorders) in children. There are relatively consistent patterns of relations between paternal and maternal characteristics in relation to children's and adolescents' psychopathology.

TABLE 5.1.   Findings from Research on Paternal Factors in Child and Adolescent Psychopathology: Studies of Referred or Diagnosed Children

Problem	Findings
ADHD	Fathers of ADHD children scored higher on nonclinical measures than controls (5 studies); no differences between fathers of ADHD children and controls on paternal psychopathology (3 studies). No differences between paternal and maternal psychopathology (8 studies), equivocal findings on differences between fathers and mothers (2 studies). Few differences in comparisons between fathers of ADHD children and fathers of children with other diagnoses (3 studies).
Conduct Disorder (CD)	Fathers of CD children showed higher rates of antisocial personality disorder and alcoholism than fathers of controls (2 studies). No studies that compared fathers and mothers directly, higher associations between mother-CD daughter than father-CD daughter characteristics (1 study). Fathers of CD sons showed higher rates of psychopathology than fathers of sons with other diagnoses (7 studies).
Delinquency	Mixed findings comparing fathers of delinquents with controls (2 studies). No studies that compared fathers and mothers directly, higher conflict shown by fathers and mothers of delinquent daughters than fathers and mothers of delinquent sons (1 study). Consistent evidence of associations between paternal psychopathology or other characteristics and delinquency in adolescents (3 reviews, 8 studies).
Nonspecific Behavior Problems	Fathers showed less realistic beliefs than fathers of controls (2 studies). Mixed findings comparing fathers and mothers (6 studies). Equivocal findings about associations between paternal psychopathology and children's behavior problems (3 studies show significant associations, 3 studies show no association).
Alcohol/Substance Abuse	Mixed findings about associations between paternal psychopathology and adolescents' substance abuse (6 studies). Retrospective studies show somewhat stronger associations between paternal characteristics and offspring's substance abuse (9 studies).

(Continued)

TABLE 5.1. *(Continued)*

Problem	Findings
Depression	Concurrent studies: Stronger link between childhood depression and maternal depression than paternal depression (10 studies). Retrospective studies: Somewhat strong associations between adult depression and paternal characteristics (4 studies).
Suicidal Behavior	Fathers of suicidal children showed higher levels of depression than controls (2 studies). Fathers of attempters were more physically abusive than clinical comparison, but showed few differences in psychopathology (2 studies).
Anxiety Disorders	Fathers of children with an anxiety disorder showed higher rates of obsessive compulsive disorder and general obsessional characteristics than fathers of controls (2 studies). Few differences found between fathers and mothers of children with an anxiety disorder (2 studies). Retrospective reports of low paternal care and high overprotection were associated with mixed anxiety-depression and other anxiety disorders (5 studies).
Eating Disorders	More maladaptive paternal behavior and interactions in families of eating-disordered adolescents (10 studies). Mixed findings comparing fathers and mothers (3 studies). Psychiatrically referred (non-eating-disordered) adolescents reported less paternal care than anorexic adolescents (1 study).
Learning Disabilities (LD) and Language Disorders	Fathers of LD boys showed higher levels of anxiety than nonclinical controls (1 study). Mothers of LD children reported higher levels of stress than fathers (1 study). Fathers of LD children reported lower levels of depression than fathers of CD children (1 study). Fathers and mothers of language-disordered children showed linguistic differences when compared with parents of non-language-disordered children (1 study).
Personality Disorders	Paternal overprotection and low levels of care are associated with borderline personality disorder and low socialization scores in clients with personality disorders (2 studies).

TABLE 5.1. *(Continued)*

Problem	Findings
Schizophrenia	Fathers of schizophrenics showed lower intelligence and more problems in their interactions and personality than fathers of controls (1 study). Compared with mothers, fathers of schizophrenics showed higher levels of sociability, dominance, suspiciousness, and tension (1 study). Paternal hostility and harsh discipline were correlated with schizophrenia in offspring (3 studies).
Autism	Comprehensive reviews suggest that fathers and mothers of autistic children do not differ from nonclinical controls in psychological adjustment or personality functioning (2 reviews).
Referral Status	Fathers of children referred for services showed higher levels of psychopathology and disturbed interactions with their children (6 studies).
Physical Illness	Equivocal findings about paternal characteristics, depending on the type of childhood illness (15 studies).

CHAPTER 6

Referred Fathers and
Characteristics of Their Children

This chapter will review the empirical research that has investigated the children of fathers who have been referred for psychiatric or psychological services or who have received a psychiatric diagnosis. As in the previous chapter, the diagnostic terminology will reflect the nomenclature found in the studies that are reviewed. This chapter will follow the convention of noting significance when the p-level is equal to or below .05. This means that sometimes the chapter will review research findings that were written up as "significant" when in fact the significance level was higher than .05 (e.g., $p < .07$ or $p < .10$). If the authors of the research used statistical corrections for the number of analyses that were conducted (e.g., a Bonferroni correction), those results will be reported as the authors reported them.

Parental psychopathology has been investigated in relation to child adjustment for more than three decades (Sameroff, Seifer, & Zax, 1982; Rolf, Masten, Cicchetti, Neuchterlein, & Weintraub, 1990). With most diagnoses that have been investigated, such as major depressive disorder and schizophrenia, parental psychopathology has been found to be associated with increased levels of psychopathology in children (Downey & Coyne, 1990; Rolf et al., 1990). However, the base of knowledge is limited due to the overreliance on psychiatrically disturbed mothers, and not fathers, in these investigations (Phares, 1992; Phares & Compas, 1992). Although fathers have been underrepresented in investigations into the role of parental psychopathology, a number of studies have been conducted that have yielded important findings.

PATERNAL ANTISOCIAL PERSONALITY
DISORDER AND CRIMINALITY

Surprisingly little research has been completed that investigates the children of fathers with antisocial personality disorder (APD) or the children of fathers who have a history of criminality. Much of the research into APD fathers has used the research strategy reviewed in Chapter 5; investigators have identified children and adolescents who are referred for clinical problems and then have investigated the prevalence of APD in their fathers. For example, Loeber and Dishion (1983, 1987) reviewed research that showed a strong connection between fathers' antisocial behavior and delinquent behavior in their offspring; however, nearly all of these studies identified delinquent youth and then investigated the characteristics of their fathers. Although this is a valid research design, it is also important to investigate the offspring of fathers diagnosed with APD because different associations of paternal-child or paternal-adolescent behavior may be identified with the alternate research design. The offspring of APD fathers may experience a number of problems, but if only delinquent and conduct-disordered youth are investigated, then this precludes the ability to establish other disorders for which the youth are at risk. Thus, the few studies that have been completed with adjudicated or APD fathers and the characteristics of their children and adolescents provide the basis for an important area of research that is in need of attention.

In an investigation of a Danish birth cohort, Kandel and colleagues (1988) compared the IQ of offspring who were at high risk for antisocial behavior and who avoided criminal behavior and those offspring at high risk for antisocial behavior who evidenced criminal behavior. They found that offspring who avoided criminal behavior had significantly higher intelligence than offspring who were involved in criminal activities. Thus, IQ apparently served as a protective factor for children and adolescents who were at high risk for antisocial behavior due to their fathers' criminal history. However, because public records (e.g., arrests and convictions) were used to identify criminal behavior in youth, it may be that offspring with higher IQ were less likely to get caught for criminal behavior rather than actually being less likely to commit criminal behavior.

Lanier (1991) investigated the proximal interactions (face-to-face) and the distal interactions (phone calls, letters) of fathers who were incarcerated in a maximum-security prison and their children. Based on the responses of over 300 inmates, 32.8% reported that they have had no face-to-face contact with their children while in prison, 37.1% reported that their children visited them less than once a month, and the remaining 30.1% reported seeing their children at least once or more per month. Regarding distal communication, 77.4% of the fathers reported receiving mail from their children, 84.9% reported sending mail to their children, and 78.4% reported that they interact with their children via telephone. These patterns of interaction were somewhat influenced by whether or not the fathers lived with their children before the incarceration. Face-to-face visitation and telephone calls were more likely for fathers who lived with children before incarceration than for fathers who did not live with their children before incarceration. However, interaction through the mail did not differ according to preincarceration residential status. Lanier concluded that the families of fathers who were imprisoned often did not take advantage of visitation opportunities, such as Family Day picnics or daily visits. However, this study did not address the beneficial or deleterious impact of visitation between imprisoned fathers and their children.

In a similar prison population, Hairston (1989) investigated fathers' visitation with their children and the desire for improved parenting skills. The sample consisted of 96 men who were incarcerated in a maximum-security prison, 70% of whom had sentences of 20 years or more. The fathers averaged 2.4 children each and the ages of the children ranged from under 5 years old (15%) to adult children (22%). Approximately one-third of the fathers reported that they visited with their children while imprisoned. In a questionnaire assessing men's interest in learning better parenting skills, 91% of the fathers responded that they would like to improve their parenting skills. In addition, 65% of nonfathers who were questioned reported that they would like to learn better parenting skills for the future in case they choose to have children. Hairston suggested that prison administrators should allow access to parenting classes while men are incarcerated so that these skills might translate to more effective parenting while the men are in prison and once they are released.

The two studies of parenting issues with fathers who are imprisoned (Hairston, 1989; Lanier, 1991) provide intriguing data that illustrate children's contact with fathers who are imprisoned. Further research is needed to establish the impact on children, fathers, and mothers when children interact with their imprisoned fathers. Presumably, the interactions would have beneficial effects for some families and deleterious effects in other families. Overall, there is a limited amount of research on the children of fathers with histories of criminal and antisocial behavior. None of these studies investigated the overall psychological functioning of the offspring of incarcerated fathers.

PATERNAL ALCOHOLISM AND SUBSTANCE ABUSE

The investigation of children of alcoholics is unique in that it is the one area of parental psychopathology that has studied paternal characteristics significantly more than maternal characteristics. Although alcoholism is more prevalent in men than women (Helzer, 1987), children of alcoholic fathers have been investigated almost to the exclusion of children of alcoholic mothers (West & Prinz, 1987). In addition, sons of alcoholic fathers have been studied to a much larger extent than daughters of alcoholic fathers. When available, research on alcoholic mothers and daughters of alcoholic parents will be discussed. For interesting discussions of theoretical models of paternal transmission of alcohol abuse, see Fitzgerald, Davies, Zucker, and Klinger (1994), Maguin, Zucker, and Fitzgerald (1994), and Ullman and Orenstein (1994).

A number of reviews summarizing the research on children of alcoholic fathers have concluded that children of alcoholic fathers are at increased risk for a variety of cognitive (Peterson & Pihl, 1990), affective (Kumpfer & DeMarsh, 1985), and psychological problems (Velleman, 1992; West & Prinz, 1987) when compared with children of nonclinical fathers. The long-term effects of paternal drinking have been less consistent and less well documented with regard to the functioning of adult children of alcoholics (Sher, 1991; Velleman, 1992). Nonetheless, it appears that there is consistent evidence for some increased risk of psychopathology in relation to paternal drinking behavior.

When children and adolescents of alcoholic fathers are compared with children and adolescents of nonclinical fathers, paternal alcoholism is found to be associated with a variety of problems in the children and adolescents, including internalizing problems such as depression, anxiety, self-deprecation (e.g., Berkowitz & Perkins, 1988; Callan & Jackson, 1986; Herjanic, Herjanic, Penick, Tomelleri, & Armbruster, 1977); externalizing behavior problems such as hyperactivity, impulsivity, and conduct disorder (e.g., Benson & Heller, 1987; Fine, Yudin, Holmes, & Heinemann, 1976; Fitzgerald, Sullivan, Ham, & Zucker, 1993; Goodwin, 1986; Knop, Teasdale, Schulsinger, & Goodwin, 1985); alcohol/substance abuse (e.g., Chassin, Rogosch, & Barrera, 1991; Herjanic et al., 1977; Merikangas, Weissman, Prusoff, Pauls, & Leckman, 1985); delinquency (e.g., Offord, Allen, & Abrams, 1978; Rimmer, 1982); greater problems with Type A behaviors (Manning, Balson, & Xenakis, 1986); personality problems (Benson & Heller, 1987; Whipple & Noble, 1991); low levels of agreeableness and conscientiousness (Martin & Sher, 1994); poor perceptions of the family environment and more conflict in the family environment (Barrera, Chassin, & Rogosch, 1993; Callan & Jackson, 1986); poor hierarchical family structure (Preli & Protinsky, 1988); greater biological vulnerability (Berman, Whipple, Fitch, & Noble, 1993; Cowley, Roy-Byrne, Godon, & Greenblatt, 1992; Polich, Pollock, & Bloom, 1994); and greater likelihood of postneonatal mortality (Borges, Garrido, Cardenas, Ibarra, & Bobadilla, 1993). There is some evidence to suggest that African American children and adolescents are more at risk than their Caucasian peers for substance abuse due to paternal alcohol abuse (Luthar, Merikangas, & Rounsaville, 1993). Interestingly, the place of paternal drinking (in the home vs. out of the home) appears not to have an impact on the relation between paternal alcoholism and adolescents' maladaptive functioning (Seilhamer, Jacob, & Dunn, 1993).

Although the majority of studies have found significant risk for child and adolescent psychopathology associated with paternal alcoholism, a few studies were identified that did not find differences between children of alcoholic and nonclinical fathers. For example, Murphy, O'Farrell, Floyd, and Connors (1991) compared the academic functioning of young adolescent children of alcoholic fathers and of fathers in a nonclinical control group. The two groups of young adolescents did not differ significantly in their grade-point average nor in their attendance at school. In another series of studies that investigated the adolescent sons of alcoholic fathers and nonclinical fathers, Tarter and colleagues (Tarter, Hegedus, & Gavaler, 1985; Tarter, Hegedus, Goldstein, Shelly,

& Alterman, 1984) found very few differences in neuropsychological functioning, personality characteristics, and hyperactivity. However, all the adolescent boys in the studies by Tarter and colleagues (1984, 1985) were receiving psychiatric services on an inpatient unit. Therefore, although the comparison was between sons of alcoholic and of nonclinical fathers, all the adolescent boys showed significant levels of psychopathology. With the exception of the three studies just reviewed, the majority of studies have found that children and adolescents of fathers who abuse alcohol are at increased risk for psychopathology.

There is somewhat less consistent evidence regarding the functioning of adult children of alcoholic fathers (Velleman, 1992). However, a number of studies have shown adult children to be at increased risk for cognitive deficits (Peterson, Finn, & Pihl, 1992) and psychopathology (Alford, Jouriles, & Jackson, 1991; el-Guebaly et al., 1991; Jarmas & Kazak, 1992; Mathew, Wilson, Blazer, & George, 1993; Sher, Walitzer, Wood, & Brent, 1991). Alford and colleagues (1991) found that male alcoholics who had a father who was alcoholic were more likely to have begun drinking at an earlier age, to prefer the taste of beer, and to become more emotional when drinking than male alcoholics who did not have a father who was alcoholic. There were no significant differences between the two groups on retrospective reports of delinquent behavior or on frequency of drinking. Peterson and colleagues (1992) compared nonalcoholic sons of alcoholic fathers and of fathers in a nonclinical control group and found that the former group showed significantly more cognitive deficits than the latter based on a battery of neuropsychological tests.

In a sample of psychiatric inpatients, el-Guebaly et al. (1991) found that 80 out of 250 inpatients (32%) could be classified as adult children of alcoholics. A total of 88% of the "ACOA" group had an alcoholic biological father, 37% had an alcoholic biological mother, 12% had an alcoholic nonbiological father, and 3% had an alcoholic nonbiological mother. These percentages were not mutually exclusive. In comparing the ACOA group with the non-ACOA psychiatrically disturbed group, el-Guebaly and colleagues (1991) found that the ACOA inpatients were younger at first psychiatric hospitalization and were more likely to be diagnosed with substance abuse or phobic disorders. Unfortunately, there were no analyses of paternal versus maternal alcoholic status. In addition, because there was not a nonclinical control group, it is difficult to establish whether the prevalence of 32% of the inpatient sample that met criteria for ACOA is elevated from what might be found in the general population.

Two empirically rigorous studies using large samples of male and female college students found a variety of differences between adult children of alcoholic fathers and adult children of parents did not have problems with alcohol (Jarmas & Kazak, 1992; Sher et al., 1991). When compared with college students who did not have a family history of alcoholism, college students who had an alcoholic father showed significantly more self-criticism and felt that their families showed greater inconsistency, less cohesion, lower expressiveness, more conflict, less organization, and poorer communication (Jarmas & Kazak, 1992). Sher and colleagues (1991) also found that college students with an alcoholic father showed lower academic achievement, lower verbal ability, more alcohol and drug problems, more major depression, more anxiety disorders, greater behavioral undercontrol, higher levels of neuroticism, and stronger alcohol expectancies than college students without an alcoholic father. Overall, there is somewhat consistent evidence that children, adolescents, and adults of alcoholic fathers are at increased risk for a variety of cognitive, affective, social, and psychological problems. Further work is needed to thoroughly investigate gender differences in relation to paternal alcoholism.

As mentioned earlier, the research on children of alcoholic mothers is limited, and therefore few studies have investigated the differential associations between having an alcoholic mother in contrast to an alcoholic father. One large-scale study of children and adolescents aged 5 to 17 years found that 8% of the children were living with an alcoholic father and 2% were living with an alcoholic mother (Dawson, 1992). This shows that, although there is a higher prevalence of children exposed to paternal alcoholism, there is still a significant portion of children who experience maternal alcoholism. The few studies that evaluate paternal and maternal alcoholism provide inconsistent findings regarding the risk associated with paternal versus maternal alcoholism. Two studies (el-Guebaly, Offord, Sullivan, & Lynch, 1978; Steinhausen, Gobel, & Nestler, 1984) found that children of alcoholic fathers did not differ from children of alcoholic mothers in their emotional/behavioral functioning and psychiatric status. One study (Werner, 1986) found that maternal alcoholism was associated with higher child psychosocial problems than paternal alcoholism. Conversely, another study (Levenson, Oyama, & Meek, 1987) found that children of alcoholic fathers showed greater responsivity to stress than children of alcoholic mothers. In an attempt to establish whether drinking within the family might span three generations, Harford and Grant (1990) studied alcohol abuse among grandsons of paternal versus maternal alcoholic grandfathers. They found that there was greater alcohol abuse by the grandsons of maternal than paternal grandfathers. Because no other family characteristics were assessed, it is difficult to draw any conclusions from the study by the Harford and Grant study.

The relations between paternal and maternal alcoholism and children's functioning may be influenced by child gender and parental behavior. Orford and Velleman (1991) conducted a study with males and females, aged 16 to 35 years old, who had one non-problem-drinking parent and either an alcoholic father or an alcoholic mother. For both males and females, a positive parent-child relationship with an alcoholic father (but not an alcoholic mother) was associated with more alcohol consumption. For females (but not males), a stronger perceived similarity with their alcoholic father was associated with greater problem drinking and greater problem drug use. Ironically, for females (but not males), a stronger perceived similarity with their alcoholic mother was associated with fewer drinking problems. Children in families with an alcoholic father are also at increased risk to experience a family environment in which their mother is showing high levels of depression and low levels of social support (Tubman, 1993). Orford and Velleman suggest that future investigations of paternal and maternal alcoholism must consider the family environment and parent-child relationship to establish the mechanisms of intergenerational transmission of alcohol problems.

Very few studies were identified that compared paternal alcoholism with other types of paternal psychopathology, and none of these studies showed greater risk for problems due to paternal alcoholism than to paternal depression (el-Guebaly et al., 1978; Jacob, Krahn, & Leonard, 1991; Jacob & Leonard, 1986) or paternal schizophrenia (el-Guebaly et al., 1978). For example, after controlling for family size, el-Guebaly and colleagues (1978) did not find differences in parents' reports of children's emotional/behavioral problems in families with an alcoholic father, a depressed father, or a schizophrenic father. Similarly, Jacob and Leonard (1986) did not find differences between children of alcoholic fathers and children of depressed fathers based on parents' reports and teachers' reports of children's emotional/behavioral functioning. In addition, no significant differences in dyadic father-child interactions were found between families with an alcoholic father and families with a depressed father. However, when triadic father-mother-child interactions were assessed, families with a depressed father engaged in significantly less smiling, laughing, and humor than families with an alcoholic father or a nonclinical father. There was not a significant difference between families with an alcoholic father and families in the nonclinical control group with regard to these congeniality behaviors.

There has been extensive research with the children, adolescents, and adult children of alcoholic fathers. There is relatively consistent evidence that children and adolescents, and to a lesser extent adult children, of alcoholic fathers show greater levels of psychopathology and more cognitive deficits than the offspring of nondisturbed fathers. There are far fewer studies, and thus fewer firm conclusions, regarding the risk associated with having an alcoholic father versus an alcoholic mother. Because there is evidence of assortative mating with regard to alcoholism (Gleiberman, Harburg, DiFranceisco, & Schork, 1992), it is important for researchers to assess the psychological functioning of both parents even if the family was recruited into the research based on the father's alcoholism. Further research is also needed that compares the specific risk associated with paternal alcoholism compared with the risk associated with other psychiatric disorders in fathers. The few studies that have investigated other paternal disorders in relation to paternal alcoholism have suggested that the risk for psychopathology associated with paternal alcoholism is similar to the risk associated with other paternal psychiatric disorders. However, more studies with larger sample sizes of psychiatrically disturbed fathers are needed before a firm conclusion can be drawn. No studies were identified that investigated paternal substance abuse other than the abuse of alcohol.

PATERNAL DEPRESSION

The diagnosis of major depressive disorder provides an interesting and important comparison between paternal and maternal effects on child functioning. Depression is one of the most extensively researched parental diagnoses in relation to risk factors for child maladjustment (Downey & Coyne, 1990; Kaslow, Deering, & Racusin, 1994). Given the substantially higher rate of depression in adult women than in adult men, it is not surprising that the vast majority of this research has examined the functioning of children of depressed mothers. It is interesting to note that several reviews of "parents" who were depressed did not specifically mention fathers (as opposed to mothers) who were depressed (e.g., Beardslee, 1986; Beardslee, Bemporad, Keller, & Klerman, 1984; Cytryn, McKnew, Zahn-Waxler, & Gershon, 1986; Orvaschel, Weissman, & Kidd, 1980; Weintraub, Winters, & Neale, 1986). Even though there are substantially more depressed women than depressed men, epidemiological studies provide evidence that a substantial number of men suffer from depression at some point in their lives. The Epidemiological Catchment Area (ECA) study suggested that 3.5% of men and 7.9% of women could be diagnosed with major depressive disorder at some point in their lives (Robins et al., 1984). The one-month prevalence rates from the ECA study suggested that at any given time 1.6% of men and 2.9% of women could be diagnosed with depression (Regier et al., 1988; summarized in Robins & Regier, 1991). Although the prevalence rates of depression are twice as high for women as for men in both lifetime and one-month prevalence, substantial numbers of men appear to experience major depressive disorder. This suggests that research with depressed fathers is warranted.

Thirteen studies were identified that directly assessed the psychological functioning of children of depressed fathers (Atkinson & Rickel, 1984; Beardslee, Schultz, & Selman, 1987; Billings & Moos, 1983, 1985; el-Guebaly et al., 1978; Harjan, 1992; Jacob & Leonard, 1986; Klein, Clark, Dansky, & Margolis, 1988; Klein, Depue, & Slater, 1985; Orvaschel, Walsh-Allis, & Ye, 1988; Radke-Yarrow, Cummings, Kuczynski, & Chapman, 1985; Radke-Yarrow, Nottelmann, Martinez, Fox, & Belmont, 1992; Zahn-Waxler, Cummings, McKnew, & Radke-Yarrow, 1984). Nine of these studies compared children of depressed fathers with children of nonclinical fathers and found that children of depressed fathers were at increased risk for child psychopathology (Atkinson & Rickel, 1984; Beardslee et al., 1987; Billings & Moos, 1983, 1985; el-Guebaly et al., 1978; Harjan, 1992; Jacob & Leonard, 1986; Klein et al., 1988; Orvaschel et al., 1988). For example, Orvaschel and colleagues (1988) used structured clinical interviews to assess the psychopathology in children whose fathers or mothers were diagnosed with unipolar depression. They found that children of depressed fathers and mothers were significantly more psychologically distressed than children of nonclinical fathers and mothers. Billings and Moos (1983, 1985) found that children of depressed fathers and mothers showed significantly more psychopathology than children of nonclinical fathers and mothers at the initial point of assessment and at the 1-year follow-up. In a study that compared children of depressed fathers, alcoholic fathers, and non-clinical fathers, Jacob and Leonard (1986) found that children of depressed or alcoholic fathers showed significantly higher rates of emotional/behavioral problems than children of nonclinical fathers.

When children of depressed fathers are compared with children of depressed mothers, differences in psychological functioning rarely are found (Atkinson & Rickel, 1984; Beardslee et al., 1987; Billings & Moos, 1983, 1985; Harjan, 1992; Klein et al., 1988; Orvaschel et al., 1988). Billings and Moos (1983, 1985) found that children of depressed fathers and children of depressed mothers showed equivalent rates of increased emotional/behavioral problems, academic problems, social problems, and physical problems. Orvaschel and colleagues (1988) found that children of depressed fathers and children of depressed mothers showed similar increased risk for child psychopathology, including affective disorders, attention deficit/hyperactivity disorder, and anxiety disorders. The lack of differences between children of depressed fathers and of depressed mothers appears to be specific to unipolar affective disorders rather than bipolar affective disorders. Klein and colleagues (1988) found similar levels of heightened psychopathology in children of fathers and mothers diagnosed with unipolar depression. However, Klein and colleagues (1985) found significantly higher rates of psychopathology in the adolescent children of mothers diagnosed with bipolar depression (69%) than in the adolescent children of fathers so diagnosed (27%). Thus, the lack of differences in rates of psychopathology of children of depressed fathers and depressed mothers appears to be specific to unipolar depression rather than bipolar depression.

Although differences are rarely found in the psychological adjustment of children of unipolar depressed fathers and children of unipolar depressed mothers, the sample sizes of depressed fathers in many of these studies limits the certainty of this conclusion. The small sample sizes of depressed fathers may be because few researchers have specifically targeted paternal depression for investigation. Samples of depressed fathers have most often been included with samples of depressed mothers, and it appears that few researchers have intentionally recruited depressed fathers. For example, Klein et al. (1988) had a sample of 19 depressed mothers and only 5 depressed fathers. Orvaschel and colleagues (1988) had a sample of 26 mothers and only 8 fathers who were diagnosed with depression. In addition, some researchers have not determined paternal depression directly, but rather have administered a structured interview to the depressed mother to establish the psychiatric status of the father (e.g., Beardslee et al., 1987). Structured diagnostic interviews administered directly to the father would undoubtedly provide a more valid diagnosis.

Another way of investigating the functioning of children of depressed fathers and mothers has been to investigate the increased risk associated with having both parents who are depressed. When one parent (e.g., the mother) is identified as depressed, there is evidence to suggest that there may be significant psychopathology in the other parent due to patterns of assortative mating (McLeod, 1993; Merikangas & Spiker, 1982; Merikangas, Weissman et al., 1988) or due to the increased burdens and stressors associated with living with a depressed person (Coyne et al., 1987). It appears that children are at an even greater risk for the development of psychopathology when both parents have a psychiatric diagnosis. Merikangas, Weissman et al. (1988) found that when neither parent was diagnosed, one-third of their children were diagnosed. When one parent was diagnosed, the numbers increased to over one-half of the children who were diagnosed. When both parents were diagnosed, the numbers increased to three-quarters of children who met diagnostic criteria. This pattern of increased risk was found for a variety of parental diagnoses, including depression, as well as for a variety of child diagnoses, including depression.

However, the evidence suggesting an increased risk for psychopathology in children based on the number of parents who are depressed is somewhat equivocal. One study found that presence of a depressed father did not increase the likelihood of child insecure attachment with depressed mothers, but emotional/behavioral problems of these children were not assessed (Radke-Yarrow et al., 1985). In a follow-up to this study that included assessments of children's emotional/behavioral functioning, Radke-Yarrow et al. (1992) found that the presence of a depressed father did not increase the likelihood of children's problematic levels of disruptive, depressed, or anxious behavior.

Another layer of complexity must be addressed when the residential status (living in the home or out of the home) of depressed fathers is considered. In a sample of depressed mothers, Hammen and her colleagues (summarized in Hammen, 1991) found that children were more likely to meet diagnostic criteria for a variety of disorders when fathers were absent from the home, regardless of whether mothers or fathers were disordered or not disordered. Additionally, children of psychiatrically disordered fathers showed increased levels of diagnoses, regardless of whether the father resided with the children or not. However, there was not an additive effect of paternal disorder and paternal absence. Regardless of maternal status, children who lived with a nondisordered father were least likely to meet diagnostic criteria, whereas the other three groups of children (those who lived with a disordered father, those whose disordered father was absent, those whose nondisordered father was absent) showed approximately equal levels of increased psychopathology. A small sample size precluded analyses of the differential impact of specific paternal diagnosis (e.g., alcohol abuse vs. unipolar depression). Hammen (1991) argued that further analyses of larger samples of families who are specifically recruited for paternal depression (as well as maternal depression) are necessary to more fully address the consequences of maternal versus paternal dysfunction.

There is fairly high comorbidity between major depression and a variety of disorders, especially anxiety disorders. Epidemiological research has found that 25% of depressed patients have a lifetime history of panic disorder and between 40% and 80% of panic disorder patients have experienced a major depressive episode at some point in their lives (Katon & Roy-Byrne, 1991). The rates of comorbidity in clinically referred samples are even higher than in community epidemiological samples. For example, in a sample of clinically referred parents, Merikangas, Prusoff, and Weissman (1988) found that 89% of those diagnosed with major depression also had lifetime diagnoses of anxiety disorders. In addition, Clark (1989) summarized 15 studies of subjects who were clinically referred for depression, and found that the percentage overlap between depression and a variety of anxiety disorders ranged from 11% to 74% (depending on the diagnostic criteria used).

Numerous researchers have noted the importance of investigating comorbidity of psychiatric disorders (Achenbach, 1990–1991; Caron & Rutter, 1991; Lewinsohn, Rohde, Seeley, & Hops, 1991; Rohde, Lewinsohn, & Seeley, 1991). Because of the apparent high comorbidity between depression and anxiety disorders, field trials for DSM-IV were conducted to assess a possible new diagnostic category of mixed anxiety-depressive disorder (Clark & Watson, 1991; Katon & Roy-Byrne, 1991). However, a diagnostic category of mixed anxiety-depressive disorder was not included in the final draft of DSM-IV, but rather was listed in the Appendix as a diagnosis in need of further study (American Psychiatric Press, 1994).

To investigate the effects of comorbidity of depression and an anxiety disorder, Weissman, Leckman, Merikangas, Gammon, and Prusoff (1984) compared the psychological functioning of children of fathers and mothers diagnosed solely with depression and children of fathers and mothers diagnosed with both depression and an anxiety disorder. They found that the presence of an anxiety disorder (agoraphobia, generalized anxiety disorder, panic disorder) in a parent increased the risk for disorder in children when compared with children of normal control parents and children whose parents were diagnosed with only depression. There were no differences in the levels of children's psychological functioning when comparing diagnosed fathers and mothers. However, the authors suggested that this failure to find a difference between children of diagnosed fathers and mothers may have been due to the small samples of children in some of the groups.

Overall, children of depressed fathers appear to be at increased risk for psychopathology when compared with children of nonclinical fathers. There appear to be no differences in the risk for psychopathology associated with unipolar depression in fathers and unipolar depression in mothers. Children of depressed fathers and of depressed mothers have been found to have higher rates of both externalizing problems and internalizing problems when compared with children of nonclinical parents. Because of the small sample sizes of depressed fathers in many of these studies, there is a need to conduct research that specifically targets the children of depressed fathers. There is also a need to investigate the children of depressed fathers compared with children of fathers with other psychiatric disorders.

PATERNAL ANXIETY DISORDERS

There has been surprisingly little research on the children of fathers who experience a variety of anxiety disorders. Anxiety disorders have been identified as one of the most frequently occurring psychiatric disorder in epidemiological studies in the community (Regier et al., 1984; summarized in Robins & Regier, 1991). In addition, Barlow (1988) noted that some types of anxiety disorders have a high prevalence among adult men. For example, social phobia has a prevalence rate of 1.7% and rates of simple phobias range from 2.3% to 7.3% (Robins & Regier, 1991). Therefore, it is surprising to find so few studies that investigate the children of fathers who experience these disorders. The only anxiety disorder in fathers that has received a lot of attention in relation to their children's functioning is posttraumatic stress disorder (PTSD).

Only one study (reported in Weissman, Gershon et al., 1984; Weissman, Leckman et al., 1984) could be identified that provided separate analyses of children of fathers who were diagnosed with an anxiety disorder other than PTSD. Other studies (such as Turner, Beidel, & Costello, 1987) investigated the children of adults with anxiety disorders but did not detail how many fathers and mothers were in the sample nor did they provide separate analyses for the children of fathers versus mothers who were diagnosed with an anxiety disorder. As noted in the section on paternal depression, the study by Weissman, Leckman et al. (1984) investigated the functioning of children who had parents diagnosed with depression and an anxiety disorder. There was not a separate group of families in which the parent was diagnosed with an anxiety disorder to the exclusion of any other psychiatric disorder. Given the high rates of comorbidity with other psychiatric disorders, especially depression (Robins & Regier, 1991), this research design was not surprising. When children of nonclinical parents and children of depressed parents were compared with children of parents diagnosed with both an anxiety disorder (such as agoraphobia, panic disorder, generalized anxiety disorder) and depression, the latter group showed higher rates of psychopathology (Weissman, Leckman et al., 1984). Thus, the presence of a parental anxiety disorder, in addition to parental depression, showed that children had an increased risk for a psychiatric disorder. When the rates of psychopathology in children of diagnosed fathers were compared with the rates in children of diagnosed mothers, no significant differences emerged. This suggested that there was equivalent risk associated with having a father or a mother with an anxiety disorder. However, the researchers cautioned that this lack of significant differences in the rates of psychopathology in either parent may have been due to inadequate statistical power due to small sample sizes.

In contrast to the research on other types of anxiety disorders, children of fathers diagnosed with PTSD have received far more attention. One study (Rosenheck, 1986) investigated the offspring of fathers who served in World War II, and two studies (Jordan et al., 1992; Parsons, Kehle, & Owen, 1990) investigated the children of fathers who served in the Vietnam War. Rosenheck (1986) investigated 12 offspring (ranging in age from 18 to 42) of five fathers who experienced PTSD as a result of their combat experience in World War II. Although the small sample size precluded statistical analysis, the findings provided intriguing information about families of fathers who had experienced chronic symptoms of PTSD for over four decades. Nine of the 12 participants continued to feel that the combat experience was responsible for their father's continued psychological distress. When asked the extent that their father's war experience and resultant psychological disorder had affected them, 6 participants said it had little to no impact on them, 4 participants said it continued to have some impact on their current functioning, and 2 participants said that it continued to have a major influence on their current functioning. Unfortunately, no standardized measures of psychological functioning were administered to the offspring of the World War II veterans who continued to experience PTSD. Rosenheck noted that the impact of paternal PTSD seemed to vary across families. When offspring were compared with their siblings and then compared with offspring in other families, there appeared to be more between-family differences than within-family differences. Thus, certain families with fathers diagnosed with PTSD may have experienced more disruption in relation to the PTSD than other families. However, these tentative conclusions must be tested out empirically in larger samples.

The next two studies compared the children and adolescents of male Vietnam veterans who were experiencing PTSD with the children and adolescents of male Vietnam veterans who were not experiencing PTSD (Jordan et al., 1992; Parsons et al., 1990). Both studies assessed children's and adolescents' functioning with the Child Behavior Checklist (CBCL; Achenbach, 1991), but Parsons and colleagues (1990) had fathers complete the CBCL whereas Jordan and colleagues (1992) had mothers complete the CBCL. Because parental psychological symptoms are associated with their reports of their children's emotional/behavioral problems (Phares, Compas, & Howell, 1989), it is important to have multiple informants of children's emotional/behavioral problems. Therefore, the combined results of these two studies should serve as a strong basis for understanding children's behavioral functioning in families with a father who has been diagnosed with PTSD.

Parsons and colleagues (1990) found that fathers with PTSD rated their children as experiencing higher levels of externalizing problems (e.g., aggression, hyperactivity, and delinquency) than did fathers who were not experiencing PTSD and in fact who had not been exposed to combat during their service in the Vietnam War. Although there were some differences based on age and gender of the child, the results indicated that children of fathers with PTSD showed greater behavioral problems than children of fathers who served in Vietnam but who were not diagnosed with PTSD. Jordan and colleagues (1992) found a similar pattern of results. Based on maternal reports on the CBCL, school-age children of fathers with PTSD were significantly more likely to experience clinical levels of emotional/behavioral problems than were children of fathers who were not experiencing PTSD. More specifically, when overall behavioral problems were broken down into the normative range and the clinical range, a greater percentage of children of fathers with PTSD (34.8%) than children of fathers without PTSD (14.2%) showed behavioral problems in the clinical range. Jordan and colleagues also found that the families of fathers with PTSD showed greater levels of family violence, marital distress, and family maladjustment than did the families of fathers without PTSD. The findings of both studies appear to be robust because both fathers' and mothers' reports of children's functioning showed the same patterns of child maladjustment. Interested readers are referred to Jurich (1983) for a discussion of the unique therapeutic issues that arise in working with families in which the father is experiencing PTSD in response to the Vietnam War.

The lack of research into the children of anxiety-disordered fathers (other than those experiencing PTSD), combined with the fairly high prevalence rates of anxiety disorders in men, suggests that this area is in need of further research. Care should be taken in attempting to analyze children who have fathers diagnosed solely with an anxiety disorder compared with children who have fathers diagnosed with other psychiatric disorders. In addition, further research is needed into the children of fathers who experience PTSD in reaction to stressors other than war (e.g., car accidents, violent crime). Jensen, Lewis, and Xenakis (1986) provided a review of families of military men and concluded that children in military families may be exposed to a variety of risk factors other than paternal PTSD. For example, frequent paternal absence due to being stationed overseas, geographic and residential instability, and the authoritarian military structure may all affect children in addition to the PTSD that some fathers in the military may experience.

PATERNAL SCHIZOPHRENIA

Schizophrenia is another parental diagnosis that has been studied predominantly in mothers rather than fathers even though Lidz et al. (1956) noted the importance of the father's role in the development of schizophrenia many years ago. The overreliance on studies of children of mothers diagnosed with schizophrenia may be due to two reasons. First, it appears that schizophrenic men are unlikely to marry and to have children and therefore schizophrenic fathers are somewhat atypical (Watt, 1986). Second, many of the schizophrenic mothers who are investigated are unmarried and, typically, can provide little information about the psychological adjustment of their children's father (Walker & Emory, 1983). Thus, it is difficult for researchers to identify and recruit children of fathers with schizophrenia.

Several large-scale prospective research projects have included children of schizophrenic fathers in their samples with schizophrenic mothers (for reviews of these studies, see Rolf et al., 1990; Watt, 1986; Watt, Anthony, Wynne, & Rolf, 1984). Most of these studies have not provided separate analyses of paternal and maternal effects in relation to parental schizophrenia and child psychopathology. Often the sample sizes of schizophrenic fathers were prohibitively small and therefore statistical analyses were not completed. However, some studies have been completed that investigated schizophrenic fathers and provided separate analyses for paternal effects. Results from these studies, however, do not provide a clear picture of the risk for child psychopathology associated with having a schizophrenic father.

Studies of EEG functioning and brain abnormalities in children of schizophrenic fathers have been conducted. Itil, Huque, Shapiro, Mednick, and Schulsinger (1983) compared children in families with a schizophrenic father, a schizophrenic mother, both a schizophrenic father and schizophrenic mother, or a nondisturbed father and a nondisturbed mother. Children of schizophrenic fathers differed from children of nonclinical controls on only 4 of 22 EEG measures and differed from children of schizophrenic mothers on 11 of 22 EEG measures. Children of schizophrenic mothers differed from children of nonclinical controls on 13 of the 22 EEG measures. Itil and colleagues concluded that children of schizophrenic mothers were more at risk for EEG abnormalities than were children of schizophrenic fathers. Conversely, Silverton, Mednick, Schulsinger, Parnas, and Harrington (1988) found that fathers' schizophrenia was associated with increased risk for brain abnormalities (e.g., cerebral ventricular enlargement) and low birthweight in their offspring. Their sample consisted of offspring of schizophrenic mothers, some of whom also had schizophrenic fathers and some nondisturbed fathers. The association between low birthweight and ventricular enlargement was more pronounced in the offspring of both schizophrenic fathers and schizophrenic mothers when compared with the offspring of schizophrenic mothers and nondisturbed fathers. Silverton and colleagues concluded that paternal schizophrenia is associated with greater risk for brain abnormalities and for the development of schizophrenia.

Turning to the psychological functioning of children with schizophrenic fathers, Erlenmeyer-Kimling and colleagues (1984) investigated the referral status of children of schizophrenic fathers, children of schizophrenic mothers, and children with two schizophrenic parents. There were no significant differences in children's psychiatric hospitalization or psychological treatment based on the gender of the disturbed parent. A study by el-Guebaly and colleagues (1978) compared the children's psychological functioning in relation to paternal versus maternal schizophrenia. Initially, the investigators found that children of schizophrenic fathers showed more parent-reported emotional/behavioral problems than children of schizophrenic mothers. However, this difference was no longer significant when family size was controlled. Thus, there appeared to be no greater risk for emotional/behavioral problems in children of schizophrenic fathers than in children of schizophrenic mothers.

With regard to parental behavior, children seemed to perceive schizophrenic fathers to be less accepting and less involved than fathers who were not diagnosed with a psychiatric disorder (Weintraub & Neale, 1984). Children of schizophrenic mothers rated their mothers as more involved, more lax in discipline, and more child-centered than did children of nondisturbed mothers. Based on a study of direct observations in a free-play situation with families of schizophrenic parents and their nondisordered spouses, fathers were found to be more active with their children than were mothers regardless of their psychiatric status (Baldwin, Baldwin, Cole, & Kokes, 1984). In addition, nondisturbed spouses were significantly more active with their children than were schizophrenic parents regardless of their gender.

Overall, the increased risk for brain abnormalities and for emotional/behavioral problems in children of schizophrenic fathers is unclear. Children of schizophrenic fathers may be at increased risk for development of neurological and psychological disturbances when compared with children of nonclinical fathers; however, they may not have the same degree of risk as children of schizophrenic mothers. In future research, care should be taken to investigate how much contact children have with their schizophrenic fathers and schizophrenic mothers before discussing solely genetic or environmental mechanisms.

FATHERS WHO PHYSICALLY AND SEXUALLY ABUSE THEIR CHILDREN

The research literatures on fathers who physically abuse or sexually abuse their children are very different from one another. Studies on paternal physical abuse are similar to many other areas of research in which the role of mothers has been investigated almost to the exclusion of the role of fathers (Martin, 1984). The research literature on sexual abuse of children is limited by the reverse problem. Sexually abusive fathers and father figures have been investigated to the near exclusion of potentially sexually abusive mothers, and it has been suggested that maternal sexual abuse of children has been severely underdetected (Banning, 1989).

Paternal Physical Abuse of Children

Even though there is evidence that children are approximately equally likely to be physically abused by their father as by their mother (Martin, 1984), most research on physical abuse of children has focused on mothers (Wolfe, 1985). There is some suggestion that mothers more often commit acts of mild violence toward children (e.g., pushing, grabbing, shoving, slapping, spanking the child), whereas acts of severe violence (e.g., kicking, hitting with a fist, hitting with an object, biting, burning, scalding, threatening with a gun or a knife, using a gun or a knife) are more likely to be committed by fathers (Sariola & Uutela, 1992; Wolfner & Gelles, 1993). A frustrating characteristic of much of this research is that samples of "physically abused children" are identified but the perpetrator of the abuse is often not noted. For example, in many studies (e.g., Reid, Kavanagh, & Baldwin, 1987; Rogeness, Amrung, Macedo, Harris, & Fisher, 1986; Whipple & Webster-Stratton, 1991), the researchers do not provide information as to the proportions of children who were physically abused by their fathers, by their mothers, or by both parents. It may be that the identity of the perpetrator was not established, and therefore the children are classified as having been physically abused without information as to the identity of the perpetrator. Often when this information is provided, statistical analyses are not provided for abusive versus nonabusive parents (Wolfe, 1985). This lack of specificity may be due to the small sample sizes that are often recruited.

Even with these research design problems and the overreliance on samples of mothers, there have been a few studies that have investigated paternal characteristics in relation to child physical abuse or that have investigated characteristics of children who were abused by their fathers. Not surprisingly, the fathers and mothers of physically abused children often show higher rates of psychopathology than the fathers and mothers of children who have not been physically abused (Reid et al., 1987; Rogeness et al., 1986; Whipple & Webster-Stratton, 1991). Fathers who physically abused their children reported higher rates of their own conduct problems compared with fathers of nonabused children, and mothers who physically abused their children reported higher rates than controls on a number of self-reported psychological symptoms, such as hostile-withdrawn, disposition, aggression, conduct problems, and intellectual inefficiency (Reid et al., 1987). Fathers' aggressive behavior appears to be related to paternal alcohol consumption (Diacatou, Mamalakis, Kafatos, & Vlahonikolis, 1993).

Rogeness and colleagues (1986) found that fathers of abused or neglected children were more likely to meet diagnostic criteria for a psychiatric disorder and to show evidence of an antisocial personality disorder when compared with the fathers of nonabused or neglected children. Greater rates of alcoholism were also evident for fathers of abused or neglected boys (but not girls) when compared with fathers of boys who were not abused or neglected (Rogeness et al., 1986). In the same study, Rogeness and colleagues found that mothers of neglected children showed greater psychiatric disturbance than mothers of children who were not abused or neglected, but that the rates of alcoholism and antisocial personality disorder did not differ between the two groups.

In a sample of conduct-disordered children who had either been or not been physically abused, Whipple and Webster-Stratton (1991) found evidence of increased psychopathology in mothers of abused children but little evidence in fathers. However, the nonsignificant findings related to paternal psychopathology may be due to the small sample size of fathers. The total sample consisted of 29 conduct-disordered children who had been physically abused and 94 who apparently had not. Because fathers were no longer in the homes of 14 of the 29 physically abused children, the sample included only 15 fathers of abused children. Thus, the nonsignificant findings for fathers should be interpreted with caution. Overall, Whipple and Webster-Stratton found that mothers of abused conduct-disordered children reported greater levels of stress, depression, state anxiety, marital dissatisfaction, and social isolation than mothers of conduct-disordered children who had not been physically abused. Although fathers of abused conduct-disordered children were not found to show greater levels of psychological distress, they reported that they spanked their children significantly more often than fathers of conduct-disordered children who were not physically abused.

Physically abusive fathers showed more coercive influence and more negative behavior in response to other family members, even during conflict negotiation tasks that were laboratory based (Silber, Bermann, Henderson, & Lehman, 1993). In addition, children of abusive fathers showed more criticism toward their fathers and less agreement with their fathers than nonabused children.

Other studies have investigated the families and family histories of children who are at risk for physical abuse (Garbarino, Sebes, & Schellenbach, 1984; Simons, Whitbeck, Conger, & Chyi-In, 1991). Garbarino and colleagues found that enmeshment, chaos, low paternal supportive behavior, and high maternal punitiveness characterized families in which there was high risk for physical abuse of children. Abusive fathers and mothers reported that their fathers and mothers were less nurturing, and their mothers were more restrictive than reported by nonabusive parents (Wiehe, 1992).

In a study of intergenerational transmission of harsh parenting, Simons and colleagues (1991) provided complex path analyses to investigate gender-based links in parenting behavior characterized by severe discipline between three generations. The parenting styles of grandfathers, grandmothers, fathers, and mothers were analyzed in relation to their male and female offspring who were attending the seventh grade at the time of the study. Initial correlational analyses suggested that both fathers' and mothers' self-reported harsh parenting with their sons and their daughters was significantly related to the harsh parenting that they had received from both their father and their mother. Path analyses provided a more detailed analyses of these processes. Grandmothers' (but not grandfathers') harsh parenting was strongly linked to fathers' harsh parenting of their adolescent sons and to mothers' harsh parenting of their adolescent sons and daughters. Grandfathers' (but not grandmothers') harsh parenting was strongly linked to fathers' harsh parenting of their adolescent daughters. In addition, for both fathers and mothers of both sons and daughters, a hostile personality and a belief in physical discipline were strongly related to harsh parenting. This study provides a good example of the complexity that is needed in research on parenting styles that are associated with physical abuse of children.

Two issues that have received recent attention regarding abusive parenting are Munchausen syndrome by proxy and murder of one's own children. Munchausen syndrome by proxy is identified when a parent or primary caregiver fabricates a medical problem or induces physical symptoms in his or her child to gain medical attention for the child. Although mothers appear to be guilty of Munchausen syndrome by proxy more often than fathers (Mercer & Perdue, 1993), there is evidence that fathers sometimes create illness and physical symptoms in their children (Jones, Badgett, Minella, & Schuschke, 1993). With regard to the extremes of abuse when a child actually dies at the hands of a parent, Plass (1993) documented that African American children are more likely to be killed by their father than by their mother.

Along with the research that specifically addresses the fathers of physically abused children, there is also research that has investigated children's functioning in relation to paternal aggression toward children's mothers (Holden & Ritchie, 1991; Jouriles & LeCompte, 1991; Langhinrichsen-Rohling, Heyman, Schlee, & O'Leary, 1993; Sternberg et al., 1993). Even before the birth of children, it appears that husbands' aggression is associated with both marital partners' expectations regarding parenting. Specifically, Langhinrichsen-Rohling and colleagues (1993) investigated a sample of recently married, childless couples, to determine the relation between marital functioning and expectations regarding children's behavior. Couples in which husband-to-wife aggression was evident expected significantly more problems with their future children than couples in which aggression was not evident. In addition, maritally distressed couples expected more problems from children than did nondistressed couples.

This research suggests that marital aggression and dissatisfaction precede the birth of children and are associated with the expectations of problems once children are born into the family. Langhinrichsen-Rohling and colleagues noted that the results of this study call into the question the assumption that children's behavior problems create problems within the marital dyad and negatively influence marital satisfaction. Distressed and aggressive couples may benefit from preventive efforts, such as parenting skills training before the birth of children, to prevent increased aggression and distress once children are born.

The impact of marital violence on children has also been investigated. In a sample of families in which the mother had been battered by the child's father, Holden and Ritchie (1991) found that young children from families with paternal violence showed higher levels of internalizing behavior problems, more aggression, and more difficult temperaments than children from families in which no paternal violence was evident. O'Keefe (1994) found that children's witnessing of marital violence and their own experience of maternal but not paternal aggression were associated with greater internalizing and externalizing behavioral problems. In the group of violent families, maternal stress and paternal irritability were significantly associated with children's total behavior problems. Jouriles and LeCompte (1991) investigated families in which there was evidence of spouse abuse and found that aggression within the family was associated with child gender. Regression analyses showed that husbands' aggression toward wives interacted with child gender (but not child age) in predicting paternal and maternal aggression toward children. Further correlational analyses suggested that husbands' aggression toward wives was related to paternal and maternal aggression toward sons but not daughters. It is important to note that boys and girls in this sample did not differ in their experience of paternal or maternal aggression.

In an intriguing study of the effects of domestic violence on children's emotional/behavioral functioning in Israel, Sternberg and colleagues (1993) characterized children into one of four groups: Child was physically abused, child witnessed parental abuse (usually mother was physically abused by father) but did not experience physical abuse him- or herself, child was physically abused and also witnessed the physical abuse of his or her parent, and child neither experienced physical abuse nor witnessed parental abuse. Children who had been physically abused themselves, those who witnessed abuse of their parent, and those who were both physically abused and witnessed abuse of their parent reported significantly higher levels of depressive symptoms than nonabused children.

Many of these studies (e.g., Holden & Ritchie, 1991; Jouriles & LeCompte, 1991; Simons et al., 1991) have attempted to address the complexity in violent families. To date, the research literature on physically abused children tends to focus more on mothers than on fathers, with little attention to who perpetrated the abuse. These issues will need to be addressed in future research.

Paternal Sexual Abuse of Children

Because the majority of intrafamilial sexual abuse of children is perpetrated by fathers and father figures, most research investigating childhood sexual abuse has studied paternal characteristics and children's characteristics in relation to paternal sexual abuse. However, it should be noted that sexual abuse by female perpetrators (including mothers) occurs. Finkelhor and Russell (1984) found that the sexual abuse of 13% of girl victims and 24% of boy victims had been perpetrated by an adult female. Although these incidence rates were not broken down into mothers versus other adult women, it is important to acknowledge that childhood sexual abuse can be perpetrated by mothers in addition to fathers. Banning (1989) suggested that professionals often do not consider maternal sexual abuse as a possibility and therefore provide assessments that are not thorough enough to detect child sexual abuse by mothers. Thus, the lack of research into maternal sexual abuse may be due to inadequate assessment rather than an absence of the occurrence of child sexual abuse by mothers. With regard to the epidemiological factors related to child sexual abuse, the following risk factors have been noted: being female, being a preadolescent or young adolescent, having a stepfather, living without a biological parent, having a psychiatrically disturbed mother, experiencing poor paternal and maternal parenting, and witnessing family conflict (Finkelhor, 1993). Socioeconomic status, race, and ethnicity were not associated with greater risk for childhood sexual abuse (Finkelhor, 1993).

The research literature on intrafamilial sexual abuse of children has focused a lot of attention on the effects of paternal sexual abuse, especially in relation to whether the child was sexually abused by the biological father or by a nonbiologically related father figure (e.g., a stepfather or mother's boyfriend who is supposed to serve in a paternal role). A number of reviews of the literature (Beitchman et al., 1992; Browne & Finkelhor, 1986; Finkelhor, 1990; Russell, 1986) and empirical studies (Harter, Alexander, & Neimeyer, 1988; Scott & Stone, 1986a, 1986b; Sirles, Smith, & Kusama, 1989) have concluded that sexual abuse by fathers or father figures is associated with significantly greater short- and long-term psychological maladjustment than sexual abuse by perpetrators who were not supposed to serve in the paternal role. For example, in a sample of children receiving psychiatric outpatient services, those who had been sexually abused by their father or stepfather were significantly more likely to receive a psychiatric diagnosis than children who had been sexually abused by another relative (Sirles et al., 1989). Children can also be at risk of sexual abuse by their grandfathers. Margolin (1992) identified a sample of children who had been sexually abused by their grandfather and found that the sexually abusive grandfathers had often been sexually abusive as fathers and that stepgrandchildren appear to be at greater risk for physically violent sexual abuse than biologically related grandchildren.

Turning back to paternal sexual abuse, when compared with participants in a control group who had not been sexually abused, paternal sexual abuse has been related to elevated psychopathology and poorer adjustment in adolescent girls (Scott & Stone, 1986b) and adult women (Bigras, Leichner, Perreault, & Lavoie, 1991; Edwards & Alexander, 1992; Scott & Stone, 1986a). A total of 53.8% of children aged 3 to 16 years who had been sexually abused by their father met criteria for posttraumatic stress disorder (McLeer, Deblinger, Henry, & Orvaschel, 1992). In a retrospective study of adult women who had experienced overt sexual abuse by their father or who had experienced paternal seductiveness without overt sexual abuse, Herman and Hirschman (1981) found that women who had experienced overt sexual abuse were more likely to report running away, suicide attempts, or pregnancy during adolescence. These studies all point to the increased maladjustment in girls and women who were sexually abused by their fathers.

Turning to characteristics of fathers who sexually abuse their daughters, Parker and Parker (1986) conducted a study to compare the familial background of men who were found guilty of sexually abusing their daughters and men who apparently had not sexually abused their daughters. Both biological fathers and stepfathers were included in this study, with approximately equal numbers across both the sexually abusive and nonabusive groups. Sexually abusive fathers reported significantly more parental mistreatment in their own childhoods when compared with nonabusive fathers. Specifically, 20% of sexually abusive fathers reported mistreatment by both parents, 29% reported mistreatment by only their father, and 10% reported mistreatment by only their mother. These figures were 2%, 11%, and 4%, respectively, for the nonabusive fathers' reports of their own upbringing. Parker and Parker also assessed these fathers' experience with their daughters during the daughters' early years. Sexually abusive fathers were significantly more likely than nonabusive fathers to have been partially or fully absent from the home during the first 3 years of their daughter's life. Specifically, 34% of the sexually abusive fathers and 70% of the nonabusive fathers reported being at home "almost all the time" during the first 3 years of their daughter's life. Similarly, sexually abusive fathers were less involved in child care and nurturing activities than were nonabusive fathers. Considering only fathers who were present in the home during the first 3 years of life, 8% of sexually abusive fathers and 39% of nonabusive fathers reported being involved in three or more caretaking activities with their daughters.

This study suggests that early involvement by fathers may decrease the likelihood of later sexual abuse of their daughters. Alternatively, it may be that fathers who are more responsible in their fathering role early in their daughter's life may also be less likely to sexually abuse their daughters. In either case, Parker and Parker noted that fathers' perceptions of maltreatment in their own childhood and lack of involvement in caretaking their infant daughters are associated with increased likelihood of sexual abuse. These data could be used to target preventive interventions at fathers who might be at increased risk for sexually abusing their daughters.

In a sample of men who had all sexually abused one or more of their daughters, Langevin and Watson (1991) compared biological fathers and stepfathers on a variety of characteristics of sexual history and personality. There were few differences between the two groups, which showed that biological fathers and stepfathers who sexually abuse their daughters did not differ in their penile responses to pictures (regardless of age and gender of the person in the picture), their sexual history, or their level of psychopathology based on the MMPI. Both groups of fathers showed a greater likelihood of penile response to pictures of children (pedophilia was indicated in 21.2% of the sample), higher rates of anxiety, and more disturbances in the family of origin than would be expected in a nonclinical control group. Overall, there were strikingly few differences between biological fathers and stepfathers who sexually abused their daughters.

Research has also addressed the perceptions of children's credibility when they report sexual abuse and the perceptions of responsibility for sexual abuse. In a study using vignettes that described children reporting sexual abuse by either their father or a stranger who denied the allegations, college students were most likely to believe that the child was telling the truth (O'Donohue, Elliott, Nickerson, & Valentine, 1992). Perceptions of believability were similar whether the alleged perpetrator was the father or a stranger, whether the hypothetical victim was female or male, and whether the victim was aged 5, 10, or 15 years. Female subjects were significantly more likely than male subjects to believe the child's allegations.

With regard to perceptions of responsibility for childhood sexual abuse, a number of studies have found that victims (Collings & Payne, 1991) and mothers (Bigras et al., 1991; Pierce, 1987; Ringwalt & Earp, 1988) are often held accountable for paternal sexual abuse. In a study of college students' reactions to vignettes that described father-daughter sexual abuse, Collings and Payne (1991) found that victims were held more responsible for the abuse if they reacted in a passive manner as opposed to a resistive manner, and older victims (15 years old) were consistently held more responsible for the sexual abuse than were younger victims (7 years old). Professionals often hold mothers responsible for paternal sexual abuse, with the implication that mothers either overtly or covertly facilitate the sexual abuse of their daughters (Bigras et al., 1991; Pierce, 1987; Ringwalt & Earp, 1988). Although mental health professionals may acknowledge that the primary fault lies with the abusive father, mothers are often held responsible for not preventing the sexual abuse of their daughters (Reidy & Hochstadt, 1993).

These examples of blaming the victim and blaming the mother for actions that are obviously under the control of fathers is quite disturbing. Because the culpability of victims of sexual abuse and the mothers of victims of father-daughter sexual abuse has not been empirically investigated and therefore not empirically established, researchers and clinicians should refrain from drawing implications of child or maternal culpability for paternal sexual abuse. In an interesting study that tested directly the assumptions about nonoffending mothers of sexually abused children, Deblinger, Hathaway, Lippmann, and Steer (1993) found that psychological symptoms and psychosocial characteristics did not differ for mothers whose child was sexually abused by the child's father, by another relative, or by a nonrelative. The only characteristic that differentiated these three groups of mothers was that mothers of children who were sexually abused by the child's father were more likely to have been physically abused by the child's father than were the mothers in the other two groups. This study highlights the risk that both mothers and children experience in a household with a sexually abusive father.

In summary, children who are sexually abused by their father or by their stepfather are at increased risk for the development of psychological problems. There is a need to investigate the effects of childhood sexual abuse in contrast to other types of physical abuse and neglect during childhood. In addition, to prevent such abuse, more research should be completed that addresses the mechanisms that lead to a child being at risk for paternal sexual abuse.

PATERNAL PHYSICAL ILLNESS

Along with investigating the functioning of children whose fathers experience psychological problems, it is also important to investigate the functioning of children whose fathers experience physical problems. However, only two studies were identified that specifically recruited fathers with a physical illness and assessed their children's psychological functioning (Baer, 1983; Rickard, 1988). Rickard (1988) recruited samples of fathers with chronic low back pain (CLBP), fathers with diabetes, and fathers with no known physical illness. When comparing the emotional/behavioral problems of the children of fathers in these three groups, children of fathers with CLBP were found to have higher self-reported and teacher-reported emotional/behavioral problems than children of either diabetic or physically healthy fathers. The heightened emotional/behavioral problems in children of CLBP fathers included increased levels of externalizing behavior problems, crying, whining, avoidance, physical complaints, dependency, greater external health locus of control, more days absent from school, and more visits to the school nurse.

In another study of children of fathers experiencing chronic physical illness, Baer (1983) assessed the parent-child interactions in families of fathers with and without hypertension. Overall, families with hypertensive fathers showed greater levels of negative nonverbal behaviors than control families in laboratory-based interactions. However, these differences appeared to be due to mother-child interactions rather than father-child interactions. For example, when gaze aversion was investigated, mothers, but not fathers or children, in families with a hypertensive father showed higher rates of gaze aversion than their counterparts in families without a hypertensive father. This heightened likelihood of maternal gaze aversion was evident prior to and after, but not during, negative and critical remarks made by the hypertensive father.

Although no empirical research has been conducted to date, an important issue for further research is children's physical and emotional health when their father is HIV-positive or is diagnosed with acquired immune deficiency syndrome (AIDS). Melvin and Sherr (1993) provided case studies of 18 children whose father and/or mother was diagnosed with AIDS or HIV infection. All these children were also HIV-positive or were diagnosed with AIDS. The case studies described the physical and emotional toll that this disease takes on family members. Until a vaccine or a cure is found for AIDS, children's coping with paternal or maternal AIDS as well as coping with their own AIDS will be an important area of research. Although there are too few studies to draw any overall conclusion about the psychological functioning of children with physically ill fathers, these studies indicate that this is a meaningful area for further research.

SUMMARY

Children of psychiatrically disturbed fathers are at increased risk for a variety of different types of psychopathology when compared with children whose fathers are not psychiatrically disturbed. This was found to be true for disorders that are more prevalent in men, such as alcohol abuse, as well as disorders that are more prevalent in women, such as major depressive disorder. In most cases, the degree of risk associated with paternal psychopathology has been found to be comparable to that associated with maternal psychopathology (Phares & Compas, 1992). Overall, it appears that paternal psychopathology represents a *sufficient* but not *necessary* condition for the development of psychopathology in children and adolescents. These results are summarized in Table 6.1.

TABLE 6.1. Findings from Research on Paternal Factors in Child and Adolescent Psychopathology: Studies of Referred or Diagnosed Fathers

Problem	Findings
Antisocial Personality Disorder	No studies were identified that compared APD fathers with controls, mothers, or other diagnostic groups.
Alcohol/Substance Abuse	Offspring of alcoholic fathers showed higher disturbance than offspring of control fathers (6 reviews, 23 studies with children and adolescents, 7 studies with adult offspring). Equivocal findings when comparing children of alcoholic fathers and mothers (7 studies). No differences identified between children of alcoholic fathers and children of fathers with other disorders (4 studies).

(Continued)

TABLE 6.1   *(Continued)*

Problem	Findings
Depression	Children of depressed fathers showed higher psychopathology than children of controls (9 studies); no differences found when compared with controls (4 studies). No differences in disturbance found between children of depressed fathers and children of depressed mothers (7 studies). Comorbidity of depression and another disorder, or having two disordered parents may raise the likelihood of child psychopathology (4 studies).
Anxiety Disorders	Children of anxious-depressed fathers showed more psychopathology than children of controls (1 study); children of fathers with PTSD showed more disturbance than children of fathers in control groups (2 studies). No differences between children of fathers and mothers who were anxious-depressed (1 study). No studies with other diagnostic groups.
Schizophrenia	Schizophrenic fathers perceived as less accepting and less involved than control fathers (1 study); equivocal evidence on EEG, brain abnormalities, and psychopathology (2 studies). Equivocal evidence on differences between children of schizophrenic fathers and mothers (3 studies). No studies with other diagnostic groups.
Physical and Sexual Abuse	Children who were physically abused by their father or mother and children who witnessed paternal aggression showed more disturbance than nonabused controls (4 studies); fathers and mothers who physically abuse their children showed more psychological disturbance than nonabusive parents (3 studies). Children who were sexually abused by their father or a father figure showed more disturbance than children who were sexually abused by a nonfather (4 reviews, 8 studies). No studies with other diagnostic groups.
Physical Illness	Children of physically ill fathers showed more disturbance than children of physically healthy fathers (2 studies). No other studies.

CHAPTER 7

Nonreferred Fathers and Children

Chapters 5 and 6 reviewed empirical research on paternal characteristics in clinical populations of children and fathers. However, a number of investigations have explored clinical issues in nonclinical populations in which neither the father nor the child has been referred for services. This chapter will review the empirical research literature investigating characteristics of nonreferred samples of fathers and their children. Unless otherwise noted, samples of children usually consist of approximately half boys and half girls. Nomenclature found within the studies will be used. A number of investigators do not follow the convention of denoting statistical significance at $p < .05$ and do not provide an explanation for using higher significance levels (such as $p < .07$ or $p < .10$). However, this chapter will only review findings that were significant at the $p < .05$ level, or lower if the authors used corrections to control for the number of analyses that were conducted.

DELINQUENCY

A number of behaviors associated with delinquency have been investigated in nonreferred samples of children and adolescents (Rothbaum & Weisz, 1994). The majority of research has been completed with boys, undoubtedly due to the assumption that aggressive and delinquent behaviors are more problematic for boys than for girls, and that boys are at greater risk for delinquency than girls (Elliot, Huizinga, & Ageton, 1985). Although it may be the case, this rationale should not preclude investigation of delinquency in both boys and girls. Of the six studies that were identified that investigated paternal characteristics in relation to children's and adolescents' delinquent behaviors, all but one investigated boys only.

In the study that included both boys and girls, Johnson (1987) surveyed over 700 high school sophomores in a community-based sample. Adolescents in the sample represented a wide range of socioeconomic status and ethnicity. For this study, delinquent behaviors that were assessed included different types of theft, property destruction, and personal assault. Drug and status offenses were not included in the assessment of delinquent behavior. Johnson found that girls as well as boys reported delinquent behavior although boys reported significantly more. Boys reported an average 6.6 delinquent acts and girls an average of 2.7 delinquent acts during the past year. A total of 65% of the boys and 40% of the girls reported at least one violation of the law within the last year, and 36% of the boys and 16% of the girls reported more than three law violations within the last year. Self-reported acts of delinquent behavior did not differ according to adolescents' ethnicity or socioeconomic status.

Johnson also investigated the adolescents' report of father-child and mother-child closeness and expression of anger in relation to adolescents' self-reported delinquency. He found that the father-child relationship had a greater association with adolescents' delinquent behavior than the mother-child relationship, especially for boys. Girls' delinquent behavior was inversely related to their perceptions of love from their mother and their father, and positively related to their anger toward their father. Girls' delinquent behavior was not significantly related to anger toward their mother, nor to perceptions of maternal or paternal attachment to the adolescent. Boys' delinquent behavior was inversely related to their perceptions of love from their mother, perceptions of love from their father, and feelings of closeness from their father. Boys' delinquent behavior was positively related to the anger they felt toward both their mother and father. Overall, boys and girls who felt low amounts of love from their mothers or fathers, boys and girls who felt high amounts of anger toward their father, boys who felt high amounts of anger toward their mother, and boys who felt low levels of closeness with their father were all involved in higher levels of delinquent behavior than other adolescents. Johnson summarized the findings by suggesting that, although there were no clear patterns of same-gender or opposite-gender effects for parents and children, both mothers' and fathers' relationships with their adolescents were significantly related to their sons' and daughters' delinquent behavior.

A number of other paternal and maternal characteristics have been investigated in relation to boys' delinquent and predelinquent behaviors. For example, in a sample of primarily Caucasian high school boys, Neapolitan (1981) found that both fathers' and mothers' support for aggressive behavior (teaching adolescents how to fight, encouraging the use of aggression, and teaching the importance of defending oneself) was associated with adolescents' self-reports of aggressive behavior. In a study of father-son relationships and adolescents' self-reported violent behavior, Brownfield (1987) found that paternal employment and adolescents' ability to share thoughts, feelings, and future plans with their fathers were associated with decreased levels of fighting and assault in both African American and Caucasian American adolescents. In fact, even when fathers had a history of unemployment, if boys were able to share their future plans with their fathers, they showed somewhat lower levels of violent behavior.

The previous studies all relied on adolescents' own reports of parental characteristics and their own delinquent behavior. In a series of studies conducted by Loeber and colleagues (Loeber & Dishion, 1984; Stouthamer-Loeber &

Loeber, 1986), parent and teacher reports of the behavior of 4th-, 7th-, and 10th-grade boys were utilized to investigate the relation between parental characteristics and boys' delinquent behavior. Loeber and Dishion (1984) found that boys who fight at both school and home received lower levels of paternal and maternal acceptance than boys who fight only at school, boys who fight only at home, and boys who did not fight at all. Paternal and maternal rejection were associated with higher levels of lying in 4th- and 7th-grade boys, and maternal but not paternal rejection was associated with higher levels of lying in 10th-grade boys. Boys' lying was significantly related to the socioeconomic status of the family. Because the majority (99.4%) of the boys in this sample were Caucasian American, analyses of racial and ethnic similarities and differences were not feasible. These studies suggest that paternal and maternal rejection (or lack of acceptance) is associated with the delinquent behaviors of fighting and lying. In addition, fathers' and mothers' effective parenting was significantly related to their sons' self-restraint, which in turn was related to decreased delinquent behavior up to 4 years later (Feldman & Weinberger, 1994).

Overall, paternal and maternal characteristics appear to show similar patterns of relations to children's and adolescents' predelinquent and delinquent behavior in nonreferred samples. As noted in reference to Johnson's (1987) research, although boys showed more delinquent behavior than girls, a total of 40% of girls in the sample reported violating at least one law within the past year. Although the prevalence of law violations may be higher in boys, Johnson's study suggested that the prevalence of girls' delinquent behavior is high enough to warrant investigation in its own right. As with any self-reports, adolescents' self-reports of delinquent behavior must be viewed with caution. Even though adolescents provided responses anonymously in the samples that used self-reports, it is possible that the adolescents' self-reports were not accurate. However, for the purposes of comparing paternal and maternal characteristics in relation to children's and adolescents' delinquent behavior, there is no reason to believe that adolescents' potentially inaccurate self-reports would differ in relation to the paternal and maternal characteristics that were assessed.

In contrast to studies that used self-reports and parental reports of delinquent behavior, an alternative strategy can be used to observe directly behavior that is related to delinquency in adolescents. In an observational study of aggressive behavior in young adolescents and their families, Inoff-Germain et al. (1988) assessed hormonal levels in adolescents to determine fluctuations in aggressiveness toward their fathers and mothers. They found that, for girls, higher levels of estradiol and androstenedione were associated with higher levels of aggressiveness toward their parents, including showing explosiveness, trying to dominate, showing defiance, and expressing anger toward their fathers and mothers. Hormonal levels were not meaningfully related to boys' aggressiveness toward their parents. This study highlights the possibility of using alternative research strategies to investigate behaviors related to delinquency in nonreferred samples of adolescents.

ALCOHOL AND SUBSTANCE USE

Similar to the studies of referred children and referred fathers, there have been quite a number of investigations into fathers' characteristics and their children's drinking behavior. Research on the relations between parents and children seems to follow along gender lines of behavior, with huge numbers of studies conducted with mothers and children on depression and quite a number of studies conducted with fathers and children on drinking behavior (Phares, 1992). This pattern seems to reflect the base lines of these characteristics in adult women and men (and therefore mothers and fathers). Although this explanation may help make sense out of the large numbers of depression studies completed with mothers and alcohol studies completed with fathers, it is no excuse to continue this pattern of research.

Of the studies that have investigated paternal characteristics and the use of alcohol by their children and adolescents, a number have shown significant relations between fathers' drinking and children's drinking. In a study of alcohol consumption by sixth and eighth graders, Forney and colleagues (1984) found that adolescents who showed excessive amounts of drinking tended to have fathers who also showed excessive amounts of drinking. Kafka and London (1991) found similar results in a sample of high school students who were from working-class and middle-class families. Similar results of father-son connections for heavy drinking were found in a sample of nearly 4,000 adolescents in Australia (Cumes-Rayner, Lucke, Singh, & Adler, 1992). Fathers' alcohol use was significantly correlated with adolescents' self-reported alcohol use, as well as adolescents' use of cigarettes, marijuana, cocaine, and "other drugs." In an ethnically diverse sample from Los Angeles, Fawzy, Coombs, and Gerber (1983) found that paternal drinking of beer, wine, and hard liquor were all associated with greater substance use in adolescents. Interestingly, the association with drinking hard liquor appeared to be curvilinear, with the highest percentage of substance-using adolescents having fathers who drink moderate amounts rather than large or small amounts of hard liquor. In a series of studies by Barnes and colleagues (Barnes, 1984; Barnes, Farrell, & Cairns, 1986), adolescents' drinking was not significantly related to paternal alcohol use; however, there were significant relations between adolescents' drinking and fathers' socialization practices. Adolescents who showed high rates of drinking tended to have fathers who provided low amounts of support and nurturance to their children. The same pattern of maternal socialization practices was also found, whereby adolescents with higher levels of drinking had mothers who showed lower levels of support and nurturance to their children. Heavy drinking by male college students was associated with growing up with a father who was a heavy drinker (Barnes, Welte, & Dintcheff, 1992).

In a similar study of parental socialization practices and adolescents' substance use, Coombs and Landsverk (1988) found a similar pattern of results as

Barnes and colleagues. The sample consisted of over 400 children and adolescents, ranging from 9 to 17 years, with a wide representation of socioeconomic classes and ethnicities. The study investigated "substance use" and collapsed children's and adolescents' use of alcohol and drugs into one variable. A stepwise multiple regression was conducted to ascertain the predictive relations of fathers' and mothers' parenting style (closeness to parent, wanting to be like parent, parental trust, parental encouragement and praise, talking with parent about personal problems, parental rules, parental strictness, and dependence on parent for advice and guidance) and demographic variables (age, sex, ethnicity, and social class) on children's and adolescents' substance use. Of all of the variables just noted, only four explained more than 1% of the variance in adolescents' substance use: age, positive father sentiment, number of conduct rules, and dependence on mother's advice. These four variables accounted for 31% of the variance in adolescents' substance use. Children's and adolescents' substance use is higher when the children are older, when their fathers show little positive sentiment, when there are lower numbers of conduct rules, and when they show lower levels of dependence on their mothers for advice. The pattern of findings was similar regardless of the ethnicity of the child or adolescent.

In a nationally representative sample of Latino and Latina adolescents aged 12 to 17, fathers' and mothers' use of licit and illicit drugs was related to their adolescents' drug use (Gfroerer & delaRosa, 1993). There was also evidence to suggest that adolescents were at higher risk for drug use when their parents were more acculturated into American society.

Kandel (1990) provided an interesting study that examined fathers' and mothers' history of alcohol and substance abuse and their current child-rearing practices. Because most of the children in this study were less than 11 years old, the investigator did not analyze children's drinking or drug use. However, children's emotional and behavioral functioning was examined in relation to fathers' and mothers' substance abuse history. Fathers' heavy drinking and drug use during the past year were significantly related to fathers' reports of greater amounts of discussion with their children, and greater levels of positive involvement with their children. Fathers' drug use during the past year was also correlated with children's positive behavioral relations and low levels of detachment. Kandel noted that these correlations were in the opposite direction as might be expected, but could not provide a reason why this might have occurred in this sample. More in line with what might be expected, fathers' lifetime drug use was associated with lower levels of affection toward their children, lower levels of children's positive behavior toward their fathers, and lower levels of child independence. Mothers' patterns of drinking and drug use were more consistent with the hypotheses of the study. For example, mothers' heavy drinking during the past year was associated with less expression of closeness toward their children and more control problems exhibited by their children. Mothers' drug use during the past year was associated with lower levels of supervision of their children and more control problems exhibited by their children. Mothers' lifetime drug use was associated with lower levels of positive involvement with their children and more control problems exhibited by their children.

Although Kandel summarized these data by suggesting that maternal drinking and substance abuse were more consistently related to poor parenting and poor behavior on the part of the children, the conflicting results based on fathers' reports of drinking, drug use, parenting behavior, and children's functioning should not be dismissed. There are a growing number of studies with paternal findings that are counterintuitive based on previous results that were established with mothers (e.g., see the Depression section in this chapter for the discussion of results by Thomas & Forehand, 1991). Before these counterintuitive results are discarded, further research should attempt to replicate these studies and to investigate the meaning of these findings.

Along with these investigations of alcohol and substance use in samples of children and their parents, a number of studies have been conducted to ascertain the relations between paternal characteristics and marijuana use in male and female college students. Brook and colleagues (Brook, Whiteman, Brook, & Gordon, 1982; Brook, Whiteman, Gordon, & Brook, 1983, 1984a, 1984b, 1986) provided a series of papers based on a study of 403 female college students and 246 male college students and their fathers. Overall, Brook and colleagues found that daughters' and sons' marijuana use showed similar patterns in relation to their fathers' characteristics. Paternal child-rearing practices and paternal personality characteristics showed direct and indirect relations to daughters' and sons' marijuana use, with different patterns emerging depending on the other predictor variables included in the analyses. Specifically, even after controlling for the mother-son relationship, Brook, Whiteman et al. (1983) found that fathers' personality and child-rearing practices were significantly related to their son's marijuana use. However, fathers' personality and child-rearing practices also interacted with sons' peer relationships in the prediction of sons' marijuana use (Brook et al., 1982). These patterns have also been found between fathers' characteristics and their daughters' marijuana use (Brook et al., 1984b, 1986).

Taken together, these studies show relatively consistent associations between fathers' drinking, fathers' parenting behavior, and adolescents' substance use in community samples. Most notably, higher levels of positive paternal sentiment, support, and nurturance have been associated with lower levels of drug and alcohol use in children and adolescents. Most of these findings are similar to those reported in Chapters 5 and 6 with samples of referred children and referred fathers. Therefore, even when children or fathers do not show clinically significant levels of substance use, or when they are not referred for their substance use, fathers' characteristics likely are still important in understanding children's and adolescents' alcohol and drug use.

NONSPECIFIC BEHAVIOR PROBLEMS

A variety of characteristics of fathers and mothers have been investigated in relation to children's and adolescents' emotional/behavioral functioning. Because these are nonreferred samples, the studies have often been conducted without a specific diagnostic focus. The studies in this area can be categorized into three different areas of focus: Parental behavior and children's sociometric status, parental behavior and children's emotional/behavioral problems, and parental psychological symptoms and children's emotional/ behavioral problems.

Parental Behavior and Children's Sociometric Status

A number of studies have investigated paternal and maternal behavior in relation to children's peer ratings of sociometric status in preschools and elementary schools. MacDonald (1987) measured the sociometric status of preschool boys and then videotaped the boys at home with their fathers and mothers for 20 minutes each. Physical play behavior between parents and boys was a primary focus of this investigation, so if play behavior was not elicited within the first 10 minutes of the observation session, the research assistant told the parent-child dyad "I am interested also in physical play between parents and children, activities like tickling, wrestling, or chasing, if that is something you normally do with your child. If not, you can continue with your present activity or switch to an activity of your choice" (MacDonald, 1987, p. 706). The videotapes were coded for eight categories of parent and child behavior: Parent and child verbal behavior, parent and child direct commands, parent and child suggestions, parent and child questions, physical play, approach stimulation, avoid stimulation, and overstimulation.

The overall comparisons between fathers and mothers showed that fathers scored higher than mothers on all of the variables related to physical play. This finding is consistent with the research discussed in Chapters 1 and 2 (e.g., Parke & Tinsley, 1981) that suggested fathers relate to their children through more playful means than do mothers. With regard to children's sociometric status and parental behavior, MacDonald (1987) found a number of differences in fathers' and mothers' behaviors during the observation session that were related to boys' peer-rated sociometric status. Fathers of neglected boys were less likely than fathers of rejected or popular boys to have boys seek "approach stimulation" (boys initiated play behaviors with their father), and conversely fathers of neglected boys were more likely to be avoided by their neglected boys than were fathers of rejected or popular boys. Fathers of rejected boys were more likely to overstimulate their sons than were fathers of neglected or popular boys. In general, fathers of neglected boys showed significantly less affectively arousing physical play than fathers of rejected or popular boys. Only two significant findings were related to mothers' behavior and their sons' so-ciometric status. Mothers, but not fathers, showed higher levels of parental di-recting with their rejected boys than with their neglected or popular boys, and mothers of neglected boys asked significantly more questions of their children than mothers of rejected or popular boys. The remaining studies that investi-gated children's sociometric status were conducted with boys and girls.

In contrast to observing play interactions between preschool children and their parents as just described, Roopnarine and Adams (1987) observed par-ents' teaching strategies during a puzzle task with their children. They found that fathers and mothers of moderately popular and unpopular children used fewer suggestions and explanations during the puzzle task than fathers and mothers of popular children. For both unpopular children and moderately pop-ular children, mothers were significantly more likely to use explanations and to ask questions to aid their children during the puzzle task than were fathers. With regard to the questions that were asked and the suggestions that were made by parents, children were more likely to respond in an "off-task" man-ner after their mothers' questions than after their fathers' questions. This "off-task" behavior in response to mothers was evident for unpopular, moderately popular, and popular children.

Peery, Jensen, and Adams (1985) conducted a study that investigated how fathers' and mothers' child-rearing attitudes differed according to their pre-school childrens' sociometric status. The findings for fathers and mothers showed somewhat different patterns of child-rearing attitudes. Fathers of iso-lated and rejected children were more likely than fathers of popular and amiable children to show child-rearing attitudes that reflected low levels of interaction with children, dislike of children's intrusive behavior, definite expectations about their children's behavior, and a strong belief that child rearing is a mother's duty. In contrast, mothers of isolated and rejected children were more likely than mothers of popular and amiable children to show child-rearing atti-tudes that failed to promote a sense of independence in their children, that showed infrequent praise for children's good conduct, and that showed poor self-concepts about the maternal role. Based on a discriminant function analysis, fa-thers' child-rearing attitudes correctly identified children's sociometric status in 44% of the cases and mothers' child-rearing attitudes correctly categorized children in 49% of the cases. Overall, the four sociometric categories accounted for 62% of the variance in paternal child-rearing attitudes and 42% of the vari-ance in maternal child-rearing attitudes. This study highlighted the relations between fathers' and mothers' perceptions of their child-rearing role and their preschool children's peer-rated sociometric status.

To investigate the relations between parent-child relationships and socio-metric ratings of children older than preschool age, Patterson, Kupersmidt, and Griesler (1990) investigated children from the third and fourth grades. The sample of over 500 children was ethnically diverse. The researchers assessed sociometric status, and children's self-reported relationships with their father, mother, best friend, and teacher. Significant relations between sociometric status and children's relationships with their father and best friend were found. However, significant relations did not emerge between sociometric status and children's self-reported relationships with their mother or their teacher.

Children who were classified as rejected reported significantly less affection from their father, less companionship with their father, and less satisfaction in the father-child relationship than did popular children. In addition, rejected children reported feeling less satisfied with the father-child relationship than did neglected children. There were no differences based on sociometric status with regard to perceived instrumental aid from fathers, intimacy with fathers, or conflict with fathers. Patterson and colleagues highlighted the importance of the father-child relationship in children's sociometric status vis-à-vis their peers.

Dekovic and Janssens (1992) conducted a study of sociometric status in children attending first, third, or fifth grade in the Netherlands. Parents' child-rearing styles were measured according to the amount of authoritative/democratic behaviors they used with their children (e.g., positive remarks, support suggestions, warmth, and responsiveness) and the amount of authoritarian/restrictive behaviors they used with their children (e.g., negative remarks, prohibitions, directives, power assertion, and restrictiveness). Children's sociometric status was assessed by peer ratings of their social preference (e.g., positive nominations). Children were perceived as more popular by their peers when their fathers and mothers showed greater levels of authoritative/democratic parenting behaviors and children were perceived as less popular by their peers when their fathers and mothers showed greater levels of authoritarian/restrictive parenting behaviors. This study suggested a robust connection between parenting style and children's sociometric status with their peers.

In another study of sociometric status in elementary school, East (1991) conducted a study of sixth graders and their parents. The sample was primarily middle class and represented a variety of ethnicities. The peer-reported sociometric ratings classified children into one of three groups: withdrawn, aggressive, and sociable. Fathers, mothers, and children reported on the parent-child relationship, which was assessed on three dimensions: Warmth/closeness, support, and satisfaction. In a comprehensive analysis of parents' and children's perspectives on these issues, East provided fathers', mothers', and children's ratings of the parent-child relationship for boys and girls separately. Based on children's reports of their fathers, withdrawn girls reported lower levels of warmth/closeness than aggressive and sociable girls and lower levels of support than sociable girls. Girls' ratings of their satisfaction with their fathers did not differ according to children's sociometric status. Aggressive boys reported lower levels of paternal warmth/closeness, support, and satisfaction than withdrawn and sociable boys. Girls' and boys' ratings of their relationship with their mother did not differ according to children's sociometric categorization.

Somewhat similar results were found when fathers' and mothers' reports of the parent-child relationship were analyzed in the same study. Mothers of withdrawn children reported lower levels of support for their children than mothers of aggressive and sociable children, and mothers of withdrawn and aggressive children showed lower levels of satisfaction with the parent-child relationship than mothers of sociable children. Mothers' reports of warmth/closeness with their children did not differ according to their children's sociometric status. Fathers of aggressive children showed lower levels of warmth/closeness with their children than fathers of sociable children and also showed lower levels of satisfaction with the parent-child relationship than fathers of withdrawn and sociable children. Fathers' ratings of support for their children did not differ according to their children's sociometric status.

In summary, these studies of peer ratings of children's sociometric status suggest that many aspects of fathers' and mothers' behavior and attitudes are related to children's sociometric status. There were significant associations for fathers' and mothers' play behavior, teaching strategies, parental child-rearing attitudes, and parent-child relationships with regard to children's relationships with peers. Although it is tempting to interpret these data as causal in nature (parental behavior leads to children's sociometric status), the parental behavior elicited in the observation sessions and the parental attitudes and behavior that were reported through questionnaires may have been in response to their children's behavior, rather than the reverse. More research is needed to ascertain the causal link between children's sociometric status and parents' attitudes and behavior. These studies suggest that paternal and maternal characteristics are related to children's sociometric status in somewhat similar ways. However, there are enough differences in the relations between fathers' and mothers' behavior and their children's sociometric status that it appears worthwhile to continue to investigate fathers and mothers separately, rather than assuming that one parent can serve as a proxy for the other.

Parental Behavior and Children's Emotional/Behavioral Problems

Fathers' and mothers' parenting behavior and parental style have been investigated in relation to children's and adolescents' maladjustment. In a study of preschool children's temperament and parental behavior, Nelson and Simmerer (1984) found that fathers' parenting behavior was related to their children's temperament. Fathers' involvement, reasoning guidance, limit setting, responsiveness, and intimacy were positively correlated with their children's adaptability and negatively correlated with their children's intensity. In addition, fathers' level of intimacy as a parent was positively associated with children's tendency to approach their father. Fathers' parenting behavior was not related to their children's activity level, mood, or persistence. None of the child temperament behaviors that were assessed in this study were significantly associated with any of mothers' parenting behavior.

Based on teachers' and peers' reports of children's psychosocial adjustment, Stollak and colleagues (1982) found that fathers' but not mothers' interpersonal perceptual style (degree of inaccuracy in perceptions of children's behavior) was associated with their third grader's adjustment. Fathers of "adequate" or "highly adjusted" children showed lower levels of negatively biased perceptions than fathers of "problem" children. In contrast, Kendall and Fischler (1984) found that neither fathers' nor mothers' interpersonal cognitive problem-solving skills (means-end thinking, consequential thinking, generation of alternative solutions, and identified obstacles) were significantly related to their 6- to 11-year-old children's emotional/behavioral problems. This lack of significant associations was true whether teachers or parents reported on the children's emotional/behavioral problems.

Parenting behavior has also been investigated through retrospective reports of college students using either the Children's Report of Parental Behavior Inventory (CRPBI; Schludermann & Schludermann, 1970) to assess college students' recollections of paternal and maternal parenting behavior, or the Parental Authority Questionnaire that was derived from Baumrind's (1971) parental authority prototypes. In a study of female college undergraduates and their parents, Phares (in press) investigated risk and protective factors related to daughters' psychological adjustment and reports of parenting behavior on the CRPBI. Daughters' psychological symptoms were significantly related to fathers' and mothers' parenting behavior of psychological control and paternal and maternal psychological symptoms, and inversely related to paternal and maternal acceptance. Daughters' global self-worth was significantly related to paternal acceptance and inversely related to paternal and maternal psychological control. In regression analyses, daughters' psychological symptoms were significantly predicted by higher paternal and maternal psychological control, lower paternal global self-worth, and higher paternal and maternal psychological symptoms. Daughters' self-worth was predicted by higher levels of paternal acceptance and lower levels of maternal psychological control. This study suggested that paternal and maternal psychological control and paternal and maternal psychological symptoms were significant risk factors in the development of daughters' psychological problems. Additionally, fathers' global self-worth was found to be a protective factor against development of their daughters' psychological problems, and paternal acceptance appeared to enhance the development of global self-worth in daughters.

In contrast to these results, Eastburg and Johnson (1990) found that daughters' recollections of their mothers' parenting behavior, but not their fathers' parenting behavior, were related to daughters' current level of social reticence

and shyness. Maternal acceptance and encouragement of psychological autonomy were associated with lower levels of daughters' shyness during their first
year in college. Daughters' ratings of maternal control when they were growing up were not related to their current level of shyness. None of the three factors of parenting behavior exhibited by fathers (acceptance, encouragement of
psychological autonomy, control) were significantly related to daughters' ratings of shyness. Because male college students did not participate in this study,
it is difficult to determine whether same-gender parent-child associations were
more prevalent. Although the study by Eastburg and Johnson suggested that fathers' parenting behavior was not associated with their daughters' shyness,
Musser and Fleck (1983) found that fathers' parenting behavior was associated
with their college student daughters' personality adjustment. Based on retrospective reports of parenting behavior and current reports of daughters' personality adjustment, fathers' greater acceptance and control were positively
correlated with daughters' better personality adjustment. Fathers' encouragement of psychological autonomy was not analyzed and no ratings of mothers'
parenting behavior were collected for this sample.

In a study that used the Parental Authority Questionnaire with a sample of
both female and male undergraduate students, Buri, Louiselle, Misukanis, and
Mueller (1988) found somewhat stronger associations between parental behavior and daughters' self-esteem in contrast to sons' self-esteem. For both
daughters and sons, paternal and maternal authoritarianism were associated
with lower levels of self-esteem, whereas both paternal and maternal authoritativeness were associated with higher levels of self-esteem. When regression
analyses were conducted, paternal and maternal authoritarianism and authoritativeness accounted for over twice the variance in daughters' self-esteem than
in sons' self-esteem.

Taken together, these studies suggest that fathers' parenting behavior is important to consider at any stage of children's development, from preschool
through college. It is interesting to note that fathers' parenting behavior had a
stronger relation to children's behavioral adjustment than mothers' parenting
behavior when young children were investigated (Nelson & Simmerer, 1984;
Stollak et al., 1982). However, when samples of college students were used,
both fathers' and mothers' parenting behavior were associated with their offsprings' adjustment. There are too few studies to suggest differing influence of
parenting behavior at different developmental levels.

Parental Psychological Symptoms and Children's
Emotional/Behavioral Problems

In Chapters 5 and 6, a number of studies were reviewed that investigated
the connection between fathers' and children's psychological functioning in

samples of referred children and referred fathers. There has also been research into the connection between fathers', mothers' and children's psychological functioning in samples of nonreferred families.

In an investigation into the impact of fathers' and mothers' psychological symptoms on their ratings of their young adolescents' emotional/behavioral problems, Phares and colleagues (1989) found that fathers' and mothers' symptoms were modestly associated with their own reports of their children's emotional/behavioral problems as well as their children's self-reports of their emotional/behavioral problems. In addition, both fathers' and mothers' symptoms were significant predictors of their ratings of their children's emotional/behavioral problems. Jensen, Traylor, Xenakis, and Davis (1988) also found that both fathers' and mothers' self-reported psychological symptoms were associated with their children's emotional/behavior problems.

Compas, Phares, Banez, and Howell (1991) investigated the correlates of internalizing and externalizing problems in young adolescents and found that fathers of adolescents in the clinical range of self-reported adolescent internalizing and externalizing behavior problems reported more psychological symptoms than fathers of adolescents in a normative control group. Maternal psychological symptoms significantly differentiated between groups only when maternal reports of adolescent internalizing and externalizing behavior problems were utilized as the criterion, and not when adolescents' self-reports were used as the criterion.

In contrast to these studies that found consistent relations between fathers', mothers', and children's psychological symptoms, Forehand, Long, Brody, and Fauber (1986) found that children's conduct problems were related to their mothers' but not their fathers' self-reported depressive symptoms. They did find however, that both fathers' and mothers' reports of conflict with their children were significantly related to their children's conduct problems.

In a series of studies completed with a community-based sample in Puerto Rico, conflicting findings as to the strength of paternal and maternal psychological symptoms and children's psychological functioning emerged. Bird, Gould, Yager, Staghezza, and Canino (1989) found that children's impaired adaptive functioning and their propensity to meet criteria for a psychiatric diagnosis were associated with mothers', but not fathers', psychiatric history. Paternal psychiatric history was found to be associated with children's diagnoses of overanxious disorder when socioeconomic status (SES) and the mothers' psychiatric history were statistically controlled (Velez, Johnson, & Cohen, 1989). Maternal psychiatric history was found to be associated with children's diagnoses of oppositional disorder and major depression when SES and the fathers' psychiatric history were statistically controlled.

In summary, these studies show that fathers' and mothers' psychological symptoms are related to children's emotional/behavioral problems. Fathers' and mothers' psychological symptoms seemed to act as risk factors for children's adjustment problems, even when the psychological symptoms in the family were not severe enough to warrant therapeutic intervention.

DEPRESSION

There have been a number of investigations into the relation between fathers' characteristics and depression in their offspring. The bulk of this research has been completed with college students or retrospective reports of young adults, rather than by actually assessing depression in young children and adolescents. No studies were identified that investigated paternal characteristics in relation to depressive symptoms in children younger than 11 years old.

Studies of Adolescents

Nine studies were identified that investigated paternal characteristics and adolescents' depressive symptoms. Of these nine studies, six showed significant relations between paternal characteristics and adolescents' depressive-type symptoms (Forehand & Smith, 1986; Gallimore & Kurdek, 1992; Koestner, Zuroff, & Powers, 1991; Tannenbaum & Forehand, 1993; Thomas & Forehand, 1991; Wright, 1985); one study showed weak effects between fathers' depressive symptoms and adolescents' depressive symptoms (Hops, 1992); and two did not show significant relations between paternal characteristics and adolescents' depressive symptoms (Kashani, Burbach, & Rosenberg, 1988; Seligman et al., 1984). In a study of depressive symptoms within the families of young adolescent girls, Forehand and Smith (1986) found that fathers' reports of depressive symptoms on the Beck Depression Inventory (BDI) were significantly related to their daughters' reports of depressive symptoms on the Children's Depression Inventory (CDI). Mothers' BDI scores were not significantly related to their daughters' depressive symptoms. Similar results were found by Gallimore and Kurdek (1992) who studied depressive symptoms in young adolescents aged 13 or 14 years. Although they included both boys and girls in their sample, 26 of the 35 adolescents who took part in the study were girls. For the entire sample of adolescents, Gallimore and Kurdek found that adolescents' self-reported depressive symptoms on the CDI were significantly related to fathers' self-reported depressive symptoms on the BDI but only showed a nonsignificant trend in relation to mothers' self-reported depressive symptoms on the BDI.

Thomas and Forehand (1991) investigated parental depressive symptoms in relation to adolescents' functioning based on teachers' reports. Mothers and fathers provided their own self-reports of depressive symptoms and teachers provided reports of young adolescents' conduct problems, anxiety/withdrawal, and cognitive competence. Based on parental reports of depressive symptoms, 9%

of the mothers and 21% of the fathers fell in the clinical range of the BDI. For adolescent boys, fathers' depressive symptoms were positively related to their sons' anxiety/withdrawal problems and were negatively associated with their sons' cognitive competence. Fathers who showed higher levels of depressive symptoms had sons who showed higher levels of anxiety and withdrawal, and lower levels of cognitive competence. There were no significant relations between mothers' depressive symptoms and their sons' behavior or cognitive competence. Mothers' depressive symptoms were positively related to their daughters' problems with anxiety/withdrawal, but not to their daughters' levels of conduct problems or cognitive competence. Fathers' depressive mood was positively associated with their daughters' cognitive competence but was not significantly related to their daughters' emotional and behavioral functioning. Thus, higher levels of depressive mood in fathers were associated with greater cognitive competence in adolescent females. Although this may appear counterintuitive, Thomas and Forehand (1991) discuss the research by Radin (1981b; see Chapter 2 for discussion) that suggests fathers' greater involvement with their daughters may serve to limit their daughters cognitive functioning. This explanation is only speculative and requires further examination. In additional regression analyses of these data, Thomas and Forehand found that fathers' depressive symptoms accounted for 7% of unique variance to the explanation of girls' conduct problems, added 22% of unique variance to the explanation of boys' cognitive competence, and added 7% of unique variance to boys' levels of anxiety and withdrawal. Thomas and Forehand summarized these findings by highlighting the importance of paternal rather than maternal depressive symptoms in relation to adolescents' behavioral and cognitive functioning.

Tannenbaum and Forehand (1993) provided an interesting investigation into the possible buffering effects of a good father-child relationship on the potentially maladaptive effects of maternal depression. They found that when young adolescents were exposed to heightened levels of maternal depression, they did not show increased internalizing and externalizing behavioral problems if they also had a close and stable relationship with their father. This buffering effect of a positive father-child relationship will be important to consider in future research on children's functioning in the context of maternal psychopathology. In addition, parallel studies should be conducted that investigate the possible buffering effect of a positive mother-child relationship when children are exposed to paternal psychopathology.

Suicidal ideation and self-criticism are often associated with depressive symptoms in adolescents. To study the specific symptom of suicidal ideation, Wright (1985) investigated the relation between high school seniors' self-reports of suicidal ideation and their reports of poor father-child relationship, poor mother-child relationship, and fathers' and mothers' drinking problems and permissiveness. A total of 10.6% of the sample of 207 high school seniors responded "yes" to the question, "Have you seriously considered a suicide attempt during the last 6 months?" Based on a chi-square analysis, there was not a significant difference in the number of boys versus girls who reported suicidal thoughts. Parental characteristics of adolescents who experienced suicidal ideation were compared with parental characteristics of adolescents who did not report experiencing suicidal ideation. Adolescents who reported suicidal ideation were significantly more likely to have a poor father-child relationship and to have a father with an alcohol problem than adolescents who did not report suicidal ideation. Suicidal thoughts were not related to a poor mother-child relationship, maternal drinking problems, nor to mothers' or fathers' permissiveness. Suicidal ideation has also been found to be related to low levels of paternal and maternal social support in both male and female adolescents (deMan, Labreche-Gauthier, & Leduc, 1993).

To determine the origins of self-criticism in young adolescents, Koestner and colleagues (1991) investigated the relation between parenting behavior that was assessed when the adolescents were 5 years old and self-criticism when the adolescents were 12 years old. Ratings of fathers' and mothers' parenting behavior were provided by mothers. Based on these ratings, paternal restrictiveness and paternal rejection were significantly related to boys' but not girls' self-criticism that was assessed 7 years later. Maternal restrictiveness and maternal rejection were significantly related to girls' but not boys' self-criticism. These patterns were still evident when children's early temperaments were controlled through partial correlations. Koestner and colleagues summarized the study by highlighting the apparent impact of negative parenting on same-gender children. Although the pattern of same-gender parent-child influences is evident in this study and is suggested by the results of Thomas and Forehand (1991), other studies also show cross-gender parent-child influences (e.g., Forehand & Smith, 1986).

Taken together, these studies show strong relations between paternal characteristics and adolescent depressive symptoms, suicidal ideation, and self-critical feelings. The longitudinal study by Hops (1992) found a strong connection between mothers' and daughters' fluctuations in depressive symptoms but found a weaker connection in the fluctuations of fathers' and sons' depressive symptoms. Two studies that investigated paternal characteristics and young adolescents' depressive symptoms failed to find significant associations. Seligman and colleagues (1984) did not find significant relations between young adolescents' depressive symptoms and their fathers' depressive symptoms or attributional styles. Conversely, young adolescents' depressive symptoms were significantly related to their mothers' depressive symptoms and attributional styles. Kashani and colleagues (1988) found a similar pattern of nonsignificant relations between young adolescents and their fathers with significant relations between young adolescents and their mothers. Adolescents' depressive symptoms were not significantly related to their fathers' methods of conflict resolution in the family, but were significantly related to adolescents' and mothers' methods of conflict resolution. Based on these studies that investigated depressive symptoms in nonclinical adolescent populations, there is relatively strong evidence for a link between fathers' and adolescents' depressive symptoms.

Studies of Older Adolescents and Young Adults

A number of studies have been completed with "older adolescents" (college students) and young adults as informants of their depressive symptoms. In a longitudinal study that assessed maternal and paternal rejection of children at the age of 8 and then assessed children's depressive symptoms 11 years later, significant relations were found for fathers but not mothers. Lefkowitz and Tesiny (1984) found that paternal rejection when children were 8 years old significantly predicted older adolescents' depressive symptoms when they were 19 years old. This predictive association remained significant even when characteristics of the mother-child relationship were controlled. Lefkowitz and Tesiny reported on two additional cross-sectional studies; however, only maternal and not paternal data were collected in those studies.

Richman and Flaherty (1987) combined a longitudinal approach with retrospective reports in a sample of first-year medical students. They had the students provide current reports of their depressive symptoms and retrospective reports of parental behavior during their childhood. Data were collected at the beginning and the end of the academic year. After controlling for depressive symptoms at the beginning of the academic year, depressive symptoms at the end of the academic year were significantly related to retrospective recollections of paternal affection, paternal overprotection, and maternal overprotection. This study showed a somewhat stronger association between paternal rather than maternal parenting characteristics and later depressive symptoms in a sample of medical school students.

To investigate self-criticism and dependency as sources of vulnerability to depression, McCranie and Bass (1984) obtained retrospective reports of parental behavior during childhood and current reports of self-criticism and dependency in a sample of young women. They found that fathers' use of strict control, inconsistency of love, and achievement control during childhood were correlated with self-criticism in young adulthood. No paternal parental behaviors were significantly associated with current levels of dependency. Both self-criticism and dependency were related to some aspects of maternal parenting behavior.

Turning now to cross-sectional studies of college students, additional analyses in the previously discussed study by Wright (1985) should be mentioned. Wright not only investigated high school students' levels of suicidal ideation in relation to paternal and maternal characteristics (as already stated), but also investigated these issues within a sample of college students. In a sample of 901 college students, Wright found that 6.4% reported having serious suicidal ideation within the past 6 months. There were no gender differences in the reports of suicidal ideation. Students who reported suicidal thoughts were significantly more likely to have a poor relationship with their father than were students who did not report suicidal thoughts. Paternal permissiveness and paternal problem drinking did not differ between suicidal and nonsuicidal students. No significant differences were evident when mother-child relationship, maternal permissiveness, and maternal drinking problems were analyzed.

In a sample of women from the United States and from India, Luthar and Quinlan (1993) found that both groups of women showed more depressive symptoms when they reported higher levels of paternal intrusiveness and lower levels of maternal caring when they were growing up. Similar results were found in a sample from the Netherlands (Kerver, Van-Son, & deGroot, 1992). Low levels of paternal affection and high levels of maternal overinvolvement were associated with later development of depressive symptoms.

Through prescreening of large numbers of college students, Edell and Kaslow (1991) identified a group of anhedonic participants and a group of nondistressed participants who served as a control group. Participants completed a retrospective measure of paternal and maternal acceptance of childhood dependent and independent behaviors. Participants were also asked to represent symbolically their family structure with the Kvebaek Family Sculpture Technique (Cromwell, Fournier, & Kvebaek, 1980). When compared with the control group, anhedonic participants reported lower levels of support and approval from their mothers, and they felt greater disinterest from their mothers with regard to dependent behaviors. No differences were found in reports of maternal criticism, or paternal support, disinterest, or criticism. There were also no significant differences between the anhedonic group and the control group in their symbolic representation of family structure. This lack of differences may reflect that the anhedonic group was not showing significantly elevated levels of depression and thus, as a group, might not have been all that different from the control group.

In a series of studies investigating male and female college students, Brook and colleagues (Brook, Brook, Whiteman, & Gordon, 1983; Brook, Whiteman, Brook, & Gordon, 1988) attempted to ascertain the relations between fathers' personality attributes, fathers' socialization techniques, and their older adolescents' level of depressive mood. Maternal characteristics were not assessed in these studies. For both males and females, Brook and colleagues found evidence of a mediation model suggesting that paternal personality attributes and socialization techniques influence children's personality, which in turn is related to children's depressive mood. Brook, Brook et al. (1983) found that male college students' depressive mood was associated with certain personality attributes (interpersonal aggression, rebelliousness, impulsivity, obsessiveness, low responsibility, and low paternal identification) that could be predicted from certain paternal socialization practices (low levels of affection and encouragement, use of power-assertive and guilt-inducing discipline techniques) and certain paternal personality characteristics (poor object relations, poor interpersonal relatedness, stereotyped masculinity, and low responsibility). For female college students, Brook and colleagues (1988) found that depressive mood was associated with their personality characteristics (introversion, guilt, low paternal identification, interpersonal difficulty), which appeared to be predicted from paternal parenting practices (low child-centeredness, low time spent with the child, conflicted father-daughter relationship) and certain paternal personality characteristics (interpersonal difficulty, low self-esteem, depression, and anxiety). In comparing the results of male and female college students, Brook and colleagues (1988) noted that rebelliousness and impulsivity were more salient in the development of depressive mood in males, whereas introversion and guilt were more meaningful in relation to females' depressive mood. Brook and colleagues (Brook, Brook et al., 1983; Brook et al., 1988) point out that the cross-sectional design of these studies precludes predictive interpretations. There is evidence, however, to suggest that for both male and female college students, they found consistent support for the mediational model whereby paternal attributes and parenting techniques are associated with students' personality characteristics, which in turn are related to levels of depressive symptoms. This series of studies points out the complexity that is necessary to investigate fathers' influences on their children's depressive symptoms.

Overall, there is a relatively strong connection between fathers' characteristics and their adolescent or young adult children's depressive symptoms. Although there appears to be a stronger genetic link between maternal depression and offsprings' depression than between paternal depression and offsprings' depression (Tambs & Moum, 1993), there does appear to be a link between paternal depressive symptoms and children's development of depressive symptoms. As noted, more research needs to be completed with children below the age of 11. In addition, Thomas and Forehand (1991) and Levant (1991) argue that additional work needs to be completed to ascertain the etiologic mechanisms in the development of depressive symptoms in nonclinical samples of children and adolescents. Specifically, Levant (1991) argues that the amount of paternal contact and involvement with children should be assessed to thoroughly investigate the impact of paternal versus maternal behavior on children's and adolescents' functioning. Overall, the link between fathers' characteristics and their adolescents' depressive symptoms in nonreferred samples is stronger than the link found between fathers' characteristics and their children's and adolescents' depressive symptoms in samples of clinically referred children. In future studies, it will be important to investigate the severity of depressive symptoms in both children and fathers to establish whether different mechanisms are at work for clinical levels of depressive symptoms in contrast to subclinical levels of depressive symptoms.

TYPE A BEHAVIOR PATTERN

Type A behavior in children has been investigated in relation to their mothers' and fathers' Type A behavior; however results are inconsistent due to differing measurement scales and ages of the children. For example, teachers' reports of children's Type A behavior on the Matthews Youth Test for Health (MYTH; Matthews & Angulo, 1980) were associated with both maternal and paternal impatience in a sample of preschool children (Vega-Lahr & Field, 1986); were associated with lower levels of maternal anxiety for Japanese preschool boys and girls and lower levels of paternal anxiety for Japanese preschool boys, but not girls (Yamasaki, 1990); were associated with maternal and paternal Type A scores for boys but not girls in the second and fourth grades (Matthews, Stoney, Rakaczky, & Jamison, 1986); were associated with maternal but not paternal Type A scores in boys and girls in the fourth through sixth grades (Sweda, Sines, Lauer, & Clarke, 1986); were not associated with maternal or paternal Type A scores for children in the sixth and eighth grades (Matthews et al., 1986); and were not associated with maternal or paternal aspirations in boys and girls in the fourth through sixth grades (Kliewer & Weidner, 1987).

More consistent results were found when utilizing children's self-reports rather than teacher-reports of children's Type A behavior patterns. Fathers' aspirations and Type A scores, but not mothers', were found to be associated with boys', but not girls', self-reported Type A behavior pattern in samples of children ranging in age from 7 to 17 years old (Kliewer & Weidner, 1987; Weidner, Sexton, Matarazzo, Pereira, & Friend, 1988). In a study of college students, with a mean age of 19, Forgays and Forgays (1991) found some evidence for a cross-gender pattern between parents' and students' self-reported Type A behavior. Specifically, they used three measures of Type A behavior and found that two of the nine correlations were significant for mother-son pairs, none of the nine correlations were significant for father-son pairs, one of the nine correlations was significant for mother-daughter pairs, and four of the correlations were significant for father-daughter pairs. Although these results are somewhat suggestive of a cross-gender pattern, they should be interpreted with care given the large number of correlational analyses and the possibility of significant findings by chance.

Only one study was identified that used an observational measure of children's Type A behavior in relation to fathers' Type A behavior. Using performance tasks designed to elicit Type A behavior, Bortner, Rosenman, and Friedman (1970) found that the 15-year-old sons of Type A fathers showed significantly higher Type A behavior than the sons of Type B fathers.

The relations between fathers' and mothers' Type A behavior and their children's Type A behavior to remain unclear. The most consistent findings to date suggest that fathers' Type A behavior may be most closely associated with their sons' Type A behavior pattern in samples of children and adolescents, but not in samples of college students.

PATERNAL UNEMPLOYMENT

Research findings regarding fathers' employment and children's functioning were discussed in Chapter 1. The current section will briefly discuss fathers' unemployment and the ramifications on children's functioning. As noted in Chapter 1, most studies on the effects of employment have investigated mothers, whereas most of the studies on the effects of unemployment have focused on fathers (Barling, 1990). There is an association between fathers' unemployment and their children's maladjustment; however, the association appears to be indirect rather than direct. McLoyd (1989) provided an excellent review of the effects on children of paternal unemployment and reported that paternal job and economic loss have negative effects on children's functioning. However, McLoyd argued that there was an indirect relation between paternal unemployment and children's adjustment. Paternal job loss appears to lead to increased paternal negativity and pessimism, which leads to poorer father-child relationships, which eventually leads to increases in children's somatic symptoms and socioemotional problems, with decreases in children's aspirations and personal expectations. The same relations between paternal negativity, but not maternal negativity, and children's increased emotional/behavioral problems have been found in families under economic pressure (Elder, Conger, Foster, & Ardelt, 1992). Economic hardship also appears to impact negatively on the marital relationship, which in turn can impact negatively on the father-child and mother-child relationship (Conger, Conger, Elder, & Lorenz, 1993; Ge, Conger, Lorenz, & Elder, 1992; Simons, Lorenz, Conger, & Wu, 1992).

McLoyd (1989) suggested that a number of moderating variables may influence the connection between paternal unemployment and children's functioning. Child gender, child temperament, the mother-child relationship, the degree of contact with the father, and the child's attractiveness as rated by the father were all variables that seemed to influence the association between paternal job loss and children's maladjustment. For example, Elder, Nguyen, and Caspi (1985) analyzed data on fathers and children during the Great Depression and found that adolescent boys' adjustment seemed directly affected by paternal job loss, whereas adolescent girls' adjustment was negatively influenced by fathers' rejecting behavior due to paternal job loss. A study of adolescents living in a farm community that was experiencing severe economic loss found somewhat similar results. In a series of path analyses, Lempers and Clark-Lempers (1990) found that economic loss was related to fathers' decreased support for their daughters which was in turn related to their daughters' increased drug use and delinquent behaviors. The direct path from paternal economic stress to daughters' drug use and delinquent behavior was not significant. For sons, fathers' economic stress and decreased support both had a direct link to sons' increased drug use and delinquent behaviors. However, paternal support did not moderate the path between paternal economic stress and sons' drug use and delinquency. With regard to adolescents' depression and loneliness, there was no evidence that paternal support moderated the impact of paternal economic stress. For both boys and girls, fathers' increased economic stress and fathers' decreased support were directly related to children's increased feelings of depression and loneliness. Lempers and Clark-Lempers cautioned that further investigation, with children at various developmental stages, should be completed to clarify what types of paternal behaviors buffer the effects of paternal economic loss.

McLoyd (1990) provided an intriguing review of the effects of economic hardship on African American families and children. There is strong evidence to suggest that in families exposed to economic hardship, the father-child relationship is significantly impacted by the quality of the father-mother relationship. Thus, families in which there is a poor father-mother relationship tend to be the families in which there is a poor father-child relationship. Conversely, even with the burden of economic hardship, a good father-mother relationship seems to be associated with a good father-child relationship.

In addition to the studies that investigated fathers' unemployment and economic stress in relation to children's maladjustment, one study also investigated violence within families exposed to paternal unemployment and economic stress. Cantrell, Carrico, Franklin, and Grubb (1990) studied 15- to 17-year-olds who lived in an impoverished rural community in the Appalachians. They studied adolescents' reports of physical violence and physical abuse within families with either an unemployed or an employed father. Although Wolfe (1991) categorized frequent spanking as inappropriate parental discipline, it should be noted that Cantrell and colleagues (1990) did not include spanking in the categorization of physical violence or abuse because they reported that it was a common disciplinary technique in this sample. The results of the study showed that there was significantly more physical violence and physical abuse in families with unemployed fathers than in families with employed fathers. Specifically, 34% of adolescents' with an unemployed father reported parent-to-child physical violence and abuse, whereas 19% of adolescents with an employed father reported parent-to-child physical violence and abuse. Across the entire sample, boys were more likely to report parent-to-child physical violence and abuse than girls. Because there was no indication of whether fathers or mothers committed the physical violence and physical abuse, no conclusions can be made about the perpetrators of the violent acts.

Overall, this line of research suggests that fathers' unemployment has both indirect and direct effects on children's and adolescents' functioning. Further research will be needed to identify the moderating factors related to the effects of paternal unemployment and to tease out the differential impact of employment status and economic hardship from the changes to relationships within the family.

STRESSFUL EVENTS

A number of studies have investigated the relations between stressful events and psychological symptoms for fathers', mothers', and children. Handford, Mayes, Mattison, Humphrey, Bagnato, Bixler, and Kales (1986) studied fathers', mothers', and children's reactions to the Three Mile Island nuclear incident. They investigated the coping styles and psychological symptoms of local families over an 18-month period. The total sample included 35 families. Handford et al. found that fathers' and mothers' reactions were not directly related to their children's level of anxiety about the nuclear incident, but that the discrepancy between fathers' and mothers' reactions to the incident was related to children's level of anxiety. In other words, when fathers and mothers showed similar reactions and mood related to the incident, their children did not show elevated levels of anxiety. However, when fathers and mothers differed in their mood and reaction to the incident, children showed higher levels of self-reported anxiety. Breton, Valla, and Lambert (1993) studied another industrial disaster (an industrial fire that necessitated evacuation for over 2 weeks). They found that fathers' and mothers' greater level of psychological symptoms were significantly related to their children's increased experience of psychological symptoms. In a study of the responses of families in Lebanon to the constant threat of violence from war, children, fathers, and mothers appeared to show higher levels of stress in relation to the economic impact of war, daily hassles due to the breakdown of community services, and restricted contact from their support system (e.g., friends and relatives) rather than in relation to the constant threat of violence (Farhood, Zurayk, Chaya, & Saadeh, 1993).

Turning to major life events that are not life-threatening, in an investigation of children who showed difficulty in adjusting to the transition to elementary school, Elizur (1986) found that parents' coping responses were related to children's subsequent adjustment to elementary school. For example, children's improved adjustment over the first 2 years of school were related to supportive paternal and maternal attitudes toward the child, cooperation in paternal and maternal coping behaviors, maternal efforts to stimulate paternal coping behavior, and paternal coping behavior. Young adolescents' adaptive responses to major life events appear to be related to mothers', but not fathers', greater nurturance (Wyman, Cowen, Work, & Raoff, 1992).

Turning to the study of daily hassles and major life events that were not specified as the same for the entire sample, a number of studies have conducted both cross-sectional and prospective analyses. In an investigation of the relation between stress and psychological symptoms within families of young adolescents, causal modeling analyses of cross-sectional data indicated that the relation between paternal stress and children's emotional/behavioral problems was mediated by paternal (but not maternal) psychological symptoms (Compas, Howell, Phares, Williams, & Ledoux, 1989). In prospective analyses with the same sample, fathers' symptoms were not predictive of their children's self-reports of maladjustment at follow-up (Compas, Howell, Phares, Williams, & Giunta, 1989). Maternal psychological symptoms but not paternal psychological symptoms were a significant predictor when maternal reports of children's emotional/behavioral problems were used as the criterion.

Similar significant findings with cross-sectional analyses combined with a lack of findings in prospective analyses were found in two other studies of parents' and children's stress and psychological symptoms. Studies by Cohen, Burt, and Bjork (1987) and by Holahan and Moos (1987) found evidence of significant correlations between fathers' stress and children's maladjustment in cross-sectional analyses but did not find evidence of any connection in prospective analyses. Overall, these studies suggest that fathers' stress and psychological functioning, as well as mothers' stress and psychological functioning, are related to children's and adolescents' stress and psychological functioning. However, these relations seem to be more consistent when stress and psychological symptoms are compared at the same point in time rather than at different points in time.

INTERPARENTAL CONFLICT AND DIVORCE

Interparental Conflict

A number of studies have investigated the impact of interparental conflict on children's functioning (reviewed by Cummings & Davies, 1994). In general, interparental conflict appears to have a greater impact on children's maladjustment than the actual family constellation in which the children live (Amato & Keith, 1991; Grych & Fincham, 1990; Jouriles & Farris, 1992; Kelly, 1993; Westerman & Schonholtz, 1993). Most of the studies in this area that included fathers as participants used them primarily to report on interparental conflict or to report on children's functioning. Burman, John, and Margolin (1987) had fathers and mothers report on perceptions of marital conflict and perceptions of their relationship with their 6- to 14-year-old child. They found that fathers' higher levels of withdrawal in the marriage were associated with a poorer father-child relationship with both sons and daughters. Fathers' lower levels of marital satisfaction were associated with a poorer father-son relationship but not with a poorer father-daughter relationship. For mothers, all three measures of marital distress (lower satisfaction, higher overt aggression, and higher withdrawal from the marriage) were associated with a poorer mother-child relationship with their sons but not their daughters. None of the correlations between mothers' reports of marital distress and the mother-daughter relationship were significant.

In a study of preschool children and their parents, Kerig, Cowan, and Cowan (1993) had fathers and mothers report on marital satisfaction and then they observed the father-child and mother-child in structured tasks and unstructured playtime. They found that fathers who were dissatisfied with their marriage were more negative in their interactions with their daughters than with their sons. Daughters of fathers who were dissatisfied with their marriage showed less compliant behavior with their father than daughters whose fathers were satisfied with their marriage. Mothers who were unhappy with their marriage showed less tolerance for their daughters' assertiveness in the observational sessions and were more likely to show negative affect with their sons.

Feldman, Wentzel, Weinberger, and Munson (1990) assessed the relation between marital satisfaction and preadolescent boys' academic functioning, family functioning, and paternal and maternal parenting behaviors. All the families were intact. They found different patterns of significance for fathers and mothers. Fathers' reports of marital satisfaction were not significantly related to any characteristics that were assessed during direct observations of family interactions. However, fathers' perceptions of marital satisfaction were significantly related to their sons' improved school achievement, and their own consistency as a parent. Conversely, mothers' perceptions of marital satisfaction were not significantly related to their sons' school achievement or their own parenting behavior. However, based on direct observations of family interactions, maternal marital satisfaction was significantly related to overall functioning within the family, connectedness, task engagement, warmth, and lack of hostility in family interactions.

In a sample of young adolescents and their families, mothers, fathers, and adolescents reported on parental conflict while teachers reported on adolescents' academic, cognitive, social, and psychological functioning (Wierson, Forehand, & McCombs, 1988). Nearly half of the families were intact (56%), and the remaining families had experienced a parental divorce (44%). The ratings were completed at two points in time, with 1 year separating the two data collection points. In the cross-sectional analysis at Time 1, mothers' and adolescents' (but not fathers') reports of parental conflict were inversely associated with adolescents' grade point average (GPA) and cognitive competence, and were positively associated with teachers' reports of adolescents' conduct problems. Mothers' (but not adolescents' or fathers') reports of parental conflict were inversely related to adolescents' social competence. The only variable that was significantly related to fathers' reports of parental conflict was teachers' reports of adolescents' anxiety-withdrawal. Fathers', mothers', and adolescents' reports of parental conflict were positively related to adolescents' anxiety-withdrawal.

To assess the impact of parental conflict over time, adolescents', mothers', and fathers' ratings of parental conflict at Time 1 were correlated with the teacher-reported measures of adolescent functioning at Time 2. Adolescents' GPA and cognitive competence were inversely related to adolescents', mothers', and fathers' reports of parental conflict, and adolescents' social competence was inversely related to mothers' and fathers' reports of parental conflict. Only mothers' reports of conflict were related to adolescents' anxiety-withdrawal at Time 2 and none of the reports of parental conflict were significantly related to adolescents' conduct problems at Time 2. Overall, this study suggested that parental conflict was associated with lower cognitive and social competence, GPA, and behavioral functioning in young adolescents. The associations are somewhat more consistent for internalizing problems (anxiety-withdrawal) than for externalizing problems (conduct problems). However, the association between parental conflict and adolescent functioning depends on whose report of parental conflict is used. Therefore, it is important to assess multiple perspectives of parental conflict to capture the conflict that exists in the family.

In a series of studies by Jenkins and Smith (1990, 1991; Smith & Jenkins, 1991), fathers, mothers, and children reported on marital disharmony and children's behavior problems. In addition, mothers were interviewed about the mother-child relationship, the father-child relationship, children's hobbies, children's friendships, and children's relationships with adults outside the immediate family (Jenkins & Smith, 1990). Children ranged in age from 9 to 12 years old, and the majority of parents (86%) were still married to each other. When families were split into two categories of "good marriages" and "poor marriages" based on interviewers' ratings of the marriage, significant differences were found for childrens' and mothers' (but not fathers') reports of psychological symptoms and mothers' (but not fathers' or teachers') reports of children's behavior. Children who lived with parents who had a poor marriage showed significantly higher levels of psychological symptoms based on children's and mothers' reports, and higher levels of behavior problems based on mothers' reports (Smith & Jenkins, 1991).

Protective factors were investigated to ascertain whether or not children could be buffered from the effects of an adverse environment of a poor parental marriage. Jenkins and Smith (1990) found that children from both good and poor marriages showed higher levels of psychological symptoms when the mother-child or the father-child relationship was poor. Conversely, a good mother-child relationship and a good father-child relationship were associated with lower levels of children's psychological symptoms, even when their parents' marriages were poor. Jenkins and Smith suggested that a good parent-child relationship could act as a protective factor even in strongly disharmonious homes. Other protective factors that were found to protect children from the adverse effects of disharmonious parental marriages were close relationships with adults outside the family, positive recognition for children's activities, good sibling relationships, presence of a best friend, and high-quality friendships.

The previous two studies analyzed marital disharmony with a global categorization of good and bad marriages. To provide a fine-grained analysis of the type of marital disharmony, Jenkins and Smith (1991) analyzed the impact of three different types of marital disharmony in this sample: Overt parental conflict, covert tension, and discrepancy in child-rearing practices. When controlling for the other types of marital disharmony, only overt parental conflict was significantly related to children's psychological symptoms. Thus, for both mothers' and fathers' reports of marital disharmony and children's psychological functioning, overt parental conflict was associated with children's psychological symptoms above and beyond the contributions of covert tension and discrepancy in child-rearing practices. Overall, the series of studies by Jenkins and Smith (1990, 1991; Smith & Jenkins, 1991) showed significant associations between marital disharmony and children's psychological functioning, especially when overt parental conflict is assessed. In addition, the findings of these studies are similar to the findings from Wierson and colleagues (1988) in showing somewhat greater significance between parental conflict and children's psychological functioning when mothers' rather than fathers' reports are used.

In contrast to the stronger associations between mothers' reports of conflict and children's adjustment just noted, Johnston, Gonzalez, and Campbell (1987) found that interviewers' ratings of paternal characteristics were associated with children's functioning during custody disputes, whereas maternal characteristics were not significantly associated. Specifically, Johnston and colleagues assessed children aged 4 to 12 whose parents were involved in a dispute over custody. The families represented a wide range of socioeconomic status and ethnicity. Families were assessed at two points in time: During the custody dispute and over 2 years later. Children's emotional and behavioral functioning was assessed by the combination of mothers' and fathers' reports on the Child Behavior Checklist (Achenbach, 1991). Mothers and fathers were interviewed separately to assess verbal and physical aggression between parents, the amount to which each parent involved the child in the custody dispute (e.g., using the child as a weapon against the other parent by asking the child to spy on the other parent or encouraging the child to harass the other parent), and the amount to which there was a role reversal with each parent (e.g., child acts as a confidant to parent or admonishes parent for "bad" behavior). Interviewers provided separate ratings of these variables for mothers and fathers after the interview.

The cross-sectional analysis at the time of the custody dispute showed that fathers' involvement of their children in the dispute was significantly related to children's total level of emotional/behavioral problems and to increased levels of aggression. In addition, the more children showed a role reversal with their fathers, the more they showed overall levels of emotional/behavioral problems and greater levels of withdrawal/uncommunicativeness. Verbal/physical aggression between parents, mothers' involvement of children in the custody dispute, and mothers' role reversal with children were not significantly related to children's emotional/behavioral problems.

When children's emotional/behavioral problems were assessed at the 2-year follow-up, verbal/physical aggression between parents and mothers' role reversal with children showed predictive associations in addition to fathers' involvement of children in the dispute and fathers' role reversal with children. Higher levels of verbal and physical aggression between parents at the time of the dispute significantly predicted greater total emotional/behavioral problems, depression, withdrawal/uncommunicativeness, and aggression in children 2 years later. Fathers' involvement of children in the custody dispute was predictive of children's aggression 2 years later. Mothers' role reversal with their children significantly predicted children's higher levels of withdrawal/uncommunicativeness 2 years later. Fathers' role reversal with children showed a nonsignificant trend toward predicting children's withdrawal and uncommunicativeness 2 years later. Finally, greater levels of verbal and physical aggression between the parents at the time of the 2-year follow-up were associated with greater levels of total emotional/behavioral problems, withdrawal/uncommunicativeness, and somatic complaints in children at the 2-year follow-up. Girls were more likely than boys to show higher levels of somatic complaints at the 2-year follow-up. There were no other main effects for children's gender or age at either data collection point. There were no significant interaction effects at the time of the custody dispute, but at the 2-year follow-up, girls in highly conflictual families showed higher levels of depression and withdrawal and older children in high-conflict families showed higher levels of somatic complaints and aggression. The lack of findings that boys showed greater problems due to the divorce is worth noting because researchers (e.g., Hetherington & Clingempeel, 1992; Wenk et al., 1994) have begun to call into question the previously held belief that parental divorce has a greater negative impact on boys than on girls. Overall, this study showed that fathers' involvement of children in custody disputes and role reversals with children, in addition to high levels of verbal and physical aggression between parents, were associated with greater emotional/behavioral problems in children. Johnston and colleagues (1987) speculated on the mechanisms through which parental conflicts influence children, including modeling, family stress, and a breakdown in the role structure within the family. However, they noted that further work is needed to ascertain the theoretical mechanism that best explains the impact of parental conflict on children's functioning.

In addition to the research into the impact of parental conflict on children's emotional and behavioral functioning, interparental conflict also has been investigated in relation to parental teaching techniques and parental discipline strategies. Brody, Pillegrini, and Sigel (1986) found that mother-child and father-child teaching strategies with their school-age children were influenced by marital quality but in different directions. Mothers in distressed marriages used effective and involved teaching strategies with their children, whereas fathers in distressed marriages used ineffective teaching strategies with their children. Regarding discipline strategies, Dadds, Sheffield, and Holbeck (1990) investigated the impact of marital discord on children's perceptions of parental discipline that was experienced in their families as well as the parental discipline that should be used in their families. Children ranged in age from 8 to 13 years old, and they all were from intact families. Children were split into high, moderate, and low perceived parental discord based on their reports of parental discord. Three discipline situations were presented to children in the form of a drawing—child noncompliance, child aggression, and child temper tantrum— and children were asked what *would* happen in their family and what *should* happen in their family. Overall, children showed a preference for time-out or parent-child discussion for both maternal and paternal discipline strategies. However, there were a number of interesting effects when maternal and paternal coercion were analyzed. Boys reported that they would and should receive more coercive discipline (such as punishment) than did girls, especially for child noncompliance and child aggression. Both boys and girls felt that fathers would and should use more punishment than mothers in situations of child noncompliance. Most children felt that they should receive less coercive punishment than they actually received, especially in situations of noncompliance and aggression. With regard to how parental discord impacts these ratings, the only significant interaction effect regarding parental discord was found for child aggression. In their responses to this situation, children from moderate- and high-discord families reported that both their mothers and their fathers would and should use more coercive discipline and punishment techniques than reported by children from low-discord families. This study highlights the importance of considering children's perceptions of maternal and paternal discipline in regard to parental discord.

One problem with a number of studies of children's functioning and interparental conflict is the possibility of autocorrelations within informants (parents' reports of parental conflict correlate with their own report of children's functioning). The Wierson et al. (1988) study is an exception to this problem because they used teacher ratings of children's academic, cognitive, social, and psychological functioning. A number of studies, however, have investigated interparental conflict and children's psychological and behavioral functioning based on fathers' and mothers' reports of these variables. For example, Klein and Shulman (1980) found that fathers' and mothers' reports of poor marital quality were associated with fathers' and mothers' reports of increased child behavior problems. Parents who reported poor marital adjustment also reported that their children had elevated behavioral problems. Goldberg (1990) found that mothers and fathers who were more satisfied with their marriages perceived their children to show more positive behavior and less negative behavior than mothers and fathers who were less satisfied.

Because of the cross-sectional nature of many of these studies, it is difficult to tease out the effects of using the same informants on parental discord and children's functioning. There is fairly consistent evidence that interparental discord is associated with higher children's emotional and behavioral problems (e.g., Amato & Keith, 1991; Emery, 1982; Grych & Fincham, 1990; Shaw & Emery, 1988) although much of the early work in this area only utilized mothers' reports. The inclusion of fathers' ratings in the studies discussed here is a decided improvement to the designs of the studies. Interestingly, a number of studies have found that the relations between parental discord and children's maladaptive behavior are more consistent for mothers' reports than they are for fathers' reports. Some investigators have speculated that the lack of associations between fathers' reports of parental conflict and children's functioning shows that fathers are less aware of family functioning and less willing to acknowledge interparental conflict and children's maladaptive behavior (e.g., Burman et al., 1987; Wierson et al., 1988). However, it may be that fathers' perspectives are as legitimate as mothers' and children's perspectives, but that they are perceiving different levels of conflict and children's maladaptive behavior than are mothers. In addition, Simons, Whitbeck, Beaman, and Conger (1994) highlight the importance of considering the reciprocal nature of conflict, visitation, and psychological distress in children, mothers, and fathers.

Parental Separation or Divorce

Along with the studies of the effects of interparental conflict, a number of studies have investigated different patterns of children's functioning after divorce. Few studies utilize fathers as informants on their own or their children's functioning, and even fewer studies directly assess paternal characteristics. A few studies have investigated fathers' and mothers' reactions to divorce (e.g., Block, Block, & Gjerde, 1988; Jacobs, 1982, 1983). Fine, McKenry, and Chung (1992) found that African American fathers and mothers were more satisfied with their parental role after divorce than were Caucasian American fathers and mothers, even after controlling for SES and time since divorce. Although it is important to assess parents' coping with divorce, it is also essential to connect parents' reactions to divorce with their children's adjustment after divorce. The majority of studies have investigated children's maladjustment in relation to their perceptions of the divorce or in relation to different family constellations after divorce. Parish (1991) found lower levels of self-esteem in children aged 10 to 18 years old when they lived in divorced-remarried households than in intact households. Similar results were found in a sample of adolescents (Studer, 1993). Kurdek and Berg (1987) utilized a measure called the

"Children's Beliefs about Parental Divorce Scale" to ascertain which maladaptive beliefs about divorce were associated with maladjustment in children whose parents had divorced. Children ranged in age from 6 to 17 years old with a mean age of 11.06. The majority of the participants were Caucasian. Kurdek and Berg found that the scale consisted of six factors, including two that are relevant here: paternal blame and maternal blame. When considering children's self-reported psychological functioning (anxiety, control beliefs, self-concept, social support, interpersonal problem-solving), paternal blame was not related to any areas of children's psychological functioning and maternal blame was only correlated with children's control beliefs about powerful others. This correlation suggested that children who showed greater maternal blame about the divorce also held more beliefs that outcomes occur because of other people's behavior or attributes. Paternal blame and maternal blame were not related to parents' or teachers' reports of children's internalizing or externalizing behavior problems. This study suggests that the degree to which children blame their fathers and mothers for divorce is not strongly related to children's psychological functioning.

To ascertain the impact of children's feelings of being caught between their divorced parents, Buchanan, Maccoby, and Dornbusch (1991) interviewed over 500 adolescents 4 years after their parents' separation. Adolescents ranged in age from 10 to 18 and represented a wide variety of races and ethnicities. Buchanan and colleagues found that the more adolescents felt caught in the middle between their divorced parents, the more depressed and anxious they felt and the more they exhibited deviant behavior. Feeling caught between parents also was related to the closeness that adolescents felt with their parents. Adolescents who reported feeling close to their mother were less likely to feel caught between their divorced parents. There was a nonsignificant trend in this direction for adolescents' feelings of closeness to their fathers. Parental reports of interparental discord were not related to adolescents' maladjustment directly, but were mediated by adolescents' feelings of being caught between their divorced parents. This study provides an important addition to the research on children of divorced parents. It suggests that it is important to assess childrens' and adolescents' perceptions of being caught between their divorced parents in addition to measuring interparental conflict and children's and adolescents' psychological functioning.

There have been a number of investigations to determine the effects of living in various family constellations before and after parental divorce. Downey (1994) found that children from single-mother and single-father households did more poorly in school than children from two-parent households, but the factors relating to poor school performance varied according to family constellation. Children who lived with their single mothers appeared to do poorly in school because of economic deprivation and lack of economic resources, whereas children who lived with their single father appeared to do poorly because of interpersonal deprivation and the lack of interpersonal parental resources.

Dornbusch and colleagues (1985) conducted a study to compare the functioning of adolescents living with both biological parents and adolescents living in mother-only households. The sample consisted of over 7,500 participants from a nationally representative database that was collected between 1966 and 1970. Dornbusch and colleagues found that adolescents who lived with both biological parents showed lower levels of deviant behavior than adolescents living in a mother-only household. Adolescents in two-parent households were also more likely than adolescents in mother-only households to make decisions with parental input. These results remained consistent even after controlling for parental education and family income. Dornbusch and colleagues did not analyze the effects of children and adolescents who lived in stepparent families.

In a study of adolescents aged 10 to 18, Buchanan, Maccoby, and Dornbusch (1992) investigated the impact of residential arrangements 4 years after parental separation and divorce. Adolescents lived either with their mother, their father, or in "dual residence," which means they alternated living with their father and their mother on a routine basis (usually on a weekly basis). In general, there were few differences in adolescents' psychological adjustment (e.g., psychological symptoms, academic functioning) based on residential status. However, adolescents who lived with their father showed somewhat poorer adjustment when they had shifted residences at least once since parental separation and when their parents continued to show high levels of hostility after separation. The poorer adjustment in adolescents who lived with their fathers appeared to be related to fathers' lower levels of monitoring their children's behavior. These patterns were true for both boys and girls. Overall, there was no evidence of better adjustment when the adolescents lived with the same-gender parent.

Rickel and Langner (1985) compared the functioning of children and adolescents who lived with their biological father (usually because the parents were still married), those who lived with a surrogate father (usually due to mothers' cohabitation or marriage to a new man), or those who lived with no father or father figure in the household. They studied the family constellations of a large community sample from New York City. Participants in the study were representative of the population of New York City, including the race and socioeconomic distribution. Children's functioning was assessed at two points in time, 5 years apart. At both Time 1 and Time 2, results of the study showed that children who lived with their biological father exhibited the least amount of psychopathology, especially related to delinquency. Children who lived with a surrogate father showed greater psychopathology than children living with their biological father or children living without a father, especially in self-destructive tendencies and lack of compulsiveness and carefulness. When the total symptom scores and total impairment scores were compared at Time 1, children living with a father surrogate showed significantly greater problems than children living either with no father or with their biological father. However, family constellation did not show a significant main effect on children's total symptom scores or their total impairment scores 5 years later. Although there was strong evidence of the stability of antisocial behavior over a 5-year period (especially in surrogate father households), this study suggested that the influences of family constellation may be more specific to antisocial behavior rather than to overall psychological functioning. In addition, this study suggested that the impact of parental separation and divorce may be most salient soon after the separation and divorce and has less of an impact 5 years later, at least as related to family constellation.

Similar results were found by Marsh (1990) in a study of over 10,000 high school students. He compared the psychological functioning of students in their sophomore year and again in their senior year of high school to ascertain the effects of living with two biological parents, a biological parent and a stepparent, or a single parent. Due to the large sample size, a wide variety of family configurations were analyzed, including adolescents who lived with both biological parents, their biological mother and stepfather, their biological father and stepmother, their single mother, or their single father. After controlling for gender, race, SES, and level of functioning during the sophomore year, Marsh found that adolescents' functioning during their senior year was not related to family configuration. This lack of significant findings due to family configuration was consistent for both boys and girls of all races and SES levels. Marsh argued that family configuration has little effect on senior high school students' psychological functioning.

Children's and adolescents' ability to cope with parental divorce and alternative family household arrangements appear to be related to their relationships with their parents. Thomas and Forehand (1993) found that adolescents had fewer problems after parental divorce when they had a good relationship with their father. Notably, the father-adolescent relationship was the strongest predictor of postdivorce adolescent adjustment, to the exclusion of other variables such as paternal and maternal depressive symptoms, paternal visitation, and the father-mother relationship. Even when there were high levels of interparental conflict, adolescents who had a close relationship with their noncustodial father showed fewer internalizing psychological problems than did adolescents who reported a poor relationship with their father (Brody & Forehand, 1990). Adolescents and young adults appear to have poorer relationships with their fathers than their mothers after parental divorce (Booth & Amato, 1994; Cooney, 1994). The poor father-adolescent relationship appears to account for the problems in adjustment that many adolescents and young adults experience after parental divorce (Swartzman-Schatman & Schinke, 1993).

In summary, these studies suggest that family constellation has some influence on children's and adolescents' psychological well-being, but it may not have as much of an impact when previous levels of functioning are controlled. In addition, care should be taken in interpreting significant findings based on family configuration. These studies obviously did not randomly assign the family constellation in which children will live, and therefore the results of these studies might still be influenced by other factors that were not assessed. For example, children showing greater adjustment problems at parental divorce may be sent to live with the parent who is considered the better disciplinarian or the parent who will also have a second coparent in the house. Therefore, any significant results that are found for family constellation should be interpreted with caution due to other extraneous variables that might actually account for the significant associations that were found. In addition, family constellation cannot be considered separate from the level of interparental conflict to which children are exposed, and therefore studies should include measures of interparental conflict to provide a comprehensive assessment of children's experiences in different family constellations (Demo & Acock, 1988). Finally, because marriages with only daughters are perceived by mothers to be at greater risk for separation and divorce than marriages with at least one son (Katzev et al., 1994) and are in fact at greater risk for divorce in Caucasian families (Mott, 1994), research in this area must continue to investigate gender differences in children and adolescents who experience parental separation and divorce.

SUMMARY

Table 7.1 provides a review of the results discussed in this section. Overall, the studies with nonreferred children and their fathers are consistent with the studies with referred children and referred fathers in showing significant associations between fathers' and children's psychological functioning. In general, the associations between fathers' characteristics and their children's functioning are similar to the associations between mothers' characteristics and their children's functioning.

TABLE 7.1.   Findings from Research on Paternal Factors in Child and Adolescent Psychopathology: Studies of Nonreferred Fathers and Children

Problem	Findings
Delinquency	Consistent associations are found between paternal factors and delinquent behaviors in children and adolescents (6 studies).
Alcohol/Substance Use	Consistent associations are found between paternal factors and adolescent alcohol and substance use (15 studies).
Nonspecific Behavior Problems	More studies find significant associations between paternal factors and child adjustment, symptoms, and behavior (16 studies) than do not (4 studies).
Depression	More studies find significant associations between paternal factors and children's depressive symptoms (15 studies) than do not (3 studies).
Type A	Stronger associations are found between father-child Type A behavior when using children's self-reports or direct observations (4 out of 4 studies) than teachers' reports (4 out of 6 studies).
Paternal Unemployment	Fathers' unemployment is associated indirectly with children's maladjustment (1 review, 8 studies).
Paternal Stress	Strong and consistent associations found between fathers' stress and/or psychological symptoms and children's maladjustment (8 studies).
Interparental Conflict	Consistent associations between interparental conflict and children's maladjustment (7 reviews, 12 studies).
Parental Divorce	Equivocal evidence on children's maladjustment based on family constellation after divorce (8 studies).

PART IV

How Should Investigators Study Fathers and Developmental Psychopathology?

CHAPTER 8

Methodological Issues and Research Hints

I once included a review by Woollett, White, and Lyon (1982) in a manuscript on fathers and developmental psychopathology. This review suggested that fathers were no more difficult to recruit into research than mothers. When a colleague was providing me with feedback on the manuscript, he drew a circle around the sentence on the Woollett et al. (1982) study and wrote "I don't believe it." Although there may be a widely held assumption that fathers are more difficult than mothers to recruit into developmental research, this chapter will critically evaluate this assumption and will outline practical considerations in paternal research involvement. The emphasis will be on practical issues of completing research on fathers and developmental psychopathology.

FATHERS' PARTICIPATION IN RESEARCH

Let's begin with the infamous article that was just mentioned. Woollett and colleagues (1982) reviewed paternal and maternal participation rates in research on child development and concluded that fathers were no more difficult to recruit than mothers. Woollett et al. reviewed articles that cited maternal refusal rates and found refusal rates ranging from zero to 76%, with an average refusal rate of 28.57%. They then reviewed 85 studies of child development that included fathers and found refusal rates ranging from zero to 73%, with an average refusal rate of 19.5%. This review of parental refusal rates suggests that fathers were no more difficult to recruit into research projects than were mothers. The researchers went on to evaluate participation rates based on the methodology employed. They found that both fathers and mothers were more likely to take part in research that required limited participation (one data collection point rather than multiple points and a small amount of time rather than a large amount) and research that was convenient (home-based rather than laboratory-based). Both fathers and mothers showed these tendencies in research participation.

Because there may be some readers who just made an "I don't believe it" notation in the margins, I will provide more details on paternal and maternal participation rates. In their classic book *The Volunteer Subject,* Rosenthal and Rosnow (1975) reviewed characteristics of participants and nonparticipants in research. In research with adults, Rosenthal and Rosnow found that participants were more likely than nonparticipants to be better educated, higher in socioeconomic status, more intelligent, more sociable, and more in need of social approval. They also included information related to male and female participation rates. Based on a review of 45 studies, Rosenthal and Rosnow concluded that adult women were somewhat more likely than adult men to participate in research. This conclusion, however, was limited to specific types of research. For example, adult males were more likely than adult females to participate in research that was potentially stressful, anxiety provoking, or potentially physically harmful through use of electric shock. Although Rosenthal and Rosnow did not specifically evaluate paternal versus maternal research participation rates, their review suggests that women are slightly more likely to participate in research that is not perceived to be stressful.

Historically, males have been used as research participants much more than females (Basow, 1992). For example, in health research, the majority of research on risk for heart attack was conducted on men (e.g., Menotti & Seccareccia, 1985; Ramamurti, Jamuna, & Ramamurti, 1984; Seraganian, Roskies, Hanley, & Oseasohn, 1987). The National Institutes of Health and other funding agencies have been criticized for neglecting women's health care concerns and for allowing research findings on men's health risk factors to be applied to women. The research on health risk factors, as well as other research that has relied primarily on adult male participants, such as achievement motivation (e.g., McClelland, 1955; McClelland, Atkinson, Clark, & Lowell, 1953), employment stress, (e.g., Repetti, 1989), and leadership (Eagly, Makhijani, & Klonsky, 1992; Gable, Hollon, & Dangello, 1992; Long, 1993; Podsakoff, MacKenzie, Moorman, & Fetter, 1990) suggests that men are willing to participate in research when they are asked. Men's participation in these studies suggests that men are neither uninterested nor "too busy" to participate in research. However, there may be differential willingness to participate in research based on its content area. Much of the research that has been completed with men has involved stereotypically male topics (e.g., heart attacks, achievement motivation, leadership qualities). There is often speculation that fathers may be less willing than mothers to participate in research on their children. However, it is difficult to say whether fathers are less willing to participate in child-focused research than other types of research or whether researchers are less likely to expect fathers to participate in such research. This is not an easy question to answer because, to my knowledge, no study has directly compared participation rates of fathers and mothers in different types of research content areas.

One study was identified that showed fathers are less likely to participate in research on family interactions (Hops & Seeley, 1992). In two-parent families, when mothers but not fathers participated, they reported lower family cohesion and more marital dissatisfaction, and when fathers but not mothers participated, they reported higher levels of depression. Thus, further research is needed on the determinants of paternal versus maternal participation as well as the representativeness of participating fathers and mothers.

To address differential paternal and maternal rates further, Phares (1995) conducted a study using the fathers and mothers of college students. This was a "low commitment" study in which parents of older adolescents (who also completed measures) were sent a packet of research measures (psychological symptoms, perceived competence, drinking behavior) and were asked to complete the measures anonymously and return the completed forms to the principal investigator in a business-reply envelope. Fathers and mothers received separate packets of forms (marked "father" or "mother") and separate business-reply envelopes. Completed, returned forms were used to assess paternal and maternal research participation. To test participation directly of both parents, only married couples were used. Including single-parent families in the analyses would have been an unfair test of participation rates because noncustodial parents could not have completed forms they had never received.

Out of the 125 parental dyads who were sent research questionnaires, 74 fathers (59.2%) and 82 mothers (65.5%) completed and returned their forms. Based on a chi-square analysis, this difference in participation rates was not statistically significant. These return rates were surprisingly similar to those found by Sarason, Pierce, Bannerman, and Sarason (1993), who received 55% of fathers' and 65% of mothers' completed questionnaires in a study of parental relationships and social support in college students. Phares (1995) conducted further analyses to compare participating and nonparticipating parents based on their older adolescents' perceptions. Participating fathers were rated by their offspring as significantly more intrusive than nonparticipating fathers; however, this difference was no longer significant after Bonferroni correction. Participating fathers and nonparticipating fathers did not differ significantly on any other measures (older adolescents' reports of paternal psychological symptoms, drinking, and other aspects of parenting behavior). Based on older adolescents' perceptions, participating mothers were reported to be significantly more intrusive than nonparticipating mothers on a parenting behavior measure (the Children's Report of Parenting Behavior Inventory), and this difference remained significant after Bonferroni correction. Participating and nonparticipating mothers did not differ significantly on any of the other research measures completed by their college student offspring (maternal psychological symptoms, drinking behavior, and other aspects of parenting behavior).

As a side note, participation rates of divorced fathers and mothers were also analyzed. In the larger sample of older adolescents, a total of 18 students reported that their parents were divorced, but they were willing to have questionnaire packets sent to both households. These older adolescents provided the addresses of both their father and mother, and questionnaires were sent to both parents separately. In these 18 families, the return rates for fathers and mothers were identical to one another (55.6%). These return rates suggest that there was no difference in paternal and maternal participation rates, nor was there any difference between the return rates in divorced couples versus married couples. It should be acknowledged that these divorced couples may not be representative of all families in which parents have divorced. Older adolescents' willingness to have questionnaires sent to both households may reflect their continued involvement with both father and mother, and possibly may reflect a lower amount of animosity between households. Further studies need to be conducted that specifically assess the participation rates of fathers and mothers who are still married versus fathers and mothers who are divorced.

An additional aspect of the study of participation rates was the assessment of fathers' and mothers' reasons for participating in the research project. Fathers and mothers were asked to report why they participated in this research project and what type of incentives would help them choose to participate in future research projects. These parents checked as many of the following reasons for participation as were applicable (numbers in parentheses denote the percentage of fathers and mothers, respectively, who endorsed each reason): I wanted to help out (66.2%; 78.0%); I think research is important (48%; 63%); It wasn't too much of a bother (37.8%; 43.9%); The questionnaires seemed interesting (23.0%; 28.0%); I enjoy filling out questionnaires (6.8%; 11.0%); Other (parents usually filled in responses related to wanting to help out their child or help out the university—13.5%; 13.4%). There were no significant differences in the paternal and maternal patterns of reasons for participation in research.

When participating parents were asked what might influence them to participate in research projects in the future, they endorsed the following characteristics (again, numbers in parentheses represent the percentage of fathers and mothers, respectively, who endorsed each statement): If I felt that my participation was benefiting my children or family (63.5%; 75.6%); If I felt my participation was benefiting myself (25.7%; 43.9%); If I had more time (14.9%; 8.5%); If I received monetary compensation (13.5%; 11.0%); If the questionnaires were shorter (9.5%; 4.9%); If the topics were interesting to me (4.1%; 14.6%); Other (parents usually made statements about perceiving themselves as usually wanting to help out, regardless of incentives—9.5%; 13.4%). Again, fathers and mothers showed similar motivations to participate in future research.

Overall, this study supported Woollett and colleagues' (1982) conclusion that fathers in married couples were no more difficult to recruit than mothers in married couples. Because of the sample and methodology, a few caveats should be mentioned. The sample was well educated (fathers' average education was 15.06 years and mothers' average education was 14.22 years); the research was tied to a popular state university; and parents perceived the research to be indirectly helping their sons and daughters. All these reasons may have helped increase research participation of both fathers and mothers. Because the research was relatively low in commitment (a one-time completion of questionnaires that took approximately 45 minutes), both fathers and mothers may have been more willing to participate than if the research had required more of a time commitment or more than one data collection point. Finally, because the research measures were completed at home, there is a slight possibility that some of the "paternal" participation may actually have been maternal participation based on mothers' completion of fathers' measures. There was a significant pattern of similarity in marital dyads' completion of forms. In 57.6% of the intact families, both parents completed their questionnaires; in 32.8%, neither parent completed their questionnaires; in 1.6%, fathers completed their questionnaires but mothers did not; and in 8.0%, mothers completed their questionnaires and fathers did not. This pattern of parents in the same household showing similar rates of response or nonresponse was statistically significant. There were absolutely no incentives for mothers to complete fathers' forms because neither parents nor students received compensation for parental participation and the research was completely anonymous so that no indirect compensation (e.g., social approval) could be given to students' whose parents completed the forms. Thus, it is assumed that the paternal participation rate reflected fathers' completion of forms.

Overall, this study suggested that fathers and mothers were equally likely to participate in this research project. Even with the caveats mentioned by Phares (1995), there is growing evidence that fathers are not significantly more difficult than mothers to recruit into research participation. It is still unclear whether noncustodial fathers are more difficult than custodial mothers to recruit for research on their children. However, the plethora of studies that have included noncustodial fathers in the research design (e.g., Emery et al., 1991, 1994; Jacobs, 1982, 1983) suggest that data can be collected from fathers who do not live with their children.

Given the growing body of evidence of fathers' willingness to participate in research related to their child (including the Woollett et al., 1982 review, the empirical study just reviewed, and the research on divorced fathers), do you still find yourself wanting to write in the margins, "I don't believe it"? At this point, it is hard to imagine what type of evidence would convince a skeptic that fathers can be recruited into child and family research. And even if it were the case that fathers are more difficult to recruit than mothers—is that any reason to dismiss them from the research process?

Admittedly, psychological research has been influenced often by the ease of subject recruitment rather than importance of the targeted research sample. This can be seen in the rampant use of college student "subject pools" for research in psychology. Sieber and Saks (1989) noted that 74% of the studies reported in the *Journal of Personality and Social Psychology* during 1987 were conducted with captive "subject pool" samples of college students. This undoubtedly has more to do with the ease of subject recruitment rather than the greater importance of college students when compared with same-age peers who do not attend college.

Participant recruitment in psychology has been criticized from many angles. In his aptly titled book *Even the Rat Was White,* Guthrie (1976) criticized the tendency for psychology to be a science dedicated to Caucasians, to the detriment of non-Caucasians. He noted that first-year college students (most of whom are Caucasian) and Norwegian white rats have been favorite research subjects because of their ready availability. More recently, Graham (1992) noted that the field of psychology is still ethnocentric with too much attention given to white middle-class subjects and not enough attention given to people of color and people of lower-than-middle class socioeconomic status. In a content analysis of six journals published by the American Psychological Association (including *Developmental Psychology* and *Journal of Consulting and Clinical Psychology*), Graham found that there was actually a decline in articles pertaining to African Americans from 1970 to 1989. She noted that psychology remains a field in which "most of the subjects were white and middle class" (p. 629). These patterns of participant recruitment based on ease and interest of the researcher are problematic to say the least. When researchers focus on the perceived ease of access to participants (e.g., research with undergraduate students), they neglect one of the basic tenets of good research: the requirement of representative samples.

The tendency to use mothers due to their easier access (whether real or imagined) is consistent with the history of "easy access to participants" in psychological research. Although it may be understandable, it is not defensible nor should it be continued. The failure to include fathers in developmental research on psychopathology leaves a huge source of variance unaccounted for in factors that may relate to children's emotional/behavioral problems. As noted in Chapter 2, meaningful findings have been unearthed when fathers are included along with mothers in studies of child development. As noted in Chapters 5, 6, and 7, meaningful associations have been established when fathers are included in research on developmental psychopathology. So, how can we as researchers increase the amount of studies conducted on paternal influences on child and adolescent psychopathology?

WHAT RESEARCHERS CAN DO IN THEIR RESEARCH DESIGNS

Researchers can do a variety of things in designing their studies to facilitate the research knowledge base on fathers and developmental psychopathology. These methods can be placed on a continuum of passive inclusion of paternal characteristics to aggressive recruitment of fathers into research projects. To begin at the easiest, albeit "sloppiest," level, a cursory review of method sections in print as well as those heard in research colloquia suggests that considerable paternal data have been inadvertently collected but never analyzed. For example, when researchers have targeted maternal-child interactions at the dinner table (e.g., Crockenberg & Litman, 1990) paternal-child interactions often occur. However, if these interactions are not coded and subsequently analyzed, then no paternal-child information can be gained from them. Undoubtedly, a number of researchers have not targeted fathers in their research and therefore have no inclination to analyze the paternal data that they have inadvertently collected. It may also be that the N's of paternal data are smaller than the N's of maternal data because fathers were not targeted by the researchers. Given these limitations, researchers may want to consider presenting these data in the form of "Brief Reports" rather than full research articles. Although it may be sloppy to analyze such inadvertently collected paternal data, this strategy can be a first step to increasing the knowledge base of fathers and developmental psychopathology.

The next strategy for investigation of paternal characteristics would be to invite fathers to participate in research whenever inviting mothers to participate. Fathers cannot even begin to take part unless researchers invite them; doing so should be another beginning step to recruiting fathers.

Merely inviting fathers' participation will not be sufficient in the long run for a clear research agenda that includes fathers. Although information will be added to the research knowledge base, paternal characteristics and fathers themselves need to be targeted specifically for inclusion if the field is to move forward in any meaningful way. Historically, maternal perceptions of paternal characteristics were used in lieu of collecting data from fathers (Boyd, 1985). Although important information was gained, this method will no longer suffice for research on fathers. An alternative would be to include children's perceptions of paternal characteristics (e.g., with the use of the Children's Report of Parental Behavior Inventory by Schaefer, 1965, or the Parental Bonding Inventory by Parker et al., 1979). In addition to children's reports of their fathers' behavior, researchers have begun using older adolescents and young adults to report on their fathers' psychological functioning. For example, Benson and Heller (1987) had young adults report on their fathers' and mothers' psychological and psychiatric history. A number of researchers (e.g., Crews & Sher, 1992; Mulinski, 1989; O'Malley, Carey, & Maisto, 1986; Sher, 1985) have had older adolescents and young adults report on their fathers' drinking behavior and have found these reports to significantly correlate with fathers' self-reported drinking behavior. The advantage of using children's and adolescents' reports of their fathers' behavior is that paternal characteristics can be assessed even when the father is not available for research participation. However, children's perceptions of paternal characteristics—like mothers' perceptions—are limited because neither method allows for fathers' direct assessment.

A goal for researchers should be to target the involvement of fathers in developmental research and to include them officially in the design whether or not the fathers live with their children. Obviously, the more participants that are required to qualify as a complete case (e.g., mother, child, and father), the more difficult the research. Mackey (1985) noted that when mother-child interactions are investigated, only one dyad must be considered. When the researcher adds a father to this design, three dyads (father-child, mother-child, father-mother) must be examined. When another child is added, for example in a four-person family, then 11 relationships (dyads, triads, and quadrads) must be considered. For a five-person family, this number increases to 46 relationships. Mackey noted this exponential increase in interactions with the addition of every family member, not to dissuade researchers from investigating the entire family, but rather to point out the alluring nature of doing research with only one dyad from the family. However, thoroughly investigating all relationships within families will be the only way to thoroughly investigate the father's role in child and adolescent psychopathology.

Merely increasing the amount of research that includes fathers will not be enough; the quality and type of research also must be improved. Belsky (1981) suggested that including fathers in research designs does more than just add a person to the research design. Including fathers in research designs necessitates that researchers consider marital functioning, husband-wife interactions, father-mother-child triadic relationships, and other contextual features within the family. Belsky and Volling (1987) argued that researchers must move away from the assumption that families are simply sets of individuals who live in the same dwelling. Instead, researchers must acknowledge that families (including residential and nonresidential fathers) consist of an interconnected system that may represent more than the sum of the individuals within it.

In addition to reconceptualizing the constellations of individuals within families, research on the roles of fathers in the development of psychopathology would benefit from additional nonsexist theory-driven research. Although theory-driven research based on sexist theories has been cited as a reason for the failure to include fathers in developmental psychopathology research (Phares, 1992), theory-driven research is needed to delineate the role of fathers in child and adolescent psychopathology. Researchers need to reevaluate theories that solely address maternal influences and therefore need to develop new theories of etiology that include nonmaternal factors (e.g., paternal factors, environmental factors, genetic factors, sibling relationships). An excellent example of a study that was conducted after reevaluating traditional theories found that fathers and mothers experienced similar levels of separation anxiety when leaving their children at a child care center (Deater-Deckard, Scarr, McCartney, & Eisenberg, 1994). Chapter 4 reviewed a number of theories of etiology in reference to the role of fathers. These theories should be tested out further to ascertain fathers' roles in the development of psychopathology.

In addition, as researchers begin to collect more data on fathers, they should take care to analyze paternal and maternal variables separately. As noted by Phares and Compas (1992), 25% of the child psychopathology research that was reviewed included both fathers and mothers but did not provide separate paternal and maternal analyses or else discussed "parents" without reference as to whether the parents were fathers or mothers. Therefore, whenever researchers collect data on fathers and mothers, it is important to provide separate analyses. Likewise, researchers should provide separate analyses of sons and daughters. These research strategies should help clarify the roles of fathers in child and adolescent psychopathology and should contribute to the knowledge base of both paternal and maternal influences on abnormal development.

Eventually, it may be useful to retreat from the focus on paternal versus maternal variables. There is a growing body of evidence that fathers and mothers influence their children in similar ways (see Chapters 2, 5, 6, and 7). However, there is also evidence that fathers contribute unique and significant variance in the explanation of some child characteristics (e.g., conduct disorder, Type A behavior), and therefore the current emphasis on research with fathers and mothers seems warranted. Eventually, it may be appropriate to focus more on characteristics of *parents* rather than fathers and mothers separately. Gilbert (1981) emphasized that future research should look beyond the polarity of paternal versus maternal characteristics and address qualities of parenting. However, the possible differential effects of fathers and mothers are not yet well enough established to suggest ignoring the unique contributions of each parent.

This discussion of increased investigation of fathers has consistently included mothers in the suggested research design. To investigate thoroughly fathers' roles in child and adolescent psychopathology, it seems important to include mothers in the investigation. Phares and Compas (1992) noted that 48% of the research they reviewed included mothers without fathers, whereas only 1% included fathers without mothers. A perusal of research on fathering will show the same pattern with almost all research on fathering including mothers in the design (e.g., Biller, 1993; Bronstein & Cowan, 1988; Lamb, 1981, 1986, in press). It is to the credit of fatherhood researchers that they include mothers in their investigations rather than trying to equalize the research literature by only including fathers. This trend may accelerate the rate of knowledge that is gained about the similarities and differences in fathers' and mothers' roles in developmental psychopathology. Both fathers and mothers (whether or not they are physically present) appear to be important in the psychological development of their children. Therefore, neither fathers nor mothers should be ignored in the research process.

PRACTICAL TIPS ON IMPLEMENTATION

Now that the research design issues have been discussed, the next step is to review the practical issues of how to recruit fathers into research on developmental psychopathology. These recommendations are for investigators with a strong commitment to recruiting fathers into their research projects.

Scheduling Issues

The scheduling of data collection has often assumed that parents (mothers) were available during the day. With the majority of fathers and mothers employed outside the household (Roberts, 1993), this assumption is no longer true for either mothers or fathers. To access employed parents, data collection may need to be scheduled during evenings and weekends. Because of the limited amount of time (due to evening meal, children's baths, etc.), data collection may need to be completed over a series of sessions rather than in one session. Research on therapy intake interviews (see Chapter 9) shows that fathers (and mothers) are much more likely to participate when appointments are convenient to their schedules (Churven, 1978).

With the addition of fathers (and possibly multiple siblings) to the research design, it may be necessary to have a team of research assistants (RAs) conduct the data collection rather than just one or two research assistants. If the design used to call for two RA's to conduct interviews with a mother and a child, then three RA's could be scheduled at the same time to interview the mother, father, and child (or children) without adding to the family's time commitment in absolute hours.

Sample Selection

In addition to providing flexible times for data collection, researchers can also target subject recruitment sites in which fathers are likely to be evident. For example, clinical research populations with men can be found in Veteran's Administration hospitals (e.g., Mulinski, 1989), and nonclinical populations can be found through the military (e.g., Jensen et al., 1986) or places of employment (e.g., Repetti, 1989). It appears that researchers assume fathers will not participate in research as fathers but will participate in research as employees and business managers. This may again point to the importance of considering the scheduling of research appointments. Many research projects in the industrial/organization area (e.g., Gable et al., 1992; Long, 1993) take place at the work site, rather than requiring additional time outside that site. Family researchers who are particularly interested in employed fathers and mothers may have to begin recruiting families through work sites and corporations as a way of increasing fathers' (and mothers') participation. This option points out the need for creative recruitment strategies to make research projects available to fathers.

Topic Selection

For research in both normative and nonnormative development, there are numerous ways to encourage investigations of a broader range of topics relating to fathers and their children. For example, Thompson and Walker (1989) noted that there is a fair amount of research on paternal characteristics and skills associated with fathers' increased involvement with children, but these issues have been ignored for mothers. Researchers seemingly continue to conceptualize paternal involvement as "helping out" rather than being necessary, whereas maternal involvement is seen as mandatory and unquestioned. It would be helpful to look at the system level of the family to investigate the quantity and quality of fathers' and mothers' involvement with their children.

Regarding parents' desired levels of involvement with their children, Margolin and Larson (1988) provided an interesting study of parents' involuntary participation in family work and violence toward children. Involuntary participation in family work was defined as a large disparity between the amount of responsibility parents would like to assume in the home and the actual amount of work they perform in the home. The researchers conceptualized involuntary participation as a type of role strain and hypothesized that it would have a greater impact on mothers than on fathers. This hypothesis was confirmed. Mothers' level of involuntary family work was more strongly associated with maternal violence toward children than the same relation in fathers. Margolin and Larson suggested that future research into family division of labor and children's functioning should consider fathers' and mothers' role strain to get a better understanding of the family as a system.

Another important topic that deserves attention is the actual institution of fatherhood and motherhood and the roles that these institutions encourage. Russo (1979) argued that we need to begin studying fatherhood and motherhood, rather than just fathers and mothers. The process of parenting, including developmental and systemic changes within the family, should be investigated as reflected in the parental roles. Russo encouraged researchers to look beyond the individual characteristics of participants in specific research projects to gain a more complete understanding of fatherhood and motherhood as these roles impact on individual parents.

As noted in Chapter 6 regarding nonnormative development, a majority of research on referred fathers has been conducted with fathers who sexually abused their children. Anecdotally, I cannot count the amount of times that I have been involved in social conversations in which, after hearing that I am interested in fathers and developmental psychopathology, the other person says something like, "Oh you mean fathers who sexually abuse their children?" It appears that both in the lay public and in the field of psychology, one of the most salient issues related to paternal influences is that of sexually abusive fathers. The same emphasis can also be said for fathers who abuse alcohol. Researchers interested in the development of psychopathology must move beyond these areas of research to better understand paternal influences in children's psychological functioning.

Family Constellation Issues

With only 61.1% of U.S. children under 18 living with both biological parents, researchers who are dedicated to studying fathers must acknowledge family constellations other than the traditional nuclear family. In any random sample of children and adolescents, a large number of children will not live with their biological fathers. Therefore, it is crucial for researchers to recruit fathers regardless of whether or not they live with their children. This means that noncustodial fathers must be contacted and recruited to participate in research projects. With the inclusion of custodial and noncustodial fathers in samples of family research, researchers will have to include brief analyses to investigate the effects of custodial and noncustodial fathers. It would be beneficial if some researchers choose specifically to investigate fathers' influences when they live with versus do not live with the child. Some of this work already has been conducted (e.g., Biller & Solomon, 1986); however, care must be taken to tease out the impact of paternal absence and subsequent decrements in socioeconomic status. Biller (1981a) noted that early research findings on paternal absence were confounded with the impact of lower SES. Although children whose fathers were absent were found to have decrements in social and emotional functioning, these decrements were later discovered to be due to loss in socioeconomic status rather than paternal absence per se.

Because the history of research on "paternal absence" is so well entrenched in the study of paternal influences on the development of psychopathology, a few additional comments should be made about this research strategy (see also Chapter 2 for a discussion of father absence research). There appears to be an assumption that after a father leaves the family residence because of parental divorce, he is completely uninvolved with his children. Although this is true in some families, it appears to be the exception rather than the rule. As discussed in Chapter 1, Seltzer and Bianchi (1988) found that the majority of children and adolescents who no longer live with their father still have some contact with him. Even if there is no physical contact, fathers may still have some type of an emotional impact on their children, depending on how children understand their father's absence. An interesting question when considering "father absence" is how "absence" should be defined. Nearly all the work on "father absence" or "paternal deprivation" has focused on fathers who no longer live with their children. Thus, absence is meant to signify physical absence. In contrast, Bernard (1987) notes that an equally important research topic is the impact of emotional absence on children's functioning, regardless of whether the father still resides with his children. Lee and Gotlib (1991) conceptualized the same characteristics when referring to emotional unavailability: To understand the development of psychopathology in children and adolescents, researchers should investigate emotional desertion in addition to physical desertion.

Aside from considering the physical and emotional presence of fathers, researchers should be willing to explore nontraditional family constellations that include fathers. For example, Wilson and colleagues (1990) investigated family functioning in single- and dual-parent families in relation to the presence or absence of the grandmother both in and outside the home. Bozett (1985, 1988) has noted the need for research on gay fathers. An excellent review of children of homosexual parents (Patterson, 1992) suggested that children raised by homosexual parents show similar levels of psychological adjustment, gender identity functioning, and peer relationships as children raised by heterosexual parents. However, the majority of the studies in Patterson's review included children of lesbian mothers rather than gay fathers. Bozett (1988) suggests that further research is needed into the psychosocial functioning and stressors of gay fathers and their children.

A number of researchers have noted the importance of evaluating paternal influences in families of different ethnicities and socioeconomic classes. For example, McAdoo (1988) highlighted the need to focus research on African American fathers who are active in their children's upbringing, rather than always focusing on the "absent" African American father and the "matricentric" African American family. McAdoo also noted that there are more similarities than differences between African American fathers and Caucasian American fathers. Mirande (1988) noted that Latino and Latina families used to be considered extremely patriarchal, but that more recent research has found these families to be more egalitarian than earlier thought. Like McAdoo, Mirande also noted that Latino and Latina families show more similarities than differences in their values, parenting styles, and family functioning when compared with Caucasian American families. Additional cross-cultural research needs to be conducted that investigates differential paternal effects in different cultures (Lamb, 1987).

Measurement Issues

Including fathers in developmental research on psychopathology adds a level of depth and complexity to statistical analyses that is both exciting and anxiety provoking. In a meta-analysis of different informants on children's emotional/behavioral problems, Achenbach, McConaughy, and Howell (1987) found that different informants provide different information in child assessments. For example, rating of informants in similar roles (e.g., mother-father dyads or teacher-teacher dyads) correlated at an average of .60, whereas ratings of informants in different roles (such as parent-teacher) averaged .28, and ratings of an informant with the child (e.g., parent-child or teacher-child) averaged .22. They also found that correlations were higher when informants rated children's externalizing behavior problems compared with internalizing problems, and that correlations between informants were higher when rating children aged 6 to 11 years compared with rating adolescents aged 12 to 18.

In more recent individual studies (that do not reflect the breadth of a meta-analysis), there is conflicting evidence as to fathers' and mothers' correspondence in their behavioral ratings of their sons and daughters. For example, Christensen, Margolin, and Sullaway (1992) found that mothers reported significantly more emotional/behavioral problems than fathers for both their sons and daughters. However, Thurber and Osborn (1993) found that fathers and mothers had a high degree of correspondence in their reports of their daughters' emotional/behavioral problems, but that mother-son convergence was higher than father-son convergence. Overall, evidence suggests that no single informant of children's or adolescents' behavior can reflect the different perspectives that are obtained from multiple informants of children's emotional and behavioral problems (Stanger & Lewis, 1993).

When utilizing parents' reports of children's emotional/behavioral problems, researchers need to be cognizant that parents' own psychological distress can influence their ratings of their children's emotional/behavioral problems. Griest, Wells, and Forehand (1979) found that maternal reports of children's emotional/behavioral problems were more strongly related to maternal depression than were observers' ratings of children's emotional/behavioral problems. Brody and Forehand (1986) found that the combination of high levels of child emotional/behavioral problems (as judged by an observer) with high levels of maternal depression resulted in higher maternal ratings of child maladjustment than any other constellation of maternal and child characteristics (high maternal depression/low child noncompliance, low maternal depression/high child noncompliance, and low maternal depression/low child noncompliance). Fathers were not investigated in either of the studies by Griest and colleagues (1979) or Brody and Forehand (1986).

In a study that included fathers, Schaughency and Lahey (1985) found the same connection between maternal depression and maternal ratings of children's externalizing (but not internalizing) behavior problems, but did not find the same significant associations between paternal depression and paternal ratings of children's externalizing or internalizing behavior problems. Conversely, Phares and colleagues (1989) investigated fathers' and mothers' levels of global psychological symptoms (not just depression) and found that both fathers' and mothers' psychological symptoms were significantly related to their reports of children's emotional/behavioral problems. In addition, fathers' reports of children's emotional/behavioral problems appeared to provide unique and significant variance to an overall assessment of children's emotional/behavioral problems above and beyond mothers' and teachers' reports of those problems.

Parents' ratings of children's functioning also seem to be related to characteristics of the family and of the child him or herself. For example, Christensen and colleagues (1992) found that father-mother correspondence in their reports of children's emotional/behavioral problems decreased as the level of family distress increased. In another study of family factors and parents' ratings of children's behavior, Shulman and Zohar (1991) categorized families of toddlers in Israel into three types: environment-sensitive (ES), distance-sensitive (DS), and consensus-sensitive (CS). The ES families displayed problem solving in which family members were aware of others' needs without ignoring their own needs. The DS families showed problem-solving strategies in which independence was valued and the acceptance of another's opinion was seen as a personal weakness. In CS families, cohesiveness and consensus within the family were valued, even if this consensus led to inadequate solutions to problems.

Shulman and Zohar suggested that the DS and CS family types were considered less optimal than the ES family type. The researchers then calculated correlations of paternal and maternal ratings of children's emotional/behavioral problems and found that correlations differed depending on family type. Parents in ES families showed significant correlations in their reports of children's anxiety, but not children's aggressiveness or hyperactivity. In contrast, parents in DS families showed significant agreement in ratings of their children's aggressiveness and hyperactivity, but not anxiety. Parents from CS families showed significant correlations in their ratings of all three types of children's behavioral problems (anxiety, aggressiveness, and hyperactivity). Because of the value placed on consensus in the CS families, it is not surprising to find that fathers and mothers provided similar ratings of their children, even though the ratings were done independently. Shulman and Zohar summarized these results by pointing out the importance of considering family functioning and family type when utilizing fathers' and mothers' ratings of their children's emotional/behavioral problems.

In a study of adolescent substance use in a community sample, Langhinrichsen and colleagues (1990) compared the congruence of fathers', mothers', and adolescents' reports of adolescents' use of marijuana, alcohol, and cigarettes. Congruence was defined as exact agreement as to whether the adolescent was a current user, an exuser, or a never-user. A total of 80% of fathers were congruent with their adolescents regarding marijuana use, 55% were congruent for alcohol use, and 70% were congruent for cigarette use. Mother-adolescent congruence showed a similar pattern, with 78% congruence on marijuana use, 54% congruence on alcohol use, and 70% congruence on cigarette use. When fathers' and mothers' congruence with their adolescents were compared for parents in the same families, there were no differences in congruence for alcohol use or cigarette use, but mothers were significantly more congruent with their adolescents than were fathers regarding adolescents' marijuana use.

To ascertain whether rates of congruence were associated with any characteristics of the adolescent, Langhinrichsen and colleagues (1990) compared congruence rates depending on adolescents' grade level, grade point average (GPA), gender, ethnicity, and after-school employment status. When compared with younger adolescents, father-adolescent congruence was significantly lower for older adolescents regarding marijuana and cigarette use, but father-adolescent congruence was significantly higher for older adolescents regarding alcohol use. Age differences were only significant for mother-adolescent congruence regarding marijuana use, where congruence was lower for older adolescents when compared with younger adolescents. Father-adolescent congruence and mother-adolescent congruence were significantly correlated with adolescents' GPA with regard to congruence of reports of marijuana use, but not alcohol or cigarette use. Adolescents' gender, ethnicity, and after-school employment were not significantly related to congruence with fathers or mothers for any of the three substances that were studied. These data suggest that parent-adolescent agreement may be influenced by characteristics of the adolescents themselves as well as the type of substance that is being measured. Overall, these studies of parent-child correspondence on ratings of children's emotional/behavioral problems suggest that individual characteristics (such as parental psychological symptoms, age, and academic functioning of the child) as well as familial characteristics (such as family type) must be taken into account when using fathers' and mothers' ratings of their children's functioning. Achenbach (1985) argues that utilizing multiple informants, in addition to assessing multiple characteristics (e.g., behavioral functioning, cognitive functioning, academic functioning) can help provide a comprehensive assessment of children's and adolescents' functioning.

In addition to having fathers serve as another informant of children's emotional/behavioral problems, another reason to include fathers in research is to assess paternal characteristics. To facilitate research on paternal characteristics, measures that emphasize paternal characteristics will be reviewed. Special attention is paid to measures that provide separate scales for fathers and mothers. For other measures that can be used in research on families, interested readers are referred to an excellent compilation of family measurement techniques by Touliatos, Perlmutter, and Straus (1990). In addition to the measures reviewed in this chapter, Touliatos and colleagues (1990) compiled a thorough listing of measures related to marital and family interaction, intimacy and family values, parenthood, roles and power, and adjustment. They provide information on the subscales of the measures, the formats of the measures, and the psychometric properties of the measures. The authors include ordering information and describe source materials for interested researchers and clinicians. Holden and Edwards (1989) also provided an excellent review of measures that assess parental attitudes toward child rearing. They found 83 measures of parental attitude that were published between 1899 and 1986. Holden and Edwards argued that many of the measures they reviewed showed marginally acceptable psychometric properties, and thus they discuss alternative ways of assessing parental attitudes toward child rearing.

Table 8.1 details measures that might interest researchers of fathers and developmental psychopathology. As can be seen in Table 8.1, measures are grouped by subject matter (parental behavior and attitudes, parent-child and parent-adolescent interactions and communication, paternal participation in the family, and feelings toward parenthood). Although psychometric properties are not listed in the table, only measures with adequate psychometrics were selected for mention. Also, all these measures were published originally in peer-reviewed journals or academic publications, rather than being published directly through a testing corporation.

A number of other measures can be given to both fathers and mothers, but they do not provide separate subscales for paternal and maternal functioning. Realistically, nearly any measure of adult functioning can be given to both fathers and mothers to assess the target characteristics. For example, broad-based psychological symptoms can be assessed by the Brief Symptom Inventory (BSI; Derogatis & Spencer, 1982). Paternal as well as maternal personality functioning can be assessed with the Minnesota Multiphasic Personality Inventory-2 (MMPI-2; Butcher, Dahlstrom, Graham, Tellegen, & Kaemmer, 1989), the Millon Multiaxial Clinical Inventory (MMCI; Widiger, Williams, Spitzer, & Frances, 1986), the Personality Assessment Inventory (PAI; Morey, 1991), or the NEO Personality Inventory, which is based on the five-factor model of personality (Costa & McCrae, 1992). Paternal and maternal functioning (including psychological symptoms, personality traits, stress, and role performance) can be measured with the Parenting Stress Index (PSI; Abidin, 1990). A thorough evaluation of fathers' and mothers' levels of stress might include an assessment of major life events via the Life Events Survey (LES; Sarason, Johnson, & Seigel, 1978), the assessment of daily hassles and uplifts via the Hassles and Uplifts Scale (DeLongis, Folkman, & Lazarus, 1988), and a measure of coping strategies such as the Ways of Coping Questionnaire (Folkman & Lazarus, 1988).

Numerous other characteristics of fathers and mothers can be evaluated such as perceived competence and global self-worth (Adult Self-Perception Profile; Messer & Harter, 1986) and gender roles (Bem Sex Role Inventory; Bem, 1981). Parents' reports of their own parenting practices can also be assessed through the use of the Modified Child Rearing Practices Report, which measures restrictiveness and nurturance in fathers and mothers (Rickel & Biasatti, 1982). Nearly any measure of adult characteristics can be given to both fathers and mothers to provide parallel data sets from both parents.

In addition to these measures that provide paternal and maternal characteristics, many researchers use measures that assess the family environment or family dynamics. Thus, rather than assessing the characteristics of all the individuals in a family, the entire family system is assessed. The Draw-A-Family technique has been used to assess the psychological presence or absence of fathers based on young adolescents' drawings of their families (Spigelman, Spigelman, & Englesson, 1992). With regard to psychometrically

TABLE 8.1. Research Measures of Paternal Characteristics

Authors	Name of Measure	Variables Assessed	Informant	Notes
Parental Behavior and Attitudes				
Bach (1946)	Father-Typing Rating Scale	View of father given to children by mother	Interview & observation of mother	
Buri (1991)	Parental Authority Questionnaire	Father's & mother's level of permissive, authoritarian, or authoritative authority	Adolescent	
Chang & Block (1960)	Parent Identification Adjective Checklist	Identification with father & mother	Adolescent	Available from NAPS-1
Daniels & Plomin (1985)	Sibling Inventory of Differential Experience (SIDE)	Paternal and maternal differential control & affection toward siblings	Older child Adolescent Young adult	Reprinted in Dunn & Plomin (1990)
Elder (1980)	Index of Parental Socialization Styles	Father's & mother's parenting behavior	Adolescent	
Hazzard, Christensen, & Margolin (1983)	Parent Perception Inventory (PPI)	Positive and negative perceptions of fathers & mothers	Child Adolescent	
Kelly & Worell (1977)	The Parent Behavior Form (PBF)	Father's & mother's warmth, control, & cognitive mediation	Child Adolescent Adult—Retrospective	Available from NAPS-3
Majoribanks (1987)	Perceived Family Environment Scale	Father's & mother's interest & encouragement of educational goals	Adolescent	Available from NAPS-3
McKinley (1964)	Father's Hostility Measure	Perception of father's hostility	Child Adolescent	
Parker, Tupling, & Brown (1979)	Parental Bonding Inventory (PBI)	Father's & mother's parenting behavior	Adolescent Adult—Retrospective	
Schaefer (1965)	Child's Report of Parental Behavior Inventory (CRPBI)	Father's & mother's parenting behavior	Child Adolescent Adult—Retrospective	Available from NAPS-3 See also Kawash & Clewes (1988)

TABLE 8.1. *(Continued)*

Authors	Name of Measure	Variables Assessed	Informant	Notes
Scheck (1979)	Inconsistent Parental Discipline Scale	Father's & mother's consistency of disciplinary actions	Adult— Retrospective	
Scheck (1979)	Parental Disagreement on Expectations of the Child Scale	Father's & mother's consistency of expectations for child	Adult— Retrospective	
Schwarz & Zuroff (1979)	Schwarz-Zuroff Love Inconsistency Scale	Father's & mother's inconsistency in love & affection	Adolescent Young adult Father, Mother	Available from NAPS-3
Siegelman (1981)	Parent-Child Relations Questionnaire—II	Father's & mother's actions toward 12 y.o. child	Adult— Retrospective	Available from NAPS-3
Spence & Helmreich (1978)	Parental Attitudes Questionnaire	Father's & mother's attitudes, actions, & the family environment	Child Adolescent	

Parent-Child and Parent-Adolescent Interactions and Communication

Authors	Name of Measure	Variables Assessed	Informant	Notes
Bowerman & Irish (1962)	Closeness to Parent	Perceived closeness to father, mother, stepfather, & stepmother	Child Adolescent	Updated version in Ganong & Coleman (1987)
Fine Moreland, & Schwebel (1983)	Parent-Child Relationship Survey	Father's & mother's trust, closeness, acceptance, & communication	Adult— Retrospective	
Heilbrun (1964)	Parent-Child Interaction Rating Scales	Father's & mother's nurturance and interactions	Adolescent	
Henggeler et al. (1986)	Family Relationship Questionnaire	Dyadic interactions of warmth, conflict, & dominance between fathers, mothers, & adolescent	Adolescent Father Mother	Available from NAPS-3
Olson et al. (1985)	Inventory of Parent-Adolescent Communication	Father's & mother's openness & style of communication	Adolescent Father Mother	
Prinz, Foster, Kent, & O'Leary (1979)	Conflict Behavior Questionnaire	Father's, mother's, & adolescent's conflict & communication style	Adolescent Father Mother	Available from NAPS-3 See also Roehling & Robin (1986)

(Continued)

TABLE 8.1. *(Continued)*

Authors	Name of Measure	Variables Assessed	Informant	Notes
Small (1988)	Child's Non-Adherence to Parental Advice Scale	Willingness to follow father's & mother's advice	Older child Adolescent	Available from NAPS-3
Paternal Participation in the Family				
Bigner (1977)	Father-Child Activity Scale	Degree of father's involvement in parenting activities	Father	Available from NAPS-3
Cowan & Cowan (1988)	Pie	Father's & mother's sense of major life roles and relationships	Father Mother	Available from NAPS-3
Cowan & Cowan (1988)	"Who Does What?"	Father's & mother's involvement in family tasks & responsibilities	Father Mother	Available from NAPS-3
Small (1988)	Adolescent's Participation in Activities with Parents	Father's & mother's time spent in recreational & leisure activities	Older child Adolescent	Available from NAPS-3
Feelings toward Parenthood				
Bigner (1977)	Attitudes Toward Fathering Scale	Father's orientation to the fathering role	Father	Available from NAPS-3
Condon (1993)	Antenatal Emotional Attachment	Expectant father's & mother's attachment to fetus	Father Mother	
Palkovitz (1984)	Role of the Father	Perception of importance of father for infant	Father Mother	
Rabin & Greene (1968)	Child Study Inventory	Father's & mother's motivation for becoming a parent	Father Mother	Available from NAPS-2 See also Reading & Amatea (1986)
Scanzoni & Arnett (1987)	Role of Wife, Husband, Father, and Mother Scales	Father's & mother's rewards & costs of paid work & child care	Father Mother	

Notes: Unless otherwise noted, the measures are paper-and-pencil questionnaires. NAPS = National Auxiliary Publications Service (P. O. Box 3513, Grand Central Station, New York, NY 10163-3513).

sound questionnaires, four of the most notable examples of family measures will be discussed: the Family Environment Scale (FES; Moos, 1990), the Family Cohesiveness and Adaptiveness Scale (FACES-III; Olson, 1986), the Family Assessment Measure (FAM-III; Skinner et al., 1983), and the McMaster Family Assessment Device (FAD; Epstein et al., 1983).

All these family measures are paper-and-pencil questionnaires that can be filled out by each family member separately. The FES (Moos, 1990) consists of 10 subscales: conflict, independence, achievement orientation, intellectual-cultural orientation, active-recreational orientation, moral-religious emphasis, organization, control, family cohesion, and expressiveness. Three forms of the FES exist: The "real form" assesses family members' perceptions of their current family environment; the "ideal form" asks family members to report on their ideal perceptions of a family environment; and the "expectations form" assesses family members' expectations about new family constellations (such as asking couples who are expecting their first child what their expectations are related to the family environment after the birth of the child). For all three of these forms, family members' responses on the FES can be graphed on a profile that allows comparison across different subscales. Adequate psychometric properties have been established and normative data are presented in the manual from a number of family constellations and families from different ethnicities (e.g., single parent families, intact families, African American families). The Family Adaptability and Cohesion Evaluation Scales (FACES-III; Olson, 1986) consists of three subscales: adaptability, cohesion, and expressivity. The FACES-III is based on the circumplex model of family functioning. Psychometric properties of the FACES-III are adequate.

The FAM-III (Skinner et al., 1983) and the FAD (Epstein et al., 1983) do not appear to be used as often as the FES or the FACES; however, the FAM-III and the FAD provide alternative options in measuring family functioning. The FAM-III consists of seven subscales: task accomplishment, role performance, communication, affective expression, involvement, control, and values and norms. In addition, the FAM-III includes two response-style subscales: social desirability and denial. The FAM-III is based on a process model of family functioning that assesses strengths and weaknesses within families. Reliability and validity of the FAM-III have been well established (Steinhauer, Santa-Barbara, & Skinner, 1984). For an investigation of the factor structure within and across the FES, FACES, and FAM, refer to Gondoli and Jacob (1993). Finally, the FAD is based on the McMaster model, which assumes that family functioning is related to accomplishing essential tasks and functions with the family. Seven dimensions are measured on the FAD: problem solving, communication, roles, affective responsiveness, affective involvement, behavioral control, and general family functioning. The FAD has adequate internal reliability and factorial validity (Kabacoff, Miller, Bishop, Epstein, & Keitner, 1990).

In addition to these questionnaires, many research projects with families in which one member is diagnosed with schizophrenia have focused on communication deviance (CD) and expressed emotions (EE) in these families (e.g., Hahlweg & Goldstein, 1987; Hahlweg et al., 1989). More recently, this assessment technique has been used in families with a depressed child (Asarnow, Tompson, Hamilton, Goldstein, & Guthrie, 1994). CD and EE are measured by observing family members interacting with one another and then quantifying the levels of CD and EE that are present between family members.

Overall, these different measures of family functioning tend to focus on the family as a system rather than focusing on the individuals within the family system. Assessing different perspectives of the family environment and of family functioning is important to thoroughly assess the family as a whole. However, to investigate characteristics that are specific to fathers and mothers, it is also important to assess individuals (as individuals) within the family. Because of the concern about "biased" reports of family members, Cook and Goldstein (1993) conducted a thorough evaluation of the reliability and validity of fathers', mothers', and children's reports of parent-child negativity. They found that each family member's report contained "true-score" variance, systematic variance that was unique to the rater's perspective, and error variance. They suggested that the latent variables approach should be used to control statistically for individual rater effects when multiple informants are used to assess the parent-child relationship.

Informant/Participant Issues

Along with considering what type of measures will be used in the study, researchers must also be cognizant of their choices of informants on questionnaires and the constellation of participants in observational techniques. With regard to paper-and-pencil questionnaires, there is a debate as to whether the reports of individual informants should remain separate or should be aggregated. For example, when multiple informants are used to measure children's emotional/behavioral problems, many researchers analyze fathers' and mothers' reports separately (e.g., Compas, Howell, Phares, Williams, & Ledoux, 1989), whereas other researchers choose to average fathers' and mothers' reports of their children's functioning (e.g., Johnston et al., 1987). Turning to parenting behavior, many researchers choose to consider children's reports of paternal and maternal behavior as indicative of children's perceptions of their parents, and thus the children's reports of their fathers and mothers are considered separately (e.g., Eastburg & Johnson, 1990). Other researchers (e.g., Schwarz, Barton-Henry, & Pruzinsky, 1985) argue that aggregating scores from multiple informants of parental behavior, such as the child's, sibling's, father's, and mother's reports of the father's parenting behavior, will provide a more realistic measurement of the parental behavior. Both strategies have their advantages and disadvantages, and researchers must consider how these advantages and disadvantages influence their own research project. In terms of research with fathers, it appears to be important to maintain separate measurements of paternal perceptions and maternal perceptions to establish how these perceptions are related to children's functioning.

When conducting behavioral observations, researchers must carefully choose the participants who will be involved in the observations. Hops and Seeley (1991) noted that different data are collected when the interactions of different constellations of dyads and triads are observed. For example, Gjerde (1986) studied families recruited from the community who had a young adolescent child. Families were observed in dyads (father-child, mother-child) as well as triads (father-mother-child), and observations were completed in a laboratory setting. In families with a son, the presence of the father in triadic interactions enhanced the mother's interactions with her son (e.g., mothers were more consistent, less bored, more relaxed, and more able to express their own opinions in the presence of fathers as opposed to during the absence of fathers). Conversely, the presence of the mother in triadic interactions decreased the quality of the father's interactions with his son (e.g., fathers were less responsive, participated less, and were more critical and hostile in the presence of mothers as opposed to during the absence of mothers). In families with an adolescent daughter, fathers were less egalitarian and less likely to explain things to their daughters in the presence of mothers. There were no significant differences based on father presence or absence in the interactions for mothers and their daughters. Overall, this study highlights the care that must be taken when conducting observational research with families. Not only must the presence or absence of each parent in the observational session be considered, but the gender of the child also must be taken into account.

Russell, Russell, and Midwinter (1992) conducted a somewhat different study that used naturalistic home-based observations of fathers, mothers, and their 6- or 7-year-old children. Rather than assessing the impact of the other parent's presence on parent-child interactions, Russell and colleagues studied the impact of the presence of an observer (reactivity) on fathers' and mothers' interactions with their children. In this study of intact, middle-class families who were recruited from the community, families were observed for 90 minutes in the early evening and behaviors were coded by two female research assistants. Families were asked to "just do the things you normally do," but they were asked not to watch television while the observer was present and they were also asked not to interact with the observer. Families were also asked to play a ring-toss game at some point during the evening. The ring-toss game was utilized to provide a playful but potentially competitive situation in which to observe the family members interact. Fathers' and mothers' behaviors were coded according to the following categories: affectionate/supportive, child-centered/responsive, control/influence, and competition. After the behavioral observations, fathers and mothers were interviewed separately to assess their perceptions of how much the observer had influenced their interactions with their children.

Over 80% of parents in the study acknowledged that the observer's presence had influenced their behavior to some degree. Based on the self-reports of perceived observer influence, there were no differences between fathers and mothers in their perceptions of influence, nor were there significant differences based on the gender of the child with whom the parents were interacting. However, when the behavioral observations were analyzed in relation to paternal and maternal perceptions of influence, observers appeared to have influenced fathers more than mothers. Fathers and mothers were divided into two groups each: those who perceived little to no influence on their behavior from observers and those who perceived moderate to high influence on their behavior due to the observer's presence. Multivariate analyses of variance (MANOVAs) were conducted for parent-initiated interactions and child-initiated parental reactions for fathers and mothers separately. When the percentage of father-initiated behaviors was analyzed, fathers who reported greater perceived influence from observers showed significantly fewer affectionate/supportive behaviors with both their sons and their daughters. This suggests that fathers may have decreased their affectionate and supportive behaviors in response to the observer's presence. There were no significant differences based on perceived influence when fathers' child-centered, control/influence, or competitive behaviors were analyzed. None of these parent-initiated behaviors differed for mothers based on their perceptions of influence from the observer.

When parental reactions to child-initiated behaviors were analyzed, fathers' positive reactions to their children's affectionate/supportive behaviors and fathers' negative reactions to their children's control/influence behaviors differed according to paternal perceptions of influence from observers. However, fathers' reactions differed according to the gender of their child. In reaction to their children's affectionate/supportive behaviors, fathers who perceived themselves to be influenced by the observer showed lower rates of positive reactions to their sons and higher rates of positive reactions to their daughters than did fathers who did not appear to be influenced by being observed. In reaction to their children's behaviors of control/influence, fathers who were influenced by observers showed greater levels of negative behaviors toward their sons and lower levels of negative behavior toward their daughters than did fathers who perceived little influence from observers. There were no significant differences in fathers' reactions to their children's behaviors of responsive/involved, seeking approval/support, or competition. Although the MANOVA for mothers' reactions to their children's behavior was significant, the subsequent ANOVA results for specific behaviors did not reach significance at the $p < .05$ level.

Overall, this study suggests that parents (especially fathers) may alter their behavior in response to knowing that they are being observed. For the most part, these alterations in behavior appear to be in the more "traditional" direction (with fathers initiating less affectionate/supportive behaviors when they are self-conscious about being observed). Russell and colleagues (1992) pointed out that the results of this study might have been different had both observers not been female and had the observers not been in view of the family (e.g., behind a one-way mirror or not present because of use of videotaping). The researchers point out that these issues must be considered when utilizing observational techniques and especially when investigating differences between fathers and mothers. The data collection techniques that are used may in fact have an impact on the data that are collected. When using audiotape recordings in the home, Jacob, Tennenbaum, Seilhamer, Bargiel, and Sharon (1994) found few differences between fathers' and mothers' reactivity to the method of data collection. Further research is needed to ascertain whether fathers are more reactive to observational methods or whether mothers might have been more reactive to male observers.

CONCLUSIONS

In addition to the suggestions provided in this chapter, Russell and Radojevic (1992) provided a compelling discussion of the need to include fathers in research on child development. In future research, they suggested that researchers must recognize the diversity among men as fathers, pay more attention to fathers' feelings and needs for support, critically evaluate arguments about the nature of time spent with children, develop family-enhancing employment policies that enable fathers and mothers to achieve a satisfactory balance between work and family, develop and enhance parenting education programs for new fathers, provide a greater focus on the relationships between fathers and mothers, and critically evaluate services that are provided to fathers and their families.

In concluding this review regarding the inclusion of fathers in research on the development of psychopathology, it might be helpful to look back to the early stages of the inclusion of fathers in normative developmental research. Barnett and Baruch (1988) noted that there have been three stages of research into fathers' participation with their children. First, researchers clearly ignored fathers, and fathers were not represented in research or clinical writings on parenting and children's development. The next stage seemed to glorify fatherhood so that any paternal involvement was seen as extraordinary and increased paternal involvement was perceived as a panacea for exhausted mothers who were employed. Barnett and Baruch suggested that the field has now moved into a third stage in which increased paternal involvement has been acknowledged to have both beneficial as well as maladaptive effects on the family system. They noted that increased (or decreased) paternal involvement should be studied in ways that are similar to increased (or decreased) maternal involvement in child rearing and family household management.

Another reflection on the history of research on normative child development was provided by Parke (1990) in a description of his own personal odyssey through research on fathers. He acknowledged that his own work into fatherhood began for several different reasons. First, he noted that he wanted to provide a "corrective" to the emphasis on mothers and the lack of attention to fathers in children's development. Second, Parke noted that in the early 1970s, the roles of men and women in the family and the workplace were being reexamined and he perceived the study of fathers as having both social and scientific relevance. Third, he acknowledged his own personal interest in research topics that had been neglected or ignored and thus offered many opportunities for innovative and meaningful research that would make significant contributions to the research knowledge base. In considering the present state of research on fathers and developmental psychopathology, all Parke's initial interests in the field of normative development still appear relevant today. Although many excellent research programs have been instituted that investigate fathers and the development of psychopathology, this continues to be a wide-open field in which much work is needed. Like Parke, I invite interested researchers to join the search and to help build a research knowledge base that meaningfully addresses the roles of fathers in the development of psychopathology.

PART V

Where Do We Go from Here?

CHAPTER 9

Future Directions in Therapy

As noted throughout this book, the field of clinical psychology has generally ignored the contributions of fathers in the development of child and adolescent psychopathology as well as family dysfunction. This oversight has included a tendency toward mother-blaming in clinical literature (Caplan & Hall-McCorquodale, 1985a; Cook, 1988) and a concomitant lack of inclusion of fathers in empirical studies of child and adolescent psychopathology (Phares & Compas, 1992). One area within clinical psychology that has received some, albeit limited, empirical attention in relation to fathers has been interventions and therapy for child and family problems. This chapter will review empirical outcome studies that investigate the effectiveness of including fathers in child and family treatment. Because there may be differences between the therapy practices that occur in the context of outcome studies and therapy that occurs in normal clinical practice (Weisz & Weiss, 1989), a review of fathers' participation in clinic-based therapy will also be included. Most of the work in the area of fathers' involvement in therapy pertains to intact families; however, issues related to nonintact families with a noncustodial father will be addressed as well. Suggestions will be provided for future directions in research regarding the role of fathers in the treatment of family and child psychological problems.

THERAPEUTIC EFFECTIVENESS

Before beginning the discussion of the effectiveness of fathers' involvement in child and family therapy, a brief summary of child and family therapy outcome studies will be given to establish the effectiveness of child and family therapy regardless of fathers' (or mothers') participation. Very little empirical research has been conducted that systematically assesses therapeutic outcome of systems-oriented therapy (e.g., family systems therapy) especially in relation to the impact of fathers' involvement in systems-oriented therapy (Lebow & Gurman, 1995). Therefore, unless otherwise noted, the majority of therapies that are discussed can be considered "child-oriented" due to the focus on alleviation of problem behaviors rather than an attempt to restructure the family system.

Effectiveness of Therapy with Children and Adolescents

A number of meta-analyses have been conducted to ascertain the effectiveness of psychological treatment of child and adolescent problems (Casey & Berman, 1985; Weisz, Weiss, Alicke, & Klotz, 1987). Although these meta-analyses have not addressed the issue of differential effectiveness due to fathers' involvement in treatment, it might be helpful to first review the research on treatment effectiveness in general before addressing the specific question of effectiveness due to paternal involvement in therapy with children and adolescents. Overall, psychotherapy with children and adolescents has been found to be more effective than no intervention in the reduction of all types of emotional/behavioral problems (Casey & Berman, 1985; Weisz et al., 1987). However, there is only limited support for differential effectiveness due to the type of therapy conducted. For example, although there is some support for the greater effectiveness of behavioral therapies in contrast to nonbehavioral therapies (Weisz et al., 1987), these findings may be due to the measures used and referral problems studied in behavioral outcome studies (Casey & Berman, 1985). In fact, Kazdin (1991) argues that it is nearly impossible to draw conclusions about the superiority of alternative types of therapies due to the paucity of rigorous empirical studies that investigate differential effectiveness of alternative therapeutic techniques with children and adolescents. In addition, Barrnett, Docherty, and Frommelt (1991) suggest that research on nonbehavioral child psychotherapy is so limited by methodological flaws that conclusions cannot be made about the effectiveness of nonbehavioral child psychotherapy.

Therapeutic outcome studies with children and adolescents, and subsequent meta-analyses of these outcome studies, have been criticized for not accurately representing the therapy done in actual clinical practice (Kazdin, 1991; Weisz & Weiss, 1989). For example, parents and families are frequently not included in therapy conducted in therapeutic outcome studies, whereas parents and families are usually included in therapy conducted in actual clinical practice with children and adolescents (Kazdin, 1991). In their meta-analysis, Casey and Berman (1985) identified 55 studies that treated the child individually and only 9 studies that included parents in the treatment. Although the inclusion of parents in child-oriented therapy was not shown to produce significantly more improvement in the child (Casey & Berman, 1985), this finding may have been due to the limited statistical power of the analyses because of the small number of studies that included parents.

To conduct a meta-analysis of outcome studies that included therapies with at least one parent and one child, Hazelrigg, Cooper, and Borduin (1987) were able to identify 20 studies of family therapy outcome. They concluded that family therapy was more effective than no treatment; however, the results were somewhat mixed when family therapy was compared with alternative treatments. Therefore, it remains unclear whether the inclusion of parents in therapy significantly improves on therapeutic gains achieved when parents are not in-cluded in child-oriented therapy. Outcome studies and subsequent meta-analyses have been limited in investigating differential effectiveness of including parents in child-oriented therapy, and there has been even less emphasis on the differ-ential effectiveness of including fathers, as opposed to mothers, in treatment of children's emotional/behavioral problems. The rare outcome studies that have been conducted to ascertain differential effectiveness of including fathers in therapy will be reviewed now to ascertain whether enough research has been con-ducted to draw conclusions about the gains or drawbacks of paternal inclusion.

Effectiveness of Fathers' Involvement in Therapy

For the purposes of this review, the term "fathers' involvement" means that the father was included in the treatment and was present for the therapy. Although there is undoubtedly a wide range of *actual* therapeutic participation encom-passed in this usage of the term involvement (e.g., fathers who are in the therapy session but do not actively participate vs. fathers who fully participate), the pres-ent usage is consistent with the definition of paternal involvement used in the studies that are reviewed. Relatively few studies have investigated whether fa-thers' involvement is related to therapeutic effectiveness, and almost no studies have investigated the effectiveness of amount and quality of fathers' participa-tion in the therapy session. Therefore, for the time being, the term involvement will be used as a gross indicator of fathers' presence or absence from the ther-apy sessions.

The inclusion of fathers in research or therapy is guided by the researcher's or clinician's theoretical orientation and hypothesized etiology of child and fam-ily problems (Phares, 1992). Many theories of personality and child develop-ment, such as Freudian theory and attachment theory, have focused primarily on the mother (Lamb, 1981, 1986). There are a few examples of Freud's atten-tion to the role of fathers, such as Little Hans's fear of horses that was inter-preted as displaced fear of his father related to the oedipal complex (Freud, 1955). However, the majority of Freud's theoretical work and the work of at-tachment theorists dealt with mothers (Lamb, 1981). Conversely, researchers and clinicians with a wide variety of theoretical orientations have supported the inclusion of fathers in therapy for child and family problems. The importance of including fathers in the treatment of child emotional/behavioral problems and family problems has been noted in the psychoanalytic therapy literature (e.g., Atkins & Lansky, 1986; Cath, Gurwitt, & Gunsberg, 1989; Galenson, 1989; Lansky, 1992; McWilliams, 1991), behavioral parent training literature (e.g., Bernal, Kinnert, & Schultz, 1980; Budd & O'Brien, 1982; Horton, 1984), and family therapy literature (e.g., Guillebeaux et al., 1986; LeCroy, 1987). How-ever, with the exception of the behavioral parent training literature, empirical investigation of the importance of including fathers in child-oriented therapy has been limited. The empirical investigations of effectiveness of fathers' involvement in therapy that have been conducted will be reviewed and presented in two ways. First, empirical studies that investigate the effectiveness of fathers' inclusion versus exclusion from treatment will be discussed. Second, empirical studies that investigate differential maternal versus paternal outcomes in therapy will be discussed.

Treatment Outcome Based on Fathers' Inclusion versus Exclusion from Therapy

Although there has been a pattern of either including only mothers in investigations of treatment effectiveness with children's emotional/behavioral problems (Budd & O'Brien, 1982) or not addressing maternal versus paternal involvement in studies of the efficacy of family therapy (Hazelrigg et al., 1987), there has been some research on the impact of fathers' inclusion versus exclusion in therapy for child problems. The four studies done in this area all evaluated the impact of paternal involvement in behavioral parent training (Adesso & Lipson, 1981; Firestone, Kelly, & Fike, 1980; Martin, 1977; Webster-Stratton, 1985). Overall, there is not strong support for the necessity of including fathers (as opposed to mothers) in behavioral parent training, but a number of problems exist in these studies that make such a conclusion tentative at best. Sample characteristics and results from these four studies are summarized in Table 9.1.

In a study of behavioral parent training in groups of parents, Adesso and Lipson (1981) randomly assigned parents to one of four different groups: (a) mother-only training, (b) father-only training, (c) couples training that included mothers and fathers, and (d) no-treatment control. Analyses of direct observations of child behavior showed that there were no significant differences in treatment gains between the three treatment groups, but all three treatment groups showed significant decreases in child misbehavior compared with the no-treatment control group. These findings suggest that either parent individually, or both parents together, can be effectively taught child behavior management skills, and that neither parent appears to have a natural superiority due to involvement in parent training.

Firestone et al. (1980) investigated the question, "Are fathers necessary in parent training groups?" They randomly assigned families of conduct problem boys to one of three groups: (a) mother-only, (b) mother and father together, and (c) no-treatment control; the investigators found that treatment effects differed according to the subscale on the Behavior Problem Checklist (BPC) that was used and the informant that was used. Children in the mother-only group, but not the mother and father group, showed significant decreases on the Personality Problem factor of the parents' BPC. Children in the mother and father group, but not the mother-only group, showed significant decreases on the Conduct Problem factor of the parents' BPC. Neither group of children, however, showed significant therapeutic changes based on the teachers' reports of child behavior

**TABLE 9.1.   Empirical Studies of Treatment Outcome Based on Fathers'
Inclusion or Exclusion from Therapy**

Researchers	N	Child Characteristics	Referral Problem	Group Assignment[a]	Findings
Adesso & Lipson (1981)	16	2–10 y.o. Boys & Girls	Variety of problems	Random: Mother only Father only Mother & Father Control	No difference between 3 treatment groups. All 3 treatment groups showed more decreases in problem child behavior than control group.
Firestone et al. (1980)	18	3–11 y.o. Boys	Conduct problems	Random: Mother only Mother & Father Control	No differences between 2 treatment groups when compared with each other at follow-up. Both treatment groups showed more decreases in some problem child behaviors compared with control group based on parent reports but not teacher reports.
Martin (1977)	43	5–10 y.o. Boys & Girls	Mother-child problems	Random: Mother only Mother & Father Control	Both treatment groups showed greater decreases in mother-child problem interactions than control group. Father-child problem interactions were not assessed.
Webster-Stratton (1985)	30	3–8 y.o. Boys & Girls	Conduct problems	Not Random: Father-absent Father-involved	No differences between treatment groups in mother-child interactions immediately after treatment. At 1-year follow-up, greater maintenance of treatment gains in father-involved families.

[a] All studies used behavioral parent training as the primary therapeutic modality. Control groups were all no-treatment wait-list controls.

problems. At 4-month follow-up, therapeutic gains were maintained and treatment groups did not differ from each other on any measures. Based on this research, Firestone and colleagues suggested that fathers are not necessary for inclusion in parent training.

Another interpretation of these findings is that treatment gains do differ somewhat depending on the inclusion versus exclusion of the father from parent training. Mother-only training appeared more effective in reducing child personality problems, whereas mother-and-father training appeared more effective in reducing child conduct problems. This study also highlights the necessity of taking into account information from different informants (e.g., Achenbach et al., 1987) as well as the possible problem of lack of treatment generalization from the home environment to the school environment.

The two previous studies investigated behavioral parent training for child behavior problems. Martin (1977) investigated the effectiveness of behavioral parent training in families referred for mother-child interaction problems. Just as in the study by Firestone et al. (1980), Martin randomly assigned families to father-included treatment, father-not-included treatment, and a wait-list control group. He found that both treatment groups showed greater reductions in problematic mother-child interactions than did the control group, but that there were no differences in problem reduction based on the fathers' involvement. The primary dependent variable, however, was frequency of mother-child problems, not frequency of father-child problems, so it was unclear what effects paternal involvement had on problematic father-child interactions. Although the random assignment to treatment groups is a strength of this study, the failure to investigate father-child problems severely limits the conclusions that can be drawn with regard to the effect of therapy on the father-child relationship. Although including fathers in treatment did not improve in the mother-child relationship, it may be that the father-child relationship would show significant gains due to the fathers' involvement in treatment. This hypothesis has yet to be directly investigated.

In a study investigating parent training in father-involved and father-absent families, Webster-Stratton (1985) found that children in both treatment groups showed decreased levels of emotional/behavioral problems, and mothers showed increased levels of praise and decreased levels of critical statements at post-treatment. All these treatment gains were also evident in both treatment groups at 1-year follow-up except for mothers' decreased levels of critical statements, which was only evident in the father-involved treatment group. Therefore, at post-treatment and to a lesser extent at 1-year follow-up, treatment gains appeared to be relatively similar regardless of whether fathers were involved or were absent from the therapy. At 1-year follow-up, a chi-square analysis showed significantly more families in the father-involved treatment were "favorable responders" to therapy when compared with families in the father-absent treatment. Father-child interactions were not assessed and compared for father-presence versus father-absence in therapy. Unlike the three other studies discussed here (Adesso & Lipson, 1981; Firestone et al., 1980; Martin, 1977), the treatment groups in the Webster-Stratton (1985) study were not randomly assigned, but were based on naturally occurring groups (if the father was present in the home, the family was placed in the father-involved treatment group; if the father was not in the home, the family was placed in the father-absent treatment group). Therefore, these results may have been confounded by the differences of having a father present in versus absent from the home, and may not have been solely due to the fathers' involvement in treatment. Given this qualification on the results, it is notable that father-present and father-absent families appeared to have relatively similar treatment gains, except for the greater number of favorable treatment responders at 1-year follow-up. This suggests that behavioral parent training can be conducted effectively in single-parent families in which there is no contact from the other parent.

Overall, these studies provide equivocal evidence for the inclusion versus exclusion of fathers in behavioral parent training. Although there is no evidence that the inclusion of fathers in any way deters from treatment gains, there is also little evidence that inclusion of fathers significantly improves treatment gains. Only one study included a father-only training group (Adesso & Lipson, 1981), whereas the three other studies primarily compared mother-only training with mother and father training. Researchers may assume that fathers are more difficult to recruit into outcome studies (Phares, 1992) or into therapy itself (see later section), and therefore they may want to establish that treatments can be effective regardless of paternal participation. The Adesso and Lipson (1981) study suggests that either mothers or fathers can be effectively taught behavioral parent training skills without inclusion of the other parent. Thus, rather than asking whether or not fathers are necessary for effective treatment, the question might be appropriately changed to how many parents are needed for effective parent training. The answer to this question appears to be one—either mother or father.

Research on the inclusion versus exclusion of fathers in therapy is notable for the primary focus on behavioral parent training. No studies could be found that specifically addressed the inclusion or exclusion of fathers in any type of therapy other than behavioral parent training. Although clinicians of many different therapeutic orientations (e.g., Atkins & Lansky, 1986; Cath et al., 1989; Doherty, 1981; Gaines, 1981; Galenson, 1989; Guillebeaux et al., 1986; LeCroy, 1987; Sachs, 1986) have advocated including fathers in therapy for child and family problems, apparently no empirical work outside the behavioral parent training literature investigates this question. This lack of empirical investigation may be related to the reservations that many nonbehavioral clinicians have about therapeutic outcome studies of any kind (Strupp, 1989). Although there is not strong empirical support for the additional benefits of inclusion of fathers in behavioral parent training, the question remains whether similar or different treatment effects are found for mothers and fathers when both are included in different types of therapy.

Differential Effects of Maternal versus Paternal Therapeutic Involvement

A number of studies have investigated therapeutic gains of mothers and fathers involved in a variety of different therapeutic interventions. Overall, more similarities than differences are found in the therapeutic gains made by mothers and fathers. Studies are summarized in Table 9.2.

In an attempt to reduce blaming attributions in families of delinquent adolescents, Alexander et al. (1989) used positive relabeling of adolescents' negative behavior when negative family interactions were taking place. They found that neither mothers' nor fathers' blaming attributions were significantly reduced by these interventions. This therapeutic intervention, however, was done in an experimental context (interventions were completed after the family interacted in a negative context for 5 minutes), not in a prolonged therapeutic relationship.

Dadds, Sanders, Behrens, and James (1987) investigated the relation between marital discord and children's oppositional behavior and found that including both fathers and mothers in treatment of oppositional children was essential for addressing concomitant marital discord. They found that child management training was effective in decreasing children's problematic behavior but did not decrease fathers' and mothers' aversive verbal exchanges with each other. Although subsequent partner support training helped to decrease fathers' and mothers' aversive behavior and to increase problem-solving behavior, it did not increase supportive behaviors. Because of the interdependence of interparental conflict and children's behavioral problems (Erel & Burman, 1995), the study by Dadds and colleagues (1987) showed the importance of addressing both parent-child and parent-parent interactions. Henggeler and colleagues (1986) also support the inclusion of both mothers and fathers in therapy to address marital discord. However, they found a greater number of improvements in mother-adolescent relations and in marital relations than in father-adolescent relations due to a family-ecological treatment with juvenile offender adolescents and their mothers and fathers. Although there were significant improvements in the father-adolescent relationship, there were a greater number of significant effects for the mother-adolescent relationship. Overall, family-ecological treatment brought about a significant decrease in maladaptive behavior exhibited by the delinquent adolescent.

In a study examining treatment with fathers, mothers, and their physically abused children in a coercive family system, a focused casework approach with the entire family was found to be more effective than structured child play therapy in decreasing coercive behaviors and increasing positive behaviors for fathers, mothers, and children (Nicol et al., 1988). The focused casework approach included a social worker establishing rapport with the family, the family having

TABLE 9.2.   Empirical Studies of Differential Maternal and Paternal Treatment Outcomes

Researchers	N	Child Characteristics	Referral Problem	Type of Intervention	Findings[a]
Alexander et al. (1989)[b]	61	13–17 y.o. Boys & Girls	Delin-quency	Reattribution (such as rela-beling blaming attributions)	No significant dif-ferences between mothers and fathers due to intervention. No significant reduction in either parent's blaming attributions due to intervention.
Dadds et al. (1987)	4	3–4 y.o. Boys	Opposi-tional	Parent training & partner sup-port training	No differences between mothers and fathers due to intervention. Parent training reduced child mis-behavior but not aversive parental exchanges. Subsequent partner support reduced aversive parental exchanges and increased problem solving.
Henggeler et al. (1986)	57	Mean age—14.8 y.o.[c] Boys	Delin-quent	Family ecolog-ical treatment	Greater number of improvements in mother-adolescent relations than father-adolescent relations. Significant decrease in adolescent misbehavior.
Nicol et al. (1988)	38	1–14 y.o. Boys & Girls	Coercive Family System	Focused case-work or child play therapy	No differences between mothers and fathers due to inter-vention. Greater decreases in coercive behavior for both mothers and fathers due to focused casework compared with child play therapy.

(Continued)

TABLE 9.2.   *(Continued)*

Researchers	N	Child Characteristics	Referral Problem	Type of Intervention	Findings[a]
Reisinger (1982)	4	2–4 y.o. Boys & Girls	Opposi-tional	Parent training	Although parent training was pro-vided only to moth-ers, both mothers and fathers showed increased differen-tial attention skills due to intervention. Fathers' improve-ments attributed to unprogrammed learning.
Webster-Stratton et al. (1988)	114	3–8 y.o. Boys & Girls	Conduct Problems	Parent training (videotape or discussion groups)	Similar pattern of improvements for mothers' and fathers' behavior (e.g., decreased criticisms, increased positive affect).
Webster-Stratton et al. (1989)	94	4–9 y.o. Boys & Girls	Conduct Problems (Follow-up)	Parent training (videotape or discussion groups)	1-year follow-up showed similar pattern of improve-ments for mothers' and fathers' behavior as at posttreatment (Webster-Stratton et al., 1988).

[a] Findings are first summarized for differences in mothers' versus fathers' improve-ments due to the intervention, then overall results are given for the study.
[b] Study 3 is the only study reported here. Therapeutic interventions were not reported in Studies 1 and 2.
[c] The age range of adolescents was not provided in this study.

a consultation with a multidisciplinary team regarding desirable and undesirable parenting techniques, and home visits by members of the team for direct observation and support for parenting skills. Overall, both fathers and mothers seemingly benefited to a similar degree based on the focused casework approach.

In a study that investigated unprogrammed learning in fathers who did not receive parent training, Reisinger (1982) found that father-child interactions improved even when they were not directly involved in treatment. Mothers received behavioral management training and showed significant improvement in differential attention skills (paying attention to good behavior and withdrawing attention from bad behavior), and these skills also improved in untrained fathers. It appeared that both mothers and fathers showed similar levels of differential attention skill acquisition due to the intervention, even though only mothers received direct training. This study has ramifications for studies presented in the previous section (e.g., Martin, 1977) that found no difference between father-involved and father-not-involved treatment. Reisinger's (1982) study suggests that the parent who receives the training in child management may teach the other parent those skills (either overtly or simply by modeling new behaviors), thereby suggesting that even when only one parent is involved in parent training, both parents may benefit. It remains to be seen whether this type of unprogrammed learning occurs for therapeutic interventions other than parent training. Because parent training teaches specific and tangible skills, it may be that unprogrammed learning to the other parent is more likely to happen in behavioral parent training than in other types of therapies.

In a study of parent training delivered by videotape and/or discussion groups to parents of children with conduct problems, Webster-Stratton, Kolpacoff, and Hollinsworth (1988) found that the patterns of improvement were very similar for father-child and mother-child interactions when both fathers and mothers were included in treatment. They found that both mothers' and fathers' criticisms decreased and positive affect increased after the intervention. Similar patterns of improvements were evident for both mothers and fathers at 1-year follow-up (Webster-Stratton, Hollinsworth, & Kolpacoff, 1989). Interested readers are also referred to other follow-up studies of these families (Webster-Stratton, 1990, 1992; Webster-Stratton & Hammond, 1990).

Overall, the studies summarized in Table 9.2 suggest that there are more similarities than differences in the therapeutic gains of mothers and fathers involved in a variety of therapeutic interventions for a variety of child problems. Although one study (Henggeler et al., 1986) found more significant maternal than paternal effects, the remainder of the studies found similar therapeutic effects (or lack thereof) for mothers and fathers. Although there was not strong evidence in the previous section (summarized in Table 9.1) that fathers' therapeutic involvement significantly improved treatment gains, these studies suggest that mothers and fathers can achieve similar levels of treatment gains from therapeutic involvement.

There have also been investigations into how maternal and paternal attitudes toward therapy and the identified problem affect the outcome of therapy. For example, Watson (1986) found that mothers' but not fathers' degree of self-held responsibility for their child's emotional disturbance was associated with better therapeutic outcome. Families in which the mother blamed herself for her child's emotional problems tended to have better outcomes in structural/strategic family therapy, but there was no such association with fathers' self-blame.

In a study of psychiatric inpatients, Greenman, Gunderson, and Canning (1989) found that fathers' concerns about their hospitalized children's separation and anger were associated with their children's resistance to treatment, and that mothers' concerns about separation and anger were associated with their children's impulsive behavior during hospitalization. This study suggested that fathers' attitudes toward therapy and their children could have negative ramifications for their children's therapeutic involvement. Similar results were found in a sample of adolescents hospitalized for eating disorders. Inpatients who prematurely dropped out of treatment had fathers who were significantly more emotionally overinvolved with their child than fathers of inpatients who completed treatment (Szmukler, Eisler, Russell, & Dare, 1985).

Conversely, fathers' positive attitudes toward therapy can also have positive ramifications on therapeutic outcome. For example, Shapiro and Budman (1973) found that families in which fathers were most enthusiastic about therapy were the least likely to prematurely terminate the family therapy. Additionally, in an outpatient sample receiving family therapy, Bennun (1989) found that fathers', but not mothers', perceptions of a competent and directive therapist were positively associated with treatment outcome. This finding is further supported by Newberry, Alexander, and Turner (1991), who found that fathers responded more positively to therapy than mothers when therapists provided structuring behaviors (task oriented and implicitly controlling behaviors) during therapy sessions.

Although these studies assessed different attitudinal characteristics, they suggest that fathers' attitudes can have an impact on treatment outcome and often have a different association to therapeutic outcome than mothers' attitudes. Heubeck, Watson, and Russell (1986) summarized attitudinal and therapeutic research with fathers and concluded that fathers' active participation in therapy and their willingness to accept some responsibility for the family's problem is associated with more positive therapeutic outcome.

In an interesting retrospective study with young adult clients, Mallinckrodt (1991) found that the father-client relationship had a significant impact on the therapeutic alliance. Clients' perceptions of social support were most strongly associated with their ratings of the client-therapist working alliance. Clients' reports of higher levels of paternal warmth and concern were significantly related to the therapists' ratings of the client-therapist working alliance.

Overall, both outcome studies and attitude studies provide some, albeit limited, evidence that supports the inclusion of fathers in child and family therapy when they are involved in the child's or adolescent's life. In a review of parent training literature, Horton (1984) concluded that although inclusion of fathers in treatment did not prove to be unequivocally superior, fathers do learn parenting skills and their skill acquisition may be different from mothers' skill acquisition. The question remains whether fathers are involved in therapy in the clinical setting, as opposed to therapy that occurs in the outcome research setting.

FATHERS' INVOLVEMENT IN CLINIC-BASED
CHILD AND FAMILY THERAPY

Many clinicians have acknowledged the "well-known" fact that fathers are reluctant to become involved in therapy for child and family problems (Berg & Rosenblum, 1977; Doherty, 1981; Gaines, 1981; Guillebeaux et al., 1986; Horton, 1984; LeCroy, 1987; Renouf, 1991; Sachs, 1986). Although empirical data are rarely cited to establish this fact, data support the notion of fathers' comparatively lower involvement in child and family treatment. Most of these data are relevant to intact, two-parent families; however, the issue of whether or not noncustodial fathers from nonintact families should participate in therapy will also be addressed.

Intact Families

In an investigation of the effect of initial family assessments conducted in the home, Churven (1978) found that all mothers attended the first clinic visit, but few fathers attended that visit. Only 6.5% of the fathers in the control group (no preclinic home visit) attended the first clinic appointment, and 43.5% of the fathers in the preclinic home visit group attended the first clinic appointment. This study was conducted with a working-class sample that was noted to be hostile toward authority, including helping professionals, so this may represent a lower-than-average rate of father involvement in treatment. In a study of adolescent drug abusers in which 90% of the initial contacts for treatment were made by the mother, Szapocznik et al. (1988) found that 6% of fathers actively resisted family treatment and in an additional 10% of the families, both the father and the adolescent resisted treatment. In another 62% of the families, the adolescent alone resisted treatment.

These researchers subsequently introduced a strategic structural-systems engagement (SSSE) treatment that was shown to be effective in engaging resistant families to participate in treatment when compared with engagement as usual (EAU) procedures. For the initial clinic intake appointment, only 7.1% of the fathers in the SSSE condition failed to show up for the appointment, whereas 57.7% of the fathers in the EAU condition did not show up for the first appointment. The engagement process also had an impact on successful termination of therapy, where 77% in the SSSE condition and only 25% in the EAU condition successfully terminated therapy and did not prematurely drop out. These data provide empirical support that it is worthwhile to attempt to engage fathers who appear to be resistant to treatment.

These studies were not designed specifically to investigate paternal participation in child and family therapy. However, they provide empirical evidence to support many clinicians' beliefs that, without an engagement intervention such as the one just described, fathers are less likely than mothers to be involved in child and family therapy. It is important to acknowledge that therapists and researchers may not even have access to families where the mother is not willing or able to become involved in treatment. Since mothers are often the first person to make contact with a clinic, families whose mothers are uninterested in treatment or who are unable to take part in treatment are not easily identified for therapeutic interventions or research investigations. For example, in Churven's (1978) study, the clinic appointments occurred only when the mother brought the child to the clinic (regardless of the father's attendance), so families whose mothers were completely uninterested or unable to attend therapy would not have been identified for the study.

Overall, there appears to be some empirical as well as clinical evidence of the lower involvement of fathers in child and family treatment when compared with mothers. This pattern is similar to the differential gender rates of participation found in individual psychological treatment. Women greatly outnumber men in outpatient therapy clinics (Russo, 1990), and even with similar levels of symptoms, women are significantly more likely to seek therapy than men (Padesky & Hammen, 1981). This differential utilization of services is assumed to be related to sex-role socialization because women are socialized to talk about their problems whereas men are socialized not to disclose their psychological concerns (Basow, 1992). This style of self-disclosure could be the reason for the differential maternal and paternal rates of participation in child and family therapy. Mothers may be more willing than fathers to disclose family problems, just as women appear more willing than men to disclose their own emotional problems.

As has been discussed in regard to research participation (Phares, 1992), the differential participation rate in child and family therapy exhibited by mothers and fathers may be related to practical time constraints that relate to lifestyle and sociocultural factors. These lifestyle factors include, but are not limited to, time constraints based on inflexibility of employment schedules, providing child care for other (nonreferred) children, and the need to coordinate the schedules of two adults rather than one (see Barling, 1990; Biller & Solomon, 1986; Bozett & Hanson, 1991, for discussions of these issues in men's vs. women's lives). The need to have both parents present at a therapy session may add time pressures at an exponential rate compared with what is required for only one parent's presence. However, if this were the primary factor in parental involvement in therapy, then one might expect a relatively equal distribution between mothers and fathers since the majority of fathers *and* mothers of U.S. children under the age of 18 years old are employed (Roberts, 1993). As is evident from participation rates in therapy, this is not the case.

Another possible reason for fathers' low rates of therapeutic involvement might relate to an institutional problem in the expectations of therapists and the structure of therapy as it exists currently. That is, low paternal involvement in therapy could also be due to the possibility that fathers are not required or even overtly encouraged to be involved in child and family treatment. In a review of outcome studies of parent training over a 12-year period (from 1970 to 1981), Budd and O'Brien (1982) found that fathers were involved in only 13% of the families in these studies, and there was a decline over time in the percentage of these studies that included fathers. It is unclear whether this low involvement reflected the fathers' reluctance (or inability) to participate or the researchers' and therapists' reluctance to have them participate. It could be that the "well-known" fact of fathers' lower therapeutic participation rates is at least partially due to therapists' and clinical researchers' lower expectations for such involvement. For example, Churven (1978) found that 24 out of 25 fathers (96%) participated in a pretherapy assessment interview when the interviews were conducted in the family's home during evening hours. Although the feasibility of in-home sessions is limited, these results suggest that scheduling flexibility on the part of therapists and clinical researchers may allow more paternal involvement in child and family therapy. In fact, based on clinical experience, Feldman (1990) argued that the most important barrier to paternal involvement in therapy is the therapist's failure to include fathers in the initial stages of therapy. Similarly, Doherty (1981) provided anecdotal evidence that when the fathers' participation in treatment was explained as "automatic" at the time of the initial intake phone call, fathers nearly always participated in treatment.

Survey research suggests that therapists' attitudes toward paternal influences on children's behavior, the perceived importance of paternal involvement in therapy, and therapist characteristics are related to fathers' lack of involvement in therapy. In a survey of 148 social workers and school psychologists, Lazar, Sagi, and Fraser (1991) measured therapists' attitudes toward familial role responsibilities and therapists' actual practices of including fathers in therapy sessions. They found that therapists were maternally oriented with regard to child-care capabilities and expectations regarding traditional divisions of roles within the family. With regard to inclusion of fathers in therapy sessions, therapists included fathers in an average of 6.27% of therapy sessions and mothers in an average of 38.01% of therapy sessions.

Regression equations were used to establish which therapist characteristics were associated with the inclusion of fathers in therapy sessions. These analyses showed that male therapists were more likely than female therapists to include fathers in therapy sessions with their children. In addition, therapists who had been at their present job for a shorter rather than longer time were more likely to include fathers in therapy sessions. Also, therapists were more likely to include both fathers and mothers in family therapy sessions if they had more academic coursework related to family therapy, if they held more egalitarian beliefs about division of labor within the family, if they were employed by an agency that espoused family involvement and that provided child welfare services, and if they were able to offer flexible hours for therapy appointments such as evening and weekend hours. This study is an important first step toward understanding the therapist's role in inclusion versus exclusion of fathers in therapy related to their child's emotional/behavioral problems. Another line of research that can illuminate the process of involving fathers in therapy is to ask fathers themselves.

Surveys of fathers' attitudes toward therapy should help elucidate the reasons for participation or nonparticipation in therapy. Guillebeaux and colleagues (1986) surveyed men who had been involved in marriage and family therapy, some of whom started out reluctantly. They found that men were more likely to be receptive to therapy if they had prior therapy experience or had been threatened by their wife with divorce if they did not take part in therapy, if they had nontraditional sex role socialization, and if they perceived their family problems to be serious. Men who perceived a high degree of marital conflict tended to be less receptive to therapy than those who did not perceive a high degree of marital conflict. Guillebeaux and colleagues also found that fathers who were initially resistant to therapy became less resistant after attending one session. Therefore, they suggest that therapists should insist on the father's presence in the first one or two sessions, and they predict that fathers will attend willingly after the therapeutic process is demystified.

A related issue for therapists to consider is parental perception of the acceptability of different treatment interventions. Miller and Kelley (1992) used the Treatment Evaluation Inventory (TEI; Kazdin, 1984) to measure fathers' and mothers' ratings of the acceptability of different therapeutic interventions with children. Parents were also asked to respond to a hypothetical vignette that described an 8-year-old boy who showed occasional noncompliant behavior toward his parents' instructions and who showed aggression toward his younger sister. The vignettes also described six different responses to the child's behavior: positive reinforcement, chair time-out, response cost, spanking, room time-out, and medication. When comparing fathers' and mothers' ratings of acceptability of these different interventions, fathers rated spanking and medication as significantly more acceptable than did mothers, and mothers rated positive reinforcement, response cost, and room time-out as significantly more acceptable than did fathers. Fathers and mothers did not differ significantly in their ratings of chair time-out.

It is interesting to note that there were more differences between fathers and mothers (significant differences on five out of six interventions) than there were when comparing maritally distressed and nondistressed parents or when comparing parents of clinically referred children with parents of nonreferred children. Miller and Kelley (1992) suggest that perceptions of treatment acceptability and preference must be taken into account, especially when both fathers and mothers are included in therapeutic interventions.

Although there is consensus on the limited participation rates of fathers in treatment when compared with mothers, there are undoubtedly a variety of underlying reasons for this lower paternal participation rate including some or all the issues just discussed. Low paternal involvement in therapy may be due to personal factors (e.g., self-disclosure), sociocultural factors (e.g., employment schedules), institutional factors (e.g., therapist expectations or structure of the therapy session), or familial factors (e.g., marital conflict). Further research will need to address these and other factors that might relate to fathers' participation in therapy.

Children of Separated, Divorced, or Never-Married Parents

Most of this review has dealt with the therapeutic involvement of fathers in intact families. However, special issues of paternal involvement in therapy need to be addressed in families where there has been a separation or divorce. Approximately 61.1% of U.S. children live with both biological parents, 10.8% live in stepfamilies, 24.2% live in single-parent families headed by mother, and 3.9% live in single-parent families headed by father (Roberts, 1993). The majority of children who live with only one biological parent have at least some contact with their noncustodial biological parent (Seltzer & Bianchi, 1988). Because so many children have noncustodial fathers with whom they have at least some contact, therapists should be open to the possibility of including noncustodial fathers in therapy with distressed children. Based on clinical experience and a literature review, Feldman (1990) argues that the noncustodial father's involvement in therapy should at least be considered when treating a child from a nonintact family, even if the child's referral question is not specifically related to the separation or divorce. Similarly, in stepfamilies and joint custody families, therapists should involve all interested parties, including fathers, to provide comprehensive treatment to the two-family system (Halperin & Smith, 1983; Richards & Goldenberg, 1985).

In the case of adolescent fathers, Kiselica, Stroud, Stroud, and Rotzien (1992) argue that teen fathers have been ignored by the mental health field. They noted that adolescent fathers often desire help to deal with their child's mother, to deal with their own family of origin, to assist in daily living (such as help with housing, education, and employment), to learn parenting skills, to learn about their children's health care needs, and to gain emotional support.

Greif and Kristall (1993) provided an interesting discussion of clinical issues and themes in a series of group therapy sessions with noncustodial parents. Common themes for many fathers in the group were issues regarding children's rejection of parents, parents' rejection of children, difficulties with holiday visitation schedules, emotional triangulation, children's adjustment to divorce and visitation, and dealing with the grandparent-grandchild relationship. Greif and Kristall noted that these issues apply to work with noncustodial parents in a variety of therapeutic modalities, including individual therapy with parents or children, family therapy, and group therapy for noncustodial parents, custodial parents, and children.

Jacobs (1982, 1983) has also highlighted the need to attend to fathers' adjustment after the divorce, especially in relation to the father's relationship with his children. In a sample of fathers who sought psychotherapy after a divorce, nearly all the fathers expressed severe distress about separation from their children (Jacobs, 1983). Jacobs (1982, 1983) suggests that divorced fathers should be involved in family therapy with their children and exspouse to help the entire family adjust to life after the divorce. Additionally, Feldman (1990) argues that (when appropriate) therapists should facilitate as much contact as possible between noncustodial fathers and their children to benefit both fathers and children. In general, clinical evidence suggests that fathers' involvement in family therapy after divorce is helpful no matter which family member is referred for treatment (Jacobs, 1983). However, empirical study of the efficacy of involving divorced fathers in family therapy has yet to be conducted.

In addition to the issues regarding the therapeutic needs of children and noncustodial fathers, Tillitski (1992) discussed the therapist's role with regard to custodial fathers. He argued that therapists must educate themselves about the importance of parental adjustment and parenting skills, regardless of whether the primary parent is a father or a mother. In addition, Tillitski noted that therapists can help families who are dealing with separation and the renegotiation of paternal and maternal roles vis-à-vis the custody of children.

CLINICAL ISSUES

Three additional clinical issues will be discussed based on clinicians' experiences. First, a number of clinicians have written about the unique clinical issues that arise when working with families in which fathers were sexually or physically abusive. In cases of incest, Lipovsky (1991) discussed the difficult therapeutic issues that surface when children report sexual abuse by their father or stepfather and the accused perpetrator denies the abuse. She noted that the family structure cannot maintain both an accusing child and a denying father. Often mothers' growing belief in their child's accusations serves as a crucial source of resolution regarding the family structure. Lipovsky noted that therapists should serve a supportive role for the family's struggle to deal with these issues and to serve as an advocate to the child in cases where no one in the family believes the child's report of sexual abuse. In addition, Zuskin (1992) noted the importance of helping the sexually abusive father gain insight into his actions to prevent the recurrence of abuse. He noted that none of 26 offenders who received therapy with a focus on the development of insight had experienced recidivism.

Therapy with physically abusive fathers has not received the same amount of attention as therapy with sexually abusive fathers. However, Peled and Edleson (1992) described therapy groups with children of mothers who had been battered. They found that the group was effective in helping children deal with their mothers' experience of physical abuse. Simms and Bolden

(1991) described a family reunification project that dealt with families in which sexual abuse, physical abuse, and neglect were responsible for the child's temporary placement in foster care. The 16-week program was developed to facilitate children's contact with their biological families and their foster families in a structured and therapeutic environment. Children were provided with structured visits with their biological and foster parents, foster parents were provided with a support group, and biological parents were provided with a support group. The program was not evaluated empirically because of the small numbers involved in data collection and the lack of a control group, but the authors noted that the program seemed to be successful in fostering communication between children, foster parents, and biological parents. Similar discussions have been provided for father-child reunification when children were given up for adoption at an early age (Jerome, 1993; Pacheco & Eme, 1993).

Regarding the second clinical issue, Dickstein and colleagues (1991) summarized a number of issues related to therapeutic interventions with men, regardless of whether or not they are fathers. They encouraged therapists to be cognizant of men's changing social roles and to be aware of how these roles might influence men from different cultural backgrounds and different family constellations. They noted the importance in addressing fathers' responses when adult children move out of or back into the family home. In addition, therapists must remain sensitive to the needs of gay male couples and gay fathers to help them with distress related to personal and sociocultural influences. Overall, Dickstein and colleagues reminded clinicians to be aware of the way in which social forces affect fathers' psychological functioning and the need for therapeutic interventions that are sensitive to these social forces.

The third clinical issue that has been discussed throughout this chapter refers to the ways in which therapists can encourage paternal involvement in therapy. Based on her own clinical experience and that of other clinicians, Hecker (1991) delineated 21 ways to involve fathers in family therapy. Although many of these 21 suggestions have already been mentioned in this chapter, a few additional suggestions will be discussed. Hecker recommended that therapists talk directly to the father and make it clear that all family members (including the father) are expected to take part in the therapeutic interventions. If the father shows reluctance at attending the initial therapy session, therapists can normalize this reluctance by acknowledging that many fathers feel equally reluctant about initial visits but then grow to find the therapy helpful. If a busy work schedule is used as an excuse to not attend therapy, Hecker suggested challenging the father's priorities or conversely using a positive reframe to reconceptualize the father's reluctance. Finally, Hecker provided a sample letter that she often uses in an attempt to engage reluctant fathers into treatment. Although she did not test these strategies empirically, Hecker noted that these strategies have been found to be effective in enticing even the most reluctant father into therapy.

FUTURE DIRECTIONS

Although fathers participate in child and family therapy at lower rates than do mothers, evidence suggests that it is important and feasible for therapists to engage fathers in the treatment of child and family dysfunction for both intact and nonintact families. Although many issues have been addressed in the empirical literature, numerous questions remain unanswered about fathers' involvement in therapy.

First of all, there is still somewhat equivocal evidence with regard to differential effectiveness of fathers' involvement in child and family therapy. Although a number of studies found no additional improvements based on paternal involvement in therapy, limitations such as only assessing mother-child interactions (Martin, 1977) or lack of random assignment to groups (Webster-Stratton, 1985) suggest that a conclusive statement about therapeutic effectiveness based on fathers' inclusion versus exclusion is not warranted. In addition, studies that specifically addressed paternal inclusion versus exclusion only assessed the effectiveness of behavioral parent training, which may lead to more gains than other therapies due to easier transfer of skills from the participating parent to the nonparticipating parent (Reisinger, 1982). In some respects, it is beneficial to ascertain that behavioral parent training needs to be conducted with only one parent to establish maximal treatment effects. This finding might lead to greater access to services and greater therapeutic gains when only one parent is able to take part in parent training sessions. There is some evidence to suggest that either mothers *or* fathers could be the parent to receive the training with equivalent amounts of treatment gains (Adesso & Lipson, 1981). However, it is unclear whether any of these results hold true for therapies other than behavioral parent training.

To clarify these issues, studies are needed that have more comprehensive designs than the ones that have already been conducted. For example, an ideal study would randomly assign groups based on the following dimensions: parent involvement (mother-only, father-only, mother and father, neither mother or father), type of therapy (behavioral, nonbehavioral), and type of child problem (internalizing, externalizing), in addition to including a contact-control group and wait-list control group. This design obviously is not feasible for a single study because it would require an exorbitant number of cells. However, outcome studies that move in this direction are needed to ascertain whether or not it is beneficial to include fathers and/or mothers in therapy for child and family problems. Eventually, greater specificity will be needed. Studies that address fathers' involvement in different types of therapy (other than just the broad categorization of behavioral and nonbehavioral) as well as involvement in the treatment of different child referral problems (beyond the broad categorization of internalizing and externalizing) will need to be conducted. In addition, investigation of personal, sociocultural, institutional, and family contextual factors, such as patterns of self-disclosure, employment schedules, therapists' expectations, and familial conflict, should be included in empirical research on fathers' involvement in therapy. To date, very little research has been completed to ascertain the impact of these factors on paternal participation in child and family therapy.

The studies reviewed in this chapter referred to fathers' involvement as fathers' presence for therapy. Few researchers have looked beyond the mere presence or absence of the father in the therapy room to actually investigate the paternal and maternal factors that relate to positive therapeutic outcomes. Coplin and Houts (1991) provided an excellent review of the issues involved in research on fathers' involvement in parent training and noted that father-mother similarities as well as differences should be investigated and individual characteristics of fathers and mothers must be addressed in relation to therapeutic effectiveness. Fauber and Long (1991) also highlighted the need to investigate family process variables, including paternal and maternal involvement, in relation to children's developmental difficulties and the treatment of these difficulties. In addition, factors such as fathers' appropriate emotional involvement (Szmukler et al., 1985), fathers' enthusiasm for family therapy (Shapiro & Budman, 1973), and fathers' perceptions of a competent therapist (Bennun, 1989) have all been found to be associated with positive therapeutic outcome. However, very little research has been completed to investigate the mechanisms of improvement related to paternal involvement in therapy. If the mechanisms of change could be established, then more effective interventions could be integrated into already existing therapies for child and family dysfunction.

One step toward investigating mechanisms of change within therapeutic interventions is to carefully assess changes in the parent-child dyad as a result of therapy. Mann, Borduin, Henggeler, and Blaske (1990) conducted a study with 45 delinquent adolescents and their families in addition to 16 nonclinical control adolescents and their families. Delinquent adolescents were randomly assigned to either individual therapy or multisystemic therapy that involved their fathers and mothers in the therapeutic process. Father-adolescent, mother-adolescent, and father-mother interactions were assessed pre- and posttherapy. At the pretreatment assessment, father-adolescent interactions showed greater amounts of hostility and conflict in the delinquent group compared with the nonclinical control group. The fathers and mothers of delinquent adolescents also showed higher levels of hostility and conflict with each other than did fathers and mothers of nondisturbed adolescents. There were no differences between groups when mother-adolescent interactions were assessed before treatment.

When the effectiveness of the two types of treatment were compared, most of the analyses showed that the multisystemic therapy was superior to individual treatment of delinquent adolescents. When psychological symptoms were analyzed, fathers, mothers, and adolescents who received multisystemic therapy showed greater reductions in global levels of symptoms than did families in which the adolescent received individual therapy. For dyadic interactions, multisystemic therapy was associated with greater increases in father-adolescent supportiveness and greater decreases in hostility and conflict than individual therapy. Mother-adolescent verbal interactions showed greater improvement with multisystemic therapy. Finally, multisystemic therapy was responsible for greater improvements in father-mother verbal activity, supportiveness, and decreased hostility and conflict than individual therapy with the adolescent.

Mann and colleagues pointed out that multisystemic therapy can be conceptualized not only as helping the individual delinquent adolescent but also as helping family interactions. These improvements in family interactions are expected to be associated with stronger maintenance of treatment gains after completion of treatment. This study provides a nice example of a thorough research design that addresses treatment outcome along with dyadic parent-child and parent-parent interactions within the family.

As this study illustrates, it will be important for family therapy researchers to investigate separate paternal and maternal effects in family therapy. Two empirical studies suggest that parent-child interactions may differ depending on the psychiatric status and/or presence of each parent. Dumas and Gibson (1990) found that children of depressed mothers were more compliant and less aversive with their mothers than with their fathers. Conversely, children of nondepressed mothers were less compliant and more aversive with their mothers than with their fathers. In addition, Hops and Seeley (1991) found that mother-adolescent interactions were influenced by the presence or absence of the father. When either mothers or fathers interacted alone with their adolescent, parents were more distressed and less aggressive than they were during interactions in the presence of the other parent. These studies suggest that the presence of both parents in family therapy may alter familial interactions, and therefore further investigation to determine the therapeutic ramifications of having both parents involved in family therapy should be conducted.

There are examples of clinical anecdotal literature (Doherty, 1981; Gaines, 1981; Kaslow, 1981; Sachs, 1986) as well as research literature (Szapocznik et al., 1988) that blame mothers for fathers' noninvolvement in therapy. Doherty (1981) observed from clinical experience that if the mother is not able to get the father to agree to therapy, then the mother herself is ambivalent about therapy. Although this may be true in some families, it may be inaccurate for others, especially in view of the power and status differentials that exist in many families. This type of unquestioned belief in mothers' culpability may be further evidence of the "mother-blaming" in clinical journals that was documented by Caplan and Hall-McCorquodale (1985a). Ironically, although the clinical and research literature on child sexual abuse may neglect mothers as perpetrators due to inadequate assessment techniques (Banning, 1989), there is still a noticeable amount of mother-blaming for maternal culpability in discussions of therapy for father-child incest (Kinzl & Biebl, 1992; Pierce, 1987; Ringwalt & Earp, 1988; Swanson & Biaggio, 1985).

Assumptions of maternal culpability for child and family problems, especially those that are perpetrated by the father, need to be empirically examined. Bernard (1981) noted that mothers are assumed to have responsibility for family well-being and child caretaking, whereas fathers seem to be given a dispensation against any familial participation other than financial responsibility. In addition, personal gains may be associated with being less emotionally involved in the well-being and day-to-day care of the family. In discussing the advantages to being a distant father figure, Caplan (1989) suggested that the parent (usually the father) who exposes less to the family has less of a chance of being criticized or questioned by other family members. Ironically, sometimes therapists' attempts to engage fathers in the therapeutic process can influence the perceptions of culpability within the family. In their discussion of family therapy, Goodrich et al. (1988) noted that therapists often employ the father's help in the amelioration of family problems. Thus, the implication is that the therapist and the father can work in a collegial manner to help the family thereby suggesting that the mother is to blame for the family's problems. Bernard (1981) cautions that professionals should not allow these inequities to be mirrored in clinical practice and research.

Overall, although numerous clinicians have noted the importance of fathers' involvement in child and family therapy based on their clinical experience (e.g., Atkins & Lansky, 1986; Cath et al., 1989; Doherty, 1981; Gaines, 1981; Galenson, 1989; Guillebeaux et al., 1986; LeCroy, 1987; Sachs, 1986), there is only limited empirical support at this time for the importance of fathers' involvement in child and family therapy. Although conclusions based on empirical evidence can only be considered tentative due to methodological weaknesses of the studies that have investigated fathers' involvement in child and family therapy, a wide gap remains between empirical research and publications based on clinical practice. Is this an example of clinicians not reading empirical research literature (Strupp, 1981, 1989) and researchers not attending to published material based on clinical experience? It could be. However, it also may reflect the relative lack of attention to fathers in many aspects of the clinical process, including etiology, assessment, and treatment of child and family dysfunction (Phares, 1992).

In sum, empirical findings suggest that neither mothers nor fathers are the superior parent who is needed for child therapy, and further that when both mothers and fathers are included in therapy, they tend to show similar patterns of treatment gains. Further empirical work will need to be completed before a conclusive statement can be made about the importance of fathers' involvement in child and family therapy. In addition, further research is needed to ascertain the factors that affect fathers' involvement in therapy and the subsequent outcome of the therapy for child and family problems.

CHAPTER 10

Future Directions in Research

This chapter will outline the research that is needed to more clearly investigate the roles of fathers in developmental psychopathology. Consideration is needed at a number of different levels: issues within families (e.g., gender differences within the family that are evident in gender of child and gender of parent interactions, developmental level of children and their fathers), issues within the legal system (e.g., establishment of paternity and child support payment), political and social issues (e.g., the "men's movement" and institutional barriers against paternal involvement with children), and research design issues (e.g., questioning biased theories and investigating mechanisms of paternal and maternal involvement in the development of psychopathology, and the need for research on families of different ethnicities and different constellations).

RESEARCH ISSUES WITHIN FAMILIES

Gender Differences within Families

At the most basic level, three levels of gender differences can be explored within families: (a) gender differences between boys and girls (sons and daughters); (b) gender differences between men and women (fathers and mothers); (c) gender differences in child × parent interaction effects. One way to assess child × parent interaction effects is to break families down into four distinct dyadic relationships: father-daughter, father-son, mother-daughter, mother-son. Similarities and differences in these four dyads have been noted throughout this book when researchers investigated child × parent interaction effects of gender differences. However, attention should be paid to a special issue of the *Journal of Youth and Adolescence* (1987, vol. *16,* no. 3) that was devoted to gender differences within families of adolescents.

As editor of the special issue, Steinberg (1987) provided an overview of research in this area that culminated in three impressions. First of all, he noted the surprising lack of gender differences between adolescent boys and adolescent girls. For example, Hauser and colleagues (1987) found few differences between the family interaction patterns of adolescent boys and adolescent girls. Additionally, no gender differences were found in parental reports of disagreement about rules with sons versus daughters (Hill & Holmbeck, 1987), adolescent boys' and adolescent girls' satisfactions with their activities with their parents (Montemayor & Brownlee, 1987), or boys' and girls' reports of how much they value their parents' opinions or how much their parents know about them (Youniss & Ketterlinus, 1987).

The second impression that Steinberg (1987) discussed was the preponderance of gender differences between fathers and mothers in relation to their children. The time that adolescents spent with their fathers was characterized by play activities, whereas the time that adolescents spent with their mothers was more evenly divided between play activities and household chores or caretaking matters (Montemayor & Brownlee, 1987). In addition, mothers' psychological functioning was more adversely influenced than fathers' psychological functioning by parent-child conflict (Silverberg & Steinberg, 1987) and the mother-child relationship was less distant than the father-child relationship, especially in households in which parents held blue-collar jobs (Youniss & Ketterlinus, 1987).

The third impression that Steinberg (1987) noted was the importance of investigating child × parent interaction effects for gender differences. For example, maternal psychological functioning was significantly related to both mother-daughter and mother-son relationships but paternal psychological functioning was significantly related to only the father-son relationship (Silverberg & Steinberg, 1987). Conversely, father-daughter conflict appeared to be more strongly related to parental acceptance when compared with the other three dyads (Hill & Holmbeck, 1987). Overall, Steinberg (1987) summarized this research by noting both the low levels of communication and affective involvement (positive or negative) in the father-daughter dyad and the emotional intensity (both positive and negative) in the mother-daughter dyad. Father-son and mother-son dyads seemed to fall in between these two ends of the continuum of emotional involvement and communication. These series of studies highlight the importance of investigating gender differences, as well as gender similarities, within families. In addition, Kavanagh and Hops (1994) provided a compelling discussion of gender differences and developmental psychopathology.

Developmental Level of Children, Fathers, Mothers, and the Family

It is important to consider the developmental level of fathers (and mothers) in addition to the developmental levels of their children (Parke, 1990). Anecdotally, a 20-year-old father might interact with his infant in ways that differ from the ways a 50-year-old father would interact with his infant. In the same way, the meaning of fatherhood may be different for a 20-year-old versus a 50-year-old father. Aside from anecdotal evidence supporting the importance of this issue, empirical data show that fathers' and mothers' developmental level interacts with their children's developmental level. For example, Mac-Donald and Parke (1986) found that fathers and mothers engage in progressively less physical play as they grow older, even after controlling for the child's age. This suggests that investigating paternal and maternal effects is not enough to capture the complexities of the father-child and mother-child relationships. Researchers should be dedicated to following individuals (father, mother, child), dyads (father-child, mother-child, father-mother), triads (father-mother-child), and entire families (father-mother-child-child or biological father-biological mother-stepfather-stepmother-child-child) over the developmental course of the life span (Parke, 1990).

RESEARCH ISSUES WITHIN THE LEGAL SYSTEM

Establishment of Paternity and Payment of Child Support

In September 1993, I attended a conference entitled "America's Fathers: Abiding and Emerging Roles in Family and Economic Support Policies." The conference was sponsored by the National Research Council of the Institute of Medicine and the National Academy of Sciences. Along with the prestigious surroundings of the National Academy of Sciences building, there were a number of well-respected psychologists (e.g., Levine, 1993; Majors, 1992; McAdoo, 1993; Parke, 1990; Phillips of Scarr, Phillips, & McCartney, 1990; Sonenstein, 1993; Turnbull, 1988; Wertlieb of Wertlieb, Weigel, & Feldstein, 1988), sociologists (e.g., Anderson, 1990; Cherlin, 1988; Kimmel, 1992; Marsiglio, 1992; Seltzer, 1991), attorneys (e.g., Fineman, 1989; Mnookin of Maccoby & Mnookin, 1992), and community activists (e.g., Ballard, discussed in Santoli, 1994; May of Davis & May, 1991), who were all actively involved in working with fathers and their children. There were also a number of politicians and political assistants who ensured that the social policy aspects of fatherhood were addressed.

One of the first topics on the agenda was the discussion of how to increase fathers' payment of child support when it was awarded after divorce or separation. Interestingly, there has been a major emphasis on the establishment of paternity, especially immediately after the birth of the child, to later enable the enforcement of payment of paternal child support (see Krawczak & Schmidtke, 1992, for discussion of paternity establishment techniques). Only 15% of children born outside marriage are awarded child support from their biological father after paternity is established and many of these awards go unpaid (Nichols-Casebolt & Garfinkel, 1991). Overall, 51.4% of mothers with physical custody received the full amount of child support that was due to them, 23.8% received partial payment, and 24.8% received no payment of the child support agreement (U.S. Bureau of the Census, 1992). These numbers varied according to the way that child support awards were determined, with fathers who received court-ordered payments being much less likely than fathers who received voluntary child support awards to pay the full amount of the award (U.S. Bureau of the Census, 1992). It should also be noted that fathers and mothers do not differ significantly in their reports of average monthly child support payments that are given (Seltzer & Brandreth, 1994).

It was interesting and somewhat disturbing that the entire discussion at the conference of establishment of paternity and child support was based on a punitive system, rather than a cooperative system. Undoubtedly, many fathers would not and do not pay child support even with this punitive system. However, the punitiveness of the system seems to add to what are often acrimonious family situations, and it is hard to believe that the best interests of the child are being met even when fathers make their enforced child support payment.

Ironically, much of the focus on payment of child support was to recoup costs that were paid out by local, state, and federal governmental agencies, rather than trying to improve the lives of children whose fathers did not pay child support. It was surprising to learn that if a mother and her children are receiving support from Aid to Families with Dependent Children (AFDC) and the children's father pays any amount of child support, the family only receives $50 per month of the father's payment and the rest of the child support payment goes to the state and federal government to help cover AFDC funds (Solomon, 1993). It is hard to imagine that a father would be motivated to pay child support when he learns that the majority of the money is not being used to enhance his children's lives directly. From the children's perspective, it is hard to believe that they feel any difference in their daily life whether or not paternal child support is paid.

This discussion is not to question the propriety of mandated child support payments. Noncustodial fathers (and mothers) should pay whatever award has been mandated, and if they are unhappy with the arrangement, they should seek legal recourse to find an arrangement that they perceive as more equitable. However, the focus on establishment of paternity and the enforcement of child support payments may inadvertently be making noncustodial fathers less likely to be involved with their children. The current system seems to imply that the only use for a father is for financial support and that the only reason fathers should provide financial support is because it has been court-mandated. It would be helpful to see some of the focus turn to other advantages of paternal involvement with children, rather than focusing on the mandated aspects of monetary involvement. In addition, it would be helpful to see research that focuses on what fathers get out of parenting and providing financial support, as a way of possibly tapping into some fathers' intrinsic motivation to help their children.

Research should also be completed that assesses the psychological impact on children of voluntary versus mandated payment of child support from their father. Regardless of the actual benefit of the financial support, children probably have different perceptions of the meaning of their father's monetary support. It would not be surprising to find that children's perception of their father's voluntary payment of child support might be associated with feeling more psychologically supported and cared for by the father. Conversely, it may be that the more legally mandated and punitive the child support payment system becomes, the less children will perceive the money to be a sign of caring from their fathers. This type of research could be used to inform social policy in a way that serves the best interests of children.

Legal and Physical Custody after Parental Separation and Divorce

As noted in Chapter 7, a lot of research has been done on the effects of different custody arrangements on children's psychological functioning after parental divorce. Thompson (1986) discussed the issue of the use of the "best interests" of the child in judicial decision making. More recently, Maccoby and Mnookin (1992) provided a thorough discussion of the social and legal issues related to custody decisions in their aptly titled book *Dividing the Child*. They noted that most states continue to use the "best interests of the child" standard when contested custody cases come before a judge. Hypothetically, this standard does not provide an advantage to either parent based on gender, but focuses solely on which parent would provide the most stable and nurturing environment for the child after parental divorce. Because the majority of developmental research suggests that both fathers and mothers can learn the skills that are necessary for parenting (e.g., Parke & Tinsley, 1981), the genderless standard can be supported by empirical research. However, Maccoby and Mnookin (1992) noted that few custody cases actually make it to a judge and there seems to be an informal standard used by families and lawyers that focuses on who served the role of the primary parent before the divorce. In most cases, the mother served the primary caretaking role before the divorce and this factor is presumably somewhat responsible for the fact that maternal physical custody is maintained in nearly 90% of parental divorce cases.

There continues to be a debate as to how "the best interests of the child" can be defined. In fact, the increasing reliance on child advocates who serve to ensure that the child's best interest is served in legal proceedings has been questioned. For example, Fineman (1989) questions whether the child's best interests can really be identified separately from the best interests of the father and the mother. At the same time, fathers' rights groups are becoming increasingly organized and vocal about the child's "right" to have access to both parents after divorce and about fathers' "right" to equal involvement in decision-making after the divorce (for discussion, see Coltrane & Hickman, 1992; Lamb & Sagi, 1983; Thompson, 1986). The legal system has been criticized for aggressively enforcing child support orders but not enforcing visitation agreements when fathers wish to visit their children (Pearson & Anhalt, 1994). With regard to fathers' rights organizations, Bertoia and Drakich (1993) provided an interesting discussion of fathers involved in fathers' rights groups and suggested that many of these fathers are motivated more by a desire to improve their own personal situation than by a firm belief in the equality of parenting responsibilities. Undoubtedly, researchers and clinicians will continue to be involved closely in decisions regarding custody and visitation arrangements. Just as with research regarding the development of psychopathology, researchers will need to be vigilant about collecting data from both fathers and mothers as well as children who are involved in the process of custody evaluation and determination. Sonenstein and Calhoun (1990) provided a model research design when they evaluated both custodial parents' and noncustodial parents' reports of court-mandated child support payments. Interestingly, they found a fair amount of convergence in the reports of payments and in the factors that were related to payment of child support. This type of research design, where fathers, mothers, and children are asked their perspectives on the custody process should become a standard in research with families in which the parents are seeking divorce (Maccoby & Mnookin, 1992). However, researchers must remain cognizant that custody and support payments remain highly emotionally charged issues, with both men's rights groups and women's rights groups feeling that their constituency is not receiving adequate attention (Chesler, 1991; Coltrane & Hickman, 1992).

RESEARCH ISSUES WITHIN THE POLITICAL AND SOCIAL STRUCTURE

Fathers in the Media

In 1992, then-Vice President Dan Quayle sparked a national debate about the importance of fathers in children's lives. He commented that *Murphy Brown,* a television situation comedy, was mocking the importance of fathers by having the lead character give birth to and raise a child on her own. Given that a vast number of mothers in the United States are raising their children without the help of fathers, the debate appeared to focus on whether mothers should be able to choose single motherhood as opposed to being forced into it if the father were to leave the family and discontinue his participation with the children. Along with the ensuing debates related to keeping abortion safe and legal to ensure that pregnant single girls and women would not be forced into single motherhood, Dan Qualye's comments seemed to hit a nerve as to how important fathers really are in children's lives and how families are defined currently.

The popular press focused on both extremes of father involvement. In April 1993, *Atlantic Monthly* published an article with the premise "Dan Quayle was right" (Whitehead, 1993). In June 1993, *Time* did a cover story that explored fathers' involvement with their children, with special attention to fathers who have sole custody (Gibbs, 1993). In August 1993, *Newsweek* did a cover story on the absence of fathers, with special attention to the absence of fathers and father figures in African American families (Ingrassia, 1993). Interested readers should also note Atkinson and Blackwelder's (1993) fascinating account of how fathers have been portrayed in the popular press over the past 90 years.

Hollywood has also seemed to discover the different variants of fatherhood. On the big screen, there are images of fathers serving in the "maternal" role (e.g., *Mr. Mom, Mrs. Doubtfire*), sons reconnecting with their previously absent fathers (*Getting Even with Dad, Indiana Jones and the Last Crusade, In the Name of the Father*), and men reluctantly serving a paternal role for children who are not their own (*Jurassic Park, A Perfect World*). On the small screen, situation comedies are devoted to fathers who have either primary responsibility or a significant amount of responsibility for the care of their children (e.g., *Full House, Who's the Boss*) as well as fathers who are absent from their children's lives (e.g., *Grace under Fire*).

These national debates, movies, and cultural trends make for interesting dinner conversations, but the role of researchers should not be lost here. Investigators are still uncertain whether popular culture and the media shape our perceptions of reality or simply reflect a reality that already exists (Field, 1987). Nevertheless, researchers could conduct studies that investigate the relation between these trends in the media and changing perceptions of the importance of fathers in children's lives. Although I don't suggest these types of studies will significantly alter interventions that are ultimately provided for children and families in need, these studies might suggest preventive efforts that could be conducted through the mass media. For example, because so many children grow up in homes without a father or father figure, might it be helpful for them to see other families who live with similar circumstances? Conversely, if relatively uninvolved fathers continue to see highly involved fathers in the media, might they use these fathers as realistic role models and attempt to increase contact with their own children? Some of this work might be more in the domain of sociologists and communication studies researchers, but it would be informative for psychologists and others in the mental health field who work closely with distressed families that are inundated with these media images every day.

Men's Movement

With the publication of *Iron John: A Book about Men* by Bly in 1990 and the subsequent publication of *Fire in the Belly: On Being a Man* by Keen in 1991, the contemporary "men's movement" brought issues of fathers and masculinity to the forefront of our culture (Gilbert, 1992). Ironically, the contemporary men's movement is nothing new. In the early 1900s, significant numbers of men in the United States were involved in fraternal lodges and significant numbers of boys were involved in Boy Scouts, apparently to reinforce a strong bond between men and masculinity (Kimmel, 1993). In 1946, Wylie wrote of the need for male involvement (and less female involvement) in boys' and men's lives. In his history of fatherhood in America, Griswold (1993) noted that the connection between fathers and their children, or more specifically fathers and their sons, has been evident in a number of different eras throughout history. For example, many middle-class fathers in the 18th and 19th centuries were heavily involved in their sons' educational endeavors. Before the Civil War in the United States, male soldiers routinely addressed their letters home to their fathers, whereas after the war, letters home were more often directed toward their mothers (Griswold, 1993).

Regarding the contemporary men's movement, much of what Bly has focused on relates to men's yearning for a father who is both physically present and emotionally engaged. Although the men's movement has been criticized for its androcentric, antifemale nature and the concomitant emphasis on men's desire for power in their own lives (e.g., Faludi, 1991), Bly's attempt to help men find the "positive father substance" is potentially quite beneficial. It will be interesting to see whether men's reaching back to connect with their own fathers will also translate into their reaching ahead to their own children. In the Foreword to their child-rearing book *The Father Factor,* Biller and Trotter (1994) noted, "The immediate goal of the men's movement is to heal the wounds inflicted by the missing father, but the ultimate goal of the movement must be to ensure that the sins of the father are not visited on the next generation" (p. 8). Bowman (1993) described a one-day retreat for grandfathers, fathers, and sons that was based on Keen's (1991) image of the "wounded healer." Men were given the opportunity to discuss their painful experiences of yearning for their father or yearning for their son. They were encouraged to reflect on these experiences and then work on these issues in their own personal therapy. Empirical data were not evaluated. Notably, the focus of this retreat was on the "male" experience of the family (grandfather, father, son), and issues regarding women in families were not given a priority. It would be interesting to conduct a study of men who are and men who are not engaged in the men's movement to see whether their involvement with their own children differs. Given the recency of the current men's movement, it is still too early to establish whether the focus on lost fathers will prevent the loss of fathers in the future.

Institutional Barriers against Increased Paternal Involvement

Levine, Murphy, and Wilson (1993) suggested that institutional barriers have worked against fathers' involvement in children's lives. They argue that institutions (such as Head Start programs, schools, and community organizations) must actively seek paternal involvement to overcome the tradition of either overtly or covertly dissuading fathers to participate in their children's lives. In addition, Greenberger, Goldberg, Hamill, O'Neil, and Payne (1989) and Pleck (1993) highlighted the importance of family-responsive benefits and policies in the workplace for both fathers and mothers. As already discussed in Chapter 8, researchers of developmental psychopathology must discontinue the practice of not inviting fathers to take part in research relevant to their children. As noted in Chapter 9, there is also a need for therapeutic institutions (e.g., psychological clinics and individual practitioners) to include fathers in therapeutic interventions involving their children.

The role of the legal system with regard to noncustodial fathers' contact with their children must also be considered. Kruk (1991, 1992) attempted to ascertain the factors associated with fathers' disengagement from their children after divorce. Fathers who were disengaged from their children after divorce and who had little to no contact with their children reported a number of factors that led to their disengagement, including obstruction from their former wife (90%), their own decision to cease contact (33%), practical difficulties such as geographic distance, finances, or work schedule (28%), children not wanting contact (18%), legal injunction (16%), and an early pattern of no contact that prohibited future contact (5%). In addition, fathers who were disengaged from their children were significantly more likely than fathers who were still involved in their children's lives to report that their lawyer in some way hindered the relationship with their children. Kruk (1992) argues that the legal system must become more sensitive to the needs of fathers when devising custodial and visitation arrangements to avoid inadvertently causing children's loss of their fathers in both a physical and an emotional sense.

Groskind (1991) provided an interesting study of the general public's support of financial assistance to poor families with and without fathers. Although this study did not directly assess attitudes regarding fathers' custodial rights or payment of child support, the findings that emerged about fathers' presence or absence from the family are relevant to the topic of institutional barriers to fathers' involvement with their children. Groskind surveyed 1,470 adults from across the United States and provided them with a variety of vignettes that described poor families in either a single-mother household or a two-parent household. The vignettes also varied according to the level of income, the number of children, and the work motivation of the parent(s). Participants were asked to rate these vignettes according to how much public assistance the family should receive.

Results showed that when mother-only families were rated, the most important characteristic that influenced participants' decision was financial need. However, when two-parent families were rated, participants focused on the employment status and the work motivation of the father when considering appropriate amounts of public assistance. For example, a two-parent family with two children in which the father was disabled and unable to work and in which the mother was unemployed but looking for work was rated as deserving

$18,720 per year in public assistance. However, a two-parent family with two children in which both the father and the mother were unemployed and not looking for work because only minimum wage jobs were available was rated as deserving $8,008 per year in public assistance. Overall, results suggested that public opinion supports less financial support for families when there is an adult male in the household.

Aside from public opinion, it is important to consider whether federally funded support programs (such as AFDC) actually discourage adult male involvement in children's lives. For example, if families receive less money when an adult male is living in the household, then this policy would discourage fathers and father figures from living with their children. Erickson and Gecas (1991) noted that in most states, public assistance is reduced or even eliminated to AFDC families if an adult male is living in the household, regardless of whether or not he is employed. Overall, Groskind's (1991) study suggests that many adults are similar to many legislators in considering the presence of a father or father figure in the household, and also in considering the work motivation of fathers with regard to the public assistance that is made available to needy families.

Increasing Paternal Involvement in Children's Lives

A number of researchers and clinicians (e.g., Cowan & Cowan, 1988; Davis & May, 1991; Levant, 1988; Levine, 1993; Levine et al., 1993; Silverstein, 1993a) have called for increased involvement of men, and specifically fathers, in the lives of children. In Chapter 2, Levant's (1988) work toward education for fatherhood was described. There has also been an effort to include fathers in the parenting and educational process through institutionals. For example, Levine (1993) called for the need to involve fathers in Head Start programs. He argued that the little empirical research that has investigated "parent" involvement in Head Start programs has focused almost solely on mother involvement. Although many children in Head Start programs do not have a father or father figure in their lives, a large majority do have contact with a father or father figure. In the only empirical study that investigated fathers' involvement in Head Start programs (Gary, Beatty, & Weaver's 1987 final report for grant funding from the Department of Health and Human Services; cited in Levine, 1993), nearly three-fourths of the 118 African American fathers who took part in the study stated that they had either never been involved in Head Start activities or had only participated in activities a few times a year. In this same study, however, the majority of fathers (97%), mothers (98%), and staff (100%) stated that it was either important or very important for fathers to be involved in their children's Head Start program.

Because of the perceived importance of getting fathers involved in Head Start programs, Levine (1993) outlined a number of practical suggestions for helping to increase paternal involvement. From previous efforts to increase maternal involvement, Levine suggested that training is needed for staff members to become more supportive of parental involvement; multiple approaches (e.g., offering refreshments, calling parents, sending reminder notes to parents, providing transportation) are needed for increased parental involvement; and financial incentives (e.g., a small stipend for parents who volunteered a certain number of hours per month) might be used to increase parental involvement. All these approaches have been found to increase maternal involvement and would probably increase paternal involvement as well.

In addition, Levine (1993) suggested approaches that are specifically meant to target paternal involvement in Head Start programs. First, the definition of father should not be restricted to biological fathers or legal stepfathers but should also include father figures such as grandfathers, uncles, older brothers, the mother's boyfriend, or any other male who serves in a parental role. Davis and May (1991) made a similar suggestion by pointing out that a child's family should be defined in terms of who touches the child emotionally through caretaking and support. Second, the initial attempts at increasing father involvement should focus on reaching fathers and father figures as men first rather than as fathers first. Levine suggested that because many men feel inadequate regarding their parenting skills, they may be uninterested in taking part in activities that might highlight their inadequacies. Therefore, Head Start programs may want to first offer opportunities in which most men would be interested, such as sporting events or outdoor outings. Fathers may be more willing to take part in activities in which they feel competent and then later may be more willing to get involved in activities in which they feel less competent.

Levine also argued that staff members and mothers play a crucial gate-keeping role in fathers' involvement in Head Start programs. Many staff members and mothers involved in Head Start programs may feel ambivalent about increased paternal involvement in their programs and therefore their concerns need to be addressed and resolved to provide an accepting environment for fathers. Levine argued that once trust is established and fathers are hooked into the Head Start program, increased paternal involvement will benefit the fathers, the children, and the programs as well. Finally, Levine suggested that future research projects on Head Start should always include a component to investigate paternal involvement unless it is contraindicated by the research design or the design of the specific Head Start program.

Beyond the need for fathers' involvement in Head Start programs, Levine and colleagues (1993) also provided a practical guide to getting fathers involved in children's lives through educational, community, and institutional efforts. Their book is geared toward professionals and nonprofessionals alike and emphasizes ways to engage fathers in their children's activities. In addition, Levine and colleagues provided a compelling description of how fathers benefit from increased involvement with their children.

RESEARCH ISSUES FOR CONSIDERATION

In the discussion section of their review article, Phares and Compas (1992) highlighted the need for researchers to conduct separate analyses of maternal and paternal factors, to investigate variables that might moderate paternal effects on the development of psychopathology, to try to identify mechanisms through which paternal factors exert their influence, to study paternal and maternal protective factors that decrease the risk for the development of psychopathology in children, and to provide explicit acknowledgment of conceptual models that guide research. They also identified four methodological issues that needed to be addressed in future research with fathers: (a) the use of different types of assessment and different informants to assess child and adolescent psychopathology; (b) the use of diverse methods of assessment and different criteria in the identification of psychopathology in fathers and the identification of correlates of specific paternal diagnoses; (c) the need for research designs that investigate paternal and child functioning from a prospective standpoint rather than a cross-sectional perspective; and (d) the need for research with representative samples of fathers and children.

In addition to these suggestions for future research, Phares (1992) noted the importance of investigating similarities as well as differences in paternal and maternal effects in relation to the development of psychopathology, questioning sexist or "mother-blaming" theories in developmental psychopathology, and exploring parenting factors such as caretaking behaviors and career versus family orientation for both fathers and mothers in relation to the development of psychopathology.

Although this book has focused on fathers and developmental psychopathology, an ultimate goal in this research is to have enough information on both paternal and maternal mechanisms related to the development of psychopathology that research could move to the next level and focus on *parental* mechanisms related to the development of psychopathology. Because there is still so little known about fathers as opposed to mothers in relation to child and adolescent psychopathology, researchers are encouraged to investigate and report separate paternal and maternal analyses. However, once researchers have collected a significant portion of data about paternal and maternal influences, the field may be able to move on to higher-order analyses, such as characteristics, behaviors, and emotions of parents (and children) that are associated with heightened risk for the development of psychopathology. Researchers will need to remain cognizant of the reciprocal nature of the family environment and to investigate factors related to both parents and their offspring and the development of psychopathology (see Hinde & Stevenson-Hinde, 1988, for review).

Throughout the book, studies that investigated similarities and differences in families of different races or ethnicities have been included. As is too often the case, the majority of research on fathers and developmental psychopathology has either been conducted with primarily Caucasian samples or has not investigated race or ethnic differences within an ethnically diverse sample. Graham (1992) documented the preponderance of research in psychology that has been conducted with nonrepresentative samples. For example, she noted that from 1985 through 1989, only 2.6% of the empirical articles in *Developmental Psychology* focused on African Americans. The percentage was even lower (2.0%) for articles published in the *Journal of Consulting and Clinical Psychology*. With the added emphasis on college student populations in many areas of psychology such as social psychology (Sieber & Saks, 1989), the field leaves much to be desired in conducting relevant research with representative samples. Thus, it will be important for researchers of fathers and developmental psychopathology to recruit representative samples and to investigate similarities and differences between families of different ethnicities and races. Although there is mounting evidence that socioeconomic status plays a more important role in functioning within families than does race or ethnicity (Erickson & Gecas, 1991), there continues to be a need to investigate diversity among and between families.

McAdoo (1993) argued eloquently that African American fathers are no different from fathers of other ethnicities in the roles they play within the family, despite the educational, economic, and employment barriers that many of these fathers face. McAdoo (1988) called for a stop to the assumption that African American families are solely matricentric and that fathers are invisible, inactive, powerless, and uninterested in the family system. Rather, he argued that researchers should investigate how African American fathers interface with various institutions (such as the school system, the mental health care system) to gain a better understanding of the functioning of fathers within African American families (McAdoo, 1993). Therefore, not only is more research needed, but rather, more relevant research is needed to increase the ecological validity of studies of fathers from various ethnic and socioeconomic backgrounds. An excellent example of this type of research was provided by Bowman (1990) who conducted a nationwide study of the provider role strain and adaptive cultural resources among married African American fathers.

Throughout this book, individual references have been included where work has been completed with fathers of different ethnicities and racial backgrounds, as well as with fathers from different cultures. Interested readers are also referred to a number of excellent discussions of these issues for fathers (Bozett & Hanson, 1991; Erickson & Gecas, 1991; McLoyd, 1990; Tripp-Reimer & Wilson, 1991). Mirande (1991) reviewed research findings about fathers who were African American, Latino, Chinese American, Japanese American, Southeast Asian American, and Native American. A fascinating study of fathering in Chinese families from mainland China, Taiwan, and Hong Kong was provided by Berndt, Cheung, Lau, and Hau (1993). Ishii-Kuntz (1994) provided an intriguing cross-national study of fathers in Japan and the United States. In addition,

Lamb's (1987) book includes discussions of fathers from Great Britain (Jackson, 1987), France (delaisi de Parseval & Hurstel, 1987), West Germany (Nickel & Kocher, 1987), Sweden (Hwang, 1987), Italy (New & Benigni, 1987), Ireland (Nugent, 1987), Israel (Sagi, Koren, & Weinberg, 1987), China (Ho, 1987), Japan (Schwalb, Imaizumi, & Nakazawa, 1987), West Africa (Nsamenang, 1987), the Central African Republic (Hewlett, 1987), and Australia (Russell, 1987). Morelli and Tronick (1992) discuss Efe fathers from northeastern Zaire.

Overall, Mirande (1991) concluded that within the United States, there are more similarities than differences between fathers of different racial and ethnic backgrounds. He cautions researchers not to fall into an ethnocentric trap of using Caucasian American fathers as the "gold standard" from which to compare all other fathers. Rather, care should be taken to discover the different and similar meanings of fatherhood and the roles that fathers play in their children's lives across diverse samples of fathers.

CONCLUSIONS

Rather than attempting to present the final word on fathers and developmental psychopathology, I hope this book (and the research discussed in these pages) will serve as a foundation for a productive and important avenue of research. Initially, it appears to be necessary to focus on fathers vis-à-vis mothers. However, once researchers have established a firmer knowledge base about fathers and developmental psychopathology, they can move to the next level of analysis by focusing on characteristics of "parents" (*both* fathers and mothers) rather than fathers and mothers as separate entities. At present, not enough is known about fathers and developmental psychopathology, especially in relation to the research literature on mothers and developmental psychopathology. Researchers must make the investigation of fathers and developmental psychopathology a research priority.

I could close by using Biller and Solomon's (1986) call for "a manifesto for research." I could also refer to Parke's (1990) "invitation to join the search" (p. 183). Instead, as an encouragement for researchers to include fathers in investigations of developmental psychopathology, I will make reference to a popular athletic shoe advertising campaign and suggest that you "just do it."

References

Abidin, R. R. (1990). *Parenting Stress Index: Test manual.* Charlottesville, VA: Pediatric Psychology Press.

Abidin, R. R. (1992). The determinants of parenting behavior. *Journal of Clinical Child Psychology, 21,* 407–412.

Achenbach, T. M. (1982). *Developmental psychopathology* (2nd ed.). New York: Wiley.

Achenbach, T. M. (1985). *Assessment and taxonomy of child and adolescent psychopathology.* Newbury Park, CA: Sage.

Achenbach, T. M. (1990–1991). "Comorbidity" in child and adolescent psychiatry: Categorical and quantitative perspectives. *Journal of Child and Adolescent Psychopharmacology, 1,* 271–278.

Achenbach, T. M. (1991). *Manual for the Child Behavior Checklist/4–18 and 1991 Profile.* Burlington, VT: University of Vermont Department of Psychiatry.

Achenbach, T. M., McConaughy, S. H., & Howell, C. T. (1987). Child/adolescent behavioral and emotional problems: Implications of cross-informant correlations for situational specificity. *Psychological Bulletin, 101,* 213–232.

Achenbach, T. M., Phares, V., Howell, C. T., Rauh, V. A., & Nurcombe, B. (1990). Seven-year outcome of the Vermont intervention program for low-birthweight infants. *Child Development, 61,* 1672–1681.

Ackerman, N. (1958). *The psychodynamics of family life.* New York: Basic Books.

Adesso, V. J., & Lipson, J. W. (1981). Group training of parents as therapists for their children. *Behavior Therapy, 12,* 625–633.

Ahrentzen, S., Levine, D. W., & Michelson, W. (1989). Space, time, and activity in the home: A gender analysis. *Journal of Environmental Psychology, 9,* 89–101.

Ahrons, C. R., & Miller, R. B. (1993). The effect of the postdivorce relationship on paternal involvement: A longitudinal analysis. *American Journal of Orthopsychiatry, 63,* 441–450.

Ainsworth, M. D. S., Blehar, M. C., Waters, E., & Wall, S. (1978). *Patterns of attachment: A psychological study of the strange situation.* Hillsdale, NJ: Erlbaum.

Alberts-Corush, J., Firestone, P., & Goodman, J. T. (1986). Attention and impulsivity characteristics of the biological and adoptive parents of hyperactive and normal control children. *American Journal of Orthopsychiatry, 56,* 413–423.

Alexander, J. F., Waldron, H. B., Barton, C., & Mas, C. H. (1989). The minimizing of blaming attributions and behaviors in delinquent families. *Journal of Consulting and Clinical Psychology, 57,* 19–24.

Alford, G. S., Jouriles, E. N., & Jackson, S. C. (1991). Differences and similarities in development of drinking behavior between alcoholic offspring of alcoholics and alcoholic offspring of non-alcoholics. *Addictive Behaviors, 16,* 341–347.

Alnaes, R., & Torgersen, S. (1990). Parental representation in patients with major depression, anxiety disorder and mixed conditions. *Acta Psychiatrica Scandinavica, 81,* 518–522.

Amato, P. R. (1987). Family processes in one-parent, stepparent, and intact families: The child's point of view. *Journal of Marriage and the Family, 49,* 327–337.

Amato, P. R., & Keith, B. (1991). Parental divorce and the well-being of children: A meta-analysis. *Psychological Bulletin, 110,* 26–46.

American Psychiatric Association. (1994). *Diagnostic and statistical manual of mental disorders* (4th ed.). Washington, DC: Author.

Anderson, E. (1990). *Streetwise: Race, class and change in an urban community.* Chicago: University of Chicago Press.

Anderson, R. E. (1968). Where's Dad?: Paternal deprivation and delinquency. *Archives of General Psychiatry, 18,* 641–649.

Andrews, J. A., & Lewinsohn, P. M. (1992). Suicidal attempts among older adolescents: Prevalence and co-occurrence with psychiatric disorders. *Journal of the American Academy of Child and Adolescent Psychiatry, 31,* 655–662.

Angermeyer, M. C. (1982). The association between family atmosphere and hospital career of schizophrenic patients. *British Journal of Psychiatry, 141,* 1–11.

Aradine, C. R., & Ferketich, S. (1990). The psychological impact of premature birth on mothers and fathers. *Journal of Reproductive and Infant Psychology, 8,* 75–86.

Archer, R. P., Stolberg, A. L., Gordon, R. A., & Goldman, W. R. (1986). Parent and child MMPI responses: Characteristics among families with adolescents in inpatient and outpatient settings. *Journal of Abnormal Child Psychology, 14,* 181–190.

Arditti, J. A. (1992). Differences between fathers with joint custody and noncustodial fathers. *American Journal of Orthopsychiatry, 62,* 186–195.

Arditti, J. A., Godwin, D. D., & Scanzoni, J. (1991). Perceptions of parenting behavior and young women's gender role traits and preferences. *Sex Roles, 25,* 195–211.

Arendell, T. (1992). After divorce: Investigations into father absence. *Gender and Society, 6,* 562–586.

Arendell, T. (1995). *Fathers and divorce.* Thousand Oaks, CA: Sage.

Asarnow, J. R., Tompson, M., Hamilton, E. B., Goldstein, M. J., & Guthrie, D. (1994). Family-expressed emotion, childhood-onset depression, and childhood-onset schizophrenia spectrum disorders: Is expressed emotion a nonspecific correlate of child psychopathology or a specific risk factor for depression? *Journal of Abnormal Child Psychology, 22,* 129–146.

Atkins, R. N., & Lansky, M. R. (1986). The father in family therapy: Psychoanalytic perspectives. In M. E. Lamb (Ed.), *The father's role: Applied perspectives* (pp. 167–190). New York: Wiley.

Atkinson, A. K., & Rickel, A. U. (1984). Postpartum depression in primiparous parents. *Journal of Abnormal Psychology, 93,* 115–119.

Atkinson, A. M. (1987). Fathers' participation and evaluation of family day care. *Family Relations, 36,* 146–151.

Atkinson, A. M. (1991). Fathers' participation in day care. *Early Child Development and Care, 66,* 115–126.

Atkinson, M. P., & Blackwelder, S. P. (1993). Fathering in the 20th century. *Journal of Marriage and the Family, 55,* 975–986.

Atwood, R., Gold, M., & Taylor, R. (1989). Two types of delinquents and their institutional adjustment. *Journal of Consulting and Clinical Psychology, 57,* 68–75.

Auslander, W. F., Bubb, J., Rogge, M., & Santiago, J. V. (1993). Family stress and resources: Potential areas of intervention in children recently diagnosed with diabetes. *Health and Social Work, 18,* 101–113.

Bach, G. R. (1946). Father-fantasies and father-typing in father-separated children. *Child Development, 17,* 63–79.

Bacon, M. K., Child, I. L., & Barry, H. (1963). A cross-cultural study of correlates of crime. *Journal of Abnormal and Social Psychology, 66,* 291–300.

Baer, P. E. (1983). Conflict management in the family: The impact of paternal hypertension. *Advances in Family Intervention, Assessment and Theory, 3,* 161–184.

Bahr, S. J., Hawks, R. D., & Wang, G. (1993). Family and religious influences on adolescent substance abuse. *Youth and Society, 24,* 443–465.

Bailey, J. M., Bobrow, D., Wolfe, M., & Mikach, S. (1995). Sexual orientation of adult sons of gay fathers. *Developmental Psychology, 31,* 124–129.

Bailey, W. T. (1991). Fathers' involvement in their children's healthcare. *Journal of Genetic Psychology, 152,* 289–293.

Baker, D. B. (1994). Parenting stress and ADHD: A comparison of mothers and fathers. *Journal of Emotional and Behavioral Disorders, 2,* 46–50.

Baldwin, C. P., Baldwin, A. L., Cole, R. E., & Kokes, R. F. (1984). Free play family interaction and the behavior of the patient in free play. In N. F. Watt, E. J. Anthony, L. C. Wynne, & J. E. Rolf (Eds.), *Children at risk for schizophrenia: A longitudinal perspective* (pp. 376–387). New York: Cambridge University Press.

Bandura, A. (1977). *Social learning theory.* Englewood Cliffs, NJ: Prentice-Hall.

Bandura, A., & Walters, R. H. (1963). *Social learning and personality development.* New York: Holt, Rinehart & Winston.

Banning, A. (1989). Mother-son incest: Confronting a prejudice. *Child Abuse and Neglect, 13,* 563–570.

Barak, A., Feldman, S., & Noy, A. (1991). Traditionality of children's interests as related to their parents' gender stereotypes and traditionality of occupations. *Sex Roles, 24,* 511–524.

Baranowski, M. D. (1985). Men as grandfathers. In S. M. H. Hanson & F. W. Bozett (Eds.), *Dimensions of fatherhood* (pp. 217–238). Beverly Hills, CA: Sage.

Barglow, P., Vaughn, B. E., & Molitor, N. (1987). Effects of maternal absence due to employment on the quality of infant-mother attachment in a low-risk sample. *Child Development, 58,* 945–954.

Barling, J. (1986). Fathers' work experiences, the father-child relationship and children's behaviour. *Journal of Occupational Behaviour, 7,* 61–66.

Barling, J. (1990). *Employment, stress and family functioning.* New York: Wiley.

Barlow, D. H. (1988). *Anxiety and its disorders: The nature and treatment of anxiety and panic.* New York: Guilford.

Barnes, G. M. (1984). Adolescent alcohol abuse and other problem behaviors: Their relationships and common parental influences. *Journal of Youth and Adolescence, 13,* 329–348.

Barnes, G. M., Farrell, M. P., & Cairns, A. (1986). Parental socialization factors and adolescent drinking behaviors. *Journal of Marriage and the Family, 48,* 27–36.

Barnes, G. M., Welte, J. W., & Dintcheff, B. (1992). Alcohol misuse among college students and other young adults: Findings from a general population study in New York State. *International Journal of the Addictions, 27,* 917–934.

Barnett, M. A., Sinisi, C. S., Jaet, B. P., Bealer, R., Rodell, P., & Saunders, L. D. (1990). Perceived gender differences in children's help-seeking. *Journal of Genetic Psychology, 151,* 451–460.

Barnett, R. C., & Baruch, G. K. (1987). Determinants of fathers' participation in family work. *Journal of Marriage and the Family, 49,* 29–40.

Barnett, R. C., & Baruch, G. K. (1988). Correlates of fathers' participation in family work. In P. Bronstein & C. P. Cowan (Eds.), *Fatherhood today: Men's changing role in the family* (pp. 66–78). New York: Wiley.

Barnett, R. C., & Marshall, N. L. (1993). Men, family-role quality, job-role quality, and physical health. *Health Psychology, 12,* 48–55.

Barnett, R. C., Marshall, N. L., & Pleck, J. H. (1992a). Adult son-parent relationships and their associations with sons' psychological distress. *Journal of Family Issues, 13,* 505–525.

Barnett, R. C., Marshall, N. L., & Pleck, J. H. (1992b). Men's multiple roles and their relationship to men's psychological distress. *Journal of Marriage and the Family, 54,* 358–367.

Barrera, M., Chassin, L., & Rogosch, F. (1993). Effects of social support and conflict on adolescent children of alcoholic and nonalcoholic fathers. *Journal of Personality and Social Psychology, 64,* 602–612.

Barrnett, R. J., Docherty, J. P., & Frommelt, G. M. (1991). A review of child psychotherapy research since 1963. *Journal of the American Academy of Child and Adolescent Psychiatry, 30,* 1–14.

Barry, H., Bacon, M. K., & Child, I. L. (1957). A cross-cultural survey of some sex differences in socialization. *Journal of Abnormal and Social Psychology, 55,* 327–332.

Bartle, S. E., & Anderson, S. A. (1991). Similarity between parents' and adolescents' levels of individuation. *Adolescence, 26,* 913–924.

Barton, M. E., & Tomasello, M. (1994). The rest of the family: The role of fathers and siblings in early language development. In C. Gallaway & B. J. Richards (Eds.), *Input and interaction in language acquisition* (pp. 109–134). New York: Cambridge University Press.

Baruch, G. K., & Barnett, R. C. (1986a). Consequences of fathers' participation in family work: Parents' role strain and well-being. *Journal of Personality and Social Psychology, 51*, 983–992.

Baruch, G. K., & Barnett, R. C. (1986b). Fathers' participation in family work and children's sex-role attitudes. *Child Development, 57*, 1210–1223.

Baruch, G. K., Biener, L., & Barnett, R. C. (1987). Women and gender in research on work and family stress. *American Psychologist, 42*, 130–136.

Basow, S. A. (1992). *Gender stereotypes and roles* (3rd ed.). Pacific Grove, CA: Brooks/Cole.

Bates, J. E. (1980). The concept of difficult temperament. *Merrill-Palmer Quarterly, 26*, 299–319.

Bateson, G., Jackson, D. D., Haley, J., & Weakland, J. (1956). Toward a theory of schizophrenia. *Behavioral Science, 1*, 251–264.

Baumrind, D. (1971). Current patterns of parental authority. *Developmental Psychology Monographs, 4*, 2.

Beal, C. R. (1994). *Boys and girls: The development of gender roles.* New York: McGraw-Hill.

Beardslee, W. R. (1986). The need for the study of adaptation in the children of parents with affective disorders. In M. Rutter, C. E. Izard, & P. B. Read (Eds.), *Depression in young people: Developmental and clinical perspectives* (pp. 189–204). New York: Guilford.

Beardslee, W. R., Bemporad, J., Keller, M. B., & Klerman, G. L. (1984). Children of parents with major affective disorder: A review. *Annual Progress in Child Psychiatry and Child Development*, pp. 390–404.

Beardslee, W. R., & Podorefsky, D. (1988). Resilient adolescents whose parents have serious affective and other psychiatric disorders: Importance of self-understanding and relationships. *American Journal of Psychiatry, 145*, 63–69.

Beardslee, W. R., Schultz, L. H., & Selman, R. L. (1987). Level of social-cognitive development, adaptive functioning, and DSM-III diagnoses in adolescent offspring of parents with affective disorders: Implications of the development of the capacity for mutuality. *Developmental Psychology, 23*, 807–815.

Becker, J. A., & Hall, M. S. (1989). Adult beliefs about pragmatic development. *Journal of Applied Developmental Psychology, 10*, 1–17.

Becvar, D. S., & Becvar, R. J. (1993). *Family therapy: A systemic integration* (2nd ed.). Needham Heights, MA: Allyn and Bacon.

Behrman, R. E. (1992). *Nelson textbook of pediatrics* (14th ed.). Philadelphia: Saunders.

Beitchman, J. H., Zucker, K. J., Hood, J. E., DaCosta, G. A., Akman, D., & Cassavia, E. (1992). A review of the long-term effects of child sexual abuse. *Child Abuse and Neglect, 16*, 101–118.

Belsky, J. (1981). Early human experience: A family perspective. *Developmental Psychology, 17*, 3–23.

Belsky, J., Gilstrap, B., & Rovine, M. (1984). The Pennsylvania Infant and Family Development Project: I. Stability and change in mother-infant and father-infant interaction in a family setting at one, three, and nine months. *Child Development,* *55,* 692–705.

Belsky, J., Lang, M., & Rovine, M. (1985). Stability and change in marriage across the transition to parenthood: A second study. *Journal of Marriage and the Family,* *47,* 855–866.

Belsky, J., & Rovine, M. J. (1988). Nonmaternal care in the first year of life and the security of infant-parent attachment. *Child Development, 59,* 157–167.

Belsky, J., Steinberg, L., & Draper, P. (1991). Childhood experience, interpersonal development, and reproductive strategy: An evolutionary theory of socialization. *Child Development, 62,* 647–670.

Belsky, J., & Volling, B. L. (1987). Mothering, fathering, and marital interaction in the family triad during infancy: Exploring family systems processes. In P. W. Berman & F. A. Pedersen (Eds.), *Men's transition to parenthood: Longitudinal studies of early family experience* (pp. 37–63). Hillsdale, NJ: Erlbaum.

Bem, S. L. (1974). The measurement of psychological androgyny. *Journal of Consulting and Clinical Psychology, 42,* 155–162.

Bem, S. L. (1981). *Bem Sex-Role Inventory: Professional manual.* Palo Alto, CA: Consulting Psychologist Press.

Bennun, I. (1989). Perceptions of the therapist in family therapy. *Journal of Family Therapy, 11,* 243–255.

Benson, C. S., & Heller, K. (1987). Factors in the current adjustment of young adult daughters of alcoholic and problem drinking fathers. *Journal of Abnormal Psychology, 96,* 305–312.

Benson, M. J., Harris, P. B., & Rogers, C. S. (1992). Identity consequences of attachment to mothers and fathers among late adolescents. *Journal of Research on Adolescence, 2,* 187–204.

Bentley, K. S., & Fox, R. A. (1991). Mothers and fathers of young children: Comparison of parenting styles. *Psychological Reports, 69,* 320–322.

Berg, B., & Rosenblum, N. (1977). Fathers in family therapy: A survey of family therapists. *Journal of Marriage and Family Counseling, 3,* 85–91.

Berg-Cross, L., Kidd, F., & Carr, P. (1990). Cohesion, affect, and self-disclosure in African-American adolescent families. *Journal of Family Psychology, 4,* 235–250.

Berger, K. S. (1994). *The developing person through the life span* (3rd ed.). New York: Worth Publishers.

Bergman, A. G. (1989). Informal support systems for pregnant teenagers. *Social Casework, 70,* 525–533.

Berkowitz, A., & Perkins, H. W. (1988). Personality characteristics of children of alcoholics. *Journal of Consulting and Clinical Psychology, 56,* 206–209.

Berman, P. W. (1980). Are women more responsive than men to the young? A review of developmental and situational variables. *Psychological Bulletin, 88,* 668–695.

Berman, P. W., & Pedersen, F. A. (Eds.). (1987). *Men's transitions to parenthood: Longitudinal studies of early family experience.* Hillsdale, NJ: Erlbaum.

Berman, S. M., Whipple, S. C., Fitch, R. J., & Noble, E. P. (1993). P3 in young boys as a predictor of adolescent substance use. *Alcohol, 10,* 69–76.

Bernal, M. E., Kinnert, M. D., & Schultz, L. A. (1980). Outcome evaluation of behavioral parent training and client-centered parent counseling for children with conduct problems. *Journal of Applied Behavior Analysis, 13,* 677–691.

Bernard, J. (1974). *The future of motherhood.* New York: Dial Press.

Bernard, J. (1975). *Women, wives, mothers: Values and options.* Chicago: Aldine.

Bernard, J. (1981). Societal values and parenting. *The Counseling Psychologist, 9,* 5–11.

Bernard, J. (1982). *The future of marriage.* New Haven, CT: Yale University Press.

Bernard, J. (1987). Re-viewing the impact of women's studies on sociology. In C. Farnham (Ed.), *The impact of feminist research in the academy* (pp. 193–216). Bloomington: Indiana University Press.

Berndt, T. J., Cheung, P. C., Lau, S., & Hau, D. T. (1993). Perceptions of parenting in mainland China, Taiwan, and Hong Kong: Sex differences and societal differences. *Developmental Psychology, 29,* 156–164.

Bernstein, G. A., Svingen, P. H., & Garfinkel, B. D. (1990). School phobia: Patterns of family functioning. *Journal of the American Academy of Child and Adolescent Psychiatry, 29,* 24–30.

Bertoia, C., & Drakich, J. (1993). The fathers' rights movement: Contradictions in rhetoric and practice. *Journal of Family Issues, 14,* 592–615.

Bettelheim, B. (1965). The commitment required of a woman entering a scientific profession in present-day American Society. In J. A. Mattfield & C. G. Van Aken (Eds.), *Women and the scientific professions* (pp. 3–19). Cambridge, MA: M. I. T. Press.

Bezirganian, S., & Cohen, P. (1992). Sex differences in the interaction between temperament and parenting. *Journal of the American Academy of Child and Adolescent Psychiatry, 31,* 790–801.

Bhatnagar, J. K., & Sharma, M. (1992). A study of the relationship between parental education and academic achievement in a semi-rural setting. *Psychological Studies, 37,* 126–129.

Bigelow, B. J., Tesson, G., & Lewko, J. H. (1992). The social rules that children use: Close friends, other friends, and "other kids" compared to parents, teachers, and siblings. *International Journal of Behavioral Development, 15,* 315–331.

Bigner, J. J. (1977). Attitudes toward fathering and father-child activity. *Home Economics Research Journal, 6,* 98–106.

Bigner, J. J., & Jacobsen, R. B. (1992). Adult responses to child behavior and attitudes toward fathering: Gay and nongay fathers. *Journal of Homosexuality, 23,* 99–112.

Bigras, J., Leichner, P., Perreault, M., & Lavoie, R. (1991). Severe paternal sexual abuse in early childhood and systematic aggression against the family and the institution. *Canadian Journal of Psychiatry, 36,* 527–529.

Biller, H. B. (1971). *Father, child and sex role.* Lexington, MA: Lexington Books.

Biller, H. B. (1974). *Paternal deprivation.* Lexington, MA: Lexington Books.

Biller, H. B. (1981a). Father absence, divorce, and personality development. In M. E. Lamb (Ed.), *The role of the father in child development* (rev. ed., pp. 489–532). New York: Wiley.

Biller, H. B. (1981b). The father and sex role development. In M. E. Lamb (Ed.), *The role of the father in child development* (rev. ed., pp. 319–358). New York: Wiley.

Biller, H. B. (1993). *Fathers and families: Paternal factors in child development.* Westport, CT: Auburn House.

Biller, H. B., & Meredith, D. (1974). *Father power.* New York: David McKay Company.

Biller, H. B., & Solomon, R. S. (1986). *Child maltreatment and paternal deprivation: A manifesto for research, prevention, and treatment.* Lexington, MA: Lexington Books.

Biller, H. B., & Trotter, R. J. (1994). *The father factor: What you need to know to make a difference.* New York: Pocket Books.

Billings, A. G., & Moos, R. H. (1983). Comparisons of children of depressed and non-depressed parents: A social-environmental perspective. *Journal of Abnormal Child Psychology, 11,* 463–486.

Billings, A. G., & Moos, R. H. (1985). Children of parents with unipolar depression: A controlled 1-year follow-up. *Journal of Abnormal Child Psychology, 14,* 149–166.

Binion, V. J. (1990). Psychological androgyny: A Black female perspective. *Sex Roles, 22,* 487–507.

Bird, G. W., & Ratcliff, B. B. (1990). Children's participation in family tasks: Determinants of mothers' and fathers' reports. *Human Relations, 43,* 865–884.

Bird, H. R., Gould, M. S., Yager, T., Staghezza, B., & Canino, G. (1989). Risk factors for maladjustment in Puerto Rican children. *Journal of the American Academy of Child and Adolescent Psychiatry, 28,* 847–850.

Bjorkqvist, K., & Osterman, K. (1992). Parental influence on children's self-estimated aggressiveness. *Aggressive Behavior, 18,* 411–423.

Block, J., Block, J. H., & Gjerde, P. F. (1988). Parental functioning and the home environment in families of divorce: Prospective and concurrent analyses. *Journal of the American Academy of Child and Adolescent Psychiatry, 27,* 207–213.

Bloom-Feshbach, J. (1981). Historical perspectives on the father's role. In M. E. Lamb (Ed.), *The role of the father in child development* (rev. ed., pp. 71–112). New York: Wiley.

Bloom-Feshbach, J., & Bloom-Feshbach, S. (1987). Introduction: Psychological separateness and experiences of loss. In J. Bloom-Feshbach & S. Bloom-Feshbach (Eds.), *The psychology of separation and loss: Perspectives on development, life transitions, and clinical practice* (pp. 1–59). San Francisco: Jossey-Bass.

Bly, R. (1990). *Iron John: A book about men.* Reading, MA: Addison-Wesley.

Boose, L. E., & Flowers, B. S. (Eds.). (1989). *Daughters and fathers.* Baltimore: The Johns Hopkins University Press.

Booth, A., & Amato, P. R. (1994). Parental marital quality, parental divorce, and relations with parents. *Journal of Marriage and the Family, 56,* 21–34.

Bordens, K. S., & Abbott, B. B. (1988). *Research design and methods: A process approach.* Mountain View, CA: Mayfield Publishing Company.

Borduin, C. M., Henggeler, S. W., & Pruitt, J. A. (1985). The relationship between juvenile delinquency and personality dimensions of family members. *Journal of Genetic Psychology, 146,* 563–565.

Borduin, C. M., Pruitt, J. A., & Henggeler, S. W. (1986). Family interactions in Black, lower-class families with delinquent and nondelinquent adolescent boys. *The Journal of Genetic Psychology, 147,* 333–342.

Borges, G., Garrido, F., Cardenas, V., Ibarra, J., & Bobadilla, J. L. (1993). Parental alcohol consumption and postneonatal mortality. *Journal of Community and Applied Social Psychology, 3,* 17–27.

Bortner, R. W., Rosenman, R. H., & Friedman, M. (1970). Familial similarity in pattern A behavior: Fathers and sons. *Journal of Chronic Diseases, 23,* 39–43.

Bowen, M. (1965). Family psychotherapy with schizophrenics in the hospital and in private practice. In I. Boszormenyi-Nagy & J. Framo (Eds.), *Intensive family therapy* (pp. 213–243). New York: Harper & Row.

Bowen, M. (1966). The use of family theory in clinical practice. *Comprehensive Psychiatry, 7,* 345–374.

Bowerman, C. E., & Irish, D. P. (1962). Some relationships of stepchildren to their parents. *Marriage and Family Living, 24,* 113–121.

Bowlby, J. (1951). *Maternal care and mental health.* Geneva: World Health Organization.

Bowlby, J. (1969). *Attachment.* New York: Basic Books.

Bowman, P. J. (1990). Coping with provider role strain: Adaptive cultural resources among Black husband-fathers. *The Journal of Black Psychology, 16,* 1–21.

Bowman, T. (1993). The father-son project. *Families in Society, 74,* 22–27.

Boyd, S. T. (1985). Study of the father: Research methods. *American Behavioral Scientist, 29,* 112–128.

Bozett, F. W. (1985). Gay men as fathers. In S. M. H. Hanson & F. W. Bozett (Eds.), *Dimensions of fatherhood* (pp. 327–352). Beverly Hills, CA: Sage.

Bozett, F. W. (1987a). Children of gay fathers. In F. W. Bozett (Ed.), *Gay and lesbian parents* (pp. 39–57). New York: Praeger.

Bozett, F. W. (Ed.). (1987b). *Gay and lesbian parents.* New York: Praeger.

Bozett, F. W. (1988). Gay fatherhood. In P. Bronstein & C. P. Cowan (Eds.), *Fatherhood today: Men's changing role in the family* (pp. 214–235). New York: Wiley.

Bozett, F. W., & Hanson, S. M. H. (Eds.). (1991). *Fatherhood and families in cultural context.* New York: Springer.

Bradbard, M. R., Endsley, R. C., & Mize, J. (1992). The ecology of parent-child communications about daily experiences in preschool and day care. *Journal of Research in Childhood Education, 6,* 131–141.

Braverman, L. B. (1989). Beyond the myth of motherhood. In M. McGoldrick, C. M. Anderson, & F. Walsh (Eds.), *Women and families* (pp. 227–243). New York: Free Press.

Brent, D. A., Johnson, B., Bartle, S., & Bridge, J. (1993). Personality disorder, tendency to impulsive violence, and suicidal behavior in adolescents. *Journal of the American Academy of Child and Adolescent Psychiatry, 32,* 69–75.

Breton, J. J., Valla, J. P., & Lambert, J. (1993). Industrial disaster and mental health of children and their parents. *Journal of the American Academy of Child and Adolescent Psychiatry, 32,* 438–445.

Brodkin, A. M. (1980). Family therapy: The making of a mental health movement. *American Journal of Orthopsychiatry, 50,* 4–17.

Brody, G. H., & Forehand, R. (1986). Maternal perceptions of child adjustment as a function of the combined influence of child behavior and maternal depression. *Journal of Consulting and Clinical Psychology, 54,* 237–240.

Brody, G. H., & Forehand, R. (1990). Interparental conflict, relationship with the noncustodial father, and adolescent post-divorce adjustment. *Journal of Applied Developmental Psychology, 11,* 139–147.

Brody, G. H., Pillegrini, A. D., & Sigel, I. E. (1986). Marital quality and mother-child and father-child interactions with school-aged children. *Developmental Psychology, 22,* 291–296.

Brody, G. H., Stoneman, Z., Flor, D., McCrary, C., Hastings, L., & Conyers, O. (1994). Financial resources, parent psychological functioning, parent co-caregiving, and early adolescent competence in rural two-parent African-American families. *Child Development, 65,* 590–605.

Brody, G. H., Stoneman, Z., & McCoy, J. K. (1992). Associations of maternal and paternal direct and differential behavior with sibling relationships: Contemporaneous and longitudinal analyses. *Child Development, 63,* 82–92.

Brody, G. H., Stoneman, Z., McCoy, J. K., & Forehand, R. (1992). Contemporaneous and longitudinal associations of sibling conflict with family relationship assessments and family discussions about sibling problems. *Child Development, 63,* 391–400.

Bron, B., Strack, M., & Rudolph, G. (1991). Childhood experiences of loss and suicide attempts: Significance in depressive states of major depressed and dysthymic or adjustment disordered patients. *Journal of Affective Disorders, 23,* 165–172.

Bronstein, P. (1984). Differences in mothers' and fathers' behaviors toward children: A cross-cultural comparison. *Developmental Psychology, 20,* 995–1003.

Bronstein, P. (1988). Father-child interaction: Implications for gender-role socialization. In P. Bronstein & C. P. Cowan (Eds.), *Fatherhood today: Men's changing role in the family* (pp. 107–124). New York: Wiley.

Bronstein, P., & Cowan, C. P. (Eds.). (1988). *Fatherhood today: Men's changing role in the family.* New York: Wiley.

Brook, J. S., Brook, D., Whiteman, M., & Gordon, A. S. (1983). Depressive mood in male college students. *Archives of General Psychiatry, 40,* 665–669.

Brook, J. S., Whiteman, M., Brook, D. W., & Gordon, A. S. (1982). Paternal and peer characteristics: Interactions and association with male college students' marijuana use. *Psychological Reports, 51,* 1319–1330.

Brook, J. S., Whiteman, M., Brook, D. W., & Gordon, A. S. (1988). Depressive mood in female college students: Father-daughter interactional patterns. *Journal of Genetic Psychology, 149,* 485–504.

Brook, J. S., Whiteman, M., Gordon, A. S., & Brook, D. W. (1983). Paternal correlates of adolescent marijuana use in the context of the mother-son and parental dyads. *Genetic Psychology Monographs, 108,* 197–213.

Brook, J. S., Whiteman, M., Gordon, A. S., & Brook, D. W. (1984a). Identification with paternal attributes and its relationship to the son's personality and drug use. *Developmental Psychology, 20,* 1111–1119.

Brook, J. S., Whiteman, M., Gordon, A. S., & Brook, D. W. (1984b). Paternal determinants of female adolescent's marijuana use. *Developmental Psychology, 20,* 1032–1043.

Brook, J. S., Whiteman, M., Gordon, A. S., & Brook, D. W. (1986). Father-daughter identification and its impact on her personality and drug use. *Developmental Psychology, 22,* 743–748.

Brown, J. E., & Mann, L. (1991). Decision-making competence and self-esteem: A comparison of parents and adolescents. *Journal of Adolescence, 14,* 363–371.

Brown, R. T., Kaslow, N. J., Madan-Swain, A., & Doepke, K. J. (1993). Parental psychopathology and children's adjustment to leukemia. *Journal of the American Academy of Child and Adolescent Psychiatry, 32,* 554–561.

Browne, A., & Finkelhor, D. (1986). Impact of child sexual abuse: A review of the literature. *Psychological Bulletin, 99,* 66–77.

Brownfield, D. (1987). Father-son relationships and violent behavior. *Deviant Behavior, 8,* 65–78.

Buchanan, C. M., Eccles, J. S., Flanagan, C., Midgley, C., Feldlaufer, H., & Harold, R. D. (1990). Parents' and teachers' beliefs about adolescents: Effects of sex and experience. *Journal of Youth and Adolescence, 19,* 363–394.

Buchanan, C. M., Maccoby, E. E., & Dornbusch, S. M. (1991). Caught between parents: Adolescents' experience in divorced homes. *Child Development, 62,* 1008–1029.

Buchanan, C. M., Maccoby, E. E., & Dornbusch, S. M. (1992). Adolescents and their families after divorce: Three residential arrangements compared. *Journal of Research on Adolescence, 2,* 261–291.

Budd, K. S., & O'Brien, T. P. (1982). Father involvement in behavioral parent training: An area in need of research. *The Behavior Therapist, 5,* 85–89.

Buffo, K. A., & Gustafson, G. E. (1994, April). *Caregiving experience and behavior in young men.* Paper presented at the Biennial Conference on Human Development, Pittsburgh, PA.

Buhrmester, D., Camparo, L., Christensen, A., Gonzalez, L. S., & Hinshaw, S. P. (1992). Mothers and fathers interacting in dyads and triads with normal and hyperactive sons. *Developmental Psychology, 28,* 500–509.

Bulik, C. M., & Sullivan, P. F. (1993). Comorbidity of bulimia and substance abuse: Perceptions of family of origin. *International Journal of Eating Disorders, 13,* 49–56.

Burbach, D. J. & Borduin, C. M. (1986). Parent-child relations and the etiology of depression: A review of methods and findings. *Clinical Psychology Review, 6,* 133–153.

Buri, J. R. (1991). Parental authority questionnaire. *Journal of Personality Assessment, 57,* 110–119.

Buri, J. R., Louiselle, P. A., Misukanis, T. M., & Mueller, R. A. (1988). Effects of parental authoritarianism and authoritativeness on self-esteem. *Personality and Social Psychology Bulletin, 14,* 271–282.

Burman, R., John, R. S., & Margolin, G. (1987). Effects of marital and parent-child relations on children's adjustment. *Journal of Family Psychology, 1,* 91–108.

Butcher, J. N., Dahlstrom, W. G., Graham, J. R., Tellegen, A., & Kaemmer, B. (1989). *Manual for the restandardized Minnesota Multiphasic Personality Inventory:*

MMPI-2. An administrative and interpretive guide. Minneapolis: University of Minnesota Press.

Calam, R., Waller, G., Slade, P. D., & Newton, T. (1990). Eating disorders and perceived relationships with parents. *International Journal of Eating Disorders, 9,* 479–485.

Callahan, C. M., Comell, D. G., & Loyd, B. (1990). Perceived competence and parent-adolescent communication in high ability adolescent females. *Journal for the Education of the Gifted, 13,* 256–269.

Callan, V. J., & Jackson, D. (1986). Children of alcoholic fathers and recovered alcoholic fathers: Personal and family functioning. *Journal of Studies on Alcohol, 47,* 180–182.

Cantrell, P. J., Carrico, M. F., Franklin, J. N., & Grubb, H. J. (1990). Violent tactics in family conflict relative to familial and economic factors. *Psychological Reports, 66,* 823–828.

Caplan, P. J. (1986, October). Take the blame off mother. *Psychology Today,* pp. 70–71.

Caplan, P. J. (1989). *Don't blame mother: Mending the mother-daughter relationship.* New York: Harper & Row.

Caplan, P. J., & Hall-McCorquodale, I. (1985a). Mother-blaming in major clinical journals. *American Journal of Orthopsychiatry, 55,* 345–353.

Caplan, P. J., & Hall-McCorquodale, I. (1985b). The scapegoating of mothers: A call for change. *American Journal of Orthopsychiatry, 55,* 610–613.

Caplan, R., & Guthrie, D. (1992). Communication deficits in childhood schizotypal personality disorder. *Journal of the American Academy of Child and Adolescent Psychiatry, 31,* 961–967.

Carlson, C. I., Cooper, C. R., & Spradling, V. Y. (1991). Developmental implications of shared versus distinct perceptions of the family in early adolescence. *New Directions for Child Development: Shared views in the family during adolescence, 51,* 13–32.

Caron, C., & Rutter, M. (1991). Comorbidity in child psychopathology: Concepts, issues and research strategies. *Journal of Child Psychology and Psychiatry, 32,* 1063–1080.

Casey, R. J., & Berman, J. S. (1985). The outcome of psychotherapy with children. *Psychological Bulletin, 98,* 388–400.

Cath, S. H., Gurwitt, A., & Gunsberg, L. (Eds.). (1989). *Fathers and their families.* Hillsdale, NJ: Analytic Press.

Cervera, N. (1991). Unwed teenage pregnancy: Family relationships with the father of the baby. *Families in Society: The Journal of Contemporary Human Services, 72,* 29–37.

Chang, J., & Block, J. (1960). A study of identification in male homosexuals. *Journal of Consulting Psychology, 24,* 307–310.

Chassin, L., Rogosch, F., & Barrera, M. (1991). Substance use and symptomatology among adolescent children of alcoholics. *Journal of Abnormal Psychology, 100,* 449–463.

Chatwin, S. L., & MacArthur, B. A. (1993). Maternal perceptions of the preterm infant. *Early Child Development and Care, 87,* 69–82.

Cherlin, A. (Ed.). (1988). *The changing American family and public policy*. Washington, DC: Urban Institute.

Chesler, P. (1972). *Women and madness*. New York: Avon Books.

Chesler, P. (1991). Mothers on trial: The custodial vulnerability of women. *Feminism and Psychology, 1*, 409–425.

Chess, S. (1964). Mal de mere. *American Journal of Orthopsychiatry, 34*, 613–614.

Chess, S. (1982). The "blame the mother" ideology. *International Journal of Mental Health, 11*, 95–107.

Chess, S., & Thomas, A. (1982). Infant bonding: Mystique and reality. *American Journal of Orthopsychiatry, 52*, 213–222.

Chira, S. (1993, September 22). Census data show rise in child care by fathers. *New York Times*, p. 1.

Christensen, A., Margolin, G., & Sullaway, M. (1992). Interparental agreement on child behavior problems. *Psychological Assessment, 4*, 419–425.

Christensen, A., Phillips, S., Glasgow, R. E., & Johnson, S. M. (1983). Parental characteristics and interactional dysfunction in families with child behavior problems: A preliminary investigation. *Journal of Abnormal Child Psychology, 11*, 153–166.

Christmon, K. (1990a). Parental responsibility and self-image of African American fathers. *Families in Society: The Journal of Contemporary Human Services, 71*, 563–567.

Christmon, K. (1990b). Parental responsibility of African American unwed adolescent fathers. *Adolescence, 25*, 645–653.

Churven, P. G. (1978). Families: Parental attitudes to family assessment in a child psychiatry setting. *Journal of Child Psychology and Psychiatry, 19*, 33–41.

Cicirelli, V. G. (1994). The individual in the family life cycle. In L. L'Abate (Ed.), *Handbook of developmental family psychology and psychopathology* (pp. 27–43). New York: Wiley.

Clark, D. A., & Bolton, D. (1985). Obsessive-compulsive adolescents and their parents: A psychometric study. *Journal of Child Psychology and Psychiatry, 26*, 267–276.

Clark, L. A. (1989). The anxiety and depressive disorders: Descriptive psychopathology and differential diagnosis. In P. C. Kendall & D. Watson (Eds.), *Anxiety and depression: Distinctive and overlapping features* (pp. 83–129). New York: Academic Press.

Clark, L. A., & Watson, D. (1991). Tripartite model of anxiety and depression: Psychometric evidence and taxonomic implications. *Journal of Abnormal Psychology, 100*, 316–336.

Clark-Lempers, D. S., Lempers, J. D., & Ho, C. (1991). Early, middle, and late adolescents' perceptions of their relationships with significant others. *Journal of Adolescent Research, 6*, 296–315.

Clarke-Stewart, K. A. (1978). And daddy makes three: The father's impact on mother and young child. *Child Development, 49*, 466–478.

Clarke-Stewart, K. A. (1989). Infant day care: Maligned or malignant? *American Psychologist, 44*, 266–273.

Claxton-Oldfield, S. (1992). Perceptions of stepfathers: Disciplinary and affectionate behavior. *Journal of Family Issues, 13,* 378–389.

Clingempeel, W. G., & Segal, S. (1986). Stepparent-stepchild relationships and the psychological adjustment of children in stepmother and stepfather families. *Child Development, 57,* 474–484.

Cohen, L. H., Burt, C. E., & Bjork, J. P. (1987). Effects of life events experienced by young adolescents and their parents. *Developmental Psychology, 23,* 583–592.

Cohn, D. A., Cowan, P. A., Cowan, C. P., & Pearson, J. (1992). Mothers' and fathers' working models of childhood attachment relationships parenting styles, and child behavior. *Development and Psychopathology, 4,* 417–431.

Coie, J. D., & Jacobs, M. R. (1993). The role of social context in the prevention of conduct disorder. *Development and Psychopathology, 5,* 263–275.

Cole, D. A., & Rehm, L. P. (1986). Family interaction patterns and childhood depression. *Journal of Abnormal Child Psychology, 14,* 297–314.

Collings, S. J., & Payne, M. F. (1991). Attribution of causal and moral responsibility to victims of father-daughter incest: An exploratory examination of five factors. *Child Abuse and Neglect, 15,* 513–521.

Collins, F. L., & Thompson, J. K. (1993). The integration of empirically derived personality assessment data into a behavioral conceptualization and treatment plan: Rationale, guidelines, and caveats. *Behavior Modification, 17,* 58–71.

Collins, W. A., & Russell, G. (1991). Mother-child and father-child relationships in middle childhood and adolescence: A developmental analysis. *Developmental Review, 11,* 99–136.

Coltrane, S., & Hickman, N. (1992). The rhetoric of rights and needs: Moral discourse in the reform of child custody and child support laws. *Social Problems, 39,* 400–420.

Coltrane, S., & Ishii-Kuntz, M. (1992). Men's housework: A life course perspective. *Journal of Marriage and the Family, 54,* 43–57.

Compas, B. E., Howell, D. C., Phares, V., Williams, R. A., & Giunta, C. T. (1989). Risk factors for emotional/behavioral problems in young adolescents: A prospective analysis of adolescent and parental stress and symptoms. *Journal of Consulting and Clinical Psychology, 57,* 732–740.

Compas, B. E., Howell, D. C., Phares, V., Williams, R. A., & Ledoux, N. (1989). Parent and child stress and symptoms: An integrative analysis. *Developmental Psychology, 25,* 550–559.

Compas, B. E., Phares, V., Banez, G. A., & Howell, D. C. (1991). Correlates of internalizing and externalizing behavior problems: Perceived competence, causal attributions, and parental symptoms. *Journal of Abnormal Child Psychology, 19,* 197–218.

Condon, J. T. (1993). The assessment of antenatal emotional attachment: Development of a questionnaire instrument. *British Journal of Medical Psychology, 66,* 167–183.

Conger, R. D., Conger, K. J., Elder, G. H., & Lorenz, F. O. (1993). Family economic stress and adjustment of early adolescent girls. *Developmental Psychology, 29,* 206–219.

Cook, J. A. (1988). Who "mothers" the chronically mentally ill? *Family Relations, 37,* 42–49.

Cook, J. A., Hoffschmidt, S., Cohler, B. J., & Pickett, S. (1992). Marital satisfaction among parents of the severely mentally ill living in the community. *American Journal of Orthopsychiatry, 62,* 552–563.

Cook, W. L., & Goldstein, M. J. (1993). Multiple perspectives on family relationships: A latent variables model. *Child Development, 64,* 1377–1388.

Cook, W. L., Kenny, D. A., & Goldstein, M. J. (1991). Parental affective style risk and the family system: A social relations model analysis. *Journal of Abnormal Psychology, 100,* 492–501.

Coombs, R. H., & Landsverk, J. (1988). Parenting styles and substance use during childhood and adolescence. *Journal of Marriage and the Family, 50,* 473–482.

Cooney, T. M. (1994). Young adults' relations with parents: The influence of recent parental divorce. *Journal of Marriage and the Family, 56,* 45–56.

Coplin, J. W., & Houts, A. C. (1991). Father involvement in parent training for oppositional child behavior: Progress or stagnation? *Child and Family Behavior Therapy, 13,* 29–51.

Corley, C. J., & Woods, A. Y. (1991). Socioeconomic, sociodemographic and attitudinal correlates of the tempo of divorce. *Journal of Divorce and Remarriage, 16,* 47–68.

Cosby, B. (1986). *Fatherhood.* New York: Berkley Books.

Costa, P. T., & McCrae, R. R. (1992). Normal personality assessment in clinical practice: The NEO Personality Inventory. *Psychological Assessment, 4,* 5–13.

Coverman, S., & Sheley, J. F. (1986). Change in men's housework and child-care time, 1965–1975. *Journal of Marriage and the Family, 48,* 413–422.

Cowan, C. P. (1988). Working with men becoming fathers: The impact of a couples group intervention. In P. Bronstein & C. P. Cowan (Eds.), *Fatherhood today: Men's changing role in the family* (pp. 276–298). New York: Wiley.

Cowan, C. P., & Cowan, P. A. (1988). Who does what when partners become parents: Implications for men, women, and marriage. *Marriage and Family Review, 12,* 105–131.

Cowan, C. P., Cowan, P. A., Heming, G., Garrett, E., Coysh, W. S., Curtis-Boles, H., & Boles, A. J. (1985). Transitions to parenthood: His, hers, and theirs. *Journal of Family Issues, 6,* 451–481.

Cowan, C. P., Cowan, P. A., Heming, G., & Miller, N. B. (1991). Becoming a family: Marriage, parenting, and child development. In P. A. Cowan & M. Hetherington (Eds.), *Family transitions* (pp. 79–109). Hillsdale, NJ: Erlbaum.

Cowley, D. S., Roy-Byrne, P. P., Godon, C., & Greenblatt, D. J. (1992). Response to diazepam in sons of alcoholics. *Alcoholism: Clinical and Experimental Research, 16,* 1057–1062.

Cox, M. J., Owen, M. T., Henderson, V. K., & Margand, N. A. (1992). Prediction of infant-father and infant-mother attachment. *Developmental Psychology, 28,* 474–483.

Cox, M. J., Owen, M. T., Lewis, J. M., & Henderson, V. K. (1989). Marriage, adult adjustment, and early parenting. *Child Development, 60,* 1015–1024.

Coyne, J. C., Kessler, R. C., Tal, M., Turnbull, J., Wortman, C. B., & Greden, J. F. (1987). Living with a depressed person. *Journal of Consulting and Clinical Psychology, 55,* 347–352.

Crandall, V., Dewey, R., Katkovsky, W., & Preston, A. (1964). Parents' attitudes and behaviors and grade-school children's academic achievements. *Journal of Genetic Psychology, 104,* 53–66.

Crawford, D. W., & Huston, T. L. (1993). The impact of the transition to parenthood on marital leisure. *Personality and Social Psychology Bulletin, 19,* 39–46.

Creasey, G. L., & Koblewski, P. J. (1991). Adolescent grandchildren's relationships with maternal and paternal grandmothers and grandfathers. *Journal of Adolescence, 14,* 373–387.

Crews, T. M., & Sher, K. J. (1992). Using adapted short MASTs for assessing parental alcoholism: Reliability and validity. *Alcoholism: Clinical and Experimental Research, 16,* 576–584.

Crockenberg, S., & Litman, C. (1990). Autonomy as competence in 2-year-olds: Maternal correlates of child defiance, compliance, and self-assertion. *Developmental Psychology, 26,* 961–971.

Cromwell, R., Fournier, D., & Kvebaek, D. (1980). *The Kvebaek Family Sculpture Technique: A diagnostic and research tool in family therapy.* Jonesboro, TN: Pilgrimage.

Crook, T., Raskin, A., & Eliot, J. (1981). Parent-child relationships and adult depression. *Child Development, 52,* 950–957.

Crouter, A. C., & Crowley, M. S. (1990). School-age children's time alone with fathers in single- and dual-earner families: Implications for the father-child relationship. *Journal of Early Adolescence, 10,* 296–312.

Crouter, A. C., MacDermid, S. M., McHale, S. M., & Perry-Jenkins, M. (1990). Parental monitoring and perceptions of children's school performance and conduct in dual- and single-earner families. *Developmental Psychology, 26,* 649–657.

Crouter, A. C., & McHale, S. M. (1993). Temporal rhythms in family life: Seasonal variation in the relation between parental work and family processes. *Developmental Psychology, 29,* 198–205.

Cullari, S., & Mikus, R. (1990). Correlates of adolescent sexual behavior. *Psychological Reports, 66,* 1179–1184.

Cumes-Rayner, D. P., Lucke, J. C., Singh, B., & Adler, B. (1992). A high-risk community study of paternal alcohol consumption and adolescents' psychosocial characteristics. *Journal of Studies on Alcohol, 53,* 626–635.

Cummings, E. M., & Davies, P. (1994). *Children and marital conflict: The impact of family dispute and resolution.* New York: Guilford.

Cunningham, C. E., Benness, B. B., & Siegel, L. S. (1988). Family functioning, time allocation, and parental depression in the families of normal and ADDH children. *Journal of Clinical Child Psychology, 17,* 169–177.

Cusinato, M. (1994). Parenting over the family life cycle. In L. L'Abate (Ed.), *Handbook of developmental family psychology and psychopathology* (pp. 83–115). New York: Wiley.

Cytryn, L., McKnew, D. H., Zahn-Waxler, C., & Gershon, E. S. (1986). Developmental issues in risk research: The offspring of affectively ill parents. In M. Rutter,

C. E. Izard, & P. B. Read (Eds.), *Depression in young people: Developmental and clinical perspectives* (pp. 163–188). New York: Guilford.

Dadds, M. R., Sanders, M. R., Behrens, B. C., & James, J. E. (1987). Marital discord and child behavior problems: A description of family interactions during treatment. *Journal of Clinical Child Psychology, 16*, 192–203.

Dadds, M. R., Sheffield, J. K., & Holbeck, J. F. (1990). An examination of the differential relationship of marital discord to parents' discipline strategies for boys and girls. *Journal of Abnormal Child Psychology, 18*, 121–129.

Dahlquist, L. M., Czyzewski, D. I., Copeland, K. G., & Jones, C. L. (1993). Parents of children newly diagnosed with cancer: Anxiety, coping, and marital distress. *Journal of Pediatric Psychology, 18*, 365–376.

Daniels, D., & Plomin, R. (1985). Differential experience of siblings in the same family. *Developmental Psychology, 21*, 747–760.

Daniels, P., & Weingarten, K. (1988). The fatherhood click: The timing of parenthood in men's lives. In P. Bronstein & C. P. Cowan (Eds.), *Fatherhood today: Men's changing role in the family* (pp. 36–52). New York: Wiley.

Danziger, S. K., & Radin, N. (1990). Absent does not equal uninvolved: Predictors of fathering in teen mother families. *Journal of Marriage and the Family, 52*, 636–642.

Davis, P. B., & May, J. E. (1991). Involving fathers in early intervention and family support programs: Issues and strategies. *Children's Health Care, 20*, 87–92.

Davison, G. C., & Neale, J. M. (1990). *Abnormal psychology* (5th ed.). New York: Wiley.

Dawson, D. A. (1992). The effect of parental alcohol dependence on perceived children's behavior. *Journal of Substance Abuse, 4*, 329–340.

Deal, J. E., Halverson, C. F., & Wampler, K. S. (1989). Parental agreement on child-rearing orientations: Relations to parental, marital, family, and child characteristics. *Child Development, 60*, 1025–1034.

Dean, R. S., & Jacobson, B. P. (1982). MMPI characteristics for parents of emotionally disturbed and learning-disabled children. *Journal of Consulting and Clinical Psychology, 50*, 775–777.

Dearden, K., Hale, C., & Alvarez, J. (1992). The educational antecedents of teen fatherhood. *British Journal of Educational Psychology, 62*, 139–147.

Dearden, K., Hale, C., & Blankson, M. (1994). Family structure, function, and the early transition to fatherhood in Great Britain: Identifying antecedents using longitudinal data. *Journal of Marriage and the Family, 56*, 844–852.

Deater-Deckard, K., Scarr, S., McCartney, K., & Eisenberg, M. (1994). Paternal separation anxiety: Relationships with parenting stress, child-rearing attitudes, and maternal anxieties. *Psychological Science, 5*, 341–346.

Deblinger, E., Hathaway, C. R., Lippmann, J., & Steer, R. (1993). Psychosocial characteristics and correlates of symptom distress in nonoffending mothers of sexually abused children. *Journal of Interpersonal Violence, 8*, 155–168.

DeFrain, J. (1977). Sexism in parenting manuals. *Family Coordinator, 26*, 245–251.

DeJong, C. A. J., Harteveld, F. M., & van de Wielen, G. E. M. (1991). Memories of parental rearing in alcohol and drug addicts: A comparative study. *The International Journal of the Addictions, 26*, 1065–1076.

Dekovic, M., & Janssens, J. M. A. M. (1992). Parents' child-rearing style and child's sociometric status. *Developmental Psychology, 28,* 925–932.

delaisi de Parseval, G., & Hurstel, F. (1987). Paternity "a la Francaise." In M. E. Lamb (Ed.), *The father's role: Cross cultural perspectives* (pp. 59–87). Hillsdale, NJ: Erlbaum.

deLong, J. A., & Roy, A. (1993). Paternal lineage of alcoholism, cohort effects, and alcoholism criteria. *Addiction, 88,* 623–629.

DeLongis, A., Folkman, S., & Lazarus, R. S. (1988). The impact of daily stress on health and mood: Psychological and social resources as mediators. *Journal of Personality and Social Psychology, 54,* 486–495.

DeLuccie, M. F., & Davis, A. J. (1991). Father-child relationships from the preschool years through mid-adolescence. *Journal of Genetic Psychology, 152;* 225–238.

deMan, A. F., Labreche-Gauthier, L., & Leduc, C. P. (1993). Parent-child relationships and suicidal ideation in French-Canadian adolescents. *Journal of Genetic Psychology, 154,* 17–23.

DeMaris, A., & Greif, G. L. (1992). The relationship between family structure and parent-child relationship problems in single father households. *Journal of Divorce and Remarriage, 18,* 55–77.

Demo, D. H. (1992). Parent-child relations: Assessing recent changes. *Journal of Marriage and the Family, 54,* 104–117.

Demo, D. H., & Acock, A. C. (1988). The impact of divorce on children. *Journal of Marriage and the Family, 50,* 619–648.

Denmark, F., Russo, N. F., Frieze, I. H., & Sechzer, J. A. (1988). Guidelines for avoiding sexism in psychological research: A report of the ad hoc committee on nonsexist research. *American Psychologist, 43,* 582–585.

Der-Karabetian, A., & Preciado, M. (1989). Mother-blaming among college students. *Perceptual and Motor Skills, 68,* 453–454.

Derogatis, L. R., & Spencer, P. M. (1982). *Brief Symptom Inventory: Administration, scoring and procedures manual.* Towson, MD: Clinical Psychometric Research.

Deutsch, H. (1944). *The psychology of women* (Vol. 1). New York: Grune and Stratton.

Deykin, E. Y., Buka, S. L., & Zeena, T. H. (1992). Depressive illness among chemically dependent adolescents. *American Journal of Psychiatry, 149,* 1341–1347.

Diacatou, A., Mamalakis, G., Kafatos, A., & Vlahonikolis, J. (1993). Alcohol, tobacco, and father's aggressive behavior in relation to socioeconomic variables in Cretan low versus medium income families. *International Journal of the Addictions, 28,* 293–304.

Dickson, L. (1993). The future of marriage and family in Black America. *Journal of Black Studies, 23,* 472–491.

Dickstein, L. J., Stein, T. S., Pleck, J. H., Myers, M. F., Lewis, R. A., Duncan, S. F., & Brod, H. (1991). Men's changing social roles in the 1990s: Emerging issues in the psychiatric treatment of men. *Hospital and Community Psychiatry, 42,* 701–705.

Dixon, S., Yogman, M. W., Tronick, E., Als, H., Adamson, L., & Brazelton, T. B. (1981). Early social interaction of infants with parents and strangers. *Journal of the American Academy of Child Psychiatry, 20,* 32–52.

Dodge, K. (Ed.). (1990). Developmental psychopathology in children of depressed mothers. *Developmental Psychology, 26,* 3–6.

Dodson, F. (1974). *How to father.* New York: Signet.

Doherty, W. J. (1981). Involving the reluctant father in family therapy. In A. S. Gurman (Ed.), *Questions and answers in the practice of family therapy* (Vol 1., pp. 23–26). New York: Brunner/Mazel.

Dornbusch, S. M., Carlsmith, J. M. Bushwall, S. J., Ritter, P. L., Leiderman, H., Hastorf, A. H., & Gross, R. T. (1985). Single parents, extended households, and the control of adolescents. *Child Development, 56,* 326–341.

Dor-Shav, N. K., & Horowitz, Z. (1984). Intelligence and personality variables of parents of autistic children. *Journal of Genetic Psychology, 144,* 39–50.

Downey, D. B. (1994). The school performance of children from single-mother and single-father families: Economic or interpersonal deprivation? *Journal of Family Issues, 14,* 129–147.

Downey, G., & Coyne, J. C. (1990). Children of depressed parents: An integrative review. *Psychological Bulletin, 108,* 50–76.

Downs, W. R., & Robertson, J. F. (1991). Random versus clinical samples: A question of inference. *Journal of Social Service Research, 14,* 57–83.

Dragonas, T. G. (1992). Greek fathers' participation in labour and care of the infant. *Scandinavian Journal of Caring Sciences, 6,* 151–159.

Dumas, J. E., & Gibson, J. A. (1990). Behavioral correlates of maternal depressive symptomatology in conduct-disorder children: II. Systemic effects involving fathers and siblings. *Journal of Consulting and Clinical Psychology, 58,* 877–881.

Dunaway, R. G., & Cullen, F. T. (1991). Explaining crime ideology: An exploration of the parental socialization perspective. *Crime and Delinquency, 37,* 536–554.

Duncan, P., & Kilpatrick, D. L. (1991). Parent ratings of the behaviors of normal male and female children with one child per family versus cross-sex siblings. *Child Study Journal, 21,* 95–115.

Dunn, C. W., & Tucker, C. M. (1993). Black children's adaptive functioning and maladaptive behavior associated with quality of family support. *Journal of Multicultural Counseling and Development, 21,* 79–87.

Dunn, J., & Plomin, R. (1990). *Separate lives: Why siblings are so different.* New York: Basic Books.

Dworkin, R. J., Harding, J. T., & Schreiber, N. B. (1993). Parenting or placing: Decision making by pregnant teens. *Youth and Society, 25,* 75–92.

Eagly, A. H. (1990). On the advantages of reporting sex comparisons. *American Psychologist, 45,* 756–757.

Eagly, A. H. (1993, June). *The science and politics of comparing women and men.* Invited address at the meeting of the American Psychological Society, Chicago, IL.

Eagly, A. H. (1995). The science and politics of comparing women and men. *American Psychologist, 50,* 145–158.

Eagly, A. H., Makhijani, M. G., & Klonsky, B. G. (1992). Gender and the evaluation of leaders: A meta-analysis. *Psychological Bulletin, 111,* 3–22.

Earls, F. (1976). The fathers (not the mothers): Their importance and influence with infants and young children. *Psychiatry, 39,* 209–226.

East, P. L. (1991). The parent-child relationships of withdrawn, aggressive, and sociable children: Child and parent perspectives. *Merrill-Palmer Quarterly, 37,* 425–443.

Eastburg, M., & Johnson, W. B. (1990). Shyness and perceptions of parental behavior. *Psychological Reports, 66,* 915–921.

Easterbrooks, M. A. (1989). Quality of attachment to mother and to father: Effects of perinatal risk status. *Child Development, 60,* 825–830.

Eastman, A. M., & Moran, T. J. (1991). Multiple perspectives: Factors related to differential diagnosis of sex abuse and divorce trauma in children under six. *Child and Youth Services, 15,* 159–175.

Edell, W. S., & Kaslow, N. J. (1991). Parental perception and psychosis proneness in college students. *American Journal of Family Therapy, 19,* 195–205.

Edwards, J. J., & Alexander, P. C. (1992). The contribution of family background to the long-term adjustment of women sexually abused as children. *Journal of Interpersonal Violence, 7,* 306–320.

Eiden, R. D., Leonard, K. E., & McLaughlin, I. G. (1994, April). *Paternal alcohol use, parenting, and infant temperament: The mediating role of maternal depression.* Paper presented at the Biennial Conference on Human Development, Pittsburgh, PA.

Eiser, C., & Havermans, T. (1992). Mothers' and fathers' coping with chronic childhood disease. *Psychology and Health, 7,* 249–257.

Elder, G. H. (1980). *Family structure and socialization.* New York: Arno.

Elder, G. H., Conger, R. D., Foster, E. M., & Ardelt, M. (1992). Families under economic pressure. *Journal of Family Issues, 13,* 5–37.

Elder, G. H., Nguyen, T., & Caspi, A. (1985). Linking family hardship to children's lives. *Child Development, 56,* 361–375.

el-Guebaly, N., Offord, D. R., Sullivan, K. T., & Lynch, G. W. (1978). Psychosocial adjustment of the offspring of psychiatric inpatients: The effect of alcoholic, depressive and schizophrenic parentage. *Canadian Psychiatric Association Journal, 23,* 281–289.

el-Guebaly, N., Staley, D., Rockman, G., Leckie, A., Barkman, K., O'Riordan, J., & Koensgen, S. (1991). The adult children of alcoholics in a psychiatric population. *American Journal of Drug and Alcohol Abuse, 17,* 215–226.

Eliopoulos, C., Klein, J., Phan, M. K., Knie, B., Greenwald, M., Chitayat, D., & Koren, G. (1994). Hair concentrations of nicotine and cotinine in women and their newborn infants. *Journal of the American Medical Association, 271,* 621–623.

Elizur, J. (1986). The stress of school entry: Parental coping behaviors and children's adjustment to school. *Journal of Child Psychology and Psychiatry, 27,* 625–638.

Elliot, D. S., Huizinga, D., & Ageton, S. S. (1985). *Explaining delinquency and drug use.* Beverly Hills, CA: Sage.

Ellwood, D. (1988). *Poor support: Poverty in the American family.* New York: Basic Books.

Emery, R. E. (1982). Interparental conflict and the children of discord and divorce. *Psychological Bulletin, 92,* 310–330.

Emery, R. E., Matthews, S. G., & Kitzmann, K. M. (1994). Child custody mediation and litigation: Parents' satisfaction and functioning one year after settlement. *Journal of Consulting and Clinical Psychology, 62,* 124–129.

Emery, R. E., Matthews, S. G., & Wyer, M. M. (1991). Child custody mediation and litigation: Further evidence on the differing views of mothers and fathers. *Journal of Consulting and Clinical Psychology, 59,* 410–418.

Englander, S. W. (1984). Some self-reported correlates of runaway behavior in adolescent females. *Journal of Consulting and Clinical Psychology, 52,* 484–485.

Entwisle, D. R., & Doering, S. (1988). The emergent father role. *Sex Roles, 18,* 119–141.

Epstein, N. B., Baldwin, L. M., & Bishop, D. S. (1983). The McMaster Family Assessment Device. *Journal of Marital and Family Therapy, 9,* 171–180.

Erel, O., & Burman, B. (1995). Interrelatedness of marital relations and parent-child relations: A meta-analytic review. *Psychological Bulletin, 118,* 108–132.

Erickson, R. J., & Gecas, V. (1991). Social class and fatherhood. In F. W. Bozett & S. M. H. Hanson (Eds.), *Fatherhood and families in cultural context* (pp. 114–137). New York: Springer.

Erlenmeyer-Kimling, L., Marcuse, Y., Cornblatt, B., Friedman, D., Rainer, J. D., & Rutschmann, J. (1984). The New York High-Risk Project. In N. F. Watt, E. J. Anthony, L. C. Wynne, & J. E. Rolf (Eds.), *Children at risk for schizophrenia: A longitudinal perspective* (pp. 169–189). New York: Cambridge University Press.

Facchino, D., & Aron, A. (1990). Divorced fathers with custody: Method of obtaining custody and divorce adjustment. *Journal of Divorce, 13,* 45–56.

Fagot, B. I., & Hagan, R. (1991). Observations of parent reactions to sex-stereotyped behaviors: Age and sex effects. *Child Development, 62,* 617–628.

Fagot, B. I., & Kavanagh, K. (1993). Parenting during the second year: Effects of children's age, sex, and attachment classification. *Child Development, 64,* 258–271.

Fairbanks, L. A. (1993). What is a good mother? Adaptive variation in maternal behavior of primates. *Current Directions in Psychological Science, 2,* 179–183.

Faludi, S. (1991). *Backlash: The undeclared war against American women.* New York: Crown.

Farhood, L., Zurayk, H., Chaya, M., & Saadeh, F. (1993). The impact of war on the physical and mental health of the family: The Lebanese experience. *Social Science and Medicine, 36,* 1555–1567.

Fauber, R. L., & Long, N. (1991). Children in context: The role of the family in child psychotherapy. *Journal of Consulting and Clinical Psychology, 59,* 813–820.

Fawzy, F. I., Coombs, R. H., & Gerber, B. (1983). Generational continuity in the use of substances: The impact of parental substance use on adolescent substance use. *Addictive Behaviors, 8,* 109–114.

Fedele, N. M., Golding, E. R., Grossman, F. K., & Pollack, W. S. (1988). Psychological issues in adjustment to first parenthood. In G. Michaels & W. Goldberg (Eds.), *The transition to parenthood: Current theory and research.* New York: Cambridge University Press.

Fein, R. A. (1978). Research on fathering: Social policy and an emergent perspective. *Journal of Social Issues, 34,* 122–135.

Feldman, L. B. (1990). Fathers and fathering. In R. L. Meth & R. S. Pasick (Eds.), *Men in therapy: The challenge of change* (pp. 88–107). New York: Guilford.

Feldman, S. S., & Weinberger, D. A. (1994). Self-restraint as a mediator of family influences on boys' delinquent behavior: A longitudinal study. *Child Development, 65,* 195–211.

Feldman, S. S., & Wentzel, K. R. (1990). The relationship between parenting styles, sons' self-restraint, and peer relations in early adolescence. *Journal of Early Adolescence, 10,* 439–454.

Feldman, S. S., Wentzel, K. R., Weinberger, D. A., & Munson, J. A. (1990). Marital satisfaction of parents of preadolescent boys and its relationship to family and child functioning. *Journal of Family Psychology, 4,* 213–234.

Felson, R. B. (1990). Comparison processes in parents' and children's appraisals of academic performance. *Social Psychology Quarterly, 53,* 264–273.

Field, M. (1987). Media violence: Closing one door—opening another. *Communications, 13,* 55–63.

Field, T., Adler, S., Vega-Lahr, N., & Scafidi, F. (1987). Temperament and play interaction behavior across infancy. *Infant Mental Health Journal, 8,* 156–165.

Fielding, D., Moore, B., Dewey, M., Ashley, P., McKendrick, T., & Pinkerton, P. (1985). Children with end-stage renal failure: Psychological effects on patients, siblings and parents. *Journal of Psychosomatic Research, 29,* 457–465.

Fine, E., Yudin, L., Holmes, J., & Heinemann, S. (1976). Behavioral disorders in children with parental alcoholism. *Annals of the New York Academy of Sciences, 273,* 507–517.

Fine, M. A., McKenry, P. C., & Chung, H. (1992). Post-divorce adjustment of Black and White single parents. *Journal of Divorce and Remarriage, 17,* 121–134.

Fine, M. A., McKenry, P. C., Donnelly, B. W., & Voydanoff, P. (1992). Perceived adjustment of parents and children: Variations by family structure, race, and gender. *Journal of Marriage and the Family, 54,* 118–127.

Fine, M. A., Moreland, J. R., & Schwebel, A. I. (1983). Long-term effects of divorce on parent-child relationships. *Developmental Psychology, 19,* 703–713.

Fineman, M. L. (1989). The politics of custody and the transformation of American custody decision making. *U.C. Davis Law Review, 22,* 829–864.

Finkelhor, D. (1990). Early and long-term effects of child sexual abuse: An update. *Professional Psychology: Research and Practice, 21,* 325–330.

Finkelhor, D. (1993). Epidemiological factors in the clinical identification of child sexual abuse. *Child Abuse and Neglect, 17,* 67–70.

Finkelhor, D., & Russell, D. (1984). Women as perpetrators. In D. Finkelhor (Ed.), *Child sexual abuse: New theory and research* (pp. 171–185). New York: Free Press.

Firestone, P., Kelly, M. J., & Fike, S. (1980). Are fathers necessary in parent training groups? *Journal of Clinical Child Psychology, 9,* 44–47.

Firestone, S. (1971). *The dialectic of sex: The case for feminist revolution.* New York: Bantam.

Fish, L. S., New, R. S., & VanCleave, N. J. (1992). Shared parenting in dual-income families. *American Journal of Orthopsychiatry, 62,* 83–92.

Fitzgerald, H. E., Davies, W. H., Zucker, R. A., & Klinger, M. (1994). Developmental systems theory and substance abuse: A conceptual and methodological framework for analyzing patterns of variation in families. In L. L'Abate (Ed.), *Handbook of developmental family psychology and psychopathology* (pp. 350–372). New York: Wiley.

Fitzgerald, H. E., Sullivan, L. A., Ham, H. P., & Zucker, R. A. (1993). Predictors of behavior problems in three-year-old sons of alcoholics: Early evidence for the onset of risk. *Child Development, 64,* 110–123.

Fitzpatrick, K. M., & Boldizar, J. P. (1993). The prevalence and consequences of exposure to violence among African-American youth. *Journal of the American Academy of Child and Adolescent Psychiatry, 32,* 424–430.

Fleck, J. R., Fuller, C. C., Malin, S. Z., Miller, D. H., & Acheson, K. R. (1980). Father psychological absence and heterosexual behavior, personal adjustment and sex-typing in adolescent girls. *Adolescence, 15,* 847–860.

Folkman, S., & Lazarus, R. S. (1988). *Manual for the Ways of Coping Questionnaire.* Palo Alto, CA: Consulting Psychologist Press.

Forehand, R. (1987). Parental roles in childhood psychopathology. In C. L. Frame & J. L. Matson (Eds.), *Handbook of assessment in childhood psychopathology* (pp. 489–507). New York: Plenum.

Forehand, R., Long, N., Brody, G. H., & Fauber, R. (1986). Home predictors of young adolescents' school behavior and academic performance. *Child Development, 57,* 1528–1533.

Forehand, R., & Smith, K. A. (1986). Who depresses whom? A look at the relationship of adolescent mood to maternal and paternal mood. *Child Study Journal, 16,* 19–23.

Forehand, R., Wierson, M., Thomas, A. M., Armistead, L., Kempton, T., & Fauber, R. (1990). Interparental conflict and paternal visitation following divorce: The interactive effect on adolescent competence. *Child Study Journal, 20,* 193–202.

Forgays, D. K., & Forgays, D. G. (1991). Type A behavior within families: Parents and older adolescent children. *Journal of Behavioral Medicine, 14,* 325–339.

Forney, M. A., Forney, P. D., Davis, H., Van Hoose, J., Cafferty, T., & Allen, H. (1984). A discriminant analysis of adolescent problem drinking. *Journal of Drug Education, 14,* 347–355.

Forston, M. T., & Stanton, A. L. (1992). Self-discrepancy theory as a framework for understanding bulimic symptomatology and associated distress. *Journal of Social and Clinical Psychology, 11,* 103–118.

Fox, N. A., Kimmerly, N. L., & Schafer, W. D. (1991). Attachment to mother/attachment to father: A meta-analysis. *Child Development, 62,* 210–225.

Frank, S. J., Olmsted, C. L., Wagner, A. E., Laub, C. C., Freeark, K., Breitzer, G. M., & Peters, J. M. (1991). Child illness, the parenting alliance, and parenting stress. *Journal of Pediatric Psychology, 16,* 361–371.

Free, M. D. (1991). Clarifying the relationship between the broken home and juvenile delinquency: A critique of the current literature. *Deviant Behavior: An Interdisciplinary Journal, 12,* 109–167.

Freeman, N. L., Perry, A., & Factor, D. C. (1991). Child behaviours as stressors: Replicating and extending the use of the CARS as a measure of stress: A research note. *Journal of Clinical Psychology and Psychiatry, 32,* 1025–1030.

Freud, S. (1949). *A general introduction to psychoanalysis.* New York: Garden City Publishing.

Freud, S. (1955). *Standard edition of the complete psychological works of Sigmund Freud* (Vol. 10). London: Hogarth Press.

Frick, P. J., Lahey, B. B., Christ, M. A. G., Loeber, R., & Green, S. (1991). History of childhood behavior problems in biological relatives of boys with attention-deficit hyperactivity disorder and conduct disorder. *Journal of Clinical Child Psychology, 20,* 445–451.

Frick, P. J., Lahey, B. B., Loeber, R., Stouthamer-Loeber, M., Christ, M. A. G., & Hanson, K. (1992). Familial risk factors to oppositional defiant disorder and conduct disorder: Parental psychopathology and maternal parenting. *Journal of Consulting and Clinical Psychology, 60,* 49–55.

Fromm-Reichmann, F. (1948). Notes on the development of treatment of schizophrenics by psychoanalytic psychotherapy. *Psychiatry, 11,* 263–273.

Frost, R. O., Steketee, G., Cohn, L., & Griess, K. (1994). Personality traits in subclinical and non-obsessive-compulsive volunteers and their parents. *Behavior Research and Therapy, 32,* 47–56.

Fry, P. S. (1982). Paternal correlates of adolescents' running away behaviors: Implications for adolescent development and considerations for intervention and treatment of adolescent runaways. *Journal of Applied Developmental Psychology, 3,* 347–360.

Fuller, T. L., & Fincham, F. D. (1994). The marital life cycle: A developmental approach to the study of marital change. In L. L'Abate (Ed.), *Handbook of developmental family psychology and psychopathology* (pp. 60–82). New York: Wiley.

Furman, W., & Buhrmester, D. (1992). Age and sex differences in perceptions of networks of personal relationships. *Child Development, 63,* 103–115.

Furstenberg, F. F. (1988). Good dads-bad dads: Two faces of fatherhood. In A. Cherlin (Ed.), *The changing American family and public policy* (pp. 193–217). Washington, DC: Urban Institute.

Gabel, S. (1992). Behavioral problems in sons of incarcerated or otherwise absent fathers: The issue of separation. *Family Process, 31,* 303–314.

Gable, M., Hollon, C., & Dangello, F. (1992). Managerial structuring of work as a moderator of the Machiavellianism and job performance relationship. *Journal of Psychology, 126,* 317–325.

Gaines, T. (1981). Engaging the father in family therapy. In A. S. Gurman (Ed.), *Questions and answers in the practice of family therapy* (Vol 1., pp. 20–22). New York: Brunner/Mazel.

Galenson, E. (1989). Factors affecting the pre-oedipal and oedipal paternal relationship in girls. In S. H. Cath, A. Gurwitt, & L. Gunsberg (Eds.), *Fathers and their families* (pp. 491–505). Hillsdale, NJ: Analytic Press.

Gallimore, M., & Kurdek, L. A. (1992). Parent depression and parent authoritative discipline as correlates of young adolescents' depression. *Journal of Early Adolescence, 12,* 187–196.

Gannon, L., Luchetta, T., Rhodes, K., Pardie, L., & Segrist, D. (1992). Sex bias in psychological research: Progress or complacency? *American Psychologist, 47,* 389–396.

Ganong, L. H., & Coleman, M. (1987). Stepchildren's perceptions of their parents. *Journal of Genetic Psychology, 148,* 5–17.

Gantman, C. A. (1978). Family interaction patterns among families with normal, disturbed, and drug-abusing adolescents. *Journal of Youth and Adolescence, 7,* 429–440.

Garbarino, J. (1993). Reinventing fatherhood. *Families in Society, 74,* 51–54.

Garbarino, J., Sebes, J., & Schellenbach, D. (1984). Families at risk for destructive parent-child relations in adolescents. *Child Development, 55,* 174–183.

Garfinkel, B. D., Froese, A., & Hood, J. (1982). Suicide attempts in children and adolescents. *American Journal of Psychiatry, 139,* 1257–1261.

Garfinkel, P. E., Garner, D. M., Rose, J., Darby, P. L., Brandes, J. S., O'Hanlon, J., & Walsh, N. (1983). A comparison of characteristics in the families of patients with anorexia nervosa and normal controls. *Psychological Medicine, 13,* 821–828.

Garmezy, N. (1989). The role of competence in the study of children and adolescents under stress. In B. H. Schneider, G. Attili, J. Nadel, & R. P. Weissberg (Eds.), *Social competence in developmental perspective* (pp. 25–39). Norwell, MA: Kluwer.

Garmezy, N., & Tellegen, A. (1984). Studies of stress-resistant children: Methods, variables and preliminary findings. In F. Morrison, C. Lord, & D. Keating (Eds.), *Advances in applied developmental psychology* (Vol. 1, pp. 231–287). New York: Academic Press.

Garralda, M. E. (1983). Child psychiatric emergencies: A research note. *Journal of Child Psychology and Psychiatry, 24,* 261–267.

Ge, X., Conger, R. D., Lorenz, F. O., & Elder, G. (1992). Linking family economic hardship to adolescent distress. *Journal of Research on Adolescence, 2,* 351–378.

Gelfand, D. M., & Teti, D. M. (1990). The effects of maternal depression on children. *Clinical Psychology Review, 10,* 329–354.

Gerlsma, C., Emmelkamp, P. M. G., & Arrindell, W. A. (1990). Anxiety, depression, and perception of early parenting: A meta-analysis. *Clinical Psychology Review, 10,* 251–277.

Gerson, K. (1993). *No man's land: Men's changing commitments to family and work.* New York: Basic Books.

Gfroerer, J., & delaRosa, M. (1993). Protective and risk factors associated with drug use among Hispanic youth. *Journal of Addictive Diseases, 12,* 87–107.

Gibbs, N. R. (1993, June 28). Bringing up father. *Time,* pp. 52–61.

Gilbert, L. A. (1981). Impediments to research on parenting. *The Counseling Psychologist, 9,* 63–68.

Gilbert, L. A., & Rachlin, V. (1987). Mental health and psychological functioning of dual-career families. *The Counseling Psychologist, 15,* 7–49.

Gilbert, R. K. (1992). Revisiting the psychology of men: Robert Bly and the mytho-poetic movement. *Journal of Humanistic Psychology, 32,* 41–67.

Gjerde, P. F. (1986). The interpersonal structure of family interaction settings: Parent-adolescent relations in dyads and triads. *Developmental Psychology, 22,* 297–304.

Gleiberman, L., Harburg, E., DiFranceisco, W., & Schork, A. (1992). Familial transmission of alcohol use: V. Drinking patterns among spouses. Tecumseh, Michigan. *Behavior Genetics, 22,* 63–79.

Glick, P. C. (1988). Fifty years of family demography: A record of social change. *Journal of Marriage and the Family, 50,* 861–873.

Goetting, A. (1994). The parenting-crime connection. *Journal of Primary Prevention, 14,* 169–186.

Goldberg, W. A. (1990). Marital quality, parental personality, and spousal agreement about perceptions and expectations for children. *Merrill-Palmer Quarterly, 36,* 531–556.

Goldsmith, E. B., Hoffman, J. J., & Hofacker, C. F. (1993). Insights into the long-term effects of parents' careers on reported parent-offspring closeness. *Journal of Employment Counseling, 30,* 50–54.

Gondoli, D. M., & Jacob, T. (1993). Factor structure within and across three family-assessment procedures. *Journal of Family Psychology, 6,* 278–289.

Goodman, R., & Stevenson, J. (1989). A twin study of hyperactivity: II. The aetiological role of genes, family relationships and perinatal adversity. *Journal of Child Psychology and Psychiatry, 30,* 691–709.

Goodnow, J. J., & Bowes, J. M. (1994). *Men, women and household work.* New York: Oxford University Press.

Goodnow, J. J., Bowes, J. M., Warton, P. M., Dawes, L. J., & Taylor, A. J. (1991). Would you ask someone else to do this task? Parents' and children's ideas about household work requests. *Developmental Psychology, 27,* 817–828.

Goodrich, T. J. (1991). Women, power, and family therapy: What's wrong with this picture? In T. J. Goodrich (Ed.), *Women and power: Perspectives for family therapy* (pp. 3–35). New York: Norton.

Goodrich, T. J., Rampage, C., Ellman, B., & Halstead, K. (1988). *Feminist family therapy: A casebook.* New York: Norton.

Goodwin, D. W. (1986). Heredity and alcoholism. *Annals of Behavioral Medicine, 8,* 3–6.

Graham, S. (1992). "Most of the subjects were white and middle class": Trends in published research on African Americans in selected APA journals, 1979–1989. *American Psychologist, 47,* 629–639.

Greenberger, E., & Goldberg, W. A. (1989). Work, parenting, and the socialization of children. *Developmental Psychology, 25,* 22–35.

Greenberger, E., Goldberg, W. A., Crawford, T. J., & Granger, J. (1988). Beliefs about the consequences of maternal employment for children. *Psychology of Women Quarterly, 12,* 35–59.

Greenberger, E., Goldberg, W. A., Hamill, S., O'Neil, R., & Payne, C. K. (1989). Contributions of a supportive work environment to parents' well-being and orientation to work. *American Journal of Community Psychology, 17,* 755–783.

Greenberger, E., & O'Neil, R. (1990). Parents' concerns about their child's development: Implications for fathers' and mothers' well-being and attitudes toward work. *Journal of Marriage and the Family, 52,* 621–635.

Greenberger, E., & O'Neil, R. (1992). Maternal employment and perceptions of young children: Bronfenbrenner et al. revisited. *Child Development, 63,* 431–448.

Greene, B. (1985). *Good morning, merry sunshine: A father's personal journey of his child's first year.* New York: Viking Penguin.

Greenman, D. A., Gunderson, J. G., & Canning, D. (1989). Parents' attitudes and patients' behavior: A prospective study. *American Journal of Psychiatry, 146,* 226–230.

Greif, G. L. (1987). A longitudinal examination of single custodial fathers: Implications for treatment. *American Journal of Family Therapy, 15,* 253–260.

Greif, G. L. (1992). Lone fathers in the United States: An overview and practice implications. *British Journal of Social Work, 22,* 565–574.

Greif, G. L., & DeMaris, A. (1990). Single fathers with custody. *Families in Society: The Journal of Contemporary Human Services, 71,* 259–266.

Greif, G. L., & DeMaris, A. (1991). When a single custodial father receives child support. *American Journal of Family Therapy, 19,* 167–176.

Greif, G. L., & Kristall, J. (1993). Common themes in a group for noncustodial parents. *Families in Society, 74,* 240–245.

Greif, G. L., & Zuravin, S. J. (1989). Fathers: A placement resource for abused and neglected children? *Child Welfare, 68,* 479–490.

Griest, D., Wells, K. C., & Forehand, R. (1979). An examination of predictors of maternal perceptions of maladjustment in clinic-referred children. *Journal of Abnormal Psychology, 88,* 277–281.

Griswold, R. L. (1993). *Fatherhood in America: A history.* New York: Basic Books.

Grolnick, W. S., & Slowiaczek, M. L. (1994). Parents' involvement in children's schooling: A multidimensional conceptualization and motivational model. *Child Development, 65,* 237–252.

Groskind, F. (1991). Public reactions to poor families: Characteristics that influence attitudes toward assistance. *Social Work, 36,* 446–453.

Grossman, F. K., Pollack, W. S., & Golding, E. (1988). Fathers and children: Predicting the quality and quantity of fathering. *Developmental Psychology, 24,* 82–91.

Grossman, K. E., & Vollkner, H. J. (1984). Fathers' presence during birth of their infants and paternal involvement. *International Journal of Behavioral Development, 7,* 157–165.

Grych, J. H., & Fincham, F. D. (1990). Marital conflict and children's adjustment: A cognitive-contextual framework. *Psychological Bulletin, 108,* 267–290.

Guillebeaux, F., Storm, C. L., & Demaris, A. (1986). Luring the reluctant male: A study of males participating in marriage and family therapy. *Family Therapy, 13,* 215–225.

Guisinger, S., Cowan, P.A., & Schuldberg, D. (1989). Changing parent and spouse relations in the first years of remarriage of divorced fathers. *Journal of Marriage and the Family, 51,* 445–456.

Gussman, K., & Harder, D. (1990). Offspring personality and perceptions of parental use of reward and punishment. *Psychological Reports, 67,* 923–930.

Guthrie, R. V. (1976). *Even the rat was white: A historical view of psychology.* New York: Harper & Row.

Hafner, R. J., & Miller, R. M. (1991). Predicting schizophrenia outcome with self-report measures of family interaction. *Journal of Clinical Psychology, 47,* 33–41.

Hahlweg, K., & Goldstein, M. J. (Eds.). (1987). *Understanding major mental disorder: The contribution of family interaction research.* New York: Family Process Press.

Hahlweg, K., Goldstein, M. J., Nuechterlein, K. H., Magana, A. B., Mintz, J., Doane, J. A., Miklowitz, D. J., & Snyder, K. S. (1989). Expressed emotion and patient-relative interaction in families of recent onset schizophrenics. *Journal of Consulting and Clinical Psychology, 57,* 11–18.

Hairston, C. F. (1989). Men in prisons: Family characteristics and parenting views. *Journal of Offender Counseling, Services and Rehabilitation, 14,* 23–30.

Halperin, S. M., & Smith, T. A. (1983). Differences in stepchildren's perceptions of their stepfathers and natural fathers: Implications for family therapy. *Journal of Divorce, 7,* 19–30.

Hamburg, D. A., Nightingale, E. O., & Takanishi, R. (1987). Facilitating the transitions of adolescence. *Journal of the American Medical Association, 257,* 3405–3406.

Hamdan-Allen, G., Stewart, M. A., & Beeghly, J. H. (1989). Subgrouping conduct disorder by psychiatric family history. *Journal of Child Psychology and Psychiatry, 30,* 889–897.

Hamilton, M. L. (1977). *Father's influence on children.* Chicago: Nelson-Hall.

Hammen, C. (1991). *Depression runs in families: The social context of risk and resilience in children of depressed mothers.* New York: Springer-Verlag.

Handford, H. A., Mayes, S. D., Bagnato, S. J., & Bixler, E. O. (1986). Relationships between variations in parents' attitudes and personality traits of hemophilic boys. *American Journal of Orthopsychiatry, 56,* 424–434.

Handford, H. A., Mayes, S. D., Mattison, R. E., Humphrey, F. J., Bagnato, S., Bixler, E. O., & Kales, J. D. (1986). Child and parent reaction to the Three Mile Island nuclear accident. *Journal of the American Academy of Child Psychiatry, 25,* 346–356.

Hansen, L. B., & Jacob, E. (1992). Intergenerational support during the transition to parenthood: Issues for new parents and grandparents. *Families in Society, 73,* 471–479.

Hanson, C. L., Henggeler, S. W., Haefele, W. F., & Rodick, J. D. (1984). Demographic, individual, and family relationship correlates of serious and repeated crime among adolescents and their siblings. *Journal of Consulting and Clinical Psychology, 52,* 528–538.

Hanson, S. M. H., & Bozett, F. W. (Eds.). (1985). *Dimensions of fatherhood.* Beverly Hills, CA: Sage.

Harford, T. C., & Grant, B. F. (1990). Alcohol abuse among grandsons of alcoholics: Some preliminary findings. *Alcoholism: Clinical and Experimental Research, 14,* 739–740.

Harjan, A. (1992). Children of parents with affective disorders: The role of an ill mother or an ill father. *European Journal of Psychiatry, 6,* 74–87.

Harlow, H. F. (1958). The nature of love. *American Psychologist, 13,* 673–685.

Harlow, H. F., Harlow, M. K., & Hansen, E. W. (1963). The maternal affectional system of rhesus monkeys. In H. L. Rheingold (Ed.), *Maternal behavior in mammals* (pp. 254–281). New York: Wiley.

Hart, C. H., DeWolf, D. M., Wozniak, P., & Burts, D. C. (1992). Maternal and paternal disciplinary styles: Relations with preschoolers' playground behavioral orientations and peer status. *Child Development, 63,* 879–892.

Harter, S., Alexander, P. C., & Neimeyer, R. A. (1988). Long-term effects of incestuous child abuse in college women: Social adjustment, social cognition, and family characteristics. *Journal of Consulting and Clinical Psychology, 56,* 5–8.

Hauser, S. T., Book, B. K., Houlihan, J., Powers, S., Weiss-Perry, B., Follansbee, D., Jacobson, A. M., & Noam, G. G. (1987). Sex differences within the family: Studies of adolescent and parent family interactions. *Journal of Youth and Adolescence, 16,* 199–220.

Hauser, S. T., Powers, S. I., Noam, G. G., Jacobson, A. M., Weiss, B., & Follansbee, D. J. (1984). Familial contexts of adolescent ego development. *Child Development, 55,* 195–213.

Haver, B. (1986). Female alcoholics: II. Factors associated with psycho-social outcome 3–10 years after treatment. *Acta Psychiatrica Scandinavica, 74,* 597–604.

Hazelrigg, M. D., Cooper, H. M., & Borduin, C. M. (1987). Evaluating the effectiveness of family therapies: An integrative review and analysis. *Psychological Bulletin, 101,* 428–442.

Hazzard, A., Christensen, A., & Margolin, G. (1983). Children's perceptions of parental behaviors. *Journal of Abnormal Child Psychology, 11,* 49–60.

Healy, J. M., Malley, J. E., & Stewart, A. J. (1990). Children and their fathers after parental separation. *American Journal of Orthopsychiatry, 60,* 531–543.

Heavey, C. L., Shenk, J. L., & Christensen, A. (1994). Marital conflict and divorce: A developmental family psychology perspective. In L. L'Abate (Ed.), *Handbook of developmental family psychology and psychopathology* (pp. 221–242). New York: Wiley.

Hebb, D. O. (1980). *Essay on mind.* Hillsdale, NJ: Erlbaum.

Hecker, L. L. (1991). Where is Dad?: 21 ways to involve fathers in family therapy. *Journal of Family Psychotherapy, 2,* 31–45.

Heide, K. M. (1992). *Why kids kill parents: Child abuse and adolescent homicide.* Columbus: Ohio State University Press.

Heide, K. M. (1993). Parents who get killed and the children who kill them. *Journal of Interpersonal Violence, 8,* 531–544.

Heilbrun, A. B. (1964). Parental model attributes, nurturant reinforcement, and consistency of behaviors in adolescents. *Child Development, 35,* 151–167.

Heilbrun, A. B. (1965). An empirical test of the modelling theory of sex-role learning. *Child Development, 36,* 789–799.

Heinowitz, J. (1982). *Pregnant fathers: Making the best of the father's role before, during, and after childbirth.* Englewood Cliffs, NJ: Prentice-Hall.

Helzer, J. E. (1987). Epidemiology of alcoholism. *Journal of Consulting and Clinical Psychology, 55,* 284–292.

Henderson, J. (1980a). On fathering (The nature and functions of the father role) Part I: Acquiring an understanding of the father role. *Canadian Journal of Psychiatry, 25,* 403–412.

Henderson, J. (1980b). On fathering (The nature and functions of the father role) Part II: Conceptualization of fathering. *Canadian Journal of Psychiatry, 25,* 413–431.

Hendricks, L. E. (1980). Unwed adolescent fathers: Problems they face and their sources of social support. *Adolescence, 15,* 860–869.

Henggeler, S. W., Cohen, R., Edwards, J. J., Summerville, M. B., & Ray, G. E. (1991). Family stress as a link in the association between television viewing and achievement. *Child Study Journal, 21,* 1–10.

Henggeler, S. W., Edwards, J., & Borduin, C. M. (1987). The family relations of female juvenile delinquents. *Journal of Abnormal Child Psychology, 15,* 199–209.

Henggeler, S. W., Melton, G. B., & Smith, L. A. (1992). Family preservation using multisystemic therapy: An effective alternative to incarcerating serious juvenile offenders. *Journal of Consulting and Clinical Psychology, 60,* 953–961.

Henggeler, S. W., Rodick, J. D., Borduin, C. M., Hanson, C. L., Watson, S. M., & Urey, J. R. (1986). Multisystemic treatment of juvenile offenders: Effects on adolescent behavior and family interaction. *Developmental Psychology, 22,* 132–141.

Herjanic, B., Herjanic, M., Penick, E., Tomelleri, C., & Armbruster, R. (1977). Children of alcoholics. In F. A. Seixas (Ed.), *Currents in alcoholism* (Vol. 2, pp. 445–455). New York: Grune and Stratton.

Herman, J., & Hirschman, L. (1981). Families at risk for father-daughter incest. *American Journal of Psychiatry, 138,* 967–971.

Herman, M. A., & McHale, S. M. (1993). Coping with parental negativity: Links with parental warmth and child adjustment. *Journal of Applied Developmental Psychology, 14,* 121–130.

Hesselbrock, M. N. (1991). Gender comparison of antisocial personality disorder and depression in alcoholism. *Journal of Substance Abuse, 3,* 205–219.

Hetherington, E. M. (1966). Effects of paternal absence on sex-typed behaviors in Negro and White preadolescent males. *Journal of Personality and Social Psychology, 4,* 87–91.

Hetherington, E. M., & Clingempeel, W. G. (1992). Coping with marital transitions. *Monographs of the Society for Research in Child Development, 57* (Serial No. 227), 1–229.

Hetherington, E. M., Reiss, D., & Plomin, R. (Eds.). (1994). *Separate social worlds of siblings: Importance of nonshared environment on development.* Hillsdale, NJ: Erlbaum.

Heubeck, B., Watson, J., & Russell, G. (1986). Father involvement and responsibility in family therapy. In M. E. Lamb (Ed.), *The father's role: Applied perspectives* (pp. 191–226). New York: Wiley.

Hewlett, B. S. (1987). Intimate fathers: Patterns of paternal holding among Aka pygmies. In M. E. Lamb (Ed.), *The father's role: Cross-cultural perspectives* (pp. 295–330). Hillsdale, NJ: Erlbaum.

Hibbs, E. D., Hamburger, S. D., Lenane, M., Rapoport, J. L., Kruesi, M. J. P., Keysor, C. S., & Goldstein, M. J. (1991). Determinants of expressed emotion in families of disturbed and normal children. *Journal of Child Psychology and Psychiatry, 32,* 757–770.

Hiew, C. C. (1992). Separated by their work: Families with fathers living apart. *Environment and Behavior, 24,* 206–225.

Hill, E. M., & Hill, M. A. (1990). Gender differences in child care and work: An interdisciplinary perspective. *Journal of Behavioral Economics, 19,* 81–101.

Hill, J. P., & Holmbeck, G. N. (1987). Disagreements about rules in families with seventh-grade girls and boys. *Journal of Youth and Adolescence, 16,* 221–246.

Hill, S. Y. (1992). Absence of paternal sociopathy in etiology of severe alcoholism: Is there a type III alcoholism? *Journal of Studies on Alcohol, 53,* 161–169.

Hillenbrand, E. D. (1976). Father absence in military families. *The Family Coordinator, 25,* 451–458.

Hilliard, J. P., Fritz, G. K., & Lewiston, N. J. (1985). Levels of aspiration of parents for their asthmatic, diabetic, and healthy children. *Journal of Clinical Psychology, 41,* 587–597.

Hinde, R. A. (1991). When is an evolutionary approach useful? *Child Development, 62,* 671–675.

Hinde, R. A., & Stevenson-Hinde, J. (Eds.). (1988). *Relationships within families: Mutual influences.* Oxford: Oxford University Press.

Hinshaw, S. P. (1987). On the distinction between attention deficits/hyperactivity and conduct problems/aggression in child psychopathology. *Psychological Bulletin, 101,* 443–463.

Ho, D. Y. F. (1987). Fatherhood in Chinese culture. In M. E. Lamb (Ed.), *The father's role: Cross-cultural perspectives* (pp. 227–245). Hillsdale, NJ: Erlbaum.

Hobbs, D. (1965). Parenthood as crisis: A third study. *Journal of Marriage and the Family, 27,* 367–372.

Hobbs, D., & Cole, S. (1976). Transition to parenthood: A decade replication. *Journal of Marriage and the Family, 38,* 723–731.

Hobhouse, L. (1916). *Morals in evolution.* New York: Holt.

Hodges, K., Kline, J. J., Barbero, G., & Woodruff, C. (1985). Anxiety in children with recurrent abdominal pain and their parents. *Psychosomatics, 26,* 859–866.

Hoffman, L. W. (1977). Changes in family roles, socialization, and sex differences. *American Psychologist, 32,* 644–657.

Holahan, C. J., & Moos, R. H. (1987). Risk, resistance, and psychological distress: A longitudinal analysis with adults and children. *Journal of Abnormal Psychology, 96,* 3–13.

Holden, G. W., & Edwards, L. A. (1989). Parental attitudes toward child rearing: Instruments, issues, and implications. *Psychological Bulletin, 106,* 29–58.

Holden, G. W., & Ritchie, K. L. (1991). Linking extreme marital discord, child rearing, and child behavior problems: Evidence from battered women. *Child Development, 62,* 311–327.

Holder, D. P., & Anderson, C. A. (1989). Women, work, and the family. In M. McGoldrick, C. M. Anderson, & F. Walsh (Eds.), *Women and families* (pp. 357–380). New York: Free Press.

Holmes, G. R., Sabalis, R. F., Chestnut, E., & Khoury, L. (1984). Parent MMPI critical item and clinical scale changes in the 1970s. *Journal of Clinical Psychology, 40,* 1194–1198.

Honig, A. S., & Pfannenstiel, A. E. (1991). Difficulties in reaching low-income new fathers: Issues and cases. *Early Child Development and Care, 77,* 115–125.

Honzik, M. P. (1963). A sex difference in the age of onset of the parent-child resemblance in intelligence. *Journal of Educational Psychology, 54,* 231–237.

Honzik, M. P. (1967). Environmental correlates of mental growth: Prediction from the family setting at 21 months. *Child Development, 38,* 337–364.

Hops, H. (1992). Parental depression and child behavior problems: Implications for behavioural family intervention. *Behaviour Change, 9,* 126–138.

Hops, H., & Seeley, J. R. (1991, November). *Father-presence effects in studies of mother-adolescent interaction: Methodological and substantive considerations.* Paper presented at the convention of the Association for Advancement of Behavior Therapy, New York.

Hops, H., & Seeley, J. R. (1992). Parent participation in studies of family interaction: Methodological and substantive considerations. *Behavioral Assessment, 14,* 229–243.

Horton, L. (1984). The father's role in behavioral parent training: A review. *Journal of Clinical Child Psychology, 13,* 274–279.

Humphrey, L. L. (1986). Structural analysis of parent-child relationships in eating disorders. *Journal of Abnormal Psychology, 95,* 395–402.

Humphrey, L. L. (1987). Comparison of bulimic-anorexic and nondistressed families using structural analysis of social behavior. *Journal of the American Academy of Child and Adolescent Psychiatry, 26,* 248–255.

Humphrey, L. L. (1989). Observed family interactions among subtypes of eating disorders using structural analysis of social behavior. *Journal of Consulting and Clinical Psychology, 57,* 206–214.

Humphrey, L. L., Apple, R. F., & Kirschenbaum, D. S. (1986). Differentiating bulimic-anorexic from normal families using interpersonal and behavioral observational systems. *Journal of Consulting and Clinical Psychology, 54,* 190–195.

Hutchinson, E. O. (1992). *Black fatherhood: The guide to male parenting.* Los Angeles: Impact Publications.

Hwang, C. P. (1987). The changing role of Swedish fathers. In M. E. Lamb (Ed.), *The father's role: Cross-cultural perspectives* (pp. 115–138). Hillsdale, NJ: Erlbaum.

Hyde, J. S., & Linn, M. C. (1988). Gender differences in verbal ability: A meta-analysis. *Psychological Bulletin, 104,* 53–69.

Ingrassia, M. (1993, August 30). Endangered family. *Newsweek*, pp. 17–27.

Inoff-Germain, G., Arnold, G. S., Nottelmann, E. D., Susman, E. J., Cutler, G. B., & Chrousos, G. P. (1988). Relations between hormone levels and observational measures of aggressive behavior of young adolescents in family interactions. *Developmental Psychology, 24*, 129–139.

Ishii-Kuntz, M. (1994). Paternal involvement and perception toward fathers' roles: A comparison between Japan and the United States. *Journal of Family Issues, 14*, 30–48.

Itil, T. M., Huque, M. F., Shapiro, D. M., Mednick, S. A., & Schulsinger, F. (1983). Computer-analyzed EEG findings in children of schizophrenic parents ("high risk" children). *Integrative Psychiatry, 1*, 71–79.

Ivens, C. & Rehm, L. P. (1988). Assessment of childhood depression: Correspondence between reports by child, mother, and father. *Journal of the American Academy of Child and Adolescent Psychiatry, 27*, 738–741.

Jackson, S. (1987). Great Britain. In M. E. Lamb (Ed.), *The father's role: Cross cultural perspectives* (pp. 29–57). Hillsdale, NJ: Erlbaum.

Jacob, T., Krahn, G. L., & Leonard, K. (1991). Parent-child interactions in families with alcoholic fathers. *Journal of Consulting and Clinical Psychology, 59*, 176–181.

Jacob, T., & Leonard, K. (1986). Psychosocial functioning in children of alcoholic fathers, depressed fathers and control fathers. *Journal of Studies on Alcohol, 47*, 373–380.

Jacob, T., Tennenbaum, D., Seilhamer, R. A., Bargiel, K., & Sharon, T. (1994). Reactivity effects during naturalistic observation of distressed and nondistressed families. *Journal of Family Psychology, 8*, 354–363.

Jacobs, J. W. (1982). The effect of divorce on fathers: An overview of the literature. *American Journal of Psychiatry, 139*, 1235–1241.

Jacobs, J. W. (1983). Treatment of divorcing fathers: Social and psychotherapeutic considerations. *American Journal of Psychiatry, 140*, 1294–1299.

Jarmas, A. L., & Kazak, A. E. (1992). Young adult children of alcoholic fathers: Depressive experiences, coping styles, and family systems. *Journal of Consulting and Clinical Psychology, 60*, 244–251.

Jarvis, P. A., & Creasey, G. L. (1991). Parental stress, coping, and attachment in families with an 18-month-old infant. *Infant Behavior and Development, 14*, 383–395.

Jary, M. L., & Stewart, M. A. (1985). Psychiatric disorder in the parents of adopted children with aggressive conduct disorder. *Neuropsychobiology, 13*, 7–11.

Jenkins, J. M., & Smith, M. A. (1990). Factors protecting children living in disharmonious homes: Maternal reports. *Journal of the American Academy of Child and Adolescent Psychiatry, 29*, 60–69.

Jenkins, J. M., & Smith, M. A. (1991). Marital disharmony and children's behaviour problems: Aspects of a poor marriage that affect children adversely. *Journal of Child Psychology and Psychiatry, 32*, 793–810.

Jensen, P. S., Bloedau, L., Degroot, J., Ussery, T., & Davis, H. (1990). Children at risk: I. Risk factors and child symptomatology. *Journal of the American Academy of Child and Adolescent Psychiatry, 29*, 51–59.

Jensen, P. S., Lewis, R. L., & Xenakis, S. N. (1986). The military family in review: Context, risk, and prevention. *Journal of the American Academy of Child Psychiatry, 25,* 225–234.

Jensen, P. S., Traylor, J., Xenakis, S. N., & Davis, H. (1988). Child psychopathology rating scales and interrater agreement: I. Parents' gender and psychiatric symptoms. *Journal of the American Academy of Child and Adolescent Psychiatry, 27,* 442–450.

Jerome, L. (1993). A comparison of the demography, clinical profile and treatment of adopted and non-adopted children at a children's mental health centre. *Canadian Journal of Psychiatry, 38,* 290–294.

Jewsuwan, R., Luster, T., & Kostelnik, M. (1993). The relation between parents' perceptions of temperament and children's adjustment to preschool. *Early Childhood Research Quarterly, 8,* 33–51.

Jiloha, R. C. (1986). Psycho-social factors in adolescent heroin addicts. *Child Psychiatry Quarterly, 19,* 138–142.

John, K., Gammon, G. D., Prusoff, B. A., & Warner, V. (1987). The Social Adjustment Inventory for Children and Adolescents (SAICA): Testing of a new semi-structured interview. *Journal of the American Academy of Child and Adolescent Psychiatry, 26,* 898–911.

Johnson, B. M., Shulman, S., & Collins, W. A. (1991). Systemic patterns of parenting as reported by adolescents: Developmental differences and implications for psychosocial outcomes. *Journal of Adolescent Research, 6,* 235–252.

Johnson, J. H., & Fennell, E. B. (1992). Aggressive, antisocial, and delinquent behavior in childhood and adolescence. In C. E. Walker & M. C. Roberts (Eds.), *Handbook of clinical child psychology* (2nd ed., pp. 341–358). New York: Wiley.

Johnson, M. M. (1963). Sex role learning in the nuclear family. *Child Development, 34,* 315–333.

Johnson, P. L., & O'Leary, K. D. (1987). Parental behavior patterns and conduct disorders in girls. *Journal of Abnormal Child Psychology, 15,* 573–581.

Johnson, R. E. (1987). Mother's versus father's role in causing delinquency. *Adolescence, 22,* 305–315.

Johnson, S. M., & Lobitz, G. K. (1974). The personal and marital adjustment of parents as related to observed child deviance and parenting behaviors. *Journal of Abnormal Child Psychology, 2,* 193–207.

Johnston, C. (1991). Predicting mothers' and fathers' perceptions of child behaviour problems. *Canadian Journal of Behavioural Science, 23,* 349–357.

Johnston, C., & Patenaude, R. (1994). Parent attributions for inattentive-overactive and oppositional-defiant child behaviors. *Cognitive Therapy and Research, 18,* 261–275.

Johnston, J. R., Gonzalez, R., & Campbell, L. E. G. (1987). Ongoing postdivorce conflict and child disturbance. *Journal of Abnormal Child Psychology, 15,* 493–509.

Jones, L. C., & Heermann, J. A. (1992). Parental division of infant care: Contextual influences and infant characteristics. *Nursing Research, 41,* 228–234.

Jones, V. F., Badgett, J. T., Minella, J. L., & Schuschke, L. A. (1993). The role of the male caretaker in Munchausen syndrome by proxy. *Clinical Pediatrics, 32,* 245–247.

Jordan, B. K., Marmar, C. R., Fairbank, J. A., Schlenger, W. E., Kulka, R. A., Hough, R. L., & Weiss, D. S. (1992). Problems in families of male Vietnam veterans with posttraumatic stress disorder. *Journal of Consulting and Clinical Psychology, 60,* 916–926.

Jouriles, E. N., & Farris, A. M. (1992). Effects of marital conflict on subsequent parent-son interactions. *Behavior Therapy, 23,* 355–374.

Jouriles, E. N., & LeCompte, S. H. (1991). Husbands' aggression toward wives and mothers' and fathers' aggression toward children: Moderating effects of child gender. *Journal of Consulting and Clinical Psychology, 59,* 190–192.

Julian, T. W., McKenry, P. C., & McKelvey, M. W. (1991). Mediators of relationship stress between middle-aged fathers and their adolescent children. *Journal of Genetic Psychology, 152,* 381–386.

Jung, C. G. (1949). *The significance of the father in the destiny of the individual.* Zurich: Rascher.

Juni, S., & Grimm, D. W. (1993). Sex-role similarities between adults and their parents. *Contemporary Family Therapy: An International Journal, 15,* 247–251.

Jurich, A. P. (1983). The Saigon of the family's mind: Family therapy with families of Vietnam veterans. *Journal of Marital and Family Therapy, 9,* 355–363.

Jurich, A. P., White, M. B., White, C. P., & Moody, R. A. (1991). Internal culture of the family and its effect on fatherhood. In F. W. Bozett & S. M. H. Hanson (Eds.), *Fatherhood and families in cultural context* (pp. 237–262). New York: Springer.

Kabacoff, R. I., Miller, I. W., Bishop, D. S., Epstein, N. B., & Keitner, G. I. (1990). A psychometric study of the McMaster Family Assessment Device in psychiatric, medical and non-clinical samples. *Journal of Family Psychology 3,* 431–439.

Kafka, R. R., & London, P. (1991). Communication in relationships and adolescent substance use: The influence of parents and friends. *Adolescence, 26,* 587–598.

Kandel, D. B. (1990). Parenting styles, drug use, and children's adjustment in families of young adults. *Journal of Marriage and the Family, 52,* 183–196.

Kandel, E., Mednick, S. A., Kirkegaard-Sorensen, L., Hutchings, B., Knop, J., Rosenberg, R., & Schulsinger, F. (1988). IQ as a protective factor for subjects at high risk for antisocial behavior. *Journal of Consulting and Clinical Psychology, 56,* 224–226.

Kanner, L. (1943). Autistic disturbances of affective contact. *Nervous Child, 2,* 217–250.

Kashani, J. H., Burbach, D. J., & Rosenberg, T. K. (1988). Perception of family conflict resolution and depressive symptomatology in adolescents. *Journal of the American Academy of Child and Adolescent Psychiatry, 27,* 42–48.

Kaslow, F. W. (1981). Involving the peripheral father in family therapy. In A. S. Gurman (Ed.), *Questions and answers in the practice of family therapy* (Vol. 1, pp. 27–31). New York: Brunner/Mazel.

Kaslow, N. J., Deering, C. G., & Racusin, G. R. (1994). Depressed children and their families. *Clinical Psychology Review, 14,* 39–59.

Kaslow, N. J., Rehm, L. P., Pollack, S. L., & Siegel, A. W. (1988). Attributional style and self-control behavior in depressed and nondepressed children and their parents. *Journal of Abnormal Child Psychology, 16,* 163–175.

Katon, W., & Roy-Byrne, P. P. (1991). Mixed anxiety and depression. *Journal of Abnormal Psychology, 100,* 337–345.

Katzev, A. R., Warner, R. L., & Acock, A. C. (1994). Girls or boys?: Relationship of child gender to marital instability. *Journal of Marriage and the Family, 56,* 89–100.

Kavanagh, K., & Hops, H. (1994). Good girls? Bad boys? Gender and development as contexts for diagnosis and treatment. In T. H. Ollendick and R. J. Prinz (Eds.), *Advances in clinical child psychology* (Vol. 16, pp. 45–79). New York: Plenum.

Kawash, G. F., & Clewes, J. L. (1988). A factor analysis of a short form of the CRPBI: Are children's perceptions of control and discipline multidimensional? *Journal of Psychology, 122,* 57–67.

Kazdin, A. E. (1984). Acceptability of aversive procedures and medication as treatment alternatives for deviant child behavior. *Journal of Abnormal Child Psychology, 12,* 289–301.

Kazdin, A. E. (1991). Effectiveness of psychotherapy with children and adolescents. *Journal of Consulting and Clinical Psychology, 59,* 785–798.

Kazdin, A. E., Mazurick, J. L., & Bass, D. (1993). Risk for attrition in treatment of antisocial children and families. *Journal of Clinical Child Psychology, 22,* 2–16.

Keen, S. (1991). *Fire in the belly: On being a man.* New York: Bantam.

Kelley, M. L., Sanchez-Hucles, J., & Walker, R. R. (1993). Correlates of disciplinary practices in working- to middle-class African-American mothers. *Merrill-Palmer Quarterly, 39,* 252–264.

Kelly, J. A., & Worell, L. (1976). The joint and differential perceived contribution of parents to adolescents' cognitive functioning. *Developmental Psychology, 13,* 282–283.

Kelly, J. B. (1993). Current research on children's post divorce adjustment: No simple answers. *Family and Conciliation Courts Review, 31,* 29–49.

Kendall, P. C., & Fischler, G. L. (1984). Behavioral and adjustment correlates of problem solving: Validational analyses of interpersonal cognitive problem-solving measures. *Child Development, 55,* 879–892.

Kendler, K. S., MacLean, C., Neale, M. C., Kessler, R. C., Heath, A. C., & Eaves, L. (1991). The genetic epidemiology of bulimia nervosa. *American Journal of Psychiatry, 148,* 1627–1637.

Kendler, K. S., Neale, M. C., Kessler, R. C., Heath, A. C., & Eaves, L. J. (1992). Childhood parental loss and adult psychopathology in women: A twin study perspective. *Archives of General Psychiatry, 49,* 109–116.

Kendler, K. S., Silberg, J. L., Neale, M. C., Kessler, R. C., Heath, A. C., & Eaves, L. (1991). The family history method: Whose psychiatric history is measured? *American Journal of Psychiatry, 148,* 1501–1504.

Kendziora, K. T., & O'Leary, S. G. (1993). Dysfunctional parenting as a focus for prevention and treatment of child behavior problems. In T. H. Ollendick & R. J. Prinz (Eds.), *Advances in clinical child psychology* (Vol. 15, pp. 175–206). New York: Plenum.

Kerig, P. K., Cowan, P. A., & Cowan, C. P. (1993). Marital quality and gender differences in parent-child interaction. *Developmental Psychology, 29,* 931–939.

Kerver, M. J., Van-Son, M. J., & deGroot, P. A. (1992). Predicting symptoms of depression from reports of early parenting: A one-year prospective study in a community sample. *Acta Psychiatrica Scandinavica, 86,* 267–272.

Khanobdee, C., Sukratanachaiyakul, V., & Gay, J. T. (1993). Couvade syndrome in expectant Thai fathers. *International Journal of Nursing Studies, 30,* 125–131.

Kimmel, M. S. (1992). *Against the tide: Pro-feminist men in the United States.* New York: Beacon Press.

Kimmel, M. S. (1993). What do men want? *Harvard Business Review, 71,* 50–63.

Kinnell, H. G. (1983). Parental age in schizophrenia. *British Journal of Schizophrenia, 142,* 204–214.

Kinzl, J., & Biebl, W. (1992). Long-term effects of incest: Life events triggering mental disorders in female patients with sexual abuse in childhood. *Child Abuse and Neglect, 16,* 567–573.

Kiselica, M. S., Stroud, J., Stroud, J., & Rotzien, A. (1992). Counseling the forgotten client: The teen father. *Journal of Mental Health Counseling, 14,* 338–350.

Kiselica, M. S., & Sturmer, P. (1993). Is society giving teenage fathers a mixed message? *Youth and Society, 24,* 487–501.

Klaus, M. H., & Kennell, J. H. (1976). *Maternal-infant bonding.* St. Louis: Mosby.

Klein, D. N., Clark, D. C., Dansky, L., & Margolis, E. T. (1988). Dysthymia in the offspring of parents with primary Unipolar Affective Disorder. *Journal of Abnormal Psychology, 97,* 265–274.

Klein, D. N., Depue, R. A., & Slater, J. F. (1985). Cyclothymia in the adolescent offspring of parents with Bipolar Affective Disorder. *Journal of Abnormal Psychology, 94,* 115–127.

Klein, M. (1957). *Envy and gratitude.* London: Tavistock.

Klein, M. M., & Shulman, S. (1980). Behavior problems of children in relation to parental instrumentality-expressivity and marital adjustment. *Psychological Reports, 47,* 11–14.

Klein, R. H., & Nimorwicz, P. (1982). The relationship between psychological distress and knowledge of disease among hemophilia patients and their families: A pilot study. *Journal of Psychosomatic Research, 26,* 387–391.

Kliewer, W., & Weidner, G. (1987). Type A behavior and aspirations: A study of parents' and children's goal setting. *Developmental Psychology, 23,* 204–209.

Klinge, V., & Piggott, L. R. (1986). Substance use by adolescent psychiatric inpatients and their parents. *Adolescence, 21,* 323–331.

Knop, J., Teasdale, T., Schulsinger, F., & Goodwin, D. (1985). A prospective study of young men at high risk for alcoholism: School behavior and achievement. *Journal of Studies on Alcohol, 46,* 273–278.

Koestner, R., Zuroff, D. C., & Powers, T. A. (1991). Family origins of adolescent self-criticism and its continuity into adulthood. *Journal of Abnormal Psychology, 100,* 191–197.

Kohlberg, L., & Kramer, R. (1969). Continuities and discontinuities in childhood and adulthood moral development. *Human Development, 12,* 93–120.

Konstantareas, M. M., & Homatidis, S. (1989a). Assessing child symptom severity and stress in parents of autistic children. *Journal of Child Psychology and Psychiatry, 30,* 459–470.

Konstantareas, M. M., & Homatidis, S. (1989b). Parental perception of learning-disabled children's adjustment problems and related stress. *Journal of Abnormal Child Psychology, 17,* 177–186.

Kotelchuck, M. (1976). The infant's relationship to the father: Experimental evidence. In M. E. Lamb (Ed.), *The role of the father in child development* (1st ed., pp. 329–344). New York: Wiley.

Kraemer, S. (1991). The origins of fatherhood: An ancient family process. *Family Process, 30,* 377–392.

Krawczak, M., & Schmidtke, J. (1992). The decision theory of paternity disputes: Optimization considerations applied to multilocus DNA fingerprinting. *Journal of Forensic Sciences, 37,* 1525–1533.

Krinsley, K. E., & Bry, B. H. (1991). Sequential analyses of adolescent, mother, and father behaviors in distressed and nondistressed families. *Child and Family Therapy, 13,* 45–62.

Kruk, E. (1991). Discontinuity between pre- and post-divorce father-child relationships: New evidence regarding paternal disengagement. *Journal of Divorce and Remarriage, 16,* 195–227.

Kruk, E. (1992). Psychological and structural factors contributing to the disengagement of noncustodial fathers after divorce. *Family and Conciliation Courts Review, 30,* 81–101.

Kruk, E. (1994). The disengaged noncustodial father: Implications for social work practice with the divorced family. *Social Work, 39,* 15–25.

Krupnick, J. L., & Solomon, F. (1987). Death of a parent or sibling during childhood. In J. Bloom-Feshbach & S. Bloom-Feshbach (Eds.), *The psychology of separation and loss: Perspectives on development, life transitions, and clinical practice* (pp. 345–371). San Francisco: Jossey-Bass.

Kuebli, J., & Fivush, R. (1992). Gender differences in parent-child conversations about past emotions. *Sex Roles, 27,* 683–698.

Kumpfer, K. L., & DeMarsh, J. (1985). Family environmental and genetic influences on children's future chemical dependency. *Journal of Children in Contemporary Society, 18,* 49–91.

Kurdek, L. A. (1981). An integrative perspective on children's divorce adjustment. *American Psychologist, 36,* 856–866.

Kurdek, L. A., & Berg, B. (1987). Children's beliefs about parental divorce scale: Psychometric characteristics and concurrent validity. *Journal of Consulting and Clinical Psychology, 55,* 712–718.

Kurdek, L. A., & Sinclair, R. J. (1988). Adjustment of young adolescents in two-parent nuclear, stepfather, and mother-custody families. *Journal of Consulting and Clinical Psychology, 56,* 91–96.

L'Abate, L. (Ed.). (1994). *Handbook of developmental family psychology and psychopathology.* New York: Wiley.

Lackovic-Grgin, K., & Dekovic, M. (1990). The contribution of significant others to adolescents' self-esteem. *Adolescence, 25,* 839–846.

Lacoursiere, R. B. (1972). Fatherhood and mental illness: A review and new material. *Psychiatric Quarterly, 46,* 109–124.

Lahey, B. B., Piacentini, J. C., McBurnett, K., Stone, P., Hartdagen, S., & Hynd, G. (1988). Psychopathology in the parents of children with Conduct Disorder and Hyperactivity. *Journal of the American Academy of Child and Adolescent Psychiatry, 27,* 163–170.

Lamb, M. E. (1975). Fathers: Forgotten contributors to child development. *Human Development, 18,* 245–266.

Lamb, M. E. (Ed.). (1976). *The role of the father in child development.* New York: Wiley.

Lamb, M. E. (1979). Paternal influences and the father's role: A personal perspective. *American Psychologist, 34,* 938–943.

Lamb, M. E. (Ed.). (1981). *The role of the father in child development* (rev. ed.). New York: Wiley.

Lamb, M. E. (Ed.). (1986). *The father's role: Applied perspectives.* New York: Wiley.

Lamb, M. E. (Ed.). (1987). *The father's role: Cross-cultural Perspectives.* New York: Wiley.

Lamb, M. E. (Ed.). (in press). *The role of the father in child development* (3rd ed.). New York: Wiley.

Lamb, M. E., Frodi, A. M., Hwang, C. P., Frodi, M., & Steinberg, J. (1982). Mother- and father-infant interaction involving play and holding in traditional and nontraditional Swedish families. *Developmental Psychology, 18,* 215–221.

Lamb, M. E., & Oppenheim, D. (1989). Fatherhood and father-child relationships: Five years of research. In S. H. Cath, A. Gurwitt, & L. Gunsberg (Eds.), *Fathers and their families.* Hillsdale, NJ: Analytic Press.

Lamb, M. E., Pleck, J. H., & Levine, J. A. (1985). The role of the father in child development: The effects of increased paternal involvement. In B. B. Lahey & A. E. Kazdin (Eds.), *Advances in clinical child psychology* (Vol. 8, pp. 229–266). New York: Plenum.

Lamb, M. E., & Sagi, A. (Eds.). (1983). *Fatherhood and family policy.* Hillsdale, NJ: Erlbaum.

Lampert, A., & Friedman, A. (1992). Sex differences in vulnerability and maladjustment as a function of parental investment: An evolutionary approach. *Social Biology, 39,* 65–81.

Lang, A. R., Pelham, W. E., Johnston, C., & Gelernter, S. (1989). Levels of adult alcohol consumption induced by interactions with child confederates exhibiting normal versus externalizing behaviors. *Journal of Abnormal Psychology, 98,* 294–299.

Langevin, R., & Watson, R. (1991). A comparison of incestuous biological and stepfathers. *Annals of Sex Research, 4,* 141–150.

Langhinrichsen, J., Lichtenstein, E., Seeley, J. R., Hops, H., Ary, D. V., Tildesley, E., & Andrews, J. (1990). Parent-adolescent congruence for adolescent substance use. *Journal of Youth and Adolescence, 19,* 623–635.

Langhinrichsen-Rohling, J., Heyman, R. E., Schlee, K. A., & O'Leary, K. D. (1993, November). *The influence of relationship distress and husband aggression on early married spouses' expectations regarding parenting.* Poster presented at the convention of the Association for the Advancement of Behavior Therapy. Atlanta, GA.

Lanier, C. S. (1991). Dimensions of father-child interaction in a New York state prison population. *Journal of Offender Rehabilitation, 16,* 27–42.

Lansky, M. R. (1992). *Fathers who fail: Shame and psychopathology in the family system.* Hillsdale, NJ: Analytic Press.

Last, C. G., & Strauss, C. C. (1989). Panic disorder in children and adolescents. *Journal of Anxiety Disorders, 3,* 87–95.

Lau, S., Lew, W. J. F., Hau, K. T., Cheung, P. C., & Berndt, T. J. (1990). Relations among perceived parental control, warmth, indulgence, and family harmony of Chinese in Mainland China. *Developmental Psychology, 26,* 674–677.

Lawton, L., Silverstein, M., & Bengtson, V. (1994). Affection, social contact, and geographic distance between adult children and their parents. *Journal of Marriage and the Family, 56,* 57–68.

Lazar, A., Sagi, A., & Fraser, M. W. (1991). Involving fathers in social services. *Children and Youth Services Review, 13,* 287–300.

Lebow, J. L., & Gurman, A. S. (1995). Research assessing couple and family therapy. *Annual Review of Psychology, 46,* 27–57.

LeCroy, C. W. (1987). A model for involving fathers in family treatment. *Family Therapy, 14,* 237–245.

Lee, C. M., & Gotlib, I. H. (1991). Family disruption, parental availability and child adjustment. In R. J. Prinz (Ed.), *Advances in behavioral assessment of children and families* (Vol. 5, pp. 171–199). London: Jessica Kingsley Publishers.

Lefkowitz, M. M., & Tesiny, E. P. (1984). Rejection and depression: Prospective and contemporaneous analyses. *Developmental Psychology, 20,* 776–785.

Leinbach, M. D., & Fagot, B. I. (1991). Attractiveness in young children: Sex-differentiated reactions of adults. *Sex Roles, 25,* 269–284.

LeMasters, E. E. (1957). Parenthood as crisis. *Marriage and Family Living, 19,* 352–355.

Lempers, J. D., & Clark-Lempers, D. S. (1990). Family economic stress, maternal and paternal support and adolescent distress. *Journal of Adolescence, 13,* 217–229.

Lempers, J. D., & Clark-Lempers, D. S. (1992). Young, middle, and late adolescents' comparisons of the functional importance of five significant relationships. *Journal of Youth and Adolescence, 21,* 52–96.

Lenane, M. C., Swedo, S. E., Leonard, H., Pauls, D. L., Sceery, W., & Rapoport, J. L. (1990). Psychiatric disorders in first degree relatives of children and adolescents with Obsessive Compulsive Disorder. *Journal of the American Academy of Child and Adolescent Psychiatry, 29,* 407–412.

Leon, C. A., & Leon, A. (1990). Panic disorder and parental bonding. *Psychiatric Annals, 20,* 503–508.

Leon, G. R., Lucas, A. R., Colligan, R. C., Ferdinande, R. J., & Kamp, J. (1985). Sexual, body-image, and personality attitudes in anorexia nervosa. *Journal of Abnormal Child Psychology, 13,* 245–258.

Lesieur, H. R., Blume, S. B., & Zoppa, R. M. (1986). Alcoholism, drug abuse, and gambling. *Alcoholism: Clinical and Experimental Research, 10,* 33–38.

Lessin, S., & Jacob, T. (1984). Multichannel communication in normal and delinquent families. *Journal of Abnormal Child Psychology, 12,* 369–384.

Lester, D. (1991a). Childhood predictors of later suicide: Follow-up of a sample of gifted children. *Stress Medicine, 7,* 129–131.

Lester, D. (1991b). Physical abuse and physical punishment as precursors of suicidal behavior. *Stress Medicine, 7,* 255–256.

Levant, R. F. (1984). *Family therapy: A comprehensive overview.* Englewood Cliffs, NJ: Prentice-Hall.

Levant, R. F. (1988). Education for fatherhood. In P. Bronstein & C. P. Cowan (Eds.), *Fatherhood today: Men's changing role in the family* (pp. 253–275). New York: Wiley.

Levant, R. F. (1991). Changes in fathers' role complicates the relationship between parental mood and adolescent functioning. *Journal of Family Psychology, 4,* 272–275.

Levant, R. F., Slattery, S. C., & Loiselle, J. E. (1987). Fathers' involvement in housework and child care with school-aged daughters. *Family Relations, 36,* 152–157.

Levant, R. F., Slattery, S. C., Loiselle, J. E., Sawyer-Smith, V. K., & Schneider, R. J. (1990). Non-traditional paternal behaviour with school-aged daughters: A discriminant analysis. *Australian Journal of Marriage and Family, 11,* 28–35.

Levenson, R. W., Oyama, O. N., & Meek, P. S. (1987). Greater reinforcement from alcohol for those at risk: Parental risk, personality risk, and sex. *Journal of Abnormal Psychology, 96,* 242–253.

Leventhal-Belfer, L., Cowan, P. A., & Cowan, C. P. (1992). Satisfaction with child care arrangements: Effects on adaptation to parenthood. *American Journal of Orthopsychiatry, 62,* 165–177.

Levine, J. A. (1993). Involving fathers in Head Start: A framework for public policy and program development. *Families in Society: The Journal of Contemporary Human Services, 74,* 4–21.

Levine, J. A., Murphy, D. T., & Wilson, S. (1993). *Getting men involved: Strategies for early childhood programs.* New York: Scholastic.

Levy-Shiff, R., Sharir, H., & Mogilner, M. B. (1989). Mother- and father-preterm infant relationship in the hospital preterm nursery. *Child Development, 60,* 93–102.

Lewinsohn, P. M., Rohde, P., Seeley, J. R., & Hops, H. (1991). Comorbidity of unipolar depression: I. Major depression with dysthymia. *Journal of Abnormal Psychology, 100,* 205–213.

Lewis, C. (1986). *Becoming a father.* Philadelphia: Open University Press.

Lewis, C., & O'Brien, M. (1987). Constraints on fathers: Research, theory, and clinical practice. In C. Lewis & M. O'Brien (Eds.), *Reassessing fatherhood: New observations on fathers and the modern family* (pp. 1–22). Newbury Park, CA: Sage.

Lewis, D. O., Pincus, J. H., Lovely, R., Spitzer, E., & Moy, E. (1987). Biopsychosocial characteristics of matched samples of delinquents and nondelinquents. *Journal of the American Academy of Child and Adolescent Psychiatry, 26,* 744–752.

Lewis, D. O., Shanok, S. S., Grant, M., & Ritvo, E. (1983). Homicidally aggressive young children: Neuropsychiatric and experiential correlates. *American Journal of Psychiatry, 140,* 148–153.

Lewis, R. A., & Salt, R. E. (Eds.). (1986). *Men in families.* Beverly Hills, CA: Sage.

Lidz, T., Parker, B., & Cornelison, A. (1956). The role of the father in the family environment of the schizophrenic patient. *American Journal of Psychiatry, 113,* 126–132.

Lindsay, J. W. (1993). *Teen dads: Rights, responsibilities, and joys.* Buena Park, CA: Morning Glory Press.

Lipovsky, J. A. (1991). Disclosure of father-child sexual abuse: Dilemmas for families and therapists. *Contemporary Family Therapy, 13,* 85–101.

Lisak, D. (1991). Sexual aggression, masculinity, and fathers. *Signs: Journal of Women in Culture and Society, 16,* 238–262.

Lisak, D., & Roth, S. (1990). Motives and psychodynamics of self-reported, unincarcerated rapists. *American Journal of Orthopsychiatry, 60,* 268–280.

Loeber, R. (1990). Development and risk factors of juvenile antisocial behavior and delinquency. *Clinical Psychology Review, 10,* 1–41.

Loeber, R., & Dishion, T. J. (1983). Early predictors of male delinquency: A review. *Psychological Bulletin, 94,* 68–99.

Loeber, R., & Dishion, T. J. (1984). Boys who fight at home and school: Family conditions influencing cross-setting consistency. *Journal of Consulting and Clinical Psychology, 52,* 759–768.

Loeber, R., & Dishion, T. J. (1987). Antisocial and delinquent youths: Methods for their early identification. In J. D. Burchard & S. N. Burchard (Eds.), *Prevention of delinquent behavior* (pp. 75–89). Newbury Park, CA: Sage.

Loeber, R., Weissman, W., & Reid, J. B. (1983). Family interactions of assaultive adolescents, stealers, and nondelinquents. *Journal of Abnormal Child Psychology, 11,* 1–14.

Long, B. C. (1993). Coping strategies of male managers: A prospective analysis of predictors of psychosomatic symptoms and job satisfaction. *Journal of Vocational Behavior, 42,* 184–199.

Luthar, S. S., Merikangas, K. R., & Rounsaville, B. J. (1993). Parental psychopathology and disorders in offspring: A study of relatives of drug abusers. *Journal of Nervous and Mental Disease, 181,* 351–357.

Luthar, S. S., & Quinlan, D. M. (1993). Parental images in two cultures: A study of women in India and America. *Journal of Cross Cultural Psychology, 24,* 186–202.

Lytton, H., & Romney, D. M. (1991). Parents' differential socialization of boys and girls: A meta-analysis. *Psychological Bulletin, 109,* 267–296.

McAdoo, J. L. (1988). Changing perspectives on the role of the Black father. In P. Bronstein & C. P. Cowan (Eds.), *Fatherhood today: Men's changing role in the family* (pp. 79–92). New York: Wiley.

McAdoo, J. L. (1990). Understanding African-American teen fathers. In P. E. Leone (Ed.), *Understanding troubled and troubling youth* (pp. 229–245). Beverly Hills, CA: Sage.

McAdoo, J. L. (1993). The roles of African-American fathers: An ecological perspective. *Families in Society: The Journal of Contemporary Human Services, 74,* 28–35.

McBride, B. A. (1991a). Parent education and support programs for fathers: Outcome effects on paternal involvement. *Early Child Development and Care, 67,* 73–85.

McBride, B. A. (1991b). Parental support programs and paternal stress: An exploratory study. *Early Childhood Research Quarterly, 6,* 137–149.

McBride, B. A., & Ferguson, P. (1992). Parental expectations for young children: Day care versus preschool. *Early Child Development and Care, 79,* 47–53.

McBride-Chang, C., & Jacklin, C. N. (1993). Early play arousal, sex-typed play, and activity level as precursors to later rough-and-tumble play. *Early Education and Development, 4,* 99–108.

McCartney, K., Phillips, D., & Scarr, S. (1993). On using research as a tool. *American Psychologist, 48,* 691–692.

McClelland, D. C. (Ed.). (1955). *Studies in motivation.* New York: Appleton-Century-Crofts.

McClelland, D. C., Atkinson, J. W., Clark, R. A., & Lowell, E. G. (1953). *The achievement motive.* New York: Appleton-Century-Crofts.

Maccoby, E. E. (1991). Different reproductive strategies in males and females. *Child Development, 62,* 676–681.

Maccoby, E. E., Depner, C. E., & Mnookin, R. H. (1990). Coparenting in the second year after divorce. *Journal of Marriage and the Family, 52,* 141–155.

Maccoby, E. E., & Mnookin, R. H. (1992). *Dividing the child: Social and legal dilemmas of custody.* Cambridge, MA: Harvard University Press.

McCord, J. (1979). Some child-rearing antecedents of criminal behavior in adult men. *Journal of Personality and Social Psychology, 37,* 1477–1486.

McCord, J. (1988). Alcoholism: Toward understanding genetic and social factors. *Psychiatry, 51,* 131–141.

McCord, J., McCord, W., & Thurber, E. (1962). Some effects of paternal absence on male children. *Journal of Abnormal and Social Psychology, 64,* 361–369.

McCranie, E. W., & Bass, J. D. (1984). Childhood family antecedents of dependency and self-criticism: Implications for depression. *Journal of Abnormal Psychology, 93,* 3–8.

McCranie, E. W., Hyer, L. A., Boudewyns, P. A., & Woods, M. G. (1992). Negative parenting behavior, combat exposure, and PTSD symptom severity: Test of a person-event interaction model. *Journal of Nervous and Mental Disease, 180,* 431–438.

McCready, W. C. (1985). Styles of grandparenting among White ethnics. In V. L. Bengtson & J. F. Robertson (Eds.), *Grandparenthood* (pp. 49–60). Beverly Hills, CA: Sage.

McDevitt, T. M., Lennon, R., & Kopriva, R. J. (1991). Adolescents' perceptions of mothers' and fathers' prosocial actions and empathic responses. *Youth and Society, 22,* 387–409.

MacDonald, K. (1987). Parent-child physical play with rejected, neglected, and popular boys. *Developmental Psychology, 23,* 705–711.

MacDonald, K. (1992). Warmth as a developmental construct: An evolutionary analysis. *Child Development, 63,* 753–773.

MacDonald, K., & Parke, R. D. (1986). Parent-child physical play: The effects of sex and age of children and parents. *Sex Roles, 7–8,* 367–378.

McGreal, C. E. (1994). The family across generations: Grandparenthood. In L. L'Abate (Ed.), *Handbook of developmental family psychology and psychopathology* (pp. 116–131). New York: Wiley.

McGue, M., Bacon, S., & Lykken, D. T. (1993). Personality stability and change in early adulthood: A behavioral genetic analysis. *Developmental Psychology, 29,* 96–109.

McGue, M., & Lykken, D. T. (1992). Genetic influence on risk of divorce. *Psychological Science, 3,* 368–373.

McHale, S. M., Crouter, A. C., McGuire, S. A., & Updegraff, K. A. (1995). Congruence between mothers' and fathers' differential treatment of siblings: Links with family relations and children's well-being. *Child Development, 66,* 116–128.

McKenry, P. C., Price, S. J., Fine, M. A., & Serovich, J. (1992). Predictors of single, noncustodial fathers' physical involvement with their children. *Journal of Genetic Psychology, 153,* 305–319.

McKenry, P. C., Price, S. J., Gordon, P. B., & Rudd, N. M. (1986). Characteristics of husbands' family work and wives' labor force involvement. In R. A. Lewis & R. E. Salt (Eds.), *Men in families* (pp. 73–83). Beverly Hills, CA: Sage.

McKenry, P. C., Tishler, C. L., & Kelley, C. (1982). Adolescent suicide: A comparison of attempters and nonattempters in an emergency room population. *Clinical Pediatrics, 21,* 266–270.

Mackey, W. C. (1985). *Fathering behaviors: The dynamics of man-child bond.* New York: Plenum.

Mackey, W. C., White, U., & Day, R. D. (1992). Reasons American men become fathers: Men's divulgences, women's perceptions. *Journal of Genetic Psychology, 153,* 435–445.

McKinley, D. (1964). *Social class and family life.* New York: Free Press.

McLeer, S. V., Deblinger, E. B., Henry, D., & Orvaschel, H. (1992). Sexually abused children at high risk for post-traumatic stress disorder. *Journal of the American Academy of Child and Adolescent Psychiatry, 31,* 875–879.

McLeod, J. D. (1993). Spouse concordance for depressive disorders in a community sample. *Journal of Affective Disorders, 27,* 43–52.

McLinden, S. E. (1990). Mothers' and fathers' reports of the effects of a young child with special needs on the family. *Journal of Early Intervention, 14,* 249–259.

McLoyd, V. C. (1989). Socialization and development in a changing economy: The effects of paternal job and income loss on children. *American Psychologist, 44,* 293–302.

McLoyd, V. C. (1990). The impact of economic hardship on Black families and children: Psychological distress, parenting, and socioemotional development. *Child Development, 61,* 311–346.

McWilliams, N. (1991). Mothering and fathering processes in the psychoanalytic art. *Psychoanalytic Review, 78,* 525–545.

Maddux, J. E. (1993). Social science, social policy, and scientific research. *American Psychologist, 48,* 689–691.

Maguin, E., Zucker, R. A., & Fitzgerald, H. E. (1994). The path to alcohol problems through conduct problems: A family-based approach to very early intervention with risk. *Journal of Research on Adolescence, 4,* 249–269.

Mahler, M. (1952). On child psychosis in schizophrenia: Autistic and symbiotic infantile psychosis. In R. S. Eissler, H. Hartmann, A. Freud, & E. Kris (Eds.), *Psychoanalytic study of the child* (Vol. 7, pp. 286–305). New York: International University Press.

Main, M., & Weston, D. R. (1981). The quality of the toddlers' relationship to mother and to father: Related to conflict behavior and the readiness to establish new relationships. *Child Development, 52,* 932–940.

Maine, M. (1991). *Father hunger: Fathers, daughters and food.* Carlsbad, CA: Gurze Books.

Majoribanks, K. (1987). Gender-social class, family environments and adolescents' aspirations. *Australian Journal of Education, 31,* 43–54.

Majors, R. (1992). *Cool pose: The dilemmas of Black manhood in America.* Lexington, MA: Lexington Books.

Mallinckrodt, B. (1991). Clients' representations of childhood emotional bonds with parents, social support, and formation of the working alliance. *Journal of Counseling Psychology, 38,* 401–409.

Mann, B. J., Borduin, C. M., Henggeler, S. W., & Blaske, D. M. (1990). An investigation of systemic conceptualizations of parent–child coalitions and symptom change. *Journal of Consulting and Clinical Psychology, 58,* 336–344.

Manning, D. T., Balson, P. M., & Xenakis, S. (1986). The prevalence of Type A personality in the children of alcoholics. *Alcoholism: Clinical and Experimental Research, 10,* 184–189.

Marett, K. M., Sprenkle, D. H., & Lewis, R. A. (1992). Family members' perceptions of family boundaries and their relationship to family problems. *Family Therapy, 19,* 233–242.

Margalit, M. (1985). Perception of parents' behavior, familial satisfaction, and sense of coherence in hyperactive children. *Journal of School Psychology, 23,* 355–364.

Margalit, M., & Heiman, T. (1986a). Family climate and anxiety in families with learning disabled boys. *Journal of the American Academy of Child Psychiatry, 25,* 841–846.

Margalit, M., & Heiman, T. (1986b). Learning-disabled boys' anxiety, parental anxiety, and family climate. *Journal of Clinical Child Psychology, 15,* 248–253.

Margalit, M., Leyser, Y., & Avraham, Y. (1989). Classification and validation of family climate subtypes in kibbutz fathers of disabled and nondisabled children. *Journal of Child Psychology, 17,* 91–107.

Margolin, L. (1992). Sexual abuse by grandparents. *Child Abuse and Neglect, 16,* 735–741.

Margolin, L., & Larson, O. W. (1988). Assessing mothers' and fathers' violence toward children as a function of their involuntary participation in family work. *Journal of Family Violence, 3,* 209–224.

Marone, N. (1988). *How to father a successful daughter.* New York: Fawcett Crest.

Marsh, H. W. (1990). Two-parent, stepparent, and single-parent families: Changes in achievement, attitudes, and behaviors during the last two years of high school. *Journal of Educational Psychology, 82,* 327–340.

Marshall, C. (1992). *Expectant father: Helping the father-to-be understand and become a part of the pregnancy experience.* New York: Prima Publishers.

Marsiglio, W. (1986). Teenage fatherhood: High school completion and educational attainment. In A. B. Elster & M. E. Lamb (Eds.), *Adolescent fatherhood* (pp. 67–88). Hillsdale, NJ: Erlbaum.

Marsiglio, W. (1991). Paternal engagement activities with minor children. *Journal of Marriage and the Family, 53,* 973–986.

Marsiglio, W. (1992). Stepfathers with minor children living at home: Parenting perceptions and relationship quality. *Journal of Family Issues, 13,* 195–214.

Marsiglio, W. (Ed.). (1993). Fatherhood. *Journal of Family Issues, 14*(4).

Marsiglio, W. (Ed.). (1994). Fatherhood: Results from national surveys. *Journal of Family Issues, 15*(1).

Marsiglio, W. (Ed.). (1995). *Fatherhood: Contemporary theory, research, and social policy.* Thousand Oaks, CA: Sage.

Martin, B. (1977). Brief family intervention: Effectiveness and the importance of including the father. *Journal of Consulting and Clinical Psychology, 45,* 1002–1010.

Martin, B. (1987). Developmental perspectives on family theory and psychopathology. In T. Jacob (Ed.), *Family interaction and psychopathology: Theories, methods, and findings* (pp. 163–202). New York: Plenum.

Martin, E. D., & Sher, K. J. (1994). Family history of alcoholism, alcohol use disorders and the five-factor model of personality. *Journal of Studies on Alcohol, 55,* 81–90.

Martin, J. A. (1984). Neglected fathers: Limitations in diagnostic and treatment resources for violent men. *Child Abuse and Neglect, 8,* 387–392.

Martin, T. R., & Bracken, M. B. (1986). Association of low birth weight with passive smoke exposure in pregnancy. *American Journal of Epidemiology, 124,* 633–642.

Mash, E. J., & Johnston, C. (1983). Parental perceptions of child behavior problems, parenting self-esteem, and mothers' reported stress in younger and older hyperactive and normal children. *Journal of Consulting and Clinical Psychology, 51,* 86–99.

Mathew, R. J., Wilson, W. H., Blazer, D. G., & George, L. K. (1993). Psychiatric disorders in adult children of alcoholics: Data from the epidemiologic catchment area project. *American Journal of Psychiatry, 150,* 793–800.

Matthews, K. A., & Angulo, J. (1980). Measurement of the Type A behavior pattern in children: Assessment of children's competitiveness, impatience-anger, and aggression. *Child Development, 51,* 466–475.

Matthews, K. A., & Rodin, J. (1989). Women's changing work roles: Impact on health, family, and public policy. *American Psychologist, 44,* 1389–1393.

Matthews, K. A., Stoney, C. M., Rakaczky, C. J., & Jamison, W. (1986). Family characteristics and school achievements of Type A children. *Health Psychology, 5,* 453–467.

Mayle, P. (1990). *How to be a pregnant father.* New York: Carol Publishing Group.

Mead, M. (1949). *Male and female: A study of the sexes in a changing world.* New York: William Morrow.

Mebert, C. J. (1991). Dimensions of subjectivity in parents' ratings of infant temperament. *Child Development, 62,* 352–361.

Melvin, D., & Sherr, L. (1993). The child in the family: Responding to AIDS and HIV. *AIDS Care, 5,* 35–42.

Menon, M. S., Balakrishnan, S., Sujatha, D., Rajalakshmi, A. L., & Lulla, R. (1982). The father in the family of the schizophrenic. *International Journal of Family Psychiatry, 3,* 301–316.

Menotti, A., & Seccareccia, F. (1985). Physical activity at work and job responsibility as risk factors for fatal coronary disease and other causes of death. *Journal of Epidemiology and Community Health, 39,* 325–329.

Mercer, S. O., & Perdue, J. D. (1993). Munchausen syndrome by proxy: Social work's role. *Social Work, 38,* 74–81.

Merikangas, K. R., Prusoff, B. A., & Weissman, M. M. (1988). Parental concordance for affective disorders: Psychopathology in offspring. *Journal of Affective Disorders, 15,* 279–290.

Merikangas, K. R., & Spiker, D. G. (1982). Assortative mating among inpatients with primary affective disorder. *Psychological Medicine, 12,* 753–764.

Merikangas, K. R., Weissman, M., Prusoff, B. A., & John, K. (1988). Assortative mating and affective disorders: Psychopathology in offspring. *Psychiatry, 51,* 48–57.

Merikangas, K. R., Weissman, M., Prusoff, B. A., Pauls, D., & Leckman, J. (1985). Depressives with secondary alcoholism: Psychiatric disorders in offspring. *Journal of Studies on Alcohol, 46,* 199–204.

Messer, B., & Harter, S. (1986). *Manual for the Adult Self-Perception Profile.* Denver, CO: University of Denver.

Metzger, D. S., & Platt, J. J. (1987). Methadone dose levels and client characteristics in heroin addicts. *International Journal of the Addictions, 22,* 187–194.

Miklowitz, D. J., Goldstein, M. J., Doane, J. A., Nuechterlein, K. H., Strachan, A. M., Snyder, K. S., & Magana-Amato, A. (1989). Is expressed emotion an index of a transactional process? I. Parents' affective style. *Family Process, 28,* 153–167.

Miklowitz, D. J., Strachan, A. M., Goldstein, M. J., Doane, J. A., Snyder, K. S., Hogarty, G. E., & Falloon, I. R. H. (1986). Expressed emotion and communication deviance in the families of schizophrenics. *Journal of Abnormal Psychology, 95,* 60–66.

Miles, M. S., Funk, S. G., & Kasper, M. A. (1992). The stress response of mothers and fathers of preterm infants. *Research in Nursing and Health, 15,* 261–269.

Miletic, A. (1986). The interpersonal values of parents of normal and learning disabled children. *Journal of Learning Disabilities, 19,* 362–367.

Miller, D. L., & Kelley, M. L. (1992). Treatment acceptability: The effects of parent gender, marital adjustment, and child behavior. *Child and Family Behavior Therapy, 14,* 11–23.

Miller, J. B., & Lane, M. (1991). Relations between young adults and their parents. *Journal of Adolescence, 14,* 179–194.

Miller, P. H. (1989). *Theories of developmental psychology* (2nd ed.). New York: Freeman.

Miller, S. A., Davis, T. L., Wilde, C. A., & Brown, J. (1993). Parents' knowledge of their children's preferences. *International Journal of Behavioral Development, 16,* 35–60.

Mills, R. S. L., & Rubin, K. H. (1990). Parental beliefs about problematic social behaviors in early childhood. *Child Development, 61,* 138–151.

Minuchin, S. (1974). *Families and family therapy.* Cambridge, MA: Harvard University Press.

Mirande, A. (1988). Chicano fathers: Traditional perceptions and current realities. In P. Bronstein & C. P. Cowan (Eds.), *Fatherhood today: Men's changing role in the family* (pp. 93–106). New York: Wiley.

Mirande, A. (1991). Ethnicity and fatherhood. In F. W. Bozett & S. M. H. Hanson (Eds.), *Fatherhood and Families in Cultural Context* (pp. 53–82). New York: Springer.

Mitchell, J., McCauley, E., Burke, P., Calderon, R., & Schloredt, K. (1989). Psychopathology in parents of depressed children and adolescents. *Journal of the American Academy of Child and Adolescent Psychiatry, 28,* 352–357.

Mitchell, J., McCauley, E., Burke, P., & Moss, S. J. (1988). Phenomenology of depression in children and adolescents. *Journal of the American Academy of Child and Adolescent Psychiatry, 27,* 12–20.

Moes, D., Koegel, R. L., Schreibman, L., & Loos, L. M. (1992). Stress profiles for mothers and fathers of children with autism. *Psychological Reports, 71,* 1272–1274.

Money, J., & Ehrhardt, H. A. (1972). *Man and woman, boy and girl.* Baltimore: Johns Hopkins University Press.

Montemayor, R., & Brownlee, J. R. (1987). Fathers, mothers, and adolescents: Gender-based differences in parental roles during adolescence. *Journal of Youth and Adolescence, 16,* 281–291.

Moos, R. H. (1990). Conceptual and empirical approaches to developing family-based assessment procedures: Resolving the case of the Family Environment Scale. *Family Process, 29,* 199–208.

Moran, M. S. (1992). Attachment or loss within marriage: The effect of the medical model of birthing on the marital bond of love. *Pre- and Peri-Natal Psychology Journal, 6,* 265–279.

Morelli, G. A., & Tronick, E. Z. (1992). Efe fathers: One among many? A comparison of forager children's involvement with fathers and other males. *Social Development, 1,* 36–54.

Moreno, A., & Thelen, M. H. (1993). Parental factors related to bulimia nervosa. *Addictive Behaviors, 18,* 681–689.

Morey, L. C. (1991). *Personality Assessment Inventory manual.* Odessa, FL: Psychological Assessment Resources.

Mott, F. L. (1990). When is a father really gone? Paternal-child contact in father-absent homes. *Demography, 27,* 499–517.

Mott, F. L. (1994). Sons, daughters and fathers' absence: Differentials in father-leaving probabilities and in home environments. *Journal of Family Issues, 14,* 97–128.

Mowrer, O. (1950). *On learning theory and personality dynamics.* New York: Ronald.

Mulinski, P. (1989). Male alcoholics' perceptions of their fathers. *Journal of Nervous and Mental Disease, 177,* 101–104.

Mullis, R. L., & Mullis, A. K. (1990). The effects of context on parent-child interactions. *Journal of Genetic Psychology, 15,* 411–413.

Murphy, R. T., O'Farrell, T. J., Floyd, F. J., & Connors, G. J. (1991). School adjustment of children of alcoholic fathers: Comparison to normal controls. *Addictive Behaviors, 16,* 275–287.

Mussen, P., & Rutherford, E. (1963). Parent-child relations and parental personality in relation to young children's sex-role preferences. *Child Development, 34,* 589–607.

Musser, J. M., & Fleck, J. R. (1983). The relationship of paternal acceptance and control to college females' personality adjustment. *Adolescence, 18,* 907–916.

Myers, K. M., Burke, P., & McCauley, E. (1985). Suicidal behavior by hospitalized preadolescent children on a psychiatric unit. *Journal of the American Academy of Child Psychiatry, 24,* 474–480.

Nash, J. (1965). The father in contemporary culture and current psychological literature. *Child Development, 36,* 261–297.

Neapolitan, J. (1981). Parental influences on aggressive behavior: A social learning approach. *Adolescence, 16,* 831–840.

Nelson, C., & Valliant, P. M. (1993). Personality dynamics of adolescent boys where the father was absent. *Perceptual and Motor Skills, 76,* 435–443.

Nelson, J. N., & Simmerer, N. J. (1984). A correlational study of children's temperament and parent behavior. *Early Child Development and Care, 16,* 231–250.

Neufeldt, V. (Ed.). (1994). *Webster's New World dictionary of American English* (3rd ed.). New York: Prentice-Hall.

New, R. S., & Benigni, L. (1987). Italian fathers and infants: Cultural constraints on paternal behavior. In M. E. Lamb (Ed.), *The father's role: Cross-cultural perspectives* (pp. 139–167). Hillsdale, NJ: Erlbaum.

Newberry, A. M., Alexander, J. F., & Turner, C. W. (1991). Gender as a process variable in family therapy. *Journal of Family Psychology, 5,* 158–175.

NICHD Early Child Care Network. (1993). Child-care debate: Transformed or distorted? *American Psychologist, 48,* 692–693.

Nichols-Casebolt, A., & Garfinkel, I. (1991). Trends in paternity adjudications and child support awards. *Social Science Quarterly, 72,* 83–97.

Nickel, H., & Kocher, E. M. T. (1987). West Germany and the German-speaking countries. In M. E. Lamb (Ed.), *The father's role: Cross cultural perspectives* (pp. 89–114). Hillsdale, NJ: Erlbaum.

Nicol, A. R., Smith, J., Kay, B., Hall, D., Barlow, J., & Williams, B. (1988). A focused casework approach to the treatment of child abuse: A controlled comparison. *Journal of Child Psychology and Psychiatry, 29*, 703–711.

Nolin, M. J., & Petersen, K. K. (1992). Gender differences in parent-child communication about sexuality: An exploratory study. *Journal of Adolescent Research, 7*, 59–79.

Noller, P., & Callan, V. J. (1990). Adolescents' perceptions of the nature of their communication with parents. *Journal of Youth and Adolescence, 19*, 349–362.

Noppe, I. C., Noppe, L. D., & Hughes, F. P. (1991). Stress as a predictor of the quality of parent-infant interactions. *Journal of Genetic Psychology, 152*, 17–28.

Nsamenang, A. B. (1987). A West African perspective. In M. E. Lamb (Ed.), *The father's role: Cross-cultural perspectives* (pp. 273–293). Hillsdale, NJ: Erlbaum.

Nugent, J. K. (1987). The father's role in early Irish socialization: Historical and empirical perspectives. In M. E. Lamb (Ed.), *The father's role: Cross-cultural perspectives* (pp. 169–193). Hillsdale, NJ: Erlbaum.

Nydegger, C. N., & Mitteness, L. S. (1991). Fathers and their adult sons and daughters. *Marriage and Family Review, 16*, 249–256.

O'Donohue, W. T., Elliott, A. N., Nickerson, M., & Valentine, S. (1992). Perceived credibility of children's sexual abuse allegations: Effects of gender and sexual attitudes. *Violence and Victims, 7*, 147–155.

Offord, D., Allen, N., & Abrams, N. (1978). Parental psychiatric illness, broken homes, and delinquency. *Journal of the American Academy of Child Psychiatry, 17*, 224–238.

O'Keefe, M. (1994). Linking marital violence, mother-child/father-child aggression, and child behavior problems. *Journal of Family Violence, 9*, 63–78.

Okin, S. M. (1989). *Justice, gender, and the family.* New York: Basic Books.

Olson, D. H. (1986). Circumplex model: VII. Validation studies and FACES III. *Family Process, 25*, 337–351.

Olson, D. H., McCubbin, H. I., Barnes, H., Larsen, A., Muxem, M., & Wilson, M. (1985). *Family inventories.* St. Paul: University of Minnesota, Family Social Science.

O'Malley, S. S., Carey, K. B., & Maisto, S. A. (1986). Validity of young adults' reports of parental drinking practices. *Journal of Studies on Alcohol, 47*, 433–435.

O'Neil, R., & Greenberger, E. (1994). Patterns of commitment to work and parenting: Implications for role strain. *Journal of Marriage and the Family, 56*, 101–118.

Onstad,.S., Skre, I., Torgersen, S., & Kringlen, E. (1993). Parental representation in twins discordant for schizophrenia. *Psychological Medicine, 23*, 335–340.

O'Reilly, B. (1992, January 1). Why grade "A" executives get an "F" as parents. *Fortune,* pp. 36–46.

Orford, J., & Velleman, R. (1991). The environmental intergenerational transmission of alcohol problems: A comparison of two hypotheses. *British Journal of Medical Psychology, 64*, 189–200.

Orvaschel, H., Walsh-Allis, G., & Ye, W. (1988). Psychopathology in children of parents with recurrent depression. *Journal of Abnormal Child Psychology, 16,* 17–28.

Orvaschel, H., Weissman, M. M., & Kidd, K. K. (1980). Children and depression: The children of depressed parents, the childhood of depressed patients, depression in children. *Journal of Affective Disorders, 2,* 1–16.

Oyserman, D., Radin, N., & Benn, R. (1993). Dynamics in a three-generational family: Teens, grandparents, and babies. *Developmental Psychology, 29,* 564–572.

Oz, S., & Fine, M. (1991). Family relationship patterns: Perceptions of teenage mothers and their non-mother peers. *Journal of Adolescence, 14,* 293–304.

Paasch, K. M., & Teachman, J. D. (1991). Gender of children and receipt of assistance from absent fathers. *Journal of Family Issues, 12,* 450–466.

Pacheco, F., & Eme, R. (1993). An outcome study of the reunion between adoptees and biological parents. *Child Welfare, 72,* 53–64.

Padesky, C. A., & Hammen, C. L. (1981). Sex differences in depressive symptom expression and help-seeking among college students. *Sex Roles, 7,* 309–320.

Palkovitz, R. (1984). Parental attitudes and fathers' interactions with their 5-month-old infants. *Developmental Psychology, 20,* 1054–1060.

Papini, D. R., Roggman, L. A., & Anderson, J. (1991). Early-adolescent perceptions of attachment to mother and father: A test of the emotional-distancing and buffering hypotheses. *Journal of Early Adolescence, 11,* 258–275.

Parish, T. S. (1991). Ratings of self and parents by youth: Are they affected by family status, gender, and birth order? *Adolescence, 26,* 105–112.

Parish, T. S., & McCluskey, J. J. (1992). The relationship between parenting styles and young adults' self-concepts and evaluations of parents. *Adolescence, 27,* 915–918.

Parke, R. D. (1981). *Fathers.* Cambridge, MA: Harvard University Press.

Parke, R. D. (1990). In search of fathers: A narrative of an empirical journey. In I. E. Sigel & G. H. Brody (Eds.), *Methods of family research: Biographies of research Projects. Volume I: Normal families* (pp. 153–188). Hillsdale, NJ: Erlbaum.

Parke, R. D., MacDonald, K. B., Beitel, A., & Bhavnagri, N. (1988). The role of the family in the development of peer relationships. In R. Peters & R. J. McMahan (Eds.), *Social learning systems: Approaches to marriage and the family* (pp. 17–44). New York: Brunner/Mazel.

Parke, R. D., & Tinsley, B. R. (1981). The father's role in infancy: Determinants of involvement in caregiving and play. In M. E. Lamb (Ed.), *The role of the father in child development* (2nd ed., pp. 429–458). New York: Wiley.

Parker, G., Tupling, H., & Brown, L. B. (1979). A parental bonding instrument. *British Journal of Medical Psychology, 52,* 1–10.

Parker, H., & Parker, S. (1986). Father-daughter sexual abuse: An emerging perspective. *American Journal of Orthopsychiatry, 56,* 531–549.

Parsons, J., Kehle, T. J., & Owen, S. V. (1990). Incidence of behavior problems among children of Vietnam war veterans. *School Psychology International, 11,* 253–259.

Parsons, T., & Bales, R. (1955). *Family socialization and interaction process.* Glencoe, IL: Free Press.

Patterson, C. J. (1992). Children of lesbian and gay parents. *Child Development, 63,* 1025–1042.

Patterson, C. J., Kupersmidt, J. B., & Griesler, P. C. (1990). Children's perceptions of self and of relationships with others as a function of sociometric status. *Child Development, 61,* 1335–1349.

Patterson, G. R. (1982). *Coercive family process.* Eugene, OR: Castaglia.

Patterson, G. R. (Ed.). (1990). *Depression and aggression in family interaction.* Hillsdale, NJ: Erlbaum.

Paulson, S. E. (1994). Relations of parenting style and parental involvement with ninth-grade students' achievement. *Journal of Early Adolescence, 14,* 250–267.

Paulson, S. E., Hill, J. P., & Holmbeck, G. N. (1991). Distinguishing between perceived closeness and parental warmth in families with seventh-grade boys and girls. *Journal of Early Adolescence, 11,* 276–293.

Paulson, S. E., Koman, J. J., & Hill, J. P. (1990). Maternal employment and parent-child relations in families of seventh graders. *Journal of Early Adolescence, 10,* 279–295.

Payne, D. E., & Mussen, P. H. (1956). Parent–child relations and father identification among adolescent boys. *Journal of Abnormal and Social Psychology, 52,* 358–362.

Pearson, J., & Anhalt, J. (1994). Examining the connection between child access and child support. *Family and Conciliation Courts Review, 32,* 93–109.

Pedersen, F. A. (1976). Does research on children reared in father-absent families yield information on father influences? *Family Coordinator, 25,* 459–464.

Peery, J. C., Jensen, L., & Adams, G. R. (1985). The relationship between parents' attitudes toward child rearing and the sociometric status of their preschool children. *Journal of Psychology, 119,* 567–574.

Peled, E., & Edleson, J. L. (1992). Multiple perspectives on groupwork with children of battered women. *Violence and Victims, 7,* 327–346.

Penfold, P. S. (1985). Parent's perceived responsibility for children's problems. *Canadian Journal of Psychiatry, 30,* 255–258.

Peters, R. D., & McMahon, R. J. (1988). Converging models of family functioning. In R. D. Peters & R. J. McMahon (Eds.), *Social learning and systems approaches to marriage and the family* (pp. 3–14). New York: Brunner/Mazel.

Peterson, J. B., Finn, P. R., & Pihl, R. O. (1992). Cognitive dysfunction and the inherited predisposition to alcoholism. *Journal of Studies on Alcohol, 53,* 154–160.

Peterson, J. B., & Pihl, R. O. (1990). Information processing, neuropsychological function, and the inherited predisposition to alcoholism. *Neuropsychology Review, 1,* 343–369.

Pfannenstiel, A. E., & Honig, A. S. (1991). Prenatal intervention and support for low-income fathers. *Infant Mental Health Journal, 12,* 103–115.

Pfeffer, C. R., Newcorn, J., Kaplan, G., Mizruchi, M. S., & Plutchik, R. (1989). Subtypes of suicidal and assaultive behaviors in adolescent psychiatric inpatients: A research note. *Journal of Child Psychology and Psychiatry, 30,* 151–163.

Pfeffer, C. R., Plutchik, R., Mizruchi, M. S., & Lipkins, R. (1987). Assaultive behavior in child psychiatric inpatients, outpatients, and nonpatients. *Journal of the American Academy of Child and Adolescent Psychiatry, 26,* 256–261.

Pfeffer, C. R., Solomon, G., Plutchik, R., Mizruchi, M. S., & Weiner, A. (1985). Variables that predict assaultiveness in child psychiatric inpatients. *Journal of the American Academy of Child Psychiatry, 26,* 775–780.

Phares, V. (1992). Where's Poppa?: The relative lack of attention to the role of fathers in child and adolescent psychopathology. *American Psychologist, 47,* 656–664.

Phares, V. (1993a). Father absence, mother love, and other family issues that need to be questioned. *Journal of Family Psychology, 7,* 293–300.

Phares, V. (1993b). Perceptions of mothers' and fathers' responsibility for children's behavior. *Sex Roles, 11/12,* 839–851.

Phares, V. (1995). Fathers' and mothers' participation in research. *Adolescence, 30,* 593–602.

Phares, V., & Compas, B. E. (1992). The role of fathers in child and adolescent psychopathology: Make room for daddy. *Psychological Bulletin, 111,* 387–412.

Phares, V., Compas, B. E., & Howell, D. C. (1989). Perspectives on child behavior problems: Comparisons of children's self-reports with parent and teacher reports. *Psychological Assessment: A Journal of Consulting and Clinical Psychology, 1,* 68–71.

Pierce, L. H. (1987). Father-son incest: Using the literature to guide practice. *Social Casework, 68,* 67–74.

Pihl, R. O., Peterson, J., & Finn, P. R. (1990). Inherited predisposition to alcoholism: Characteristics of sons of male alcoholics. *Journal of Abnormal Psychology, 99,* 291–301.

Piotrkowski, C. S., & Gornick, L. K. (1987). Effects of work-related separations on children and families. In J. Bloom-Feshbach & S. Bloom-Feshbach (Eds.), *The psychology of separation and loss: Perspectives on development, life transitions, and clinical practice* (pp. 267–299). San Francisco: Jossey-Bass.

Piotrkowski, C. S., Rapaport, R. N., & Rapaport, R. (1987). Families and work. In M. B. Sussman & S. K. Steinmetz (Eds.), *Handbook of marriage and the family* (pp. 251–283). New York: Plenum.

Plass, P. S. (1993). African-American family homicide: Patterns in partner, parent, and child victimization, 1985–1987. *Journal of Black Studies, 23,* 515–538.

Pleck, J. H. (1985). *Working wives/working husbands.* Beverly Hills, CA: Sage.

Pleck, J. H. (1993). Are "family-supportive" employer policies relevant to men? In J. C. Hood (Ed.), *Men, work, and family* (pp. 217–237). Newbury Park, CA: Sage.

Plimpton, E. H., & Rosenblum, L. A. (1987). Maternal loss in nonhuman primates: Implications for human development. In J. Bloom-Feshbach & S. Bloom-Feshbach (Eds.), *The psychology of separation and loss: Perspectives on development, life transitions, and clinical practice* (pp. 63–86). San Francisco: Jossey-Bass.

Plomin, R., & Daniels, D. (1987). Why are children in the same family so different from one another? *Behavioral and Brain Sciences, 10,* 1–60.

Plomin, R., DeFries, J. C., & McClearn, G. E. (1990). *Behavioral genetics: A primer* (2nd ed.). New York: Freeman.

Plomin, R., Reiss, D., Hetherington, E. M., & Howe, G. W. (1994). Nature and nurture: Genetic contributions to measures of the family environment. *Developmental Psychology, 30,* 32–43.

Podsakoff, P. M., MacKenzie, S. B., Moorman, R. H., & Fetter, R. (1990). Transformational leader behaviors and their effects on followers' trust in leader, satisfaction, and organizational citizenship behaviors. *Leadership Quarterly, 1,* 107–142.

Pogrebin, L. C. (1980). *Growing up free.* New York: Bantam.

Polich, J., Pollock, V. E., & Bloom, F. E. (1994). Meta-analysis of P300 amplitude from males at risk for alcoholism. *Psychological Bulletin, 115,* 55–73.

Pollock, V. E., Schneider, L. S., Gabrielli, W. F., & Goodwin, D. W. (1987). Sex of parent and offspring in the transmission of alcoholism: A meta-analysis. *Journal of Nervous and Mental Disease, 175,* 668–673.

Pratt, M. W., Kerig, P. K., Cowan, P. A., & Cowan, C. P. (1992). Family worlds: Couple satisfaction, parenting style, and mothers' and fathers' speech to young children. *Merrill-Palmer Quarterly, 38,* 245–262.

Preli, R., & Protinsky, H. (1988). Aspects of family structures in alcoholic, recovered, and nonalcoholic families. *Journal of Marital and Family Therapy, 14,* 311–314.

Price-Bonham, S., & Skeen, P. (1979). A comparison of Black and White fathers with implications for parent education. *Family Coordinator, 28,* 53–59.

Prinz, R. J., Foster, S. L., Kent, R. N., & O'Leary, K. D. (1979). Multivariate assessment of conflict in distressed and nondistressed mother-adolescent dyads. *Journal of Applied Behavior Analysis, 12,* 691–700.

Pruett, K. D. (1987). *The nurturing father: Journey toward the complete man.* New York: Warner Books.

Pruett, K. D. (1989). The nurturing male: A longitudinal study of primary nurturing fathers. In S. H. Cath, A. Gurwitt, & L. Gunsberg (Eds.), *Fathers and their families* (pp. 389–405). Hillsdale, NJ: Analytic Press.

Pruett, K. D. (1993). The paternal presence. *Families in Society, 74,* 46–50.

Puig-Antich, J., Kaufman, J., Ryan, N. D., & Williamson, D. E. (1993). The psychosocial functioning and family environment of depressed adolescents. *Journal of the American Academy of Child and Adolescent Psychiatry, 32,* 244–253.

Puig-Antich, J., Lukens, E., Davies, M., Goetz, D., Brennan-Quattrock, J., & Todak, G. (1985a). Psychosocial functioning in prepubertal Major Depressive Disorders: I. Interpersonal relationships during the depressive episode. *Archives of General Psychiatry, 42,* 500–507.

Puig-Antich, J., Lukens, E., Davies, M., Goetz, D., Brennan-Quattrock, J., & Todak, G. (1985b). Psychosocial functioning in prepubertal Major Depressive Disorders: II. Interpersonal relationships after sustained recovery from an affective episode. *Archives of General Psychiatry, 42,* 511–517.

Quinton, D., & Rutter, M. (1984a). Parents with children in care: I. Current circumstances and parenting. *Journal of Child Psychology and Psychiatry, 25,* 211–229.

Quinton, D., & Rutter, M. (1984b). Parents with children in care: II. Intergenerational continuities. *Journal of Child Psychology and Psychiatry, 25,* 231–250.

Quittner, A. L., DiGirolamo, A. M., Michel, M., & Eigen, H. (1992). Parental response to cystic fibrosis: A contextual analysis of the diagnosis phase. *Journal of Pediatric Psychology, 17,* 683–704.

Rabin, A. I., & Greene, R. J. (1968). Assessing motivation for parenthood. *Journal of Psychology, 69,* 39–46.

Radin, N. (1976). The role of the father in cognitive, academic, and intellectual development. In M. E. Lamb (Ed.), *The role of the father in child development* (pp. 237–276). New York: Wiley.

Radin, N. (1981a). Childrearing fathers in intact families: An exploration of some antecedents and consequences. *Merrill-Palmer Quarterly, 27,* 489–514.

Radin, N. (1981b). The role of the father in cognitive, academic, and intellectual development. In M. E. Lamb (Ed.), *The role of the father in child development* (rev. ed., pp. 379–427). New York: Wiley.

Radin, N. (1982). Primary caregiving and role-sharing fathers. In M. E. Lamb (Ed.), *Non-traditional families: Parenting and child development* (pp. 173–204). Hillsdale, NJ: Erlbaum.

Radin, N., Oyserman, D., & Benn, R. (1991). Grandfathers, teen mothers and children under two. In P. K. Smith (Ed.), *The psychology of grandparenthood: An international perspective* (pp. 85–99). New York: Rutledge.

Radke-Yarrow, M., Cummings, E. M., Kuczynski, L., & Chapman, M. (1985). Patterns of attachment in two- and three-year-olds in normal families and families with parental depression. *Child Development, 56,* 884–893.

Radke-Yarrow, M., Nottelmann, E., Martinez, P., Fox, M. B., & Belmont, B. (1992). Young children of affectively ill parents: A longitudinal study of psychosocial development. *Journal of the American Academy of Child and Adolescent Psychiatry, 31,* 68–77.

Ramamurti, P. V., Jamuna, D., & Ramamurti, S. (1984). A study of coronary prone behaviour among a sample of executives and non-executives. *Indian Journal of Clinical Psychology, 11,* 75–77.

Rangaswamy, K. (1983). Personality dimensions of parents of schizophrenic children. *Indian Journal of Clinical Psychology, 10,* 391–397.

Reading, J., & Amatea, E. S. (1986). Role deviance or role diversification: Reassessing the psychosocial factors affecting the parenthood choice of career-oriented women. *Journal of Marriage and the Family, 48,* 255–260.

Reed, R. (1923). Changing conceptions of the maternal instinct. *Journal of Abnormal Psychology and Social Psychology, 18,* 78–87.

Reese, E., & Fivush, R. (1993). Parental styles of talking about the past. *Developmental Psychology, 29,* 596–606.

Reeves, J. C., Werry, J. S., Elkind, G. S., & Zametkin, A. (1987). Attention Deficit, Conduct, Oppositional, and Anxiety Disorders in children: II. Clinical characteristics. *Journal of the American Academy of Child and Adolescent Psychiatry, 26,* 144–155.

Regier, D. A., Boyd, J. H., Burke, J. D., Rae, D. S., Myers, J. K., Kramer, M., Robins, L. N., George, L. K., Karno, M., & Locke, B. Z. (1988). One-month prevalence of mental disorders in the United States. *Archives of General Psychiatry, 45,* 977–986.

Regier, D. A., Meyers, J. K., Kramer, M., Robins, L. N., Blazer, D. G., Hough, R. L., Eaton, W. W., & Locke, B. Z. (1984). The NIMH Epidemiologic Catchment Area program. *Archives of General Psychiatry, 41,* 934–941.

Reid, J. B., Kavanagh, K., & Baldwin, D. V. (1987). Abusive parents' perceptions of child problem behaviors: An example of parental bias. *Journal of Abnormal Child Psychology, 15,* 457–466.

Reidy, T. J., & Hochstadt, N. J. (1993). Attribution of blame in incest cases: A comparison of mental health professionals. *Child Abuse and Neglect, 17,* 371–381.

Reilly, T., Entwisle, D., & Doering, S. (1987). Socialization into parenthood: A longitudinal study of the development of self evaluations. *Journal of Marriage and the Family, 49,* 295–308.

Reisinger, J. J. (1982). Unprogrammed learning of differential attention by fathers of oppositional children. *Journal of Behavior Therapy and Experimental Psychiatry, 13,* 203–208.

Rende, R. D., Slomkowski, C. L., Stocker, C., Fulker, D. W., & Plomin, R. (1992). Genetic and environmental influences on maternal and sibling interaction in middle childhood: A sibling adoption study. *Developmental Psychology, 28,* 484–490.

Renouf, E. M. (1991). Always on your mind but not always on your hands: Perspectives on parenting, particularly fatherhood. *Australian Journal of Marriage and Family, 12,* 39–45.

Repetti, R. L. (1989). Effects of daily workload on subsequent behavior during marital interaction: The roles of social withdrawal and spouse support. *Journal of Personality and Social Psychology, 57,* 651–659.

Resnick, S. M., Gottesman, I. I., & McGue, M. (1993). Sensation seeking in opposite-sex twins: An effect of prenatal hormones? *Behavior Genetics, 23,* 323–329.

Retterstol, N., & Opjordsmoen, S. (1991). Fatherhood, impending or newly established, precipitating delusional disorders: Long term course and outcome. *Psychopathology, 24,* 232–237.

Rheingold, J. (1967). *The mother, anxiety, and death: The catastrophic death complex.* Boston: Little Brown.

Richards, C. A., & Goldenberg, I. (1985). Joint custody: Current issues and implications for treatment. *American Journal of Family Therapy, 13,* 33–40.

Richards, M. H., Gitelson, I. B., Petersen, A. C., & Hurtig, A. L. (1991). Adolescent personality in girls and boys. *Psychology of Women Quarterly, 15,* 65–81.

Richman, J. A., & Flaherty, J. A. (1987). Adult psychosocial assets and depressive mood over time: Effects of internalized childhood attachments. *Journal of Nervous and Mental Disease, 175,* 703–712.

Rickard, K. (1988). The occurrence of maladaptive health-related behaviors and teacher-rated conduct problems in children of chronic low back pain patients. *Journal of Behavioral Medicine, 11,* 107–116.

Rickel, A. U., & Biasatti, L. L. (1982). Modification of the Block Child Rearing Practices Report. *Journal of Clinical Psychology, 38,* 129–134.

Rickel, A. U., & Langner, T. S. (1985). Short- and long-term effects of marital disruption on children. *American Journal of Community Psychology, 13,* 599–611.

Riesch, S. K., Tosi, C. B., Thurston, C. A., & Forsyth, D. M. (1993). Effects of communication training on parents and young adolescents. *Nursing Research, 42,* 10–16.

Rimmer, J. (1982). The children of alcoholics: An exploratory study. *Children and Youth Services Review, 4,* 365–373.

Ringwalt, C., & Earp, J. (1988). Attributing responsibility in cases of father-daughter sexual abuse. *Child Abuse and Neglect, 12,* 273–281.

Risman, B. J. (1987). Intimate relationships from a microstructural perspective: Men who mother. *Gender & Society, 1,* 6–32.

Ritchie, I. B., & Ross, G. F. (1992). Fathering response patterns: A non-metropolitan study of demographic and behavioural associations. *Australian Journal of Marriage and Family, 13,* 158–165.

Roberts, N. S. (1986). Teratology. In W. W. Beck (Ed.), *Obstetrics and gynecology* (pp. 135–139). New York: Wiley.

Roberts, S. (1993). *Who we are: A portrait of America based on the latest U.S. Census.* New York: Random House.

Robins, L. N., Helzer, J. E., Weissman, M. M., Orvaschel, H., Gruenberg, E., Burke, J. D., & Regier, D. A. (1984). Lifetime prevalence of specific psychiatric disorders in three sites. *Archives of General Psychiatry, 41,* 949–958.

Robins, L. N., & Regier, D. A. (1991). *Psychiatric disorders in America: The Epidemiologic Catchment Area Study.* New York: Free Press.

Robinson, B. E. (1988a). *Teenage fathers.* Lexington, MA: Lexington Books.

Robinson, B. E. (1988b). Teenage pregnancy from the father's perspective. *American Journal of Orthopsychiatry, 58,* 48–51.

Robinson, B. E., & Barret, R. L. (1986). *The developing father: Emerging roles in contemporary society.* New York: Guilford.

Rode, S. S., Chang, P., Fisch, R. O., & Sroufe, L. A. (1981). Attachment patterns of infants separated at birth. *Developmental Psychology, 17,* 188–191.

Roehling, P. V., & Robin, A. L. (1986). Development and validation of the Family Beliefs Inventory: A measure of unrealistic beliefs among parents and adolescents. *Journal of Consulting and Clinical Psychology, 54,* 693–697.

Rogeness, G. A., Amrung, S. A., Macedo, C. A., Harris, W. R., & Fisher, C. (1986). Psychopathology in abused or neglected children. *Journal of the American Academy of Child Psychiatry, 25,* 659–665.

Roggman, L. A. (1992). Fathers with mothers and infants at the mall: Parental sex differences. *Early Child Development and Care, 79,* 65–72.

Rohde, P., Lewinsohn, P. M., & Seeley, J. R. (1991). Comorbidity of unipolar depression: II. Comorbidity with other mental disorders in adolescents and adults. *Journal of Abnormal Psychology, 100,* 214–222.

Rolf, J., Masten, A. S., Cicchetti, D., Neuchterlein, K. H., & Weintraub, S. (Eds.). (1990). *Risk and protective factors in the development of psychopathology.* New York: Cambridge University Press.

Roopnarine, J. L., & Adams, G. R. (1987). The interactional teaching patterns of mothers and fathers with their popular, moderately popular, or unpopular children. *Journal of Abnormal Child Psychology, 15,* 125–136.

Roopnarine, J. L., & Ahmeduzzaman, M. (1993). Puerto Rican fathers' involvement with their preschool-age children. *Hispanic Journal of Behavioral Sciences, 15,* 96–107.

Rosen, K. S., & Rothbaum, F. (1993). Quality of parental caregiving and security of attachment. *Developmental Psychology, 29,* 358–367.

Rosenheck, R. (1986). Impact of posttraumatic stress disorder of World War II on the next generation. *Journal of Nervous and Mental Disease, 174,* 319–327.

Rosenthal, K. M., & Keshet, H. F. (1981). *Fathers without partners: A study of fathers and the family after marital separation.* Totowa, NJ: Rowman & Littlefield.

Rosenthal, R., & Rosnow, R. L. (1975). *The volunteer subject.* New York: Wiley.

Rothbaum, F., & Weisz, J. R. (1994). Parental caregiving and child externalizing behavior in nonclinical samples: A meta-analysis. *Psychological Bulletin, 116,* 55–74.

Rotter, J. B. (1954). *Social learning and clinical psychology.* Englewood Cliffs, NJ: Prentice-Hall.

Russell, A., Russell, G., & Midwinter, D. (1992). Observer influences on mothers and fathers: Self-reported influence during a home observation. *Merrill-Palmer Quarterly, 38,* 263–283.

Russell, D. E. H. (1986). *The secret trauma: Incest in the lives of girls and women.* New York: Basic Books.

Russell, G. (1983). *The changing role of fathers?* St. Lucia, Queensland, Australia: University of Queensland Press.

Russell, G. (1986a). Grandfathers: Making up for lost opportunities. In R. A. Lewis & R. E. Salt (Eds.), *Men in families* (pp. 233–259). Beverly Hills, CA: Sage.

Russell, G. (1986b). Primary caretaking and role-sharing fathers. In M. E. Lamb (Ed.), *The father's role: Applied perspectives* (pp. 29–57). New York: Wiley.

Russell, G. (1987). Fatherhood in Australia. In M. E. Lamb (Ed.), *The father's role: Cross-cultural perspectives* (pp. 333–358). Hillsdale, NJ: Erlbaum.

Russell, G., & Radojevic, M. (1992). The changing role of fathers?: Current understandings and future directions for research and practice. *Infant Mental Health Journal, 13,* 296–311.

Russell, G., & Russell, A. (1987). Mother-child and father-child relationships in middle childhood. *Child Development, 58,* 1573–1585.

Russell, J. D., Kopec-Schrader, E., Rey, J. M., & Beumont, P. J. (1992). The Parental Bonding Instrument in adolescent patients with anorexia nervosa. *Acta Psychiatrica Scandinavica, 86,* 236–239.

Russo, N. F. (1979). Overview: Sex roles, fertility and the motherhood mandate. *Psychology of Women Quarterly, 4,* 7–15.

Russo, N. F. (1990). Overview: Forging research priorities for women's mental health. *American Psychologist, 45,* 368–373.

Saarnio, D. A. (1994, April). *Recollections of adolescence: Conflict and closeness with mothers and fathers.* Paper presented at the Biennial Conference on Human Development, Pittsburgh, PA.

Sachs, B. (1986). Mastering the resistance of working-class fathers to family therapy. *Family Therapy, 13,* 121–132.

Sagi, A. (1982). Antecedents and consequences of various degrees of parental involvement in childrearing: The Israeli project. In M. E. Lamb (Ed.), *Nontraditional families: Parenting and child development* (pp. 205–232). Hillsdale, NJ: Erlbaum.

Sagi, A., Koren, N., & Weinberg, M. (1987). Fathers in Israel. In M. E. Lamb (Ed.), *The father's role: Cross-cultural perspectives* (pp. 197–226). Hillsdale, NJ: Erlbaum.

Sameroff, A. J., Seifer, R., & Zax, M. (1982). Early development of children at risk for emotional disorder. *Monographs of the Society for Research in Child Development, 47*(7, Serial No. 199).

Santoli, A. (1994, May 29). They turn young men with children into fathers. *Parade Magazine,* pp. 16–19.

Santrock, J. W., & Warshak, R. A. (1986). Development, relationships, and legal/clinical considerations in father-custody families. In M. E. Lamb, *The father's role: Applied Perspectives* (pp. 135–163). New York: Wiley.

Santrock, J. W., Warshak, R. A., & Elliott, G. L. (1982). Social development and parent-child interaction in father-custody and stepmother families. In M. E. Lamb (Ed.), *Nontraditional families: Parenting and child development* (pp. 289–314). Hillsdale, NJ: Erlbaum.

Sanua, V. D. (1961). Sociocultural factors in families of schizophrenics: A review of the literature. *Psychiatry: Journal for the Study of Interpersonal Processes, 24,* 246–265.

Sanua, V. D. (1963). The sociocultural aspects of schizophrenia: A comparison of Protestant and Jewish schizophrenics. *International Journal of Social Psychiatry, 9,* 27–36.

Sanua, V. D. (1986a). The personality and psychological adjustment of family members with autistic children: I. A critical review of the research in Britain. *International Journal of Family Psychiatry, 7,* 221–260.

Sanua, V. D. (1986b). The personality and psychological adjustment of family members of autistic children: II. A critical review of the literature research in the United States. *International Journal of Family Psychiatry, 7,* 331–358.

Sarason, B. R., Pierce, G. R., Bannerman, A., & Sarason, I. G. (1993). Investigating the antecedents of perceived social support: Parents' views of and behavior toward their children. *Journal of Personality and Social Psychology, 65,* 1071–1085.

Sarason, I., Johnson, H., & Seigel, M. (1978). Assessing the impact of life changes: Development of the life experiences survey. *Journal of Consulting and Clinical Psychology, 46,* 932–946.

Sariola, H., & Uutela, A. (1992). The prevalence and context of family violence against children in Finland. *Child Abuse and Neglect, 16,* 823–832.

Sawin, D. B., & Parke, R. D. (1979). Father's affectionate stimulation and caregiving behaviors with newborn infants. *Family Coordinator, 28,* 509–513.

Sawyer, M. G., Sarris, A., Baghurst, P. A., Cross, D. G., & Kalucy, R. S. (1988). Family assessment device: Reports from mothers, fathers, and adolescents in community and clinic families. *Journal of Marital and Family Therapy, 14,* 287–296.

Scanzoni, J., & Arnett, C. (1987). Enlarging the understanding of marital commitment via religious devoutness, gender role preferences, and locus of marital control. *Journal of Family Issues, 8,* 136–156.

Scarr, S., Phillips, D., & McCartney, K. (1989). Working mothers and their families. *American Psychologist, 44,* 1402–1409.

Scarr, S., Phillips, D., & McCartney, K. (1990). Facts, fantasies and the future of child care in the United States. *Psychological Science, 1,* 26–35.

Schachar, R., & Wachsmuth, R. (1990). Oppositional disorder in children: A validation study comparing conduct disorder, oppositional disorder and normal control children. *Journal of Child Psychology and Psychiatry, 31,* 1089–1102.

Schaefer, E. S. (1965). Children's Reports of Parental Behavior: An inventory. *Child Development, 36,* 413–424.

Schaffer, H. R. (1971). *The growth of sociability.* Harmondsworth: Penguin.

Schaughency, E. A., & Lahey, B. B. (1985). Mothers' and fathers' perceptions of child deviance: Roles of child behavior, parental depression, and marital satisfaction. *Journal of Consulting and Clinical Psychology, 53,* 718–723.

Scheck, D. C. (1979). Two measures of parental consistency. *Psychology, 16,* 37–39.

Schludermann, S., & Schludermann, E. (1970). Replicability of factors in Children's Report of Parent Behavior (CRPBI). *Journal of Psychology, 76,* 239–249.

Schobinger, R., Florin, I., Zimmer, C., & Lindemann, H. (1992). Childhood asthma: Paternal critical attitude and father-child interaction. *Journal of Psychosomatic Research, 36,* 743–750.

Schodorf, J. K., & Edwards, H. T. (1983). Comparative analysis of parent-child interactions with Language-Disordered and linguistically normal children. *Journal of Communication Disorders, 16,* 71–83.

Schor, E. L. (1988). Families, family roles, and psychological diagnoses in primary care. *Journal of Developmental and Behavioral Pediatrics, 9,* 327–332.

Schuckit, M. A. (1984). Relationship between the course of primary alcoholism in men and family history. *Journal of Studies on Alcohol, 45,* 334–338.

Schuldberg, D., & Guisinger, S. (1991). Divorced fathers describe their former wives: Devaluation and contrast. *Journal of Divorce and Remarriage, 14,* 61–87.

Schwalb, D. W., Imaizumi, N., & Nakazawa, J. (1987). The modern Japanese father: Roles and problems in a changing society. In M. E. Lamb (Ed.), *The father's role: Cross-cultural perspectives* (pp. 247–269). Hillsdale, NJ: Erlbaum.

Schwartz-Bickenbach, D., Schulte-Hobein, B., Abt, S., Plum, C., & Nau, H. (1987). Smoking and passive smoking during pregnancy and early infancy: Effects on birth weight, lactation period, and cotinine concentrations in mother's milk and infant's urine. *Toxicology Letters, 35,* 73–81.

Schwarz, J. C., Barton-Henry, M. L., & Pruzinsky, T. (1985). Assessing child-rearing behaviors: A comparison of ratings made by mother, father, child, and sibling on the CRPBI. *Child Development, 56,* 462–479.

Schwarz, J. C., & Zuroff, D. C. (1979). Family structure and depression in female college students: Effects of parental conflict, decision-making power, and inconsistency of love. *Journal of Abnormal Psychology, 88,* 398–406.

Scott, R. L., & Stone, D. A. (1986a). MMPI measures of psychological disturbance in adolescent and adult victims of father-daughter incest. *Journal of Clinical Psychology, 42,* 251–259.

Scott, R. L., & Stone, D. A. (1986b). MMPI profile constellations in incest families. *Journal of Consulting and Clinical Psychology, 54,* 364–368.

Scull, C. S. (Ed.). (1992). *Fathers, sons, and daughters: Exploring fatherhood, renewing the bond.* Los Angeles: Jeremy P. Tarcher, Inc.

Sears, R. R. (1957). Identification as a form of behavior development. In P. B. Harris (Ed.), *The concept of development* (pp. 149–161). Minneapolis: University of Minnesota Press.

Sears, R. R., Maccoby, E. E., & Levin, H. (1957). *Patterns in child rearing.* Evanston, IL: Row-Peterson.

Sebald, H. (1976). *Momism: The silent disease of America.* Chicago: Nelson-Hall.

Secunda, V. (1992). *Women and their fathers: The sexual and romantic impact of the first man in your life.* New York: Delacorte Press.

Seghorn, T. K., Prentky, R. A., & Boucher, R. J. (1987). Childhood sexual abuse in the lives of sexually aggressive offenders. *Journal of the American Academy of Child and Adolescent Psychiatry, 26,* 262–267.

Seilhamer, R. A., Jacob, T., & Dunn, N. J. (1993). The impact of alcohol consumption on parent-child relationships in families of alcoholics. *Journal of Studies on Alcohol, 54,* 189–198.

Seligman, M. E. P., Peterson, C., Kaslow, N. J., Tanenbaum, R. L., Alloy, L. B., & Abramson, L. Y. (1984). Attributional style and depressive symptoms among children. *Journal of Abnormal Psychology, 93,* 235–238.

Seltzer, J. A. (1991). Relationships between fathers and children who live apart: The father's role after separation. *Journal of Marriage and the Family, 53,* 79–101.

Seltzer, J. A., & Bianchi, S. M. (1988). Children's contact with absent parents. *Journal of Marriage and the Family, 50,* 663–677.

Seltzer, J. A., & Brandreth, Y. (1994). What fathers say about involvement with children after separation. *Journal of Family Issues, 14,* 49–77.

Seraganian, P., Roskies, E., Hanley, J. A., & Oseasohn, R. (1987). Failure to alter psychophysiological reactivity in Type A men with physical exercise or stress management programs. *Psychology and Health, 1,* 195–213.

Shapiro, J. L. (1987, January). The expectant father. *Psychology Today,* pp. 36–42.

Shapiro, J. L. (1993). *The measure of a man: Becoming the father you wish your father had been.* New York: Delacorte Press.

Shapiro, R. J., & Budman, S. H. (1973). Defection, termination, and continuation in family and individual therapy. *Family Process, 12,* 55–67.

Shaw, D. S., & Emery, R. E. (1988). Chronic family adversity and school-age children's adjustment. *Journal of the American Academy of Adolescent Psychiatry, 27,* 200–206.

Shaw, E., & Burns, A. (1993). Guilt and the working parent. *Australian Journal of Marriage and Family, 14,* 30–43.

Shaw, M. E., & Costanzo, P. R. (1982). *Theories of social psychology* (2nd ed.). New York: McGraw-Hill.

Sher, K. J. (1985). Excluding problem drinkers in high-risk studies of alcoholism: Effect of screening criteria on high-risk versus low-risk comparisons. *Journal of Abnormal Psychology, 94,* 106–109.

Sher, K. J. (1991). *Children of alcoholics: A critical appraisal of theory and research.* Chicago: University of Chicago Press.

Sher, K. J., Walitzer, K. S., Wood, P. K., & Brent, E. E. (1991). Characteristics of children of alcoholics: Putative risk factors, substance use and abuse, and psychopathology. *Journal of Abnormal Psychology, 100,* 427–448.

Shields, S. A. (1975). Functionalism, Darwinism, and the psychology of women: A study of social myth. *American Psychologist, 30,* 739–754.

Shrier, D. K., Simring, S. K., Shapiro, E. T., Greif, J. B., & Lindenthal, J. J. (1991). Level of satisfaction of fathers and mothers with joint or sole custody arrangements: Results of a questionnaire. *Journal of Divorce and Remarriage, 16,* 163–169.

Shulman, S., & Collins, W. A. (Eds.). (1993). *Father-adolescent relationships.* San Francisco: Jossey-Bass.

Shulman, S., Collins, W. A., & Dital, M. (1993). Parent-child relationships and peer-perceived competence during middle childhood and preadolescence in Israel. *Journal of Early Adolescence, 13,* 204–218.

Shulman, S., & Zohar, D. (1991). Family type and behavior problems of three-year-olds. *American Journal of Family Therapy, 19,* 266–276.

Sieber, J. E., & Saks, M. J. (1989). A census of subject pool characteristics and policies. *American Psychologist, 44,* 1053–1061.

Siegal, M. (1987). Are sons and daughters treated more differently by fathers than by mothers? *Developmental Review, 7,* 183–209.

Siegelman, M. (1981). Parental backgrounds of homosexual and heterosexual women: A cross national replication. *Archives of Sexual Behavior, 10,* 371–378.

Sigel, I. E., & Parke, R. D. (1987). Structural analysis of parent-child research models. *Journal of Applied Developmental Psychology, 8,* 123–137.

Sigelman, C. K., & Adams, R. M. (1990). Family interactions in public: Parent-child distance and touching. *Journal of Nonverbal Behavior, 14,* 63–75.

Silber, S., Bermann, E., Henderson, M., & Lehman, A. (1993). Patterns of influence and response in abusing and nonabusing families. *Journal of Family Violence, 8,* 27–38.

Silverberg, S. B., & Steinberg, L. (1987). Adolescent autonomy, parent-adolescent conflict, and parental well-being. *Journal of Youth and Adolescence, 16,* 293–312.

Silverstein, L. B. (1991). Transforming the debate about child care and maternal employment. *American Psychologist, 46,* 1025–1032.

Silverstein, L. B. (1993a). Primate research, family politics, and social policy: Transforming "cads" into "dads." *Journal of Family Psychology, 7,* 267–282.

Silverstein, L. B. (1993b). Reply to comments on the child-care debate. *American Psychologist, 48,* 694.

Silverton, L., Mednick, S. A., Schulsinger, F., Parnas, J., & Harrington, M. E. (1988). Genetic risk for schizophrenia, birthweight, and cerebral ventricular enlargement. *Journal of Abnormal Psychology, 97,* 496–498.

Simeonsson, R. J., & Rosenthal, S. L. (1992). Developmental models and clinical practice. In C. E. Walker & M. C. Roberts (Eds.), *Handbook of clinical child psychology* (2nd ed., pp. 19–31). New York: Wiley.

Simms, M. D., & Bolden, B. J. (1991). The Family Reunification Project: Facilitating regular contact among foster children, biological families, and foster families. *Child Welfare, 70,* 679–690.

Simon, R. W. (1992). Parental role strains, salience of parental identity and gender differences in psychological distress. *Journal of Health and Social Behavior, 33,* 25–35.

Simonds, P. E. (1974). *The social primates.* New York: Harper & Row.

Simons, R. L., Lorenz, F. O., Conger, R. D., & Wu, C. I. (1992). Support from spouse as mediator and moderator of the disruptive influence of economic strain on parenting. *Child Development, 63,* 1282–1301.

Simons, R. L., Whitbeck, L. B., Beaman, J., & Conger, R. D. (1994). The impact of mothers parenting, involvement by nonresidential fathers, and parental conflict on the adjustment of adolescent children. *Journal of Marriage and the Family, 56,* 356–374.

Simons, R. L., Whitbeck, L. B., Conger, R. D., & Chyi-In, W. (1991). Intergenerational transmission of harsh parenting. *Developmental Psychology, 27,* 159–171.

Singhal, S., & Dutta, A. (1990). Who commits patricide? *Acta Psychiatrica Scandinavica, 82,* 40–43.

Sirles, E. A., Smith, J. A., & Kusama, H. (1989). Psychiatric status of intrafamilial sexual abuse victims. *Journal of the American Academy of Child and Adolescent Psychiatry, 28,* 225–229.

Skinner, H. A., Steinhauser, P. D., & Santa-Barbara, J. (1983). The Family Assessment Measure. *Canadian Journal of Community Mental Health, 2,* 91–105.

Small, S. A. (1988). Parental self-esteem and its relationship to childrearing practices, parent-adolescent interaction and adolescent behavior. *Journal of Marriage and the Family, 50,* 1063–1072.

Smith, M. A., & Jenkins, J. M. (1991). The effects of marital disharmony on prepubertal children. *Journal of Abnormal Child Psychology, 19,* 625–644.

Smith, T. E. (1991). Agreement of adolescent educational expectations with perceived maternal and paternal educational goals. *Youth and Society, 23,* 155–174.

Snarey, J. (1993). *How fathers care for the next generation: A four-decade study.* Cambridge, MA: Harvard University Press.

Sobol, M. P., Ashbourne, D. T., Earn, B. M., & Cunningham, C. E. (1989). Parents' attributions for achieving compliance from Attention-Deficit Disordered children. *Journal of Abnormal Child Psychology, 17,* 359–369.

Solomon, C. D. (1993, January 6). The Child Support Enforcement Program: A fact sheet. *Congressional Research Service Report for Congress,* pp. 1–2.

Sonenstein, F. L. (1993, Summer). Linking children to their fathers. *The Urban Institute: Policy and Research Report,* p. 24.

Sonenstein, F. L., & Calhoun, C. A. (1990). Determinants of child support: A pilot survey of absent parents. *Contemporary Policy Issues, 8,* 75–94.

Speechley, K. N., & Noh, S. (1992). Surviving childhood cancer, social support, and parents' psychological adjustment. *Journal of Pediatric Psychology, 17,* 15–31.

Spence, J. T., & Helmreich, R. L. (1978). *Masculinity and femininity: Their psychological dimensions, correlates, and antecedents.* Austin: University of Texas Press.

Spigelman, G., Spigelman, A., & Englesson, I. L. (1992). Analysis of family drawings: A comparison between children from divorce and non-divorce families. *Journal of Divorce and Remarriage, 18,* 31–54.

Spitze, G. (1988). Women's employment and family relations: A review. *Journal of Marriage and the Family, 50,* 595–618.

Spitze, G., & Logan, J. R. (1989). Gender differences in family support: Is there a payoff? *Gerontologist, 29,* 108–113.

Spitze, G., & Logan, J. R. (1992). Helping as a component of parent-adult child relations. *Research on Aging, 14,* 291–312.

Spitze, G., & Miner, S. (1992). Gender differences in adult child contact among Black elderly parents. *Gerontologist, 32,* 213–218.

Spock, B., & Rothenberg, M. B. (1992). *Dr. Spock's baby and child care.* New York: Pocket Books.

Standage, K. (1986). Socialization scores in psychiatric patients and their implications for the diagnosis of personality disorders. *Canadian Journal of Psychiatry, 31,* 138–141.

Stanger, C., & Lewis, M. (1993). Agreement among parents, teachers, and children on internalizing and externalizing behavior problems. *Journal of Clinical Child Psychology, 22,* 107–115.

Starrels, M. E. (1994). Gender differences in parent-child relations. *Journal of Family Issues, 14,* 148–165.

Stattin, H., & Klackenberg-Larsson, I. (1991). The short- and long-term implications for parent-child relations of parents' prenatal preferences for their child's gender. *Developmental Psychology, 27,* 141–147.

Stearns, P. N. (1991). Fatherhood in historical perspective: The role of social change. In F. W. Bozett & S. M. H. Hanson (Eds.), *Fatherhood and families in cultural context* (pp. 28–52). New York: Springer.

Steinberg, L. (1987). Recent research on the family at adolescence: The extent and nature of sex differences. *Journal of Youth and Adolescence, 16,* 191–197.

Steinhauer, P. D. (1987). The family as a small group: The process model of family functioning. In T. Jacob (Eds.), *Family interaction and psychopathology: Theories, methods, and findings* (pp. 67–115). New York: Plenum.

Steinhauer, P. D., Santa-Barbara, J., & Skinner, H. A. (1984). Clinical applications of the process model of family functioning. *Canadian Journal of Psychiatry, 29,* 98–111.

Steinhausen, H. C., Gobel, D., & Nestler, V. (1984). Psychopathology in the offspring of alcoholic parents. *Journal of the American Academy of Child Psychiatry, 23,* 465–471.

Sternberg, K. J., Lamb, M. E., Greenbaum, C., Cicchetti, D., Dawud, S., Cortes, R. M., Krispin, O., & Lorey, F. (1993). Effects of domestic violence on children's behavior problems and depression. *Developmental Psychology, 29,* 44–52.

Stevenson, M. B., Leavitt, L. A., Thompson, R. H., & Roach, M. A. (1988). A social relations model analysis of parent and child play. *Developmental Psychology, 24,* 101–108.

Stevenson, M. R., & Black, K. N. (1988). Paternal absence and sex-role development: A meta-analysis. *Child Development, 59,* 793–814.

Stewart, M. A., & deBlois, C. S. (1983). Father-son resemblances in aggressive and antisocial behaviour. *British Journal of Psychiatry, 142,* 78–84.

Stewart, M. A., deBlois, C. S., & Cummings, C. (1980). Psychiatric disorder in the parents of hyperactive boys and those with Conduct Disorder. *Journal of Child Psychology and Psychiatry, 21,* 283–292.

Stifter, C. A., & Fox, N. A. (1990). Infant reactivity: Physiological correlates of newborn and five month temperament. *Developmental Psychology, 26,* 582–588.

Stollak, G. E., Messe, L. A., Michaels, G. Y., Buldain, R., Catlin, R. T., & Paritee, F. (1982). Parental interpersonal perceptual style, child adjustment, and parent-child interactions. *Journal of Abnormal Child Psychology, 10,* 61–76.

Stouthamer-Loeber, M., & Loeber, R. (1986). Boys who lie. *Journal of Abnormal Child Psychology, 14,* 551–564.

Strachan, A. M., Feingold, D., Goldstein, M. J., Miklowitz, D. J., & Nuechterlein, K. H. (1989). Is expressed emotion an index of a transactional process? II. Patient's coping style. *Family Process, 28,* 169–181.

Strupp, H. H. (1981). Clinical research, practice, and the crisis of confidence. *Journal of Consulting and Clinical Psychology, 49,* 216–219.

Strupp, H. H. (1989). Psychotherapy: Can the practitioner learn from the researcher? *American Psychologist, 44,* 717–724.

Studer, J. (1993). A comparison of the self-concepts of adolescents from intact, maternal custodial, and paternal custodial families. *Journal of Divorce and Remarriage, 19,* 219–227.

Suinn, R. (1984). *Fundamentals of abnormal psychology.* Chicago: Nelson-Hall.

Sullivan, S. A. (1992). *The father's almanac* (rev. ed.). New York: Doubleday.

Suppal, P. (1994, April). *Maternal employment status and men's involvement in childcare: Perspectives from North India.* Paper presented at the Biennial Conference on Human Development, Pittsburgh, PA.

Swanson, L., & Biaggio, M. K. (1985). Therapeutic perspectives on father-daughter incest. *American Journal of Psychiatry, 142,* 667–674.

Swartzman-Schatman, S. B., & Schinke, S. P. (1993). The effect of mid life divorce on late adolescent and young adult children. *Journal of Divorce and Remarriage, 19,* 209–218.

Sweda, M. G., Sines, J. O., Lauer, R. M., & Clarke, W. R. (1986). Familial aggregation of Type A behavior. *Journal of Behavioral Medicine, 9,* 23–32.

Swigart, J. (1991). *The myth of the bad mother: The emotional realities of mothering.* New York: Doubleday.

Szapocznik, J., Perez-Vidal, A., Brickman, A. L., Foote, F. H., Santisteban, D., Hervis, O., & Kurtines, W. M. (1988). Engaging adolescent drug abusers and their families in treatment: A strategic structural systems approach. *Journal of Consulting and Clinical Psychology, 56,* 552–557.

Szmukler, G. I., Eisler, I., Russell, G. F. M., & Dare, C. (1985). Anorexia nervosa, parental "expressed emotion" and dropping out of treatment. *British Journal of Psychiatry, 147,* 265–271.

Tallmadge, J., & Barkley, R. A. (1983). The interactions of hyperactive and normal boys with their fathers and mothers. *Journal of Abnormal Child Psychology, 11,* 565–579.

Tambs, K., & Moum, T. (1993). Low genetic effect and age-specific family effect for symptoms of anxiety and depression in nuclear families, halfsibs and twins. *Journal of Affective Disorders, 27,* 183–195.

Tannenbaum, L., & Forehand, R. (1993, November). *Maternal depressed mood and adolescent functioning: Fathers do make a difference.* Poster presented at the convention of the Association for the Advancement of Behavior Therapy, Atlanta, GA.

Tarter, R. E., Hegedus, A. M., & Gavaler, J. S. (1985). Hyperactivity in sons of alcoholics. *Journal of Studies on Alcohol, 46,* 259–261.

Tarter, R. E., Hegedus, A. M., Goldstein, G., Shelly, C., & Alterman, A. I. (1984). Adolescent sons of alcoholics: Neuropsychological and personality characteristics. *Alcoholism: Clinical and Experimental Research, 8,* 216–222.

Tarter, R. E., Hegedus, A. M., Winsten, N. E., & Alterman, A. I. (1984). Neuropsychological, personality, and familial characteristics of physically abused delinquents. *Journal of the American Academy of Child Psychiatry, 23,* 668–674.

Tarter, R. E., Laird, S., & Bukstein, O. (1991). Multivariate comparison of adolescent offspring of substance abuse parents: Community and treatment samples. *Journal of Substance Abuse, 3,* 301–306.

Teachman, J. D. (1991). Contributions to children by divorced fathers. *Social Problems, 38,* 358–371.

Telerant, A., Kronenberg, J., Rabinovitch, S., & Elman, I. (1992). Anorectic family dynamics. *Journal of the American Academy of Child and Adolescent Psychiatry, 31,* 990–991.

Thomas, A. M., & Forehand, R. (1991). The relationship between paternal depressive mood and early adolescent functioning. *Journal of Family Psychology, 4,* 260–271.

Thomas, A. M., & Forehand, R. (1993). The role of paternal variables in divorced and married families: Predictability of adolescent adjustment. *American Journal of Orthopsychiatry, 63,* 126–135.

Thompson, L., & Walker, A. J. (1989). Gender in families: Women and men in marriage, work, and parenthood. *Journal of Marriage and the Family, 51,* 845–871.

Thompson, R. A. (1986). Fathers and the child's "best interests": Judicial decision making in custody disputes. In M. E. Lamb (Ed.), *The father's role: Applied perspectives* (pp. 61–102). New York: Wiley.

Thomson, E., McLanahan, S. S., & Curtin, R. B. (1992). Family structure, gender, and parental socialization. *Journal of Marriage and the Family, 54,* 368–378.

Thurber, S., & Osborn, R. A. (1993). Comparisons of parent and adolescent perspectives on deviance. *Journal of Genetic Psychology, 154,* 25–32.

Tiedje, L. B., & Darling-Fisher, C. S. (1993). Factors that influence fathers' participation in child care. *Health Care for Women International, 14,* 99–107.

Tienboon, P., Wahlqvist, M. L., & Rutishauser, I. H. (1992). Self-reported weight and height in adolescents and their parents. *Journal of Adolescent Health, 13,* 528–532.

Tillitski, C. J. (1992). Fathers and child custody: Issues, trends, and implications for counseling. *Journal of Mental Health Counseling, 14,* 351–361.

Timko, C., Stovel, K. W., & Moos, R. H. (1992). Functioning among mothers and fathers of children with juvenile rheumatic disease. *Journal of Pediatric Psychology, 17,* 705–724.

Tinsley, B. J., & Parke, R. D. (1987). Grandparents as interactive and social support agents for families with young infants. *International Journal of Aging and Human Development, 25,* 261–279.

Tinsley, B. J., & Parke, R. D. (1988). The role of grandfathers in the context of the family. In P. Bronstein & C. P. Cowan (Eds.), *Fatherhood today: Men's changing role in the family* (pp. 236–250). New York: Wiley.

Tomlinson-Keasey, C., Warren, L. W., & Elliott, J. E. (1986). Suicide among gifted women: A prospective study. *Journal of Abnormal Psychology, 95,* 123–130.

Touliatos, J., Perlmutter, B. F., & Straus, M. A. (Eds.). (1990). *Handbook of family measurement techniques.* Newbury Park, CA: Sage.

Trice, A. D., & Knapp, L. (1992). Relationship of children's career aspirations to parents' occupations. *Journal of Genetic Psychology, 153,* 355–357.

Tripp-Reimer, T., & Wilson, S. E. (1991). Cross-cultural perspectives on fatherhood. In F. W. Bozett & S. M. H. Hanson (Eds.), *Fatherhood and families in cultural context* (pp. 1–27). New York: Springer.

Tronick, E. (1989). Emotions and emotional communications in infants. *American Psychologist, 44,* 112–119.

Truscott, D. (1992). Intergenerational transmission of violent behavior in adolescent males. *Aggressive Behavior, 18,* 327–335.

Tubman, J. G. (1993). A pilot study of school-age children of men with moderate to severe alcohol dependence: Maternal distress and child outcomes. *Journal of Child Psychology and Psychiatry and Allied Disciplines, 34,* 729–741.

Turnbull, A. P. (1988). The challenge of providing comprehensive support to families. *Education and Training in Mental Retardation, 23,* 261–272.

Turner, S. M., Beidel, D. C., & Costello, A. (1987). Psychopathology in the offspring of anxiety disorders patients. *Journal of Consulting and Clinical Psychology, 55,* 229–235.

Ullman, A. D., & Orenstein, A. (1994). Why some children of alcoholics become alcoholics: Emulation of the drinker. *Adolescence, 29* 1–11.

U.S. Bureau of the Census. (1987). *Who's minding the kids? Child Care arrangements: Winter 1984–1985* (P70, No. 9). Washington, DC: U.S. Government Printing Office.

U.S. Bureau of the Census. (1992). *Households, families, and children: A 30-year perspective* (P23-181). Washington, DC: U.S. Government Printing Office.

Vandenberg, S. G., & Crowe, L. (1990). Genetic factors in childhood psychopathology: Implications for clinical practice. In B. B. Lahey & A. E. Kazdin (Eds.), *Advances in clinical child psychology* (Vol. 12, pp. 139–177). New York: Plenum.

Vandenberg, S. G., Singer, S. M., & Pauls, D. L. (1986). *The heredity of behavior disorders in adults and children.* New York: Plenum.

Vanyukov, M. M., Moss, H. B., Plail, J. A., & Blackson, T. (1993). Antisocial symptoms in preadolescent boys and in their parents: Associations with cortisol. *Psychiatry Research, 46,* 9–17.

Vasta, R., Haith, M. M., & Miller, S. A. (1992). *Child psychology: The modern science.* New York: Wiley.

Vega-Lahr, N., & Field, T. M. (1986). Type A behavior in preschool children. *Child Development, 57,* 1333–1348.

Velez, C. N., Johnson, J., & Cohen, P. (1989). A longitudinal analysis of selected risk factors for childhood psychopathology. *Journal of the American Academy of Child and Adolescent Psychiatry, 28,* 861–864.

Velleman, R. (1992). Intergenerational effects—A review of environmentally oriented studies concerning the relationship between parental alcohol problems and family disharmony in the genesis of alcohol and other problems: I. The intergenerational effects of alcohol problems. *International Journal of the Addictions, 27,* 253–280.

Vitulli, W. F., & Holland, B. E. (1993). College students' attitudes toward relationships with their parents as a function of gender. *Psychological Reports, 72,* 744–746.

Volger, A., Ernst, G., Nachreiner, F., & Hanecke, K. (1988). Common free time of family members under different shift systems. *Applied Ergonomics, 19,* 213–218.

Volling, B. L., & Belsky, J. (1992a). The contributions of mother-child and father-child relationships to the quality of sibling interaction: A longitudinal study. *Child Development, 63,* 1209–1222.

Volling, B. L., & Belsky, J. (1992b). Infant, father, and marital antecedents of infant-father attachment security in dual-earner and single-earner families. *International Journal of Behavioral Development, 15,* 83–100.

Von Der Heydt, V. (1964). The role of the father in early mental development. *British Journal of Medical Psychology, 37,* 123–131.

Voydanoff, P. (1988). Women, work, and family: Bernard's perspective on the past, present, and future. *Psychology of Women Quarterly, 12,* 269–280.

Wachs, T. D., & Weizmann, F. (1992). Prenatal and genetic influences upon behavior and development. In C. E. Walker & M. C. Roberts (Eds.), *Handbook of clinical child psychology* (2nd ed., pp. 183–198). New York: Wiley.

Wagner, B. M., & Phillips, D. A. (1992). Beyond beliefs: Parent and child behaviors and children's perceived academic competence. *Child Development, 63,* 1380–1391.

Walker, E., & Emory, E. (1983). Infants at risk for psychopathology: Offspring of schizophrenic parents. *Child Development, 54,* 1269–1285.

Wall, J. C. (1992). Maintaining the connection: Parenting as a noncustodial father. *Child and Adolescent Social Work Journal, 9,* 441–456.

Wallander, J. L. (1988). The relationship between attention problems in childhood and antisocial behavior eight years later. *Journal of Child Psychology and Psychiatry, 29,* 53–61.

Waller, G., Slade, P., & Calam, R. (1990). Who knows best? Family interaction and eating disorders. *British Journal of Psychiatry, 156,* 546–550.

Ward, R. A., & Spitze, G. (1992). Consequences of parent-adult child coresidence: A review and research agenda. *Journal of Family Issues, 13,* 553–572.

Warren, J. K., Gary, F., & Moorhead, J. (1994). Self-reported experiences of physical and sexual abuse among runaway youths. *Perspectives in Psychiatric Care, 30,* 23–28.

Watson, J. (1986). Parental attributions of emotional disturbance and their relation to the outcome of therapy: Preliminary findings. *Australian Psychologist, 21,* 271–282.

Watson, J. B. (1926). Experimental studies on the growth of the emotions. In M. - Bentley, K. Dunlap, W. S. Hunter, K. Koffka, W. Kohler, W. McDougall, M. Prince, J. B. Watson, & R. S. Woodworth (Eds.), *Psychologies of 1925* (pp. 37–57). Worcester, MA: Clark University Press.

Watt, N. F. (1986). Risk research in schizophrenia and other major psychological disorders. In M. Kessler & S. E. Goldston (Eds.), *A decade of progress in primary prevention* (pp. 115–153). Hanover, NH: University Press of New England.

Watt, N. F., Anthony, E. J., Wynne, L. C., & Rolf, J. E. (Eds.). (1984). *Children at risk for schizophrenia: A longitudinal perspective.* New York: Cambridge University Press.

Webster-Stratton, C. (1985). The effects of father involvement in parent training for conduct problem children. *Journal of Child Psychology and Psychiatry, 26,* 801–810.

Webster-Stratton, C. (1988). Mothers' and fathers' perceptions of child deviance: Roles of parent and child behaviors and parent adjustment. *Journal of Consulting and Clinical Psychology, 56,* 909–915.

Webster-Stratton, C. (1990). Long-term follow-up of families with young conduct problem children: From preschool to grade school. *Journal of Clinical Child Psychology, 19,* 144–149.

Webster-Stratton, C. (1992). Individually administered videotape parent training: "Who benefits?" *Cognitive Therapy and Research, 16,* 31–35.

Webster-Stratton, C., & Hammond, M. (1990). Predictors of treatment outcome in parent training for families with conduct problem children. *Behavior Therapy, 21,* 319–337.

Webster-Stratton, C., Hollinsworth, T., & Kolpacoff, M. (1989). The long-term effectiveness and clinical significance of three cost-effective training programs for families with conduct-problem children. *Journal of Consulting and Clinical Psychology, 57,* 550–553.

Webster-Stratton, C., Kolpacoff, M., & Hollinsworth, T. (1988). Self-administered videotape therapy for families with conduct-problem children: Comparison with two cost-effective treatments and a control group. *Journal of Consulting and Clinical Psychology, 56,* 558–566.

Weidner, G., Sexton, G., Matarazzo, J. D., Pereira, C., & Friend, R. (1988). Type A behavior in children, adolescents, and their parents. *Developmental Psychology, 24,* 118–121.

Weintraub, S., & Neale, J. M. (1984). The Stony Brook High-Risk Project. In N. F. Watt, E. J. Anthony, L. C. Wynne, & J. E. Rolf (Eds.), *Children at risk for schizophrenia: A longitudinal perspective* (pp. 243–263). New York: Cambridge University Press.

Weintraub, S., Winters, K. C., & Neale, J. M. (1986). Competence and vulnerability in children with an affectively disordered parent. In M. Rutter, C. E. Izard, & P. B. Read (Eds.), *Depression in young people: Developmental and clinical perspectives* (pp. 205–220). New York: Guilford.

Weisner, T. S., Garnier, H., & Loucky, J. (1994). Domestic tasks, gender egalitarian values and children's gender typing in conventional and nonconventional families. *Sex Roles, 30,* 23–54.

Weisner, T. S., & Wilson-Mitchell, J. E. (1990). Nonconventional family styles and sex typing in 6-year-olds. *Child Development, 61,* 1915–1933.

Weissman, M. M., Gershon, E. S., Kidd, K. K., Prusoff, B. A., Leckman, J. F., Dibble, E., Hamovit, J., Thompson, D., Pauls, D. L., & Guroff, J. J. (1984). Psychiatric disorders in the relatives of probands with affective disorders. *Archives of General Psychiatry, 41,* 13–21.

Weissman, M. M., Leckman, J. F., Merikangas, K. R., Gammon, G. D., & Prusoff, B. A. (1984). Depression and anxiety disorders in parents and children. *Archives of General Psychiatry, 41,* 845–852.

Weisz, J. R., & Weiss, B. (1989). Assessing the effects of clinic-based psychotherapy with children and adolescents. *Journal of Consulting and Clinical Psychology, 57,* 741–746.

Weisz, J. R., Weiss, B., Alicke, M. D., & Klotz, M. L. (1987). Effectiveness of psychotherapy with children and adolescents: A meta-analysis for clinicians. *Journal of Consulting and Clinical Psychology, 55,* 542–549.

Weitzman, L. J. (1988). Women and children last: The social and economic consequences of divorce law reforms. In S. M. Dornbusch & M. H. Strober (Eds.), *Feminism, children, and the new families* (pp. 212–248). New York: Guilford.

Welldon, E. V. (1988). *Mother, madonna, whore: The idealization and denigration of motherhood.* London: Free Association Books.

Weller, R. A., Kapadia, P., Weller, E. B., Fristad, M., Lazaroff, L. B., & Preskorn, S. H. (1994). Psychopathology in families of children with major depressive disorders. *Journal of Affective Disorders, 31,* 247–252.

Wenk, D., Hardesty, C. L., Morgan, C. S., & Blair, S. L. (1994). The influence of parental involvement on the well-being of sons and daughters. *Journal of Marriage and the Family, 56,* 229–234.

Werner, E. E. (1986). Resilient offspring of alcoholics: A longitudinal study from birth to age 18. *Journal of Studies on Alcohol, 47,* 34–40.

Werrbach, G. B., Grotevant, H. D., & Cooper, C. R. (1992). Patterns of family interaction and adolescent sex role concepts. *Journal of Youth and Adolescence, 21,* 609–623.

Wertlieb, D., Weigel, C., & Feldstein, M. (1988). The impact of stress and temperament on medical utilization by school-age children. *Journal of Pediatric Psychology, 13,* 409–421.

West, M. O., & Prinz, R. J. (1987). Parental alcoholism and childhood psychopathology. *Psychological Bulletin, 102,* 204–218.

Westerman, M. A., & Schonholtz, J. (1993). Marital adjustment, joint parental support in a triadic problem-solving task, and child behavior problems. *Journal of Clinical Child Psychology, 22,* 97–106.

Whipple, E. E., & Webster-Stratton, C. (1991). The role of parental stress in physically abusive families. *Child Abuse and Neglect, 15,* 279–291.

Whipple, S. C., & Noble, E. P. (1991). Personality characteristics of alcoholic fathers and their sons. *Journal of Studies on Alcohol, 52,* 331–337.

Whitehead, B. D. (1993, April). Dan Quayle was right. *Atlantic Monthly,* pp. 47–50.

Widiger, T. A., Williams, J. B. W., Spitzer, R. L., & Frances, A. (1986). The MCMI as a measure of DSM-III. *Journal of Personality Assessment, 49,* 366–378.

Wiehe, V. R. (1992). Abusive and nonabusive parents: How they were parented. *Journal of Social Service Research, 15,* 81–93.

Wierson, M., Armistead, L., Forehand, R., Thomas, A. M., & Fauber, R. (1990). Parent-adolescent conflict and stress as a parent: Are there differences between being a mother or a father? *Journal of Family Violence, 5,* 187–197.

Wierson, M., Forehand, R., & McCombs, A. (1988). The relationship of early adolescent functioning to parent-reported and adolescent-perceived interparental conflict. *Journal of Abnormal Child Psychology, 16,* 707–718.

Williams, E., & Radin, N. (1993). Paternal involvement, maternal employment, and adolescents' academic achievement: An 11-year follow-up. *American Journal of Orthopsychiatry, 63,* 306–312.

Williams, E., Radin, N., & Allegro, T. (1992). Sex role attitudes of adolescents reared primarily by their fathers: An 11-year follow-up. *Merrill-Palmer Quarterly, 38,* 457–476.

Willis, D. J., & Walker, C. E. (1989). Etiology. In T. H. Ollendick & M. Hersen (Eds.), *Handbook of child psychopathology* (2nd ed., pp. 29–51). New York: Plenum.

Wilson, M. N., Tolson, T. F. J., Hinton, I. D., & Kiernan, M. (1990). Flexibility and sharing of childcare duties in Black families. *Sex Roles, 22,* 409–425.

Winnicott, D. W. (1958). *Collected papers.* London: Tavistock Publications.

Wolchik, S. A. (1983). Language patterns of parents of young autistic and normal children. *Journal of Autism and Developmental Disorders, 13,* 167–180.

Wolfe, D. A. (1985). Child-abusive parents: An empirical review and analysis. *Psychological Bulletin, 97,* 462–482.

Wolfe, D. A. (1991). *Preventing physical and emotional abuse of children.* New York: Guilford.

Wolff, S., Narayan, S., & Moyes, B. (1988). Personality characteristics of parents of autistic children: A controlled study. *Journal of Child Psychology and Psychiatry, 29,* 143–153.

Wolfner, G. D., & Gelles, R. J. (1993). A profile of violence toward children: A national study. *Child Abuse and Neglect, 17,* 197–212.

Wolk, S., Zeanah, C. H., Garcia-Coll, C. T., & Carr, S. (1992). Factors affecting parents' perceptions of temperament in early infancy. *American Journal of Orthopsychiatry, 62,* 71–82.

Woollett, A., White, D. G., & Lyon, M. L. (1982). Studies involving fathers: Subject refusal, attrition and sampling bias. *Current Psychological Reviews, 2,* 193–212.

Wright, L. S. (1985). Suicidal thoughts and their relationship to family stress and personal problems among high school seniors and college undergraduates. *Adolescence, 20,* 575–580.

Wylie, P. (1946). *Generation of vipers.* New York: Rinehart & Company.

Wyman, P. A., Cowen, E. L., Work, W. C., & Raoff, A. (1992). Interviews with children who experienced major life stress: Family and child attributes that predict resilient outcomes. *Journal of the American Academy of Child and Adolescent Psychiatry, 31,* 904–910.

Yamasaki, K. (1990). Parental child-rearing attitudes associated with Type A behaviors in children. *Psychological Reports, 67,* 235–239.

Yesavage, J. A., Becker, J. M. T., Werner, P. D., Patton, M. J., Seeman, K., Brunsting, D. W., & Mills, M. J. (1983). Family conflict, psychopathology, and dangerous behavior by schizophrenic inpatients. *Psychiatry Research, 8,* 271–280.

Yogman, M. W., Cooley, J., & Kindlon, D. (1988). Fathers, infants, and toddlers: A developing relationship. In P. Bronstein & C. P. Cowan (Eds.), *Fatherhood today: Men's changing role in the family* (pp. 53–65). New York: Wiley.

Youniss, J., & Ketterlinus, R. D. (1987). Communication and connectedness in mother- and father-adolescent relationships. *Journal of Youth and Adolescence, 16,* 265–280.

Youniss, J., & Smollar, J. (1985). *Adolescent relations with mothers, fathers, and friends.* Chicago: The University of Chicago Press.

Zahner, G. E., Jacobs, J. H., Freeman, D. H., & Trainor, K. F. (1993). Rural-urban child psychopathology in a northeastern U.S. state: 1986–1989. *Journal of the American Academy of Child and Adolescent Psychiatry, 32,* 378–387.

Zahn-Waxler, C., Cummings, E. M., McKnew, D. H., & Radke-Yarrow, M. (1984). Altruism, aggression, and social interactions in young children with a manic-depressive parent. *Child Development, 55,* 112–122.

Zeanah, C. H., Keener, M. A., & Anders, T. F. (1986). Developing perceptions of temperament and their relation to mother and infant behavior. *Journal of Child Psychology, Psychiatry, and Allied Disciplines, 27,* 499–512.

Ziller, R. C., & Stewart-Dowdell, B. J. (1991). Life after parental death: Monitoring a child's self-concept before and after family violence. *Death Studies, 15,* 577–586.

Zuskin, R. E. (1992). Developing insight in incestuous fathers. *Journal of Offender Rehabilitation, 18,* 205–216.

Zweig-Frank, H., & Paris, J. (1991). Parents' emotional neglect and overprotection according to the recollections of patients with Borderline Personality Disorder. *American Journal of Psychiatry, 148,* 648–651.

Author Index

Subject Index